Peggy.

adj. Prof.

Quest. fer Int. Eval.

COLLEGE

Law

FOR BUSINESS

TENTH EDITION

JOHN D. ASHCROFT, J.D.

Governor, State of Missouri
Member of the Missouri Bar

JANET E. ASHCROFT, J.D.

Member of the Missouri Bar

Published by

L92 **SOUTH-WESTERN PUBLISHING CO.**

CINCINNATI   WEST CHICAGO, IL   DALLAS   LIVERMORE, CA

ISBN: 0-538-12920-4

Library of Congress Catalog
Card Number: 85-63103

3 4 5 6 7 D 2 1 0 9 8 7

Printed in the United States of America

Preface

Society is becoming more and more litigious. Judgments are reaching levels which can wipe out even the largest enterprise. Everyone doing business faces the risk of being sued. While *College Law for Business*, Tenth Edition, is not designed to make lawyers of students, it should help individuals deal with legal concepts in the context of modern business. Ideally, students can learn to avoid most lawsuits and expand their awareness of their rights in business situations. With the proper care, major legal problems can be prevented. *College Law for Business*, Tenth Edition, will help business students learn to exercise that care.

By addressing the most important areas of business law, this book is designed to aid college students. The numerous examples and cases demonstrate the everyday application of legal principles without delving into the subject matter in the great detail used to train lawyers.

A new chapter on government regulation of business enhances this Tenth Edition. The rapid growth in the number of regulations and laws requiring compliance makes it essential for business persons to be aware of their legal responsibilities. Included in the new Chapter Three are discussions of topics from antitrust law to environmental regulations which have substantial impact on the business world.

The fifty chapters of the text are grouped into ten parts. Following the three general introductory chapters, the book has a nine-chapter part dealing with the foundation of business law—contracts. Because every area of business law is based, to some degree, on the law of contracts, it is essential that students understand the concepts in this part before covering subsequent chapters.

From the part on contracts, the text proceeds to other fundamental concepts: sales, bailments, commercial paper, and agency and employment.

Following the part on agency and employment, the business organization, an agency-related area, is addressed. The concluding sections cover principles involved in ownership—risk-bearing devices and property.

A number of helpful learning aids are presented at both the beginning and end of the various parts and chapters. Each part of the book begins by listing important "Learning Objectives" to help the student identify major principles to be studied. Preview cases highlight the beginning of all but the introductory chapters. These cases, along with additional case examples strategically placed within the chapters, demonstrate the application of the concepts being addressed. At the end of each part, "Summary Cases" prompt students to reinforce the major concepts explored in that part. Citations to the actual cases refer interested students to the legal reports if further, in-depth study is desired. Questions and case problems at the end of the chapters promote recall of the text and reinforce the concepts learned from the material.

Because the later chapters build, to some extent, on concepts presented in previous chapters, it would be best for students to have a firm grasp on the earlier material before moving on to subsequent chapters. The questions and case problems at the end of each chapter are designed to and should be used to determine if further review is needed before continuing with additional material.

In addition to the text, supplementary items are available which enhance the textbook's use. The Study Reports are designed for student use, while the Instructor's Manual and the tests provide teaching assistance and assessment opportunities for instructors.

The separate Study Reports reinforce student understanding by requiring review of the concepts and application of them to factual situations. A variety of learning exercises: true–false questions, fill-in-the-blank statements, yes–no questions, questions referring to fact situations, and definitional exercises are used, along with various legal forms, to inventory learning and identify weaknesses. The opportunity to fill in legal forms gives valuable experience to students by familiarizing them with commonly used forms.

The Instructor's Manual includes a lesson outline and answers to the questions and case problems for each chapter. This edition adds suggestions to assist in teaching the concepts explained in the text. A reference section suggests additional resource materials for use by instructors if expanded treatment of any topic is desired.

The bank of twelve tests includes separate testing for each part of the text. The longer parts covering negotiable instruments and contracts are the subjects of two tests each. Additionally, there are two term examinations, each covering approximately one-half of the book and a comprehensive final examination for the entire text.

The authors both received their *Juris Doctor* degrees from the University of Chicago School of Law. They have been members of the Missouri Bar for almost twenty years. Both practiced law and taught business law at Southwest Missouri State University in Springfield, Missouri. Both are also admitted to practice law in the Federal Court for the Western District of Missouri. Mrs. Ashcroft has taught additional law courses at other colleges and served as General Counsel for the Missouri Department of Revenue. Governor Ashcroft was an assistant attorney general and later served as Attorney General of Missouri for eight years. He has presented cases in every state and federal appellate court in Missouri and in the United States Supreme Court and has authored numerous articles for legal publications.

Everyday living is full of business dealings. Products are purchased, facilities are rented, checks are cashed. No one escapes the need to identify and avoid the legal pitfalls in modern life. *College Law for Business*, Tenth Edition, can help students learn to protect their interests on their own and, when necessary, with the help of legal professionals.

Contents

Part One — The Legal System and the Legal Environment of Business

Learning Objectives for Part One

The Legal System and the Legal Environment of Business

After studying this part you should be able to:

1. Define law.
2. Explain why we have laws.
3. List four sources of law.
4. Distinguish crimes from torts.
5. Explain the function of the courts.
6. Explain how the court systems operate in our society.
7. Describe the procedure for filing a lawsuit.
8. Describe the basic procedure for a jury trial.
9. Explain why government regulates business.
10. Discuss the types and powers of administrative agencies.

1
Introduction to Law

Nothing so complex as law could be completely described in one short definition. Many authors have tried to define law. Blackstone's definition is famous: "*Law* is a rule of civil conduct, commanding what is right and prohibiting what is wrong." There are many rules of civil conduct commanding what is right and condemning what is wrong, but rules are not necessarily laws. Only when a sovereign state issues rules prescribing what is right and what is wrong can a rule be called a law. Even then rules are not effective unless penalties are applied when the rules are broken.

Religious teachings, the mores of society, habit, and group pressures to conform all contribute to social control of conduct, but only the rules of law are all-pervasive, applying with equal force to every member of society. A breach of some of these rules is a crime, and the penalty is a fine, a jail sentence, or both. A breach of other rules is a civil wrong and the penalty is, for the most part, an award of money called "damages." Every deviation from prescribed rules of conduct has an appropriate penalty.

Business law is concerned primarily with those rules of conduct prescribed by government for the performance of business transactions. The laws governing business transactions in America did not come into existence overnight. Law is an evolutionary process. Laws are the result of society's changing concepts of what is right and what is wrong. For example, for several centuries in England and America an individual who owned land owned the soil and minerals below the topsoil and the air above the land "all the way to heaven." The law prohibited trespassing on a person's land *or* air. A telephone company that wanted to string a telephone wire through the air had to buy a right of way. When airplanes were invented, this law became a millstone around society's neck. Under this law, a transcontinental airline would have to buy a right of way through the air of every property owner in its path from New York to San Francisco. The modification of this rule by judicial decree is one example of the law changing when circumstances change.

3

Objectives of Law

We live in a very complex society. We are constantly dealing with other people—when doing our jobs, making a purchase, starting a business, traveling, renting an apartment, or trying to insure against loss. Every time we have dealings with others, there is a potential for dispute. The law seeks to establish rules so that we will be able to resolve any disputes. The law also sets the rules of conduct for many transactions so we can know what we must do to avoid disputes with those with whom we associate. The law thus tries to establish a stable framework to keep society operating as smoothly as possible.

The Common Law

Common law is, in reality, custom which has come to be recognized by the courts as binding on the community. In eleventh-century England, there were no laws prescribing the proper rule of conduct in hundreds of situations. When a dispute was brought before the judge, the court prescribed a rule of its own based on the customs of the time. Over a period of several centuries, these court decisions developed into a body of law. The American colonists brought this body of law to America. After the United States became a sovereign nation, most of these common laws were either enacted as statutory laws or continued as judge-made laws. This common law is the source of much of our law today.

Equity

Uniformity in the common law spread throughout England because judges tended to decide cases the same way other judges had decided them. This led to severe rigidity in the common law. Wrongs existed for which law provided no remedy. In the law courts practically the only remedy available was a judgment for money damages. In some cases, this was not an appropriate remedy. To obtain a suitable remedy, the parties began to petition the Sovereign for justice. The Sovereign delegated these matters to the chancellor, who did not decide the cases on the basis of recognized legal principles, but on the basis of "equity"—what in good conscience ought to be done. Eventually an additional system of justice evolved which granted judicial relief when there was no adequate remedy at law. This system was called *equity*.

Courts of equity, although they sometimes recognized legal rights, also provided new types of relief. For example, instead of merely ordering a person who had breached a contract to sell real estate to pay money damages, they would order "specific performance"—that is, require compliance with the terms of the contract. They also would provide for preventive action to protect individuals from a harm which was very likely to occur. In this type of case a court with equity powers might initially issue a *restraining order,* a temporary order forbidding a certain action; and, upon a complete hearing, the court might issue an *injunction,* a permanent order forbidding activities which would be detrimental to others. Today, however, only a few states maintain separate equity courts, or, as they are frequently called, Chancery Courts. In most states, legal and equitable principles are applied to each case as the facts justify, without making any formal distinction between law and equity.

Sources of Law

Our laws are derived from several sources. These sources include the decisions of judges in cases they hear, federal and state constitutions, statutes, and administrative agency orders.

Judicial Decisions. Judicial interpretation is still an important element of the legal process. Interpretations by the highest courts become precedents and under the doctrine of *stare decisis* (stand by the decision) are binding upon the lower courts. These interpretations may concern a situation not previously brought before the court, or the court may decide to reverse a previous decision. Any state supreme court or the Supreme Court of the United States can reverse a decision of a lower court. If the law is to attain stability so that we can know what our rights are before we undertake a transaction, courts must generally adhere to the judicial precedents set by earlier decisions. However, changing situations or practices sometimes make it necessary for the previous case law to be overturned and a new rule or practice to be established.

Constitutions. A *constitution* is the document which defines the relationships of the parts of the government to each other and the relationship of the government to its citizens or subjects. The United States Constitution is the supreme law of the land. State constitutions, as well as all other laws, must agree with it. The Supreme Court of the United States is the final arbiter in disputes about whether a state or federal law violates the Constitution of the United States. A state supreme court is the final judge as to whether a state law violates the constitution of that state.

Statutes. *Statutes* are laws enacted by legislative bodies. The three chief classes of legislative bodies in the United States are the federal Congress, the state legislatures, and city councils. The laws of city councils are called *ordinances,* a specific type of statutory law.

In some cases statutes enacted by one legislative body conflict with statutes enacted by another legislative body. If there is a conflict between a state statute and a constitutional federal statute, the latter prevails.

Unlike constitutions, which are difficult to amend and are designed to be general rather than specific, statutes may be enacted, repealed, or amended at any regular or special session of the lawmaking body. Thus, statutes are more responsive to the changing demands of the people.

In the field of business law the most important statute is the Uniform Commercial Code (UCC).[1] The UCC regulates the fields of sales of goods; commercial paper, such as checks; secured transactions; and particular aspects of banking, letters of credit, warehouse receipts, bills of lading, and investment securities.

Administrative Agency Orders. Many of our governmental functions today are carried on by means of administrative agencies set up by our legislative bodies. The heads of federal administrative agencies are appointed by the President of the United States with the consent of the Senate. Administrative agencies are given wide latitude in setting up rules of procedure. They issue orders and decrees that have the force of law unless set aside by the courts after being challenged.

Criminal Law

Criminal law is that branch of the law which has to do with crimes and the punishment of wrongdoers. A *crime* is an offense that tends to injure society as a whole. There are certain criminal offenses, such as arson, forgery, fraudulent conveyances, and embezzlement, that are closely related to business activities.

Crimes are usually classified according to the nature of the punishment as felonies and misdemeanors. Generally speaking, *felonies* are the more serious crimes and are usually punishable by death or by imprisonment in a penitentiary for more than one year. *Misdemeanors* are offenses of a less serious character and are punishable by a fine or imprisonment in a county or local jail. Committing a forgery is a felony, but driving an automobile in excess of the speed limit is a misdemeanor. The criminal statutes define the acts that are felonies and those that are misdemeanors.

Tort Law

A *tort* is a private or civil wrong or injury for which there may be an action for damages. A tort may be intentional or it may be caused by negligence. *Negligence* is the failure to exercise reasonable care toward someone. It is tort law which allows an innocent motorist who is the victim of a careless or negligent driver to sue the negligent driver for damages. Other

---

[1]The UCC has been adopted at least in part in every state. The UCC has also been adopted in the Virgin Islands and for the District of Columbia.

torts include fraud, trespass, assault, slander, and interference with contracts.

A tort action must be brought by the injured person against the person alleged to be negligent. This contrasts with criminal actions in which an employee of the government—usually called the *prosecutor* or *district attorney*—brings the action.

Questions

1. What is *law*? What is *business law*?

2. Why do we have laws?

3. What is *common law*?

4. Why did the equity courts develop?

5. Why are we justified in classifying law by judicial decision as a source of law? What are three other sources of law?

6. Describe the relationship between the United States Constitution, state constitutions, and state statutes.

7. What is the legal effect of an order issued by an administrative agency?

8. Classify the following crimes into felonies and misdemeanors: murder, theft of one dollar, drunkenness, robbery, overtime parking, and forgery.

9. Distinguish crimes from torts.

10. Who brings a tort action? Who brings a criminal action?

2 Courts and Court Procedure

In each state there are two distinct court systems—federal courts and state courts. While the systems are largely independent of each other, they have a similar function.

Function of the Courts

The function of a court is to declare and apply judicial precedents, or case law, and to apply laws passed by the legislative arm of the government. This is not the whole story, however. Constitutions by their very nature must be couched in generalities. Statutes are less general than constitutions; however, they could not possibly be worded to apply to every situation which may arise. Thus, the chief function of the courts is to interpret and apply the law from whatever source to a given situation. For example, the federal Constitution gives the federal Congress power to regulate commerce among the several states. Under this power Congress passes a law requiring safety devices on trains. If the law is challenged, the court must decide whether this is a regulation of interstate commerce.

Similarly, an Act of Congress regulates minimum wages for the vast majority of workers. A case may arise as to whether this applies to the wages paid in a sawmill located in a rural section of the country. The court must decide whether or not the sawmill owner is engaged in interstate commerce. The court's decision may become a judicial precedent that will be followed in the future unless the court changes its decision in a subsequent case.

Jurisdiction of Courts

The power or authority which each court has to hear cases is called its *jurisdiction*. Courts must have jurisdiction over the subject matter of the case and jurisdiction over the persons involved. If a claim is made for damages due to an automobile accident, a probate court does not have jurisdiction over the subject matter since a probate court deals with wills and the distribution of property of deceased persons. The damage action would have to be brought in a court of general jurisdiction. A court may have jurisdiction over the subject matter but not over the person. If a resident of Ohio is charged with trespassing on a neighbor's property in the same state, a court in Indiana does not have jurisdiction over the person of the accused. Nor does a court in Ohio have jurisdiction over the person of the accused if the accused has not been properly served with notice of the trial. Before any court can try a case, it must be established that the court has jurisdiction over both the subject matter and the person in the case at issue.

Classification of Courts

Courts are classified for the purpose of determining their jurisdiction. This classification can be made in a variety of ways. One classification can be made according to the governmental unit setting up the court. Under this classification system, courts are divided into (1) federal courts, (2) state courts, and (3) municipal courts.

The same courts may be classified according to the method of hearing cases. Under this system they are classified as trial courts and appellate courts. *Trial courts* conduct the original trial of cases and render their decisions. *Appellate courts* review cases appealed from the decisions of lower courts. Appellate courts include courts of appeals and supreme courts. Appellate courts exercise considerable authority over the courts under them. Lower courts are bound by the decisions of their appellate courts.

Federal Courts. The federal courts (see Illustration 2-1) are classified as:

1. Federal district courts
2. Federal courts of appeals
3. United States Supreme Court
4. Special federal courts

Federal District Courts. By far the largest class of federal courts consists of the district courts. These courts are strictly trial courts in which all criminal cases involving a violation of the federal law are tried. The district courts also have jurisdiction of civil suits which (1) are brought by the United States; (2) arise under the federal Constitution, federal laws, or treaties; and (3) are brought by citizens of different states or between citizens of one state and a foreign nation or one of its citizens where the amount in controversy is $10,000 or more.

Federal Courts of Appeals. The United States is divided into twelve federal judicial circuits. For each circuit there is a court of appeals which hears appeals from cases arising in its circuit. The federal courts of appeals hear ap-

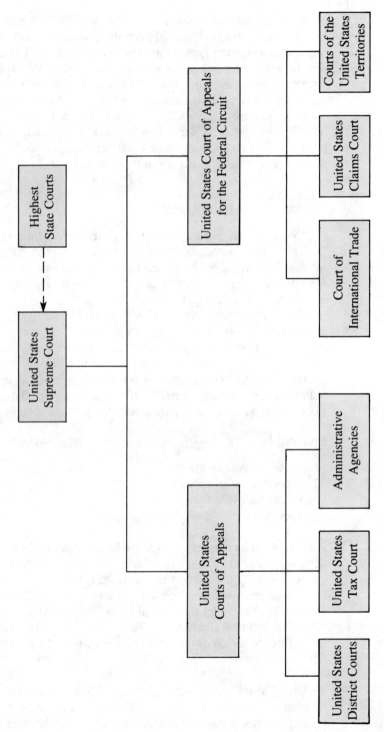

ILLUS. 2-1. The Federal Court System

peals from federal district courts and from federal administrative agencies and departments. A decision of a federal court of appeals is binding upon all lower courts within the jurisdiction of that circuit.

There is also another court of appeals called the Court of Appeals for the Federal Circuit. It reviews decisions of special federal courts (such as the Court of International Trade and the United States Claims Court), decisions of the courts of the United States territories, and appeals from district courts based on certain federal laws.

United States Supreme Court. The Supreme Court has original jurisdiction in cases affecting ambassadors, public ministers, and consuls and in cases in which a state is a party. But the majority of cases heard by the United States Supreme Court are cases appealed from the federal courts of appeals. Under certain circumstances a decision of a federal district court may be appealed directly to the Supreme Court. A state supreme court decision may also be reviewed by the United States Supreme Court if the case involves a federal constitutional question or if a federal law has been held invalid by the state court.

The United States Supreme Court is the highest tribunal in the land, and its decision is final until the Court reverses its own decision or until the effect of a given decision is changed by a constitutional amendment or an enactment by the Congress.

The Constitution created the Supreme Court and gave Congress the power to establish inferior courts.

Special Federal Courts. The special federal courts are limited in their jurisdiction by the laws of Congress creating them. For example, the Court of International Trade hears cases involving the rates of duty on various classes of imported goods, the collection of the revenues, and similar controversies. The United States Claims Court hears cases involving claims against the United States government. The Tax Court hears cases involving tax controversies.

State Courts. State courts (see Illustration 2-2) can best be classified into the following groups:

1. Inferior courts
2. Courts of original general jurisdiction
3. Appellate courts
4. Special courts

Inferior Courts. The inferior courts of the states hear only cases involving minor criminal offenses and minor disputes between citizens. In counties and smaller towns the most common inferior court is the justice-of-the-peace or magistrate court. A justice of the peace or magistrate hears cases

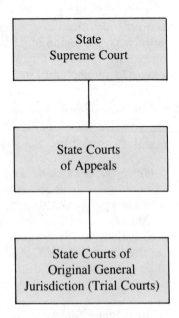

ILLUS. 2-2. Typical State Court System

between citizens with claims up to a maximum amount fixed by the state, usually $500 or less. In addition, these courts may try all criminal cases involving misdemeanors. In cities the function of the justice of the peace may be performed by the mayor, small-claims courts, police courts, or municipal courts. The loser in any of these courts may appeal to the court of original general jurisdiction.

Courts of Original General Jurisdiction. Courts of original general jurisdiction are for the average citizen the most important courts of the state. These courts have broad general jurisdiction over disputes between two or more parties as well as criminal offenses against the state. They are called *courts of original jurisdiction* because it is in them that the case is first instituted. On occasion they hear appeals from inferior courts, but this does not make them true appellate bodies because the entire case is retried at this level. Thus, such an appeal is actually treated as a case of original jurisdiction. An official, permanent record is kept of the trial showing the testimony, evidence, statements of counsel and the judge, the judgment, and the findings of the court. For this reason these courts are referred to as *courts of record*. The official name of such a court of original general jurisdiction is *Circuit Court, County Court, District Court,* or *Superior Court*.[1]

---

[1]In New York this court is known as a Supreme Court, and in Ohio it is known as a Court of Common Pleas.

Appellate Courts. In all states provision is made for an appeal to an appellate court by the party dissatisfied with the final judgment of the trial court or any of its rulings and instructions. Some states have a system of intermediate appellate courts usually called *courts of appeals,* as well as one final appellate court. Decisions of the appellate courts are binding on lower courts. The *state supreme court* is usually the highest appellate court of a state.

Special Courts. Many states have additional special courts, such as *probate courts* which handle wills and estates; *juvenile courts* which are concerned with delinquent, dependent, and neglected children; and *domestic relations courts* which handle divorce and child custody cases. These are not courts of general jurisdiction, but of special jurisdiction. In some states these courts are of the same level as the trial courts. When this is the case, they, too, are properly called trial courts and are courts of record. In other states they are on the same level as the inferior courts and are not courts of record.

Court Officers

The chief officer of an inferior court is the *justice of the peace, magistrate, trial justice,* or similar officer. The executive officer is the *constable* or *bailiff.* In a state court of record the chief officer is the *judge,* the executive officer is the *sheriff,* and the recorder is the *clerk of the court.* These titles are the same in the federal courts except that the executive officer is called a *marshal.*

Persons who are educated in the profession of the law and who are licensed to practice law are known as *lawyers* or *attorneys.* They are officers of the court and are subject to punishment for a breach of duty. Lawyers ordinarily represent the parties in a civil or a criminal action, although many states permit the parties to represent themselves. The practice of presenting one's own case, however, is usually not advisable.

Procedure in Filing Suit

Courts with but few exceptions are powerless to settle disputes between individuals unless one of the parties so requests the court. The written request is called a *complaint* or *petition* and is the beginning of a civil suit. The individual who institutes a civil action is called the *plaintiff,* and the individual against whom action is brought is called the *defendant.* The order of events in bringing an action is generally as follows:

1. The complaint or petition is filed with the clerk of the court. This petition sets forth the jurisdiction of the court, the nature of the claim, and the remedy sought.

2. As soon as the petition is filed, the clerk issues a *summons* or, as it is

sometimes called, a *process*. This gives the defendant notice of the complaint and informs the defendant of the number of days available in which to file an *answer*, admitting or denying the facts alleged in the complaint. The complaint and answer constitute the first pleadings.

3. To obtain information which is relevant to the subject matter of the action, there are a number of ways in which the parties may request unprivileged information from another party. These are called *discovery* and include:

a. Interrogatories—written questions to be answered in writing;
b. Deposition—subjecting a party or potential witness to questioning under oath;
c. Admissions—requests to agree that a certain fact is true or a matter of law is decided;
d. Medical examination by a physician; and
e. Access to real and personal property.

If a court issues an order compelling discovery, failure to comply can result in punishment. The party who does not comply may be found in contempt of court or the judge may dismiss the case.

There are other actions which the parties may take after a case has been instituted and before it goes to trial. A party may file a wide variety of motions, including a motion to dismiss the case, a motion for a judgment based solely on the pleadings, and a motion to obtain a ruling on the admissibility of certain evidence or to suppress evidence prior to trial.

4. If there are disagreements about facts of the case, a jury may be impaneled to decide these facts. If neither party requests a jury, the case may be tried before a judge alone, who would act as both judge and jury.

Trial Procedure

A typical jury trial proceeds in the following order:

1. The attorney for the plaintiff makes an opening statement to the jury indicating the nature of the action and what the plaintiff expects to prove. This is usually followed by the opening statement of the defendant's attorney.

2. The plaintiff presents evidence in the form of witnesses and exhibits. This is followed by the defendant's evidence.

3. The attorneys for each side summarize the evidence and argue their points in an attempt to win the jury to their version of the case.

4. The judge instructs the jury as to the points of law which govern the case. The judge has the sole power to determine the points of law, and the jury decides what weight is to be given to each point of evidence.

5. The jury adjourns to the jury room and in secret arrives at its decision called the *verdict*. This verdict may be set aside by the court if it is contrary to the law and the evidence. Unless this is done, the judge enters a judgment in accordance with the verdict.

Appeals

If either the plaintiff or the defendant is dissatisfied with the jury's verdict and the court's judgment and can cite an error of law by the court, an appeal may generally be taken to a higher court. When an appeal is taken, a complete transcript or written record of the trial is given to the appellate court. The appellate court reviews the entire proceedings. The attorney for each side files a brief, setting forth the reasons which warrant the appellate court to either affirm or reverse the judgment of the lower court. The decision of the appellate court becomes judicial precedent and is binding upon lower courts. The appellate court may, however, reverse itself in a future case, although this is seldom done unless the personnel of the court change, and even under those circumstances, reversals seldom occur.

Questions

1. What is the function of a court?

2. What is meant by a court's jurisdiction?

3. The decision of a federal court of appeals is binding upon whom?

4. **a.** Name the largest class of federal courts.
   b. Name two special federal courts.

5. How many court systems are there in each state?

6. Is a decision of a state supreme court binding upon all the lower courts in that state?

7. Name the court in which the following disputes would be settled:
   a. A dispute over the interpretation of a will
   b. A claim for an unpaid bill of $10
   c. The claim of a woman that her ex-husband refuses to support their child
   d. A damage suit for $2,500
   e. An appeal from the decision in the preceding suit
   f. A claim against the federal government

8. Who are the officers of
   a. An inferior court?
   b. A state court of record?
   c. A federal court?

9. **a.** What is the first step in bringing a civil suit?
   b. What is the first step in a civil suit after the jury is impaneled and the trial opens?

10. How much of the proceedings of the trial court is reviewed by an appellate court?

3

Government Regulation of Business

The operation of every business, no matter what type, is affected by governmental rules and regulations. This involvement of government, both state and federal, ranges from the way the business is operated, its prices, and the safety of any products produced to its relationship with its employees. This chapter discusses the way in which government regulates the operation of businesses. Some other aspects of governmental regulation of business are discussed in Chapter 17 (consumer protection) and in Chapters 32 and 33 (employers and employees).

Purpose of Regulation

Government has undertaken the regulation of business in order to eliminate abuses and to regulate conduct considered to be unreasonable. The goal is to enhance the quality of life for society as a whole. This is done by setting the rules under which all businesses compete.

Antitrust

One way in which government regulates business is by means of antitrust laws. These are laws which seek to promote competition among businesses.

The most important antitrust law is the federal Sherman Antitrust Act. This law declares that, "Every contract, combination in the form of trust or otherwise, or conspiracy, in restraint of trade or commerce among the several states, or with foreign nations is . . . illegal."[1] It further provides that anyone who monopolizes or tries to obtain a monopoly in interstate commerce is guilty of a felony.

The Sherman Act applies to commerce or trade between two or more

---

[1]15 U.S.C. §1

states and applies to both buyers and sellers. Most of the states also have antitrust laws, very similar to the Sherman Act, which prohibit restraints of trade within their states.

In interpreting the Sherman Act, the federal courts have said it prohibits only those activities which *unreasonably* restrain trade. This is called the *rule of reason* approach. It means that the courts examine and rule on the anticompetitive effect of a particular activity on a case-by-case basis. The effect of the activity, not the activity itself, is the most important element in deciding whether the Sherman Act has been violated.

However, there are some activities which are illegal under the Sherman Act without regard to their effect. These are called *per se* violations and include price fixing, group boycotts, and horizontal territorial restraints.

There are many activities which may lessen competition. Obviously every business firm seeks to have cooperation within its firm. This is the basis of economic productivity and this is lawful under the antitrust laws. It is only when there is a commitment to a common plan or some type of joint action by separate businesses to restrain trade that an antitrust violation exists.

In addition to the Sherman Act, the federal government has enacted three other important antitrust laws. These are the Clayton Act, the Robinson-Patman Act, and the Federal Trade Commission Act.

The Clayton Act amends the Sherman Act by prohibiting price discrimination to different purchasers where price difference is not due to differences in selling or transportation cost, agreements to sell on the condition that the purchaser shall not use goods of the seller's competitors, ownership of stock or assets in a competing business where the effect may be to substantially lessen competition, and interlocking directorates.

The Robinson-Patman Act, an amendment to the Clayton Act, prohibits price discrimination generally, and geographically for the purpose of eliminating competition. It also prohibits sales at unreasonably low prices in order to eliminate competition. Once a price discrimination has been proved, the person charged with violating the Act must prove the discrimination was justified.

The Federal Trade Commission Act prohibits "unfair methods of competition in commerce, and unfair or deceptive acts or practices in commerce."[2] In addition, this law prohibits false advertising. To prevent these unfair and deceptive practices a federal administrative agency, the Federal Trade Commission, was established.

Administrative Agencies

Many governmental functions are conducted by means of administrative agencies. At the federal level alone there are almost sixty agencies which are

---

[2]45 U.S.C. §45

involved in regulatory activity. The legislative branch of government enacts laws which prescribe the powers that may be exercised by administrative agencies, the principles which are to guide the agencies in exercising those powers, and the legal remedies which are available to those who want to question the legality of some administrative action.

Administrative agencies may be given practically the same power to make law as the legislature and almost the same power to decide cases as the courts. However, agencies are created by laws and have the power to enact law only if that power has been delegated to them by the legislature.

In most cases where administrative agencies are used to regulate, it is because of the complex nature of the area of regulation. Each administrative agency can become a specialist in its particular area of regulation. It can, if necessary, hire scientists and researchers to study industries or problems and set standards which businesses must follow. Administrative agencies conduct research on proposed drugs (the Food and Drug Administration), examine the safety of nuclear-power facilities (the Nuclear Regulatory Commission), certify the wholesomeness of meat and poultry (the Food Safety and Inspection Service), and set standards for aircraft maintenance (the Federal Aviation Administration). In all these areas, research has been necessary to determine what level is safe for the public.

Some agencies investigate industries and propose rules which are designed to promote fairness to the businesses involved and the public. This is true in the area of trading in stocks (the Securities and Exchange Commission), the granting of radio and television licenses (the Federal Communications Commission), and the regulation of banks (the Federal Deposit Insurance Corporation). The legislature thus can set up the guidelines and specify the research to be done, which is then carried out by specialists in the field.

Structure of Administrative Agencies. There are two forms of administrative agencies, depending on the way they are run. Agencies may be run by a single administrator who serves at the pleasure of the executive—either the President of the United States in the case of federal agencies, or the governor in the case of state agencies. Alternatively, agencies may be run by a commission, the members of which are appointed for staggered terms, frequently of five years.

Types of Agencies. The two types of administrative agencies are usually referred to as regulatory and nonregulatory.

Regulatory agencies govern to some degree the economic activity of businesses. They prescribe rules stating what should or should not be done in particular situations. They decide whether a law has been violated in individual cases and then proceed against those violating the law by imposing fines and, in some cases, ordering that the activity be stopped. Agencies such as the Interstate Commerce Commission, the Securities and Exchange

Commission, and the Federal Trade Commission are regulatory-type agencies.

Nonregulatory agencies are set up to dispense benefits for social and economic welfare. They are also called social regulatory agencies because they also issue regulations governing how the benefits are to be distributed. Such agencies would include the Railroad Retirement Board, the Farm Credit Administration, and the Department of Health and Human Services.

Powers of Agencies. Different regulatory agencies have different powers. However, there are three major areas of regulation: licensing power—allowing a business to enter the field being regulated; rate-making power—fixing the prices that a business may charge; and power over business practices—determining whether the activity of the entity regulated is acceptable or not. Agencies such as the Federal Communications Commission, the Nuclear Regulatory Commission, and the Securities and Exchange Commission have licensing power. The Civil Aeronautics Board, the Federal Power Commission, and the Interstate Commerce Commission all have rate-making power. The primary powers of the Federal Trade Commission and the National Labor Relations Board are to control business practices.

Rule Making. The primary way in which administrative agencies set policy is through rule making. The primary focus of the courts, when a rule is challenged, is on the procedures followed by the agency in exercising its rule-making power. The rule-making procedure followed by state agencies is similar to that which must be used by federal agencies.

After investigating a problem, an agency will develop a proposed rule. A federal agency must publish in the *Federal Register* a notice of the proposed rule. This is to allow interested parties the opportunity to comment on the proposed rule. The agency might hold formal hearings on a proposed rule, but the informal *notice and comment* rule making has been more and more common. After time for comments, the proposed rule could be published as proposed, changed, or entirely abandoned by the agency.

State Agencies. While federal administrative agencies affect businesses throughout the country, states also have administrative agencies which affect businesses operated in their states. The most common state agencies are public service commissions, state labor relations boards or commissions, and workers' compensation boards.

Environmental Protection

In recognition of the fact that the environment is the property of everyone, the federal government has enacted a number of laws to protect our environment and has established an agency, the Environmental Protection

Agency (EPA), to administer many of these laws. The most important legislation with which the EPA is concerned are the Clean Air Act, the Clean Water Act, the Safe Drinking Water Act, and the Toxic Substances Control Act.

Under the provisions of the Clean Air Act, the EPA sets minimum national standards for air quality. These standards are for the protection of public health and welfare and are applied and enforced by the states under plans approved by the EPA.

The Clean Water Act requires the states to set standards for water pollution control. However, these standards must be reviewed and approved by the EPA.

The EPA sets national standards for drinking water purity under the Safe Drinking Water Act. The states have the role of enforcing these standards under enforcement programs which must be approved by the EPA.

All three of these laws provide some degree of regulation by both the EPA and the states.

The terms of the Toxic Substances Control Act give the EPA the authority to regulate chemical substances or mixtures if the use of them "presents, or will present, an unreasonable risk of injury to health or the environment." To do this the EPA may, for example, prohibit or limit the production or distribution of the substance, require it to carry warnings, require manufacturers to keep certain data on it, or prohibit or specify disposal methods.

A large number of states have established state agencies to regulate pollution and protect the environment. Anyone contemplating establishing a business which might affect the environment should investigate the applicable laws and regulations.

Questions

1. Why does government regulate business?

2. What activity is declared illegal by the Sherman Antitrust Act?

3. Why are administrative agencies used by government to regulate?

4. Give an example of two agencies which regulate the economic activity of businesses.

5. What are the three types of powers possessed by regulatory agencies?

6. What must a federal agency do with a proposed rule before the rule can become effective?

Part Two — Contracts

Learning Objectives for Part Two

Contracts

After studying this part you should be able to:

1. Describe what a contract is and how it differs from an agreement.
2. List and describe the different types of contracts.
3. Explain the requirements for a valid offer and acceptance.
4. State what types of mistakes invalidate contracts.
5. Identify the situations in which fraud, duress, or undue influence are present.
6. Identify the situations in which parties do not have the capacity to contract.
7. Define consideration.
8. Recognize when consideration is not required.
9. Explain what types of contracts are void for illegality.
10. Identify which contracts must be in writing.
11. Distinguish adequate from inadequate writings when a written contract is required.
12. List exceptions to the requirement for written contracts.
13. Explain the difference between assignment of a contract and delegation of duties under it.
14. Explain the effects of an assignment and the difference between an assignment and a novation.
15. Describe the different types of contracts involving more than two persons.
16. List the methods of terminating contracts.
17. Explain the potential liabilities for breach of contract.

4 Contracts—Nature and Classes

Preview Cases

Mary and John promise to meet at a certain place at 6 P.M. and have dinner together. Is this an enforceable contract?

Richardson hired the J. C. Flood Co. to correct a blocked sewer line. When part of the line in the backyard was excavated, many leaks were found in a rusty, defective water pipe which ran parallel to the sewer line. To meet water district regulations the pipe had to be replaced. If Richardson did not have the pipe replaced while it was exposed for the sewer-line repair, the yard would have to be redug to replace the pipe at a later time. Flood told Richardson this and replaced the line. Richardson knew the line was being replaced but later objected to paying for it. Was there an implied contract to replace the water line?

A *contract* can be defined as a legally enforceable agreement between two or more competent persons. At first glance this seems like a very simple definition, but Chapters 4–12 are devoted exclusively to explaining and clarifying this definition. Making contracts is such an everyday occurrence that we are often inclined to overlook its importance, except when the contracts are of substantial nature. When one buys a cup of coffee during a coffee break, a contract has been made. When the purchaser agrees to pay 35¢ for the coffee, the seller agrees not only to supply one cup of coffee but also agrees by implication of law that it is safe to drink. If the coffee contains a harmful substance that makes the purchaser ill, there has been a breach of contract that may call for the payment of damages.

Business transactions are the result of agreements. Every time a person makes a purchase, buys a theater ticket, or boards a bus, an agreement is made. Each party to the agreement obtains certain rights and assumes certain duties and obligations. When such an agreement meets all the legal requirements of a contract, the law recognizes it as binding upon all parties. If one of the parties to the contract breaches it by failing or refusing to perform, the law allows the other party an appropriate action for obtaining damages or enforcing performance by the party breaching the contract.

Contracts form the very foundation upon which all modern business rests. Business consists almost entirely of the making and performing of contracts.

Contracts Contrasted with Agreements

A contract must be an agreement, but an agreement is not necessarily a contract. Whenever two or more persons' minds meet upon any subject, no matter how trivial, there is an agreement. It is only when the parties intend to be legally obligated by the terms of the agreement that a contract comes into existence. Ordinarily, the subject matter of the contract must involve a business transaction as distinguished from a purely social transaction.

Mary and John promise to meet at a certain place at 6 P.M. and have dinner together. This is an agreement, not a contract, since neither intends to be legally bound to carry out the terms of the agreement.

If Alice says to David, "I will pay you $25 to be my escort for the Spring Ball," and David replies, "I accept your offer," the agreement results in a contract. David is legally obligated to provide escort service, and Alice is legally bound to pay the $25.

Classification of Contracts

Contracts are classified by many names or terms. Unless you understand these terms, you cannot understand the law of contracts. For example, the law may state that executory contracts made on Sunday are void. You cannot understand this law unless you understand the words "executory" and "void." Every contract may be placed in one or more of the following classifications:

1. Express and implied contracts
2. Valid contracts, void agreements, and voidable contracts
3. Formal and simple contracts
4. Executory and executed contracts
5. Unilateral and bilateral contracts

Express and Implied Contracts. When contracts are classified according to the manner of their formation, they fall into two groups—express and implied contracts. An *express contract* is one in which the parties express their intentions by words, whether in writing or orally, at the time they make the agreement. Both their intention to contract and the terms of the agreement are expressly stated or written.

Osai by letter offers to purchase a particular typewriter for $300, and Sampson by letter accepts Osai's offer. This is an express contract. An analysis of the contract, however, shows that many essential parts have been omitted. Is this a cash sale or a credit sale? When is delivery to be made? Since nothing is said about credit, it is implied that the buyer will pay cash. The seller implied he would deliver the typewriter within a reasonable time. Terms which are customary need not be expressed in an express contract.

An *implied contract* is one in which the duties and the obligations which the parties assume are not expressed but are implied by their acts or conduct. The adage "actions speak louder than words" very appropriately describes this class of contracts. The parties may indicate so clearly by their conduct what they intend to do that there is no need to express the agreement by words to make it binding.

Richardson hired the J. C. Flood Co. to correct a blocked sewer line. Part of the line in the backyard was excavated and many leaks were found in a rusty, defective water pipe which ran parallel to the sewer line. To meet water district regulations the pipe had to be replaced. If Richardson did not have the pipe replaced while it was exposed for the sewer-line repair, the yard would have to be redug to replace the pipe at a later time. Flood told Richardson this and replaced the line. Richardson objected to paying for it. The court found that since Richardson inspected the work daily, knew the magnitude of the work being done, and made no objection until the work was done, there was an implied contract to replace the water line.

Valid Contracts, Void Agreements, and Voidable Contracts.

If one wishes to classify agreements according to their enforceability, then they would be valid contracts, void agreements, or voidable contracts.

A *valid contract* is one that will be enforced by the courts. Such a contract must fulfill the following definite requirements:

1. It must be based upon a mutual agreement by the parties to do or not to do a specific thing.

2. It must be made by parties who are competent to enter into a contract that will be enforceable against both parties.

3. The promise or obligation of each party must be supported by consideration (such as the payment of money, the delivery of goods, or the promise to do or refrain from doing some lawful future act) given by each party to the contract.

4. It must be for a lawful purpose; that is, the purpose of the contract must not be illegal, such as the unauthorized buying and selling of narcotics.

5. In some cases, the contract must meet certain formal requirements, such as being in writing or under seal.

These five requirements are the criteria by which one may test the validity of any contract. If the agreement fails to meet one or more of these requirements, the agreement may be void or the contract may be voidable but never valid.

An agreement that is of no legal effect is *void*. Since there is no contract in the first place, the agreement is not enforceable in a court of law and thus does not come within the definition of a contract. A void agreement (sometimes referred to as a *void contract*) must be distinguished from an *unenforceable contract*. If the law requires a certain contract to be in a particular form, such as a deed to be in writing, and it is not in that form, it is merely unenforceable, not void; but it can be made enforceable by changing the form to meet the requirements of the law. An agreement between two parties to perform an illegal act is void. Nothing the parties can do will make this agreement an enforceable contract.

Basically, a *voidable contract* would be an enforceable agreement; but, because of circumstances or the capacity of one party, it may be set aside by one of the parties. The distinguishing factor of a voidable contract is the existence of a choice by one party to abide by or to reject the contract. A contract made by an adult with a person not of lawful age (legally known as a minor or infant) is often voidable by the minor. It is enforceable against the adult but not against the minor. If both parties to an agreement are minors, either one may avoid the agreement. Until the party having the choice to avoid the contract exercises the right to set the contract aside, the contract remains in full force and effect.

Formal and Simple Contracts.

A contract which must be in a special form or be created in a certain way is a *formal contract*. Formal contracts include contracts under seal, recognizances, and negotiable instruments.

When very few people could write, contracts were signed by means of an impression in wax attached to the paper. As time passed, a small wafer pasted on the contract replaced the use of wax. The wafer seal was in addition to the written signature. This practice is still used occasionally, but the more common practice is to sign formal contracts in one of these ways:

Jane Doe (Seal); Jane Doe [L. S.]

Today, it is immaterial whether these substitutes for a seal are printed on the document, typewritten before signing, or the persons signing write them after their respective names. In jurisdictions where the use of the seal has not been abolished, the seal implies consideration.

In some states the presence of a seal on a contract allows a party a longer time in which to bring suit if the contract is broken. Other states make no distinction between contracts under seal and other written contracts. The Uniform Commercial Code abolishes the distinction with respect to contracts for the sale of goods.

Recognizances, a second type of formal contract, are obligations entered into before a court whereby persons acknowledge they will do a specified act which is required by law. The persons acknowledge that they will be indebted for a specific amount if they do not perform as they agreed. One type of recognizance is the obligation undertaken by a criminal defendant to appear in court on a particular day.

Negotiable instruments, discussed in later chapters, are a third type of formal contract. They include checks, notes, drafts, and certificates of deposit.

All contracts other than formal contracts are informal and are called *simple contracts*. A few of these, such as an agreement to sell land or to be responsible for the debt of another, must be in writing in order to be enforceable; otherwise they need not be prepared in any particular form. Generally speaking, informal or simple contracts may be in writing, may be oral, or may be implied from the conduct of the parties.

A *written contract* is one in which the terms are set forth in writing rather than expressed orally. An *oral contract* is one in which the terms are stated in spoken, not written, words. Such a contract is usually enforceable, but it is not as satisfactory as a written contract. When a contract is oral, disputes may arise between the parties as to the terms of the agreement. No such disputes need arise about the terms of a written contract if the wording is clear, explicit, and complete. For this reason most businesspeople avoid making oral contracts involving matters of very great importance.

Executory and Executed Contracts. Contracts are classified to indicate the stage of performance as executory contracts and executed contracts. An *executory contract* is one in which the terms have not been fully carried out by all parties. If a person agrees to work for another for one year in return for a salary of $950 a month, the contract is executory from its inception until the twelve months expire. Even if the employer should prepay the salary, it would still be an executory contract because the other party has not yet worked the entire year, that is, executed that part of the contract.

An *executed contract* is one that has been fully performed by all parties to the contract. The Collegiate Shop sells and delivers a dress to Benson for $85, and Benson pays the purchase price at the time of the sale. This is an executed contract because nothing remains to be done on either side; that is, each party has completed performance of each part of the contract.

Unilateral and Bilateral Contracts. When an act is done in consideration for a promise, the contract is a *unilateral contract*. If Smith loans Fink $1,000 and Fink promises to repay the loan in ninety days, this would be a unilateral contract. It is unilateral in the promise made. Fink promises to pay Smith for the act of loaning the $1,000. A *bilateral contract* consists of a mutual exchange of promises to perform some future acts—one promise is the consideration for the other promise. If Brown promises to sell a truck to Adams for $500 and Adams agrees to pay $500, then the parties have exchanged a promise for a promise—a bilateral contract.

Questions

1. Would it be possible to conduct a business if it were not for the law of contracts?

2. Explain the difference between a contract and a social agreement.

3. What is the difference between an express and an implied contract?

4. Relative to the enforceability of agreements, name the three groups into which they are classified. Define and give an example of each group.

5. Name the five requirements of a valid contract.

6. **a.** Illustrate two ways by which one may indicate that a contract is under seal.
   b. Does a seal add anything of importance to a contract?

7. Do the terms *oral, simple,* and *informal* contracts refer to the same types of agreements?

8. **a.** Define an executory contract.
   b. Define an executed contract.

9. What is the difference between a unilateral and a bilateral contract?

Case Problems

When the concluding question in a case problem can be answered simply Yes or No, state the legal principle or rule of law which supports your answer.

1. An irrigation district had a salary schedule with five steps—each step providing a higher wage. The announced practice of the district was to annually review each employee's work. Those who merited it would be advanced to the next step. This practice was adopted by the district after negotiations with the employees' union. Youngman was employed by the district and after a year was advanced one step, as were almost all the employees. The next year the district refused to advance any employees and discontinued its previously published, announced, and effected annual review. Youngman sued the district, claiming there was an implied contract for review and advancement. Was there?

2. There was an agreement between the state welfare board and the state hospital association to provide hospital care for welfare patients according to a rate schedule. In April the association told the board the schedule would have to be adjusted for all hospitals effective July 1. The welfare department prepared an adjustment. The association did not agree to it. Another adjustment was finally made and agreed to in September, but it did not cover July and August. The Bismarck Hospital Association, which had furnished hospital services to welfare patients, sued for the reasonable value of its services. The claim was for

more than the amount provided in the original schedule. Was the new schedule an implied contract for the months of July and August?

3. In a certain state all executory contracts made on Sunday are void. Bell purchased a pair of shoes from Reese on Sunday, had them wrapped, and paid for them but asked Reese to hold them until Tuesday for him. On Tuesday he refused to take the shoes and demanded a return of his money. To determine the rights of the parties it was necessary to classify this contract. Was it an executed contract or an executory contract?

4. Harper was a real estate broker. She entered into a contract with Cohen to sell Cohen's house for $65,000. Cohen was to pay Harper a commission of 5 percent "when the sale is consummated." The law required all contracts for the sale of land to be written. Must this contract be written to be enforceable?

5. Gill entered into a verbal agreement to install sound equipment at a club. A written agreement was prepared for the club to sign, but it was never executed. After the equipment was installed, the club told Gill to bill the manufacturer of the equipment, who would pay Gill. Gill billed only the manufacturer. With Gill's knowledge, in March and May the club made payments to the manufacturer. When Gill was not paid he sued the manufacturer, who then went bankrupt and never paid him anything. He sued the club. Was there an enforceable contract between Gill and the club?

6. Kathleen was invited to a formal dance. Her mother engaged Mrs. Schwartz to make an evening dress for Kathleen for $150. After the dress was finished but before it was delivered, Kathleen's boyfriend canceled the invitation. Her mother then refused to accept and pay for the dress, claiming the transaction was a social obligation, not a business transaction. Do you agree with this interpretation?

5

Offer and Acceptance

Preview Cases

Hall and Escabedo were rowing in a boat. The boat overturned. Hall could not swim. She called to Escabedo, "I will give you my sports car if you will save me." Escabedo risked her life to save Hall. Later Hall refused to give Escabedo the car. Is she obligated to do so?

Stauffer Chemical Co. had a severance pay policy embodied in instructions furnished to its management and not published or disseminated to other employees. The granting of severance pay was a voluntary, gratuitous benefit to be determined solely by Stauffer. It was not discussed with prospective employees. Stauffer sold its plant. Thirty-three former employees sued for severance pay. Was the granting of severance pay an offer which could have been accepted by the former employees?

A valid contract is created by the agreement of the parties. This agreement is reached when one party makes an offer and the other party accepts the offer.

The parties may expressly state, either orally or in writing, what they agree to do, or they may indicate their intentions by their actions. If A's conduct reasonably leads B to believe that A intends to enter into a binding contract, then A is bound as effectively as if the contract had been expressed. However, in business, a person seldom indicates every intention solely by acts. In most cases only a part of the contract is expressed and the other part is implied.

Furthermore, one may have rights and obligations imposed by law when no real contract exists. This imposition of rights and obligations is called a *quasi contract*. Rights and obligations will be imposed only when a failure to do so would result in an unjust enrichment of one person at the expense of another. For example, suppose a tenant is obligated to pay rent of $300 a month but by mistake hands the landlord $400. The law requires the landlord to return the overpayment of $100. The law creates an agreement for repayment even though no agreement exists. For the landlord to keep the money would mean an unjust enrichment at the expense of the tenant.

Two essential elements of a contract are: (1) an offer, either expressed or implied; and (2) an acceptance, either expressed or implied.

Requirements of a Valid Offer

The beginning of a contract is the offer. The *offeror* is the person who makes the offer; the *offeree* is the person to whom the offer is made. An *offer* expresses the willingness of the offeror to enter into a contractual agreement. There are three requirements of a valid offer:

1. The offer must be definite
2. It must be seriously intended
3. It must be communicated to the offeree

The Offer Must Be Definite. A contract will not be enforced unless the court can ascertain what the parties agreed to. The offeror's intentions are ascertained from the offer, and the intentions cannot be ascertained unless the offer is definite.

Diversified Contractors agreed to build a warehouse for Fritz. Diversified then negotiated with the Bank of Marion to borrow the money required for the construction. The bank told Diversified that to get the loan Fritz would have to make the checks due Diversified for the construction payable to Diversified and the bank. Diversified prepared an instrument titled "Certification of Contract" which Fritz signed. It stated it was to confirm the contract between Fritz and Diversified in the amount of $115,409 which ". . . amount . . . will be made jointly to the Bank of Marion and Diversified Contractors, Inc." Fritz was never informed that the bank was loaning money on his contract with Diversified. He issued checks payable only to Diversified, and it did not pay off its loan to the bank. The bank claimed Fritz had contracted to make the payments jointly to it and Diversified. The court held the instrument which was undated, recited no consideration, and contained no reference to anything to be done by the bank was not a definite offer so could not be the basis of a contract between the bank and Fritz.

The Uniform Commercial Code modifies this strict rule somewhat as to contracts for the sale of goods. It is not always practical for a businessperson to make an offer for the sale of merchandise that is definite as to price. The offeror may state that the price will be determined by the market price at a future date or by a third party. If the contract does not specify the price, the buyer must ordinarily pay the reasonable value of the goods.

The Offer Must Be Seriously Intended. One may make an offer in jest, banter, fear, or extreme anger; and if this fact is known or should be known by the offeree because of the surrounding circumstances, no contract is formed. A business transaction is ordinarily not entered into in jest or because of extreme fear or anger, and the offeree has no right to think that the offer is seriously intended when it is made under these circumstances. There are times, however, when the offer is not seriously intended, but the offeree has no way of knowing this. In that event, if the offer is accepted, a binding contract results. These points are illustrated in the following examples.

◆   Hall and Escabedo were rowing in a boat. The boat overturned. Hall could not swim. She called to Escabedo, "I will give you my sports car if you will save me." Escabedo risked her own life to save Hall. Hall refused to give Escabedo the sports car. She was within her rights. An offer clearly made under extreme emotional circumstances is not a valid offer.

As previously noted, the secret thoughts of a party have no effect. If the offeree has reason to think that the offer is made in earnest and accepts it, a binding contract will result even though the offer is made in jest.

◆   Lucy said to Zehmer, "I bet you wouldn't take $50,000 for . . ." the Ferguson farm. Zehmer replied, "Yes, I would, too; you wouldn't give $50." Lucy said he would and told Zehmer to write up an agreement to that effect. Zehmer took a restaurant check and wrote on the back that he agreed to sell it. Lucy told him he needed to change the "I" to "We" because Mrs. Zehmer would have to sign it, too, and add a provision for having the title examined. Zehmer wrote on another check, "We hereby agree to sell to W. O. Lucy the Ferguson Farm complete for $50,000, title satisfactory to buyer." He and his wife both signed it and Lucy took it with him. Zehmer later said he and Lucy had been drinking and the discussion about selling the farm was only a joke. The court held Zehmer's actions appeared to be a good faith acceptance of Lucy's offer, so he was bound by the contract.

The Offer Must Be Communicated to the Offeree. Until the offeror makes the offer known to the offeree, it is not certain that it is intended that the offeree may accept and thereby impose a binding contract. Accordingly, an offer cannot be accepted by the offeree until the offeror has communicated the offer to the offeree. If one writes out an offer and the offer falls into the hands of the offeree without the knowledge or consent of the offeror, it cannot be accepted. Furthermore, an offer directed to a specific individual or firm cannot be accepted by anyone else. This is true because people have a right to choose the parties with whom they deal.

◆   Stauffer Chemical Co. had a severance pay policy embodied in written instructions furnished to its management and not published or disseminated to other employees. The granting of severance pay was a voluntary, gratuitous benefit to be determined solely by Stauffer. It was not discussed with prospective employees. Stauffer sold its plant. Thirty-three former employees sued for severance pay. The court found that there had not been communication of an offer of severance pay to the former employees; thus, there was no contract to pay it.

Invitations to Make Offers

In business many apparent offers are not true offers. Instead they are treated as invitations to the public to make offers at certain terms and prices. If the invitation is accepted by a member of the public and an offer is submitted embodying all the terms set out in the invitation, the inviter may refuse to accept the offer; ordinarily, however, as a practical matter and in the interest of maintaining goodwill, such an offer will be accepted. The most common types of general invitations are advertisements, window displays, catalogs, price lists, and circular sales letters. If a merchant displays in a store window a coat for $95, there is no binding requirement to sell at this price. Most businesspeople would consider refusal to sell a very poor business policy, but it is nevertheless a protection which the law gives businesspeople who might otherwise find that they oversold their stocks of goods and would thereby be subjected to many suits for breach of contract.

◆   Morrison's Shirt Shop placed a shirt with a price tag of $8.95 in the store window. Stephen saw the shirt and offered to purchase it at that price. The price, in fact, was in error; it should have been $18.95. The store would not sell the shirt at $8.95 and raised the price in the window to $18.95. There was no contract between Morrison's and Stephen since the window display was a mere invitation to Stephen to make an offer.

The general rule is that a circular sales letter is not an offer but an invitation to the recipient to make an offer. It is often difficult however, to distinguish between a general sales letter and a personal sales letter. The fact that the letter is addressed to a particular individual does not necessarily make it a personal sales letter containing an offer. If the wording is such as to indicate that the writer is merely trying to evoke an offer on certain terms, it is an invitation to the other party to make an offer.

◆   Landis wrote Poliuka: "If I were offered $50,000 for my house, I would be delighted to sell." Poliuka immediately wrote that he accepted the offer. There was no contract because there was no offer that could be accepted. Landis was merely inviting Poliuka to make an offer.

An advertisement, however, may be an offer when it clearly shows it is intended as an offer. This is primarily true with advertisements that offer rewards.

◆ Foster placed the following ad in the newspaper: "I will pay $1,000 to anyone giving information leading to the arrest and conviction of the person who set fire to my property." Brewer saw the ad and set out to find the guilty party. As a result of Brewer's information, Dunnaway was arrested and tried. There was strong circumstantial evidence of his guilt, but the jury acquitted him. Brewer demanded her $1,000. Although his ad was an offer, Foster did not have to pay because his ad set forth two conditions, namely, that the guilty part be "arrested" and "convicted." Since Dunnaway was not convicted, Foster did not have to pay.

Duration of the Offer

There are several rules regarding the duration of an offer.
1. The offeror may revoke an offer any time prior to its acceptance.

◆ Richards, a real estate broker, found a prospective buyer, Baker, for Simpson's mining claims. Simpson had escrow instructions prepared which provided that they were to be signed by the buyer. They were not signed by Baker. However, Richards sent Simpson different escrow instructions, signed by Baker, which required an access road. Simpson did not agree to the access road. On April 2 Simpson cancelled the first escrow instructions and the listing of the property with Richards. On April 14 Baker signed new escrow instructions containing Simpson's original offer, but Simpson refused to sell. The court held Baker's acceptance of Simpson's offer was too late because the offer had been withdrawn.

2. The offer may state that it will be held open for a particular time. Ordinarily the offer may be revoked in spite of such a provision. However, if the offeror receives something in return for the promise to hold the offer open, it is said to be an option and the offer cannot be revoked. If the offer relates to the sale or purchase of goods by a merchant, a signed written offer to purchase or sell which states that it will be held open cannot be revoked during the time stated or if no time is stated, for a reasonable time, not to exceed three months.

In states in which the seal has its common-law effect, an offer cannot be revoked when it is contained in a sealed writing which states that it will not be revoked.

3. A revocation of an offer must be communicated to the offeree prior to the acceptance. Mere intention to revoke is not sufficient. This is true even though the intent is clearly shown to persons other than the offeree, as when the offeror dictates a letter of revocation.

Notice to the offeree that the subject matter of the offer has been sold to another party revokes the offer.

◆ Davis wrote the Towns Tire Company offering to lease them a building for five years for $800 a month. She gave thirty days to accept or reject the offer. Ten days later Davis leased the building to the Bell Tire Company and the Towns Tire Company learned of this lease. This revoked the offer to the Towns Tire Company. It is irrelevant how the revocation is communicated to the offeree as long as the notice is communicated before the offeree accepts.

4. An offer is revoked by the lapse of the time specified in the offer. If no time is specified in the offer, it is revoked by a lapse of a reasonable time after being communicated to the offeree. What is a reasonable length of time varies with each case depending on the circumstances. It may be ten minutes in one case and sixty days in another. Important circumstances are whether the price of the goods or services involved are fluctuating rapidly, or whether perishable goods are involved, and whether there is keen competition with respect to the subject matter of the contract.

A New Orleans cotton broker wrote the Gulf Textile Company as follows: "Because of the unstable world conditions, I am anxious to dispose of my stock of cotton. I will take $165 a bale f.o.b. New Orleans." The Gulf Textile Company waited 25 days and then accepted. The offer had lapsed since its wording clearly indicated that the offeror wanted an immediate reply.

5. Death or insanity of the offeror automatically revokes the offer. This is true even though the offeree is not aware of the death or the insanity of the offeror and communicates an acceptance of the offer. Both parties must be alive and competent to contract at the moment the acceptance is properly communicated to the offeror.

6. Rejection of the offer by the offeree and communication of the rejection to the offeror terminates the offer.

7. If, after an offer has been made, the performance of the contract becomes illegal, the offer is terminated.

The Acceptance

When an offer has been properly communicated to the party for whom it is intended and that party or an authorized agent accepts, a binding contract is formed. The acceptance must be communicated to the offeror, but no particular procedure is required. The acceptance may be made by words, oral or written, or by some act which clearly shows an intention to accept. Silence does not, except in rare cases, constitute an acceptance; nor is a mental intention to accept sufficient. If the offer stipulates a particular mode of acceptance, the offeree must meet those standards in order for a contract to be formed.

Counteroffers

An offer must be accepted without any deviation in its terms. If the intended acceptance varies or qualifies the offer, this is a *counteroffer* and is a rejection of the original offer. This rule is changed to some extent where the offer relates to the sale or purchase of goods. In any case, a counteroffer may be accepted or rejected by the original offeror.

◆   The Schoonovers offered to sell some real estate to Nance for $17,000 in cash. Nance told the Schoonovers he intended to give them a personal check in the amount of $17,000 to pay for the property. Since the offer specified payment in cash, not by personal check, Nance's statement was a counteroffer. The Schoonovers could either accept or reject this counteroffer.

Inquiries Not Constituting Rejection

The offeree may make an inquiry without rejecting the offer. For example, if the offer is for 1,000 shares of stock for $20,000 cash, the offeree may inquire as follows: "Would you be willing to wait thirty days for $10,000 and hold the stock as collateral security?" This is a mere inquiry and is not a rejection of the offer. If the inquiry is answered in the negative, the original offer may still be accepted, if it has not been revoked in the meantime.

Offers and Acceptances by Correspondence

When an offer is made by mail, the offeror may stipulate that the acceptance must be written and received by the offeror in order to be effective. However, an offer which does not specify a particular manner of acceptance may be accepted in any manner reasonable under the circumstances. If there is no requirement of delivery, a mailed acceptance is effective when the acceptance is properly mailed; this rule applies even though the acceptance is never received by the offeror.

Similarly the delivery of an acceptance to the telegraph company is effective unless the offeror specifies otherwise or unless custom or prior dealings indicate that acceptance by telegraph is improper. In former years it was held that an offer could be accepted only by the same means by which the offer was communicated. But this view is being abandoned in favor of the provision of the Uniform Commercial Code, Sec. 2-206(1)(a), relating to sales of goods: "Unless otherwise unambiguously indicated by the language or circumstances, an offer to make a [sales] contract shall be construed as inviting acceptance in any manner and by any medium reasonable in the circumstances."

Careful and prudent persons can avoid many difficulties by stipulating in the offer how it must be accepted and when the acceptance is to become effective. For example, the offer may state, "The acceptance must be sent by letter and be received by me in Chicago by 12 noon on June 15 before the

Sults for #153 - invitation not an offer

contract is complete." The acceptance is not effective unless it is sent by letter and is actually received by the offeror in Chicago by the time specified.

◆   Taul owned a negotiable option to purchase 500 shares of stock in a uranium company at $12 a share. He wrote ten letters to ten different people offering to sell the option for $1,000. Three of these parties immediately accepted. Taul could be sued by two of them for breach of contract because he can sell to only one. He should have included a protective clause in the offer such as, "contract not to become effective until acceptance acknowledged by me."

Questions

1. What is a *quasi contract*?

2. What are the three requirements of a valid offer?

3. Under what conditions may one accept an offer that is made in the form of a newspaper advertisement?

4. What is an option?

5. How is a "reasonable time" after which an offer would "lapse" determined?

6. **a.** When may an offer be revoked?
   b. What is the effect of death or insanity of the offeror?

7. What particular procedure is required for communicating an acceptance to the offeror?

8. What is the effect of a counteroffer?

9. If an offer by letter is received and the recipient wishes to accept the offer, may the acceptance be by letter or by telegram? When would the acceptance be effective?

10. If an offer is made by telegram and the acceptance is sent by letter, when is the contract formed?

Case Problems

1. Carr agreed to sell specific property to the Savins for $18,500 plus a down payment which was to be the Savins' efforts in restoring the property. The sale was to be made when the Savins had paid one-third of the purchase price. They did substantial work on restoration and made monthly payments for which Carr gave receipts reciting the payments were to apply towards purchase of the prop-

erty. Carr later claimed the agreement was too indefinite as to time of performance and price to be binding. Was it?

2. Dawson, the sales manager for the Builders Supply Company, offered to sell Dobbs Brothers 500 gallons of paint at $6 per gallon. On October 1, Dobbs Brothers accepted by letter with a stipulation that the paint was to be delivered fifty gallons a week. No reply was ever made to this acceptance. Was there a contract?

3. Carrol was arrested by the police and put in jail for an attempted robbery. Samuel saw a picture of Carrol in the local paper and recognized him as a suspect wanted for robbery in a distant city. There was a reward of $5,000 for "arrest and conviction." Samuel called the police department in the distant city and informed them that Carrol was in a local jail. She demanded the reward of $5,000. Was she entitled to it? *- must wait for Conviction*

4. Medicine Shops Inc. (MSI) offered to allow Jayco to use MSI's trademark, trade name, logo, and services. On January 18, Jayco wrote a letter to MSI accepting its offer. Although properly addressed, stamped, and mailed on January 20, the letter was never delivered. On January 19, MSI wrote and mailed a letter to Jayco revoking the offer. This letter was received by Jayco on January 21. Was there a contract?

5. A local corporation formed for the purpose of drilling for oil went out of business. The stock was considered by all the townspeople to be absolutely worthless. Hipps, the owner of 1,000 shares of this stock, offered to sell them to Hurley for 10 cents a share. Hurley accepted. A few minutes later a radio report stated that oil had been discovered on a tract of land adjoining the property of the defunct corporation. Hipps refused to sell Hurley the stock, claiming the offer was made in jest. Was there a contract?

6. Joel wrote Broadnax a letter, offering to sell him a tract of real estate owned by Joel. Twenty-four hours later Joel sold the land to Ledbetter without waiting to hear from Broadnax. As soon as Broadnax received Joel's offer, he accepted. Joel contended that his selling the land to Ledbetter was a revocation of his offer to Broadnax. Do you agree?

7. Lynch received a contract to teach for the following school year. She signed the contract and delivered it to Chinn, the vice-president of the school board, in a sealed envelope. Chinn took it to the school board meeting that evening and gave it to the secretary. Miner, the school superintendent, announced Lynch had returned the contract unsigned and recommended she be notified her services would be terminated at the end of the current school year. The board approved that recommendation. After the meeting, the secretary opened the envelope. When sued by Lynch, the board alleged there was no contract because its offer had been withdrawn before it was accepted. Was there a contract?

6

Defective Agreements

Merritt had a survey made and used the description from the survey to convey the land to McIntyre. The surveyors had made a mistake and the description included more property than Merritt had intended. McIntyre had used the survey to have the land appraised so he would know what to pay for it. Did the mistake in the description invalidate the contract?

Greenspan and Jacobsen built a duplex on a foundation which was constructed in violation of the building code. It was inadequate to sustain the weight of the building. Massive cracks and severe settlement ensued. They had plasterboard erected in the basement to cover the cracks. They then sold the duplex to Haberman and Ericksen. When the cracks and settlement were discovered, the buyers sought to invalidate the contract. May they?

As a general rule, a mistake made by one party without the knowledge of the other—a unilateral mistake—has no effect on the validity of the contract. A mistake made by both parties regarding a material fact—a mutual mistake—usually makes a contract void because there is no genuine assent.

Mistakes That Make Agreements Defective

Mistakes that make agreements defective are:

1. Mistakes as to the nature of the transaction
2. Mistakes as to the identity of the party
3. Mutual mistakes as to the identity of the subject matter
4. Mutual mistakes as to the existence of the subject matter

Mistakes as to the Nature of the Transaction. A mistake as to the nature of the transaction renders the contract void if the mistake was caused by the fraud of the other contracting party. If, through trickery, a person is induced to sign a deed under the impression it is a note, the signature is not binding. But to avoid a contract on the ground of mistake, the party attempting to avoid the contract must not have been negligent. A person signing a contract without reading it and without taking reasonable steps to learn what it means may be prevented from claiming that the contract is void. A person who is unable to read should have someone read and explain the paper.

◆ Moore and Kinnaman opened an account in a savings and loan association with $17,000 of Kinnaman's money. The signature card supplied by the association stated the signatories were "joint tenants with right of survivorship" and "any funds placed in . . . the account by any one of the parties is and shall be conclusively intended to be a gift . . . to the other signatory." Kinnaman was of sound mind and had the opportunity and ability to read the card but did not. After she died the court held that her mistake in failing to read the card did not invalidate the terms of the agreement on this card and the money went to Moore.

Mistakes as to the Identity of the Party. Freedom of contract includes among other things the freedom to choose the parties with whom one contracts. With but rare exceptions, the law does not compel people to contract with a person with whom they do not wish to deal. If one is mistaken as to the identity of the party with whom a contract is made, then the contract is void. When the mistake as to the identity of a party is induced by trick or deception, however, the contract is voidable and may be set aside by the deceived party.

If people contract with others in face-to-face relationships, they are presumed to have intended to contract with these particular individuals even though they thought they were dealing with someone else. Even if the other party said, "I am Charles Greene," when in fact he was Francis Barlow, the contract would be valid if the party was mistaken only as to the person's name, not his real identity. If the dealing is at a distance, however, and the other party falsely pretends to be someone else, the contract is void. Under these circumstances it cannot be ascertained through reasonable diligence that a mistake was made.

If the mistake as to the identity of the party involves an executory contract, then the remedy consists merely of refusing to perform the contract. If it is executed, then an innocent party may rescind the contract by returning anything of value which has been received and demanding that the other party do likewise. The law requires that, as far as possible, both parties be restored to their prior positions.

◆   Holden had once been defrauded by a salesman for the Handy Book Company. A salesman for the Handy Book Company later called on Holden to sell her a set of encyclopedias. The salesman knew of Holden's extreme distaste for the Handy Book Company. For this reason, he told Holden the encyclopedias were published by the United Book Company. Holden agreed to buy the books. When they arrived she learned the true identity of the publisher. She rescinded the contract, demanding return of her money. She was within her rights.

Mutual Mistakes as to the Identity of the Subject Matter. To make an agreement defective, mistakes as to the identity of the subject matter of a contract must be mutual. If parties do not have in mind the same subject matter, their minds can never meet; thus, there can be no contract. For example, if A offers to sell and B agrees to buy "all the pulpwood on my Barnett Shoals Road farm" and A has two farms on that road, the parties may not have the same farm in mind. This cannot become a binding contract until the farm described in the offer is clearly identified.

◆   Biddle was the purchasing agent for a steel mill. She called on the Loef Brothers Scrap Iron Company to purchase scrap iron. There were two piles of several hundred tons each, one valued at 4 cents a pound and the other at 6 cents. The seller pointed directly at the 6-cents scrap and said, "This is the 4-cents pile of scrap iron." Biddle purchased it. Later the seller learned of his error in identifying the cheaper pile of scrap. It was too late. Since there was no mistake as to the pile to which he pointed, the contract was binding.

Mutual Mistakes as to the Existence of the Subject Matter. If two parties enter into a contract relative to a specific subject matter, but at the moment of the contract this specific subject matter does not exist, the contract is void. Such a mistake most often arises when the subject matter of the contract has been destroyed by flood, fire, tornado, or other means, but its destruction is unknown to either party when the contract is formed.

◆   Smith agreed to sell 5,000 identified railroad ties to the Missouri Pacific Railroad. Prior to the contract but unknown to either party, the ties had been destroyed by a forest fire. The contract was void since the agreement was based on the assumed existence of a specific lot of 5,000 railroad ties as contrasted with a contract to supply any 5,000 ties of a particular grade.

It is evident from these four classes of mistakes that it is not the function of the law to save us from the consequences of all mistakes. These four classes of mistakes cover a very small percentage of those made in business transactions. Knowledge and diligence, not law, are the chief bulwarks against losses due to mistakes.

Mistakes That Do Not Make Agreements Defective

The types of mistakes which do not affect the validity of the contract are:

1. Mistakes as to value, quality, or price
2. Mistakes as to the terms of the contract

Mistakes as to Value, Quality, or Price. A contract is not affected by the fact that one of the parties was mistaken as to the value, quality, or price of the subject matter of the contract. If buyers do not trust their judgment, they have the right to demand a warranty from the seller as to the quality, quantity, or the value of the articles they are buying. Their ability to contract wisely is their chief protection against a bad bargain. If Snead sells Robinson a television set for $350, Robinson cannot rescind the contract merely because the set proved to be worth only $150. This is a mistake as to value and quality. Robinson should obtain as a part of the contract an express warranty as to the set's quality. Conversely, if the seller parts with a jewel for $50, thinking it is a cheap stone, a complaint cannot later be made if the jewel proves to be worth $2,500.

Even if the unilateral mistake as to price is the result of an error in typing or in misunderstanding of an oral quotation of the price, the contract is valid.

McGregor dictated an offer to the Instant Typing Service and quoted a price for a certain grade of typing paper at $.90 a ream. McGregor's secretary, by error, typed the offer at $.80 a ream. McGregor did not catch the error when signing the letters because many grades were sold. The Instant Typing Service immediately accepted the offer and ordered 1,000 reams. It was then that the error was discovered. The contract was valid.

If both parties are mistaken as to the quantity, there is no contract. However, a unilateral mistake as to quantity does not affect the contract.

Merritt had a survey made and used the description from the survey to convey the land to McIntyre. The surveyors had made a mistake and the description included more property than Merritt had intended. McIntyre had used the survey to have the land appraised so he would know what to pay for it. Merritt claimed the error in the description was a mutual mistake which should invalidate the contract. Only Merritt was mistaken; therefore, the contract was binding.

As an exception to the principles stated above, one party cannot hold the other to a contract if that party knows that the other one has made a mistake.

Svalina, foreign-born and poorly educated, paid $5,160.40 to Big Horn National Life Insurance Co. Agents of the company had told him he could make an investment. He asked what would be paid in interest and they told him 10 percent. He entered into a contract with Big Horn which he thought was primarily for the purchase of stock. It was solely for the purchase of insurance. When Svalina found out he had purchased insurance and no stock, he sued for the return of his money. The court found Svalina made a unilateral mistake caused and known by the agents. This entitled Svalina to relief.

To entitle a party to relief the mistake must be one of fact, not mere opinion. If *A* buys a painting from *B* for $10 and it is actually worth $5,000, and *A* knows *B* is mistaken as to its value, there is a valid contract. *B*'s opinion as to its value is erroneous, but there is no mistake as to a fact.

The Vaugh Lumber Company sold the Hope Construction Company 10,925 feet of lumber at $187.75 per thousand board feet. The bookkeeper prepared an invoice showing the total price to be $205.11. The correct amount was $2,051.17. After the purchaser had paid the $205.11, she received a bill for an additional $1,846.06. She must pay it because there was no error in the unit price of $187.75 and the error in calculation on the invoice should have been evident to the purchaser. There was, in fact, no error in the contract price.

Mistakes as to the Terms of the Contract. A mistake as to the terms of the contract is usually the result of a failure to read the contract if it is written or a failure to understand its meaning or significance. Such mistakes in both written and oral contracts do not affect their validity; otherwise anyone could avoid a contract merely by claiming a mistake as to its terms. However, mistake as a result of an ambiguous contract may be excused.

Lula and Martin signed a property settlement agreement giving Lula all the couple's property in California and Martin all the couple's property in Missouri. The agreement had been drawn up by Martin's lawyer. Martin later wanted the agreement voided because he had intended a note and a bank account in California to be his. Lula said she thought that property was to be hers. The court found Martin's mistake regarding the terms of the contract did not invalidate it.

Frequently contracts are entered into orally and then reduced to writing. If through an error in typing the written form does not conform to the oral form, then the parties may not be bound by the written form.

Fraud

One who induces another to enter into a contract as a result of an intentionally or recklessly false statement of a material fact is guilty of *fraud*. A contract so induced is voidable, not void, since the party defrauded intended to make the contract but was induced to do so through fraud.

Fraud may be perpetrated by:

1. Express misrepresentation
2. Concealment of material facts
3. Silence when it is one's duty to speak

Express Misrepresentation. Fraud, as a result of express misrepresentation, consists of four elements, each one of which must be present to constitute fraud:

1. A false statement of a material fact must be made.
2. The false statement must be made by one who knew it to be false, or by one who made it in reckless disregard of its truth or falsity.
3. There must be an intent to induce the innocent party to act by reason of the false statement.
4. The innocent party must have been induced to make the contract by the false statement.

If these four elements are present, the injured party may rescind the contract. If there has been damage by reason of the fraud, the injured party may, in addition, sue for damages.

Brown was the administrator of a health care clinic and a member of the board of directors of the corporation which owned the clinic. He told several stockholders that pursuant to a corporate resolution they were required to sell their stock for $500, which was less than its fair market value. After the stock was purchased by the corporation, Brown and the other remaining stockholders enjoyed a favorable income tax advantage and the retained earnings of the corporation were distributed to them. Brown was guilty of fraud.

Statements of opinion, as contrasted with statements of fact, do not, as a rule, constitute fraud. The theory here is that the person hearing the statement realizes or ought to realize that the other party is merely stating a view and not a fact. But if the speaker is an expert or has special knowledge not available to the other party and should realize that the other party relies on this expert opinion, then a misstatement of opinion or value, intentionally made, would amount to fraud.

Such expressions as "This is the best buy in town," "The price of this stock will double in the next twelve months," "This business will net you $15,000 a year" are all statements of opinion, not statements of fact. If one says, "This business has netted the owner $15,000," this is not an opinion or a prophecy, but a historical fact.

Concealment of Material Facts. If one actively conceals material facts for the purpose of preventing the other contracting party from discovering them, such concealment is fraud even though there are no false statements.

Merely refraining from disclosing pertinent facts unknown to the other party is not fraud as a rule. There must be an active concealment.

◆   Greenspan and Jacobsen built a duplex on a foundation which was constructed in violation of the building code and which was inadequate to sustain the weight of the building. Massive cracks and severe settlement ensued and they had plasterboard erected in the basement to cover the cracks. They then sold the duplex to Haberman and Ericksen. When the inadequate foundation was discovered, the contract was invalidated. The sellers' active concealment of the cracks constituted fraud.

Silence When It Is One's Duty to Speak. If one's relationship with another is that of trust and confidence, then silence may constitute fraud. Such a relationship exists between partners in a business firm, an agent and principal, a lawyer and client, a guardian and ward, a physician and patient, and in many other trust relationships. In the case of an attorney-client relationship, for example, the attorney has a duty to reveal anything that is material to the client's interests, and silence has the same effect as making a false statement that there was no material fact to be told to the client. The client could, in such a case, avoid the contract.

Silence, when one has no duty to speak, is not fraud. If Lawrence offers to sell Marconi, a diamond merchant, a gem for $500 that is actually worth $15,000, Marconi's superior knowledge of value does not, in itself, impose a duty to speak.

Duress

For a contract to be valid, all parties must enter into it of their free wills. *Duress* is a means of destroying another's free will by obtaining consent by means of a threat to do the person or family members some harm. The threat may relate to one's property (such as a threat to burn down a house) or to earning power. When the effect of the threat is to prevent the exercise of free will, duress exists. A contract made because of duress is voidable.

◆   Barrett financed the purchase of cars which Sovine then sold. They divided the profit between them. After Sovine gave Barrett two worthless checks, Barrett had two warrants issued against Sovine. Barrett repeatedly visited Sovine's seventy-year-old mother, waving the two checks at her and saying Sovine would go to jail. On February 20, Mrs. Sovine signed a note and mortgage on her home to Barrett. On March 5, the warrants were dismissed. When Barrett sought to foreclose on the home, Mrs. Sovine successfully alleged duress by Barrett.

Undue Influence

One person may exercise such influence over the mind of another that the latter does not exercise free will. Although there is no force or threat of harm (which would be duress), the contract is nevertheless regarded as voidable. If a party in a confidential or fiduciary relationship to another induces the execution of a contract against the other person's free will, the agreement is voidable because of *undue influence*. If, under any relationship, one is in a position to take undue advantage of another, undue influence may render the contract voidable. Relationships which may result in undue influence are family relationships, a guardian and ward, an attorney and client, a physician and patient, and any other relationship where confidence reposed on one side results in domination by the other. Undue influence may result also from sickness, infirmity, or serious distress.

In undue influence there are no threats to harm the person, property, or relations of the other party as in duress. The relationship of the two parties must be such that one yields because it is not possible to hold out against the superior position, intelligence, or personality of the other party. Whether undue influence exists is a question for the court (usually the jury) to determine. Not every influence is regarded as undue; for example, a nagging spouse is ordinarily not regarded as exercising undue influence. In addition, persuasion and argument are not per se undue influence. The key element is that the dominated party is helpless in the hands of the other.

Caleb Patterson, age eighty-five and in bad mental and physical health, wanted to give his home to the university. After numerous visits from employees of the university, he was told his house was wanted, but not for the use he proposed. The visits were not always cordial. At times there would be arguing and the voices would get loud. After the visitors left, Patterson would be nervous, shaky, upset, and confused. He told his housekeeper the university was going to take all his money and he did not want that. Patterson did deed his home and almost all his property to the university. The gift was held to be the result of undue influence by university employees.

Remedies for Breach of Contract Because of Fraud, Duress, or Undue Influence

Since fraud, duress, and undue influence render contracts voidable, not void, one must know what to do when a victim of one of these acts. If nothing is done, the right to avoid the contract may be lost. Furthermore, the contract may be ratified by some act or word indicating an intention to be bound. After the contract is affirmed or ratified, one is as fully bound on it as if there had been no fraud, duress, or undue influence. But still the innocent party may sue for whatever damages have been sustained.

If one elects to rescind or set aside the contract, what was received under the contract must first be returned or offered to be returned. After this is done, the innocent party is in a position to take one of three actions depending upon the circumstances:

1. Suit may be brought to recover any money, goods, or other things of value, plus damages.
2. If the contract is executory on the part of the innocent party, performance can be refused. If the other party sues, fraud, duress, or undue influence can be interposed as a complete defense.
3. A suit may be brought to have the contract judicially declared void. Damages can be sought.

Dartner, a shoe merchant, was induced through fraud to purchase some shoes for $6,500. The shoes were purchased on ninety days' credit. Dartner's best remedy in this case might be to affirm the contract but to refrain from paying for the shoes. When the seller sues him, he can set up the fraud as a counterclaim. If he could prove that he was damaged to some extent—for example, $3,000—by reason of the fraud, then he would pay the balance of the account, or $3,500.

In no case can the wrongdoer set the contract aside and thus profit from the wrong. If the agreement is void, neither party may enforce it; no special act is required for setting the agreement aside.

Questions

1. How is a contract affected by a mistake as to the nature of the transaction?

2. If one is mistaken as to the identity of the party with whom a contract is made, may the contract be avoided when the dealings were face to face?

3. Can the parties be in mutual agreement when they are honestly mistaken as to the identity of the subject matter of the contract?

4. If the subject matter of the contract did not exist at the time the contract was formed and both parties were unaware of this fact, is the contract valid or void?

5. Does a unilateral mistake as to value, quality, or price affect the validity of a contract?

6. If one does not rely on a misrepresentation, may fraud be pleaded as a defense when sued on the contract?

7. Is it possible for fraud to exist even when no false statements are made?

8. Define *duress*.

9. When does *undue influence* exist?

10. What is the effect of ratifying a contract made as a result of fraud, duress, or undue influence?

Case Problems

1. Larry and Shirley McDaniel paid American Independent Management Systems, Inc. (AIMS), $1,500 to open an AIMS agency. AIMS had told the McDaniels that it had agencies nationwide; would provide extensive training for them; offered a variety of financial management services; and would provide a monthly management bulletin and advertising material. In fact, AIMS had only 14 agents in seven states; it provided a two-day training session; supplied no advertising material and only one monthly bulletin; and did not provide the financial management services. The McDaniels sued for $1,500 and their expenses in setting up the office, alleging fraud. Was AIMS guilty of fraud?

2. The Lapp Jewelry Company had a diamond necklace for sale. The price was $7,500. McLean, a prospective purchaser, inquired of the salesperson as to the price. The salesperson looked up the price and said "$750," thinking that was the price shown on the price list. Neither the salesperson nor the buyer knew the true value of the necklace. McLean agreed to purchase it. Was the Lapp Jewelry Company bound on this contract?

3. Harris Bibb was office manager for the Griffin Wholesale Company. In this capacity he signed a contract with the Atlanta Collecting Agency to collect $50,000 of delinquent accounts receivable. The written contract with the agency contained this clause: "The Griffin Wholesale Company agrees to pay the Atlanta Collecting Agency 25% of the aggregate listing as its collection fee." Bibb thought this meant that for each $1,000 collected, the agency would take $250 and remit $750 to the Griffin Wholesale Company. The true meaning was that the agency kept the first $12,500 collected and remitted all over that. Was the Griffin Wholesale Company bound on this contract?

4. Martinez owned a deep-sea fishing boat. He agreed to sell it to Huntley for $10,000, delivery to be made as soon as the boat returned to port. At the time the contract was made, the boat had sunk during a storm. This fact was unknown by both buyer and seller. Was there a valid contract?

5. The Sailors Antique Shop displayed several old-style beds. Hargrove purchased one for $2,700, thinking it was a very valuable Louis XIV make. The seller knew Hargrove was mistaken about the antiquity of the bed but said nothing to enlighten him about his ignorance. The bed was of fairly recent make and actually worth only $150. When Hargrove learned of this fact, he attempted to rescind the contract. Can he do so?

6. The Sweetwater County School District had a rule incorporated in its contracts which read, "New teachers being hired by the district will be expected to reside in the community at least five days a week. . . ." Joseph Roush was hired to teach and did live in the community. In a subsequent year he moved to another town and commuted. Two other teachers also commuted. The district tried to terminate Roush, saying that the rule dealing with "new teachers" was meant to apply to teachers hired after the adoption of the rule. Roush had assumed that the rule applied only to first-year teachers. The superintendent testified that the rule had not been enforced. Was Roush's mistake justified?

7. Dimou advertised for sale a used car "in very good condition." McGregor took the car for a short test-drive and discovered it could start only in reverse. Dimou said it was an electrical problem and denied that the car had ever been in an accident. McGregor bought the car and took it to an auto dealer for a complete inspection and evaluation. He was told it was seriously defective, hazardous, and not repairable. The car had been "totalled" in an accident. Dimou had purchased it from a salvage operator and had done extensive work on it. Can McGregor rescind the contract of sale?

lack of clarity: contracts cannot be selectively enforced

7

Capacity to Contract

Preview Cases

When Jacqueline Flowers, who lived on welfare, was four years old she was severely injured in an automobile accident. She received medical treatment for her injuries from East Tennessee Baptist Hospital, and the unpaid bill for this treatment was $5,271.29. A settlement in the amount of $7,125 was made for Jacqueline with the person alleged to have caused the accident. The hospital tried to subject the settlement to the payment of the hospital bill. Can the hospital recover?

Sanders, a minor, owned and operated a service station. In this capacity he purchased gasoline, tires, and other merchandise amounting to $3,000. He was sued on this account, and his service station was to be sold to satisfy the debt. Sanders claimed he was not liable on his debts because of his minority. Was he?

In order that an agreement may be enforceable at law, all parties must have the legal and mental capacity to contract. This means that the parties must have the ability to understand that a contract is being made, have the ability to understand its general nature, and have the legal competence to contract. The general rule is that all parties are presumed to have this capacity. However, in the eyes of the law some parties lack such capacity because of age, physical condition, or public policy. Among those whom the law considers to be incompetent to some degree are minors, insane persons, intoxicated persons, convicts, and aliens.

Minors

The common-law rule that persons under twenty-one years of age are *minors* has been abolished by most of the states. Most states have enacted statutes making persons competent to contract at eighteen years of age. In a few other states all minors who are married are fully competent to contract. In still other states minors who are in business for themselves are bound on all their business contracts.

Contracts of Minors.

A minor may make contracts freely, and many of these contracts are fully as valid and enforceable as those of an adult. Some contracts are voidable at the minor's option. If a minor desires, voidable contracts may be performed. If a minor wishes to treat a contract made with an adult as valid, the adult is bound by it; the adult cannot disaffirm it on the ground that the minor might avoid the contract. Should the minor die, the personal representative of the estate may disaffirm the contract which the minor could have avoided.

Firms that carry on business transactions in all the states must know the law dealing with minors in each of the fifty states. Mail-order houses and correspondence schools are particularly susceptible to losses when dealing with minors. The significance of the law is that, with but few exceptions, people deal with minors at their own risk. The purpose of the law is to protect minors from unscrupulous adults, but in general the law affords the other party no more rights in scrupulous contracts than in unscrupulous ones. The minor is the sole judge as to whether a voidable contract will be binding.

Contracts of Minors for Necessaries.

A minor is fully liable for the reasonable value of necessaries. The dividing line between necessaries and luxuries is often a fine one. *Necessaries* historically included food, clothes, and shelter not already provided for the minor. But with the raising of standards of living, courts now hold that necessaries also include medical services such as surgery, dental work, and medicine; education through high school or trade school, and in some cases through college; working tools for a trade; and other goods which are luxuries to some people but necessaries to others because of peculiar circumstances.

The minor's liability is quasi-contractual in nature in that the reasonable value of what is actually received must be paid in order to prevent the minor from being unjustly enriched. The minor is not, however, required to pay the contract price.

When Jacqueline Flowers, who lived on welfare, was four years old she received severe injuries in an automobile accident. She received medical treatment for her injuries from East Tennessee Baptist Hospital, and the unpaid bill for this treatment was $5,271.29. A settlement of $7,125 was made for Jacqueline with the person alleged to have caused the accident. The hospital tried to subject the settlement to the payment of the hospital bill. The court found that the inability of Jacqueline's parents to pay for the needed medical treatment made the treatment a necessary for which she was required to pay the reasonable value.

Disaffirmance. The term *disaffirmance* means the repudiation of a contract, that is, the election to avoid it. A minor has the legal right to disaffirm a voidable contract at any time during minority or within a reasonable time after becoming of age.

If the contract is wholly executory, a disaffirmance completely nullifies the contract.

Minors, upon electing to disaffirm contracts, must return whatever they may have received under the contracts, provided they are still in possession of it. The fact that the minor is not in possession of the property, however, regardless of the reason, does not prevent the exercise of the right to disaffirm the contract, and an adult may not recover compensation from a minor who returns the property in damaged condition.

◆ Halbman, a minor, agreed to purchase a car from Lemke. He made a down payment and took possession of the car. An engine rod broke. Halbman had the car repaired at a garage. Lemke endorsed the car's title to Halbman, but shortly thereafter Halbman returned the title to Lemke, disaffirmed the contract, offered to return the car, and demanded the return of all his money. The repair bill had never been paid, so the garage removed the engine and transmission. The car was vandalized, making it unsalvageable. Halbman sued Lemke for the money he had paid him. Lemke argued that he should be entitled to recover for the damage to the vehicle up to the time of disaffirmance. Halbman was entitled to recover his payments without liability for the use, depreciation, or damage to the car.

If an adult purchases personal property from a minor, the adult has only a voidable title to the property. If the property is sold to an innocent third party before the minor disaffirms the contract, the innocent third party obtains good title to the property.

◆ Wilson, a minor, owned a 1978 automobile which he traded to Patino for a 1980 car. Wilson drove the car for two weeks and found the car not as good as the 1978 car. He asked Patino to return his car but was told that it had been sold to Forrest. Wilson then sued Forrest for return of the 1978 car. Although Wilson could avoid the sale to Patino, he could not do so against Forrest, who acquired title to the car in good faith and for value. Wilson could, however, demand the value of the car from Patino.

Ratification. A minor may ratify a voidable contract only after attaining majority. *Ratification* means indicating one's willingness to be bound by promises made during minority. It is in substance a new promise and may be oral, written, or merely implied by conduct. A minor cannot ratify part of a contract and disaffirm a part; all or none of it must be ratified. Ratification must be made within a reasonable time after majority. What is a reasonable time is a question of fact to be determined in the light of all surrounding circumstances.

It should be noted that there is a difference between a minor's executed contracts and executory contracts. After majority is reached, silence ratifies an executed contract, while it disaffirms an executory contract.

William Jones, a minor, signed a contract with Free Flight Sport Aviation allowing Jones to use an airplane ferrying skydivers. The contract included an agreement not to sue and exempting Free Flight from liability. A month later Jones attained majority. Ten months after that he was seriously injured when a Free Flight skydiving plane crashed. He sued Free Flight for his injuries. It was held that Jones had ratified the contract by accepting the benefits of it when he used Free Flight's facilities the day of the crash.

Minors' Business Contracts. Many states, either by special statutory provision or by court decisions, have made a minor's business contracts fully binding. If a minor engages in a business or employment in the same manner as a person having legal capacity, contracts that arise from such business or employment cannot be set aside.

Sanders, a minor, owned and operated a service station. In this capacity he purchased gasoline, tires, and other merchandise amounting to $3,000. He was sued on this account, and his service station was to be sold to satisfy the debt. Sanders claimed he was not liable on his debts because of his minority. He was held responsible as though he were a person having legal capacity.

Contracting Safely with Minors. Since in general one deals with minors at a risk, every businessperson must know how to be protected when contracting with minors. The safest way is to have an adult (usually parent or guardian) join in the contract as a cosigner with the minor. This does not bind the minor, but it does give the first party the right to sue the adult who became party to the contract. A merchant must run some risks when dealing with minors. If a sale is made to a minor, the minor may avoid the contract and demand a refund of the purchase price years later. Since few minors exercise this right, it is more profitable for a businessperson to run the risk of contracting with minors than to seek absolute protection against loss.

Minors' Torts. As a general rule, a minor is liable for torts as fully as an adult. If minors misrepresent their age, and the adults with whom they contract rely upon the misrepresentation to their detriment, this is a tort. The law is not uniform throughout the United States as to whether or not minors are bound on contracts induced by misrepresenting their age. In some states, when sued, they cannot avoid their contracts if they fraudulently misrepresented their age. In some states they may be held liable for any damage to or deterioration of the property they received under the contract. If minors sue on the contracts to recover what they paid, they may be denied recovery if they misrepresented their age.

Insane Persons

In determining an insane person's capacity, the intensity and duration of the insanity must be determined. In most states, if the person has been examined according to law and been formally adjudicated insane, contracts made by the person are void without regard to whether they are reasonable or for necessaries. Such a person is considered incapable of making a valid acceptance of an offer no matter how fair the offer is. If the person is insane but has not been so declared by the court, then such contracts are voidable, not void. Like a minor, the person must pay the reasonable value of necessaries that have been supplied. Upon disaffirmance, anything of value received under the contracts which the person still has must be returned.

A person who has not been declared insane and has only intervals of insanity or delusions can make a contract which is fully as binding as those of a normal person if it is made during a sane or lucid interval. The person must be able to understand that a contract is being made.

When a person has been judicially declared insane and sanity is later regained, the capacity to contract is the same as that of any other normal person after a court officially declares the person to be competent.

◆   Robert Stacey was judicially declared insane. A guardian was appointed for him. Later Stacey sold his car for $500, a fair price. His guardian sued for return of the car. The court held that the buyer had to return the car because Stacey's contract was void. Stacey had to return any money which had not been lost or spent.

Intoxicated Persons

Contracts made by people who have become so intoxicated that they cannot understand the meaning of their acts are voidable. Upon becoming sober, they may affirm or disaffirm contracts they made while drunk. If one delays unreasonably in disaffirming a contract made while intoxicated, however, the right to have the contract set aside may be lost.

That a contract is foolish and would not have been entered into if the party had been sober is not sufficient to make the contract voidable.

A person who has been legally declared to be a habitual drunkard cannot make a valid contract but is liable for the reasonable value of necessaries furnished. If a person is purposely caused to become drunk in order to be induced to contract, the agreement will be held invalid.

Convicts

While many states have repealed their former laws restricting the capacity of a *convict* (one convicted of a major criminal offense, namely, a felony or treason) to contract, there are still jurisdictions in which there are limitations. These range from depriving convicts of rights as needed to provide for the security of the penal institutions in which they are confined and for reasonable protection of the public, to classifying convicts as under a disability, as are minors and insane persons. In these instances, the disability lasts only as long as the person is imprisoned.

Aliens

An alien is a resident of the United States who is citizen or subject of a foreign country. Originally subject to disabilities to contract, an alien is in most instances able to make binding contracts. Some states have restrictions on property ownership by aliens. As a rule, an *enemy alien*—a subject or citizen of a country with which we are at war—may not make binding contracts or sue on an existing contract. Generally, the enemy alien's rights under an existing contract are suspended until peace is restored. But an enemy alien may make a defense when sued on such a contract. Contracts are not suspended where their performance disadvantages the enemy.

Questions

1. What classes of persons are considered by the law to lack full capacity to make contracts?

2. If a minor wishes to treat as binding a contract with an adult, can the adult avoid it because the other party is a minor?

3. Why is it important for business firms to know their state's and other states' laws dealing with minors?

4. Name some necessaries for which a minor may be liable for payment.

5. When can a minor disaffirm a contract?

6. If Sally purchases a car from Henry, a minor, and then sells it to Watson, can Henry demand that Watson return the car to him?

7. When can a minor ratify a voidable contract?

8. If a minor purchases two articles by the same contract, can the contract for one of the items be disaffirmed and the contract for the other one be ratified?

9. Can a minor who is in business make a binding contract?

10. If Gordon, a minor, lies about his age, is he guilty of a tort?

11. Can a person who has been judicially declared insane make a binding contract?

12. If a person judicially declared insane becomes sane, is the capacity to contract restored?

13. Is a contract made by an intoxicated person valid?

14. How long does the disability of a convict to contract last?

Case Problems

1. Holcomb was a disabled minor, unable to walk. He was working his way through college with a paper route necessitating a car. He found a car for $900 at A & H Motors. Holcomb would not agree to buy the car unless A & H Motors agreed to repair a dented fender. They finally agreed that Holcomb would purchase the car for $875 and that he would pay the A & H Motors $25 for repairing the fender. Before the car was delivered, Holcomb attempted to disaffirm. Can he do so?

2. The parents of Marilyn Calhoun, age thirteen, were divorced. Her mother and two other people came to an apartment where Marilyn was babysitting. Marilyn was told that her father was dead and that she needed to sign certain documents for the body to be picked up. She signed the documents while one person covered the written portion. She was not told they were documents which indicated her agreement to turn over the proceeds of an insurance policy for $1,944.72 and her promise to pay for her father's funeral and allow a judgment to be entered against her if the money was not paid. Eight months later an action was filed and a judgment was entered. A year after Marilyn attained majority, a prospective employer informed her that her credit record was impaired. Upon further inquiry, she first learned of the judgment. Two months later she sought to challenge it. Was this a disaffirmance of the documents she had signed and, if so, must she return anything to the holder of the note?

3. Burson, a minor, owned and operated the Red and Black Cleaners. He incurred about $5,000 in debts for rent, equipment, and cleaning materials. He failed to pay any of them, and his creditors brought suit to foreclose on the business in order to collect payment. Burson claimed that since he was a minor, he was not liable for these debts. Is this contention sound?

4. When seventeen years old, Cindy Farrar signed a form at Swedish Health Spa for a two-year membership for $324.31. As payment she used her father's Master-Card credit card. The father paid his Master-Card bill but then told the spa that Cindy was a minor and asked that the money be refunded. Cindy never used the facilities or services of the spa after signing the form. Did the payment of the Master-Card bill by the father constitute ratification?

5. Melvin Parrent was fifteen when he was injured while working for Midway Toyota. Midway accepted liability and paid temporary total disability payments for more than a year. Several months later Parrent and Midway signed a final settlement for disability benefits totaling $6,136.40. Parrent and his mother negotiated the settlement, and she was present at the time he signed. She did not object, but no one of legal age signed in Parrent's behalf. Parrent later filed a petition to reopen his claim. Midway claimed that because of the close relation and continuous awareness of the mother the settlement is enforceable. Is it?

6. Howard was declared insane by the proper court, and the court appointed Dominique as his guardian. A few days later Howard purchased a suit on credit, but the guardian refused to pay for the suit. Was this a valid contract?

7. Paris, seventeen years old, left home and rented a room in town. After one month, she refused to pay, claiming a room was not a necessary for her since she could have stayed at home. Is her contention correct?

8

Consideration

Preview Cases

Richard Runyan, age fifty-three, was advised that his employment would be terminated. Runyan felt, and told his employer, that his termination involved age discrimination. His employer disagreed, saying it was due to inadequate job performance. After discussing the terms under which Runyan's employment would be terminated, a one-year consulting agreement was signed providing a minimum monthly compensation. Later Runyan asked that the agreement be extended and the compensation increased. The company agreed to increase the monthly compensation by $1,667 in consideration for Runyan's releasing the company from all other debts and claims relating to his termination. This agreement was signed by Runyan and the company. After the consulting agreement expired, Runyan sued the company for $450,000, claiming he was terminated because of age discrimination. Did the release in the agreement bar the suit?

Kelly, along with many other communicants, pledged to a building fund for the First United Methodist Church. The finance committee of the church let a contract for the construction of the church, the cost to be met from the pledges. Kelly attempted to revoke her pledge after the church was half finished because she did not like the architecture. Is she bound on her promise?

Courts will compel compliance with an agreement only when it is supported by consideration. Consideration distinguishes mere agreements from legally enforceable obligations. *Consideration* is whatever the promisor demands and receives as the price for a promise.

Nature of Consideration

In most contracts, the parties require and are content with a promise by the other party as the price for their own promises. For example, a homeowner may promise to pay a painter $1,000 in return for the promise of the painter to paint the house. Correspondingly, the painter makes the promise to paint in return for the promise of the homeowner to make such payment. From its very nature, this exchange of a promise for a promise occurs at the one time.

For a promise to constitute consideration, the promise must impose an obligation upon the person making it. If a merchant promises to sell a businessperson all of the carbon paper ordered at a specific price in return for the businessperson's promise to pay that price for any carbon paper ordered, there is no contract. There is no certainty that any carbon paper will be needed.

Consideration may also be the doing of an act or the making of a promise to refrain from doing an act which can be lawfully done. Thus, a promise to give up smoking or drinking can be consideration for a promise to make a certain payment in return therefor. In contrast, a promise to stop driving an automobile in excess of the speed limit is not consideration because a person does not have a right to drive illegally; the promise to drive lawfully does not add anything to that which is already required.

Adequacy of Consideration

As a general rule, the adequacy of the consideration is irrelevant. The law does not prohibit bargains. Except in cases where the contract calls for a performance or the sale of goods which have a standard or recognized market value, it is impossible to fix the money value of each promise. If the consideration given by one party is grossly inadequate, this is a relevant fact in proving fraud, undue influence, duress, or mistake. Then, too, the inadequacy of the consideration may be a factor in a court of equity, where the equity judge is not bound by strict rules of law but is free to decide the case according to what is considered just.

Part Payment

A partial payment of a past-due debt is not consideration to support the creditor's promise to cancel the balance of the debt. This is because the creditor is already entitled to the part payment. Promising to give something to which the other party is already entitled is not consideration.

There are several exceptions to this rule:

1. If the amount of the debt is in dispute, the debt is canceled if a lesser sum than that claimed is accepted in full settlement.

Richard Runyan, age fifty-three, was advised that his employment would be terminated. Runyan felt, and told his employer, that his termination involved age discrimination. His employer disagreed, saying it was due to inadequate job performance. After discussing the terms under which Runyan's employment would be terminated, a one-year consulting agreement was signed providing a minimum monthly compensation. Later Runyan asked that the agreement be extended and the compensation increased. The company agreed to increase the monthly compensation by $1,667 in consideration for Runyan's releasing the company from all other debts and claims relating to his termination. This agreement was signed by Runyan and the company. After the consulting agreement expired, Runyan sued the company for $450,000, claiming he was terminated because of age discrimination. The court found a bona fide dispute existed concerning the reason for Runyan's termination. Therefore, any greater amount potentially owed by the company because of age discrimination was waived when the increased compensation was given in full settlement of any claims by Runyan regarding his termination.

2. If there are several creditors, and each one agrees to accept in full settlement a percentage of the amount due, this agreement will cancel the unpaid balance due these creditors. This arrangement is known as a *composition of creditors*.

Lind's creditors sign an agreement that they will accept 45 cents on the dollar in satisfaction of their claims. Later, Schneider, one of the creditors, sues Lind for the balance of Lind's debt to him. Schneider was not allowed to collect. When the creditors agreed to accept a fractional share of their claims against Lind, their agreements were supported by consideration. Lind's debts were discharged.

3. If the debt is evidenced by a note or other written evidence, cancellation and return of the written evidence cancels the debt.

4. If the payment of the lesser sum is accompanied by a receipt in full and some indication that a gift is made of the balance, the debt may be canceled.

5. If a secured note is given and accepted in discharge of an unsecured note for a greater amount, the difference between the two notes is discharged. The security is the consideration to support the contract to settle for a lesser sum.

Insufficient or Invalid Consideration

Many apparent considerations lack the full force and effect necessary to make enforceable agreements. Consideration of the following classes is either insufficient or invalid:

1. Performing or promising to perform what one is already obligated to do
2. Refraining from doing or promising to refrain from doing what one has no right to do
3. Past performance

Performing or Promising to Perform What One Is Already Obligated to Do. If the claim to consideration consists merely of a promise to do what one is already legally obligated to do anyway, consideration is said to be invalid. If the consideration is invalid, the contract is invalid. In such case, the promise gives nothing new to the other contracting party.

Wendell Anderson purchased a herbicide and applied it to farmland. He later became aware of a weed control problem on the farm. The company which produced the herbicide offered to settle Anderson's claim by providing an alternative herbicide equal to the value of the original herbicide plus a cash allowance for application. Anderson accepted the offer. He later sued for $10,228 for the failure of the original herbicide to control the growth of weeds, alleging that the producer's settlement offer was a promise to perform a pre-existing duty (weed control) and so the compromise agreement was invalid for lack of consideration. The court held that since the parties disputed the producer's liability for damages under the warranty accompanying the purchase of the original herbicide, the producer's act of providing an alternative herbicide plus cash and Anderson's promise not to sue provided consideration and that the compromise agreement was valid.

Parties to a contract may at any time mutually agree to cancel an old contract and replace it with a new one. For this new contract to be enforceable, there must be some added features that benefit both parties though not necessarily to an equal extent. If a contractor agrees to build a house of certain specifications for $40,000, a contract of the homeowner to pay an additional $1,000 is not binding unless the contractor concurrently agrees to do something the original contract did not require as a consideration for the $1,000. The value of the additional act by the contractor need not be $1,000. It merely must have a monetary value.

If unforeseen difficulties arise that make it impossible for the contractor to complete the house for $40,000, these unforeseen difficulties may, in rare cases, be consideration. Strikes, bad weather, and a change in prices are examples of foreseeable difficulties, which would not be consideration. Underground rock formations or a change in the law relative to the building codes and zoning laws are examples of unforeseen difficulties. The homeowner is not bound to agree to pay more because of unforeseen difficulties; but if such an agreement is made, these difficulties will constitute a consideration even though the contractor does not agree to do anything additional.

Refraining from Doing or Promising to Refrain from Doing What One Has No Right to Do. When one promises to refrain from doing something, this conduct is called *forbearance*. If the promisor had a right to do the act, forbearance is a valid consideration. Consideration is invalid when it consists of a promise to forbear doing something which one has no right to do, such as to commit an unlawful act.

Often the forbearance consists of promising to refrain from suing the other party. Promising to refrain from suing another is a good consideration if one has a reasonable right to demand damages and intends to file a suit.

Desmarais purchased a farm from Huberdeau for $40,000 down and $5,000 of principal and accrued interest yearly. Desmarais failed to make several principal payments. Huberdeau agreed to accept only the interest if Desmarais would continue farming. Then they agreed if the farm was forfeited because Desmarais breached the contract of sale, Desmarais would transfer the allotment base under which he received federal payments to Huberdeau. Huberdeau agreed to forbear suing for the timely payment of the principal installments. The agreement was not binding. Huberdeau did not have a valid ground of forbearance.

Past Performance. An act performed prior to the promise does not constitute valid consideration. If a carpenter gratuitously helps a neighbor build a house with no promise of pay, a promise to pay made after the house is completed cannot be enforced. The promise to pay must induce the carpenter to do the work, and this cannot be done if the promise is made after the work is completed.

For thirty years Virginia Sigler resided with Helen Mariotte and shared expenses. After Mariotte was hospitalized, Sigler was eager for her to return home and told Mariotte's son she would care for her at no charge. Sigler assisted in caring for Mariotte and paid $200 per month for food and rent. Three years later Mariotte signed a document in which she instructed that from the time of her return from the hospital, Sigler was to be paid $85 per week plus room and board. After a conservator was appointed for Mariotte, Sigler filed a claim for $85 per week and reimbursement for rent and food after Mariotte's return from the hospital. The claim was disallowed. Sigler agreed to care for Mariotte free of charge. Past benefits did not constitute consideration for the subsequent promise by Mariotte.

A debt that is discharged by bankruptcy may be revived under certain circumstances, usually by the debtor's agreeing, with approval from the bankruptcy court, to pay it. Such promises are enforceable even though the creditor, the promisee, gives no new consideration to support the promise. The debtor is said to have waived the defense of discharge in bankruptcy; and the original debt, therefore, is deemed to remain in force.

Exceptions to Requirement of Consideration

As a general rule, a promise is not binding unless it is supported by consideration. Certain exceptions to the rule involve voluntary subscriptions, debts of record, promissory estoppel, and modification of sales contracts.

Voluntary Subscriptions. When charitable enterprises are financed by voluntary subscriptions of many persons, the promise of each person is generally held to be enforceable. When a number of people make pledges to or subscribe to a charitable association or to a church, for example, the pledges or subscriptions are binding. One theory for enforcing the promise is that each subscriber's promise is supported by the promises of other subscribers. Another theory is that a subscription is an offer of a unilateral contract which is accepted by creating liabilities or making expenditures. Despite the fact that such promises lack the technical requirements of ordinary contracts, the courts will enforce the promises as a matter of public policy.

Kelly, along with many other communicants, pledged to a building fund for the First United Methodist Church. The finance committee of the church let a contract for the construction of the church, the cost to be met from the pledges. Kelly attempted to revoke her pledge after the church was half finished because she did not like the architecture. She is legally bound on her promise even though her promise is not supported by consideration.

Debts of Record. Consideration is not necessary to support an obligation of record, such as a judgment, on the basis that such an obligation is enforceable as a matter of public policy.

Promissory Estoppel. Although not supported by consideration, some promises are enforced by the courts on the basis of *promissory estoppel*. According to this doctrine, if one person makes a promise to another and that other person acts in reliance upon the promise, the promisor will not be permitted to claim lack of consideration. Enforcement is held to be proper when the promisor should reasonably expect to cause and does cause action by the promisee and the promisee would be harmed substantially if the promise is not enforced. The theory has gained support as a means of realizing justice.

Modification of Sales Contracts. As is detailed in Chapter 13, sales of goods are regulated by the Uniform Commercial Code. The Code provides that when a contract for the sale of goods is modified by agreement of the parties, no consideration is necessary to make it enforceable.

Questions

1. What is *consideration*?

2. Must every contract be supported by consideration to make it valid?

3. Does the adequacy of consideration determine if a contract is valid?

4. If a boy promises his father that he will not own and operate an automobile until he is eighteen in exchange for his father's promise to pay him $2,000, is this a valid contract?

5. What is a *composition of creditors*?

6. If Davis owes Dennis $10,000 and Dennis offers to settle for $7,000, what must be done to make the contract binding?

7. During Halloween night, two young men promised not to damage Jackson's car if Jackson would agree to pay them $50. Is this contract enforceable?

8. May a debt that has been discharged by bankruptcy be revived?

9. What are the four situations in which a promise not supported by consideration will be enforced?

10. What is *promissory estoppel*?

Case Problems

1. Mr. Brodie owed the Lanier National Bank $5,000. The note was past due, and the bank was on the verge of suing him. Mrs. Brodie executed a $5,000 first mortgage on the home that was in her name to secure her husband's note. She did this in return for the bank's promise not to sue her husband. Four years later the bank brought suit against Mrs. Brodie to foreclose on the mortgage since Mr. Brodie's note was still unpaid. Mrs. Brodie denied liability on the grounds of no consideration. Is this defense good?

2. Henry and Doris lived in a house owned by Henry's father. They paid a monthly rental of about 50 percent of its true rental value. Over a period of five years Henry spent $3,200 on the house and greatly improved its value. Henry's father, before he died, promised in writing that Henry should be paid from the father's estate for this $3,200. The administrator refused to pay it. Can Henry compel him to do so?

3. Branch was the bookkeeper for the Brown Lumber Company. His duties were to keep the books and to prepare and file all tax returns. One year his employer felt that the company had paid too much income tax and asked Branch to seek a refund. He promised to give Branch 50 percent of any refund. Branch worked many hours overtime preparing the application for a refund. The company received $24,000. Branch demanded $12,000, and the company refused to pay. Must it do so?

4. William Coester had a beer distributorship agreement with H.H.B. Company. The parties entered into a Termination of Business Agreement which included a full release of H.H.B. from Coester. H.H.B. agreed to purchase all Coester's inventory at retail price and pay off a $44,164.10 mortgage on a ware-

house rented by Coester from his mother for use in his business. H.H.B. performed all its obligations under the Agreement. Coester sued H.H.B., arguing that the release was invalid because it was not supported by adequate consideration because the retail price of the beer was not much and he did not receive the benefit of the $44,164.10 paid on the mortgage. Was the release valid?

5. Two corporations of which Samuel Bogley was an officer passed resolutions or motions stating ". . . in consideration of past services and services to be rendered by Samuel E. Bogley . . . the Corporation is authorized upon . . . death . . . to pay (his) estate or named beneficiary the total compensation received by the officer for the past two years prior to his death." After Bogley's death the corporations paid his estate $126,300. The IRS claimed it should be included in computing federal estate tax because the corporations made offers which were accepted by Bogley's continuing to serve as an officer of the corporations until his death. Thus, the IRS argued, the money was paid under binding contracts and it should be included in his estate for tax purposes. Were there binding contracts?

6. Carl Evans Boyd and Luther Claud Boyd died leaving two sets of wills. The beneficiaries of the earlier wills contested the later wills, claiming the Boyds did not have the testamentary capacity to make them. While the will contest was pending, all the parties entered into written agreements resolving all the questions regarding the distribution of the estates of the Boyds. They then asked the judge to enter an order confirming the agreements and disposing of the will contest in accordance with the agreements. The judge claimed he could not enter a judgment declaring the later wills void without a finding that the Boyds lacked capacity to make them. Was there sufficient consideration for the agreements? *yes - judge was right*

7. In an effort to rehabilitate Bacon, who habitually wrote checks which were not backed by funds in the bank, Abza promised Bacon $100 if he would write no insufficient-funds checks for a period of one year. Is the promise enforceable?

8. At an alumni reunion of graduates of Elay College, Barr agreed to donate $5,000 to the proposed Thomas library. Later, after a student demonstration, Barr attempted to revoke her promise. Is she bound to give the $5,000?

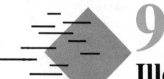

9

Illegal Agreements

Preview Cases

Alewine and Goodnoe formed a contract whereby Alewine agreed to sell Goodnoe 10,000 shares of stock one month from date at $42 a share. They did not actually intend to buy and sell the stock, but they did agree to settle for the difference between $42 a share and the closing price on the date fixed in the contract. Is the contract valid?

Before their marriage, Richard J. Reynolds executed a prenuptial agreement with Marianne O'Brien. In it he conveyed all the common stock of Sapelo Plantation, Inc., by bill of sale and agreed to transfer the stock upon the books of the corporation in consideration of $10 and O'Brien's agreement to marry him. At the time he was married to Elizabeth Dillard Reynolds. The stock was not transferred on the books of the corporation. After Reynolds's death, Marianne Reynolds claimed title to the stock. Was the agreement to marry another when already married valid?

A contract must be for a lawful purpose, and this purpose must be achieved in a lawful manner. Otherwise the contract is void. If this were not true, the court might be placed in the absurd position of compelling one party to a contract to commit a crime. If the act itself is legal, but the manner of committing the act which is stipulated in the contract is illegal, the contract is void.

A contract that is void because of illegality does not necessarily involve the commission of a crime—it may consist merely of a private wrong, for example, an agreement by two persons to slander a third.

If the contract is indivisible; that is, it cannot be performed except as an entity, then illegality in one part renders the whole contract invalid. If the contract is divisible, so that the parts which are legal can be performed separately, the legal parts of the contract are enforceable. For example, when one purchases several articles, each priced separately, and the sale of these articles is illegal because the price was illegally set by price-fixing, the whole contract will not fall because of the one article.

The Varsity Sports Center employed Strobel as an accountant at $200 a week. She was to do all the accounting and, in addition, to handle all wagers on each week's football games. The latter act is illegal. Since it was not stated how much of Strobel's salary was for her duties as an accountant and how much was for taking the wagers, the whole contract was void because of illegality. The legal part cannot be separated from the illegal part. Strobel could not collect any salary.

Contracts Prohibited by Statute

Many types of contracts are declared illegal by statute, such as:

1. Gambling contracts
2. Sunday contracts
3. Usurious contracts
4. Contracts of an unlicensed operator
5. Contracts for the sale of articles that cannot be the subject matter of an ordinary sale
6. Contracts in unreasonable restraint of trade

Gambling Contracts. A *gambling contract* is a transaction wherein the parties stand to win or to lose based on pure chance. What one gains, the other must lose. Under the early common law wagering contracts were enforceable, but they are now generally prohibited in all states by statute. In recent years certain classes of gambling contracts, such as state lotteries and pari-mutuel systems of betting on horse races and dog races, have been legalized in some states.

In general the courts will leave the parties to a gambling contract where it finds them and will not allow one party to sue the other for the breach of a gambling debt. If two parties to a gambling contract give money to a stakeholder with instructions to pay the money to the winner, the parties can demand a return of their money. If the stakeholder pays the money to the winner, then the loser may sue either the winner or the stakeholder for reimbursement. No state will permit the stakeholder, who is considered merely a trustee of the funds, to keep the money. The court in this event requires the stakeholder to return each wagerer's deposit.

Closely akin to gambling debts are loans made to enable one to gamble. If A loans B $100 and then wins it back in a poker game, is this a gambling debt? Most courts hold that it is not. If A and B bet $100 on a football game and B wins, and if A pays B by giving a promissory note for the $100, such a note may be declared void.

Trading on the stock exchange or the grain market represents legitimate business transactions. But the distinction between such trading and gambling contracts is sometimes very fine. These two sets of facts illustrate the distinction:

◆   Alewine and Goodnoe form a contract whereby Alewine agrees to sell Goodnoe 10,000 shares of stock one month from date at $42 a share. They do not actually intend to buy and sell the stock, but they do agree to settle for the difference between $42 a share and the closing price on the date fixed in the contract. This is a gambling contract.

◆   Ripetto agrees to sell Bolde 10,000 bushels of wheat to be delivered six months later at $1.70 a bushel. Ripetto does not own any wheat, but expects to buy it for delivery. If at the end of the six-month period the seller does not actually deliver the wheat, and if the price of wheat has gone up, the seller may pay the buyer the difference between the current price and the contract price. If the seller does not deliver the wheat and the price of wheat has gone down, the buyer may pay the seller the difference. Nevertheless the contract is legal because the intention was to deliver.

The primary difference between the two situations is in the intention to deliver. In the second case Ripetto intended at the time of the contract to deliver the wheat and Bolde intended to accept it. In the first case no such intention to deliver existed.

Sunday Contracts. The laws pertaining to Sunday contracts are the result of statutes and judicial interpretation. They vary considerably from state to state. Some states prohibit all Sunday contracts except those involving works of necessity and charity. In others both labor (servile or manual labor) and transactions of business on Sunday are prohibited. In some states, a contract though made on Sunday is valid if it is ratified on another day and the law permits such ratification. However, other courts hold that such contracts are invalid because one cannot ratify an illegal contract. And it has been held that an offer made on Sunday and accepted the next day constituted a valid agreement because a contract was formed when acceptance was given. In some states there is no prohibition on Sunday contracts.

The performance of an act on Sunday which is prohibited by law from being performed on Sunday is a misdemeanor, but seldom are the violators prosecuted. For this reason the types of transactions one observes being carried on on Sunday are not good guides to the restrictions in these laws.

Usurious Contracts. State laws which limit the rate of interest which may be charged for the use of money are called *usury* laws. Frequently there are two rates, the contract rate and the legal rate. The *contract rate* is the maximum rate which may be charged; any rate above that is *usurious*. The *legal rate,* which is a rate somewhat lower than the contract rate, applies to all situations in which interest may be charged but in which the parties were silent as to the rate. If merchandise is sold on thirty days' credit, the seller may collect interest from the time the thirty days expire until the debt is paid. If no rate is agreed upon in a situation of this kind, the legal rate may be charged.

The courts will ignore attempts to disguise transactions which in fact are usurious. The courts will treat transactions as usurious when there is in fact a lending of money at a usurious rate even though disguised by the lender's:

1. Requiring the borrower to execute a note for an amount in excess of the actual loan

2. Requiring the borrower to antedate the note so as to charge interest for a longer period than that agreed on

3. Requiring the borrower to perform some service or labor for the lender without charge

4. Charging a brokerage fee for lending one's own money when no broker was used

5. Requiring the borrower to purchase some article from the lender at an exorbitant price

6. Requiring the borrower to sell the lender some property at a price considerably below its market value

The penalty for usury varies from state to state. In most states the only penalty is to prohibit the lender from collecting the excess interest. In other states the entire contract is void, and in still others the borrower need not pay any interest but must repay the principal. If the borrower has already paid the usurious interest, the court will require the lender to refund to the borrower any money collected in excess of the contract rate.

In all states there are special statutes governing consumer loans by pawnbrokers, small loan companies, and finance companies. In some states these firms may charge much higher rates of interest. Frequently a loan is to be repaid in installments, and the borrower actually pays a higher interest rate than the item expressly described as the *nominal interest rate* in the loan calculation. This is so because the borrower pays interest on the full amount of the loan for the total loan period but only has the first installment of the principal borrowed for the first loan period, the second installment for two loan periods, and so on. Although the sum charged the borrower for the amount of money actually "used" is thus greater than the legal rate of interest, it is held that the usury laws are not violated by such transactions.

◆   The Walkers executed an agreement with Nationwide Financial Corporation for a loan of $15,537.64 secured by a first deed of trust against real property. The interest rate was 18 percent. In the state where they borrowed the money, the maximum permissible interest rate for loans which did not come within the Uniform Consumer Credit Code was 10 percent. The Code recited that a loan secured by an interest in land was a consumer loan and also that a loan primarily secured by an interest in land was a consumer loan if the interest rate exceeded 10 percent. Thus, the loan was a consumer loan and its rate of 18 percent was not usurious.

Contracts of an Unlicensed Operator.

Statutes make it illegal to operate certain types of businesses or professions without a license. Most of these statutes are made to protect the public from incompetent operators. The most common types of professional persons who must be licensed to operate are doctors, lawyers, certified and licensed public accountants, dentists, and insurance and real estate salespeople. A person who performs these services without license not only cannot sue to collect for the services but may also be guilty of a crime.

A licensing law may be designed solely as a revenue measure by requiring payment of a fee for a license. Contracts made by an unlicensed person operating in one of the fields or businesses covered by such a law are held valid, but the person may still be subject to fine or imprisonment for violating the law.

Contracts for Sale of Prohibited Articles.

If a druggist sells morphine or a similar drug to one who does not have a prescription, a suit to collect the price would not be successful. One who sells cigarettes or alcoholic beverages to a minor when such sale is prohibited cannot recover on the contract. In such cases, the court will not interfere to protect either party.

Contracts in Unreasonable Restraint of Trade.

It is the policy of our government to encourage competition. Any contract, therefore, intended to unreasonably restrain trade is null and void. The dividing line between reasonable and unreasonable restraint of trade is often dim, but certain acts have by judicial decision become well established as being an unreasonable restraint of trade. The most common acts in this class are:

1. Contracts not to compete
2. Contracts to restrain trade
3. Contracts to fix the resale price
4. Unfair competitive practices

Contracts Not to Compete. When one purchases a going business, not only are the physical assets purchased, but also the goodwill, which is often the most valuable asset of the firm. In the absence of a contract prohibiting the seller from attempting to retake the asset "goodwill," it may be done by engaging in the same business again and seeking to retain former customers. It is customary and highly desirable when purchasing a business to include in the contract a provision prohibiting the seller from entering the same business again in the trade territory for a specified length of time. Such a contract not to compete is legal if the restriction is reasonable as to both time and place.

The restriction as to territory should not go beyond the trade area of the business. Since the restriction is sustained to protect the buyer of the business from competition of the seller, it follows that the restriction should not reach out into areas where the buyer's reputation has not reached, nor should the seller be subjected to the restriction longer than is reasonably necessary for the buyer to become established in the new business. When the restriction goes further or longer than necessary to protect the buyer of the business, it is unlawful not only because it is oppressive to the seller but also because the business community and society in general are unnecessarily deprived of the benefit of the activities of the seller.

Closely allied to this type of contract is one whereby an employee, as a part of the employment contract, agrees not to work for a competing firm for a certain period of time after terminating employment. These contracts must be reasonable as to time and place.

James Dagata was employed by Timenterial, Inc., under a contract which provided that he would not "engage . . . in any business venture having to do with the sale or rental of mobile homes . . . in a 50-mile radius from any existing Timenterial, Inc., sales lot" for one year after leaving Timenterial. He terminated his employment with Timenterial and continued to engage in the mobile home business. Timenterial sued Dagata. The court found that the one-year restriction was reasonable, but the area covered by the 50-mile radius from Timenterial lots would include parts of six states and was unreasonable.

Contracts to Restrain Trade. Contracts to fix prices, divide up the trade territory, limit production so as to reduce the supply, or otherwise limit competition are void. Such contracts which affect interstate commerce and which are therefore subject to regulation by the federal government are specifically declared illegal by the Sherman Antitrust Act and the Clayton Act. Most of the states have similar laws applicable to intrastate commerce.

Contracts to Fix the Resale Price. An agreement between a seller and a buyer that the latter shall not resell below a stated price is generally illegal as a price-fixing agreement. The original seller (manufacturer) can, of course, control the price by selling directly to the public through outlet stores.

Unfair Competitive Practices. The Robinson-Patman Act attempted to eliminate certain unfair competitive practices in interstate commerce. Under this act it is unlawful to discriminate in price between competing buyers if the goods are of like grade, quantity, and quality. Most states have passed similar laws for intrastate commerce. Some state statutes go further and prohibit the resale of goods at a loss or below cost for the purpose of harming competition.

Contracts Contrary to Public Policy

Many contracts are unenforceable because they are contrary to public policy. The courts must determine from the nature of the contract whether or not it is contrary to public policy.

One court, in attempting to classify contracts contrary to public policy, defined them thus: "Whatever tends to injustice, restraint of liberty, restraint of a legal right, whatever tends to the obstruction of justice, a violation of a statute, or the obstruction or perversion of the administration of the law as to executive, legislative, or other official action, whenever embodied in and made the subject of a contract, the contract is against public policy and therefore void and not susceptible to enforcement." (Brooks v. Cooper, 50 N. J. Eq. 761, 26 A. 978.)

The most common types of contracts that are invalid because they are contrary to public policy are:

1. Contracts limiting the freedom of marriage
2. Contracts obstructing the administration of justice
3. Contracts injuring the public service

Contracts Limiting the Freedom of Marriage. It is contrary to public policy to enter into any contract the effect of which is to limit freedom of marriage, and such contracts are void. The following provisions in contracts have been held to render the contract a nullity: (1) an agreement whereby one party promises never to marry; (2) an agreement to refrain from marrying for a definite period of time (an agreement not to marry during minority, however, is valid); (3) an agreement not to marry certain named individuals.

Before their marriage, Richard J. Reynolds executed a prenuptial agreement with Marianne O'Brien. In it he conveyed all the common stock of Sapelo Plantation, Inc., by bill of sale and agreed to transfer the stock upon the books of the corporation in consideration of $10 and O'Brien's agreement to marry him. At the time he was married to Elizabeth Dillard Reynolds. The stock was not transferred on the books of the corporation. After Reynolds's death, Marianne Reynolds claimed title to the stock. The agreement to marry another when already married is contrary to public policy, which encourages the preservation of marriage. The agreement was void.

Also, in order to preserve and protect marriages it is held that an agreement to seek a divorce for a consideration is void as against public policy. However, property settlement agreements made in contemplation of divorces are valid.

Contracts Obstructing the Administration of Justice. Any contract that may obstruct our legal processes is null and void. It is not necessary that justice actually be obstructed. If the contract has the tendency to do so, the courts will not enforce it.

The following provisions have been held to render contracts void: (1) an agreement to pay a witness a larger fee than that allowed by law, provided the promisor wins the case; (2) an agreement by a candidate for sheriff that a certain individual will be appointed deputy sheriff in return for aid in bringing about the promisor's election; (3) an agreement to pay a prospective witness a sum of money to leave the state until the trial is over; (4) an agreement not to prosecute a thief if the stolen goods will be returned.

Contracts Injuring the Public Service. Any contract that may, from its very nature, injure public service is void. A person may contract as an attorney to appear before any public authority to obtain or oppose the passage of any bill. But a contract to use improper influence to obtain the desired results is void.

Contracts to use one's influence in obtaining a public contract which by statute must be let to the lowest responsible bidder, to obtain pardons and paroles, or to pay a public official more or less than the statutory salary are also void.

Questions

1. Does a contract which is void for illegality necessarily involve the commission of a crime?

2. What is the effect of an illegal part of a contract?

3. What are some of the types of contracts that have been declared illegal by statute?

4. May one party to a gambling contract sue the other for breach of contract?

5. If a law prohibits the making of a contract on Sunday, what effect might it have on a contract when the offer is made on Sunday and the acceptance made on Monday?

6. What is the difference between the contract rate of interest and the legal rate of interest?

7. Give three illustrations of attempts to disguise transactions to avoid the usury laws.

8. If a real estate agent who is not licensed secures a buyer for a house, is the owner bound to pay the commission?

9. What is the effect of a contract which unreasonably restrains trade?

10. If Joan purchases the Trenton Shoe Store from Mitchell, may she include an enforceable clause in the contract binding Mitchell not to enter the shoe business again in the United States?

11. Is an agreement not to marry enforceable?

12. Donald promises to pay Henry $1,000 if he will leave the state so that he cannot be called as a witness against Donald. Is this a valid contract?

Case Problems

not liable for architectural work

1. Andrews entered into a contract with the Chapman Construction Company to build a garage for $60,000. The construction price included all labor, materials, and architectural services, the architectural designs having been prepared by an employee of the Chapman Construction Company. Neither the employee nor anyone connected with the firm was a licensed architect. After the Chapman Construction Company had done about $5,000 worth of work, Andrews ordered him to stop and refused to pay for any work already done. Is Andrews liable? If the contract had called for the labor and materials to be $58,000 and the architectural fees to be $2,000, would your answer be different?

2. Barbara Weiss Lurie and Bertram S. Lurie, while married but living apart, entered into a property settlement agreement. Bertram was to give Barbara real and personal property and $23,000 cash, $750 for all attorneys' fees, support prior to any divorce, and child support and alimony thereafter. She was to release certain property rights in jointly or separately owned property and resign as requested by Bertram from any position as "Trustee, Officer and/or Director of any trust, corporation or other entity" in which he was involved. All of this was "(u)pon and in the event of the entry or issuance of a final decree in divorce . . ." within four months. The divorce was not final within four months but Barbara asked the court to require Bertram to comply with the agreement. Was the agreement against public policy and therefore illegal?

3. Lund was store manager for Downtown Sporting Goods, Inc. Boland wished to purchase an expensive pistol the store had for sale. A state law made it illegal to sell pistols to anyone who did not have a police permit to carry one. Lund did not know of this law and sold the pistol to Boland on credit. Boland never paid for it, and the seller sued. Must Boland pay for it?

4. The Akin Trucking Company was in desperate need of a loan of $10,000 but could not obtain one without collateral security. It had no acceptable collateral security. The bookkeeper owned $10,000 worth of industrial bonds. He offered to loan these to the firm to use as collateral if the firm would pay him 16 percent a year for their use. The offer was accepted. The contract rate in this state is 15 percent. Was this contract usurious?

5. George and Linda Vordenbaum contracted to sell a residence to Barry and Patricia Rubin. The contract obligated the Rubins to sign a note which would have been usurious. When the Vordenbaums refused to convey the property, the Rubins asked the court to order them to do so. May the Vordenbaums avoid the contract because of usury?

6. Haile contracted with Blank Manufacturing Company to use his influence with the proper government officials to obtain a $10,000,000 government contract for the Blank Company. Haile was to receive 5 percent of any contract he obtained, nothing if he was unsuccessful. Through bribery he obtained a $6,000,000 contract and then demanded a fee of $300,000. Was he entitled to collect?

7. Arthur Wells agreed to sell the stock he owned in Ramson, Inc., back to the corporation for $52,500. He also agreed not to compete with Ramson in the New Bedford and Fall River areas, which are in southeastern Massachusetts —between and not distant from the areas of Ramson's existing business activity. Arthur then formed a corporation which provided the same kind of services as Ramson. Both corporations contracted with regional, nonprofit corporations to provide social services to people. At the time of Arthur's agreement with Ramson no such nonprofit corporations had been organized in the Fall River or New Bedford areas, but they later were. Ramson contracted to provide services with a newly formed New Bedford corporation. Arthur's corporation advertised for a director of a New Bedford office. Ramson sought to have the agreement not to compete enforced. Is the agreement enforceable in Fall River and New Bedford?

10
Form of Contracts

Preview Cases

General Federal Construction, Inc., was awarded a contract for the construction of a hospital. James A. Federline, Inc., had submitted a bid to General for the mechanical work. Federline's bid was used by General in submitting its own bid, but Federline was not awarded the subcontract. It sued General, alleging breach of an oral agreement for it to do the mechanical work. By the terms of the contract the mechanical subcontractor was to provide all preventative maintenance for the equipment for one year after substantial completion of the contract and a complete water treatment service for one year after acceptance of the condensor water system. Was this contract enforceable?

Robertson orally promised his daughter to deed her his lakeside cottage if she would marry Moreau. After the marriage, Robertson refused to execute the deed, and the daughter sued him. Was Robertson bound on his promise?

Contracts may be in written or oral form. All contracts of importance ought to be in writing, but only a few must be written in order to be enforceable. An oral contract is just as effective and enforceable as a written contract unless it is one of the few types specifically required by statute to be in writing.

Reasons for Written Contracts

A written contract has advantages over an oral contract, provided it includes all the terms and provisions of the agreement. In the first place, the existence of a contract cannot be denied if it is in writing. If there were no witnesses when an oral contract was formed, one of the parties might successfully deny that any contract was formed. In the second place, one of the parties may die or become insane. The administrator or executor of an estate in case of death, or the committee or guardian in case of insanity, is tremendously handicapped in enforcing an oral agreement made previously by the deceased or insane person. Even when there are witnesses present at the time an oral contract is formed, the testimony may vary considerably as to the actual terms of the contract. Written evidence, composed in clear and unambiguous language, is always better than oral evidence.

For these reasons most businesspeople prefer to have contracts pertaining to matters of importance reduced to writing as a matter of caution even when this is not required by law.

Statute of Frauds

In the year 1677 the English Parliament enacted a statute known as the *Statute of Frauds*. The statute listed certain classes of contracts which could not be enforced unless their terms were evidenced by a writing. The fourth and the seventeenth sections of the Statute of Frauds contained a list of these contracts. Most of our states have adopted these two sections with but slight variations.

The general provisions of the fourth section are given below. Those in the seventeenth section relating to the sale of goods are covered by the Uniform Commercial Code and will be discussed in Chapter 14.

The Statute of Frauds applies only to executory contracts. If two parties enter into an oral contract which comes within the Statute of Frauds and both parties have fully performed according to its terms, neither party can seek to set aside the transaction on the ground that there was no writing.

The fourth section of the Statute of Frauds provides that the following types of agreements must be in writing:

1. An agreement to sell land or any interest in or concerning land.
2. An agreement the terms of which cannot be performed within one year from the time it is made.
3. An agreement to become responsible for the debts or default of another.
4. An agreement of an executor or administrator to pay debts of the estate from the executor's or the administrator's personal funds.
5. An agreement in which the promise of one person is made in consideration of marriage.

An Agreement to Sell Land or Any Interest in or Concerning Land.   An agreement to sell any interest in land comes within the Statute of Frauds. The writing which is thus required is distinct from the deed which will be executed later and by which the seller makes the actual transfer of title to the buyer.

One may wish to sell not the land itself, but only an interest in the land. The evidence of this contract also must be in writing. These sales usually involve rights of way, joint use of driveways, mineral rights, or timber. A lease for more than one year must be evidenced by a writing to be binding.

◆   The Hulbers orally agreed to sell the standing timber on their land to W. S. Hundley for $64,000. They subsequently executed a written agreement to convey the timber to J. T. Butler for $68,500. Hundley sued the Hulbers to require them to comply with the oral contract, alleging that the sale of the timber was the sale of personal, not real, property. The court held that the sale of the timber was the sale of real property. Since the contract was not in writing, it was voidable by the sellers.

Frequently, oral contracts relative to land are performed before any question of their validity is raised. For example, one leases a building by oral contract for two years. The building is occupied for that period and then the rent is not paid on the ground that the contract is invalid because it is oral. The law will compel payment of the rent orally agreed to for the time that the premises were occupied. If one has paid money or performed a service under an oral contract, the money or the value of the service may be recovered even though the executory part of the contract cannot be enforced. This recovery is not based on the terms of the contract, but on the theory of preventing the unjust enrichment of one party.

An Agreement the Terms of Which Cannot Be Performed Within One Year from the Time It Is Made. The terms of a contract that cannot be performed in one year might easily be forgotten before the contract is completed. To minimize the need to resort to the courts, the law requires all contracts that cannot be performed within one year to be in writing.

This provision of the Statute of Frauds means that if the terms of the contract are such that, by their nature, they cannot be performed within one year from the date of the contract, then the contract must be in writing. The contract can be so worded that it may not be completed for fifty years, yet if it is physically possible to complete it within one year, it need not be in writing. If John agrees in consideration of $5,000 to care for Chen for "as long as he (Chen) lives," this contract need not be in writing because there is no certainty Chen will live one year. But an agreement to manage a motel for five years will, by its terms, require more than one year for performance; therefore, it comes within the Statute of Frauds.

◆   General Federal Construction, Inc., was awarded a contract for the construction of a hospital. James A. Federline, Inc., had submitted a bid to General for the mechanical work. Federline's bid was used by General in submitting its own bid, but Federline was not awarded the subcontract. It sued General, alleging breach of an oral agreement for it to do the mechanical work. By the terms of the contract the mechanical subcontractor was to provide all preventative maintenance for the equipment for one year after substantial completion of the contract and a complete water treatment service for one year after acceptance of the condensor water system by the owner. By the terms of this contract, it could not be performed within one year; therefore, it was not enforceable.

An Agreement to Become Responsible for the Debts or Default of Another.

The term *debt* here refers to an obligation to pay money; *default* refers to a breach of contractual obligations other than money, such as a contract to build a house. Under such an agreement the promisor undertakes to make good the loss which the promisee would sustain if another person does not pay the promisee the debt owed or fails to perform a duty imposed by contract or by law. If *A* promises *C* to pay *B*'s debt to *C* if *B* fails to pay, *A*'s promise must be in writing; *A*'s promise is to be responsible for the debt of another.

The Statute of Frauds does not apply to the promise if in fact it is an original promise by the promisor rather than a promise to pay the debt of another. For example, if *A* buys on credit from *B* and tells *B* to deliver the goods to *C*, *A* is not promising to pay the debt of another; the promise is to pay *A*'s own debt. *A*'s promise does not have to be in writing.

The Statute of Frauds does not apply if the main purpose of the promise is to gain some advantage for the promisor. This provision of the Statute of Frauds was designed especially for those situations where one promises to answer for the debt of another person purely as an accommodation to that person. There are situations where one person promises to answer for the debt or default of another because it is in the promisor's personal financial interest to do so.

Modern Electric Co. contracted with Warren Reese to install heating and air conditioning equipment in Reese's building. The equipment that was installed was not at all satisfactory and did not meet the specifications in the contract. Air Engineers, Inc., told Reese that if he would delay suing Modern Electric it would correct the problem. The heating and air conditioning never became adequate.

Nearly two years after the requested delay Reese filed suit. The court found that the forbearance of suit was beneficial to Air Engineers and so was not within the Statute of Frauds.

The Statute of Frauds does not apply where the promisor promises the debtor that the promisor will pay the debt owed to the third person.

Durwood sold Kenney an air conditioner for $400 and gave him 90 days to pay for it. Kenney became ill and could not work. His Uncle Glen said to him, "Don't worry; when it falls due, I will pay it." When the uncle did not pay Durwood, Kenney demanded that he pay. The uncle claimed he was not bound because the promise was not in writing. This defense is not valid because the Statute of Frauds does not require a writing when the promise is made directly to the debtor.

An Agreement of an Executor or Administrator to Personally Pay the Debts of the Estate.

When a person dies, an executor or administrator takes over all the deceased's assets and from these assets pays all the debts of the deceased before distributing the remainder according to the terms of the decedent's will or, in the absence of a will, to the heirs. The executor or the administrator is not obligated to pay the debts of the deceased out of the executor's personal funds. For this reason, a promise to pay the debts of the estate from personal funds is in reality a contract to become responsible for the debts of another and must be in writing to be enforceable.

The Statute of Frauds does not apply when the administrator or the executor enters into an original contract relative to the estate. For example, an agreement to cover burial arrangements for the deceased does not come within the statute.

An Agreement in Which the Promise of One Person Is Made in Consideration of Marriage.

An agreement by which one person promises to pay a sum of money or to give property to another in consideration of marriage or a promise to marry must be in writing. This requirement of the Statute of Frauds does not apply to mutual promises to marry.

Robertson orally promised his daughter to deed her his lakeside cottage if she would marry Moreau. After the marriage, Robertson refused to execute the deed and the daughter sued him. Robertson was not bound to execute the transfer since his promise was oral.

Note or Memorandum

The Statute of Frauds requires either that the agreement be in writing and signed by both parties or that there be a note or memorandum in writing signed by the party against whom the claim for breach of promise is made. With the exception of the case of the sale of goods, as will be discussed in Chapter 14, the contract and the note or memorandum required by the Statute of Frauds must set forth all the material terms of the transaction. For example, in the case of the sale of an interest in real estate the memorandum must contain the names of the parties, the subject matter of the contract, the basic terms of the contract, including the price and the manner of delivery, and it must be signed by the one to be charged.

The law states that the memorandum must contain all the essential terms of the contract; yet the memorandum differs materially from a written contract. Probably the chief difference is that one may introduce oral testimony to explain or complete the memorandum. The court held the following receipt was an adequate memorandum: "Received of Sholowitz twenty-five dollars to bind the bargain for the sale of Noorigian's brick store and land at 46 Blackstone Street to Sholowitz. Balance due $1,975."

The memorandum need not be made at the time of the contract. It need be in existence only at the time suit is brought. The one who signs the memorandum need not sign with the intention of being bound. If Jones writes Smith, "Since my agreement to pay you the $500 Jacobson owes you was oral, I am not bound by it," this is a sufficient memorandum and removes the objection based on the Statute of Frauds.

Other Written Contracts

The five classes of contracts that are listed by the Statute of Frauds are not the only contracts required by law to be in writing in order to be enforceable. Every state has a few additional requirements. The more common ones are contracts for the sale of securities, agreements to pay a commission to real estate brokers, and a new promise to extend the statute of limitations.

Parol Evidence Rule

Spoken words, that is, *parol evidence*, will not be permitted to add to, modify, or contradict the terms of a written contract which appears to be complete unless there is evidence of fraud, accident, or mistake so that the writing is in fact not a contract or is incomplete. This is known as the *parol evidence rule*.

If a written contract appears to be complete, the parol evidence rule will not permit modification by oral testimony or other writing made before or at the time of executing the agreement. However, an exception is made when the contract refers to other writings and indicates they are considered as incorporated into the contract.

The parol evidence rule is based on the assumption that a written contract represents the complete agreement. If, however, the contract is not complete, the courts will admit parol evidence to clear up ambiguity or to show the existence of trade customs which are to be regarded as forming part of the contract.

A contract which appears to be complete may, in fact, have omitted a provision which ought to have been included. If the omission is due to fraud, alteration, typographical errors, duress, or other similar conduct, oral testimony may be produced to show such conduct.

Questions

1. As a general rule, an oral contract is just as enforceable as a written contract. Why, then, should all important contracts be in writing?

2. Name some types of contracts that must be in writing to be enforceable.

3. If one assumes an original obligation, even though the benefits go to another party, must the contract be in writing to be enforceable?

4. If the main purpose of a promise to answer for another's debt is to gain some advantage for the promisor, must the contract be in writing?

5. What contracts of an executor need to be in writing?

6. Does the Statute of Frauds apply to mutual promises to marry?

7. What must be included in a note or memorandum required by the Statute of Frauds?

8. Must a memorandum be made at the same time the contract is made?

9. What is the *parol evidence* rule?

10. May oral evidence ever be admitted to contradict a complete written contract?

Case Problems

1. Howard E. Johnson and Loren Ward orally contracted to form a partnership to operate a dental supply business. Johnson later sued for a dissolution of the partnership. A written contract which was never signed provided for the termination of the partnership on default, withdrawal, or death of Ward or the closing of other branches operated by Johnson. Ward asked the court to dismiss the suit because the contract was not in writing and not performed within one year. Was the contract in violation of the Statute of Frauds?

2. Kenneth Gross, the primary unsecured creditor of Wind Surfing, Inc., asked White Stag Manufacturing Co. to extend credit to Wind Surfing. White Stag said not until a past-due balance was paid. After negotiations, Gross personally sent $14,000 to White Stag to apply to the past-due account. When calling to check on whether further merchandise would be sent, Gross promised White Stag he had signed a guaranty form which was in the mail. White Stag shipped goods worth a total of $49,637.87 to Wind Surfing. Gross's guaranty never arrived and Wind Surfing never paid its accounts. In a suit by White Stag, Gross argued that he was not liable because his agreement to pay the debt of Wind Surfing was not in writing. Was he liable?

3. The Cofer Office Equipment Company entered into a written contract with the Mercurio Insurance Company to keep all the insurance company's equip-

ment repaired for the next three years for a monthly fee of $200. This written contract was signed, and each party retained a copy. Before the contract was signed, it was orally agreed that the contract was not to become effective unless Congress passed a new accelerated depreciation law. Nevertheless, the parties signed the contract and each retained a copy. This law was never passed. Cofer Office Equipment sued for breach of contract. The Mercurio Insurance Company attempted to prove by parol evidence the existence of this oral side agreement. Can it do so?

4. The Jabberwock Band contracted in writing with Jeanette Johnson to perform for two months at The Riverbend Lounge. Before the contract was signed, the leader of the band orally promised Johnson she could terminate upon giving two weeks' notice if the band did not draw well. This promise was not in the written contract. The band failed to draw patrons. Johnson gave two weeks' termination notice and then fired the band. The band sued her for the amount due for the remaining time under the written contract. Was evidence of the two-week termination agreement admissible? *No.*

5. Marcia rented a house by oral contract for two years at $425 a month. She soon became dissatisfied with the deal because she learned she could rent a better house for $375 a month. She did not learn that this oral contract was not binding on her until after two years. She then demanded that the landlord reimburse her $50 a month for two years. Can she succeed?

6. The Reed Paper Company had for some time been negotiating with Downs on a business deal of the utmost importance to the company. The parties finally reached an agreement. Paul Chapman, secretary to the president of the Reed Paper Company, made a written memorandum of the contract, and Downs signed it. Chapman filed the memorandum. Later Downs refused to conform to her agreement. The memorandum could not be found because Chapman could not remember how or where he had filed it. The contract involved the sale of several thousand acres of pulpwood and the processing of the wood into paper over a period of three years. Can this contract be enforced if the memorandum was not found?

7. Robert Sickinger owned the motion picture rights to a novel and was required to direct the first motion picture based on it. Sickinger and David Sawyer orally agreed that if the author would allow Sawyer to direct the first movie, Sickinger would give Sawyer an option to acquire a screenplay and all of Sickinger's rights under his agreements with the author. The option required Sawyer to pay Sickinger 1.5 percent of the producer's share of the net profits from the movie forever. Sawyer obtained the required permission from the author, but Sickinger refused to perform the agreement. Sawyer sued Sickinger, who alleged the agreement could not be performed within one year. Could it?

8. John Barner was sales manager for the Patterson Motor Company. Billy Seabolt, a minor, agreed to purchase a used car for $1,400. As a part of the

contract Barner stipulated that an adult must "stand good" for the payment. Steedman, an aunt of Seabolt, said, "Let him have the car, and if he does not keep up the payments, I will." Seabolt wrecked the car and refused to pay. Can Barner look to Steedman for the selling price?

9. Pat O'Halloran owned and operated the O'Halloran Barber Shop. He orally contracted with Buddy Broadnax to give Broadnax, a druggist, and his three boys all the haircuts and shaves they needed for the next two years for $400 cash. Broadnax was to pay the money the next day, but he changed his mind and refused to pay it. O'Halloran wrote Broadnax a letter and demanded that "you pay me the $550 as you promised." Broadnax immediately replied by letter, "I never agreed to pay $550. It was $400. Anyway it is an oral contract, so try to collect it." O'Holloran claimed this constituted a sufficient memorandum. Do you agree?

11

Third Parties and Contracts

Preview Cases

Equilease Corporation leased seven trucks to Henry Oil Company, Inc. To secure the lease payments, Henry Oil assigned six savings certificates issued by State Federal Savings and Loan Association to Equilease. State Federal was not notified of the assignment. Henry Oil told State Federal that the savings certificates had been lost and was allowed by State Federal to withdraw the deposits represented by the certificates. Henry Oil defaulted on its lease with Equilease, which then discovered that the funds had been withdrawn. Equilease sued State Federal for the amount of the savings certificates. Can it recover?

Hemisphere National Bank loaned Fancy Foods of Greenbank Ltd. $72,000 secured by a surety bond from Wisconsin Surety Corporation. Fancy Foods defaulted and Wisconsin Surety became insolvent. Monte and Marietta Bourjaily, the sole shareholders of Fancy Foods, then executed a deed of trust on real estate to the bank. The deed of trust was foreclosed and the bank received $30,000. During the foreclosure proceedings, the bank executed an affidavit stating the deed of trust was "to replace the surety bond provided by Wisconsin Surety." The bank sued the District of Columbia Insurance Guaranty Association for reimbursement of the debt. The Association was liable only if the bank had a claim against Wisconsin Surety. Did it?

A contract creates both rights and obligations. Initially, one who is not a party to the contract has no right to the benefits to be derived from the contract, nor responsibility for any of the duties or obligations. Third parties, however, may acquire these rights or assume these duties.

A party to a contract may wish to assign the rights or to delegate the duties under the contract, or to do both. If one party transfers the contract in its entirety, it is "an assignment of rights and a delegation of duties." An *assignment* is the means whereby one party conveys rights in a contract to another who is not a party to the original undertaking. The term *delegation* is used to describe a transfer of the duties alone without a transfer of rights. Whether rights may be assigned and duties delegated depends upon their nature and the terms of the contract.

◆   Bolliot made a contract with DeFoe whereby DeFoe was to wire Bolliot's house. For this service Bolliot agreed to pay DeFoe $925. DeFoe delegated the job to Kujath. This is a valid delegation of duties without an assignment of the right to receive the $925 upon the completion of the work.

Rights transferred by assignment and duties transferred by delegation cannot be modified by the assignment or transfer. They remain the same as though only the original parties to the contract were involved.

Assignment of Rights

As a general rule, a party's rights under a contract may be assigned. One's rights under a contract may be transferred almost as freely as property. The party making the assignment is known as the *assignor*; the one to whom the right is transferred is the *assignee*.

Statutes may impose some restrictions on the assignment of rights. Statutes in a number of states prohibit employees from assigning their wages. Statutes also prohibit the assignment of future pay by soldiers, sailors, and marines. Many states and cities also prohibit the assignment of the pay of public officials. Employees on public works are in many states prohibited by law from assigning a certain minimum percentage of their wages. This is to protect wage earners and their families from hard-pressing creditors.

Often one's right under a contract is to receive the services of the other party, such as a bookkeeper, salesperson, or other employee. A right to personal services cannot be assigned because an employee cannot be required to work for a new employer without the employee's consent.

The parties may include in the original contract a prohibition of the assignment of rights thereunder. Such a prohibition, however, is not effective in some states when only the right to money has been assigned.

Delegation of Duties

The duties under a contract cannot be delegated by a party as readily as the rights can be assigned because there is more frequently a "personal" element in the performance aspect of a contract, and it would change the obligation thereof if it were performed by another. If Allen retains Bentley, an attorney, to obtain a divorce for a fee of $350, Bentley can assign the right to receive the $350 to anyone and Allen must pay. The duty to represent Allen in the divorce proceeding, however, may not be delegated. In those contracts that involve trust and confidence, one may not delegate the duties. If one employs the Local Wonder Band to play for a dance, the contract cannot be assigned, even to a nationally known band. Taste, confidence, and trust cannot be scientifically measured. Nor is it material that a reasonable person would be satisfied or content with the substitution. But if one hires Horne to paint a house for $900, whether or not the house has been painted properly can readily be determined by recognized standards in the trade.

Only when the performance is standardized may one delegate its performance to another. In the construction industry, for example, there are many instances of delegation of duties because the correct performance can be easily ascertained. Contracts calling for unskilled work or labor may in most instances be delegated.

In all cases of delegation the delegating party remains fully liable under the contract. Suit may be brought for any breach of contract even though another party actually performed. In such an event the delegating party may in turn sue the party who performed inadequately.

The parties to the original contract may expressly prohibit the delegation of duties thereunder.

Effect of an Assignment

An assignment transfers to the assignee all the rights, title, or interest held by the assignor in whatever is being assigned. The assignee does not receive any greater right or interest than was held by the assignor.

The nonassigning party retains all rights and defenses as though there had never been an assignment. For example, if the nonassigning party was incompetent to contract or entered into the contract under duress, undue influence, fraud, or misrepresentation, these defenses may be raised by the nonassigning party against the assignee as effectively as they could have been raised against the assignor.

Most assignments involve claims for money. The Fair Deal Grocery Company assigned $10,000 worth of its accounts receivable to the First National Bank. The assignor warranted that the accounts were genuine. If a customer, therefore, refused to pay the bank and proved that no money was owed, the grocery company would be liable. If payment was not made merely because of insolvency, most courts would hold that the assignor was not liable.

Warranties of the Assignor

When one assigns rights under a contract to an assignee for value, three implied warranties are made:

1. That the assignor is the true owner of the right
2. That the right is valid and subsisting at the time the assignment is made
3. That there are no defenses available to the debtor which have not been disclosed to the assignee

If there is a breach of warranty by the assignor, the assignee may seek to recover any loss from the assignor.

In the absence of an express guarantee, an assignor does not warrant that the other party will perform the duties under the contract, that the other party will make payment, or that the other party is solvent.

The Harbottle Distributing Company owed the Norfolk Brewery $10,000. In payment Harbottle assigned $10,000 of its accounts receivable to the Norfolk Brewery in full satisfaction of the debt. The assignee was able to collect only $7,000 of these accounts because the debtors were insolvent. The brewery has no recourse to Harbottle. Had the $3,000 been uncollectible because the debtors had valid defenses to the claims, then the Harbottle Distributing Company would have had to make good the loss.

In the preceding case the Norfolk Brewery Company erred by taking these accounts receivable by assignment. In this case Harbottle Distributing Company paid its debt, not with cash, but by a transfer of title of its accounts receivable. From the brewery company's standpoint the same result could have been obtained, not by taking title to these accounts, but by taking them merely as collateral security for their debt with a provision that the brewery was to collect the accounts and apply the proceeds on the $10,000. Under this arrangement, the brewery could have looked to the distributing company for the balance of $3,000.

Form of the Assignment

An assignment may be made either by operation of law or by the act of the parties. In the event of death, the rights and duties (except for personal services) of the deceased are assigned by law to the executor or administrator of the estate. In the event of bankruptcy, the rights and duties of the bankrupt are assigned by operation of law to the trustee in bankruptcy. These two types of assignments are automatic. The assignment is effective without any act of the parties.

When the assignment is made by act of the parties, it may be either written or oral; however, it must be clear that a present assignment of an interest held by the assignor is intended. If the original contract is one which must be in writing, the assignment must be in writing; otherwise, it may be made orally. It is always preferable to make an assignment in writing. This may be done in the case of written contracts by writing the terms of the assignment on the back of the written contract. Any contract may be assigned by executing an informal written assignment. The following written assignment is adequate in most cases.

> In consideration of the Local Finance Company's canceling my debt of $500 to it, I hereby assign to the Local Finance Company $500 owed to me by the Dale Sand and Gravel Company.
>
> Signed at noon, Friday, December 16, 1985, at Benson, Iowa.
>
> (Signed) Harold Locke

While an assignment may be made for consideration, consideration is not necessary.

Notice of an Assignment

Notice need not be given to the other party in order to make the assignment effective as between the assignor and the assignee. Business prudence demands that the original promisor be notified, however. The assignee may not receive payment if notification of the assignment is not given to the original promisor. The promisor has a right to assume that the claim has not been assigned unless otherwise notified. For example, F. Gonzales promised to pay Hodges $500 in thirty days. When the account came due, Gonzales, since no notice of assignment had been given, was safe in paying Hodges. But if Hodges had assigned the account to Wilson and Wilson had not given Gonzales notice, then Wilson would not have been able to collect from Gonzales.

Equilease Corporation leased seven trucks to Henry Oil Company, Inc. To secure the lease payments, Henry Oil assigned six savings certificates issued by State Federal Savings and Loan Association to Equilease. State Federal was not notified of the assignment. Henry Oil told State Federal that the savings certificates had been lost and was allowed by State Federal to withdraw the deposits represented by the certificates. Henry Oil defaulted on its lease with Equilease, which then discovered that the funds had been withdrawn. Equilease sued State Federal for the amount of the savings certificates. Since State Federal had not been notified of the assignment, it was not liable for allowing Henry Oil to withdraw the funds.

In most jurisdictions, if a party to a contract makes more than one assignment and the assignees all give notice, priority is given in the order in which the assignments were made.

In the event the assignor assigns a larger sum than the debtor owes, there is no obligation on the debtor to pay the entire assignment. When the creditor assigns only part of a claim, there is no obligation on the debtor to make payment thereof to the assignee, although such payment may be made and the debtor's liability to the creditor reduced to the extent of such payment.

Novation

The party entitled to receive performance under a contract may agree to release the party who is bound to perform and to permit another party to render performance. When this occurs it is not just a matter of delegating the duties under the contract; rather, it is a matter of abandoning the old contract and substituting a new one in its place. The change of contract and parties is called *novation*. To be more precise, it is substituting a new party for one of the original parties at the mutual agreement of the original parties, such that the prior contract is terminated and a new one substituted for it. The terms of the contract remain the same, but the parties are different. For example, if Koslov and Burnham have a contract, they, together with Caldwell, may agree that Caldwell shall take Koslov's place. If this is done, there is a novation. Koslov is discharged from the contract, and Burnham and Caldwell are bound. It must be shown that a novation was intended. When there is a novation, the original obligor drops out of the picture, and the new party takes the original obligor's place and is alone liable for the performance.

Hemisphere National Bank loaned Fancy Foods of Greenbank Ltd. $72,000 secured by a surety bond from Wisconsin Surety Corporation. Fancy Foods defaulted and Wisconsin Surety became insolvent. Monte and Marietta Bourjaily, the only shareholders of Fancy Foods, then executed a deed of trust on real estate to the bank. The deed of trust was foreclosed and the bank received $30,000. During the foreclosure proceedings, the bank executed an affidavit stating the deed of trust was "to replace the surety bond provided by Wisconsin Surety." The bank sued the District of Columbia Insurance Guaranty Association for reimbursement of the debt. The Association was liable only if the bank had a claim against Wisconsin Surety. On the basis of the affidavit and the $30,000 from the foreclosure sale, there was a novation and the bank had no claim against Wisconsin Surety.

Third Party Beneficiary Contracts

At common law only the parties to a contract could sue upon or seek to enforce the contract. It was held that strangers to a contract had no rights under a contract. But courts began to make exceptions to the rule when it seemed evident that the contracting parties intended to benefit a third person, called a *third party beneficiary*.

The rule today is that a third person who is expressly benefited by the performance of the contract may enforce it against the promisor if benefit to the third party was intended by the contracting parties. The third person may be either a creditor beneficiary or a donee beneficiary. A *creditor beneficiary* is a person to whom the promisee owes an obligation or duty which will be discharged to the extent that the promisor performs the promise. If *A* makes a contract to pay *B*'s debt to *C*, *C* is the creditor beneficiary of the contract between *A* and *B*. A *donee beneficiary* is one to whom no legal duty is owed by the promise but to whom performance is a gift; an example is the beneficiary named in a life insurance contract.

Not everyone who benefits by the performance of a contract between others is properly considered a third party beneficiary with rights under the contract. If a person is merely incidentally benefited by the performance of a contract, suit for breach or for performance will not be successful. For example, if a town contracts with a contractor for the paving of a certain street and the contractor fails to perform, the property owners whose property would have been improved by the paving are not entitled to sue for damages for nonperformance because they were to be only incidentally benefited. The contract for the paving of the street was designed essentially to further the public interest, not to benefit individual property owners who are merely *incidental beneficiaries*.

Joint, Several, and Joint and Several Contracts

When two or more persons enter into a contract with one or more other persons, the contract may be joint, several, or joint and several. The intention of the parties determines which type of contract it is.

Joint Contracts. A *joint contract* is a contract in which two or more persons jointly promise to carry out an obligation or a contract in which two or more persons are jointly entitled to the performance of another party or parties. If Sands and Cole sign a contract stating "we jointly promise . . . ," the obligation is the joint obligation of Sands and Cole. Unless otherwise expressed, a promise by two or more persons is generally presumed to be joint and not several.

Several Contracts. A *several contract* arises when two or more persons individually agree to perform the same obligation even though the individual agreements are contained in the same document. If Sands and Cole sign a contract stating "we severally promise" or "each of us promises" to do a particular thing, the two signers are individually bound to perform.

Joint and Several Contracts. A *joint and several contract* is one in which two or more persons are bound both jointly and severally. If Sands and Cole sign a contract stating "we, and each of us, promise" or "I promise" to perform a particular act, they are jointly and severally obligated.

The other party to the contract may treat the obligation as either a joint obligation or as a group of individual obligations and may bring suit against all or any one or more of them at one time. By statute in some states, a joint contract is interpreted to be a joint and several contract.

Questions

1. What is an assignment?

2. Name and identify the parties to an assignment.

3. Why may rights to personal services not be assigned?

4. If one delegates duties under a contract, what is the delegating party's liability under the contract?

5. If a party becomes dissatisfied with a contract, does assigning it to someone else rid the party of all obligations?

6. What is the effect of an assignment upon each party involved?

7. Must assignments be in writing?

8. Is notice necessary to make an assignment effective?

9. When may a third person who is benefited by a contract enforce it?

10. Explain the meaning of *joint*, *several*, and *joint and several contracts*.

Case Problems

1. Verlin and Loretta Wippert agreed to sell Stone Ranch to the Robertsons. By a written supplemental agreement the Robertsons agreed to carry out the terms of a summer pasturage lease to Larry Whitford and the Robertsons were to ". . . be entitled to payment from Larry Whitford of the remaining $12,000 . . ." rent. The ranch was conveyed to the Robertsons. The $12,000 was not paid, and the Robertsons sought to recover the $12,000 from the Wipperts. Was the agreement an assignment? Could the Robertsons recover from the Wipperts?

2. Eugene Black was credit manager for a furniture store. Stine purchased some furniture and in payment assigned to the furniture store $800 which was owed to her by the Clarke Engineering Corporation. Since the $800 was not due until ten days after the date of the assignment, Black held the assignment until that date and presented it for payment. Payment was refused because Stine had offered the Clarke Engineering Corporation a 10-percent discount if they

would pay her before the account was due. This they did. Must the corporation also pay the furniture store?

3. A partnership, Boger-Hare Manufacturing, and its partners, Mike Boger and J. O. Hare, got a loan from American Bank of Commerce and signed a note. Hare signed a guaranty contract agreeing to pay the partnership debts. A second loan was made and note executed by Hare. Seven months later a third note in the amount due on the partnership notes was prepared to be executed by Boger-Hare, Inc., although the business had not, in fact, been incorporated. Both Hare and Boger signed it, without indicating any corporate titles. The first two notes were not cancelled. The bank sued the partnership and the partners for payment of the first two notes. They argued the third note was a novation. Was it?

4. Delaney, who owned and operated the Downtown Cafeteria, sold it to Harper for $80,000, with $30,000 cash and the balance paid by note. Sometime later Harper sold the cafeteria to Mitchell; and Mitchell, as a part of the purchase price, agreed to assume Harper's obligation to pay Delaney the $50,000. Mitchell operated the cafeteria profitably for several months during which time his net profits were $18,000, but he made no payment on the notes. He became ill, and the business declined rapidly. Delaney demanded that Harper pay the balance due on the original selling price. Was Harper obligated to pay this?

5. At a contempt of court hearing, Thomas C. Vaughn said he planned to pay his child support arrearages out of his inheritance from the estate of Marvin Everett Vaughn. Nine days later, Vaughn executed a written assignment of his interest in the estate to Homemaker's Finance and Real Estate Loans. The personal representative of the estate asked the court which of the assignments he should honor. Was Vaughn's action at the contempt hearing a present assignment of his interest in the estate or merely an agreement to transfer the funds sometime in the future?

6. The Marbut Office Supply Company had a contract with the Second National Bank to keep all its office machines repaired for $200 a month. The Marbut Company sold its business in bulk to the McGregor Corporation and assigned the repair contract to this company. The bank refused to honor the assignment. Must it do so?

12

Termination of Contracts

Preview Cases

Jerry and Ann Beachum conveyed land to Rancho Camille, S.A., which agreed to pay a note secured by a deed of trust on the property, to pay the taxes, and to keep the property insured. The Beachums sued to rescind the conveyance and for costs of court, alleging that a payment on the note was past due and unpaid, the taxes were delinquent, and the insurance policy had not been renewed. After part of the trial, Rancho Camille offered to pay the taxes, alleging the note and insurance had been paid. At the end of the trial it offered to pay the taxes and the still unpaid note payment and insurance. Was there a valid tender?

Winfred Mullen agreed to purchase Rufus Wafer's "accounting business and equipment, including all accounts in connection therewith." Wafer agreed "to remain active in the accounting business with Buyer for a period of two years" and "cooperate fully with the Buyer in effecting a satisfactory transfer of accounts . . . and giving all encouragement possible to the continuation of business relations." Wafer moved from his offices and occupied offices with Mullen. They executed a promissory note and security agreement. Less than a month later, Wafer died. Mullen asked the court to rescind the contract of sale and cancel the note claiming the contract was contingent on Wafer's providing personal services. The executrix of Wafer's estate argued the contract was for the sale of the accounting business, and the transfer was made before Wafer's death. Who was correct?

While it is important to know how a contract is formed and who is bound on it, it is also important to know when it is ended, or terminated, and when the parties are no longer bound.

Methods by Which Contracts Are Terminated

There are five common methods by which contracts may be terminated. These are (1) by performance of the contract, (2) by operation of law, (3) by voluntary agreement of the parties, (4) by impossibility of performance, and (5) by acceptance of a breach of contract.

Performance. When all the terms of a contract have been fulfilled, the contract is discharged by performance. Not all the parties, however, need to perform simultaneously. Parties are discharged from further liability as soon as they have done all that they have agreed to do. The other party or parties are not discharged, nor is the contract, if any material thing remains to be done by them.

Several factors determine whether there has been performance:

1. Time of performance
2. Tender of performance
3. Satisfactory performance
4. Substantial performance

Time of Performance. If the contract states when performance is to be rendered, the contract provisions must be followed unless under all the circumstances, performance on the exact date specified is not vital. When performance on the exact date is deemed vital, it is said that "time is of the essence." If no time for performance is stated, then performance must ordinarily be rendered within a reasonable time.

Tender of Performance. An offer to perform an obligation in satisfaction of the terms of a contract is called a *tender of performance*. If a contract calls for the performance of an act at a specified time, a tender of performance will discharge the obligation of the one making the tender so long as the tender conforms to the agreement.

An offer, along with the ability, to pay money in satisfaction of a debt or claim is a *tender of payment*. The debtor must offer the exact amount due, including interest, costs, and attorneys' fees, if any are required. If the debtor says, "I am now ready to pay you," a sufficient tender has not been made. The debtor must pay or offer the creditor the amount due.

Jerry and Ann Beachum conveyed land to Rancho Camille, S.A., which agreed to pay a note secured by a deed of trust on the property, to pay the taxes, and to keep the property insured. The Beachums sued to rescind the conveyance and for costs of court, alleging that a payment on the note was past due and unpaid, the taxes were delinquent, and the insurance policy had not been renewed. After part of the trial, Rancho Camille offered to pay the taxes, alleging the note and insurance had been paid. At the end of the trial it offered to pay the taxes and the still unpaid note payment and insurance. The court found there was not a valid tender since even after offering to pay the note payment and insurance, Rancho Camille had never offered to pay the accrued court costs.

A tender in the form of a check is not a proper tender. The payment must be made in *legal tender*. With but few minor exceptions, this is any form of United States money. If a check is accepted, the contract is performed as soon as the check is honored by the bank on which it is drawn.

If the tender is refused, the debt is not discharged. However, proper tender does stop the running of interest. In addition, if the creditor should bring suit, the person who has tendered the correct amount is not liable for court costs after the date of the tender. The debtor must, however, be in readiness to pay at any time. If a tender is made after a suit, the debtor frequently pays the money over to the court.

Satisfactory Performance. It frequently happens that contracts specifically state that the performance must be "satisfactory to" or "to the satisfaction of" a certain person. What constitutes satisfactory performance is frequently a disputed question. The courts generally have adopted the rule especially when a definite, objective measure of satisfaction exists that if the contract is performed in a manner that would satisfy an ordinary, reasonable person, the terms of the contract have been met sufficiently to discharge it. There is one exception to this rule: If the performance clearly involves the personal taste or judgment of one of the parties, it may be rejected on the ground that it is not satisfactory to that party.

Mary employed Janet, an expert seamstress, to make her wedding gown. It was to be made "to your absolute satisfaction." Mary refused to take the gown on the ground "it doesn't look exactly right on me." This was sufficient ground for refusing to pay. Clothing generally, and a wedding gown in particular, involves personal satisfaction of the customer. The seamstress had expressly agreed that it was to be made "to your absolute satisfaction."

Substantial Performance. Under the early common law, each party to a contract had to perform to the last letter of the contract before a demand for the party's rights under the contract could be made. Such a rule was often extremely inequitable. If a contractor builds a $50 million office building, it might be grossly unfair to say that none of the $50 million could be collected because of a relatively minor breach.

The law today can be stated as follows: If a construction contract is substantially performed, the party performing may demand the full price under the contract less the difference between the value if constructed according to the contract and the value as constructed. In the case of the office building, if the value of the building if constructed according to contract would be $50 million and the value of the building as constructed is $49,995,000, the contractor will be allowed to collect the contract price minus $5,000. Suppose, however, that the contractor completed the excavation and then quit. The contractor would be entitled to collect nothing. Just how far the contractor must proceed toward full performance before there has been substantial performance is often difficult to determine. The performance must be so nearly complete that it would be a great injustice to deny the contractor any compensation for the work. There must have been an honest attempt to perform without an intentional or significant deviation from the contract.

◆   Dorothy E. Converse sold her equipment-rental business to John and Beverly Zinke for cash and a note secured by a lien on the business property. The Zinkes failed to make the required note payments, so Converse sued. The Zinkes alleged failure of consideration because 71 of the 273 items of inventory purchased were in need of repair or inoperable. This was not a total failure of consideration. The contract was substantially performed by Converse. The Zinkes could be adequately compensated by damages or a setoff of the purchase price.

Discharge by Operation of Law.   Under certain circumstances the law will effect a discharge of the contract, or at least the law will bar all right of action. The most common conditions under which the law operates to discharge contracts are:

1. Discharge in bankruptcy
2. Running of the statute of limitations
3. Alteration of written contract

Bankruptcy. It is not uncommon for individuals and business firms to be overwhelmed with financial obligations. The law permits individuals and firms to petition the court for a decree of voluntary bankruptcy. Creditors may, under certain circumstances, force one into involuntary bankruptcy. In either event, after a discharge in bankruptcy creditors' rights of action to enforce the contracts of the debtor are barred.

Statute of Limitations. A person's right to sue must be exercised within the time fixed by a statute which is called the *statute of limitations*. This time varies from state to state, for different types of suits, and for different types of debts. For open accounts, accounts receivable, and ordinary loans, the time varies from two to eight years, while for notes it varies from four to twenty years.

After a person has brought suit and obtained judgment, the judgment must be enforced by having the property of the debtor levied upon and sold. If this is not done, a statute of limitations operates even against judgments in some states. In those states where a statute applies to judgments, the time varies from five to twenty-one years from date of judgment. If a payment is made on a support judgment, the payment constitutes an acknowledgment of the debt and the statute starts to run again from the date of payment.

The time is calculated from the date the obligation is due. In the case of running accounts, as purchases from department stores, the time starts from the date of the last purchase. If a part payment is made, the statute begins to run again from the date of such payment. If the promisor leaves the state, the statute ceases to run while the promisor is beyond the jurisdiction of the court.

◆   Jack Slayton purchased items from Oras Taylor on an open account. Five years after the last purchase, Slayton made two $5 payments on the account. Less than three years after the payments, Taylor sued to collect the amount owed. Slayton defended the suit on the basis of a three-year statute of limitations. The court ruled that on an open account, part payment made after the statute of limitations has barred suit starts the statute running again.

A debt that has been outlawed by a statute of limitations may be revived. This is done in some states by a written acknowledgment of or a promise to pay the debt, in others by part payment after it has been outlawed, and in still others by the mere payment of the interest. After the debt is revived the period of the statute of limitations begins to run again from the time of the revival.

Alteration of Written Contract. If one of the parties alters the written contract, it is discharged if the alteration was done intentionally and without the consent of the other party. In most states the alteration must also be material. If a contractor who has undertaken to build a house by January 15, realizing that because of winter conditions it cannot be finished by that date, erases and changes the date to March 15, there is a material alteration which will discharge the contract.

Voluntary Agreement of the Parties. A contract is a mutual agreement. The parties are as free to change their minds by mutual agreement as they are to agree in the first place. Consequently, whenever the parties to a contract agree not to carry out its terms, the contract is discharged. The contract itself may recite events or circumstances which will automatically terminate the agreement. The release of one party to the contract constitutes the consideration for the release of the other.

Impossibility of Performance. If the act called for in a contract is impossible to perform at the time the contract is made, no contract ever comes into existence. Frequently, impossibility of performance arises after a valid contract is formed. This type of impossibility discharges the contract under certain circumstances. However, the fact that performance has merely become more difficult does not discharge the contract. The most common causes of discharge by impossibility of performance occurring after the contract is made are:

1. Destruction of the subject matter.
2. New laws making the contract illegal.
3. Death or physical incapacity of person to render personal services.

Destruction of the Subject Matter. If the contract involves specific subject matter, the destruction of this specific subject matter without the fault of the parties, discharges the contract because of impossibility of performance. This rule applies only when the performance of the contract depends on the continued existence of a specified person, animal, or thing.

The contract is not discharged if an event occurs which it is reasonable to anticipate. Any payment made in advance must be returned when performance of the contract is excused.

An agreement provided that Ishikawajima-Harima Heavy Industries Co., Ltd., would manufacture and deliver "as far as it is able" small boats of particular types and sizes ordered by Charles Goddard and Roland St. Pierre. Goddard and St. Pierre transmitted a written order for a number of boats. Ishikawajima-Harima's factory where the boats were to be manufactured was completely destroyed by fire, and it was impossible to manufacture the boats in time. The court held destruction of the factory excused performance for the order.

New Laws Making the Contract Illegal. If an act is legal at the time of the contract but is subsequently made illegal, the contract is discharged.

The Gates Construction Company contracted with Segrest to build a service station on Segrest's property. After the contract was entered into, but before work began, the city council passed a zoning ordinance restricting the site of the proposed station to residential purposes. The contract was discharged by this ordinance.

Death or Physical Incapacity. If the contract calls for personal services, death or physical incapacity of the person to perform such services discharges the contract. The personal services must be such that they cannot readily be performed by another or by the personal representative of the promisor.

Such acts as the painting of a portrait, representing a client in a legal proceeding, and other services of a highly personal nature are discharged by death or incapacity. In general, if the performance is too personal to be delegated, the death or disability of the party bound to perform will discharge the contract.

Winfred Mullen agreed to purchase Rufus Wafer's "accounting business and equipment, including all accounts in connection therewith." Wafer agreed "to remain active in the accounting business with Buyer for a period of two years" and "cooperate fully with the Buyer in effecting a satisfactory transfer of accounts . . . and giving all encouragement possible to the continuation of business relations." Wafer moved from his offices and occupied offices with Mullen. They executed a promissory note and security agreement. Less than a month later, Wafer died. Mullen asked the court to rescind the contract of sale and cancel the note claiming the contract was contingent on Wafer's providing personal services. The executrix of Wafer's estate argued the contract was for the sale of the accounting business, and the transfer was made before Wafer's death. The court found the contract embodied and provided for the personal services of Wafer so his death cancelled the sale of the accounting business.

Acceptance of Breach of the Contract by One of the Parties.

When one of the parties fails or refuses to perform the obligations assumed under the contract, there is a breach of the contract.

If one party, prior to the time the other party is entitled to performance, announces an intention not to perform, there is *anticipatory breach* of the contract. If the innocent party accepts the breach of the contract, the contract is thereby discharged.

Remedies for Breach of Contract

If there is a breach of contract, the innocent party has three courses of action which may be followed:

1. Sue for damages
2. Rescind the contract
3. Sue for specific performance

Sue for Damages. The usual remedy for breach of contract is to sue for damages. In a suit for damages there are really two suits in one. The first is to prove breach of contract. The second is to prove damages. There are four kinds of damages: (1) nominal, (2) compensatory, (3) punitive, and (4) liquidated.

Nominal Damages. If the plaintiff in a breach of contract suit is able to prove that the defendant broke the contract but is unable to prove any loss was sustained because of the breach, then the court will award *nominal damages,* generally one dollar, to symbolize vindication of the wrong done to the plaintiff.

Thoben Textile Company contracted with the Panovich Warehouse to purchase 1,000 bales of cotton for $20,000. The Panovich Warehouse failed to perform, and the Thoben Textile Company purchased 1,000 bales of cotton of the same grade elsewhere for $19,975. In a suit for breach of contract by the Thoben Textile Company, the court awarded the plantiff nominal damages of $1 since it did win its case by proving a breach of contract, but it failed to prove it had sustained any loss. The defendant had to pay the court costs.

Compensatory Damages. The theory of the law of damages is that an injured party is to be compensated for any loss which may have been sustained but should not be permitted to profit from the other party's wrong-doing. The law, when there is a breach of contract, entitles the injured party to compensation for the exact amount of loss, but no more. Such damages are called *compensatory damages*. Sometimes the actual loss is easily determined, but at other times it is very difficult to determine. As a general rule, the amount of damages is a question to be decided by the jury.

Punitive, or Exemplary, Damages. In most instances the awarding of compensatory damages fully meets the ends of justice. There are cases, however, where compensatory damages are not adequate. In these instances the law may permit the plaintiff to receive punitive damages. *Punitive damages* are damages which are paid to the plaintiff in order to punish the defendant, not to compensate the plaintiff. If a tenant maliciously damages the rented property the landlord may frequently recover as damages the actual cost of repairs plus additional damages as punitive damages.

Liquidated Damages. When two parties enter into a contract, they may, in order to avoid the problems involved in proving the actual damages sustained, include a provision fixing the amount of damages to be paid in the event one party breaches the contract. Such a provision is called *liquidated damages.* Such a clause in the contract specifies recoverable damages in the event that the plaintiff establishes a breach by the defendant. Liquidated damages must be reasonable and should be provided only in those cases where actual damages are difficult or impossible to prove. If the amount of damages fixed by the contract is unreasonable and in effect the damages are punitive, the court will not enforce this provision of the contract.

◆   O'Dell employed the Puchta Construction Company to build a house for her for $60,000, to be completed by November 1. The contract stipulated that for every day the contractor was late in completing the house, $500 in damages should accrue. The house was not finished until November 11. O'Dell's only actual loss was that she had to pay one more month's rent. The liquidated damages provision was excessive and not binding since the owner of a $60,000 house would not sustain $500 damage for each day's delay.

Rescind the Contract. The aggrieved party, when a contract is breached, may elect to rescind the contract. This party then is released from all obligations not yet performed. If this party has executed the contract, the remedy is to sue for recovery of what was parted with. If the aggrieved party rescinds a contract for the sale of goods, damages for the breach may also be requested.

Sue for Specific Performance. Sometimes neither a suit for damages nor rescission will constitute an adequate remedy. The injured party's remedy under these circumstances is a suit in equity to compel *specific performance,* that is, the carrying out of the specific terms of the contract.

This remedy is available in most contracts for the sale of real estate or any interest in real estate and for the sale of rare articles of personal property, such as a painting or an heirloom, the value of which cannot readily be determined. There is no way to measure sentimental value attached to a relic. Under such circumstances mere money damages may be inadequate to compensate the injured party. The court may compel specific performance under such circumstances.

The Small Art Museum contracted with McCloud to purchase a famous work of art for $40,000. Before McCloud delivered the painting to the buyer, another museum offered her $50,000 for it. McCloud failed to deliver the painting to the Small Art Museum. The Small Art Museum's remedy was to sue for specific performance.

As a general rule, contracts for the performance of personal services will not be specifically ordered, both because of the difficulty of supervision by the courts and because of the restriction of the Constitution prohibiting involuntary servitude except as a criminal punishment.

Malpractice

A professional person, such as a lawyer, accountant, or doctor who makes a contract to perform professional services has a duty to perform with the ability and care normally exercised by others in the profession. If the contract is not so performed, the contract is breached because of *malpractice.*

An accountant is liable to a client who suffers a loss because the accountant has not complied with valid accounting practices.

Hargraves, an accountant, prepared the federal and state income tax returns for the Welcher Corporation. Hargraves advised the corporation's officers that certain payments made by the corporation were valid expenses and deductions on the income tax returns. Actually the IRS had ruled two years earlier that such payments were not valid corporation income tax deductions. The corporation was required to pay additional taxes plus a penalty and interest. It sued Hargraves for malpractice. The court held Hargraves' work did not meet the professional standard it should and Hargraves was guilty of malpractice.

In some cases, a person other than a party to the contract may sue a professional person for malpractice. In the case of a contract for accounting services, a third party may under certain circumstances recover when the negligence or fraud by the accountant causes a loss to that party.

Questions

1. What is performance of a contract?

2. If a contract contains no provision for time of performance, when must performance be rendered?

3. If a contract calls for an act, what is the effect of a refusal of a tender of performance?

4. If a debtor tenders payment of money but payment is refused, is the debt discharged?

5. What is the rule regarding satisfactory performance?

6. If one party does not perform every detail of a contract, is the other party released from the obligations under the contract?

7. What effect does bankruptcy have on the debtor's contracts?

8. If one cannot perform a contract on time because of a strike in the trucking industry, is this a legal impossibility?

9. If a singer contracts to sing at a party, is the contract released if the singer develops laryngitis just before the party starts?

10. What are *compensatory damages*?

11. Why are punitive damages awarded?

12. Under what conditions may one sue for specific performance of a contract rather than sue for damages?

Case Problems

1. The Brunswick Molasses Company contracted with the Candler Feed Company to deliver 100,000 gallons of molasses on or before April 1. Due to a strike at the Brunswick plant, the company was shut down for two months and did not fulfill its contract with the Candler Feed Company. When sued for damages, it set up the defense of impossibility of performance. Is this a good defense?

2. Lukens Tool & Die Company agreed to construct a machine to manufacture hay-rake teeth for Alliance Tractor & Implement Company. The machine was to "have capabilities to manufacture the rake teeth . . . at the average rate of 100 per hour during a period of 100 hours" and the teeth were to have "no less degree of usability and performance than rake teeth . . . produced by International Harvester Company." The machine never operated five hours. In-

ternational Harvester teeth had a sharp ninety-degree bend, and teeth manufactured by the Lukens machine had a round bend which would not fit as tightly into the clamp which fastened them to the rake frame. When sued by Alliance, Lukens alleged substantial performance. Was there substantial performance?

3. The Gentili Construction Company had a contract to erect a $2 million office building. It called for bids to supply the wire for the electrical wiring needs for the building. The invitation for bids stated that time was an extremely important factor. The Heller Copper Company submitted a bid. It wished to include a clause such as "Performance on the date specified is to be waived if performance cannot be made due to fire, flood, tornado, or other acts of God," but Heller Copper Company knew its nearest competitor would not include a similar clause in its bid. The Heller Company used this clause: "This wire to be fabricated in our plant located at Watkinsville." This plant was destroyed by a tornado before the wire was fabricated. Was the Heller Company released from its contract?

4. Daniel tendered a certified check in payment of her account. Cohen refused the check "because the amount is incorrect." Later Cohen sued Daniel on the account. Daniel proved that she had tendered a certified check for $500 as the full amount due, and she offered before the trial started to pay this amount. Cohen refused to accept it, claiming $700. The jury awarded Cohen a judgment for $500. Who must pay the court costs?

5. George Booth contracted to renovate a kitchen for Ray Parker. Parker sued Booth for failure to complete the job in a workmanlike manner, alleging recovery should be the amount paid to have the kitchen work redone by others. Booth alleged damages for defective performance should be the difference between the value of the performance contracted for and the value of the performance actually rendered. What is the correct measure of damages?

6. When Willie and Londia Weatherspoon were divorced, Willie was granted custody of their seven children, and Londia was ordered to pay $520-a-month child support. Years later Willie sued for past-due child support. More than three years before, Londia had failed to pay child support for two months. No other payments had been missed that year. She argued that the three-year statute of limitations barred recovery for the two missed payments. Did it?

7. Freeport Minerals Co. was the tenant of a lease under which it had the right to mine kaolin and bauxite in exchange for a royalty of "12½ cents per ton of 2,240 pounds of refined clay and bauxite (railroad weight) removed . . . by tenant." Freeport told Minnie Belle Dennard, the holder of the lease, that it intended to pay her 12½ cents per ton on each ton of crude ore rather than on refined kaolin or bauxite. Freeport mined and removed kaolin. Dennard sued for material breach of the lease. Did payment on the basis of crude ore rather than refined kaolin constitute substantial compliance?

8. Four college students rented a house from Duncan at $280 a month. The term was for ten months. There were several heated disputes between students and Duncan over whether or not the terms of the lease were being broken. The students, to get even with Duncan, deliberately let the bathtub overflow, causing $700 water damage to the building. What are Duncan's rights?

9. The Vaughn Paper Company contracted with the Guest Printing Company to supply the printing paper for the Guest Printing Company for ten months for $20,000. The paper was to be supplied in ten equal shipments. A clause in the contract stipulated, "If any one shipment is late in arriving by 48 hours, the Vaughn Paper Company agrees to pay damages in the amount of $20,000." One shipment was four days late in arrival, but there was no evidence the Guest Printing Company was inconvenienced since it had ample stock on hand. It sued the Vaughn Paper Company for $20,000. What amount of damages is the Guest Printing Company entitled to receive?

10. Marshall County Redi-Mix, Inc., and Wright-Denaut Construction Co. contracted to pour and finish a concrete floor for a building being constructed by La Verne and Martha Matthew. The floor was poured but not yet sealed. The concrete froze, leaving the top $\frac{1}{16}''$ of the $4''$ base in a crumbling and powdery condition. The Matthews finished the building and began to use it, although the floor was unsightly and dusty. When the Matthews refused to pay for the floor, Redi-Mix and Wright-Denaut sued. The Matthews argued that because of the destruction of the subject matter of the contract (the floor) they should not have to pay as required by the contract. Do they?

Summary Cases for Part Two

Contracts

1. McLeish Ranch signed an agreement to list land for sale with Reinhold Schauer. The agreement stated the terms would be "cash upon delivery of deed. Sale includes ½ of the mineral rights, oil, gas." Erwin Grossman signed a "contract for sale" to purchase the land for the full price in the listing agreement, subject to financing, and stating coal and gravel were included minerals. The ranch would not sell the land. Grossman sued for specific performance alleging the listing agreement constituted an offer to sell which was accepted by Grossman's signing of the "contract for sale." Was there a contract? [*Grossman v. McLeish Ranch*, 291 N.W.2d 427 (N.D.)]

2. In January, Edward Hayes, an employee of Plantations Steel Company, announced his intention to retire in July because he had worked continuously for fifty-one years. One week before his retirement, an officer of Plantations told him the company "would take care" of him. The following January and for the following three years Plantations paid Hayes $5,000. After the company refused to make any further payments, Hayes filed suit alleging an implied contract to pay him a yearly pension of $5,000. Was there an implied contract? [*Hayes v. Plantations Steel Company*, 438 A.2d 1091 (R.I.)]

3. The defendant Rosenbusch owned a 1/160 interest in an oil lease on some land in Oklahoma. Rosenbusch was a resident of Washington, D.C., and was not familiar with conditions in Oklahoma. She had never received any income from the lease. Deardorf wrote to her offering to purchase her "nonproductive royalty interest" for $10. She accepted the offer but later learned that some very productive wells had been drilled near her lease and that it was now a very valuable lease, a fact known to Deardorf when he wrote her. She brought suit to set the contract aside. Should the court grant rescission? [*Deardorf et al. v. Rosenbusch*, 206 P.2d 996 (Okla.)]

4. The Midtown Motors employed Wise as an expert automobile mechanic for three years at a stated salary which increased each year. After eight months Wise was discharged without justifiable cause. He sued for damages and obtained a judgment. He went to work in the meantime for another auto firm. To collect his judgment Wise garnisheed the Midtown Motors' bank account. The owner of the Midtown Motors went to Wise's new place of employment and engaged in considerable verbal abuse of Wise. He threatened him with legal action for garnisheeing the bank account. Wise's present employer joined in the verbal abuse and told him he was "fired" unless he accepted the proffered $200 in full settlement and signed a release for the balance. While in a state of extreme mental confusion as to what to do, he signed the release. The

next day he changed his mind and repudiated the release and demanded the full amount due him. May he repudiate the signed release? [*Wise v. Midtown Motors*, 42 N. W. 2d 404 (Minn.)]

5. American Family Life Assurance Company filed an action to prevent six former employees from violating the nondisclosure covenants in written agreements. Paragraph seven of the agreements, titled "Covenant Not To Compete," contained six subparagraphs, two of which were nondisclosure covenants and two of which were noncompetitive covenants. The two non-competitive covenants were overly broad and unenforceable. Could the non-disclosure covenants be enforced? [*American Family Life Assurance Company v. Tazelaar*, 468 N.E.2d 497 (Ill. App. Ct.)]

6. Parker sold his bakery business to Thomas. As a part of the sales agreement, this clause appeared: "together with goodwill and bakery machinery in said bakery." Another clause stipulated, "Parker agrees that he will not engage in the bakery business directly or indirectly for a period of seven years within a radius of seven miles of Boston." About one year later Parker began working as a baker for the Boston Syrian Baking Company. Thomas brought suit asking that Parker be enjoined from working for the Syrian Baking Company. Is he entitled to the injunction? [*Thomas v. Parker*, 98 N. E. 2d 640 (Mass.)]

7. Andrew Truebenbach owned two adjoining tracts of land. He sold one to Edward Pick and the deed stated, "Grantors also guarantee grantees . . . a right-of-way across the twenty-five-acre tract sold to Walter Bartel." The other tract, consisting of twenty-five acres, was sold to Bartel five days later. Since an easement is an interest in land and therefore subject to the Statute of Frauds, was the language in Pick's deed sufficient to establish an easement? [*Pick v. Bartel*, 659 S.W.2d 636 (Tex.)]

8. Babylon Associates contracted to build a water-pollution-control plant for Suffolk County. It hired Lizza Industries, Inc., as subcontractor to install re-inforced "102-inch" pipe. Lizza subcontracted with Clearview Concrete Products Corp. to manufacture the "102-inch" pipe. Clearview was convicted of making defective pipe used in the water-pollution-control plant. The EPA's reduction in its grant for the project and tests to determine the soundness of the pipes delayed construction. The contract with Suffolk County provided that the contractor agreed "to be fully and directly responsible . . . for all acts and omissions of his Subcontractors and of any other person employed directly or indirectly by the . . . Subcontractors." In claiming breach of contract the county alleged it was entitled to recission of the whole contract and all the money it had paid Babylon. Is it? [*Babylon Associates v. County of Suffolk*, 475 N.Y.S.2d 869 (N.Y. App. Div.)]

9. After a divorce decree was entered, Richard Pressley was ordered to pay $20 per week child support. He made payments directly to his ex-wife. A year later she applied for public assistance and was required to assign her right to

support to the Commonwealth of Pennsylvania, Department of Public Welfare. Pressley was never notified of the assignment and continued to make payments to his ex-wife. Four years later the Department of Public Welfare sought to collect the support payments from Pressley. Was Pressley bound on the assignment? [*Commonwealth v. Pressley*, 479 A.2d 1069 (Pa. Super. Ct.)]

10. Chevalier entered into an oral contract with Lane's, Inc., to work for the corporation for a period of twelve months, work to begin shortly after the contract was made. Chevalier began work and continued for a period of six months. According to his oral contract, Chevalier was to be paid a monthly salary plus a bonus of $1,500 at the end of six months. He was laid off without cause at the end of the first six months without receiving his $1,500 bonus, although his monthly salary had been paid. He brought suit for his $1,500 bonus plus his damages for having been discharged without cause. Is he entitled to either the $1,500 or damages? [*Chevalier v. Lane's, Inc.*, 1948, 213 S. W. 2d 530, (Tex.)]

11. Kelley entered into a contract with Hance whereby Kelley was to construct a sidewalk and curb in front of Hance's property. The price for the work was to be $3 a running foot, or $420 for the 140 feet. Kelley was to start work within one week and complete it before cold weather. Although the contract was entered into in September, Kelley did not begin work until December 4. He continued to work until he had removed dirt to a width of twelve feet. He then discontinued the work and never returned. In March the following year, Hance notified Kelley that the contract was canceled. Kelley then brought suit to recover for the value of the work he already had done at the time the contract was terminated by Hance. Is Kelley entitled to any compensation? [*Kelley v. Hance*, 142 A. 683 (Conn.)]

12. While employed at the Stardust Hotel, Gilbert Smith thought that a recreational vehicle park, built and operated as a part of the hotel, would be a profitable idea. He devised a brochure indicating his plan and met with the manager of the Stardust, Allan Sachs. After explaining his idea, Smith stated he wanted to be paid either in money or by being an executive in the operation. The only interest Sachs expressed was to suggest Smith contact him later. Smith could not arrange another meeting and finally received a note from Sachs' secretary saying he was not interested. The Stardust opened a recreational vehicle park two years later. Smith's demands for compensation were refused, so he sued, alleging an implied contract. Was there such a contract? [*Smith v. Recrion Corporation*, 541 P.2d 663 (Nev.)]

13. Silverstein and Silverstein held a three-year written lease on space in Dohoney's property to be used for cigarette vending machines. The lease provided for the payment of rent by means of a commission on all cigarettes sold, but the amount of the commission was not stated. Prior to this lease the plaintiff had a machine in Dohoney's property and had paid him commissions

on all sales of cigarettes. In a suit involving this contract, the key question was whether or not oral testimoney could be introduced to prove the amount of commissions that were to be paid. Should the oral testimony be admitted? [*Silverstein v. Dohoney*, 108 A. 2d 451 (N.J. Super. Ct. App. Div.)]

Part Three — Sales

Learning Objectives for Part Three

Sales

After studying this part, you should be able to:

1. Define movable personal property.

2. Define a sale of goods and distinguish it from a contract to sell.

3. Distinguish between existing and future goods.

4. List the requirements of the Statute of Frauds and explain the exceptions to it.

5. Describe the nature of the writing required by the Statute of Frauds.

6. Define an auction sale and describe its peculiarities to the law of sales.

7. Understand the importance of determining when title and risk of loss pass in the case of particular sales.

8. Distinguish between a sale on approval, a sale or return, and a consignment.

9. Explain the application of the law of sales to fungible goods.

10. Discuss the rules regarding attempted sales by people who do not have title to the goods.

11. Define a warranty and distinguish between express and implied warranties.

12. Specify the warranties which apply to all sellers and those which apply only to merchant sellers.

13. Explain how warranties may be excluded or surrendered.

14. Identify the different theories by which a person may be entitled to recover damages for personal injury or property damage.

15. Discuss the measures designed to protect consumers from abuse, sharp dealing, and fraud.

13

Sales of Personal Property

Preview Cases

John Van Sistine contracted with Jan Tollard to install some windows; reposition an air conditioner, a range, and a cabinet; install siding; and perform certain finishing. He was referred to in the contract as a contractor, and most of the price was for labor. They agreed to additional work but then disagreed on the value of the work. Van Sistine sued Tollard for more money. Tollard defended on the basis of the law of sales. Since Van Sistine furnished both goods and services, the test was whether the predominant factor of the contract was the rendition of a service or a sale. Which was it?

Yorio, a shoe manufacturer, contracted to sell the Mitchell Shoe Store 2,000 pairs of shoes. At the time this contract was made, the shoes had not been manufactured. After they were manufactured but before they were shipped, Yorio's creditors levied upon the shoes. Yorio claimed they were not her shoes, because she had sold them to the Mitchell Shoe Store. Was she correct?

In terms of the number of contracts as well as in the dollar volume, contracts for the sale of goods—movable personal property—constitute the largest class of contracts in our economic system. Every time one purchases a package of gum, a sales contract is made. If the gum contained some harmful substance, the sale could be the basis of a suit for thousands of dollars in damages. Sales of movable personal property are governed by Article 2 of the Uniform Commercial Code, effective in all states except Louisiana.

Property Subject to Sale

As used in the Uniform Commercial Code and in these chapters, sale applies only to the sale of movable personal property. Thus, it does not apply to (1) real property or (2) intangible personal property. *Movable personal property* consists of all physical items which are not real estate. Examples are food, vehicles, clothing, and furniture. *Real property* is land, interests in land, and things permanently attached to land. *Intangible personal property* consists of evidences of ownership of personal property, such as contracts, copyrights, certificates of stock, accounts receivable, notes receivable, and similar assets.

Sales contracts must have all the essentials of any other contract, but they also have some additional features. There are many rules pertaining to sales of personal property that would have no significance to any other type of contract, such as a contract of employment.

Sales and Contracts to Sell

A distinction is made between a sale and a contract to sell.

A *sale* of goods is the transfer of title to goods from the seller to the buyer for a consideration called the price. It is a contract in which the ownership changes hands at the moment the bargain is made regardless of who has possession of the goods.

A *contract to sell* goods is a contract whereby the seller agrees to transfer the title to goods to the buyer for a consideration called the price. In this type of contract individuals promise to buy and to sell in the future.

The important distinction between a sale and a contract to sell is that in a sale the title, or the ownership of the subject matter, is transferred at once; in a contract to sell it will be transferred at a later time. A contract to sell is not in the true sense of the word a sale; it is merely an agreement to sell.

Since in a sale title passes to the buyer immediately, and in a contract to sell title passes at some future date, it is extremely important to distinguish between the two. There can be no such thing as an intervening period during which time title rests with neither the seller nor the buyer. The risk of loss, with the exceptions set out later in this chapter, is borne by the owner. Also, any increase in the property belongs to the one who has the title. It is essential, therefore, to have definite rules to aid the courts in determining when title and risk of loss pass if the parties to the contract are silent as to these matters. If the parties specify when title or risk of loss passes, the courts will enforce this agreement.

Sales of Goods and Contracts for Services

An agreement to perform some type of service must be distinguished from a sale of goods since sales of goods are governed by Article 2 and agreements to perform services are not. Even when a contract for services includes the supplying of articles of movable personal property, the contract is not considered a contract of sale of goods. The test is whether the predominant factor is supplying a service, with the goods being incidental, or whether the predominant factor is a sale, with the labor being incidental. For example, the repair of a television set is not a sale even though new tubes are supplied.

John Van Sistine contracted with Jan Tollard to install some windows; reposition an air conditioner, a range, and a cabinet; install siding; and perform certain finishing. He was referred to in the contract as a contractor, and most of the price was for labor. They agreed to additional work but then disagreed on the value of the work. Van Sistine sued Tollard for more money. Tollard defended on the basis of the law of sales. Since Van Sistine furnished both goods and services, the test was whether the predominant factor of the contract was the rendition of a service or a sale. Since Van Sistine was referred to in the contract as a contractor, most of the money claimed was for labor, and the work was to "install," "reposition," "move," and "finish," the transaction was not a sale of goods.

Price

The consideration in a sales contract is generally expressed in terms of money or money's worth and is known as the *price*. The price may be payable in money, goods, or services.

The sales contract is ordinarily an express contract, but some of its terms may be implied. If the price is not stated, it will be held to be the reasonable price. If the goods are sold on a regulated market, such as a commodity exchange, the price on such market will be deemed the reasonable price. If the parties indicate that the price must be fixed by them or by a third person at a later date, there is no binding contract if the price is not thus fixed. If the price can be computed from the terms of the contract, the contract is valid.

A. P. Leonards employed an architect to renovate a building. While Leonards was out of the country, his wife selected bay windows for the building, and the architect ordered them from Benglis Sash & Door Co. The price of the windows was not discussed. When they arrived Leonards refused to accept them. Benglis sued for the price of the windows. Leonards argued there was no contract because the parties had never agreed on the price. Since the parties had a history of dealings in which Leonards ordered things and paid the invoice price, and since he did not object to the price charged, consent to buy at a reasonable price may be implied and the contract was enforceable.

Existing Goods

In order to be the subject of a sale, it is necessary that the goods be existing. This means that the goods must both be in existence, as contrasted with goods not yet manufactured, and be then owned by the seller. If these conditions are not met, the only transaction that can be made between the seller and the buyer will be a contract to sell goods.

Future goods are goods which are not both existing and identified. They are expected to be acquired in the future by purchase or by manufacture. Any contract purporting to sell future goods is a contract to sell and not a contract of sale. Title to the goods does not pass to the buyer when the goods come into existence. Some further action must be taken by the seller.

◆   Yorio, a shoe manufacturer, contracted to sell the Mitchell Shoe Store 2,000 pairs of shoes. At the time this contract was made, the shoes had not been manufactured. After they were manufactured but before they were shipped, Yorio's creditors levied upon the shoes. Yorio claimed they were not her shoes, since she had sold them to the Mitchell Shoe Store. Since the shoes at the time of the contract were not in existence, they were future goods. Consequently, Yorio had made a contract to sell, not of sale. The title to the shoes did not pass to Mitchell Shoe Store once they had been manufactured.

Bill of Sale

A *bill of sale* is written evidence of one's title to tangible personal property. It is generally not necessary to have such evidence of title; but if a person's title is questioned, such evidence is highly desirable. If an individual buys a stock of merchandise in bulk, a house trailer, livestock, or any other relatively expensive items, such as jewelry or furs, demand should be made to the seller for a bill of sale. The bill of sale serves two purposes:

1. If the buyer wishes to resell the goods and the prospective buyer demands proof of title, the bill of sale can be produced.

2. If any question arises as to whether or not the buyer came into possession of the goods legally, the bill of sale is proof.

◆   Howard purchased a trailer from Henderson. A few months later he contracted to sell it to Tucker. Tucker would not pay Howard for the trailer unless he could produce a bill of sale showing he had title to it. This often is a wise precaution.

Illegal Sales

Many difficulties arise over illegal sales, that is, the sale of goods prohibited by law, such as alcoholic beverages in a "dry" locality. If the sale is fully executed, the court will not intervene to aid either party. If an innocent party through fraud is induced to enter into an illegal sale, the court will compel a restoration of the goods or money the innocent party has transferred.

If the illegal sale is wholly executory, the transaction is a contract to sell and will not be enforced. If it is only partially executory, the courts will still leave the parties where it finds them unless the one who has performed is an innocent victim of a fraud.

If the sale is divisible and a part is legal and a part illegal, the court will enforce the legal part. If the individual items are separately priced, the sale is divisible. If the sale involves several separate and independent items but is a lump-sum sale, then the sale is indivisible. If any part of a sale that is indivisible is illegal, the entire sale is illegal.

Bonnot, a married minor, purchased $100 worth of groceries on credit from the Jackson Supermarket. On two occasions the purchases included two bottles of wine. A state law prohibited the sale of wine to anyone under twenty-one years of age. The wine on the sales tickets was separately priced, so the illegal part could easily be separated from the legal part. Bonnot had to pay for all groceries except the wine.

Questions

1. **a.** What is the difference between a sale and a contract to sell?
   b. Why is it important to make a distinction between a sale and a contract to sell?

2. What is the difference between an agreement to perform services and a sale of goods?

3. If the price in a sales contract is not stated, is the contract void?

4. Is an offer to sell a specified amount of wheat at the Chicago market closing price on June 7 an acceptable offer?

5. **a.** What are *future goods*?
   b. Can future goods ever constitute the subject matter of a contract of sale?

6. **a.** What is a *bill of sale*?
   b. Is a bill of sale necessary to pass title?

7. How does the court view an illegal sale that has been executed, as compared to one which is partially executory?

Case Problems

1. Harvey, Inc., agreed to sell Rudy Brown restaurant equipment. After Brown accepted the equipment there was a dispute about the price. Brown had

agreed to pay the amount owed a bank on the equipment. Harvey asserted that Brown had agreed to pay both the principal and the interest owed and sued him for this amount. Brown said the price was not fixed. The president of the bank testified that Brown agreed to pay the outstanding principal but that there was a dispute about who was to pay the outstanding interest. Was there a fixed price and, if so, what was it?

2. Bilko rented a fishing boat from a wholesale fish merchant for the purpose of a fishing expedition. He purchased provisions and supplies for the expedition from Wholesale Foods, Inc., and gave as security a bill of sale on all the fish he was to catch on the trip at 20 cents a pound. When the boat docked laden with several tons of fish, the creditors of Bilko attached the fish for the debts owed them by Bilko. Wholesale Foods produced its bill of sale to prove it had title to the fish. Who has superior rights in this case, the creditors or Wholesale Foods, Inc.?

3. Colorado Carpet Installation, Inc., negotiated with Fred and Zuma Palermo for the sale and installation of carpeting, carpet padding, tile, and vinyl floor covering. Colorado submitted a written proposal which referred to Colorado as "the seller," to the Palermos as "the customer," and set the price at $4,775.75, of which $926 was for labor. Colorado alleged Zuma orally accepted the proposal, so it ordered the carpeting and delivered the ceramic tile to the Palermos' home. Zuma disagreed with Colorado's tile person and had someone else supply and install tile. Colorado sued the Palermos for breach of contract. The Palermos contended that the transaction was an oral sale of goods for more than $500. Since the Statute of Frauds requires a contract for the sale of goods for the price of $500 or more to be in writing to be enforceable, the Palermos argued that their agreement with Colorado was unenforceable. Was it?

4. Lasher, the purchasing agent of the Hertz Company, purchased a used bookkeeping machine from the Adams Bookkeeping Service for $3,200. About two weeks later, a representative of the manufacturer of the machine demanded possession of the machine, claiming it was only rented to the Adams Bookkeeping Service. She showed Lasher the rental agreement as proof of her statement. What should Lasher have done to avoid this loss?

5. Kune Junde Haby signed a contract not to make a will which provided that if she were permitted to use her children's land then her property would pass on her death according to the plan in the contract. The plan violated the law and no element of it could be removed without destroying the whole plan. After she died her children disputed the validity of the contract, with one arguing that the illegal provisions were separable from the valid provisions. Were they?

6. Before the pecan season opened in Albany, Georgia, Thompson Brothers entered into a contract with Kahn, a pecan grower, to purchase all his pecans

"at the market price." After Kahn had delivered 20,000 pounds of pecans and had received the market price in Albany, he asked Thompson Brothers for a settlement. He produced a New York paper showing a higher market price for pecans in New York than he had been receiving. Could Kahn collect the higher price?

14

Formalities of a Sale

Preview Cases

Madson orally promised to sell Kubichek a certain article for $675 and subsequently refused to deliver the article. Kubichek sued for breach of contract. Madson's defense was that the agreement was unenforceable because it was not in writing. Was this defense successful?

Each fall, Oakland Gin Co. asked Tennessee Valley Cotton Oil Mill what it would pay for seed. Tennessee always said it would pay whatever prices and rebates were paid by its competitors. During two years Oakland was not paid the rebates the other cottonseed oil mills had paid. Oakland requested Tennessee pay the rebates, but Tennessee refused. Oakland then asked Tennessee for $15,000, which Tennessee gave it. Oakland made one delivery of seed, said it would make no more deliveries, and claimed the $15,000 as payment for the unpaid rebates and the one delivery. Tennessee sued for the $15,000. Did it recover?

The Statute of Frauds requires that all contracts for the sale of goods be evidenced by a writing when the sales price is $500 or more. If the sales price is less, the contract may be oral, written, implied from conduct, or a combination of any of these.

If a sales contract does not meet the requirements of the Uniform Commercial Code, it is unenforceable. If both parties elect to abide by its terms even though they are not legally bound to do so, neither one can later avoid the contract.

◆ Madson orally promised to sell Kubichek a certain article for $675 and subsequently refused to deliver the article. Kubichek sued for breach of contract. Madson's defense was that the agreement was unenforceable because a contract to sell or a contract for the sale of goods with the price of $500 or more needed to be in writing to be enforceable. Madson's defense was successful.

Sales Within the Statute of Frauds

Frequently one makes several purchases the same day from the same seller. The question may then be raised as to whether there is one sale or several sales. If one contracts to purchase five items from the same seller in one day, each one having a sale price of less than $500, but in the aggregate they are in excess of $500, must this contract meet the requirement of the Statute of Frauds? If the several items are part of the same sales transaction, it is one sale and must meet the requirement of the Statute. If all the contracts to purchase are made during the same shopping tour and with the same salesperson who merely adds up the different items and charges the customer with a grand total, the several items are considered to be part of the same transaction. But if a separate sales slip is written for each purchase as an individual goes through a department store and buys in different departments, each transaction is a separate sale.

When Proof of Oral Contract Permitted

In some instances the absence of a writing does not bar the proof of a sales contract for $500 or more.

Receipt and Acceptance of Goods. An oral sales contract may be enforced if it can be shown that the goods were delivered by the seller and were received and accepted by the buyer. Both a receipt and an acceptance by the buyer must be shown. *Receipt* is taking possession of the goods. *Acceptance* is the assent of the buyer to become the owner of specific goods. The contract may be enforced only insofar as it relates to the goods received and accepted.

Each fall, Oakland Gin Co. asked Tennessee Valley Cotton Oil Mill what it would pay for seed. Tennessee always said it would pay whatever prices and rebates were paid by its competitors. During two years Oakland was not paid the rebates the other cottonseed oil mills had paid. Oakland requested Tennessee pay the rebates, but Tennessee refused. Oakland then asked Tennessee for $15,000, which Tennessee gave it. Oakland made one delivery of seed, said it would make no more deliveries, and claimed the $15,000 as payment for the unpaid rebates and the one delivery. When Tennessee sued for payment of the $15,000, the court held that although the contract agreeing to pay the rebates was oral, it was enforceable because Tennessee had received and accepted the seed.

Payment. An oral contract may be enforced if the buyer has made full payment on the contract. In the case of part payment, a contract may be enforced only with respect to goods for which payment has been made and accepted.

There is some uncertainty under this rule as to the effectiveness of payment by check or a promissory note executed by the buyer. Under the law of commercial paper, a check or note is conditional payment when delivered, and it does not become absolute until the instrument is paid. The earlier decisions held that the delivery of a negotiable instrument was not such a payment as would make the oral contract enforceable unless it was agreed at that time that the instrument was to be accepted as absolute, and not conditional, payment. A modern, contrary view, based on the fact that business people ordinarily regard the delivery of a check or note as payment, holds that the delivery of such an instrument is sufficient to make the oral contract enforceable. A check or promissory note that is tendered as payment but which is refused by the seller does not constitute a payment under the Statute of Frauds.

When the buyer has negotiated or assigned to the seller a negotiable instrument that was executed by a third person and the seller has accepted the instrument, a payment has been made within the meaning of the Statute of Frauds.

Judicial Admission. No writing is required when the person against whom enforcement of the contract is sought voluntarily admits in the course of legal proceedings to having made the contract.

Nonresellable Goods. No writing is required when the goods are specifically made for the buyer and are of such an unusual nature that they are not suitable for sale in the ordinary course of the seller's business. For this exception to apply, however, the seller must have made a substantial beginning in manufacturing the goods or, if a middleman, in procuring them, before receiving notice of a repudiation by the buyer.

Nature of the Writing Required

The UCC does not have stringent requirements for the sufficiency of a writing to satisfy the Statute of Frauds for sales contracts.

Terms. The writing need only give assurance that there was a transaction. Specifically, it need only indicate that a sale or contract to sell has been made and state the quantity of goods involved. Any other missing terms may be shown by parol evidence in the event of a dispute.

Signature. When a suit is brought against an individual on the basis of a transaction, the terms of which must be in writing, the writing must be signed by the person who is being sued or an authorized agent of that person. The signature must be placed on the writing with the intention of authenticating the writing. It may consist of initials; it may be printed, stamped, or typewritten. The important thing is that it was made with the necessary intent.

When the transaction is between merchants, the Uniform Commercial Code makes an exception to the requirement of signing. It provides that the failure of a merchant to repudiate a confirming letter sent by another merchant is binding just as though the letter or other writing had been signed. This ends the possibility of a situation under which the sender of the letter was bound but the receiver could safely ignore the transaction or could hold the sender as desired depending upon which alternative gave the better financial advantage.

Time of Execution. A writing to satisfy the Statute of Frauds may be made at any time at or after the making of the sale. It may even be made after the contract has been broken or a suit brought on it, since the essential element is the existence of written proof of the transaction when the trial is held.

Particular Writings. The writing which satisfies the Statute of Frauds may be a single writing or it may be several writings considered as a group. Formal contracts, bills of sale, letters, and telegrams are common forms of writings that satisfy the Statute of Frauds. Purchase orders, cash register receipts, sales tickets, invoices, and similar papers generally do not satisfy the requirements as to a signature and sometimes they do not specify any quantity or commodity.

Auction Sales

A sale by auction for any amount is valid even though it is, by necessity, oral. In most states the auctioneer is the special agent for both the owner and the bidder. When the auctioneer or the clerk of the auction makes a memorandum of the sale and signs it, this binds both parties. The *bidder* is the one who makes the offer. There is no contract until the auctioneer accepts the offer, which may be done in several ways. The most common way is the fall of the hammer, with the auctioneer saying, "Sold" or "Sold to (a certain person)." In most auctions the final bid is preceded by several lower bids. When a person makes a bid to start the sale, the auctioneer may refuse to accept this as a starting bid. If the bid is accepted and a higher bid is requested, the auctioneer can later refuse to accept this starting bid as the selling price.

If a bid is made while the hammer is falling in acceptance of a prior bid, then the auctioneer has the choice of reopening the bid or declaring the goods sold. The auctioneer's decision is binding.

Goods may be offered for sale with reserve or without reserve. If they are *without reserve,* then the goods cannot be withdrawn after the bidding starts unless no bid is received within a reasonable time after the auctioneer calls for bids. Goods are presumed to be offered *with reserve* unless the goods are explicitly put up without reserve.

Questions

1. What contracts involving the sale of goods must be in writing to be enforceable?

2. What facts would be relevant to determining whether the purchase of a number of items is one sale or many sales?

3. **a.** What is *receipt*?
   b. What is *acceptance*?

4. Discuss the effectiveness of payment by check.

5. How does a contract for goods which are specifically manufactured for the buyer and not suitable for sale to others in the seller's ordinary course of business differ from an ordinary contract of sale?

6. May a merchant who has not signed anything be bound on an oral contract?

7. In order to satisfy the Statute of Frauds, must a writing be made at the time of sale?

8. What kind of writing meets the requirements of a written agreement for an auction sale?

Case Problems

1. Donald Fisher orally agreed to buy a sloop from Albert Cohn for $4,650. He gave Cohn a check for $2,325 on which was written, "deposit on aux. sloop, D'Arc Wind, full amount $4,650." They agreed to meet later for Fisher to pay the remainder of the purchase price and Cohn to transfer title. They had a disagreement and Fisher stopped payment on the check. Cohn readvertised the boat, sold it for the highest offer, $3,000, and sued Fisher for breach of contract. Did the check satisfy the memorandum requirements of the Statute of Frauds?

2. Joel, sales manager for the Lazzarini Building Materials Company, sold Wilson $6,000 worth of building materials. Joel wrote down the items on a purchase order as Wilson listed them. Joel agreed to take in part payment a sixty-day draft drawn by Downs Motor Company in favor of Wilson. Wilson assigned this draft in writing to the Lazzarini Building Materials Company.

Joel interpreted this to meet the requirements of a memo under the Statute of Frauds. Wilson signed nothing else and made no other payment at the time. She later canceled the order and demanded a return of the draft. Was Wilson bound on this contract?

3. Lynette Clay purchased a piano from Walden and paid for it by indorsing a check to Walden which was made to the order of Ms. Clay. On the back of the check she wrote: "Pay to the order of A. Walden but I will not be responsible if the check is not paid. Signed: Lynette Clay." Walden agreed to accept the check with this indorsement. Does this meet the modern test of payment?

4. At a stockholders' meeting, Leonard Pirilla offered to buy all the outstanding shares of stock held by the remaining shareholders in two corporations for $525,000 plus a $15,000 commission. The minutes of the meeting indicated that all the shareholders of the corporations were present in person or by proxy, all voted to accept the offer, and the officers of the corporations were authorized to implement the sale. They signed a Letter of Intent containing the terms of the sale. Pirilla tendered a Stock Purchase Agreement to the shareholders, but some refused to sign it. Pirilla sued for specific performance of the sale. The defense was the Statute of Frauds. Is there an enforceable contract?

5. Mitchell Swerdloff was the manager of a Station Managers, Inc. (SMI), service station under a written agreement which could be terminated at will by either party. He alleged that Mobil Oil Corporation, which owned SMI, orally promised him that he would be granted a dealership of the station if and when it was converted from an SMI station to a straight dealership. Was the oral promise enforceable? *no, over $500. Had to be in writing*

6. Jane Langley inspected some carpet material on display at the Sinkwich Carpet Mart. The salesperson quoted her a definite price per square foot, the carpet material to be cut individually to fit her living room. She orally agreed to purchase it. Her living room had a very unusual shape. After the carpet was cut and laid, Langley was keenly disappointed in its appearance. She had faintly remembered from her business law course that an oral sales contract under certain conditions is invalid. She refused to pay for the carpet and demanded that the seller take it up. What were the rights of the parties?

7. The Glo-Coat Paint Company offered to sell the Lull Paint Store a quantity of paint of various grades and colors. The value of the bulk lot was $5,575. The owner of the Lull Paint Store orally agreed to buy it, but the seller insisted on a written memorandum of the sale to make it comply with the Statute of Frauds. Lull was in a quandary. He really wanted the paint as it was a very good price, but there was a possibility he would sell his paint store in a few days, in which case he would not want it. He drew up a memo as follows: "It is hereby agreed that were I to buy the paint herein described, I will pay cash on the day of delivery, which is to be not later than one week from today."

Both parties signed the memo. Lull sold his paint store the next day and notified the Glo-Coat Paint Company that he would not buy the paint. The Glo-Coat Paint Company sued him for breach of contract, alleging that they were inveigled into signing a trick memo. Was the Lull Paint Store liable on this contract?

15

Transfer of Title and Risk in Sales Contracts

Preview Cases

Roger and Sharon Russell agreed to sell Robert Clouser a boat for $8,500. Clouser made an initial payment of $1,700, with the balance to be paid upon possession. The Russells were to retain the boat to replace an engine and drive train, after which Clouser was to take delivery at their marina. No documents of title were required to sell a boat. Prior to delivery to Clouser, while being tested by the Russells' employees, the boat hit a seawall and was destroyed. The Russells' insurance policy with Transamerica Insurance Company did not cover damage resulting from watercraft hazard unless the watercraft was not owned by the Russels. Transamerica refused to pay, claiming the boat was owned by the Russells at the time of the accident. Who owned the boat?

W. A. Andres rented his motor home to Philip Robertson, who was really Lewis Murphy. Murphy obtained an Alabama registration for the home under the name L. E. Boggs. Nebraska provided Boggs a certificate of title which was transferred to Murphy. Murphy traded the home to McDonald's Chevrolet, Inc., after applying for an Indiana certificate of title. Otis Johnson purchased the home from McDonald's. It was seized by the Indiana State police and given to Andres' insurer, Foremost Insurance Company. Johnson sued Foremost to recover the home. Could he recover?

When a person owns a television set, all the power to control the set is held by that owner. If desired, the set may be kept or sold. To signify ownership we say that the owner has *title* to the set. When it is sold, title to—and, normally, physical possession of—the set passes to the buyer who then has control over it. Normally, if the TV set is damaged or lost, the owner bears any loss. However, in business transactions, because of the large volume of goods dealt in and the need to arrange the sale of goods before they may even be in existence, all of which may make physical possession of the goods difficult or impossible, some problems may arise regarding title to goods and risk of loss.

Potential Problems

In the vast majority of sales transactions, the buyer receives the proper goods, makes payment, and the transaction is thus completed. However, several types of problems may arise. For the most part, problems can be avoided if the parties expressly state their intentions in their sales contract. When the parties have not specified the results they desire, however, the rules in this chapter apply.

Creditors' Claims. Creditors of the seller may seize the goods as belonging to the seller, or the buyer's creditors may seize them on the theory that they belong to the buyer. In such a case it must be determined who owns the goods. The question of ownership is also important in connection with resale by the buyer, liability for or computation of certain kinds of taxes, and liability under certain registration and criminal statutes.

Insurance. Until the buyer has received the goods and the seller has been paid, both the seller and buyer have an economic interest in the sales transaction. The question arises as to whether either or both have enough interest to entitle them to insure the property involved; that is, whether they have an insurable interest.

Damage to Goods. If the goods are damaged or totally destroyed without any fault of either the buyer or the seller, must the seller bear the loss and supply new goods to the buyer? Or must the buyer pay the seller the purchase price even though the buyer now has no goods or has only damaged goods?

Nature of the Transaction

The nature of the transaction between the seller and the buyer determines the answer to be given to each question in the preceding section. Sales transactions may be classified according to (1) the nature of the goods and (2) the terms of the transaction.

Nature of Goods. The goods may be *existing goods,* which means that they are physically in existence and are owned by the seller. It is immaterial whether the existing goods are in the condition required by the contract or whether the seller must do some act or complete the manufacture of the goods before they satisfy the terms of the contract.

In addition to existing goods, there are the classifications of identified goods and future goods. The seller and buyer may have agreed which goods are to be received by the buyer, or the seller may have picked out the goods. When such a selection has been made, the goods are *identified goods.* If the goods are either not existing or not identified at the time of the transaction, they are *future goods*.

Terms of the Transaction. The terms of the contract may require that the goods be sent or shipped to the buyer, that is, that the seller make shipment. In that case, the seller's part is performed when the goods are handed over to a carrier for shipment.

Instead of calling for actual delivery of goods, the transaction may involve a transfer of the document of title representing the goods. For example, the goods may be stored in a warehouse, the seller and the buyer having no intention of moving the goods, but intending that there should be a sale and a delivery of the warehouse receipt that stands for the goods. In this case the seller is required to produce the proper paper as distinguished from the goods themselves. The same is true when the goods are represented by a bill of lading issued by a carrier or by any other document of title.

Transfer of Title, Special Property Interests, and Risk in Particular Transactions

The kinds of goods and transaction terms may be combined in a number of ways. Only the more common types of transactions will be considered. The following rules of law apply only in the absence of a contrary agreement by the parties concerning these matters.

Existing Goods Identified at Time of Contracting. The title to such goods that are not to be transported passes to the buyer at the time and place of contracting.

Roger and Sharon Russell agreed to sell Robert Clouser a boat for $8,500. Clouser made an initial payment of $1,700, with the balance to be paid upon possession. The Russells were to retain the boat to replace an engine and drive train, after which Clouser was to take delivery at their marina. Prior to delivery to Clouser, while being tested by the Russells' employees, the boat hit a seawall and was destroyed. The Russells' insurance policy with Transamerica Insurance Company did not cover damage resulting from watercraft hazard unless the watercraft was not owned by the Russells. Transamerica refused to pay, claiming the boat was owned by the Russells at the time of the accident. The court said that since the boat had been identified at the time of contracting, no documents were to be delivered, and delivery was to be made without the boat being moved, title passed at the time of contracting.

If the existing goods are to be transported, title to the goods passes when the seller has completed delivery.

The buyer, who becomes the owner of the goods, has an insurable interest in them when title passes. Conversely, the seller no longer has an insurable interest unless by agreement a security interest has been reserved to protect the right to payment.

If the seller is a merchant, the risk of loss passes to the buyer when the goods are received from the merchant. If the seller is a nonmerchant seller, the risk passes when the seller tenders or makes available the goods to the buyer. Thus, the risk of loss remains longer on the merchant seller on the ground that the merchant seller, being in the business, can more readily arrange to be protected against such continued risk.

The fact that "title" to a motor vehicle has not been transferred because of a statute making the issuance of a title certificate essential for that purpose does not affect the transfer of the risk of loss as between the seller and buyer.

Negotiable Documents Representing Existing Goods Identified at Time of Contracting. In this case the buyer has a property interest, but not title, and an insurable interest in the goods at the time and place of contracting. But the buyer does not ordinarily acquire the title nor become subject to the risk of loss until delivery of the documents is made. Conversely, the seller has an insurable interest and title up to that time.

Seller's Marking Future Goods for Buyer. If the buyer sends an order for goods to be manufactured by the seller or to be filled from inventory or by purchases from third persons, one step in the process of filling the order is the seller's act of marking, tagging, labeling, or in some way doing an act for the benefit of the shipping department or for the seller to indicate that certain goods are the ones to be sent or delivered to the buyer under contract. This act is enough to give the buyer a property interest in the goods and the right to insure them. However, neither title nor risk of loss passes to the buyer at that time. The seller, as continuing owner, also has an insurable interest in the goods. Neither title nor liability passes to the buyer until some event, such as a shipment or delivery, occurs.

Contract for Shipment of Future Goods. In this situation the buyer has placed an order for goods that will be shipped later. The contract is performed by the seller when the goods are delivered to a carrier for shipment to the buyer. Under such a contract the title and risk of loss pass to the buyer when the goods are delivered to the carrier, that is, at the time and place of shipment.

Donohue was a local distributor for the Acme Brewing Co. Under the distribution contract, sales were made at prices set by the company "all f.o.b. Acme

Brewing Company's plant, from which shipment is made. . . . Distributor agrees
. . . to pay all freight and transportation charges from Acme Brewing Company's
place of business or to the delivery point designated by the distributor and all delivery expenses." Donohue wrote the company to deliver a quantity of beer to a
trucker by the name of Stetson as soon as the latter would accept the goods. The
company delivered the goods to Stetson. Snow delayed the transportation and
caused the beer to freeze. Donohue rejected the beer and was sued by the company for the purchase price. Judgment was for the company. As the contract
called for shipment f.o.b. the seller's plant, the risk of loss passed to the buyer at
that time and place. The fact that the goods were damaged thereafter did not affect
the buyer's duty to pay for the goods.

Damage to or Destruction of Goods

Damage to or the destruction of the goods affects the transaction as
follows:

Damage to Identified Goods before Risk of Loss Passes. When
goods that were identified at the time the contract was made suffer some
damage or are destroyed without the fault of either party before the risk of
loss has passed, the contract is avoided if the loss is total. If the loss is partial or if the goods have so deteriorated that they do not conform to the
contract, the buyer has the option, after inspecting the goods, (1) to treat
the contract as avoided, or (2) to accept the goods subject to an allowance
or deduction from the contract price. In either case, the buyer cannot assert
any claims against the seller for breach of contract.

Damage to Identified Goods after Risk of Loss Passes. If partial
damage or total destruction occurs after the risk of loss has passed, it is the
buyer's loss. The buyer may, however, be able to recover the amount of
the damages from the person in possession of the goods or from a third
person causing the loss. For example, in many instances the risk of loss
passes at the time of the transaction even though the seller is to deliver the
goods later. During the period from the transfer of the risk of loss to the
transfer of possession to the buyer, the seller has the status of a bailee of
the goods and is liable to the buyer under the circumstances for which an
ordinary bailee would be liable.

Damage to Unidentified Goods. So long as the goods are unidentified, no risk of loss has passed to the buyer. If any goods are damaged or
destroyed during this period, it is the loss of the seller. The buyer is still
entitled to receive the goods according to the contract. A seller who fails to
deliver the goods is liable to the purchaser for the breach of the contract.
The only exception arises when the parties have provided in the contract

that destruction of the seller's supply shall release the seller from liability or when it is clear that the parties contracted for the purchase and sale of part of the seller's supply to the exclusion of any other possible source of such goods.

Reservation of Title or Possession. When the seller reserves title or possession solely as security to make certain that payment will be made, the risk of loss is borne by the buyer if the circumstances are such that the buyer would bear the loss in the absence of such reservation.

Sales on Approval and with Right to Return

A sales transaction may give the buyer the privilege of returning the goods. In a *sale on approval,* the sale is not complete until the buyer approves. A *sale or return* is a completed sale with the right of the buyer to return the goods and thereby set aside the sale. The agreement of the parties determines whether the sale is a sale on approval or a sale or return. If they fail to indicate their intention, it is deemed a sale on approval if the goods are purchased for use, that is, by a consumer. It is deemed a sale or return if purchased for resale, that is, by a merchant.

Consequence of Sale on Approval. Unless agreed otherwise, title and risk of loss remain with the seller under a sale on approval. Use of the goods by the buyer consistent with the purpose of trial does not constitute approval. There is an approval, however, if the buyer acts in a manner that is not consistent with a reasonable trial, or fails to express a choice within the time specified or within a reasonable time if no time is specified. If the goods are returned, the seller bears the risk and the expense involved. Since the buyer is not the "owner" of the goods while they are on approval, the goods may not be claimed by the buyer's creditors.

Consequence of Sale or Return. In a sale or return, title and risk of loss pass to the buyer as in the case of an ordinary sale. In the absence of a contrary agreement, the buyer under a sale or return may return all of the goods or any commercial unit thereof. A *commercial unit* is any article, group of articles, or quantity commercially regarded as a separate unit or item, such as a particular machine, a suite of furniture, or a carload lot. The goods must still be in substantially their original condition, and the option to return must be exercised within the time specified by the contract or within a reasonable time if none is specified. The return under such a contract is at the buyer's risk and expense. As long as the goods are in the buyer's possession, the buyer's creditors may treat the goods as belonging to the buyer.

Other Transactions. A consignment is not a sale on approval or a sale with right to return. In the absence of any contrary provision, it is merely an agency and denotes that property is in the possession of the consignee for sale. In the absence of some restriction, the consignor may revoke the agency at will and retake possession of the property. Whether goods are sent to a person as buyer or on consignment to sell for the seller is a question of the intention of the parties.

Sales of Fungible Goods

Fungible goods are goods of a homogeneous or like nature that may be sold by weight or measure. They are goods of which any unit is from its nature or by commercial usage treated as the equivalent of any other unit. Wheat, oil, coal, and similar bulk commodities are fungible goods since any one bushel or other unit of the mass will be the same as any other bushel or similar unit.

The UCC provides that title to an undivided share or quantity of an identified mass of fungible goods may pass to the buyer at the time of the transaction, making the buyer an owner in common with the seller. For example, when one person sells to another 600 bushels of wheat from a bin which contains 1,000 bushels, title to 600 bushels passes to the buyer at the time of the transaction. This gives the buyer a $^6/_{10}$ths undivided interest in the mass as an owner in common with the seller. The courts in some states, however, have held that the title does not pass until a separation has been made.

Sale of Undivided Shares

The problem of the passage of title to a part of a larger mass of fungible goods is distinct from the problem of the passage of title when the sale is made of a fractional interest without any intention to make a later separation. In the former case the buyer is to become the exclusive owner of a separated portion. In the latter case the buyer is to become a co-owner of the entire mass. Thus, there may be a sale of a part interest in a radio, an automobile, or a flock of sheep. The right to make a sale of a fractional interest is recognized by statute.

Auction Sales

When goods are sold at an auction in separate lots, each lot is a separate transaction, and title to each passes independently of the other lots. Title to each lot passes when the auctioneer announces by the fall of the hammer or in any other customary manner that the auction is completed as to that lot.

Free on Board

A contract may call for goods to be sold f.o.b., free on board, a designated point. Goods may be sold f.o.b. the seller's plant, the buyer's plant, an intermediate point, or a specified carrier. The seller bears the risk and expense until the goods are delivered at the f.o.b. point designated.

C.O.D. Shipment

In the absence of an extension of credit, a seller has the right to keep the goods until paid, but this right is lost if possession of the goods is delivered to anyone for the buyer. However, where the goods are delivered to a carrier, the seller may keep the right to possession by making the shipment C.O.D., or by the addition of any other terms indicating that the carrier is not to surrender the goods to the buyer until the buyer has made payment. Such a provision has no effect other than to keep the buyer from obtaining possession until payment has been made. The C.O.D. provision does not affect when title or risk of loss passes.

Transfer of Title

As a general rule, people can sell only such interest or title in goods as they possess. If property is subject to a bailment (personal property temporarily in the custody of another person), a sale by the bailor is subject to the bailment. Thus, if the owner of a rented car sells the car to another person, the bailee may still use the car according to the terms of the bailment. Similarly, bailees can only transfer their individual rights under the bailments, assuming that the bailment agreements permit the rights to be assigned or transferred.

A thief or finder generally cannot transfer the title to property since only that which such a person has, namely possession, can be passed. In fact, the purchaser from the thief not only fails to obtain title but also becomes liable to the owner as a converter of the property even though it may have been purchased in good faith.

W. A. Andres rented his motor home to Phillip Robertson, who was really Lewis Murphy. Murphy obtained an Alabama registration for the motor home under the name L. E. Boggs. Nebraska provided Boggs a certificate of title which was transferred to Murphy. Murphy traded the home to McDonald's Chevrolet, Inc., after applying for an Indiana certificate of title. Otis Johnson purchased the motor home from McDonald's. It was seized by the Indiana State Police and given to Andres' insurer, Foremost Insurance Company. Johnson sued Foremost to recover the home. Since Murphy did not have title, he could not convey title to McDonald's and McDonald's could not convey title to Johnson. Even though

Johnson did not know the motor home was stolen and even though he had paid for it, Johnson was not entitled to it.

There are certain instances, however, when either because of the conduct of the owner or the desire of society to protect the bona fide purchaser for value, the law permits a greater title to be transferred than the seller possesses.

Sale by Entrustee. If the owner entrusts goods to a merchant who deals in goods of that kind, the merchant has the power to transfer the entruster's title to anyone who buys in the ordinary course of business.

It is immaterial why the goods were entrusted to the merchant. Hence the leaving of a watch for repairs with a jeweler who sells new and second-hand watches would give the jeweler the power to pass the title to a buyer in the ordinary course of business. The entrustee is, of course, liable to the owner for damages caused by the sale of the goods and may be guilty of a statutory offense such as embezzlement.

If the entrustee is not a merchant, but merely a prospective customer, there is no transfer of title when the entrustee sells to a third person.

Consignment Sales. A manufacturer or distributor may send goods to a dealer for sale to the public with the understanding that the manufacturer or distributor is to remain the owner and the dealer is, in effect, to act as an agent. When the dealer maintains a place of business at which dealings are made in goods of the kind in question under a name other than that of the consigning manufacturer or distributor, the creditors of the dealer may reach the goods as though they were owned by the dealer.

Estoppel. The owner of property may be estopped (barred) from asserting ownership and denying the right of another person to sell the property to a good-faith purchaser. A person may purchase a product and have the bill of sale made out in the name of a friend to whom possession of the product and the bill of sale is then given. This might be done in order to deceive creditors or to keep other persons from knowing that the purchase had been made. If the friend should sell the product to a bona fide purchaser who relies on the bill of sale, the true owner is estopped or barred from denying the friend's apparent ownership.

United Road Machinery Co. leased a truck scale to Consolidated Coal Co. United paid for the scale and told the supplier of the scale that Consolidated would take possession, which it did. United sent a contract for the lease to Consolidated, which never returned the contract. Consolidated took the scale to its place of business in Laurel County, added decking, and then sold it to Kentucky Mobile Homes of Pulaski County. Kentucky had had the records of Laurel and Pulaski Counties checked and found there was no encumbrance shown against the scale.

Kentucky then sold the scale to Clyde Jasper, who had also searched the records for an encumbrance on the scale. Neither Kentucky nor Jasper knew of any dispute between United and Consolidated. When it failed to receive any payment from Consolidated, United sued Jasper for the scale. The court found that there was nothing to suggest that Consolidated was not the owner of the scale as against Jasper, a good-faith purchaser. United was estopped from asserting its title against Jasper.

Documents of Title. By statute, certain documents of title, such as bills of lading and warehouse receipts, have been clothed with a degree of negotiability when executed in proper form. By virtue of such provisions, the holder of a negotiable document of title directing delivery of the goods to the holder or order, or to bearer, may transfer to a purchaser for value acting in good faith such title as was possessed by the person leaving the property with the issuer of the document. In such cases it is immaterial that the holder had not acquired the documents in a lawful manner.

Recording and Filing Statutes. In order to protect subsequent purchasers and creditors, statutes may require that certain transactions be recorded or filed and may provide that if that is not done, the transaction has no effect against a purchaser who thereafter buys the goods in good faith from the person who appears to be the owner or against the execution creditors of such an apparent owner. Thus, if a seller retains a security interest in the goods sold to the buyer but fails to file a financing statement in the manner required by the UCC, the purchaser appears to own the goods free from any security interest; subsequent bona fide purchasers or creditors of the buyer can acquire title free of the seller's security interest.

Voidable Title. If the buyer has a voidable title, as when the goods were obtained by fraud, the seller can rescind the sale while the buyer is still the owner. If, however, the buyer resells the property to a bona fide purchaser before the seller has rescinded the transaction, the subsequent purchaser acquires valid title. It is immaterial whether the buyer having the voidable title had obtained title by fraud as to identity, or by larceny by trick, or that payment for the goods had been made with a bad check, or that the transaction was a cash sale and the purchase price has not been paid.

Questions

1. **a.** What are *existing goods?*
   b. What are *identified goods?*
   c. What are *future goods?*

2. If the terms of a sales transaction require that the goods be shipped by the seller to the buyer, when is the seller considered to have completed performance?

3. When does title to existing and identified goods which are not to be transported pass?

4. What interest does a buyer have in goods which are marked to indicate they are the ones for the buyer?

5. If Judson sells 500 cases of a cola drink to Goodman "f.o.b. Judson's plant," when does risk of loss pass?

6. If damage occurs to identified goods before risk of loss passes, what options does the buyer have?

7. **a.** Distinguish between a *sale on approval* and a *sale or return*.
   b. Why is it important to make a distinction?

8. **a.** What are *fungible goods*?
   b. When does title to fungible goods pass?

9. Can a thief normally transfer title to goods?

10. If Holmes leaves a portable television set for repair with Ace TV (repair shop and dealer in new and used sets), and Ace sells the set to Lodder, would the buyer get good title?

Case Problems

1. Andrew Pruitt, a supervisor of the commissary meat department at Fort Lewis, diverted meat ordered for Fort Lewis to his two restaurants. Pruitt instructed Randy's Meats to set aside an order of meat for Fort Lewis in a "will-call" trailer to be picked up later. Randy's marked the top boxes "Fort Lewis" and entered the number on each box on the invoices for Fort Lewis. A person who told Randy's he was acting for Pruitt picked up the meat and delivered it to the restaurants. When charged with conspiracy and theft, the restaurants alleged the meat was not government property. Was it?

2. Lowell agrees to purchase a certain quantity of cotton that Sturgis, the seller, agrees to bale. The cotton is destroyed before it is baled. Upon whom does the loss fall in each of the following situations?
   a. Sturgis is an ordinary seller.
   b. Sturgis is a merchant seller.

3. Tri-State Contracting & Trading Corporation contracted with Saudi Arabian importers for the sale of Pepsi-Cola. After aluminum cans were filled with soda, they were packed on trays, covered with "shrink wrap," and shipped to

a warehouse where the trays were unloaded and hand packed into containers. The containers were sealed at the warehouse and delivered to ocean terminals to be put on ocean carriers. The ocean carriers issued negotiable bills of lading for the soda to Tri-State, which was fully paid for the sales. When the shipment arrived in Saudi Arabia the cans had sustained significant leakage and were not merchantable. Would the carriers be liable to Tri-State?

4. Russ Bullock met with Parkes Shewmake, an official of Joe Bailey Auction Company, to arrange for Shewmake to act as a bidder for Bullock at an auction. Verification of financing was received, and Shewmake successfully bid on the equipment for Bullock. The equipment was not in operable condition. It was left at the auction site until after Bullock performed extensive repairs and removed it to Utah. Bullock's financing was delayed, and he gave Shewmake a check which stated, "Not to be presented to the bank for collection until adequate financing is completed." When the check could not be negotiated, Bailey indicated he intended to reclaim the equipment, alleging there was no sale because payment had not been made. Was there a sale?

5. Anthony Coppola ordered some coins from First Coinvestors, Inc., under an agreement that the coins would be paid for or returned within ten days. Coppola was not in the business of selling coins but was a collector. The package of coins was delivered to a person on Coppola's property who signed for them, but no one knew who he was or what happened to the coins. Coinvestors sued Coppola for the value of the coins. Is he liable?

6. A manufacturer sells five vending machines of a new type to a dealer. The terms of the agreement provide that the buyer can return the machines within sixty days if he does not succeed in selling them. Twenty days later the machines are destroyed by fire. Upon whom does the loss fall? *Buyer - right of return*

7. Lindsey, who has thirty tons of coal in a bin, sells ten tons of it to Monroe. Before Monroe calls for her coal, who has title to the coal in the bin?

8. Dunham orders a specified number of sacks of cement mix from Neltner who, according to agreement, marks the goods C.O.D. and delivers them to the carrier. The goods are lost in transit. Who must suffer the loss?

9. Eastern Supply Co. purchased lawn mowers from the Turf Man Sales Corp. The purchase order stated on its face "Ship direct to 30th & Harcum Way, Pitts., Pa." Turf Man delivered the goods to Helm's Express, Inc., for shipment and delivery to Eastern at the address in question. Did title pass on delivery of the goods to Helm or upon their arrival at the specified address?

16

Warranties of the Seller

Preview Cases

Gerard Construction, Inc., executed a bill of sale for a towboat to Phillip Mossesso and Donald Fix. Paragraph 2 of the bill of sale stated, "Seller warrants title to be good and marketable and free of all debts, liens, and encumbrances." Paragraph 5 stated, "Seller states that it is its belief that the vessel is now operative and in a safe condition and is not in violation of any federal regulation." Mossesso and Fix used the boat and then tried to rescind the transaction, claiming Paragraph 5 constituted a warranty. Did the language of Paragraph 5 create a warranty?

While William Bernick was playing hockey for Georgia Tech he was struck in the face by a hockey stick. His mouthguard was shattered, his upper jaw fractured, three teeth knocked out, and a part of a fourth tooth broken off. The manufacturer of the mouthguard, Cooper of Canada, Ltd., had promoted it through hockey catalog advertisements and parent guides as giving "maximum protection to the lips and teeth." Did the advertising create an express warranty?

In making a sale, a seller often warrants or guarantees that the article will conform to a certain standard or will operate in a certain manner. By the warranty the seller agrees in effect to make good any loss or damages that the purchaser may suffer if the goods are not as they are represented.

If a warranty is made at the time of the sale, it is considered to be a part of the contract and is therefore binding. If a warranty is made after a sale has been completed, it is binding even though not supported by any consideration; it is regarded as a modification of the sales contract.

Express Warranties

The statement of the seller in which the article is warranted or guaranteed is known as an *express warranty*. The UCC specifically provides that any affirmation of fact or promise made by the seller to the buyer which relates to the goods and becomes part of the basis of the bargain creates an express warranty. It is express because the seller actually and definitely states it, either orally or in writing.

No particular words are required to constitute an express warranty. The words "warrant" or "guarantee" need not be used. If a statement or a promise is such that a reasonable interpretation of the language leads the buyer to believe there is a warranty, the courts will construe it as such. A seller is bound by the ordinary meaning of the words used, not by any unexpressed intentions.

The seller can use the word "warrant" or "guarantee" and still not be bound by it if an ordinary, prudent person would not interpret it to constitute a warranty. If the seller of a car says, "I'll guarantee that you will not be sorry if you buy the car at this price," no warranty exists; this is mere sales talk, even though the word "guarantee" is used.

Seller's Opinion

The law holds that sellers may praise their wares, even extravagantly, without being obligated on their statements or representations. A person should not be misled by such borderline expressions as "best on the market for the money," "these goods are worth $10 if they are worth a dime," "experts have estimated that one ought to be able to sell a thousand a month of these," and many others which sound very convincing but which have been held to be mere expressions of opinion and not warranties.

Gerard Construction, Inc., executed a bill of sale for a towboat to Phillip Mossesso and Donald Fix. Paragraph 2 of the bill of sale stated, "Seller warrants title to be good and marketable and free of all debts, liens, and encumbrances." Paragraph 5 stated, "Seller states that it is its belief that the vessel is now operative and in a safe condition and is not in violation of any federal regulation." Mossesso and Fix used the boat and then tried to rescind the transaction, claiming Paragraph 5 constituted a warranty. The court found the language of Paragraph 5 was clearly drafted in pursuance of the UCC provision regarding a seller's opinion not creating a warranty. Also, Paragraph 2 clearly indicated that the parties knew how to embody a warranty when they wanted to.

The rule that a statement of opinion or belief does not constitute a warranty must be qualified. Although an expression by the seller of what is clearly an opinion does not constitute either a warranty or a basis for fraud liability, the seller may be liable for fraud if, in fact, the seller does not believe the opinion which is stated.

Defects

If there are defects that are actually known to the buyer, or defects that are so apparent that no special skill or ability is required to detect them, an express warranty may not cover them. The determining factor is whether the statement becomes a part of the basis of the bargain. If it does, it is an express warranty. This would not be true if the seller used any scheme or artifice to conceal the defect such as covering the defect with an item of decoration. The seller must not do anything for the purpose of diverting the attention of the buyer from the defects.

Implied Warranties

An *implied warranty* is one that was not made by the seller but which is imposed by the law. That is, the implied warranty arises automatically from the fact that a sale has been made. Express warranties arise because they form part of the basis on which the sale has been made.

The fact that express warranties are made does not exclude implied warranties. When both express and implied warranties exist, they should be construed as consistent with each other. In case it is unreasonable to construe them as consistent, an express warranty prevails over an implied warranty as to the same subject matter, except in the case of an implied warranty of fitness for a particular purpose.

Warranties of All Sellers

The following warranties apply to all sellers:

Warranty of Title. All sellers, by the mere act of selling, make a warranty that their titles are good and that the transfers are rightful. A warranty of title may be excluded or modified by the specific language or the circumstances of the transaction. The latter situation is found when the buyer has reason to know that the seller does not claim title or that the seller is purporting to sell only such right or title as the seller or a third person may have. For example, no warranty of title arises when the seller makes the sale in a representative capacity, such as a sheriff, an auctioneer, or an administrator. Likewise no warranty arises when the seller makes the sale by virtue of a power of sale possessed as a pledgee or mortgagee.

Warranty Against Encumbrances. In addition to a warranty of title, every seller makes a warranty that the goods shall be delivered free from any security interest or any other lien or encumbrance of which the buyer at the time of making the sales contract had no knowledge. Thus, there is a breach of warranty when the automobile sold to the buyer is already subject to an outstanding claim that had been placed against it by the original owner and which was unknown to the buyer at the time of the sale.

The warranty against encumbrances applies to the goods only at the time they are delivered to the buyer and is not concerned with an encumbrance which existed before or at the time the sale was made. For example, a seller may not have paid in full for the goods which are being resold and the original supplier may have a lien on the goods. The seller may resell the goods while that lien is still on them, and the only duty is to pay off the lien before the goods are delivered to the buyer.

A warranty against encumbrances does not arise if the buyer knows of the existence of the encumbrance in question. Knowledge must be actual knowledge as contrasted with constructive notice. Constructive notice is information which the law presumes everyone knows by virtue of the fact that it is filed or recorded on the public record.

Warranty of Conformity to Description, Sample, or Model.

Any description of the goods, sample, or model which is made part of the basis of the sales contract creates an express warranty that the goods shall conform in kind and quality to the description, sample, or model. Ordinarily a *sample* is a portion of a whole mass that is the subject of the transaction. A *model* is a replica of the article in question. The mere fact that a sample is exhibited in the course of negotiations does not make the sale a sale by sample, as there must be an intent shown that the sample be part of the basis of contracting.

Warranty of Fitness for a Particular Purpose.

When the seller has reason to know at the time of contracting that the buyer intends to use the goods for a particular or unusual purpose, the seller may make an implied warranty that the goods will be fit for that purpose. Such an implied warranty arises when the buyer relies on the seller's skill or judgment to select or furnish suitable goods, and when the seller has reason to know of the buyer's reliance. This warranty does not arise when the goods are to be used for the purpose for which they are customarily sold or when goods are ordered on particular specifications and the purpose is not disclosed. For example, where a government representative inquired of the seller whether the seller has a tape suitable for use on a particular government computer system, there arose an implied warranty, unless otherwise excluded, that the tape furnished by the seller was fit for that purpose.

The fact that a seller does not intend to make a warranty of fitness for a particular purpose is immaterial. Parol evidence is admissible to show that the seller had knowledge of the buyer's intended use.

Additional Warranties of Merchant Seller

A *merchant* seller (a seller who deals in goods of the kind or who is considered, because of occupation, to have particular knowledge or skill regarding the goods involved) makes additional implied warranties.

Warranty Against Infringement. Unless otherwise agreed, a seller who is a merchant regularly dealing in goods of the kind sold warrants that the goods shall be delivered free of the rightful claim of any third person by way of patent or trademark infringement. A buyer who is sued for infringement must notify the seller. A buyer who supplies the seller with specifications must protect the seller against claims growing out of compliance with the specifications. In this case, the seller must notify the buyer of an infringement suit.

Warranty of Merchantability or Fitness for Normal Use. Unless excluded or modified, merchant sellers make an implied warranty of merchantability. The warranty is in fact a group of warranties, the most important of which is that the goods are fit for the ordinary purposes for which they are sold. Consequently, when the seller of ice-making and beverage-vending machines is a merchant of such machines, an implied warranty of fitness for use arises. Also included are implied warranties as to the general or average quality of the goods, and their packaging and labeling.

The implied warranty of merchantability relates to the condition of the goods at the time the seller is to perform under the contract. Once the risk of loss has passed to the buyer, there is no warranty as to the continuing merchantability of the goods unless such subsequent deterioration or condition is proof that the goods were in fact not merchantable when the seller made delivery.

Warranty of merchantability relates only to the fitness of the product that is made or sold. It does not impose upon the manufacturer or seller the duty to employ any particular design or to sell one product rather than another because another might be safer.

Pfahl purchased a Chevrolet station wagon made by General Motors. While driving the station wagon, he was struck on the left side by another vehicle. The left side of the station wagon collapsed and inflicted fatal injuries. An action was brought on behalf of his estate against General Motors, claiming that the station wagon had been negligently constructed in that it was built on an X-frame (of two supporting rails crossing diagonally under the body of the car) and that the collapse of the left side would have been avoided if General Motors had added side rails to the X-frame. Judgment was for General Motors. The requirement that the automobile be fit for its intended purpose did not mean that it must be made accident-proof, particularly in view of the fact that engaging in collisions is not the purpose of an automobile. The fact that some competitors put side rails on the frames, and that some expert stated that this would be safer, did not create liability for failing to do so.

Warranties in Particular Sales

Particular types of sales may involve special considerations.

Sale of Food or Drink. The sale of food or drink, whether to be consumed on or off the seller's premises, is a sale. When made by a merchant, the sale carries the implied warranty that the food is fit for its ordinary purpose, that is, human consumption. Under the prior law some authorities held that there was no breach of warranty when a harmful object found in the food was natural to the particular kind of food, such as an oyster shell in oysters, a chicken bone in chicken, and so on.

Other cases regarded the warranty as breached when the harm-causing substance in the food was such that its presence could not be reasonably expected, without regard to whether the substance was natural or foreign, as in the case of a nail or piece of glass. In these cases it is necessary to make a determination of fact, ordinarily by the jury, to determine whether the buyer could reasonably expect the object in the food. The UCC does not end the conflict between the courts applying the "foreign/natural" test and those applying the "reasonable expectation" test.

It is, of course, necessary to distinguish the foregoing situations from those in which the preparation of the foods contemplates the continued presence of some element which is not removed, such as prune stones in cooked prunes.

Ginger Lee Jeffries ordered a "crab melt" sandwich from Clark's Restaurant Enterprises, Inc. It contained a piece of crab shell one inch in diameter, which Jeffries did not see. The crab shell lodged in her esophagus and had to be removed surgically. Jeffries filed suit for damages. The court held that it was a question for the jury whether Jeffries should have reasonably expected to find such a piece of shell in the sandwich.

Sale of Article with Patent or Trade Name. The sale of a patent- or trade-name article is treated with respect to warranties in the same way as any other sale. The fact that the sale is made on the basis of the patent or trade name does not bar the existence of a warranty of fitness for a particular purpose or of merchantability when the circumstances giving rise to such a warranty otherwise exist.

It is a question of fact, however, whether the buyer relied on the seller's skill and judgment when the purchase was made. That is, if the buyer asked for a patent- or trade-name article and insisted on it, it is apparent that there was no reliance upon the seller's skill and judgment and therefore the factual basis for an implied warranty of fitness for the particular purpose is lacking. If the necessary reliance upon the seller's skill and judgment is shown, however, the warranty arises in that situation.

Sperry Rand Corp. agreed to convert the record-keeping system of Industrial Supply Corp. so that it could be maintained by a computer and to sell a computer and nine other items necessary for such a record-keeping system. The computer and the equipment were ordered by identified trade name and number. When the system did not work, Industrial Supply sued Sperry Rand for breach of implied warranty of fitness. Sperry Rand raised the defense that there was no such warranty because the equipment had been ordered by trade name and number. The court held that the fact that the equipment was ordered by trade name and number did not automatically extinguish the warranty of fitness. The circumstances showed the sale was made in reliance on the seller's skill, and with appreciation of the buyer's problems, and the sale of the particular equipment to the buyer was made as constituting the equipment needed by it. Under such circumstances, a warranty of the fitness of the equipment for such purpose was implied.

The seller of automobile parts is not liable for breach of the implied warranty of their fitness when the parts were ordered by catalog number for use in a specified vehicle and the seller did not know that the lubrication system of the automobile had been changed so as to make the parts ordered unfit for use.

Sale on Buyer's Specifications. When the buyer furnishes the seller with exact specifications for the preparation or manufacture of goods, the same warranties arise as in the case of any other sale of such goods by the particular seller. No warranty of fitness for a particular purpose can arise, however, since it is clear that the buyer is purchasing on the basis of a decision made without relying on the seller's skill and judgment.

In sales made upon the buyer's specifications, no warranty against infringement is impliedly made by the merchant seller. Conversely, the buyer in substance makes a warranty to protect the seller from liability should the seller be held liable for patent violation by following the specifications of the buyer.

Sale of Secondhand or Used Goods. No warranty arises as to fitness of used property for ordinary use when the sale is made by a casual seller. If made by a merchant seller, such a warranty may exist. A number of states follow the rule that implied warranties may apply in connection with the sale of used or secondhand goods, particularly automobiles and equipment.

Full or Limited Warranties

When a written warranty is made for a consumer product, it may be either a full warranty or a limited warranty. The seller of a product with a *full warranty* must: remedy any defects in the product in a reasonable time without charge, place no limit on the duration of implied warranties, not limit consequential damages for breach of warranty unless done conspicuously on the warranty's face, and permit the purchaser to choose a refund or replacement without charge if the product contains a defect after a reasonable number of attempts by the warrantor to remedy the defects. All other written warranties for consumer products are *limited warranties*.

Exclusion and Surrender of Warranties

Warranties can be excluded or modified by the agreement of the parties, subject to the limitation that such a provision must not be unconscionable.

It is proper for the jury to consider the purchase price in determining the scope of the warranty of fitness, as where the coal was bought for one-half or less the price of standard coal.

If a warranty of fitness is to be excluded, the exclusion must be in writing and so conspicuous as to assure that the buyer will be aware of its presence. If the implied warranty of merchantability is excluded or modified, the exclusion clause must expressly mention the word "merchantability" and if in writing must be conspicuous.

Particular Provisions. Such a statement as "there are no warranties which extend beyond the description on the face hereof" excludes all implied warranties of fitness. Normally, implied warranties are excluded by the statement "as is," "with all faults," or other language which in normal common speech calls attention to the warranty exclusion and makes it clear that there is no implied warranty. An implied warranty that a steam heater would work properly in the buyer's dry cleaning plant was effectively excluded by provisions that "the warranties and guarantees herein set forth are made by us and accepted by you in lieu of all statutory or implied warranties or guarantees, other than title. . . . This contract contains all agreements between the parties and there is no agreement, verbal or otherwise, which is not set down herein," and the contract had only a "one-year warranty on labor and material supplied by seller."

In order for a disclaimer of warranties to be a binding part of an oral sales contract, the disclaimer must be called to the attention of the buyer. When the contract as made does not disclaim warranties, a disclaimer of warranties accompanying goods delivered later is not effective because it is a unilateral attempt to modify the contract.

Examination. There is no implied warranty with respect to defects in goods that an examination should have revealed when the buyer before making the final contract has examined as fully as desired the goods, or a model or sample, or has refused to make such examination.

Dealings and Customs. An implied warranty can be excluded or modified by course of dealings, course of performance, or usage of trade.

Caveat Emptor

In the absence of fraud on the part of the seller or circumstances in which the law imposes a warranty, the relationship of the seller and the buyer is aptly described by the maxim of *caveat emptor* (let the buyer beware). Courts at common law rigidly applied this rule, requiring purchasers in ordinary sales to act in reliance upon their own judgment except when sellers gave express warranties. The trend of the earlier statutes, the Uniform Commercial Code, and decisions of modern courts has been to soften the harshness of this rule, primarily by establishing implied warranties for the protection of the buyer. The rule of caveat emptor is still applied, however, when the buyer has full opportunity to make such examination of the goods as would disclose the existence of any defect and the seller is not guilty of fraud.

Product Liability

When harm to person or property results from the use or condition of an article of personal property, the person injured may be entitled to recover damages. This right may be based on the theory that there was a breach of warranty or that the person sued was negligent.

Breach of Warranty. At common law the rule was that only the parties to a transaction had any rights relating to it. Accordingly, only the buyer could sue the immediate seller for breach of warranty. The rule was stated in the terms that there could be no suit for breach of warranty unless there was a privity of contract (a contract relationship) between the plaintiff and the defendant.

In most states an exception to the privity rule developed under which members of the buyer's family and various other remote persons not in privity of contract with the seller or manufacturer could sue for breach of warranty when injured by the harmful condition of food, beverages, or drugs. The right to sue the manufacturer of a bottled or packaged food might be denied where there is evidence that another person has or might have tampered with the item before it reached the buyer or consumer.

The UCC expressly abolished the requirement of privity against the seller by members of the buyer's family, household, and guests in actions for personal injury. Apart from the express provision made by the UCC, there is a conflict of authority as to whether privity of contract is required in other cases, with the trend being toward the abolition of that requirement. In many states, the doctrine is flatly rejected when suit is brought by a buyer against the manufacturer or a prior seller. In many instances, recovery by the buyer against the remote manufacturer or seller is based on the fact that the defendant had advertised directly to the public and therefore made a warranty to the purchasing consumer of the truth of the advertising. Although advertising by the manufacturer to the consumer is a reason for not requiring privity when the consumer sues the manufacturer, the absence of advertising by the manufacturer frequently does not bar such action by the buyer. While most jurisdictions have modified the privity requirement beyond the exceptions specified in the UCC, each state has retained limited applications of the doctrine.

◆   While William Bernick was playing hockey for Georgia Tech he was struck in the face by a hockey stick. His mouthguard was shattered, his upper jaw fractured, three teeth knocked out, and a part of a fourth tooth broken off. The manufacturer of the mouthguard, Cooper of Canada, Ltd., had promoted it through hockey catalog advertisements and parent guides as giving "maximum protection to the lips and teeth." The language was such as to induce the purchase of the mouthguard by Bernick's mother for his use while playing. Bernick did rely on an express warranty.

Recovery may also be allowed when the consumer mails to the manufacturer a warranty registration card which the manufacturer had packed with the purchased article.

Negligence. Aside from the provisions of the UCC, a person injured through the use or condition of personal property may be entitled to sue the manufacturer for the damages which are sustained on the theory that the defendant was negligent in the preparation or manufacture of the article. Historically, such suits were also limited by the concept of privity of contract so that only the buyer could sue the seller for the latter's negligence; the buyer could not sue the manufacturer for negligence. This requirement of privity has generally been abolished. The modern rule is that whenever the manufacturer as a reasonable person should foresee that, if there is negligence, a particular class of persons will be injured by the product, the manufacturer is liable to an injured member of that class without regard to whether such plaintiff purchased from the manufacturer or from anyone.

Effect of Reprocessing by Distributor. Liability of the manufacturer or supplier to the ultimate consumer, whether for warranty or negligence, does not arise when the manufacturer or supplier believes or has reason to believe that the immediate distributor or processor is to complete processing or is to take further steps that will remove an otherwise foreseeable danger. Accordingly, although the supplier of unfinished pork to a retailer should realize that it might contain trichinae and be dangerous to the ultimate consumers, there is no liability to an ultimate consumer who contracts trichinosis when the retailer in purchasing the unfinished pork told the supplier that processing would be finished. The processing would have destroyed any trichinae, and the supplier did not know or have reason to know that the retailer failed to process the meat.

Identity of Parties

The existence of product liability may be affected by the identity of the claimant or of the defendant.

Third Persons. Historically, third persons, meaning persons who were not "buyers" from anyone, such as guests, employees, or total strangers, were denied recovery because of the absence of privity. The UCC permits recovery for breach of warranty by the guests of the buyer but makes no provision for recovery by employees or strangers.

There is a conflict of authority as to whether an employee of the buyer may sue the seller or manufacturer for breach of warranty. In some jurisdictions recovery is denied on the ground that the employee is outside of the distributive chain, not being a buyer. Others allow recovery in such a case. By the latter view, an employee of a construction contractor may recover for breach of the implied warranty of fitness made by the manufacturer of the structural steel which proved defective and fell, injuring the employee.

In some states, the courts have ignored privity of contract when the injured person was not even a subpurchaser but a member of the public or a stranger at large by adopting a doctrine of strict tort liability. This doctrine makes a manufacturer liable to anyone who is injured because of a defect in the manufacture of the product when such defect makes the use of the product dangerous to the user or to persons in the vicinity of the product and the person injured or killed is such a user or person in the vicinity. There is also a growing trend to allow recovery by the "stranger" on the theory of breach of warranty. It has been held that a mechanic who is injured because of a defect in the automobile he or she is fixing may sue the manufacturer for breach of implied warranty of fitness.

Manufacturer of Component Part. Many items of goods in today's marketplace were not made entirely by one manufacturer. Thus, the harm caused may result from a defect in a component part of the finished product. Since the manufacturer of the total article was the buyer from the component-part manufacturer, it followed that the privity rule barred suit against the component-part manufacturer for breach of warranty by anyone injured. In jurisdictions in which privity of contract is not recognized as a bar to recovery, it is not material that the defendant manufactured merely a component part. In these cases, the manufacturer of a component part cannot defend from suit by the ultimate purchaser on the ground of absence of privity. Thus, the purchaser of a tractor trailer may recover from the manufacturer of the brake system of the trailer for damages sustained when the brake system failed to work. Likewise, a person injured while on a golf course when an automobile parked on the club parking lot became "unparked" and ran down hill can sue the manufacturer of the defective parking unit.

Nature and Cause of Harm

The law is more concerned in cases where the plaintiff has been personally injured as contrasted with economically harmed. That is, the law places protection of the person of the individual above protection of property rights. The harm sustained must have been "caused" by the defendant, regardless of whether suit is based on the negligence of the defendant or on breach of warranty.

There is no liability when harm is not foreseeable. For example, when the law requires that a particular product be used with a safety device, the manufacturer of the product is not negligent when an injury is sustained because the product is used without the safety device required by law. Thus, the manufacturer of grinding wheels had the right to anticipate that the danger of injury from flying fragments of the wheel would be reduced or eliminated by the use of a protective shield as was required by law. The manufacturer was therefore not under any obligation to make the wheels "accident-proof" when used without a protective shield.

In many states, an injured plaintiff has the choice of suing for breach of warranty or for damages for negligence. The importance of the distinction between the two remedies lies in the fact that to prove a case for breach of warranty only facts of which the plaintiff has direct knowledge or about which information can readily be learned need be proven. That is, the plaintiff need show only that there was a sale and a warranty, that the goods did not conform to the warranty, and that there was injury from the goods. In the case of the action for negligence against the manufacturer, the plaintiff figuratively must also go into the defendant's plant or factory and learn how the given article was made and prove in court that there was negligence. Unless the plaintiff is able to show that the design of the manufacturer's product or the general method of manufacture was faulty, it is likely that the plaintiff will be unable to prove that there was negligence. It has been the recognition of this difficulty which, to a large degree, has led the courts to expand the warranty liability under which proof of negligence is not required.

A manufacturer or seller may assume by the terms of a contract a liability broader than would arise from a mere warranty.

Spiegel purchased a jar of skin cream from Saks 34th Street. It had been manufactured by the National Toilet Co. The carton and the jar stated that it was chemically pure and absolutely safe. When Spiegel used the cream, it caused a severe skin rash. She sued Saks and National. Judgment was for Spiegel. The statements on the carton and the jar constituted an express warranty binding both the seller and the manufacturer. The statement that it was safe was an absolute undertaking that it was safe for everyone; as distinguished from merely an implied warranty of reasonable fitness, which would be subject to an exception of a particular allergy of a plaintiff.

Questions

1. What is an express warranty?

2. Can one make a warranty without intending to do so?

3. If an oral warranty is not included when the contract is written up, can the purchaser prove it by oral testimony?

4. Is the statement, "This fish bait is so good you will have to hide behind a tree to put it on a hook," a warranty?

5. Do all sellers make a warranty of good title?

6. What warranty does the seller make when there is a sale by sample?

7. Distinguish by examples the difference between an implied warranty of fitness for a particular purpose and an implied warranty of merchantability.

8. Explain the difference in the "foreign/natural" test and the "reasonable expectation" test as applied to the sale of food or drink.

Case Problems

1. While negotiating the sale of a parakeet to Heck, Sheridan states, "This bird is healthy, as far as I know." Heck purchases the parakeet in reliance on Sheridan's statement. In an action against Sheridan, Heck proves that Sheridan knew at the time of the sale that the bird was diseased. Is Heck entitled to judgment?

2. David Duff bought tongue-and-groove lumber from Bonner Building Supply, Inc., a dealer in lumber products. Bonner represented that the lumber was kiln-dried, which meant its moisture content would not exceed 19 percent. Duff installed the lumber as wall paneling and significant shrinkage occurred. Some boards shrank ½ inch, which was enough to pull the wood tongues from their grooves leaving gaps between the boards. Shrinkage for lumber with a moisture content of 19 percent would not exceed ⅜ inch. Duff sued Bonner for the cost of repair and replacement, alleging breach of implied warranty of merchantability. Was it?

3. Daniel Shaffer ordered a glass of wine at the Victoria Station restaurant. The wine glass broke in his hand, resulting in injury. Shaffer sued the restaurant for breach of warranty. Victoria Station argued the UCC did not apply because it was not a merchant with respect to wine glasses, and the glass itself was not sold. Does the UCC apply?

4. Kevin Woods purchased a car from Robert Secord. Their oral agreement stated that Woods purchased it in "as is" condition without guarantee. Woods was only willing to purchase the car "as is" based upon Secord's representation that the car was in good condition and ran properly. Immediately after the sale Woods had severe problems with the car. Secord refused to cure the problems, so Woods sold the car for salvage. Woods sued, alleging the car was not fit for its intended use at the time of sale. Can he recover?

5. The Elkhorn Motor Sales Corporation sold Kirby a car for $3,200. Kirby was given a written guarantee that stated the car was in "A-1 condition" and provided that if anything went wrong with the car within twelve months, the Elkhorn Motor Corporation would repair it, charging only the wholesale cost of parts plus labor. What is the weakness in this warranty?

6. Branch, a rancher, purchased from the Hay Seed Company 2,000 pounds of reseeding crimson clover seed. The seller said, "This is the Dixie strain of reseeding clover, and I guarantee you won't have to worry about its reseeding." There are several strains of crimson clover, some reseeding, some not. The Dixie strain is the most reliable. Branch later learned his seed was not the Dixie strain. It did reseed satisfactorily, but Branch could not market his seed as Dixie seed. He sued the Hay Seed Company for breach of warranty. Was he entitled to collect damages?

7. Lorraine Hinchliffe bought a new Jeep Wagoneer from Lipman Motors, Inc. Hinchliffe had told the seller she wanted a vehicle capable of hauling her camper trailer. The jeep was advertised as having "full-time four-wheel drive" when it had just a system for transmitting power to the wheels using a limited slip differential mechanism. Hinchliffe had many problems with the Jeep and sued, alleging breach of warranty. Could she establish a case?

8. Young sold his cement mixer to the Harris Construction Co. A short time thereafter Second State Bank claimed title to the mixer as a result of a perfected security interest it held at the time of the sale. Is Young liable to Harris for damages resulting from the bank's successful claim to the mixer?

9. The defendant wrote to the plaintiff for information and prices on a road-finishing machine. In his letter he stated that the machine must be for 16″ x 18″ finishing work on a concrete pavement and "must pass the specifications of the Michigan State Highway Department." The machine that was delivered failed to do the work. The defendant refused to pay the notes that he had given in payment of the purchase price.

    a. Did the purchaser expressly or impliedly make known the purpose for which the machine was to be used?

    b. Did the buyer rely on the seller's skill or judgment?

10. Michael Booher purchased 128 copying machines from Royal Business Machines, Inc. Royal had told Booher that: the machines were of high quality, experience and testing had shown the frequency of repairs was very low, replacement parts were readily available, experience had shown that the purchase of the machines and leasing of them to customers would give substantial profits to Booher, and that the machines were safe and could not cause fires. In a suit for breach of warranty, Booher alleged all the statements were express warranties. Were any of them warranties? *No, they were opinion*

17

Consumer Protection

Preview Cases

Porter & Dietsch, Inc., marketed "X-11" tablets, which were nonprescription, weight-reduction tablets. Advertisements for the tablets stated, "EAT WELL . . . AND LOSE THAT FAT" and "EAT WHAT YOU WANT—AND SLIM DOWN." They continued to state that "no starvation dieting" was necessary and loss of weight could be accomplished without "suffering through starvation dieting hunger" or "boring reducing diets." In fact, use of the tablets would not cause weight loss unless a severely restricted caloric diet was followed. Is the advertising deceptive?

Terry Fischl applied for credit. General Motors Acceptance Corp. (GMAC) obtained a consumer report on him. It erroneously referred to one of Fischl's jobs as past employment and an account in good standing with Sears, Roebuck & Co. as a credit inquiry. GMAC sent Fischl a form letter rejecting his application and indicating the reason was "credit references are insufficient." The section of the form designed to report the use of information from outside sources was marked "disclosure inapplicable." When sued for violation of the Fair Credit Reporting Act, GMAC argued credit was not refused because of what was in the report, but because of what was not in the report. Should Fischl have been notified of the report?

Consumer protection laws are designed to protect the parties to a contract from abuse, sharp dealing, and fraud. They are based on the awareness that the bargaining power of the parties many times is unequal. Frequently the consumer-buyer is a total novice in the area of business dealings while the seller is a virtual professional in regard to the particular transaction.

Consumer protection is more than a protection of "consumer" interests. Legitimate business interests are strengthened by it. Laws requiring fairness and full disclosure of business dealings make it more difficult for unscrupulous businesspeople to operate and thereby infringe upon the trade of those whose business practices are sound. This area of the law is still growing, and further measures attempting to protect the consumer from unfair practices are likely to be adopted.

Traditional Protection

Of the protective measures, some have been in existence for many years. Such traditional protections include: usury laws, antitrust laws, and regulatory agencies.

Usury Laws. Among the oldest measures designed to protect parties to business transactions are the laws which fix the maximum rate of interest that may be charged on loans. Such laws are called usury laws. These laws recognize that the borrower is frequently in a weak position and therefore unable to bargain effectively for the best possible rates of interest.

Most states provide for several rates of interest. The legal rate, which varies from state to state from 5 percent to 15 percent, applies when interest is to be paid but no rate has been specified. The contract rate is the maximum that can be demanded of a debtor. This rate varies from 8 percent to as much as 45 percent. Some states allow the parties to set any rate of interest. Statutes usually permit a rate higher than the maximum to be charged on small loans on the theory that the risks and costs per dollar loaned are greater in making small loans.

The laws vary regarding the damages awarded to a person charged a usurious rate of interest. Some laws allow recovery of the total interest charged and others allow recovery of several times the amount charged.

In many states, corporations are prohibited from raising the defense of usury. In an effort to reflect fluctuating market rates of interest, a number of jurisdictions have recently adopted a fluctuating maximum rate of interest based on such rates as the Federal Reserve discount rate, the prime rate, or the rate on United States Treasury Bills.

Antitrust Laws. *Antitrust laws* are designed to prevent any individual, corporation, or group from controlling too large a share of the market for a product. These laws are based on the theory that monopolists would charge higher prices than exist in a competitive market and might not seek to improve the product so as to provide the consumer with the best possible goods. The laws prohibit corporations from actions which lessen competition or result in a restraint of trade.

Two shoe companies which together would have controlled 5 percent of the United States shoe market attempted to merge. The federal government sought to prohibit the merger on the grounds that it violated the Clayton Act, which prohibits corporations from acquiring other corporations where the effect of the acquisition might substantially lessen competition or tend to create a monopoly. The United States Supreme Court prohibited the merger holding that the proposed merger would tend to lessen competition.

Regulatory Agencies. Most jurisdictions regulate a wide variety of professions which serve the public. Barbers, doctors, insurance agents, morticians, cosmetologists, fitters of hearing aids, and restauranteurs are among those supervised and regulated by governmental agencies in an effort to protect the interests of consumers. In order to be licensed to practice a regulated profession, an individual must meet the requirements set by the appropriate regulatory agency.

Public utility companies, which are granted monopoly status, are regulated to assure that fair rates are charged and that adequate service is rendered. Such businesses include natural gas, electric, and water companies. In most states these companies are subject to regulation by an agency usually called the Public Service Commission or Public Utilities Commission.

Expansion of Consumer Protection

The more recent consumer emphasis includes: product safety, disclosure and uniformity, statutes prohibiting unconscionable contracts, warranty protection, fair credit reporting, and state consumer protection agencies.

Product Safety. Laws requiring that goods meet safety standards have become increasingly widespread in recent years. Probably the most well-known of these product design requirements is found in the case of automobiles. Standards for bumpers, tires, and glass have been set by the federal government. The range of products affected by safety standards is substantial. It includes toys, television sets, insecticides, and drugs. Substandard products are often subject to recall at the instigation of federal agencies. In some instances fines and imprisonment are available against corporate executives whose businesses have distributed clearly hazardous, substandard goods.

In 1972 the federal government implemented the Consumer Product Safety Act which established the Consumer Product Safety Commission. The Commission has broad power to promulgate safety standards for many products. The Commission may order a halt to the manufacture of unsafe products. Certain products, inherently dangerous or hazardous, may be banned by the Commission if there appears to be no way to make the product safe. The law requires manufacturers, distributors, and retailers of consumer products to immediately notify the commission if a product fails to comply with an applicable safety standard or contains a defect which creates a substantial risk of injury to the public.

Medical research suggested a possible link between certain aerosol spray adhesives and birth defects. Prenatal parental exposure to the sprays was the suspected cause of chromosome damage. The Consumer Product Safety Commission ordered a halt to the manufacture and sale of thirteen aerosol spray adhesives containing the suspected ingredients.

Motor vehicles, pesticides, airplanes, boats, food and drugs, and similar items usually regulated by other federal agencies are not covered by the 1972 act.

Disclosure and Uniformity.
The objectives of disclosure and uniformity include: truth in advertising, truth in lending, and product uniformity.

Truth in Advertising. Under authorization initially granted in the Federal Fair Trade Acts shortly after the turn of the century, the Federal Trade Commission has been active in demanding that advertisements be limited to those statements which can be substantiated about products. The FTC may seek voluntary agreement from a business to stop false or deceptive advertising and in some instances to agree to corrective advertising. Such agreement is obtained by the business signing a consent order. The FTC also has the power to order businesses to "cease and desist" from unfair trade practices. The business has the right to contest an order of the FTC in court.

The FTC has the authority to require the name of a product to be changed if it misleads or tends to mislead the public regarding the nature or quality of the product. If an advertisement actually misstates the quality of a product or makes the product appear to be what it is not, the FTC can prohibit the advertising.

Porter & Dietsch, Inc., marketed "X-11" tablets, which were nonprescription, weight-reduction tablets. Advertisements for the tablets stated, "EAT WELL . . . AND LOSE THAT FAT" and "EAT WHAT YOU WANT—AND SLIM DOWN." They continued to state that "no starvation dieting" was necessary and loss of weight could be accomplished without "suffering through starvation dieting hunger" or "boring reducing diets." In fact, use of the tablets would not cause weight loss unless a severely restricted caloric diet was followed. The FTC found the advertising deceptive and required the phrase "DIETING IS REQUIRED" to be included in future advertising.

Truth in Lending. The federal Truth in Lending Act requires lenders to clearly disclose in a set, predetermined way the total amount of interest to be charged. Prior to the enactment of this law, lenders were not required to disclose the interest rate charged or could state the rate in a confusing way. Disclosures must be made prior to the extension of credit. The Truth in Lending Act also requires lenders to state the interest in terms of an annual percentage rate. Such statements facilitate "comparison shopping" when a person is seeking credit. Advertisements indicating any credit terms must also meet substantially the same requirements regarding disclosure. The law provides that when the purchase of consumer products is financed by executing a mortgage on the debtor's principal dwelling, the debtor has three days in which to rescind the mortgage agreement. Both criminal penalties and civil recovery are available against those who fail to comply with the Truth in Lending Act.

Product Uniformity. A number of practices are required which are designed to give consumers the ability to make intelligent choices when comparing competing products. For years, some states have required certain products to be packaged in specifically comparable quantities.

Some local governments require what is known as *unit pricing.* In unit pricing the price for goods sold by weight is stated as the price per ounce or other unit of measurement of the product as well as a total price for the total weight. Thus, all products sold by the ounce would be marked with not only a total price but also with a price per ounce which could be compared to competing products even if the competing products were not packaged in an equal number of ounces.

In order to allow consumers to compare various makes of automobiles more easily, the federal government requires sellers of automobiles to publish mileage test data in marketing new cars.

Statutes Prohibiting Unconscionable Contracts.
Section 2-302 of the Uniform Commercial Code provides courts with authority to refuse to enforce a sales contract or a part of it because it is "unconscionable." Some courts have described this section as an enactment into law of the community's moral awareness. If the terms of the contract are so harsh or the price so unreasonably high as to shock the conscience of the community, the courts may rule the contract to be unconscionable.

The Reynosos purchased a refrigerator-freezer from the Frostifresh Corporation for a cash price of $900 plus a credit charge of $245.88 for a total price of $1,145.88. The contract was negotiated orally in Spanish, and during the conversation Mr. Reynoso stated he had only one week left on his job and could not afford the appliance. The signed retail installment contract covering the sale was entirely in English. Frostifresh had paid $348 for the appliance. When sued for the contract price the Reynosos argued that the contract was unconscionable. The New York courts set aside the contract price and required the Reynosos to pay only the net cost of the refrigerator-freezer to Frostifresh along with a reasonable profit and trucking and service charges.

Warranty Protection.
In 1975 the Congress passed the Magnuson-Moss Warranty and Federal Trade Commission Improvement Act. The Act

does not require sellers to give written warranties for consumer goods, but if the seller chooses to give a warranty, it must meet certain requirements. Clear disclosure of all warranty provisions and statement of the legal remedies of the consumer under the warranty are required by the FTC to be a part of the warranty. According to the Act, the consumer must be informed of the warranty prior to the sale. In order to satisfy the law, the language of warranties of goods costing more than $15 must not be misleading to a "reasonable, average consumer."

The Act allows the FTC to provide for an extension of the warranty time in the event repairs require that the product be out of service for an unreasonable length of time.

Mertens purchased a lawn mower which was guaranteed for one year. After using the mower for eight months, she returned it to the seller for necessary repairs covered by the warranty. The seller retained the mower for five months in making repairs. It is within the power of the FTC to prescribe rules extending Mertens' warranty because five months exceeds a reasonable time for making repairs to the mower.

Further, when repairs take an unreasonable amount of time, incidental expenses are recoverable by the consumer. If after a reasonable number of opportunities to remedy the defect in a product the manufacturer is unable to do so, the consumer must be permitted to elect to receive a refund or a replacement when the product has been sold with a full warranty.

A significant aspect of the Act is the requirement that no written warranty may waive the implied warranties of merchantability and fitness for a particular purpose during the term of the written warranty or unreasonably soon thereafter. Thus, the previously common practice of replacing the implied warranties of fitness and merchantability with substandard written warranties has been significantly limited. The Act also curtails the limitation of implied warranties on items for which a service or maintenance contract is offered within ninety days after the initial sale. The Act also extends the coverage of a warranty to those who purchase consumer goods secondhand during the term of the warranty.

Enforcement of the Act is through civil suits authorized in the Act. Attorney fees as well as damages may be awarded to plaintiffs who successfully sue to enforce the provisions of the statute.

Fair Credit Reporting. The Fair Credit Reporting Act is another of the recent federal enactments protecting the rights of consumers. It requires creditors to notify a potential recipient of credit whenever any adverse action or denial of credit was based on a credit report. It permits the consumer about whom a credit report is written to obtain from a credit agency the substance of the credit report. If a credit report is incorrect, it must be corrected by the credit agency. In some cases, if the consumer disagrees with a creditor about the report the consumer may be permitted to add an explanation of the dispute to the report. Certain types of adverse information may not be maintained in the reports for more than seven years. The reports may be used for legitimate business purposes only.

Individuals whose rights under the Act have been violated may sue and recover ordinary damages if the harm resulted from negligent noncompliance. If the injury resulted from willful noncompliance with the Fair Credit Reporting Act, punitive damages are available to the aggrieved party.

Terry Fischl applied for credit. General Motors Acceptance Corp. (GMAC) obtained a consumer report on him. It erroneously referred to one of Fischl's jobs as past employment and an account in good standing with Sears, Roebuck & Co. as a credit inquiry. GMAC sent Fischl a form letter rejecting his application and indicating the reason was "credit references are insufficient." The section of the form designed to report the use of information from outside sources was marked "disclosure inapplicable." When sued for violation of the Fair Credit Reporting Act, GMAC argued credit was not refused because of what was in the report, but because of what was not in the report. The court held that disclosure under the Act was not conditioned on derogatory or negative information in a report, but disclosure was required when a decision is based wholly or in part on information in the report.

State Consumer Protection Agencies. A number of states have enacted laws giving either the state attorney general or a special consumer affairs office the authority to compel fairness in advertising, sales presentations, and other consumer transactions. When complaints are received from consumers, the state officials will investigate. If the complaint is found to be valid, efforts will be made to secure voluntary corrective action by the seller. Frequently these agencies have injunctive powers which means that they may issue cease and desist orders similar to those of the FTC. In a limited number of jurisdictions the agencies may prosecute the offending business, and significant criminal penalties are provided which substantially augment the operation of these efforts.

Questions

1. What is the purpose of consumer protection laws?

2. What are *usury laws*?

3. Explain how antitrust laws benefit consumers.

4. What agency may order a halt to the manufacture of unsafe products?

5. What methods may the FTC use to curtail unfair trade practices?

6. Explain how the disclosure provisions of the Truth in Lending Act benefit consumers.

7. **a.** What is *unit pricing*?
   b. Why is it considered beneficial to consumers?

8. How does the Magnuson-Moss Warranty Act assist a consumer?

9. How can a consumer correct false information contained in a credit report?

10. What state governmental agencies are usually empowered to assist with consumer complaints?

Case Problems

1. The Abernathys purchased two snowmobiles from a local snowmobile dealer who represented that the vehicles were new. Although they were unused, they were two "model-years" old. The Abernathys complained to their state office of consumer protection. What is the most likely course of action the state office might take?

2. Advance Machine Company owned Commercial Mechanisms, Inc., which manufactured automatic baseball-pitching machines for thirteen years. Later, the Consumer Product Safety Commission inspected Advance and obtained information about a possible defect in the pitching machine. Five years after the cessation of the machines' manufacture, the Commission notified Advance it had decided to issue an administrative complaint seeking a penalty for failure to immediately report the defect. Regulations defined "immediately" as twenty-four hours. Advance argued that the duty to report ended after twenty-four hours. Did it?

3. The Philips Sugar Corporation advertised its sugar as "substantially different from all other refined sugars in composition and food value." It represented that it was the official sugar of several national sports leagues on the basis of the "superior quality and nutritional value" of its sugar. In fact these claims were not substantially true. What action could have been taken against Philips and by whom?

4. The Harris Container Corporation purchased some equipment on credit from Herndon Equipment Company. The purchase price was $9,500 and the total for the twelve monthly payments was $10,700. The maximum rate of interest allowed in the state was 10 percent. After making all the payments of interest up to $950, Harris made only principal payments claiming that any amount of interest in excess of $950 would be usurious. Did Harris have to pay the additional $250 interest? *Usury laws not applicable to corp.*

5. The Flemings applied to the Federal Land Bank of Columbia for a loan on real estate which they said was not their residence. When they defaulted on

the loan, the Land Bank foreclosed on the real estate and then brought an action against the Flemings for a deficiency judgment. The Flemings argued that under the Truth in Lending Act the Land Bank wrongfully denied them the right to rescind the loan transaction. Should they have had the right to rescind?

Summary Cases for Part Three

Sales

1. Songbird Jet Ltd., Inc., and Jet Leasing Corporation, acting together, negotiated with Amax Inc. for the purchase of a jet airplane. Songbird and Jet Leasing claimed that an oral agreement was reached by which they would purchase the jet for $8,850,000. Jet Leasing sent Amax a check for $250,000 which it claimed was a deposit on the sale. Amax later notified Jet Leasing the jet was not for sale and that no contract had been made. Songbird and Jet Leasing sued Amax claiming the $250,000 check was partial performance of the alleged contract. Amax alleged that claim was barred by the Statute of Frauds. Was it? [*Songbird Jet Ltd., Inc. v. Amax Inc.*, 581 F. Supp. 912 (S.D.N.Y.)]

2. Halstead Hospital, Inc., ordered bond forms from Northern Bank Note Company. Northern was advised that the bond closing was scheduled for December 18. Northern accepted the order stating it would complete its work for shipment December 16. It arranged for the delivery of the bond forms to a specific location in New York City, the Signature Company, so that they could be inspected and signed prior to the closing. Northern printed the bonds, boxed them into four cartons, and arranged for a common carrier to deliver them to New York. One of the boxes did not arrive until after December 18, so the closing was cancelled for that day. Halstead sued for breach of contract, alleging that the contract required shipment and timely delivery by Northern. Did it? [*Halstead Hospital, Inc. v. Northern Bank Note Co.*, 680 F.2d 1307 (10th Cir.)]

3. Plummer sold a car for $800 cash to Davis. Davis paid for the car by check. Plummer delivered the car to Davis together with a certificate of title but with the understanding that there was to be no sale until the check was cleared through the bank. The check turned out to be a bad check. Davis in the meantime had sold the car to Kingsley, who knew nothing about the arrangement between Plummer and Davis. Plummer brought suit against Kingsley to recover the car, claiming that since Davis did not have good title to the car, he could not transfer good title to Kingsley. Did Kingsley obtain good title? [*Plummer v. Kingsley*, 226 P. 2d 297 (Or.)]

4. Saunders purchased a canvas tent from Cowl, a merchant, paying $250 down. Saunders inspected the tent, but at the time of inspection it was folded and not easily inspected. Furthermore, the evidence showed that Saunders would not have been able to perceive the defects in the canvas even if he had inspected it thoroughly. The seller stated, "It is to be in good condition when delivered." The tent was so defective that it was in reality worthless. Saun-

163

ders alleged a breach of warranty and sued to recover his $250. Was there a breach of warranty? [*Saunders v. Cowl et al.*, 277 N.W. 12 (Minn.)]

5. Hodge Chile Co. negotiated for the purchase of food cartons from Interstate Folding Box Co. Interstate sent samples of its boxes to Hodge without making any statement as to their qualifications. Hodge subjected the samples to various tests and then placed an order for the boxes with Interstate. Hodge did not pay for the boxes and, when sued for their purchase price, claimed that there was a breach of an implied warranty of fitness of the boxes for use for a particular purpose. It was shown that the defects of which Hodge complained had not been revealed in the tests because the cartons had been filled by hand instead of by machine and the chile put in the boxes was poured at a lower temperature than when poured by machine. Did Hodge have a valid defense? [*Interstate Folding Box Co. v. Hodge Chile Co.*, 334 S.W.2d 408 (Mo. Ct. App.)]

6. At an auction, Gaylen Bennett bought fifty-five head of cattle from Jansma Cattle Company. The next day some of the cattle were sick. Eventually nineteen of the fifty-five cattle died. Jansma regularly dealt in the buying and selling of cattle and held itself out as having knowledge peculiar to cattle transactions. Bennett sued for breach of the warranty of merchantability. Was Jansma a merchant? [*Bennett v. Jansma*, 329 N.W.2d 134 (S.D.)]

7. Central Credit Bureau issued a credit report on Barbara Johnson which contained an item relating to Johnson's outstanding obligation to Beneficial Finance Corp. The obligation had been discharged by Johnson's bankruptcy. At Johnson's request, Central had reinvestigated and made a note that the debt had been discharged. It then corrected the report. Johnson sued for damages, alleging a violation of the Fair Credit Reporting Act. Was there such a violation? [*Johnson v. Beneficial Finance Corp.*, 466 N.Y.S.2d 553 (N.Y.)]

8. Brack Barker picked up a carton of Dr. Pepper from a self-service shelf at Arlan's Food Store. While attempting to place the carton in a cart provided by Arlan's, one of the bottles exploded. A piece of glass struck Barker in the eye, causing a 90 percent loss of vision. He sued for damages, alleging breach of implied warranty of merchantability. Does the warranty of merchantability protect a person who is invited by a merchant to take possession of goods from a self-service display and make payment subsequent to taking possession? [*Barker v. Allied Supermarket*, 596 P.2d 870 (Okla.)]

9. The Standard Stevedoring Company purchased a crane from Jaffe that Jaffe had widely advertised as having a lifting capacity of fifteen to twenty tons. There was no evidence that this statement was made orally when an agent of the buyer came to inspect the crane. The seller was aware that the buyer became interested in the crane as a result of the advertising. The purchasing agent of the Standard Stevedoring Company made no attempt to verify the lifting capacity of the crane due to the impracticality of doing so. The pur-

chaser learned after he bought the crane that it would not lift anywhere near fifteen to twenty tons and brought suit to rescind the contract. Was there a breach of an express warranty? [*Standard Stevedoring Company v. Jaffe*, 302 S.W.2d 829 (Tenn. Ct. App.)]

Part Four — Bailments

Learning Objectives for Part Four

Bailments

After studying this part you should be able to:

1. Define a bailment and name the two categories of bailments.
2. Explain the three types of bailments and the characteristics of each type.
3. Discuss the duties of the bailor and bailee.
4. Explain what a carrier is and name the two categories of carriers.
5. Identify the exceptions to the normal rule of the carrier being an insurer of the safety of goods.
6. Specify the cases in which a carrier may limit its liability.
7. Explain what a bill of lading is and name the two types.
8. Describe the rights, liabilities, and duties of common carriers of persons.
9. Define baggage and discuss a carrier's liability for baggage.
10. Define hotelkeeper.
11. Name the duties and liabilities of a hotelkeeper.
12. Explain who guests are.
13. State what a hotelkeeper's lien is, and explain when it attaches and when it is lost.
14. Discuss the potential for crimes against hotels.

18

Principles of Bailments

Preview Cases

Fred Peterson asked Nathan Shay, who was in business as a jeweler, to sell some jewelry. Shay picked up the jewelry at Peterson's house and gave him a receipt listing the items and an estimated value for each. At the bottom of the receipt was written, "To be sold at the agreed prices above." Two days later Peterson told Shay to return the jewelry, but one item had been stolen. Peterson brought suit against his insurance company under his homeowner's insurance policy for the loss. The insurance company claimed it was not liable because the jewelry had been sold to Shay and was not owned by Peterson when it was stolen. Was the transaction a bailment or a sale?

Fleeman borrowed Brown's truck expressly for the purpose of hauling a load of cotton to the cotton gin. After the cotton was ginned, Fleeman drove about ten miles further to another town to get some farm machinery parts. The truck was wrecked on this part of the trip due to no fault on the part of Fleeman. Who must bear the loss for damage to the truck?

A *bailment* is the transfer of possession, but not the title, of personal property (never real property) by one party, usually the owner, to another party on condition that the identical property will be returned or appropriately accounted for either to the owner or an agent at a future date or that it will be delivered to a person designated in the agreement. The person who gives up possession is called the *bailor*. The person who acquires possession but not the title is called the *bailee*.

Characteristics of a Bailment

Bailments are generally classified as either ordinary or extraordinary. *Extraordinary bailments* are those in which the public interest is so affected that the law imposes unusual liabilities, as in the case of hotel-keepers or common carriers. *Ordinary bailments* include all other bailments.

In a bailment two conditions are always present:

1. The parties to the bailment must agree that the same property is to be returned to the bailor or accounted for as directed although the property may be greatly altered in form. The property may be delivered with the understanding that the bailee is to deliver it to a third party or sell the item for the bailor.
2. There must be both a delivery and an acceptance of property.

If either one of the preceding conditions is absent, the transaction is not a bailment.

Some typical transactions resulting in a bailment are:

1. A motorist leaves a car with the garage for repairs.
2. A family stores its furniture in a warehouse.
3. A student borrows a dinner jacket to wear to a formal dance.
4. A hunter leaves a pet with a friend for safekeeping while going on an extended hunting trip.

The Bailment Agreement

A bailment is based upon an agreement, express or implied, between the bailor and the bailee. If the agreement is the result of written or spoken words, the bailment is express. If the agreement is indicated by the conduct of the parties, the bailment is implied. When a person checks a coat upon entering a restaurant, nothing may be said, but the bailment is implied by the acts of the two parties.

Delivery and Acceptance

A bailment can be established only if there is delivery accompanied by acceptance of personal property. The delivery and acceptance may be actual or constructive. They are actual when the goods themselves are delivered and accepted. They are constructive when there is no physical delivery of the goods but when control over the goods is delivered and accepted.

There is a constructive bailment when someone finds lost property. The owner does not actually deliver the property to the finder, but the law holds this to be a bailment. A constructive bailment also occurs when property of one person is washed up on the land of another, the latter being made the bailee for the goods of the former.

Dieball had a painting on exhibit at an art show. Hauchin, a furniture merchant, offered to rent it for sixty days to place on display in her store. Dieball wrote out a statement notifying the manager of the art exhibition to deliver his painting to Hauchin. The delivery of this writing to Hauchin constituted constructive delivery.

Return of the Bailed Property

In a bailment the bailee must return to the bailor the identical goods bailed. However, in the case of fungible goods, such as wheat, a bailment exists if the bailor is to receive a like quantity and quality of goods unless the goods are to be processed in some way. If a farmer delivers wheat to a miller, a bailment is established if flour made from the same wheat is to be returned. If the farmer is to get back flour made from any wheat of like grade, there is an exchange of personal property (a sale, with the purchase price for the flour being the delivery of a certain quantity of grain), but not a bailment.

Fred Peterson asked Nathan Shay, who was in business as a jeweler, to sell some jewelry. Shay picked up the jewelry at Peterson's house and gave him a receipt listing the items and an estimated value for each. At the bottom of the receipt was written, "To be sold at the agreed prices above." Two days later Peterson told Shay to return the jewelry, but one item had been stolen. Peterson brought suit against his insurance company under his homeowner's insurance policy for the loss. The insurance company claimed it was not liable because the jewelry had been sold to Shay and was not owned by Peterson when it was stolen. The court held the transaction was a bailment because any unsold jewelry was to be returned to Peterson.

Types of Bailments

There are three types of bailments:

1. Bailments for the sole benefit of the bailor
2. Bailments for the sole benefit of the bailee
3. Bailments for the mutual benefit of both parties

Bailments for the Sole Benefit of the Bailor. If one is in possession of another's personal property for the sole benefit of the owner, a bailment for the sole benefit of the bailor exists. The bailee receives no benefits in the way of compensation or else it would not be a bailment for the sole benefit of the bailor. For example, a person asks a friend to keep a piano until the owner is able to rent larger quarters. The friend may not play the piano or otherwise receive the benefits of ownership while it is being bailed. If a farmer agrees, gratuitously, to haul a load of hay to town for a neighbor, this is clearly a bailment for the sole benefit of the bailor. Another example of a bailment for the sole benefit of the bailor occurs when one person loses an article and another person finds it. In this case the loser is the bailor, and the finder is the bailee.

The bailee assumes certain responsibilities while in possession of the goods. The bailee must use reasonable care with respect to the property. In a bailment for the sole benefit of the bailor, the bailee must exercise slight care and is liable for gross negligence with respect to the property.

Bailments for the Sole Benefit of the Bailee. If the bailee has possession of another's personal property, and the owner of the property receives no benefit or compensation for its use, a bailment for the sole benefit of the bailee exists. This type of bailment arises through borrowing someone else's property. The bailee must exercise great care over the property and is liable for even slight negligence if such care is not used. The bailee, however, is not an insurer of the bailed property since any loss or damage due to no fault whatsoever of the bailee falls upon the owner. If Petras borrows Walker's diamond ring to wear to a dance and is robbed on the way to the dance, the loss falls upon Walker, the owner, as long as Petras was not negligent.

Even though the bailor receives no benefit from a bailment for the sole benefit of the bailee, the bailee must be informed of any known defects in the bailed property. If the bailee is injured by reason of a defect, the bailor who knew of the defect and failed to inform the bailee is liable for damages.

◆   John Maurer Painting and Decorating Company contracted to paint a highway overpass bridge which was under construction. To do this, a wooden scaffold was constructed of planks from a pile of lumber at the worksite. The lumber had presumably been used by Calhoun County Contracting Corporation when it poured the concrete deck of the bridge. When the scaffold was being dismantled, the plank on which Frank Rynders, an employee of Maurer, was standing broke and Rynders fell to the ground. The board had an obvious knothole on one side. Rynder sued Calhoun for damages for his injuries. Even if Calhoun did loan the lumber to Maurer, the bailment was for the sole benefit of the bailee. Calhoun's only duty was to warn of known defects, so it was not liable.

Bailments for the Mutual Benefit of Both Parties.   Most bailments are for the mutual benefit of both the bailor and the bailee. Some common bailments of this type are: machinery left with a mechanic to be repaired; laundry and dry cleaning contracts; the rental of personal property, such as an automobile or a typewriter; and material left with a fabricator to be converted into a finished product for a price. The bailee must take reasonable care of the bailed property. The bailor must furnish safe property, not just inform the bailee of known defects.

Bellanti rented a You-Drive-It automobile from Trestle Motors Company. While driving to Denver, he collided with a car driven by Yousef, and both cars were wrecked. The roads were coated with ice, and at the time of the collision Bellanti was driving down a fairly steep grade at about forty miles an hour. Visibility because of snow was about 200 feet. Bellanti was liable to the Trestle Motors Company for damages to the car. Forty miles an hour, under the conditions described, was faster than an ordinary, prudent person would have been driving.

Had the Trestle Motors Company furnished Bellanti with a car which had a defect that caused the accident, not only would Bellanti not have been liable, but the Trestle Motors Company would have been liable to Bellanti for any damages sustained by him.

In mutual-benefit bailments, the bailee usually makes a charge for services rendered. This is true in all repair jobs, laundry, dry cleaning, shoe mending, and storage bailments. The bailee has a lien against the bailed property for the charges. If these charges are not paid, the bailee is under no obligation to return the bailed goods. After a reasonable time, the bailee may advertise and sell the property for the charges. If any money remains from the sale after expenses and the charges are paid, it must be turned over to the bailor.

If the bailee parts with possession of the property before being paid, in most states the lien is lost. If possession of the same property is later regained, the lien is not reestablished for the old charges, except where this right is given to the bailee by special statute.

The bailee in a mutual-benefit bailment may receive a benefit other than a fee or monetary payment. For example, a skating rink may offer to check shoes for its customers without charging for the service. A mutual-benefit bailment exists. The customer (bailor) receives storage service and the skating rink (bailee) gains the benefit of a neater, safer customer area.

Care of Bailed Property

As a general rule, any loss due to the theft or damage of personal property falls upon the owner. This may not be true in the case of a bailment. Thus, it is important to ascertain if there is in fact a bailment. If there is a bailment and the loss was caused by the negligence of the bailee, the owner can hold the bailee responsible for the loss.

In ordinary bailments, the standard of care required of the bailee is: *reasonable care under the circumstances,* that is, the degree of care which a reasonable person would exercise in order to protect the property from harm.

The chief factors in determining what is reasonable care in a bailment are (1) time and place of making the bailment, (2) facilities for taking care of the property, (3) nature of the property, (4) bailee's knowledge of its nature, and (5) extent of the bailee's skill and experience in taking care of goods of that kind. Bailees are also liable for the negligence of their employees or servants with respect to the property. Whether or not a bailee is negligent is ordinarily a question of fact to be decided by a jury.

Use of the Bailed Goods

The bailee in a bailment for the sole benefit of the bailor has no right to use the property for personal benefit. The bailee may, however, use the property if the use will benefit or preserve it.

In any bailment, the wrongful use of the property makes the bailee liable for any damages caused by that use. The only question is whether the bailment permits the use. For example, does a bailment to repair a car give permission to the mechanic to drive the car for the purpose of a road test? If the road test is reasonably required in order to properly fix the car, such a test is permitted.

Fleeman borrowed Brown's truck expressly for the purpose of hauling a load of cotton to the cotton gin. After the cotton was ginned, Fleeman drove about ten miles further to another town to get some farm machinery parts. The truck was wrecked on this part of the trip due to no fault of Fleeman. He must bear the loss, since he used the truck for a purpose for which it was not bailed.

Duties and Obligations of the Bailor

The bailor must always inform the bailee of any defects known to the bailor. The bailor is normally not liable if an injury is due to an unknown defect. If, however, the bailor benefits from the bailment, reasonable efforts must be made to discover the existence of any unknown defects. For example, when *A* borrows or rents *B*'s truck, *B* must inform *A* if the brakes are known to be deficient. If *B* fails to do so and *A* is injured, *B* is liable.

Bailee's Duty to Protect Property

Often bailed property is damaged or destroyed not by any negligence by the bailee in the use of it, but by some act having nothing to do with its use. In the absence of a promise supported by a consideration to insure the property, the bailee is under no obligation to insure it. But the bailor may as a part of the contract of bailment obligate the bailee to insure the bailed property. Under such circumstances the bailee is subject to full liability for all losses due to a failure to insure.

Melvin Delzer leased a paylogger from Rapid City Implement. The lease stated: "Lessee further agrees to protect the Lessor on this contract with full insurance coverage" and "Lessee agrees to pay the Lessor for all loss and damages to the equipment arising from any cause . . . during the life of this lease." During the lease, the paylogger was damaged by fire. It was returned and Rapid City's insurer paid Rapid City for the damage. The insurer then sued Delzer. The court found Delzer liable since he had failed to obtain insurance.

A bailee who fails to return bailed property on time or who returns it to the wrong party in good faith is liable to the bailor.

Sale of Bailed Property by the Bailee

Possession of property is not proof of ownership. One who purchases property from a bailee ordinarily does not get good title to it. There are situations, however, where the bailor may not deny that the bailee had the right to sell the property. This is particularly true in goods put out on consignment with a commission merchant or factor. In these cases a mutual-benefit bailment exists even though the bailor does not want to get the bailed property back. The purpose of the bailment is to have the property sold and the proceeds remitted to the bailor. The bailee has the power to sell all goods under these types of contracts regardless of any restriction upon the right to sell, unless the buyer knows of the restriction.

The bailor may mislead an innocent third person into believing that the bailee owns the property. In this situation, the bailee may convey good title.

Donovan purchased a typewriter from the Dodd Office Equipment Company. He paid for the machine but asked the seller to leave it on display until he was ready to pick it up. Dodd sold it to Dooley. Dooley got good title to it even though the seller was merely the bailee of the typewriter. Donovan's act of making it possible for the Dodd Office Equipment Company to perpetrate a fraud upon an innocent party estops him from denying that the company had a right to sell it. However, the company is liable to Donovan.

Pawn or Pledge

One type of bailment is the deposit of personal property as security for some debt or obligation. If the security is tangible property, such as livestock, a radio, or an automobile, it is a *pawn*. If the security is intangible property, such as notes, bonds, or stock certificates, it is a *pledge*. In either case the transaction is a mutual-benefit bailment.

Questions

1. In a bailment, is the owner the bailor or the bailee?

2. May a bailment exist without any verbal or written communication between the bailor and the bailee?

3. Give an example of a contract of bailment without an actual delivery of the property to the bailee.

4. If the owner of a car has it in *B*'s garage and gives the keys to *C* with the instruction to get the car, is this a bailment?

5. When there is a bailment, must the identical goods always be returned?

6. In a bailment for the sole benefit of the bailor, how may the bailee use the property?

7. What is the extent of liability of a bailor with regard to defects in property loaned for no compensation to the bailee?

8. What is the standard of care required of a bailee in an ordinary bailment?

9. In a bailment for the mutual benefit of both parties, the bailee used the property contrary to the agreement. Is the bailee liable for damages if the property is damaged due to no negligence?

10. **a.** Define a *pawn*.
    b. Define a *pledge*.

Case Problems

1. Crutchfield ran the following advertisement in a daily newspaper: "Found one palomino horse. Owner can get it by paying for the cost of this ad and a reasonable price for feed and caring for it." Must the owner pay before obtaining the horse?

2. Marzano Construction Company leased a backhoe from Ausdale Equipment Rental Corporation. On September 6, the steel cable that supported the backhoe's boom and bucket snapped. The cable was replaced, and ten days later the backhoe was being used to lower concrete pipe into a trench. The cable snapped again. The bucket fell, glanced off a section of pipe and struck Augustine Brimbau, who was working in the trench. Brimbau was severely injured and sued Ausdale. Backhoe cables generally have a useful life of three to four months. Was Ausdale liable?

3. Lucille entered an exclusive coat and dress shop intending to purchase a coat. Planning to try on a coat, she removed the one she was wearing and laid it

with her handbag on the store counter. The handbag, containing $500 in currency and a $150 watch, was stolen by an unknown customer. The owner of the dress shop contended she was not liable for the loss because there was no delivery of the articles to her or her agents. Do you agree?

4. The Dupree Garage, over a period of one month, did about $1,500 in repairs on several trucks owned by the Fajen Trucking Company. The $1,500 repair bill was past due. Two trucks were later brought in for minor repairs. Dupree refused to let Fajen have the trucks until the old bill for $1,500 plus the current repair bill was paid. Fajen paid the current repair bill and demanded possession of the trucks. Was he within his rights?

5. The Bronson Typewriter Exchange sold an electric typewriter to Holmes, who was to pick up the machine the following day. The next day Holmes telephoned the Bronson Typewriter Exchange and asked that the machine be delivered to 237 Hull Street. The secretary attached a memo to the machine showing that it was to be delivered to 237 Hull Street. Because of poor penmanship, the truck driver read it 237 Hall Street. It was delivered to that address. The machine was stolen before the error was detected. Who must bear the loss, Holmes or the Bronson Typewriter Exchange?

6. James Smith delivered his motorcycle to the main building of McRary Harley-Davidson for a warranty check and servicing. Smith knew the building had a burglar alarm system. On previous visits he had seen other motorcycles being repaired and stored in that building. McRary gave no indication the motorcycle would be stored in a separate, smaller building. The smaller building was broken into and Smith's motorcycle stolen. Smith sued McRary for failure to return the motorcycle. Smith asked the judge to instruct the jury that if there was agreement that the motorcycle was to be stored at the main building and McRary stored it at another building without the consent of Smith, McRary would be liable. Should the instruction be given?

7. Edwards took her car to Crestmont Cadillac Corporation to have a tire changed and the wheels aligned. She told the service order man that she and her family were packed and ready to leave on a vacation. She was told to wait in the outer lobby. Several hours later she was told the car had been stolen. Edwards had had personal property valued at more than $2,500 in the car's trunk. She sued Crestmont for the value of the personal property, alleging there had been a bailment of the property. Was Crestmont liable for the personal property in the trunk?

8. In danger of sinking, the MV *Harry Adams* was towed to Norfolk Shipbuilding and Drydock's wharf. Emergency repairs were made. The captain decided further repairs could be completed in Nova Scotia. Norfolk asked John Mosele, the owner, to pay for the repairs and remove the ship. Mosele replied he would. Norfolk had to install two pumps because the ship still leaked. In March, Norfolk asked Mosele to move the vessel and stated there would be a

$25-per-day storage charge. Mosele said he hoped to move the ship soon and asked if it could be left a short time longer without storage charges. In August, the pumps failed and the *Harry Adams* was partially submerged. Norfolk refloated the ship and made emergency repairs. Norfolk then sued for these repairs and dockage from the date of the repairs. Could it recover even though the pumps it installed had failed?

9. J. D. Butler borrowed a tractor from Don Shirah to help in driving cattle. Several people rode on the tractor as passengers. After going a short distance the left, rear wheel of the tractor fell off causing injuries to Butler. Butler died from these injuries and Butler's mother sued for wrongful death. Was Shirah liable?

10. Washington owned a warehouse used for storing wheat for her customers. Wheat of like grade was deposited in bins, and the owner was given a warehouse receipt showing the number of bushels and grade of wheat stored. It was the custom to return to the wheat owner the correct number of bushels of wheat of like grade that was left in the warehouse, but no promise was made to return exactly the same wheat. Rice deposited wheat with Washington, and soon thereafter the warehouse and all the wheat was destroyed. Rice demanded payment from Washington for the value of the wheat contending there was a sale, not a bailment. Do you agree?

19

Common Carriers

Preview Cases

Semi Metals, Inc., delivered two cartons of germanium to Pinter Brothers for shipment under a straight bill of lading. The germanium was worth $85 a pound, but to avoid higher freight charges Semi Metals described it as electronic material and no value was stated in the bill of lading. The tariff for electronic materials had a maximum value of $5 a pound. The two cartons were lost. Semi Metals sued Pinter for $19,280, the full value of the germanium. Could Semi Metals recover the full value or only $5 a pound?

For two weeks during the summer, Burton Fendelman was a passenger on Conrail trains which were late; overcrowded; lacking in air conditioning, water facilities, and electricity; and which had dirty toilets and noxious odors. He sued Conrail and testified that these "atrocious conditions" had existed for years. Did Conrail breach its duty to its passengers?

A *carrier* is engaged in the business of transporting either goods or persons, or both. A carrier of goods is a bailee. Since a fee is charged for such service, the bailment is one for the mutual benefit of both parties. The general law of bailments, however, does not apply to all carriers of goods.

Classification of Carriers

Carriers are usually classified into two groups:

1. Private carriers
2. Common carriers

Private Carriers. A *private carrier* is one which, for a fee, undertakes to transport goods or persons. It does not hold itself out to the public as being able and willing to serve all who apply. It transports only under special instances and special arrangements. Since a private carrier conducts its business for profit, it is eager to serve all as far as profitable. A private carrier is free to refuse service if such service is unprofitable, a freedom denied to common carriers. The most usual types of private carriers are trucks, moving vans, trains, ships, and delivery services. A carrier owned by the shipper, such as a truck from a fleet owned and operated by an industrial firm or a ship from a fleet owned by an oil company for transporting its own products, is a private carrier.

Private carriers' contracts for transporting goods are mutual-benefit bailments, and the general law of bailments as well as of contracts governs them. Thus, such carriers are liable only for loss resulting from the failure to exercise ordinary care. A private carrier may limit liability for loss to the goods whether caused by its negligence or by the fault of others. Any state or city may impose certain limitations upon these private carriers, but such limitations are seldom extensive.

Common Carriers. A *common carrier* is one which undertakes to transport goods or persons, without discrimination, for all who apply for that service, assuming that the goods to be transported are proper and that facilities are available for transport. One who ships goods by a common carrier is called the *consignor*; the one to whom the goods are shipped is called the *consignee*; and the contract between the parties is called a *bill of lading*.

A common carrier must serve without discrimination all who apply. If it fails to do so, it is liable for any damages resulting from such a refusal. A common carrier may, however, refuse service because the service is not one for which it is equipped; for example, an express company does not have to accept lumber for transportation. Also, a common carrier may refuse service if its equipment is inadequate to accommodate customers in excess of the normal demands. A common carrier of persons is not required to transport (1) any person who requires unusual attention, such as an invalid, unless that person is accompanied by an attendant, (2) any person who intends to cause an injury to the carrier or the passengers, (3) any person who is likely to harm passengers, such as a person with a contagious disease, or (4) any person who is likely to be offensive to passengers, such as an intoxicated person.

The usual types of common carriers of persons are trains, buses, airplanes, ships (both ocean and river), and subways. Common carriers are public monopolies and are subject to regulations as to prices, services, equipment, and other operational policies. This public regulation is in lieu of competition as a determinant of their prices and services.

Liability of Common Carriers of Goods for Loss

Common carriers of goods are held to a higher standard of care than are private carriers. With but five exceptions noted below, a common carrier of goods is liable for loss or damage without regard to negligence or intentional fault of the carrier, its employees, or third persons. It, thus, is an insurer of the safety of the transported goods.

The common carrier is not liable as an insurer for losses arising from:

1. Acts of God
2. Acts of a public authority
3. Inherent nature of the goods
4. Acts of the shipper
5. Acts of public enemy

These exceptions do not excuse the carrier if the carrier is also negligent in failing to safeguard the goods from harm.

Acts of God. If the loss to goods being transported is due to floods, snowstorms, tornadoes, lightning, or fire caused by lightning, the carrier is not liable since these are considered acts of God.

A flash flood weakened the pillars of a railroad bridge. Soon after the waters began to recede, a freight train started across the bridge, causing it to collapse and plunge into the raging waters. The company did not have the bridge inspected before dispatching the train across. Many carloads of freight were badly damaged by water. The railroad denied liability on the ground that this was an act of God. The railroad was not excused from liability since its negligence in failing to inspect and repair the bridge contributed to the harm.

Acts of a Public Authority. If goods being transported suffer any loss due to public authority, the loss is borne by the shipper, not the carrier. Illicit goods may be seized by public officials, or goods that are a menace to health may be seized by health officials. The carrier is not liable for such loss.

Inherent Nature of the Goods. Some goods, such as vegetables, are highly perishable. If the carrier uses proper care, it is not liable for damage due to the inherent nature of the goods. The most common types of loss due to the inherent nature of the goods are: decay of vegetables, fermentation or evaporation of liquids, and the death of livestock as a result of natural causes or the fault of other animals.

Acts of the Shipper. If the loss is due to the act of the shipper, the carrier is not liable. The most common cause of this type of loss is improper packing. If the packing is clearly improper, the carrier should refuse to accept the goods. If the improper packing cannot be detected by inspection and a loss results from the improper packing, the carrier is relieved from liability. Other instances are misdirection of the merchandise and failure to indicate fragile contents.

Semi Metals, Inc., delivered two cartons of germanium to Pinter Brothers for shipment under a straight bill of lading. The germanium was worth $85 a pound, but to avoid higher freight charges Semi Metals described it as electronic material and no value was stated in the bill of lading. The tariff for electronic materials had a maximum value of $5 a pound. The two cartons were lost. Semi Metals sued Pinter for $19,280, the full value of the germanium. The court held that the intentional misdescription of the shipper to avoid higher shipping charges limited Semi Metals' recovery to $5 a pound.

Acts of Public Enemy. If the loss or damage to goods is the result of organized warfare or border excursions of foreign bandits, the carrier is not liable. Mobs, strikers, and rioters are not classified as public enemies in interpreting this exclusion.

Limitations Upon the Carrier's Liability

A carrier may attempt to limit or escape the extraordinary liability imposed upon it by law. This is most often done by a contract between the shipper and the carrier. Since the bill of lading is the written evidence of the contract, the limitations on the carrier's liability are set out in this document. Since the shipper does not have any direct voice in the preparation of the bill of lading, the law requires all carriers to have the printed bill-of-lading form approved before it is adopted. For interstate commerce this approval is given by the Interstate Commerce Commission. The states have similar bodies to regulate purely intrastate commerce. These bodies have approved a few provisions whereby the carriers limit their liability. But in addition to the uniform limitations set out in the printed form of bill of lading, space is left for any additional limitations which the shipper and the carrier may agree upon. The Federal Bills of Lading Act governs this matter as to interstate shipments, while the Uniform Commercial Code controls with respect to intrastate shipments. In general the limitations upon the carrier's liability permitted by these acts fall into the following classes:

1. A carrier is permitted to limit by agreement its loss to a specified sum or to a specified percent of the value of the goods. To obtain the benefit for itself, a carrier must give the shipper the choice of shipping at lower rates subject to the limited liability or at a higher rate without limitation of liability.

2. Most states permit the carriers to exempt themselves from liability due to certain named hazards. The most common named hazards are: fire,

leakage, breakage, spoilage, and losses due to riots, strikes, mobs, and robbers. Some states specifically prohibit an exemption for loss by fire. Before these exemptions are valid, they must be specifically enumerated in the bill of lading or shipper's receipt. In all cases the exemptions are not effective if the loss is due to the negligence of the carrier. No consideration in the form of a reduced rate need be given to justify these limitations.

3. Livestock shipments create many problems for carriers, and delay in transportation for any cause may result in serious losses or extra expense for feed. Most states allow some form of limitation upon the carrier's liability if the loss is due to a delay over which the carrier has no control.

The Uniform Commercial Code specifically provides that the Code does not change or alter in any way those liabilities imposed upon the carrier for losses not the result of the carrier's negligence. In those cases where the carrier is held liable only for loss due to negligence, the Uniform Commercial Code provides for liability only for ordinary negligence.

Duration of the Carrier's Liability

The carrier is subject to the high degree of liability discussed in the previous sections only during transportation. If the goods are delivered to the carrier for immediate shipment and are received from the carrier promptly upon arrival, the goods are regarded as being transported during the entire transaction.

Carrier as Bailee before Transportation. Frequently, goods are delivered to the carrier before they are ready for transportation. The carrier may be instructed to hold the goods until shipping instructions are received, or the carrier may delay shipment until the freight charges are paid. In either event, the carrier is liable only as a mutual-benefit bailee. The carrier's role as an insurer, therefore, does not arise until the goods are ready to be transported.

Carrier as Bailee after Transportation. When the goods arrive at their destination, the consignee is given a reasonable time to accept delivery of the goods. Express companies must deliver the goods to the consignee's place of business, but railroads need only place the goods in the freight depot, or, in case of car lots, set the car on a siding where the consignee can unload the goods. If the consignee does not call for the goods within a reasonable time after being notified by the carrier that the goods have arrived, the carrier is liable only as a mutual-benefit bailee.

Connecting Carriers

The initial carrier and the final, or terminal, carrier are each liable for a common carrier loss occurring on the line of a connecting carrier. Whichever of these carriers has been held liable may then compel the connecting carrier to reimburse it. The connecting carrier on whose line the loss occurs is subject to liability.

Bill of Lading

A bill of lading is a document of title. It sets forth the contract between the shipper and the carrier. Title to the goods described in the bill of lading may be passed by transferring the bill of lading to the purchaser. There are two types of bills of lading:

1. Straight, or nonnegotiable, bills of lading
2. Order, or negotiable, bills of lading

Straight Bills of Lading. Under this type of bill of lading the consignee alone is designated as the one to whom the goods are to be delivered. The consignee's rights may be transferred to another, but as a rule the third party obtains no better title than the shipper or the consignee had. However, under certain circumstances the third party may get greater rights than the consignee. If the bill of lading contains a recital as to the contents, quantity, or weight of the goods, the carrier is bound to a bona fide transferee as to the accuracy of these descriptions unless the bill of lading itself indicates that the contents of packages are unknown to the carrier.

As with all assignments, the assignee should notify the carrier of the assignment when the original consignee sells the goods before receipt. The carrier is justified in delivering goods to the consignee if it has received no notice of assignment.

Richard Hightower, an army officer, shipped goods on a U.S. Government bill of lading by Bekins Van Lines Co. After shipment, some articles were missing and others were damaged. The full loss was $14,868.83. The bill of lading limited the value of the goods to 60 cents per pound "unless otherwise specifically annotated" and there was no annotation. An "Order for Services" contained a written and signed agreement by Hightower limiting losses to 60 cents per pound and a condition that in the space provided the shipper had to insert the declared value or the words "60 cents per pound" in his own handwriting or "the shipment will be deemed released to a maximum value equal to $1.25 times the weight of the shipment in pounds." An insertion of "60 cents per pound" was made but not in Hightower's handwriting. Since Bekins treated Hightower as the shipper in the Order for Service and Hightower had not written "60 cents per pound" on the Order, Hightower was allowed to recover $1.25 times the weight, or $6,650.

Order Bills of Lading. The bill of lading may set forth that the goods are shipped to a designated consignee or order, or merely "to the bearer" of the bill of lading. In such case, the bill of lading is an order, or negotiable, bill of lading and must be presented to the carrier before the carrier can safely deliver the goods. If the goods are delivered to the named consignee and later a bona fide innocent purchaser of the bill of lading demands the goods, the carrier is liable to the holder of the bill of lading.

The Clark Milling Company shipped a carload of flour to Rose and Rogers in South Carolina. The order bill of lading was attached to a draft and sent to a bank at the point of destination. The consignee, without paying the draft or obtaining the bill of lading, was permitted to receive the flour. The carrier was held liable for delivery of the flour without demanding that the consignee surrender the bill of lading.

Rights of Common Carriers of Persons

Common carriers of persons have the right to prescribe the place and time of the payment of fares, usually before boarding the plane, train, bus, or other vehicle. They also have the right to prescribe certain rules of conduct while transporting passengers so long as the rules are reasonable. They may stop the vehicle and remove any passenger who refuses to pay the fare or whose conduct is offensive to the other passengers. They also have the right to reserve certain coaches, seats, or space for special classes of passengers, as in the case of sleeper coaches on trains.

Scott boarded a ship for a coastal trip south. When the ship's master called for all tickets, Scott could not locate his. Upon his refusal to pay for his passage, he was removed at the first mooring. He sued the ship line owner for damages after he later located his ticket. He did not succeed in his claim for damages since he could not produce a ticket when required. The carrier was not required to take his word that he had a valid ticket.

Liability of Common Carriers of Persons

The carriers of passengers are not insurers of the passengers' safety, but they are required to exercise the highest degree of care possible, consistent with practical operation. The liability of the carrier begins as soon as passengers enter the station or waiting platform and does not end until they have left the station at the end of the journey. The degree of care required is only ordinary care while passengers are in the station. After passengers board the bus, train, plane, or other vehicle, the utmost care is required.

Duties of Common Carriers of Persons

A carrier's duties to its passengers consist of:

1. Duty to provide reasonable accommodations and services
2. Duty to provide reasonable protection to its passengers

Duty to Provide Reasonable Accommodations and Services.
When a traveler purchases a ticket from a common carrier, a contract is formed between the carrier and the passenger. Historically, the contract entitled the passenger to a seat. If there was no seat available, the passenger could get off at the next station and demand a refund of the fare. Suit could also be brought for damages for breach of contract. However, the better view today is that the carrier's duty is to make reasonable efforts to provide sufficient facilities so that the public can be accommodated, which may be merely standing room; and there is no guarantee that a passenger will have a seat in the absence of an express reservation. The carrier must also notify the passenger of the arrival of the train, bus, or airplane at the destination and stop long enough to permit the passenger to disembark. A personal notice is not necessary, only a general announcement. If this is not done and a passenger is carried beyond the destination, suit may be brought for any damages suffered.

For two weeks during the summer, Burton Fendelman was a passenger on Conrail trains which were late; overcrowded; lacking in air conditioning, water facilities and electricity; and which had dirty toilets and noxious odors. He sued Conrail and testified that these "atrocious conditions" had existed for years. The court found that as a common carrier, Conrail was required to furnish such service and facilities as shall be safe and adequate and in all respects just and reasonable. This it did not do and was required to pay Fendelman damages.

Duty to Provide Reasonable Protection to Its Passengers. Common carriers of passengers are not insurers of the absolute safety of passengers but must exercise extraordinary care to protect them. Any injury to the passenger by an employee or fellow passengers subjects the carrier to liability for damages, provided the passenger is without blame. The vehicle must stop at a safe place for alighting, and passengers must be assisted when necessary for alighting.

Definition of Baggage

Baggage consists of those articles necessary for personal convenience while traveling. Articles carried by travelers on similar missions and destinations constitute the test rather than what passengers in general carry. For example, fishing paraphernalia is baggage for a person on a fishing trip, but not for the ordinary traveler. Also, a lady's watch is not baggage when carried in a traveling bag by a man. Any article carried for the accommodation of one who is not a passenger is not baggage. The carrier is not held to as great a degree of care for the loss of articles other than baggage and the passenger is not entitled to have them transported without extra charge. They are freight, not baggage.

Liability for Baggage

The liability of a common carrier for baggage is the same as that of a common carrier of goods. The common carrier is an insurer of the baggage with the five exceptions noted in the section on common carriers of goods. It is necessary to distinguish between baggage retained in the possession of the traveler and that carried in the baggage car or other space. In the first type, the carrier is liable only for lack of reasonable care or for willful misconduct of its agents or employees.

A reasonable amount of baggage may be carried as a part of the cost of the passenger's fare. The carrier may charge extra for baggage in excess of a reasonable amount.

Questions

1. What standard of care must a private carrier exercise?

2. When may a common carrier refuse service?

3. Is a common carrier liable for a loss or damage to goods being transported regardless of negligence?

4. Name some events which the law calls acts of God.

5. What acts of the shipper will relieve a common carrier of liability for loss?

6. When does the common carrier's liability begin?

7. When goods must be transported by two or more carriers before reaching their destination, which carrier is liable if the goods are damaged?

8. a. What is a *bill of lading*?
   b. What is the difference between a *straight bill of lading* and an *order bill of lading*?

9. Are common carriers insurers of the safety of passengers?

10. What is the liability of a common carrier for baggage carried by a passenger?

Case Problems

1. The Hunziker Equipment Company purchased ten tractors from the Case Manufacturing Company. The tractors were shipped by railroad freight with a negotiable bill of lading. The consignee borrowed money on the tractors from Finley Finance Company and indorsed the bill of lading to the lender as security for the loan. When the tractors arrived, they were delivered to the consignee without demanding that he produce the bill of lading. The Finley Finance Company sued the railroad for its loss. Is the railroad liable?

2. Containers of plywood shipped by Masonite Corporation on Norfolk & Western Railway Company tilted so much during transit they almost fell from the flatcar and required extraordinary handling to unload. The railroad told Masonite that improper internal bracing allowed the plywood to move and subsequent containers were to be sent to an intermodal facility for inspection prior to shipment. Later, Masonite sent two containers which were poorly packed and which were not sent to the intermodal facility. The containers received only a routine inspection at the yard. They fell from the flatcar and derailed another car in the train. Masonite sued Norfolk & Western alleging that it was strictly liable for the damages because it knew of the defective bracing. Norfolk & Western alleged it had no duty to discover defects in Masonite's packing. Did it?

3. The Devon Seed Company ordered a carload of seed from the Newberry Seed Corporation. When the seed arrived, the car was placed on a siding where the consignee by agreement was to load it onto his truck and at his expense. The car was placed on the siding at 10 A.M., but the Devon Seed Company was not notified that day. During the night a riot occurred, and the seed was thrown out of the car by the rioters and destroyed by a heavy rain. Loss by riot had not been excluded in the bill of lading. Is the carrier liable for the loss?

4. The Baxter Machine Company shipped an expensive machine to the Buford Mining Company in Denver by a straight bill of lading. An agent of the Buford Mining Company called at the office of the Stern Engineering Corporation and offered to sell them the machinery, stating that their plans had been altered and they would have to return it. The Stern Corporation purchased the machinery and received the bill of lading by indorsement. Three days later they inquired of the railroad if the machinery had arrived and were told that it had already been delivered to the consignee, the Buford Mining Company. The Buford Mining Company, after it got possession of the machinery, had sold and delivered it to the Rocky Mountain Mining Company. The Stern Engineering Corporation sued the railroad for the value of the machinery, alleging it had delivered the machinery to the wrong party. Was the railroad liable?

5. Iowa Beef Processors, Inc., shipped meat to Standard Meat Company by American Trucking Company, a common carrier. The meat was loaded into a trailer which was sealed by Iowa. It was Standard's responsibility to break the seal upon arrival. When the shipment arrived, the meat was tendered to Standard but not unloaded for two days because of a lack of freezer space. It was discovered during unloading that much of the meat was spoiled. The shipment was rejected. Iowa sued American for damages, alleging American was liable as an insurer because the meat was in good condition when it was shipped. Is American liable?

6. Thomas owned a large truck in which he hauled fresh vegetables from Florida to Atlanta for a produce exchange. On the return trip he often carried freight at rates considerably below those charged by the railroad. On one of these return trips, the Glenn Jewelry Company shipped two cases of jewelry valued at $2,500 to its branch store in Orlando. The jewelry was stolen through no fault of Thomas. The Glenn Jewelry Company sued Thomas as a common carrier for the value of the jewelry. Was he liable? *private carrier; ordinary care required. truck owner not required*

7. K. C. Mah bought a full-fare ticket from New York to Radford on Greyhound Lines, Inc. She checked three pieces of baggage and was given three claim checks. Each claim check stated: "BAGGAGE LIABILITY LIMITED TO $50.00 (SEE OVER)." Language on the back stated Greyhound's liability was limited to $50 for all baggage checked on one full-fare ticket unless a greater value was declared in writing and additional charges were collected at the time of checking. It added, "This check is accepted subject to all conditions of published tariffs." The tariff had the same limitation of liability. Mah boarded a bus and upon arrival in Radford her baggage could not be found. Three days later one piece was delivered. She sued for $1,000, the value of the lost bags and their contents. For what, if anything, was Greyhound liable?

8. During the daytime Phyllis Parlato alighted from a Connecticut Transit bus and started to cross the bus-stop area. She stepped into a hole which was covered by leaves and broke her leg. The bus driver had stopped at the area five or six times previously that day and did not know there was a hole. Parlato sued for breach of Connecticut's duty of utmost care for its passengers. Did Parlato breach its duty? *Carrier not responsible*

9. The Associated Farmers Warehouse Corporation shipped a load of wheat by riverboat to St. Louis. The boat struck a tree trunk that had been washed into the river channel by a recent flood. The boat sank, and all the wheat was destroyed. Was the carrier liable for this loss?

10. Julia Hasbrouck obtained passage on a train to Natick, Massachusetts, to visit her daughter, a college student in that city. In her baggage were four rings valued at about $15,000. Mrs. Hasbrouck was socially prominent and was in the habit of wearing expensive jewelry at all social functions. The baggage

was checked with the railroad, the excess value was declared, and the charges paid. When she arrived at her destination, her baggage was returned to her, but the jewelry was missing. The railroad refused to pay her claim, contending that so much jewelry, four diamond rings, was not properly baggage, and therefore the railroad was not liable for its loss. Was the railroad liable for the loss?

20

Hotelkeepers As Bailees

Preview Cases

Jean King and Miriam Kelley were assaulted and robbed in Room 821 of the Ilikai Tower Building. The Tower Building of the Ilikai Hotel was operated by Ilikai Properties, Inc., as a hotel, but it also contained condominium units. Room 821 was a condominium owned by Melvin Shigeta, who had rented it to King. Kelley was visiting King. King and Kelley sued Ilikai Properties, alleging their injuries were caused by Ilikai's failure to make the premises safe. Did Ilikai have a duty to protect them from their assailants?

Garson registered at the Ridge Manor Hotel in Florida and incurred a hotel bill amounting to $120. He paid the bill by check and departed, taking all his baggage and jewelry. The check was returned marked "Insufficient funds." Was the hotelkeeper's lien reestablished by the return of the check?

Traditionally the innkeeper has been held to an extraordinary degree of liability for the safety of the personal property of guests, travelers, or transients. The common law is the basis of most of our laws dealing with hotelkeepers, but as conditions have changed, the law has changed. Today most states have laws permitting hotelkeepers and motel keepers to limit their liability. These statutes vary so widely that only a few general statements can be made about them. Even with statutory modifications of the common law, the hotelkeeper still owes guests a high degree of care for their property. In the absence of a valid limitation, hotelkeepers are generally insurers of the safety of goods entrusted to their care.

Who Is a Hotelkeeper?

Today "hotelkeeper" is synonymous with "innkeeper." A *hotelkeeper* is one who is regularly engaged in the business of offering living accommodations to all transient persons. The hotelkeeper may supply food or entertainment, but providing lodging to the transients is the cardinal test.

Those Who Are Not Hotelkeepers

If one provides rooms only or room and board to permanent guests, but does not behave as able and willing to accommodate transients, such a person is not a hotelkeeper and thus is not held to the strict accountability of the common law. A tourist home is not an inn if the owner does not advertise as willing to accommodate all transients who apply. Motels and tourist cabin establishments are usually classed as inns. Hotels that cater only to permanent residents are not inns, although a hotel may cater to both permanent guests and transients. If so, the hotel owes the typical duties to its transient guests; but to its permanent guests it owes the duties of a landlord.

Duties and Liabilities of a Hotelkeeper

The duties and liabilities of a hotelkeeper are:

1. To serve all who apply
2. To protect a guest's person
3. To care for the guest's property

Duty to Serve All Who Apply. The basic test of hotelkeepers is that they hold themselves out as willing to serve without discrimination all who apply. If a hotel refuses accommodations for an improper reason, it is liable for damages, including exemplary damages, to the person rejected.

In addition, a hotel may be liable for discrimination under a civil rights or similar statutory provision and may also be guilty of a crime if a court has issued an injunction prohibiting such discrimination. By virtue of the Federal Civil Rights Act of 1964, neither a hotel nor its concessionaire can discriminate against patrons nor segregate them on the basis of race, color, religion, or national origin. The federal act is limited to discrimination for the stated reasons. When there has been improper discrimination or segregation or it is reasonably believed that such action may occur, the federal act authorizes the institution of proceedings in the federal courts for an order to stop such practices.

A hotelkeeper may, however, turn people away for a number of proper reasons. For example, a drunken person who would be highly offensive to other guests, someone who is criminally violent, or someone who is not dressed in a manner required by reasonable hotel regulations applied to all persons may be turned away. If all rooms are filled, all other applicants may be turned away.

Duty to Protect a Guest's Person. A hotelkeeper is not liable as an insurer of a guest's safety. Reasonable care must be used for the safety of those who are on the premises as guests, but not for a mere visitor or a patron of the newsstand or lunchroom. The hotelkeeper's liability with respect to the condition of the premises is the same regardless of the identity of the victim. The difference in duty arises only in connection with the "property" of the victim.

A hotelkeeper must provide fire escapes and also have conspicuous notices indicating the direction of the fire escapes. There is no liability for an injury due to a fire if the hotelkeeper was in no way negligent in starting the fire. If there is negligence in preventing the spread of the fire or in directing the guests to fire escapes, the hotelkeeper is liable. Fire prevention practices, such as steel doors leading to stairways between floors, are required of all hotels. If a fire starts due to no negligence of the hotelkeeper or employees, there is no liability to the guests for their personal injuries unless they can show that the fire was not contained because of a failure to install the required fire safety features. In one case the court held the hotelkeeper was not liable for the loss of life on the floor where the fire started, but was liable for all personal injuries on the four floors to which the fire spread because of the negligence of the hotel.

Duty to Care for the Guest's Property. The hotelkeeper under prior law was an insurer of the guest's property except for losses occurring from:

1. An act of God
2. The act of a public enemy
3. An act of a public authority
4. An act of a guest
5. The inherent nature of the property

By statute in every state this liability has been modified to some extent. Most statutes limit a hotel's liability to a designated sum. Other statutes simply declare that the law of mutual-benefit bailments applies.

Some states permit the hotelkeeper to limit liability by contract with the guest, usually a notice posted in the guest's room. Some of the statutes require that the hotelkeeper, in order to escape full liability, provide a vault or other safe place of deposit for valuables such as furs and jewelry. If a guest fails to deposit valuable articles when notice of the availability of a safe is posted in the room or at the registration desk, the hotelkeeper is released from liability as an insurer.

Who Are Guests?

Before a hotelkeeper can be held to the high standard of care either for injury to the person or for loss of property, the injured party must be a guest. To be a *guest* one must be a transient, not a permanent resident. Also, the person must have been received as a transient guest. One who enters the hotel to attend a ball or other social function or to visit a guest is not a guest. Likewise, a person going to a hotel restaurant for dinner is not a "guest" of the hotel, but merely a "patron." The essential element in the definition of *guest* is that the person is a transient. A guest need not be a traveler nor come from a distance. A person living within a short distance of the hotel who engages a room and remains there overnight is a guest.

The relationship of guest and hotelkeeper does not begin until a person is received as a guest by the hotelkeeper. The relationship terminates when the guest leaves or ceases to be a transient, as when arrangements are made for a more or less permanent residence at the hotel.

Jean King and Miriam Kelley were assaulted and robbed in Room 821 of the Ilikai Tower Building. The Tower Building of the Ilikai Hotel was operated by Ilikai Properties, Inc., as a hotel, but it also contained condominium units. Room 821 was a condominium owned by Melvin Shigeta, who had rented it to King. Kelley was visiting King. King and Kelley sued Ilikai Properties, alleging their injuries were caused by Ilikai's failure to make the premises safe. The court found that King and Kelley were not guests of the hotel, so Ilikai had no duty to protect them from their assailants.

Lien of the Hotelkeeper

A hotelkeeper has a lien on the baggage of guests for the value of the services rendered. This lien extends also to all wearing apparel not actually being worn, such as an overcoat, a fur coat, or an extra suit. If the hotel knows that the property belongs to a third person, the property is not subject to the lien in some states; in other states the lien of the hotel may be asserted if the property has been entrusted to the guest by the owner with knowledge or reason to know that it might be taken to a hotel.

The lien of the hotelkeeper usually attaches only to baggage. It does not apply to an automobile, for example, in most states. If the hotel provides storage facilities for the guest's car, the car cannot be held if the guest fails to pay the hotel bill. If there is a separate charge for car storage, this charge (but not the room charge) must be paid before the car can be removed.

If the charges are not paid within a reasonable time, the hotelkeeper may sell the baggage or other goods to pay for the charges. Any residue must be returned to the guest. The lien terminates when the property is returned to the guest even though the room charges have not been paid. A minor is as fully bound by these laws as an adult.

Garson registered at the Ridge Manor Hotel in Florida and incurred a hotel bill amounting to $120. He paid the bill by check and departed, taking all his baggage and jewelry. The check was returned marked "Insufficient funds." The lien is not reestablished by a return of the check.

Boardinghouse Keepers

A *boardinghouse keeper* is a person whose business is to supply living accommodations to permanent boarders. The laws of a hotelkeeper do not apply to boardinghouse keepers. The boardinghouse keeper has no lien under the common law, but most states have given this right to boardinghouses by statute. The chief difference in the common law relating to a hotelkeeper and a boardinghouse keeper is that the latter need take only ordinary care of the property of the boarder or lodger. A boardinghouse keeper is in no way an insurer and does not have to accept all who apply.

Crimes Against Hotels

Statutes commonly make it a criminal offense for hotel guests, boardinghouse tenants, or similar lodgers to attempt to defraud the hotel or boardinghouse by intentionally leaving without paying their bills, removing their property secretly, or engaging in similar fraudulent practices.

Dobson had been a guest at the Georgian Hotel for five days. She secretly left the hotel without paying her bill. The hotel owner had her indicted "for fraudulently leaving without paying her hotel bill." She was found guilty because the act of leaving secretly without paying showed that her intent was to defraud the hotel.

Questions

1. **a.** What is a hotelkeeper?
   b. Who is a guest?

2. What are the duties of a hotelkeeper to guests?

3. Can a hotelkeeper be guilty of a crime for failure to provide accommodations?

4. Is the hotelkeeper liable for the injury to a guest by fire if the hotel was in no way negligent?

5. How may a hotelkeeper frequently limit liability for loss of a guest's property?

6. If a guest's baggage is held by the hotel as a lien for the payment of the hotel charges, what disposition may be made of the property?

7. What is the chief difference in the liability of a hotelkeeper and a boarding-house keeper?

8. May one be charged with a crime for fraudulently leaving without paying the board bill at a boardinghouse?

Case Problems

1. Burke registered at the Devon Hotel. He was a minor. He ran up a hotel bill of $175. The hotel held his baggage and a hi-fi set until the bill was paid. Burke attempted to disaffirm his contract, contending that there was no necessity for him to travel or to stay at a hotel. May he disaffirm?

2. Danner drove up to the King Cotton Motel. An attendant approached and she inquired about a room. She left two traveling bags with the attendant, stating she would return later to register. She changed her mind and returned for her bags. They could not be located. Is the motel liable? *she didn't check in so hotel wasn't liable*

3. Mr. and Mrs. Kanagawa took two rooms at a motel fixed for light housekeeping. They were to pay rent by the month and planned to spend the winter in the city. While they were out, a thief entered the room and stole a necklace worth $1,500. They sued the motel owner for the loss. Is he liable?

4. Ms. Seagraves, an actress, spent some time at an exclusive hotel in Florida. When she got ready to leave, she had an unpaid hotel bill of several hundred dollars. She was unable to pay the bill, and the hotel notified her that she could not remove her baggage from the room. Although the temperature outside was 96, she put on her expensive mink coat, adorned herself with all her expensive jewelry, and then attempted to leave without her baggage. The hotel contended it was entitled to a lien on her coat and her excess jewelry. Is its contention correct? *no, she didn't need for coat*

5. The Greenway Auto Court had signs along the highway soliciting all travelers to become guests. John L. Hewess, a labor leader, applied for accommodations. Because the owner of the auto court was violently opposed to unions, he refused Hewess accommodations although he had vacant rooms. Hewess sued for damages. Was the Greenway Auto Court liable?

6. While Douglas Margreiter was alone in his room at the Monteleone Hotel, two men unlocked the door and entered. One turned up the television, and the other struck Margreiter on the head. The men took him down the freight elevator, which was supposed to have been shut and locked. Margreiter was later found three blocks away, severely beaten and intoxicated. The security officer had gone home sick, so the only security was the assistant manager at the lobby desk and an employee who was to be at the back door. The hotel had been advised that earlier in the day fifteen rooms had been burglarized in

a hotel two blocks away. Margreiter sued the hotel for his injuries. Was the hotel liable?

7. Hawkins registered at a hotel and was assigned a room. During the night the hotel caught fire; neither the hotel nor its employees were negligent. When Hawkins was awakened, she could not leave by the stairway, so she sought the fire escape. Since there were no signs directing her to the fire escape, she could not find it. Seeing no other way out, she jumped from a second-floor window and was injured. All her baggage was destroyed. Hawkins brought suit against the hotel to collect for the value of her baggage and compensation for her injuries. Discuss the rights and obligations of the parties.

8. Mary Weaver had been staying at the Sea Esta Motel for about four months and paid a monthly rate. She was injured when a chair in her motel room collapsed. She sued the motel. Was she a guest?

9. Mr. and Mrs. Andrew Laubie were guests at the Royal Sonesta Hotel. They locked the doors and windows and secured the chain lock to their room, but during the night burglars opened the door and severed the chain lock. Valuable jewelry was stolen. The hotel provided a safety deposit vault for its guests. State law provided that an innkeeper was not liable to guests for loss of property in any sum exceeding $100 if a copy of the law was conspicuously posted in the guest's room or unless greater liability was contracted for in writing. In a suit brought by the Laubies against the hotel, the question was whether the statute limited the hotel's liability for negligence as well as its liability as a depositary. Did it?

Summary Cases for Part Four

Bailments

1. Cerreta parked his automobile in the Kinney Corporation parking lot. On the back seat of the car were some valuable drawings and sporting equipment. The articles on the back seat were not visible from the outside of the car. When Cerreta returned to pick up the car, the articles were missing. He sued the Kinney Corporation as a bailee. Decide. [*Cerreta v. Kinney Corp.*, 142 A. 2d 917 (N.J. Super. Ct. App. Div.)]

2. Georgia Best Sales Company delivered cases of Cornish hens to H & M Motor Lines, Inc., for transport from Chattanooga to South Carolina. When the truck arrived, ninety-four cases of hens were missing. The bill of lading signed by H & M stated, "WSHE L. CARRIER COUNT," which wording required the carrier to count the actual load rather than goods placed on the dock for later loading. Georgia Best sued H & M for the missing hens. Was H & M liable for the loss? [*H & M Motor Lines, Inc. v. Georgia Best Sales Company*, 253 S.E.2d 841 (Ga. Ct. App.)]

3. Tilson was a passenger on an interstate railroad to Kansas City from St. Louis. She carried two handbags with her. She gave these handbags to a red-cap in the station in St. Louis, and they were stolen. The luggage was later found and delivered to her in Kansas City, but jewelry valued at $2,885 had been taken from the luggage. The carrier operated under a rule approved by the Interstate Commerce Commission whereby a limit of $25 is set for the loss of any one piece of luggage or its contents unless a larger value is declared and an extra charge paid. She sued the carrier for $2,885. Was the carrier liable for the $2,885? [*Tilson v. Terminal Railroad Association of St. Louis*, 236 S. W. 2d 42 (Mo. Ct. App.)]

4. American Cyanamid Co. shipped twelve large boxes of heavy machinery and oil by Seatrain Lines of Puerto Rico, Inc., and then by land with Francisco Vega Otero, a common carrier. The boxes were loaded onto three platforms owned by Seatrain, and the platforms were loaded aboard Seatrain's ship. Upon arrival in Puerto Rico the platforms were unloaded and each mounted on a chassis with wheels. Later they were attached to three Vega Otero trucks. The cargo on the platforms was so high the truck drivers could not pass under a bridge on the normal route. They blocked off a one-way exit ramp and went up the ramp the wrong way intending to make a U-turn at the top. When the first driver carefully and cautiously tried to turn, the platform tipped onto its side causing the chassis and truck to overturn, damaging the cargo. It was the custom of the parties for the land carrier to accept goods in the trailers chosen by the sea carrier. Cyanamid's insurance company sued

Seatrain and Vega Otero. What is the liability of either or both carriers? [*American Foreign Insurance Association v. Seatrain Lines of Puerto Rico, Inc.*, 689 F.2d 295 (1st Cir.)]

5. Before boarding an airplane, Tremaroli was required to submit himself and his hand baggage to the security check. The hand baggage was placed by Tremaroli on a conveyor belt, and while it rolled through an X-ray machine Tremaroli went through the magnetometer. At that time he was unable to see his baggage. He immediately went to the pick-up end of the conveyor belt, picked up the only bag there, which resembled his own, and boarded the airplane. While the plane was on the ground, Tremaroli realized he did not have his baggage. He reported this to the airline, but his baggage was never found. Tremaroli sued the airline for the value of his baggage. Was the airline liable? [*Tremaroli v. Delta Airlines*, 458 N.Y.S.2d 159 (N.Y. Civ. Ct.)]

6. While she was a passenger in a motor home leased from BCJ Corporation, Jayne Miles was severely burned when the motor home caught fire. It had collided with a guard rail causing the gas tanks to rupture, and the leaking gas caught fire. Miles sued BCJ, alleging it knew the motor home was defectively designed because the only exit door was directly over the gas tanks, and the tires were overloaded and likely to rupture. The trial court dismissed the suit before any evidence was heard. Did Miles allege a cause of action against BCJ? [*Miles v. General Tire & Rubber Co.*, 460 N.E.2d 1377 (Ohio Ct. App.)]

7. After checking into his motel room late at night, Thomas Urbano went to his car in the motel parking lot to get his luggage. He was assaulted and seriously injured by unidentified people. There had been forty-two episodes of criminal activity at the motel in the prior three years, and twelve of the episodes had occurred in the previous three and one-half months. The parking lot was not enclosed, and the area of Urbano's room was dimly lighted. Urbano sued the motel, alleging it was negligent in not providing adequate lighting, not fencing the parking lot, not notifying him of criminal activity, and not monitoring and protecting the premises. The motel argued the case should be dismissed. Should it? [*Urbano v. Days Inn of America, Inc.*, 295 S.E.2d 240 (N.C. Ct. App.)]

8. Upjohn Company shipped a tank car of PAPI (a liquid plastic) to a facility in Elizabethport called Through Bulk Service (TBS), a division of the Central Railroad of New Jersey. Upjohn told TBS to hold the tank car at the Elizabethport facility and transship quantities of PAPI to tank trucks for shipment. The PAPI was to be off-loaded by the carrier. The last two shipments trucked to a customer were rejected. The PAPI was contaminated by moisture and was unsalvageable. The bill of lading used by Upjohn stated: "Claims must be filed . . . within nine months after delivery of the property. . . . When claims are not filed . . . in accordance with the foregoing provisions, no carrier hereunder shall be liable, and such claims will not be paid." Upjohn

submitted a claim for damages more than nine months after the PAPI was returned to it and sued Central, claiming the time limitation did not apply once the PAPI reached the TBS facility. It argued since the PAPI was consigned to itself "c/o TBS," TBS received the goods on Upjohn's behalf. Upon arrival the bill of lading expired and the carrier was liable as a bailee. Was it? [*Upjohn Company v. Timpany*, 402 A.2d 979 (N.J. Super. Ct. App. Div.)]

9. Gantt was a student at Aircraft Sales and Service, a privately owned flight school. The school supplied the planes in which students did their flight training. On one flight with Gantt at the controls, the plane went out of control, and the pilot was unable to bring it under control. It crashed and Gantt was seriously injured. An investigation revealed that a mechanic for the school had left a screwdriver in the control mechanism. Gantt sued the school for his personal injuries. Was the bailor liable? [*Aircraft Sales and Service v. Gantt*, 52 So. 2d 388 (Ala.)]

Part Five — Commercial Paper

Learning Objectives for Part Five

Commercial Paper

After studying this part you should be able to:

1. Explain what negotiable instruments are and how they developed.
2. Discuss how negotiable instruments are transferred.
3. Differentiate between bearer paper and order paper.
4. Name the types of negotiable instruments and the parties to them.
5. List the seven requirements of negotiability.
6. Distinguish between the different types of notes.
7. Identify the two different kinds of drafts.
8. Explain how drafts are accepted and the admissions made by acceptance.
9. Describe the characteristics of a check and name the types of checks.
10. Specify who is primarily and who is secondarily liable on commercial paper.
11. Discuss the requirements for presentment and notice of dishonor.
12. Explain the procedures for an agent to use when executing a negotiable instrument.
13. Discuss how indorsements are made and identify the different types of indorsements.
14. Describe the liabilities and warranties of an indorser.
15. Define holders and holders through a holder in due course.
16. Discuss the special rules for holders of consumer paper.
17. Distinguish between limited and universal defenses to holders.
18. Identify the defenses which may be universal or limited.

21

Nature of Commercial Paper

Preview Cases

Smithson owed Gregory $250. She gave Gregory a check payable to "bearer." Gregory had never seen bearer paper and insisted that Smithson needed to indorse it. Smithson claimed it would be illegal to indorse it. Would it?

Enterprises, Inc., and George Becker entered into a contract by which Enterprises agreed to do certain work on a residence for Becker, and he agreed to pay for it. Enterprises later sued for breach of contract, alleging Becker did not own the residence and neither the owner nor Becker allowed performance of the contract. Becker moved to dismiss the suit, arguing that the contract was subject to the Home Solicitation Sales Act and violated it. The Act stated that any "note . . . given by a buyer in respect of a home solicitation sale shall bear on its face" a statement that the sale is subject to the Act and the note is not negotiable. Did the Act apply to the contract?

A _negotiable instrument_ is a writing drawn in a special form which can be transferred from person to person as a substitute for money or as an instrument of credit. Such an instrument must meet certain definite requirements in regard to form and the manner in which it is transferred. Checks and notes are two types of negotiable instruments. Another term for negotiable instruments is _commercial paper_. Since a negotiable instrument is not money, a person is not required by law to accept one in payment of a debt.

History and Development

The need for instruments of credit that would permit the settlement of claims between distant cities without the transfer of money has existed as long as trade has existed. There were references to bills of exchange or instruments of credit as early as 50 B.C. Their widespread usage, however, began about A.D. 1200 as international trade began to flourish in the wake of the Crusades. At first these credit instruments were used only in international trade, but they gradually became common in domestic trade.

In England prior to about A.D. 1400, all disputes between merchants were settled on the spot by special courts set up by the merchants. The rules applied by these courts became known as the *law merchant*. Later the common-law courts took over the adjudication of all disputes, including those between merchants, but these courts retained most of the customs developed by the merchants and incorporated the law merchant into the common law. Most, but by no means all, of the law merchant dealt with bills of exchange or credit instruments. In the United States each state modified in its own way the common law dealing with credit instruments so that eventually the various states had different laws regarding credit instruments. A commission was appointed by the American Bar Association and the American Bankers Association to draw up a Uniform Negotiable Instruments Law. In 1896 the commission proposed a Uniform Act. This act was adopted in all the states, but it has since been displaced by Article 3 of the Uniform Commercial Code.

Negotiation

Negotiation is the act of transferring ownership of a negotiable instrument to another party. A negotiable instrument owned by and payable to a person may be negotiated by the owner merely by signing the back of it and delivering it to another party. When a person signs the back of a negotiable instrument before delivery, this is called *indorsing* the instrument.

When a negotiable instrument is transferred to one or more parties, these parties may acquire rights that are superior to those of the original owner. Parties who acquire rights superior to those of the original owner are known as *holders in due course*. It is mainly this feature of the transfer of superior rights that gives negotiable instruments a special classification all their own.

Order Paper and Bearer Paper

Commercial paper is made payable either to the order of a named person, in which case it is called *order paper*, or to bearer, in which case it is called *bearer paper*. Order paper must use the word "order," as in the phrase "pay to the order of John Doe," or some other word to indicate it may be paid to a transferee. Order paper is negotiated only by indorsement of the person to whom it is then payable and delivery of the paper to another person. In the case of bearer paper, the transfer may be made merely by handing the paper to another person.

Payment is made on a different basis with order paper than with bearer paper. Order paper may be paid only to the person to whom it is made payable on its face or the person to whom it has been properly indorsed. However, bearer paper may be paid to any person in possession of the paper.

◆ Smithson owed Gregory $250. She gave Gregory a check payable to "bearer." Gregory had never seen bearer paper and insisted that Smithson needed to indorse it. Smithson claimed it would be illegal to indorse it. Although it is not necessary to indorse bearer paper, it is not illegal to do so.

Classification of Commercial Paper

The basic negotiable instruments may be classified as follows:

1. Drafts
2. Promissory notes

Drafts. A *draft* or *bill of exchange* is a written order signed by one person and requiring the person to whom it is addressed to pay on demand or at a particular time a sum certain in money to order or to bearer. Trade acceptances and checks are special types of drafts.

Promissory Notes. A *negotiable promissory note* is an unconditional promise in writing made by one person to another, signed by the maker, engaging to pay on demand, or at a particular time, a sum certain in money to order or to bearer (see Illustration 21-1).

$ *7,000.00*   Greenfield, Missouri, _____ *April 1,* ___ 19 _ _

_____ *One (1) year* _____ after date, for value received, _____ *I* _____ promise

to pay to the order of _____ *Ana Nieves* _____

the sum of _____ *Seven Thousand Dollars ($7,000.00)* _____

with interest thereon from date at the rate of _____ *fifteen percent (15%)* _____

per annum, interest payable _____ *semiannually* _____ and if interest

is not paid _____ *semiannually* _____ , to become as principal and bear

the same rate of interest.

Payable at _____ *Northside Bank* _____

_____ *Jan L. Hendricks* _____

ILLUS. 21-1. Promissory Note
Parties: maker—Jan L. Hendricks; payee—Ana Nieves

◆   Enterprises, Inc., and George Becker entered into a contract by which Enterprises agreed to do certain work on a residence for Becker, and he agreed to pay for it. Enterprises later sued for breach of contract, alleging Becker did not own the residence and neither the owner nor Becker allowed performance of the contract. Becker moved to dismiss the suit, arguing that the contract was subject to the Home Solicitation Sales Act and violated it. The Act stated that any "note . . . given by a buyer in respect of a home solicitation sale shall bear on its face" a statement that the sale is subject to the Act and the note is not negotiable. The court held the Act did not apply to the contract because it was not a note. The contract did not contain an unconditional promise to pay, but merely a promise to pay when the other party performed.

◆   Cramer delivered a note to Anderson in the amount of $1,000 which called for the payment of 10 percent of the amount of the note as an attorney's fee if default were made in the payment of the note and it was turned over to an attorney for collection. Anderson thought this provision made the note nonnegotiable, since the sum would not be certain. It is negotiable, since an attorney's fee, interest, and such additional payments alone do not prevent a note from being negotiable.

Parties to Negotiable Instruments

Each party to a negotiable instrument is designated by a certain term, depending upon the type of instrument. Some of these terms are common to all types of negotiable instruments, while others are restricted to one type only. The same individual may be designated by one term at one stage and by another at a later stage through which the instrument passes before it is collected. These terms are payee, drawer, drawee, acceptor, maker, bearer, holder, indorser, and indorsee.

Payee. The party to whom any negotiable instrument is made payable is called the *payee*.

Drawer. The person who executes any draft is called the *drawer*.

Drawee. The person who is ordered to pay a draft is called the *drawee*.

Acceptor. A drawee who accepts a draft, that is, indicates a willingness to assume responsibility for its payment, is called the *acceptor*. Drafts which are not immediately payable are accepted by writing upon the face of the instrument these or similar words: "Accepted Jane Daws." This indicates that Jane Daws is willing to perform the contract according to its terms.

$450.00   December 25, 19 - -

Six months after date _____ PAY TO THE

ORDER OF Community Bank

Four hundred fifty dollars and no/100 _____ DOLLARS

FOR CLASSROOM USE ONLY

VALUE RECEIVED AND CHARGE TO ACCOUNT OF

TO Walter Evans

No. 27 Walden, Virginia   Lee W. Richardson

ILLUS. 21-2. Draft
Parties: drawer—Lee W. Richardson
drawee—Walter Evans; payee—Community Bank

Maker. The person who executes a promissory note is called the *maker*. This is the person who contracts to pay the amount due on the note. This obligation is similar to that of the acceptor of a draft.

Bearer. Any negotiable instrument may be made payable to whoever is in possession of it. The payee of such an instrument is the *bearer*. If the instrument is made payable to the order of "Myself," "Cash," or another similar name, these terms are equivalent to bearer.

Holder. Any person in possession of an instrument is the *holder* if it has been delivered to the person and it is either bearer paper or it is payable to that person as the payee or by indorsement. The payee is the original holder.

Holder in Due Course. A holder who takes a negotiable instrument in good faith and for value is a *holder in due course*.

Indorser. When the payee of a draft or a note wishes to transfer the instrument to another party, it must be indorsed. The payee is then called the *indorser*. The payee makes the indorsement by signing on the back of the instrument.

Indorsee. A person who becomes the holder of a negotiable instrument by an indorsement which names him or her as the person to whom the instrument is negotiated is called the *indorsee*.

Belmont executed a note in favor of Yehdego. Yehdego indorsed it to Lewis and Lewis indorsed it to Norburn. Lewis was an indorsee after Yehdego indorsed the note and became an indorser when he indorsed it to Norburn.

Negotiation and Assignment

The rights given the original parties are alike in the cases of negotiation and assignment. In the case of a promissory note, for example, the original parties are the maker (the one who promises to pay) and the payee (the one to whom the money is to be paid). Between the original parties, both a nonnegotiable and a negotiable instrument are equally enforceable. Also, the same defenses against fulfilling the terms of the instrument may be set up. For example, if one party to the instrument is a minor, the incapacity to contract may be set up as a defense against carrying out the agreement.

However, nonnegotiable and negotiable instruments are different in respect to the rights given to subsequent parties. When a nonnegotiable instrument is transferred by assignment, the assignee receives only the rights of the assignor and no more. (See Chapter 11.) If one of the original parties to the instrument has a defense that is valid against the assignor, it is also valid against the assignee. When an instrument is transferred by negotiation, however, the party who receives the instrument in good faith and for value may have rights that are superior to the rights of the original holder.

Questions

1. What is a negotiable instrument?

2. What is negotiation?

3. How does one indorse a negotiable instrument?

4. What is generally the difference in the wording of "bearer" paper and "order" paper?

5. Who is the payee of a negotiable instrument?

6. What is the difference between the drawer and the drawee of a draft?

7. What is the drawee who accepts a draft called?

8. What does the maker of a promissory note contract to do?

9. Who is the indorser of a negotiable instrument? The indorsee?

10. What is the difference in the rights of the subsequent parties in cases of negotiation and assignment?

Case Problems

1. The Lopez Company sold Huntley a hi-fi set for $400, and Huntley paid for it by giving a sixty-day nonnegotiable promissory note. Before the note became due, Huntley worked for the Lopez Company and earned $350. When the note came due, Lopez informed Huntley it had assigned his note to the Comer National Bank, an innocent purchaser, and that he would have to pay the bank. The Lopez Company refused to pay the $350 wages, and Huntley attempted to offset this $350 against the $400 when the bank demanded payment. Can he do so?

   Would your answer be different if the note was so worded that it was negotiable and the note had been negotiated instead of assigned?

2. Gregory drew a check on the Dayton National Bank for $704.50, payable to "Bearer." Before the check was delivered, it was stolen by Duppong and cashed at the bank. Gregory demanded that the bank restore the amount of the check to her checking account. Must the bank do this? *no*

3. **a.** Who is the payee in this instrument?
   b. Identify the drawer and the drawee in this instrument.

No._231_   Miami, Florida_____   April 15, 19--

To_ Red Owl Shoe Store _____   _Indianapolis, Indiana_

On_ July 4, 19-- _   Pay to the order of_ Ourselves _

One thousand no/100 ----------------------Dollars, ($ 1,000.00   )

FOR CLASSROOM USE ONLY

The obligation of the acceptor hereof arises out of the purchase of goods from the drawer. The drawee may accept this bill payable at any bank, banker, or trust company in the United States which such drawee may designate.

Accepted at _Indianapolis_ on _April_ 19--
Payable at _First National_ Bank   Smith, Caterwaul & Company
Bank Location _Indianapolis, Indiana_
Buyer's Signature _Red Owl Shoe Stre_   _____
By Agent or Officer _R. Owl, Pres._   By _C. L. Smith, Treas._

---

4. Jacobson, Inc., sued Walter Burris personally on a charge account. The application for the charge account indicated the applicant was Oak Tree Homes, but at the end it was signed by Walter Burris with no indication it was signed other than by him individually. At trial the judge entered judgment against Burris, relying on a law that referred to negotiable instruments. Was this the proper law to rely upon?

5. C. C. Lamb executed five promissory notes to Opelika Production Credit Association (OPCA), which was directly supervised by the Federal Intermediate

Credit Bank of New Orleans (FICB). The notes became in default, so OPCA made demand for payment and then filed suit. Lamb alleged that OPCA could not sue on the notes because it was not the holder of them. Although the notes remained in OPCA's vaults, they had a prestamped restrictive indorsement to the FICB. Was OPCA the holder of the notes?

22

Essentials of Negotiability

Preview Cases

George Werner, Stan Fejta, and August Werner as well as two witnesses signed the following document:

> Promissory Note
>
> Werner Enterprises, Inc., by resolution and signature acknowledges that a debt of $8000.00 is owed to Mr. Stan Fejta (Fejta Construction Company) regarding the construction of "Pontchartrain Plaza," 1930 West End Park.
>
> This note is payable at maturity on or before May 19, 1979, plus 10% (percent) interest.
>
> Date: April 4, 1979

After unsuccessful attempts to collect this indebtedness, Fejta filed suit. Werner alleged that the writing was nothing more than an acknowledgement of a preexisting debt since it did not contain an unconditional promise to pay. Was this a note?

Koyt Everhart executed a note to Jane Everhart in which he promised to pay $150,000 "in lieu of a property settlement supplementing that certain Deed of Separation and Property Settlement . . . the terms of which are incorporated herein by reference." Jane signed a document prepared by her attorneys which purported to assign one-third of the note to them. After default, they sued for collection of the note. For them to recover, the note had to be negotiable. Was it?

An important characteristic of commercial paper is its transferability or negotiability. However, commercial paper must meet certain requirements in order to be negotiable.

Requirements

There are seven requirements with which an instrument must comply in order to be negotiable. If any one of these requirements is lacking, the instrument is not negotiable even though it may be valid and enforceable as between the original parties to the instrument. These seven requirements are:

1. The instrument must be in writing and signed by the party executing it.
2. The instrument must contain either an order to pay or a promise to pay.
3. The order or the promise must be unconditional.
4. The instrument must provide for the payment of a sum certain in money.
5. The instrument must be payable either on demand or at a fixed or definite time.
6. The instrument must be payable to the order of a payee or bearer.
7. The payee (unless the instrument is payable to bearer) and the drawee must be designated with reasonable certainty.

A Signed Writing. A negotiable instrument must be written. The law does not, however, require that the writing be in any particular form. The instrument may be written with pen and ink or with pencil; it may be typed or printed; or it may be partly printed and partly typed. If an instrument is executed with a lead pencil, it meets the legal requirements of negotiability; but a person might hesitate to accept it because of the ease with which it could be altered without detection.

A signature must be placed on a negotiable instrument in order to indicate the intent of the promisor to be bound. The normal place for a signature is in the lower right-hand corner, but the location of the signature and its form are wholly immaterial if it is clear that a signature was intended. The signature may be written, typed, printed, or stamped. It may be a name, a symbol, a mark, or a trade name. The signature, however, must be on the instrument. It cannot be on a separate paper which is attached to the instrument.

The instrument may be signed by another person who has been given authority to perform this act. When an agent signs for the principal or when an officer signs for the corporation, care must be taken to avoid making the agent or officer solely liable or jointly liable with the principal or corporation.

Below are some odd but valid signatures:

1.   His
   Richard x Cooper
          Mark
2. "I, Tammy Morley," written by Morley in the body of the note but with her name typed in the usual place for the signature.
3. "Snowwhite Cleaner," the trade name under which Glendon Sutton operates his business.

An Order or a Promise to Pay. A draft, such as a trade acceptance or a check, must contain an order to pay. If the request is imperative and unequivocal, it is an order even though the word "order" is not used.

A promissory note must contain a promise to pay. The word "promise" need not be used—any equivalent words will answer the purpose—but the language used must show that a promise is intended. Thus, the words "This is to certify that we are bound to pay" were held to be sufficient to constitute a promise. A mere acknowledgment of a debt is not sufficient.

George Werner, Stan Fejta, and August Werner as well as two witnesses signed the following document:

Promissory Note

Werner Enterprises, Inc., by resolution and signature acknowledges that a debt of $8000.00 is owed to Mr. Stan Fejta (Fejta Construction Company) regarding the construction of "Pontchartrain Plaza," 1930 West End Park.

This note is payable at maturity on or before May 19, 1979, plus 10% (percent) interest.

Date: April 4, 1979

After unsuccessful attempts to collect this indebtedness, Fejta filed suit. Werner alleged that the writing was nothing more than an acknowledgment of a preexisting debt since it did not contain an unconditional promise to pay. The court held that examination of the entire writing showed a promise to pay. It was titled "Promissory Note" and stated it was "payable at maturity"; therefore, it was intended to be a promise to pay money.

Unconditional. The order or the promise must be absolute and unconditional. Neither must be contingent upon any other act or event. If Baron promises to pay Noffke $500 "in sixty days, or sooner if I sell my farm," the instrument is negotiable because the promise itself is unconditional. In any event there is a promise to pay the $500 in sixty days. The contingency pertains only to the time of payment, and that time cannot exceed sixty days. If the words "or sooner" were omitted, the promise would be conditional, and the note would be nonnegotiable. As stated previously, however, an instrument may be valid even though nonnegotiable.

If the order to pay is out of a particular fund or account, the instrument is normally nonnegotiable. For example, "Pay to the order of Leonard Cohen $5,000 out of my share of my mother's estate" would be a conditional order to pay. The order or the promise must commit the entire credit of the one primarily liable for the payment of the instrument. There is an exception made in the case of instruments issued by a government or a governmental agency or unit.

A reference to the consideration in a note that does not condition the promise does not destroy negotiability. The clause "This note is given in consideration of a typewriter purchased today" does not condition the maker's promise to pay. If the clause read, "This note is given in consideration for a typewriter guaranteed for ninety days, breach of warranty to constitute cancellation of the note," the instrument would not be negotiable. This promise to pay is not absolute, but conditional. Also, if the recital of the consideration is in such form as to make the instrument subject to another contract, the negotiability of the instrument is destroyed.

Koyt Everhart executed a note to Jane Everhart in which he promised to pay $150,000 "in lieu of a property settlement supplementing that certain Deed of Separation and Property Settlement . . . the terms of which are incorporated herein by reference." Jane signed a document prepared by James Booker and Oren McClain, her attorneys, which purported to assign one-third of the note to them. After default, they sued for collection of the note. For them to recover, the note had to be negotiable. It was not. Incorporating the Deed of Separation and Property Settlement into the note made it subject to any conditions in those documents, and therefore the promise was conditional. All the essential terms of the note could not be discovered from the face of it.

A Sum Certain in Money. The instrument must call for the payment of money. It need not be American money, but it must be some national medium of exchange. It cannot be in scrip, gold bullion, bonds, or similar assets. The instrument may provide for the payment of either money or goods. If the choice lies with the holder, such a provision does not destroy its negotiability.

Sixty days after date I promise to pay to the order of Ira Rasmussen $500 or 250 bushels of wheat at his option.

Signed—*Frances Birchmore*

This note is negotiable because it is at the option of the payee, Rasmussen, or any subsequent holder of the instrument. If the words "his option" were changed to read, "my option," the note would not be negotiable.

The sum payable must be a certain amount that is not dependent upon other funds or upon future profits.

In consideration for recommending Varney for a certain construction job, Fulton received the following instrument: ". . . we hereby agree to pay you the sum of $1,059 ninety days from date; the amount to be paid out of our profits on the 3 East 40th Street job." The statement on the note that the money was to be paid out of a particular fund destroyed its negotiability.

Not only must the contract be payable in money to be negotiable, but the amount must be certain from the wording of the instrument itself. If a note for $5,000 provides that all taxes which may be levied upon a certain piece of real estate will be paid, it is nonnegotiable. The amount to be paid cannot be determined from the note itself. A provision providing for the payment of interest or exchange charges, however, does not destroy negotiability. Other terms which have been held not to destroy negotiability are provisions for cost of collection, a 10 percent attorney's fee if placed in the hands of an attorney for collection, and installment payments.

Frequently, through error of the party writing the negotiable instrument, the words on the instrument may call for the payment of one amount of money, while the figures call for the payment of another. The amount expressed in words prevails because one is less likely to err in writing this amount. Also, if anyone should attempt to raise the amount, it would be much simpler to alter the figures than the words. By the same token, handwriting prevails over conflicting typewriting, and typewriting prevails over conflicting printed amounts.

Payable on Demand or at a Definite Time.

An instrument meets the test of negotiability as to time if it is payable on demand (as in a demand note) or at sight (as in a sight draft). If no time is specified (as in a check) the commercial paper is considered payable on demand.

If the instrument provides for payment at some future time, the due date must be fixed.

Vaughn gave Marx an instrument containing the following provision: "I promise to pay Marx the sum of $450 when my son reaches the age of twenty-one." Such a condition rendered the instrument nonnegotiable because the time of payment was dependent upon a condition that might not happen. In other words, Vaughn's son might never reach the age of twenty-one.

If Riggs promises to pay Burton $500 "sixty days after my marriage," the instrument is not payable at a fixed future time because the event is not certain to occur.

An instrument payable "thirty days after my death," is not negotiable. Even though the date is certain to arrive, the time is not definite.

In promissory notes there is often included either an acceleration clause or a prepayment clause. An acceleration clause is for the protection of the payee, and the prepayment clause is for the benefit of the party obligated to pay. A typical acceleration clause provides that in the event one installment is in default, the whole note shall become due and payable at once. This does not destroy its negotiability. Most prepayment clauses give the maker or the drawee the right to prepay the instrument in order to save interest. This does not affect the negotiability of the instrument.

Payable to Order or Bearer. The two most common words of negotiability are "order" and "bearer." The instrument is *payable to order* when some person is made the payee and the maker or drawer wishes to indicate that the instrument will be paid to the person designated or to anyone else to whom the payee may transfer the instrument by indorsement.

It is not necessary to use the word "order," but it is strongly recommended. The law looks to the intention of the maker or the drawer. If the words used clearly show an intention to pay either the named payee or anyone else whom the payee designates, the contract is negotiable. A note payable to "Smith and assigns" was held to be nonnegotiable. If it had been payable to "Smith or assigns," it would have been negotiable.

The other words of negotiability, *payable to bearer*, indicate that the maker or the acceptor of a draft is willing to pay the person who has possession of the instrument at maturity. The usual form in which these words appear is: "Pay to bearer" or "Pay to Lydia Lester or bearer." There are other types of wording that make an instrument a bearer instrument. For example, "pay to the order of cash," and "pay to the order of bearer," or any other designation which does not refer to a natural person or a corporation is regarded as payable to bearer.

Payee and Drawee Designated with Reasonable Certainty. When a negotiable instrument is payable "to order," the payee must be so named that the specific party can be identified with reasonable certainty. For example, a check which reads, "Pay to the order of the Treasurer of the Virginia Educational Association" is not payable to a specific named individual, but that person can be ascertained with reasonable certainty, and the check is negotiable. If, on the other hand, the check is payable "to the order of the Treasury of the Y.M.C.A." and there are three such organizations in the city, it would not be possible to ascertain with reasonable certainty who the payee is. This check would not be negotiable.

The drawee of a draft must likewise be named or described with reasonable certainty so that the holder will know who will accept or pay it.

Execution and Delivery

When a negotiable instrument is written by the drawer or maker, it does not have any effect until it is "issued," which ordinarily means that the drawer or maker mails it or hands it over to the payee or does some other act which releases control over it and sends it on its way to the payee. To negotiate order paper, it must be both indorsed by the person to whom the paper is then payable and delivered to the new holder. In the case of bearer paper no indorsement is required, and negotiation is effected by a physical transfer of the instrument alone.

Whenever delivery is made in connection with either the original issue or a subsequent negotiation, the delivery must be absolute, as contrasted with conditional. If it is conditional, the issuing of the instrument or the negotiation does not take effect until the condition is satisfied; although, as against a holder in due course, a defendant will be barred from showing that the condition was not satisfied.

Delivery of an Incomplete Instrument

If a negotiable instrument is only partially filled out and signed before delivery, the maker or drawer is liable if the blanks are filled in according to instructions. If the holder fills in the blanks contrary to authority, the maker or drawer is liable to the original payee or an ordinary holder for only the amount actually authorized. A holder in due course, however, can enforce the paper according to the terms as they were filled in even though they were not authorized.

Date and Place

Various matters which are not of commercial significance do not affect the negotiable character of a negotiable instrument.

The instrument need not be dated. The negotiability of the instrument is not affected by the fact it is undated, antedated, or postdated. The omission of a date may cause considerable inconvenience, but the date is not essential. The holder may fill in the correct date if the space for the date is left blank. If an instrument is due thirty days after date, and the date is omitted, the instrument is payable thirty days after it was issued or delivered. In case of dispute, the date of issue may be proved.

The name of the place where the instrument was drawn or where it is payable need not be specified. For contracts in general, one's rights are governed by the law where the contract is made or where it is to be performed. This rule makes it advisable for a negotiable instrument to stipulate the place where it is drawn and where it is payable, but neither is essential for its negotiability.

Questions

1. Must the signature of the maker on a negotiable contract be in the lower right-hand corner?

2. Must a draft contain the word *order* to be negotiable?

3. Will a reference to the consideration in a note destroy negotiability?

4. When must a negotiable instrument be payable?

5. Does an acceleration clause in a note destroy its negotiability?

6. Explain the difference between *payable to order* and *payable to bearer*.

7. Why is it important to designate the payee and drawee with reasonable certainty?

8. What does it mean to *issue* a negotiable instrument?

9. If a check is signed but not filled out and is then stolen and completed, is the drawer liable on it?

Case Problems

1. Kathryn McCain was employed near a safety deposit box to which she and other employees had access at the front desk of a motel. Money ($110) was stolen from the safety deposit box, and McCain was investigated as a suspect. Following a polygraph test, McCain was fired. She went to the motel to pick up a payroll check that was due her and was told $110 was to be withheld from her wages, pending the results of the police investigation. While there, she saw her payroll check and refused a check for the amount of her wages less $110. After being refused a written demand for the payroll check, she filed suit, alleging wrongful conversion of her payroll check. Conversion requires the taking or a detention, interference, illegal assumption of ownership, or illegal use or misuse of property. Was there a wrongful conversion?

2. An accepted time draft read as follows: "Sixty days after the presidential election, pay Adam Horton $2,700." Soon after its acceptance this draft was negotiated to the Cates Land Company as a partial payment for some timberland. When the draft came due, the drawee was bankrupt, and the Cates Land Company sought to make the drawer pay the $2,700. Was the draft properly negotiated to Cates?

3. Charles Cox, Morris Grossman, Thomas King, and Melvin Gittleman formed a partnership named G.G.C. Co. to build and operate an apartment complex. Cox, Grossman, and King then formed a corporation, also named G.G.C. Co., which was designated by the partnership as attorney-in-fact to secure financing for the complex. The corporation, Cox, Grossman, and King signed a promissory note in favor of First National Bank of St. Paul to secure a $1,250,000 loan. The corporation defaulted on the note and the Bank foreclosed on the complex. The Bank alleged that Gittleman should be liable on the note because he was a partner in the partnership which dominated the corporation which executed the note. Should he be liable?

4. Is the following note negotiable?

> Sixty days after Easter I obligate myself to pay Globe, Inc., or bearer, the sum of $5,000 out of the proceeds of the sale of my GMC stock.
>
> Glen Tinsdale

5. Is the following draft negotiable?

> To Lenox, Inc.
>
> At sixty days sight pay upon demand to John Ray $1,000 in gold bullion.
>
> Henry Adams

6. S. Gentilotti executed a check for $20,000 payable to the order of his son. It was postdated fifteen years and delivered to the boy's mother. Before his death, Gentilotti frequently asked the mother if she had the check. After his death demand for payment was made and refused. The mother and son sued the executrix of Gentilotti's estate for payment of the check. Was it negotiable?

23

Promissory Notes and Certificates of Deposit

Preview Cases

Massey made a note payable to Hess or order, and Hess indorsed the note to Frazier. Hess was a minor. When Massey refused to pay the note upon its due date, Frazier brought an action against her. Massey set up the defense that the minor was not competent to indorse the note to Frazier and therefore Frazier could not sue and recover on the note. Should Frazier be allowed to recover?

George Robinson bought a money market certificate from the West Greeley National Bank and named his stepdaughter, Loretta Wygant, as the pay-on-death (P.O.D.) beneficiary. He later married Hope Robinson and orally asked the bank to change the beneficiary to his wife. After Robinson died, Hope and Wygant both claimed the proceeds of the certificate. Wygant claimed the certificate was a negotiable instrument and her indorsement was required to change the beneficiary. Was the certificate negotiable?

Any written promise to pay money at a specified time is a promissory note, but it may not be a negotiable instrument. To be negotiable, a note must contain the essential elements discussed in Chapter 22.

It is not necessary to use the word "promise" in a note, but the substitute word or words must mean "promise." Such expressions as "I will pay" and "I guarantee to pay" have been held to constitute a "promise to pay."

The two original parties to a promissory note are the maker, the one who signs the note and promises to pay, and the payee, the one to whom the promise is made. A payee who transfers a note becomes an indorser.

Liability of the Maker

The maker of a promissory note (1) expressly agrees to pay the note according to its terms, (2) admits the existence of the payee, and (3) warrants that the payee is competent to transfer the instrument by indorsement.

Massey made a note payable to Hess or order, and Hess indorsed the instrument to Frazier. Hess was a minor. When Massey refused to pay the note upon its due date, Frazier brought an action against her. Massey set up the defense that the minor was not competent to indorse the note to Frazier and therefore Frazier could not sue and recover on the note. The court held that Frazier could recover. Massey, by making the note payable to Hess, a minor, warranted the competency of Hess to negotiate the paper.

Types of Notes

Many types of notes are known by special names. There are:

1. Bonds
2. Collateral notes
3. Real estate mortgage notes
4. Debentures

Bonds. A *bond* is a sealed, written contract obligation, generally issued by a corporation, a municipality, or a government, which contains a promise to pay a sum certain in money at a fixed or determinable future time. It will generally contain, in addition to the promise to pay, certain other conditions and stipulations. If it is issued by a corporation, it is generally secured by a deed of trust on the property of the corporation.

A bond is classified as a *security* by the Uniform Commercial Code. A bond may be a coupon bond or a registered bond.

A *coupon bond* is so called because the interest payments which will become due on the bond are represented by detachable individual coupons, which are to be presented for payment when due. Coupon bonds and the individual coupons are usually payable to the bearer; as a result, they can be negotiated by delivery, and there is no registration of the original purchaser or any subsequent holder of the bond.

A *registered bond* is a bond payable to a named person and is recorded under that name by the organization issuing it to guard against its loss or destruction. When a registered bond is sold, a record of the transfer to the new bondholder must be made under the name of the new holder of the bond. In contrast with the registered bond, a coupon bond may be payable to "bearer," in which case anyone in possession of the bond can require payment, and there is no registration of the name of the purchaser or any subsequent holder of the bond.

Collateral Notes. A *collateral note* is a note secured by personal property. The collateral usually consists of stock, bonds, or other written evidences of debt, or a security interest in tangible personal property which is given by the debtor to the payee-creditor. When the creditor is given possession of collateral, reasonable care must be taken of it, and the creditor is liable to the debtor for any loss resulting from lack of reasonable care. The transaction may vary in terms of whether the creditor keeps possession of the property as long as the debt is unpaid or whether, under some forms of security transactions, the debtor is allowed to keep possession of the property until default. Regardless of the form of the transaction, the property is freed from the claim of the creditor if the debt is paid. If the debt is not paid, the creditor may sell the property in the manner prescribed by law. The creditor must return to the debtor any excess of the sale proceeds above the debt, interest, and costs. If the sale of the collateral does not provide sufficient proceeds to pay the debt, the debtor is liable for any deficiency. If the creditor receives any interest, dividend, or other income from the property while it is held as collateral, such amount must be credited against the debt or returned to the debtor.

Real Estate Mortgage Notes. A *real estate mortgage note* is given to evidence a debt which the maker-debtor secures by giving to the payee a mortgage on real estate. As in the case of a real estate mortgage generally, the mortgagor-debtor retains possession of the property, but if the real estate is not freed by payment of the debt, the holder may proceed on the mortgage or the mortgage note to enforce the maker-mortgagor's liability as is more thoroughly described in Chapter 46.

Debentures. An unsecured bond or note issued by a business firm is called a *debenture*. A debenture, like any other bond, is nothing more nor less than a promissory note under seal. It may be embellished with gold-colored edges, but this does not in any way indicate its value. A debenture is usually negotiable in form, but like any other note, it is the wording, not its name, that determines whether or not it is negotiable.

Certificates of Deposit

While the Uniform Commercial Code does not classify a certificate of deposit as a note, it has all the elements of a note except it does not contain the word "promise." The UCC defines a *certificate of deposit* as "an acknowledgement by a bank of a receipt of money with an engagement to repay it." Normally the money is repaid with interest. A certificate of deposit is not a draft since it does not contain an order to pay.

George Robinson bought a money market certificate from the West Greeley National Bank and named his stepdaughter, Loretta Wygant, as the pay-on-death

(P.O.D.) beneficiary. He later married Hope Robinson and orally asked the bank to change the beneficiary to his wife. After Robinson died, Hope and Wygant both claimed the proceeds of the certificate. Wygant claimed the certificate was a negotiable instrument and her indorsement was required to change the beneficiary. In order to be negotiable, there must be an unconditional promise to pay. Here, the P.O.D. clause conditioned payment to Wygant on the death of Robinson; thus, it was not negotiable.

Questions

1. Must a promissory note contain the word "promise" to be enforceable?   No

2. Who are the two original parties to a note?

3. What are the obligations of the maker of a promissory note?

4. What is a bond and by whom are bonds usually issued?

5. What is the difference between a registered bond and a coupon bond?

6. (a) What is a collateral note?
   (b) Of what does the collateral usually consist?

7. Is a certificate of deposit a note?

Case Problems

1. Dolanson Company, a partnership, and the partners individually, executed a promissory note to C & S National Bank in order to finance some property. When the Bank sued them on the note, the partners alleged that C & S's president, Mills Lane, orally agreed to look solely to the property for payment of the note and not require the partners to pay until the property could be sold or refinanced. Would an oral agreement by Lane change the terms of the note?

2. Wenzel needed to repair his residence, and O'Neal, his daughter, gave him $582.20 to make the repairs. Upon receipt of the money Wenzel gave O'Neal a written instrument which stated, "Inasmuch as my daughter has put certain improvements on my house . . . I desire that she will be protected in her own right to the amount of said improvements. . . . This is to certify that O'Neal has put into said above described property (house) of her own money the sum of $582.20. [signed] H. S. Wenzel." Was this written instrument a note?

3. Peoples Protective Life Insurance Company sued to recover $50,000 deposited with the Bank of Alamo and represented by a certificate of deposit. The certificate stated:

Peoples Protective Life Insurance Company has deposited in this bank exactly $50,000 dollars payable to themselves in current funds on the return of this certificate properly endorsed 6 months after date with interest at the rate of 5½ per cent per annum for the time specified only.

s/Patricia Nolen

Authorized Signature

When the Bank was sued for payment of the certificate there was an issue as to whether it was a negotiable note. Was it?

4. Darter owned fifty $1,000 coupon bonds, the interest payable semiannually. On one of the due dates of the interest coupons, Darter detached them, intending to cash them at the bank. Before he did so, they were stolen, and the thief cashed them at the Bank of Fargo. Darter sued the bank for reimbursement, claiming it should not have paid the coupons to the thief. Was Darter correct in his contention?

24 Drafts

Preview Cases

At about three-thirty Friday afternoon, Maria Garcia purchased jewelry from Shaw's of San Antonio, Inc., by a check for $1,328.20 drawn on Groos National Bank. Before delivering the jewelry, Shaw's telephoned the Bank and was told the check was good. On Saturday Garcia returned to Shaw's and tried to buy more jewelry. Finding out that the address Garcia used on her check was nonexistent, Shaw's became suspicious and sent an employee to the Bank at nine o'clock Monday when it opened for business. There was not enough money in Garcia's account to pay the check. When Shaw's sued the Bank for payment the Bank alleged it was not liable because it had not accepted the check. Had there been a proper acceptance?

O'Kelly forged Cohen's name as drawer to a draft for $3,000 payable to Daro, who presented it to Nowicki for acceptance. Daro then transferred the draft by indorsement to Berger. Later Nowicki learned that Cohen's signature was forged and refused to pay the draft when it became due. May Nowicki avoid payment?

As mentioned previously, a draft is a written order signed by one person and requiring the person to whom it is addressed to pay on demand or at a particular time a sum certain in money to order or bearer. It must be clear that the signature is intended to be that of a drawer; otherwise the signature will be construed to be that of an indorser. A draft is drawn or executed by the drawer in favor of the payee, who has the drawer's authority to collect the amount indicated on the instrument. It is addressed to the drawee, who is the person ordered by the drawer to pay the amount of the instrument. The amount is paid to the payee or some other party to whom the payee has transferred the instrument by indorsement. The drawee, after accepting the instrument, that is, after agreeing to pay it, becomes the acceptor.

An *inland*, or *domestic, draft* is one that shows on its face that it is both drawn and payable within the United States. If the draft shows on its face that it is drawn or payable outside the United States, it is a *foreign draft*.

Forms of Drafts

There are two kinds of drafts to meet the different needs of business:

1. Sight drafts
2. Time drafts

Sight Drafts. A *sight draft* is a draft payable at sight or upon presentation by the payee or holder. By it the drawer demands payment at once. Money orders and checks are special types of sight drafts.

Time Drafts. A *time draft* has the same form as a sight draft except regarding the date of payment. The drawee is ordered to pay the money a certain number of days or months after the date on the instrument or a certain number of days or months after presentation.

In the case of a time draft, the holder cannot require payment of the paper until it has matured. The holder normally presents the draft to the drawee for acceptance. However, whether or not the draft has been accepted does not affect the time when it matures if it is payable a certain length of time after its date.

If the drawee is ordered to pay the draft a specified number of days after sight, it must be presented for acceptance because the due date is calculated from the date of the acceptance, not from the date of the draft.

Trade Acceptance

The *trade acceptance* is a type of draft. Its use is confined to the sale of goods. It is a draft drawn by the seller on the purchaser of goods sold, and accepted by such purchaser. It is drawn at the time the goods are sold. The seller is the drawer, and the purchaser is the drawee. A trade acceptance orders the purchaser to pay the face of the bill to the order of the named payee or to the order of the seller.

Use of Drafts

Negotiable instruments are called instruments of credit and instruments of collection. If *A* sells *B* merchandise on sixty days' credit, the buyer may at the time of the sale execute a sixty-day negotiable note or time draft in payment of the merchandise. This note or draft then is an instrument of credit. But negotiable instruments may also be used as credit obligations. A trade acceptance is a time draft used as a credit obligation of the drawee.

The seller fills out a trade acceptance and in most cases mails it to a bank in the buyer's hometown. The bank then presents it to the buyer for acceptance. The bank acts as an agent of the seller. When a negotiable note is used, the buyer fills out the note, signs it, and mails it to the seller. Both the trade acceptance and the note are instruments of credit.

If the seller in the transaction above is unwilling to extend the original credit to sixty days, a sight draft may be drawn on the buyer, who would be the drawee. In this case, the drawer may make a bank the payee, the bank being a mere agent of the drawer, or one of the seller's creditors may be made the payee so that an account receivable will be collected and an account payable will be paid all in one transaction. When the account receivable comes due, the buyer will mail a check, which is a particular type of sight draft, to the seller. In this example, the sight draft is an instrument of collection.

Presentment for Acceptance

All trade acceptances and all time drafts payable so many days after sight must be presented for acceptance by the payee to the drawee. In case of other kinds of drafts, presentment for acceptance is optional and is made merely to determine the intention of the drawee and to give the paper the additional credit strength of the acceptance. If an acceptance is qualified it destroys the negotiability of the instrument.

Place. The instrument should be presented at the drawee's place of business. If there is no place of business, it may be presented at the drawee's home or wherever the drawee may be found.

Party. It must be presented to the drawee or to someone authorized either by law or by contract to accept it. If there are two or more drawees, the draft must be presented to all of them unless one has authority to act for them all.

Form of Acceptance

The usual method of accepting a draft is to write on the face:
"Accepted
John Doe."
The word "accepted" and the drawee's name are all that is necessary to constitute a valid acceptance. If an acceptance on a sight draft is not dated, the holder may supply the date.

The drawee may use other words of acceptance, but the words used must indicate an intention to be bound by the terms of the instrument and must be written on the instrument.

If the drawee refused to accept the draft or to accept it in a proper way, the holder of the draft has no claim against the drawee but can return the draft to the drawer. Any credit given the drawer by the delivery of the draft is thereby canceled. If the draft is a trade acceptance, the refusal of the drawee to accept means that the buyer is refusing to go through with the financing terms of the transaction; unless some other means of financing or payment is agreed upon, the transaction falls through.

At about three-thirty Friday afternoon, Maria Garcia purchased jewelry from Shaw's of San Antonio, Inc., by a check for $1,328.20 drawn on Groos National Bank. Before delivering the jewelry, Shaw's telephoned the Bank and was told the check was good. On Saturday Garcia returned to Shaw's and tried to buy more jewelry. Finding out that the address Garcia used on her check was nonexistent, Shaw's became suspicious and sent an employee to the Bank at nine o'clock Monday when it opened for business. There was not enough money in Garcia's account to pay the check. When Shaw's sued the Bank for payment the Bank alleged it was not liable because it had not accepted the check. The court agreed saying that an acceptance must be in writing and on the instrument.

Presentment for Payment

All commercial paper must be presented either to the maker of the note or the acceptor of a draft, in order to get money for the paper. If, after presentment, the party to whom presentment was made fails to pay, it may be desirable to proceed against the drawer or indorsers.

Admissions of the Acceptor

When a draft is presented to a drawee for acceptance, it must be either accepted or returned. If it is not returned, the drawee is treated as having stolen the paper from the holder. By accepting the instrument the drawee assumes liability for the payment of the paper. This liability of the acceptor runs from the time that the paper is due until the statute of limitations bars the claim.

When the drawee accepts a draft, two admissions concerning the drawer are made:

1. That the signature of the drawer is genuine
2. That the drawer has both the capacity and the authority to draw the draft

The drawee, by accepting a draft, also admits the payee's capacity to indorse, but not the genuineness of the payee's indorsement.

Having made these admissions, the acceptor cannot later deny them against a holder of the instrument.

O'Kelly forged Cohen's name as a drawer to a draft for $3,000 payable to Daro, who presented it to Nowicki for acceptance. Daro then transferred the draft by indorsement to Berger. Later Nowicki learned that Cohen's signature was forged and refused to pay the draft when it became due. He could not avoid payment because he had admitted the genuineness of Cohen's signature when he accepted the draft. It was then too late to raise the defense of forgery against Berger. He could, of course, proceed against O'Kelly.

Acceptance by the Buyer's Financing Agency

Another financing technique employed in the sale of goods is "acceptance by the buyer's financing agency." As a variation of the pattern in which the buyer is the drawee of the trade acceptance, the buyer may arrange with a bank or finance company to accept the trade acceptance which the buyer will draw upon. When this is the case, the buyer will have worked out some loan or financing arrangements with the bank or finance company. The buyer will name the bank or finance company as drawee, and the bank or finance company will accept the draft. As in the case of any other kind of bank or finance company loan, the buyer may be required to furnish the bank or finance company with some form of security in order to induce it to make the loan and accept the instrument.

It is lawful to extend credit without any particular document being executed. For example, the corner grocery store allowing its customers to run up a bill which is paid at the end of the month and the department store which puts the purchases on a monthly charge account are both extending credit without any document. In contrast with these simple transactions, the creditor may require the debtor to sign loan papers and some form of commercial paper. The execution of commercial paper has the advantage of giving written proof of the amount due and also of giving the creditor something which can be resold more readily than an open account receivable can be assigned. That is, the manufacturer can sell a trade acceptance to a bank more readily than it can assign an account receivable which represents the purchase for which the trade acceptance is payment. The reason for this is that the holder of commercial paper is in a better legal position than the assignee of an account receivable.

Money Orders

A *money order* is an instrument issued by a bank, post office, or express company indicating that the payee may request and receive the amount indicated on the instrument. When paid for, issued, and delivered to the payee, there is a contract by the issuer to pay.

Questions

1. Name two types of drafts and indicate the characteristics of each.

2. What is a trade acceptance?

3. Must a time draft payable thirty days after sight be presented for acceptance?

4. Where and to whom should a draft be presented for acceptance?

5. Must a person write the word "accepted" on a draft in order to accept it?

6. When the drawee accepts a draft, what admissions are made concerning the drawer?

7. What technique is employed in the sale of goods which uses a bank or finance company as drawee?

Case Problems

1. National Bank of Austin sent North Valley Bank a letter authorizing North Valley to execute a sight draft on it for $75,000 within seven months. Based on that, North Valley loaned Donald Chambers $75,000 for six months. Chambers defaulted, so North Valley drew a draft on National for $75,000. The line for the signature of the drawer on the draft was blank; however, on the back was a stamp which said, "Pay to the Order of Any Bank, Banker or Trust Co. All Prior Endorsements Guaranteed. North Valley State Bank . . ." Also on the back was the signature of the vice-president of North Valley. National notified North Valley it would not honor the draft. North Valley sued. National alleged the instrument was not a draft because it did not contain a proper signature of the drawer. Did it?

2. Harold owed Jenkins $2,700. To pay it he drew a sixty-day time-sight (sixty days after sight) draft on Henderson, one of his customers. When Jenkins received the draft, dated April 2, she filed it. On June 1, she presented the draft to Henderson for payment. Henderson refused to pay it, claiming he should merely accept it since it had never been presented for acceptance. Did it need to be presented for acceptance?

3. Cotton States Mutual Insurance Company executed a draft payable to the order of B. C. Baum and drawn on First National Bank of Atlanta. When presented for payment the draft was not accepted. Baum then sued Cotton States for payment. Cotton States defended by saying the draft was conditional on acceptance, and since it was not accepted, Cotton States was not liable. Was this defense good?

4. Dalton owed Nasrabadi and Son $3,200. When the account came due, he was unable to pay it. He drew a time draft on Turner for $3,200 and sent it to

Nasrabadi and Son. Hand, the bookkeeper for Nasrabadi and Son, presented the draft to Turner for acceptance, and Turner wrote this on the draft: "The face of this draft is the correct amount I owe Nasrabadi and Son. A Turner." Was this a proper acceptance?

5. Thomas J. Granger executed the following instrument:

Chicago, Ill., April 10, 19—

At sixty days sight pay to the order of Charles Hudson five hundred dollars ($500) and charge the same to the account of
To Albert W. Morris
  St. Louis, Mo.   Thomas J. Granger

---

a. Must this draft be presented for acceptance?

b. To whom should it be presented?

c. When should it be presented?

d. If the drawee was out when it was presented and his secretary accepted it, would this be a proper acceptance?

e. The drawee took the draft, and the next day returned it by mail with this memo stapled to it: "I will pay this draft when it comes due. A. W. Morris." Was this a valid acceptance?

f. If the acceptance by Morris was not a valid acceptance, what may Hudson do to protect himself?

g. When Hudson received the draft with the acceptance written on a separate paper, he notified Granger that this was unsatisfactory and demanded that Granger pay him. Granger did this. Two months later Morris paid Hudson and Hudson accepted the money but never remitted it to Granger. Must Morris replace the $500 in Granger's account.

6. The draft on page 232 was sent by Security State Bank to Midland National Bank for collection.

Midland acknowledged receipt on October 4, but no date of presentment was written on the draft. Ronald Berklund attempted to pay on March 15 of the following year. In the lawsuit which followed, Clawson claimed that since Berklund never indicated the date of presentment, Clawson may supply the presentment date of October 4. He further alleged that since presentment was October 4, the due date was March 13 of the following year, 160 days after the 4th; therefore the draft was dishonored since payment was not attempted until March 15. Was he correct?

COLLECT DIRECTLY THROUGH MIDLAND NATIONAL BANK   559499
                                      Billings, Montana 59101

                                                        September 30, 19--

One Hundred Sixty (160) Days After Sight and Subject to Approval of Title

Pay to the
  Order of ____ Tim Clawson _____ $ 5,400.00
               ---Five Thousand Four Hundred and No/100---   DOLLARS

Consideration for Balance of bonus consideration - executing oil & gas lease

To: Ronald D. Berklund
    605 Midland Bank Bldg.   /s/ Ruth L. Berklund
    Billings, Montana 59101   Ruth L. Berklund

7. **a.** If the draft in the foregoing case read "At sight," would it require presentment for acceptance?

b. If this draft read "Ten days after date pay . . . ," would an acceptance be
necessary? If it were accepted on October 5, when would it be due?

25

Checks

Preview Cases

Mr. and Mrs. Charles Wilson signed and gave to Steven Anny, a real estate sales-man, printed forms of "offer to buy real estate" which Anny filled out. They also gave him a postdated check dated February 14 for $500 payable to the real estate company. On February 11, Anny visited Eileen Lewis, who owned the real estate the Wilsons wanted to buy, and after about two hours of discussion she accepted the offer. The offer stated the company had "Received from (the Wilsons) herein called Buyer, the sum of Five Hundred dollars ($500.00) evidenced by . . . per-sonal check" to be held as a deposit. Lewis did not examine the check and was not told that it was postdated. The next day Lewis called Anny and said she wanted to rescind. The Wilsons, the company, and Anny sued for breach of contract. Was Lewis liable?

Falk wrote out a check payable to Lytle. She later requested that her bank stop payment on it. The order was ignored and the check was paid. Falk sued the bank for the amount of the check. Will she recover?

A *check* is a draft drawn on a bank and payable on demand. It is basi-cally a sight draft, but there are differences between checks and other sight drafts. The drawee of a check is a bank instead of an individual or a busi-ness firm, as may be the case with other sight drafts. Just like a draft, a check is an order by the *drawer*, upon the *drawee*, to pay a sum of money to the order of another person, the *payee*. However, the drawer is a deposi-tor, a person who has funds deposited with a bank. A check is always drawn upon a bank as drawee and is always payable on demand.

The numbers at the bottom of a check (see Illustration 25-1) are printed in magnetic ink. The numbers identify the specific account and the bank which holds the account. Since the numbers are printed in magnetic ink, the check may be sorted by electronic data processing equipment. The

ILLUS. 25-1. Check

Federal Reserve System requires that all checks passing through its clearinghouses be imprinted with such identifying magnetic ink. In most cases, however, the drawee bank will accept checks which do not carry the magnetic ink coding. In fact, the validity of a check is not affected by the material upon which it is written.

Special Kinds of Checks

There are five special types of checks:

1. Certified checks
2. Cashier's checks
3. Bank drafts
4. Voucher checks
5. Traveler's checks

Certified Checks. A *certified check* is an ordinary check which an official of the bank, the drawee, has accepted by writing across the face of the check the word "certified," or some similar word, and signed. Either the drawer or the holder may have a check certified. The certification of the check by the bank has the same effect as an acceptance. It makes the bank liable for the payment of the check and binds it by the warranties which are made by an acceptor.

If the certification is obtained by a holder, it releases the drawer from liability. The rationale for releasing the drawer from liability is that the holder was willing to accept the obligation of the bank to pay rather than require payment at the time. Had payment been made, all other parties would have been discharged from all possible future liability. Having failed to free the other parties by accepting the certification in place of payment, the holder loses the right to proceed against the other parties.

Sherman Matney gave Garner a $10,000 check on a Grundy bank. Garner didn't want to cash the check and carry the cash while traveling, so he had it certified. Before Garner arrived at his destination, the bank failed, and its assets were insufficient to pay all its depositors. Garner received $4,000 from the bank on liquidation and sued Matney for the remaining $6,000. Garner could not recover. He chose to have the check certified and keep the money in the bank, thereby taking the risk.

Cashier's Checks. A check that a bank draws on its own funds and that is signed by the cashier or some other responsible official of the bank is called a *cashier's check*. It is accepted for payment when issued and delivered. Such a check may be used by a bank in paying its own obligations, or it may be used by anyone else who wishes to remit money in some form other than a personal check.

Bank Drafts. A *bank draft* is a check drawn by one bank on another bank. It is customary for banks to keep a portion of their funds on deposit with other banks. A bank, then, may draw a check on these funds as freely as any corporation may draw checks.

Voucher Checks. A *voucher check* is one with a voucher attached. The voucher lists the items of an invoice for which the check is means of payment. It is customary in business for the drawer of the check to write on the check such words as "In full of account," "For invoice No. 1622," or similar notations. These notations make the checks excellent receipts when they are returned to the drawer. A check on which additional space is provided for the drawer to make a notation for which the check is issued is sometimes referred to as a voucher check. A payee who indorses a check on which a notation has been made agrees to the terms of the check, which include the terms written in the notation by the drawer.

Traveler's Checks. A traveler's check is an instrument much like a cashier's check of the issuer except that it requires signature and countersignature by its purchaser. Traveler's checks are sold by banks and express companies and are payable on demand. The purchaser of traveler's checks signs each check once at the time of purchase and then countersigns it and fills in the name of the payee when the check is to be used.

◆ Charles Gray, who owned a wholesale grocery business, received an order from Ernie's Truck Stop for $4,900 worth of cigarettes. Gray delivered the cigarettes to Ernie's, which gave them to Joseph Faillance. Faillance paid Ernie's with $4,900 in American Express traveler's checks. Gray saw Faillance countersign the checks, but they were not dated or made payable to anyone. Ernie's gave the checks to Gray in payment for the cigarettes. The next day Gray turned them in to a bank and was refused payment because they were stolen. Gray sued American Express for payment. The court found that although an instrument need not be dated, the name of the payee is essential. Since the checks were incomplete, they were unenforceable.

Postdated Checks

A check which is drawn prior to the time it is dated is a *postdated check*. If it is drawn on June 21, but dated July 1, it is in effect a ten-day draft. There is nothing unlawful about a postdated check as long as it was not postdated for an illegal or fraudulent purpose. It is payable on demand on or any time after its date. As a practical matter the payee may refuse to accept it because payment is desired now rather than at a later date.

◆ Mr. and Mrs. Charles Wilson signed and gave to Steven Anny, a real estate salesman, printed forms of "offer to buy real estate" which Anny filled out. They also gave him a postdated check dated February 14 for $500 payable to the real estate company. On February 11, Anny visited Eileen Lewis, who owned the real estate the Wilsons wanted to buy, and after about two hours of discussion she accepted the offer. The offer stated the company had "Received from (the Wilsons) herein called Buyer, the sum of Five Hundred dollars ($500.00) evidenced by . . . personal check" to be held as a deposit. Lewis did not examine the check and was not told that it was postdated. The next day Lewis called Anny and said she wanted to rescind. The Wilsons, the company, and Anny sued for breach of contract. The court found a postdated check was merely a promise to pay in the future and not payment as had been recited in the offer. Lewis was entitled to rescind.

Bad Checks

If a check is drawn with intent to defraud the payee, the drawer is civilly liable, as well as subject to criminal prosecution in most states under so-called "bad check" laws. Usually these statutes state that if the check is not made good within a specific period, such as ten days, there is a presumption that the drawer originally issued the check with the intent to defraud.

Duties of the Bank

The bank owes several duties to its customer, the depositor-drawer. It must maintain secrecy regarding information acquired by the bank in connection with the depositor-bank relationship.

The bank also has the duty of comparing the signature on the depositor's checks with the signature of the depositor in the bank's files to make certain the signatures on the checks are valid. If the bank pays a check which does not have the drawer's signature, it is liable to the drawer for the loss.

Refusal of Bank to Pay. The bank is under a general contractual duty to its depositors to pay on demand all of their checks to the extent of the funds deposited to their credit. When the bank breaches this contract, it is liable to the drawer for damages. In the case of a draft other than a check, there is ordinarily no duty on the drawee to accept the draft or to make payment if it has not been accepted. Therefore, the drawee is not liable to the drawer when the draft is not paid.

Even if the normal printed form supplied by the bank is not used, the bank must pay a proper order by a depositor. Any written document which contains the substance of a normal printed check must be honored by the bank.

The liability of the drawee bank for improperly refusing to pay a check runs in favor only of the drawer. Even if the holder of the check or the payee may be harmed when the bank refuses to pay the check, a holder or payee has no right to sue the bank. However, the holder has a right of action against the person from whom the check was received. This right of action is based on the original obligation which was not discharged because the check was not paid.

A check which is presented more than six months after its date is commonly called a *stale check*, and a bank which acts in good faith may pay it; however, unless the check is certified, the bank is not required to pay it.

Stopping Payment. Drawers have the power of stopping payment of checks. After a check is issued, a drawer can notify the drawee bank not to pay it when it is presented for payment. This is a useful procedure when a check is lost or mislaid. A duplicate check can be written, and to make sure that the payee does not receive payment twice or that an improper person does not receive payment on the first check, payment on the first check can be stopped. Likewise, if payment is made by check and the payee defaults on the contract, payment on the check can be stopped, assuming that the payee has not cashed it.

A stop-payment order may be written or oral. However, if it is oral, the bank is bound by it only for fourteen calendar days unless confirmed in writing within that time. A written order is effective for no more than six months unless renewed in writing.

Unless there is a valid limitation on its liability, the bank is liable for the loss the depositor sustains when the bank makes payment on a check after receiving proper notice to stop payment. However, the depositor has the burden of proving the loss sustained.

Falk wrote out a check payable to Lytle. She later requested that her bank stop payment on it. The order was ignored and the check was paid. Falk sued the bank for the amount of the check. Falk did not recover because she was unable to show any damage as a result of the bank's payment of the check.

A depositor who stops payment without a valid reason is liable to the payee. The depositor is also liable for stopping payment with respect to any holder in due course or other party having the rights of a holder in due course unless payment is stopped for a reason that may be asserted against such a holder as a defense. The fact that the bank refuses to make payment because of the drawer's instruction does not make the case any different from any other instance in which the drawee refuses to pay, and the legal consequences of imposing liability upon the drawer are the same.

Usually it is only when the drawer has good cause with respect to the payee that payment is stopped. For example, the purchaser of goods may give the seller a check in advance payment for the goods. The seller may then declare the goods will not be delivered. The purchaser may stop payment on the check since the seller has no right to the check if the sales contract is not performed. Thus, the payee could not sue the drawer-purchaser for stopping payment on the check.

When the depositor makes use of a means of communication such as the telegraph to give a stop-payment notice, the bank is not liable if the notice is delayed in reaching the bank and the bank makes payment before receiving the notice. The depositor can, however, sue the telegraph company if negligence on its part can be shown.

A seller is always in a better position if a certified check of the buyer or a cashier's check from the buyer's bank is required because neither the buyer nor the buyer's bank can stop payment to the seller on such checks.

Payment after Depositor's Death. Usually a check is ineffective after the drawer dies. However, until the bank knows of the death and has had a reasonable opportunity to act, the bank's agency is not revoked; and the bank may even continue to pay or certify the depositor's checks for ten days unless a person claiming an interest in the estate orders it to stop.

Questions

1. What is a check?

2. Is it necessary for a check to have numbers printed in magnetic ink?

3. If the holder of a check has it certified, who is liable for its payment?

4. If one bank has some of its funds deposited in another bank and draws a check on these funds, what is this type of check called?

5. What is a *voucher check?*

6. If the drawer's signature is forged on a check and the check is cashed, must the bank reimburse the depositor?

7. Does a payee of a check have a cause of action against a bank which, without giving any reason for its refusal, refuses to honor a check when presented for payment?

8. May a stop-payment order be oral?

Case Problems

1. Hartsfield owed Caspari $1,900. She wrote on a postcard these words:

   The First National Bank
   Pay to the order of J. A. Caspari $1,900

   > Cordially yours,
   > A. W. Hartsfield.

   She put a stamp on this postcard and mailed it to Caspari. Caspari thought a check had to be written on a printed check form. He discarded the postcard and demanded Hartsfield pay $1,900. Was he correct?

2. Davison drew a check on June 7 payable to Lester Hardware Company. He dated the check June 12 and asked the Lester Hardware Company to hold the check until June 12 before cashing it, stating the money to pay it would be in the bank at that time. The Lester Hardware Company deposited the check on June 8, and it was returned marked "Insufficient Funds." Davison was indicted for giving a bad check. Was he guilty? *No*

3. Teffera orally notified her bank on February 6 to stop payment on a check. The holder of the check presented it to the bank on February 22 and the bank paid it. Teffera sued the bank for paying the check after receiving a valid stop-payment order. Decide the case. *Oral - 14 day limit*

4. Erma Brown, who owed taxes to the state, purchased from the Bank of the Commonwealth on August 29 a cashier's check payable to the state. On May 17 of the following year, the state served a warrant-notice of levy on the Bank advising it of Brown's debt. On May 22, at one of the Bank's branches, Brown indorsed the check to herself and received full payment. The state sued the Bank, alleging that once a cashier's check has been issued it cannot be countermanded. Could the cashier's check be cancelled by Brown and the Bank?

5. Robert Kaiser rented space from Northwest Shopping Center, Inc., under a lease which gave Kaiser the exclusive right to operate a pharmacy in the shopping center. The term expired on December 31, but a letter gave Kaiser the right to extend at an increased rental of $750. Another letter, dated January 22 after the original termination date, told Kaiser that he was a month-to-month tenant at $600 per month because he had not extended. Starting in January after the original termination date, Kaiser sent checks in the amount of $750, but Northwest held Kaiser's rent checks while it negotiated with another tenant which wanted to put in a pharmacy. The negotiations collapsed, so in October Northwest presented the checks to Kaiser's bank. It refused to honor some because they were stale. Northwest sued. Kaiser alleged that since the checks were held more than a reasonable time, they and the underlying debt were discharged. Were they?

26

Liabilities of the Parties to Commercial Paper

Preview Cases

Mr. and Mrs. Giarraputo executed a promissory note in favor of Dusheke, who indorsed it to Collins. The note was delivered to Peterson for collection. The Giarraputos had moved, leaving no address, so presentment for payment was not made. Notice of dishonor was given to Dusheke. Collins sued Dusheke for payment of the note. Was Dusheke liable?

Community Bank and Trust loaned Pitrolo Pontiac Company $400,000, and Paul and Janice Pitrolo executed a "Guarantee of Payment" of the promissory note. Pitrolo Pontiac defaulted and Community sued the Pitrolos as guarantors. They asserted they were not liable on the note because it was a corporate note, and they did not receive any direct consideration for signing. Did the lack of consideration relieve the Pitrolos from liability?

The law of commercial paper imposes liability upon parties to negotiable instruments based upon: the nature of the paper; the role of the party as maker, acceptor, indorser, or transferor; and the satisfaction of certain requirements of conduct by the holder of the instrument. There are two basic categories of liability incidental to commercial paper: (1) the liability created by what is written on the face of the paper (contractual liability), and (2) the liability for certain warranties regarding the instrument which, unless such warranties are specifically excluded, the law of commercial paper automatically charges every transferor of commercial paper with making.

Liability for the Face of the Paper

Two types of liability exist regarding the order or promise written on the face of the instrument: primary liability and secondary liability. Parties whose signatures do not appear on the paper are not liable for its payment.

Primary Liability. A person who is primarily liable may be called upon to carry out the specific terms indicated on the paper. Of course, the paper must be due, but no other conditions need be met by the holder of commercial paper prior to the demand being made upon one who is primarily liable. Makers of notes and drawees of drafts are the two parties who ordinarily have the potential of primary liability on commercial paper.

The maker of a note is primarily liable and may be called upon for payment. The maker has intended this by the unconditional promise to pay. Such a promise to pay contrasts sharply with the terms used by drawers of drafts who order drawees to pay.

The drawer of a draft does not expect to be called upon for payment; the drawer expects that payment will be made by the drawee. However, it would be unreasonable to expect that the drawee could be made liable by a mere order of another party, the drawer. Understandably then, the drawee of a draft who has not signed the instrument has no liability on it. Only when a drawee accepts a draft by writing "accepted" and signing it does liability on the instrument arise. By acceptance the drawee in effect says, "I promise to pay. . . ." This acceptance renders the drawee primarily liable just as the maker of a note is primarily liable.

Secondary Liability. Indorsers and drawers are the parties whose liability on commercial paper is ordinarily secondary. Generally, three conditions must be met for a party to be held secondarily liable:

1. The paper must be properly presented for payment.
2. The paper must be dishonored.
3. Notice of the dishonor must be given to the party who is to be held secondarily liable.

When the conditions of secondary liability—presentment, dishonor, and notice of dishonor—have been met, a holder may require payment by any of the indorsers who have not limited their liability by the type of indorsement used or by the drawer.

Presentment. Presentment is the demand for acceptance or payment made upon the maker, acceptor, drawee, or other payor of commercial paper. In order for indorsers to remain secondarily liable, the instrument must be properly presented. This means the instrument should be presented to the right person, in a proper and timely manner. Presentment of instruments on which there is a specified date for payment should be made on that date. Other instruments must be presented for payment within a reasonable time after a party becomes liable on the instrument. The nature of the instrument, existing commercial usage, and the particular facts of the case determine what length of time is reasonable. The Uniform Commercial Code specifies that for drawers on uncertified checks, a presentment within thirty days after the date of the check or the date it was issued, whichever is later, is presumed to be reasonable. As to indorsers, the UCC specifies presentment within seven days of the indorsement is presumed to be reasonable. Drawers and makers of instruments payable at a bank who are deprived of funds to cover the instruments because the bank fails after the time when presentment should have been made are excused from secondary liability for lack of proper presentment if the drawers or makers assign in writing to the holders their rights against the bank to the extent of the funds lost.

◆   Reynolds was the holder of a note made by Agee in favor of Gerig. On the date the note came due, Reynolds failed to demand the funds from Agee. When he later requested the money, Agee was unable to pay. Reynolds then demanded the amount from Gerig, who had indorsed the note to Reynolds. Gerig successfully defends against liability because Reynolds failed to make presentment to Agee on the due date.

Later Agee inherits a large sum from her rich uncle. At this time Reynolds can again demand payment from Agee, who, as a primary party, remains liable unless the statute of limitations has run.

Proper presentment is not a condition to secondary liability on a note when the maker has died or has been declared insolvent. In the case of a draft, presentment is not required if it is the drawee or acceptor who has died or gone into insolvency proceedings. Commercial paper may contain terms specifying that the indorsers and the drawer agree to waive their rights to the condition of presentment. Further, the holder is excused from the requirement of presentment if, after diligent effort, the drawee of a draft or the maker of a note cannot be located.

◆   Mr. and Mrs. Giarraputo executed a promissory note in favor of Dusheke, who indorsed it to Collins. The note was delivered to Peterson for collection. The Giarraputos had moved, leaving no address, so presentment for payment was not made. Notice of dishonor was given to Dusheke. Collins sued Dusheke for payment of the note. Dusheke is liable for payment because Peterson had exercised proper diligence in attempting to make presentment by going to the Giarraputos' last known address and questioning neighbors as to the Giarraputos' current address.

Finally, if the secondary party knows that the draft or note will not be paid or has no reason to believe that the paper will be honored, presentment is excused.

Dishonor. The UCC states that dishonor occurs when a presentment is made and a due acceptance or payment is refused or cannot be obtained within the prescribed time.

Notice of Dishonor. A holder desiring to press secondary liability upon an indorser or drawer must inform that party of the dishonor. Notice of dishonor must be conveyed promptly to parties who are secondarily liable. The UCC provides that such notice shall be given by midnight of the third business day following the dishonor or receipt of notice of dishonor. This time limit applies to all holders except banks. The UCC requires that a bank give notice of dishonor to those it wishes to hold liable by midnight of the next banking day following the day in which it receives notice of dishonor. In order to avoid unduly burdening holders, the UCC provides that notice may be given by mail and that proof of mailing conclusively satisfies the requirement that notice be given.

Generally, notice of dishonor does not need to be in any special form. However, if the dishonored instrument is drawn or payable outside the United States of America, notice of dishonor must be certified by a public official authorized to do so. This requirement is known as *protest*.

Delay or failure to give notice of dishonor is excused in most cases where timely presentment would not have been required. Basically, this is when notice has been waived, when notice was attempted with due diligence but was unsuccessful; or if the party to be notified had no reason to believe that the instrument would be honored.

Liability of Agents.
If certain conditions are met, a negotiable instrument may be signed by an agent, and the principal, not the agent, will be bound. If the agent, authorized by the principal, signs the instrument, "John Smith, Principal, by Jane Doe, Agent," or more simply, "John Smith by Jane Doe," the principal will be bound, but the agent will not be bound by the terms of the instrument.

There are three general types of situations in which the agent could carelessly sign the instrument. The result would be that the agent would be bound while the principal might not be bound.

1. The agent could sign the instrument in such a way that the instrument did not name the principal, nor indicate that it was signed by an agent. For example, if the agent simply signed, "Jane Doe," the principal would not be bound, since the principal's signature does not appear on the instrument. The agent would be bound because there was nothing to indicate that she did not sign in her own capacity.

2. The agent could sign the instrument in such a way that the principal was named, but it was not shown that the agent was acting merely as an agent. If the agent signed, "John Smith and Jane Doe," the agent and the principal would both be bound. The agent would be bound because she did not indicate that she was an agent, and the other party to the instrument might have relied on the signature of the agent as an individual.

3. The agent could sign the instrument in such a way that the principal was not named, but it would be clear that the agent signed as an agent. Such a case would occur if the agent signed, "Jane Doe, Agent." In this

situation, only the agent would be bound by the instrument since it would not be evident from the face of the instrument who the principal might be. However, in these last two examples, if the parties to the instrument knew that John Smith was the principal and Jane Doe was merely an agent, then only the principal would be bound on the instrument.

In the case of a corporation or other organization, the authorized agent should sign above or below the corporation or organization's name and indicate the position held after the signature. For example, Edward Rush, the president of Acme Industries should sign:

> ACME INDUSTRIES
> By Edward Rush, President.

If the instrument were signed this way, Acme Industries, not Edward Rush, would be bound.

If an individual signs an instrument as an agent, "John Smith, Principal, by Jane Doe, Agent," but the agent is not authorized to sign for the principal, the principal would not be bound. It would be as if the agent, Jane Doe, had forged John Smith's signature. However, the agent who made the unauthorized signature would be bound. This protects innocent parties to the instrument who would not be able to enforce their rights against anyone if the unauthorized agent was not bound.

Guarantors. Indorsers can escalate their liability to primary status by indorsing an instrument "Payment guaranteed." If the transferor indorses the instrument with the words "Collection guaranteed," secondary liability is preserved. However, the contingencies which must be met by the holder in order to hold this type of guarantor liable are changed from presentment, dishonor, and notice of dishonor to obtaining against the maker or acceptor a judgment which cannot be satisfied.

People usually act as guarantors in order to increase the security of commercial paper. Frequently, if someone who is liable has a poor credit rating, the instrument could not be negotiated without having an additional party sign as a guarantor of the instrument.

◆   Community Bank and Trust loaned Pitrolo Pontiac Company $400,000, and Paul and Janice Pitrolo executed a "Guarantee of Payment" of the promissory note. Pitrolo Pontiac defaulted and Community sued the Pitrolos as guarantors. They asserted they were not liable on the note because it was a corporate note, and they did not receive any direct consideration for signing. The court held that lack of consideration merely established them as accommodation guarantors. Accommodation guarantors agree to pay if the principal debtor defaults. They sign the instrument for the purpose of lending their names to the other party to it. The liability of an accommodation guarantor is supported by the consideration received by the principal debtor. The Pitrolos were, therefore, liable on the note.

Warranties of the Transferor of Commercial Paper

Every transferor of commercial paper warrants the existence of certain facts. It is significant to note that one's signature or even one's name does not have to appear on the instrument in order to be liable as a warrantor, as for example, when a person negotiates bearer paper by delivery alone.

The UCC specifies that each unqualified transferor who receives consideration warrants that:

1. The transferor has good title to the instrument, authorization to obtain acceptance or payment on behalf of the rightful owner, and that the transfer is otherwise rightful.
2. All signatures are genuine or authorized.
3. The instrument has not been materially altered.
4. No defense of any party is good.
5. The transferor has no knowledge of any insolvency proceedings instituted with respect to the maker or acceptor or the drawee of an unaccepted instrument.

Questions

1. What is the difference between primary and secondary liability?

2. What two parties to commercial paper might be primarily liable?

3. What conditions must be met in order for a party to be held secondarily liable?

4. If there is no specified date for payment, when must an instrument be presented for payment?

5. When does a dishonor occur?

6. To whom must notice of dishonor be given?

7. Under what circumstances would an agent rather than a principal be bound on a negotiable instrument?

8. If someone signs a commercial paper as guarantor, what is the effect of this act:
   a. if the words "Payment guaranteed" are used?
   b. if the words "Collection guaranteed" are used?

9. What warranties are made by a transferor of commercial paper?

Case Problems

1. Betty Jean Wright and her husband, Verlon, opened a joint checking account at the Commercial Savings Bank in the name of Level Building Supply. Either party could draw on the account with only one signature. After Betty Jean and Verlon had marital problems, Verlon instructed the Bank to remove Betty Jean's name from the account, which it did. Betty Jean went to the Bank and asked for a counter check to withdraw $500 from the account. The teller refused because her name was no longer on the account. Betty Jean sued the Bank, alleging wrongful dishonor because it refused to issue the counter check. Was there a wrongful dishonor?

2. Ashby, who was the agent of Bridges, signed a promissory note "Bridges by Ashby, agent." When the note came due, Bridges was unable to pay. Is Ashby liable on the note?

3. Gus Stathis agreed to sell real estate to Edgar, Rintz, and Grandinetti and as consideration received a promissory note for $575,000 executed by the purchasers and their wives. This debt was secured by First Arlington National Bank's letter of credit which guaranteed payment of $575,000 upon default of the note if Stathis indorsed the note to the Bank. There was default in the payment of interest. When Stathis sought payment on the letter of credit and presented the indorsed note, the Bank refused to pay. In a lawsuit over payment of the letter of credit, the Bank contended that the warranties of transferors of negotiable instruments were applicable because Stathis was required to transfer the note to it. Were they?

4. Fritz wanted to buy some new furniture but did not have an established credit rating. She and her uncle, Schmidt, decided that Fritz would execute a note for the price of the furniture in favor of Schmidt, who would then indorse it "collection guaranteed" to the furniture company. Fritz failed to pay the note. What must the furniture company do in order to make Schmidt pay the note?

5. Stancel Kirkland was an indorser on a note given by Cecil Development Company, Inc., to American Bank and Trust Company. He was an officer in the Company, owned 30 percent of its stock, and served as its attorney. The note was not paid when due, and the Bank did not present it to Cecil Development nor give written notice of dishonor to Kirkland, who knew of the default. The Bank sued Kirkland for payment of the note. Kirkland alleged that as an accommodation indorser he was discharged by the failure of the Bank to make presentment and give him notice of dishonor. Was he discharged?

6. The Harbin Hosiery Mills, Inc., was a family-owned corporation. The president, James Harbin, borrowed $50,000 from the bank on a six-month note. He signed the note:

James Harbin, Owner
Harbin Hosiery Mills, Inc.

His intention was to commit the credit of the corporation for the loan, but not his personal estate. The corporation went into bankruptcy, and the note was unpaid. The bank sued, contending that James Harbin was personally liable on this note. Is he personally liable?

27

Negotiation and Discharge

Preview Cases

Mahmoud Halloway bought an insurance policy from Home Life Insurance Company through Home's field underwriter for $2,551. He executed and delivered a note for that amount payable to Madison Bank & Trust Company, and Duane Wolfram, the manager of a branch office of Home, signed the note "without recourse" as an accommodation party. When Halloway defaulted on the note, Wolfram paid the $2,551. Halloway refused to reimburse Wolfram. Wolfram sued Halloway, who alleged that Wolfram had had no obligation to pay the note because he had indorsed it "without recourse." Did the qualified indorsement absolve the indorser from liability on the instrument?

Hale drew a check payable to Shane in the amount of $500. Shane cleverly altered the check to $2,500 and negotiated it to McFain, an innocent purchaser who had no knowledge of the alteration. The bank refused to pay the check. From whom may McFain recover?

Negotiation is the transfer of a negotiable instrument in such a way that the transferee becomes the holder of the instrument. Bearer instruments may be negotiated by delivery. Delivery effectively vests ownership in the transferee. In practice an indorsement is usually required even for bearer paper because this adds the liability of the new indorser to the paper and thus makes it a better credit risk. It also preserves a written chronological record of all negotiations. If the instrument is payable to "order," there can be a negotiation only by indorsement and delivery. By indorsing or transferring a negotiable instrument, certain liabilities are created, depending upon the nature of the indorsement or transfer.

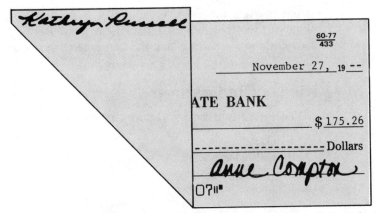

ILLUS. 27-1. An indorsed check folded to show the position of the indorsement

Place of Indorsement

The usual place to indorse a negotiable instrument is on the back of the form. (See Illustration 27-1.) If the indorser's signature appears elsewhere and it cannot be determined in what capacity the signature was made, it will be considered an indorsement. In any event, the indorsement must be on the instrument or on a paper firmly attached to it. An *allonge* is a paper so firmly attached to an instrument as to become a part of it. If a party does not wish to be liable as an indorser, the instrument can be assigned by a written assignment on a separate piece of paper.

Occasionally, the name of the payee or indorsee of an instrument is misspelled. If a paycheck intended for, and delivered to, John F. Smith is made out to "John K. Smith" through clerical error, John F. Smith may ask his employer for a new check properly made out to him or he may keep the check and indorse in any of the following ways:

1. "John K. Smith"
2. "John F. Smith"
3. "John K. Smith, John F. Smith"

If he intends to receive value for the check, the person to whom it is negotiated may require him to sign both names.

However, if a check made payable to, and intended for, John K. Smith is obtained by John F. Smith, it would be illegal for the latter to indorse it and receive payment for it. Only when the check is actually intended for John F. Smith may he make a corrective indorsement.

It is not always necessary to correct an irregularity in the name of a party to an instrument. An irregularity does not destroy negotiability. Only if it is shown that different people were actually identified by the different names, as opposed to the different names standing for one person, must the irregularity be considered. It has been held that a note was correctly negotiated when indorsed "Greenlaw & Sons by George M. Greenlaw," although it was payable to "Greenlaw & Sons Roofing & Siding Co." There was nothing to indicate that the two enterprises were not the same firm.

Kinds of Indorsements

There are four types of indorsements:

1. Blank indorsements
2. Special indorsements
3. Qualified indorsements
4. Restrictive indorsements

Blank Indorsements. As the name indicates, a *blank indorsement* is one having no words other than the name of the indorser. (See Illustration 27-2.) If the instrument is bearer paper, it remains bearer paper when a blank indorsement is made. Thus, the new holder may pass good title to another holder without indorsing the instrument. The one primarily liable on the instrument is bound to pay the person who presents it for payment on the date due, even if the person is a thief or other unauthorized party.

If the instrument is order paper, a blank indorsement converts it to bearer paper; if it is thereafter indorsed specially, it becomes order paper again. Risks involved in handling instruments originally payable to bearer or indorsed in blank can be minimized as shown in the following paragraph and in the section on special indorsements.

If the office force of a business firm is aware of these risks relative to bearer paper and paper indorsed in blank, the firm may be spared these risks in the following ways: (1) The drawer, if it is convenient, can be requested to make the instrument order paper from its inception; (2) if the firm becomes the indorsee by a blank indorsement, this indorsement may be converted to a special indorsement by writing over the indorser's signature these words: "Pay to the order of Mays, Inc." The instrument cannot now be negotiated except by indorsement and delivery. This in no way alters the contract between the indorser and the indorsee.

Special Indorsements. A *special indorsement* designates the particular person to whom payment is to be made. (See Illustration 27-2.) After such

ILLUS. 27-2. Blank Indorsement and Special Indorsement

an indorsement is made, the paper is order paper, whether or not it was originally so payable or was originally payable to bearer. The holder must indorse it before it can be further negotiated. Of course, the holder may indorse the instrument in blank, which makes it bearer paper. Each holder has the power to decide to make either a blank or a special indorsement.

Qualified Indorsements. A *qualified indorsement* has the effect of qualifying, that is, limiting the liability of the indorser. This type of indorsement is usually used when the payee of an instrument is merely collecting the funds for another. For example, if an agent receives checks in payment of the principal's claims but the checks are made payable to the agent personally, the agent can and should elect to use a qualified indorsement. This is done merely by adding to either a blank or special type of indorsement the words "without recourse" immediately before the signature. (See Illustration 27-3.) This releases the indorser from liability for payment if the instrument is not paid because of insolvency or mere refusal to pay. However, the indorser still warrants that the signatures on the instrument are genuine, that the indorser has good title to the instrument, that the instrument has not been altered, that no defenses are good against the indorser, and that the indorser has no knowledge of insolvency proceedings with respect to the maker, acceptor, or drawer (as was mentioned in Chapter 26). The agent may avoid these warranties as well by indorsing the instrument "without recourse or warranties."

ILLUS. 27-3. Qualified Indorsement and Restrictive Indorsement

Henderson was a special agent for the Cates Realty Company. One of his duties was to collect the rent from the occupants of rental properties handled by the Cates Realty Company. One of these tenants made a check for the rent payable to "John Henderson." When Henderson turned in his receipts at the end of the day, the accounting department asked him to indorse the check by special indorsement to the Cates Realty Company. This he did. The check was returned because the drawer had no funds in the bank to pay it. The Cates Realty Company demanded that Henderson make good on his special indorsement. This he must do. He should have indorsed this by a qualified indorsement.

Restrictive Indorsements. A *restrictive indorsement* is an indorsement which attempts to prevent the use of the instrument for anything except the stated use. (See Illustration 27-3.) The indorsement may state that the indorsee holds the paper for a special purpose or as an agent or trustee for another or it may impose a condition precedent to payment. Such an indorsement does not prohibit further negotiation of the instrument. As against a holder in due course, it is immaterial whether the restrictions have in fact been recognized by the indorsee.

Liability of Indorser

By indorsing a negotiable instrument, a person can become secondarily liable for payment of the face amount and responsible for certain warranties.

Liability for Payment of Instrument. By making an indorsement, an indorser, with the exception of a qualified indorser, agrees to pay any subsequent holder the face amount of the instrument if the holder presents the instrument to the primary party when it is due and the primary party refuses to pay. The holder must then give the indorser in question notice of such default. This notice may be given orally or it may be given by any other means, but it must be given before midnight of the third full business day after the day on which the default occurs.

Warranties of the Indorser. Warranties of the indorser were listed at the end of Chapter 26. They differ from liability for the face of the paper in that they are not subject to the requirements of presentment and notice. The distinction is also important for purposes of limiting liability; for an indorsement "without recourse" destroys only the liability of the indorser for the face of the instrument. It does not affect all warranties. Such an indorsement does limit the warranty that there are no good defenses. This becomes a warranty that the indorser has no knowledge of any good defenses. The indorsement does not limit the other warranties. An indorsement "without warranties" or a combined "without recourse or warranties" is required to exclude warranty liability.

Mahmoud Halloway bought an insurance policy from Home Life Insurance Company through Home's field underwriter for $2,551. He executed and delivered a note for that amount payable to Madison Bank & Trust Company, and Duane Wolfram, the manager of a branch office of Home, signed the note "without recourse" as an accommodation party. When Halloway defaulted on the note, Wolfram paid the $2,551. Halloway refused to reimburse Wolfram. Wolfram sued Halloway, who alleged that Wolfram had had no obligation to pay the note because he had indorsed it "without recourse." The court held that the qualified indorsement did not necessarily absolve the indorser from liability on the instrument because it does not protect from liability for breach of warranty.

Obligation of Negotiator of Bearer Paper

Bearer paper need not be indorsed when negotiated. Mere delivery passes title. One who negotiates a bearer instrument by delivery alone does not guarantee payment, but is liable to the immediate transferee as a warrantor of the genuineness of the instrument, of title to it, of the capacity of prior parties, and of its validity. These warranties are the same as those made by an unqualified indorser, except that the warranties of the unqualified indorser extend to all subsequent holders, not just to the immediate purchaser. But since negotiable instruments are not legal tender, no one is under any obligation to accept bearer paper without an indorsement. By requiring an indorsement even though not necessary to pass title, the holder is protected by requiring the one who wishes to negotiate it to assume all the obligations of an indorser.

Discharge of the Obligation

Negotiable instruments may be discharged by payment, by cancellation, by renunciation, or by alteration. Payment at or after the date of the maturity of the instrument by the party who is primarily liable constitutes proper payment. Cancellation consists of any act that indicates the intention to destroy the validity of the instrument. A cancellation is not effective, however, when it is made unintentionally, without authorization, or by mistake. A holder of several negotiable instruments might intend to cancel one upon its payment and inadvertently cancel an unpaid one. This does not discharge the unpaid instrument. Renunciation is a unilateral act of a holder of an instrument, usually without consideration, whereby the holder gives up rights on the instrument or against one or more parties to the instrument. A party to a negotiable instrument is discharged from liability if the instrument is materially altered without consent. If such an instrument gets into the hands of a holder in due course, however, the holder in due course may collect according to the original terms of the instrument, but not according to its altered terms.

Hale drew a check payable to Shane in the amount of $500. Shane cleverly altered the check to $2,500 and negotiated it to McFain, an innocent purchaser who had no knowledge of the alteration. The bank refused to pay the check. McFain can recover $500 from Hale, since this was the original amount of the check. He could then sue Shane for the $2,000.

The obligations of the parties may be discharged in other ways, just as in the case of a simple contract. For example, parties will no longer be held liable on instruments if their debts have been discharged in bankruptcy or if there has been the necessary lapse of time provided by a statute of limitations.

A negotiable instrument may be lost or accidentally destroyed. This does not discharge the obligation. A party obligated to pay an instrument has a right to demand its return if this is possible. If this cannot be done, then the payor has a right to demand security from the holder adequate to protect the payor from having to pay the instrument a second time. The security usually takes the form of an indemnity bond.

Questions

1. What is *negotiation?*

2. How are instruments payable to "order" negotiated?

3. Can an indorsement of an instrument be on a totally separate writing?

4. Name four kinds of indorsements and give an example of the proper use of each one.

5. Why is it usually undesirable to indorse a check in blank?

6. If an instrument that is payable to "bearer" is indorsed by special indorsement, what must the second holder do in order to negotiate it?

7. If a check is indorsed "without recourse," is the indorser absolved from all liability on the instrument?

8. If one loses a negotiable instrument, is there any way it can be collected?

Case Problems

1. Louis Chiodo filed a claim against the estate of his brother, Anthony Chiodo, for repayment of a loan of $1,000. When the estate disputed such a loan, Louis Chiodo produced a check made out to Anthony. The word "labor" was scratched out and "loan to be replaced when possible" was written on the top of the check. This had been done by Louis after the check had cleared the banking system and had been returned to him. The estate argued that the check was materially altered and therefore could be enforced only according to its original terms which bore the word "labor," indicating it was given by Louis to his brother for "labor" and not as a loan. Was this argument valid?

2. Wood was the payee of a time draft for $3,200. He mailed the draft to James Hill for collection. Wood indorsed the draft as follows: "Pay to the order of James Hill only." Hill collected the draft and placed the $3,200 in his personal checking account and mailed his personal check to Wood. Hill owed the bank a note for $5,000 that was past due. It refused to honor any more

checks on Hill's account and applied his balance to the note. Indicate specifically what errors Wood committed.

3. Richards owed Griffith $4,000. He executed a negotiable note as follows: Ninety days after date I promise to pay to Bearer $4,000 with 6% interest from date.

Signed: E. J. Richards

This note was lost by Griffith. The finder transferred it by delivery alone to Hopkins. Griffith ordered Richards not to pay the note to Hopkins, but Richards ignored this order and paid it anyway. Can Griffith compel Richards to pay her? What could Griffith have done to avoid this loss?

4. Fortson was the payee of a check for $802.63. He transferred it to Samuel for value and indorsed it as follows: "Pay to the order of A. Samuel without recourse."

Signed: Ben Fortson

The drawer of the check stopped payment on the check because she was a minor and wished to disaffirm her contract. Samuel demanded that Fortson reimburse him for the check. Must he do so?

5. To obtain a loan for George Richardson from Liberty National Bank, where he had been employed, Michael Johnson executed a standard form blank guaranty agreement. The loan was not obtained from Liberty, and Johnson was so notified. Instead, a renewal note guaranteed by Johnson was issued to Richardson by Shepherd Mall State Bank, and about seven months later another renewal note was issued to him. When there was default in the second note, the Bank sent Johnson a demand letter regarding the guaranty agreement and then sued. The letter was the first notice Johnson had that the agreement had been used for a loan from this Bank. Did the agreement impose the liability of an indorser on Johnson?

6. Paul Chapman, as the administrator of his aunt's estate, was required to collect all debts due the estate. One of the estate's debtors paid her debt of $1,100 by check made payable to Paul Chapman. Chapman indorsed this check as follows: "Pay to the order of Paul Chapman, Administrator of Leah Chapman's Estate. Paul Chapman." This check was never paid because the drawer had insufficient funds in the bank. Later demand was made on Paul Chapman that he pay this $1,100 out of his personal funds because of his special indorsement. Was he personally liable for it?

7. Corporacion Venezolana de Fomento was the guarantor of promissory notes in the total amount of $5,813,950 executed by Venezolana de Cruceros del Caribe, C.A. (Cariven), to The Merban Corporation. Merban indorsed the notes in blank and delivered them to Security Pacific International Bank. Some of the notes were then transferred to Chemical Bank to be held for the benefit of any people to whom participating interests in the notes might be

sold. Merban sold participations in the notes to four Canadian banks, and Chemical issued each one a certificate of ownership in the notes to the extent of the interest purchased. Cariven defaulted, and in the subsequent lawsuit, Corporacion alleged that the Canadian banks were not holders of the notes because Chemical and Security had physical possession of them. Were the Canadian banks holders?

8. Paul Reid contracted to sell land to Bruce Cramer. The contract stated earnest money in the form of a promissory note for $4,000 due at closing was received and the earnest money would be forfeited if Cramer failed to buy the land. The note was payable to Home Realty, the seller's agent, and indorsed to Reid. When Cramer refused to buy the land, Reid sued to enforce the note. The note had been marked "void" without authorization by an employee of Home. Cramer alleged the marking made the note unenforceable. Did it?

9. A note was indorsed "without recourse" to the Finance Trust Co. by Skyline Furniture. When the Trust Co. tried to collect on the note, the maker of the note alleged incapacity by reason of minority. The Trust Co. then sued Skyline, which defended on the basis that the indorsement was "without recourse." Who will win?

28

Holders in Due Course

Negotiable instruments would have no advantage over ordinary contracts if the remote parties could not be given immunity against many of the defenses which might be made against simple contracts. To enjoy this immunity, the holder of a negotiable instrument must be a *holder in due course*. The term "innocent purchaser" is also used to describe a person who is a holder in due course.

Holders in Due Course

Neither the term holder in due course nor innocent purchaser can be used to describe anyone but the holder of a negotiable instrument who has obtained it under these conditions:

1. The holder must take the instrument in good faith and for value.
2. The holder must have no notice the instrument is overdue or has been dishonored.
3. At the time the instrument is negotiated, the holder must have had no notice of any defense against or adverse claim to the instrument.

For Value and in Good Faith. The law of commercial paper is concerned only with persons who give something for the paper. Thus, to attain the specially favored status of being a holder in due course, it is necessary that the holder give value for the paper. Conversely, one who does not do so, as a niece receiving a Christmas check from an uncle, cannot be a holder in due course. A mere promise does not constitute value.

The requirement that value be given does not mean that one must pay full value for a negotiable instrument in order to be a holder in due course. Thus, one who purchases a negotiable contract at a discount can qualify as a holder in due course. The law states that it must be taken "for value and in good faith." If the instrument is offered at an exorbitant discount, that fact may be evidence that the purchaser did not buy it in good faith. It is the lack of good faith that destroys one's status as a holder in due course, not the amount of the discount.

If the payee of a negotiable instrument for $3,000 offered to transfer it for a consideration of $2,700, and the purchaser had no other reason to suspect any infirmity in the instrument, the purchaser can qualify as a holder in due course. The instrument was taken in good faith. If, on the other hand, the holder had offered to discount the note $1,000, the purchaser could not take it in good faith because it should be suspected that there is some fatal infirmity in the contract because of the large discount.

As often occurs, the purchaser may pay for the instrument in cash and other property. The discount is concealed in the inflated value placed on the property taken in payment. The test always is: Were there any circumstances that should have warned a prudent person that the instrument was not genuine and in all respects what it purported to be? If there were, the purchaser did not take it in good faith.

If the holder is notified of a problem with the instrument or a defect in the title of the transferor before the full purchase price has been paid, the holder will be a holder in due course to the extent of the amount paid before notification.

Farmers Insurance Group delivered a draft payable "On Acceptance of Commerce Bank of Kansas City" to the order of Deborah Crippen. Crippen indorsed the draft for deposit in her checking account at Friendly National Bank of Southwest Oklahoma City. Friendly credited her account with the amount of the draft, and Crippen wrote checks against it. When Friendly had paid out $490.15 on Crippen's checks, the draft was returned to Friendly with the notation "Payment Declined by Farmers Insurance: Payment Stopped." Friendly sued Farmers, alleging it was a holder in due course because it had given value for the draft. The court held that crediting Crippen's account for the amount of the draft and allowing her to draw checks on it meant Friendly had given value.

No Knowledge Instrument Past Due or Dishonored.

One who takes an instrument that is known to be past due cannot be an innocent purchaser. However, a purchaser of demand paper on which demand for payment has been made and refused is still a holder in due course if there is no notice of the demand. A purchaser who has reason to know that any part of the principal is overdue, that there is an uncured default in payment of an instrument in the same series, or that acceleration of the instrument has been made has notice that the instrument is overdue. A note which is dated and payable in a fixed number of days or months itself indicates whether or not it is past due.

If the instrument is transferred on the date of maturity, it is not past due but would be overdue on the day following the due date. If it is payable on demand, it is due within a reasonable time after it is issued. For checks drawn and payable in the United States, thirty days is presumed to be a reasonable time.

No Knowledge of Any Defense or Adverse Claim to the Instrument.

When one takes a negotiable instrument by negotiation, to obtain the rights of an innocent purchaser there must be no knowledge of any defense against or claim adverse to the instrument. Notice of a claim may be inferred if the holder has knowledge that a fiduciary has negotiated an instrument in payment of a personal debt. As between the original parties to a negotiable instrument, any act, such as fraud, duress, mistake, illegality, which would make any contract either void or voidable will have the same effect on a negotiable instrument. Many of these defenses, as will be seen in the next chapter, are eliminated as defenses if the instrument is negotiated to an innocent purchaser. Knowing that an instrument has been antedated or postdated, was incomplete and has been completed, that default has been made in the payment of interest, or that it was issued or negotiated in return for an executory promise or accompanied by a separate agreement does not give a holder notice of a defense or claim.

Sellers and Brizendine were engineers for an oil prospecting company. Their occupation was well known by Harley. Sellers told Harley they had discovered unmistakable signs of oil on a tract of land Sellers owned. He offered the land to Harley for $20,000. If there was no oil on it, its true value was $1,000. Brizendine knew Sellers was misrepresenting the facts to Harley, although he took no part in the deal. Harley bought the land, giving Sellers $5,000 in cash and a twelve-month negotiable note for $15,000. Sellers immediately sold the note to Brizendine for $14,000. The question is whether or not Brizendine can qualify as an innocent purchaser. He cannot because he knew at the time the note was negotiated to him that Harley, the maker, could raise the defense of fraud to his obligation to pay.

Holder Through a Holder in Due Course

The first holder in due course brings into operation for the first time all the protections which the law has placed around negotiable instruments. When these protections once accrue, they are not easily lost. Consequently, a subsequent holder may benefit from them even though not a holder in due course. Such a holder is known as a *holder through a holder in due course*. For example, Doerhoff, without consideration, gives Bryce a negotiable note due in sixty days. Before maturity, Bryce indorses it to Cordell under conditions which make Cordell a holder in due course. Thereafter, Cordell transfers the note to Otke, but Otke is not a holder in due course, since she did not give any consideration for the note. If Otke is not a party to any wrongdoing or illegality affecting this instrument, she acquires all the rights of a holder in due course. This is true because Cordell had these rights, and when Cordell transferred the note to Otke, he transferred all of his rights, which include the right to collect the amount due and the right to be free from the defense of no consideration.

Holders of Consumer Paper

The Uniform Commercial Code rules regarding the status of a holder in due course have been modified for those holders of negotiable instruments given in exchange for consumer goods or services. *Consumer goods or services* are defined as goods or services for use primarily for personal, family, or household purposes. The changes are the result of both amendment to the UCC by the states—which means that the rules vary somewhat from state to state—and the adoption of the FTC rule.

Generally, the rights of the holder of consumer paper are subject to all defenses and setoffs of the original purchaser or debtor arising from the consumer transaction. In the case of consumer sales, the FTC rule requires that consumer credit contracts contain specified language in bold print indicating that holders of the contracts are subject to all claims and defenses the debtor could assert against the seller. The state laws generally make holder in due course rules inapplicable to consumer sales or limit the cutoff of consumer rights to a specified number of days after notification of assignment.

Normally these rights of the debtor are available only when the loan was arranged by the seller or lessor of the goods or was made directly by the seller or lessor. The state laws do not apply to credit card sales on a credit card issued by someone other than the seller. However, federal law allows a credit card holder to refuse to pay credit card issuers in some cases when an earnest effort at returning the goods is made or a chance to correct a problem is given the seller.

The purpose of modifying or abolishing the special status of a holder in due course for consumer goods is to prevent frauds which were frequently practiced upon consumers by unscrupulous business people. Such individuals would sell shoddy merchandise on credit and immediately negotiate the instrument of credit to a bank or finance company. When the consumer discovered the defects in the goods, payment could not be avoided, because the new holder of the commercial paper had purchased it without knowledge of the potential defenses and was therefore a holder in due course. Further, the seller who had frequently left the jurisdiction or gone bankrupt was unavailable to be sued. Thus, the consumer would be unable to assert a defense against either the seller or the holder. Recent modifications have remedied this problem.

Copas was induced to purchase a lifetime membership in a health spa for $450. He signed a negotiable note for $450 which was negotiated to the Reliance Finance Company. The spa was in business only two weeks. Copas refused to make any of the payments on his note to the finance company, claiming he did not receive the services promised by the membership. Copas does not have to pay. He may assert this defense against Reliance, since the note was given in payment of consumer services to the seller of the services.

The reason for allowing the consumer to have such rights against a holder who would otherwise be a holder in due course is to protect consumers who usually do not have knowledge of negotiable instruments laws. It is usually easier for the bank or finance company, which may buy many instruments from the seller, to ascertain whether the seller is reliable than for individual consumers to do so.

Questions

1. What is the prime significance of negotiability?

2. Who is a holder in due course?

3. May a holder in due course obtain possession by receiving the instrument as a Christmas gift?

4. What is presumed to be a reasonable time within which checks drawn and payable in the United States are not overdue?

5. Does knowledge that an instrument was postdated constitute knowledge of a defense or adverse claim?

6. Explain how a future holder may benefit from the fact that an instrument was held in due course.

7. Under what circumstances is an innocent holder of consumer paper denied the status of a holder in due course?

Case Problems

1. Kenneth Hessler signed a promissory note payable to John Smith Grain Company for some hogs. The hogs had previously been mortgaged to Producer's Livestock Association. After Hessler signed, he was told by an officer of John Smith to sign his wife's name, Carla Hessler, to the note. Hessler did so and put his initials, K.H., after her name. John Smith assigned the note to Arcanum National Bank. Shortly thereafter, Producer's took the hogs from Hessler's farm because of financial problems of John Smith. John Smith had no money to pay the note, so Arcanum sued Hessler. It handled the Hesslers' personal finances. Hessler alleged that Arcanum was not a holder in due course because it took the note with notice of a defense since it was irregular on its face. Was the note irregular on its face?

2. The General Services Administration (GSA) contracted with Almark, Inc., to buy bulletin boards. Almark and A. C. Davenport & Son Co. agreed that Davenport would supply the bulletin boards. Davenport later had doubts about Almark's ability to pay. It insisted that Almark and the GSA modify their contract to change the payment address from "Almark, Inc., 542 South 23rd Street, Arlington, Virginia 22202" to "Almark, Inc., c/o Davson, 306 East Helen Road, Palatine, IL 60067" and provide that checks under the contract be deposited in a special account from which only Davenport could withdraw the funds. Despite the contract modification, the GSA sent checks to Almark's Virginia address. When Davenport wrote the GSA that it had not received checks for shipments, it was advised that the checks had been sent to Almark, but a stop-payment had been put on them. The GSA issued a duplicate check which was deposited in the special account, and Davenport withdrew the money. The stop order was ineffective as to checks totaling $11,822.89. The GSA demanded the money. When Davenport did not pay, the GSA withheld payments due Davenport on unrelated contracts as setoffs against the amount it claimed was owed. Davenport sued to recover the money. For Davenport to be a holder in due course it must have taken the check without notice of any defense or claim. Did Davenport have such notice?

3. Charles was the payee on a note made by Benjamin. Charles indorsed the note to his attorney, Lawrence, for the purpose of having Lawrence available for legal services in the event Charles would need services in the future. Benjamin defaulted on the note, claiming that the goods which had been given in exchange for the note were defective and failed to conform to the promises

given by Charles. Lawrence claims to be a holder in due course. Benjamin says no value was given for the note. What will be the outcome?

4. Super Discount Carpets sold carpeting to Rogain. The carpet was installed in her house. Rogain executed a note to Super Discount Carpets in return for the carpet. The note was in the amount of $1,600, but Rogain was assured in a separate agreement that her home would be used as a model home and that she would receive a $50 credit against the $1,600 for each visitor who would agree to hear a sales presentation regarding the carpet. Super Discount Carpets negotiated the note to First City Bank and then vanished, leaving Rogain with no way of gaining her $50 credits. Rogain refused to pay the note. Can the bank recover?

5. For one and a half years, Ranchers Exploration and Development Corp. made monthly payments to American Express Company (AmEx) which covered both its corporate credit card bills and unknowingly covered personal debts of Linda Rodriguez, an employee of Ranchers. After paying Ranchers for its loss, Travelers Indemnity Company sued AmEx for the payments made on Rodriguez's behalf. AmEx said the court should find for it without a trial because, on the basis of the facts, it was clearly a holder in due course of the payments, since there was no evidence it received Ranchers' payments with knowledge of the defense that the payments on Rodriguez's account were unauthorized. Was it clearly a holder in due course?

6. After making a loan, the Valley National Bank held a perfected security interest in all accounts including checks payable to Van Dyck Heating and Air Conditioning, Inc., but indorsed to a third party. Van Dyck was owned and operated by Shirley and Kenneth Horn. A loan was in default, but Valley allowed Van Dyck to operate for five months. Kenneth Horn was contacted by Fred Couch, an IRS officer, because Van Dyck's federal tax payments were slow. Couch advised Horn to pay the taxes before other creditors to avoid civil and criminal penalties for delinquent tax payments. To avoid writing bad corporate checks to the IRS because of cash flow problems, Horn indorsed checks received from customers directly to the IRS. In accord with IRS policy, because Van Dyck's tax account was not classed as delinquent, no search for security interests was made. Valley sued. Did the IRS take the checks in good faith?

29

Defenses

Preview Cases

Donald Mertens sold the personal property of a laundromat to Cliff Coffman, who sold it to Elna Phillips. The sale to Phillips was subject to a financing and security agreement between Mertens and Coffman which Phillips assumed and agreed to pay. Part of the security agreement was a promissory note. After Phillips went broke, Mertens sued for the balance on Coffman's note. Coffman had told Phillips that the business was profitable and the equipment in good working order, and Phillips relied on these representations. They were false. Phillips raised the defense of fraud in the inducement. Was this defense good?

Heritage, a blind man, was expecting delivery of goods to his home by the Atlex Delivery Service. When the goods arrived, the deliverer requested Heritage to sign papers which he maintained were needed receipts for the delivery service. In fact, they were promissory notes made out to the delivery van driver. Will Heritage be liable on these notes?

When the holder of commercial paper is refused payment, a lawsuit may be brought. An earlier chapter showed which parties are liable for the payment of the face of the paper. What defense can be raised by the defendant who is being sued? This is a question which does not arise until it has first been determined that the plaintiff is the holder of the paper and that the defendant is a person who would ordinarily have liability for payment of the face of the paper. Assuming that those two questions have been decided in favor of the plaintiff, the remaining question is whether this defendant has a particular defense which may be raised.

Assume that there are four successive indorsers and the holder who comes at the end of these four indorsers sues the first indorser. Can the first indorser raise against the holder a defense which the first indorser has against the second indorser? For example, can the defense be raised that the first indorser was induced by fraud to make the indorsement? More commonly the situation will arise in which the remote holder sues the drawer of a check. The drawer then defends on the ground that the check had been given in payment for goods or services which the drawer never got, did not work, or were not satisfactory. Can the drawer now raise against the remote holder the defense against the payee of the check, namely, the defense of failure of consideration? The answer to this depends on the nature of the defendant's defense against the person with whom the dealings were made and the character of the holder. If the defense is a *limited defense* and the remote holder is a holder in due course, the defendant cannot raise such a defense. If the defense is a *universal defense* or the holder is an ordinary holder, the defendant may raise that defense.

Classification of Defenses

Certain defenses are limited to being raised against an ordinary holder and cannot be raised against a holder in due course. Limited defenses are:

1. Ordinary contract defenses
2. Fraud which induced the execution of the instrument
3. Conditional delivery
4. Improper completion
5. Payment or part payment
6. Nondelivery
7. Theft

Other defenses—universal defenses—can be raised regardless of who is being sued or who is suing. Thus, they can be raised against the holder in due course as well as an ordinary holder. The more common universal defenses are:

1. Minority
2. Forgery
3. Fraud as to the nature of the instrument or its material terms
4. Discharge in bankruptcy proceedings

Limited Defenses. There are a significant number of defenses which cannot be raised against a holder in due course or a holder through a holder in due course. It is important to distinguish limited defenses from universal ones.

Ordinary Contract Defenses. In general the defenses available in a dispute over a contract may be raised only against holders who do not qualify as holders in due course. Accordingly, if the instrument is held by a holder in due course, the defense of failure of consideration is not effective when raised by the maker who alleges that no consideration was received for the paper. In an action on an ordinary contract, the promisor may defend on the ground that there was no consideration for the promise; or that if there was consideration in the form of a counterpromise, the promise was never performed; or that the consideration was illegal. Thus, if Smith agreed to paint Jones's house but did not do it properly, Jones would have a right of action against Smith for breach of contract, or Jones could refuse to pay Smith the price agreed upon. If Smith were to assign the right to payment, Jones would be able to raise against the assignee the defenses available against Smith.

However, if Jones were to pay Smith by check before the work was completed, and the check were negotiated to a holder in due course, Jones could not defend on the ground of failure of consideration. The check would have to be paid. Jones's only right of action would be against Smith for the loss.

Fraud Which Induced the Execution of the Instrument. When a person knows a commercial paper is being executed and knows its essential terms but is persuaded or induced to execute it because of false representations or statements, this is not a defense against a holder in due course. For example, if Drucker is persuaded to buy a car from Randolph because of false statements made by Randolph about the car, and Drucker gives Randolph a note for it which is later negotiated to a holder in due course, Drucker cannot defend on the ground that Randolph lied about the car. Drucker will have to pay the note and seek any recovery from Randolph.

◆   Donald Mertens sold the personal property of a laundromat to Cliff Coffman, who sold it to Elna Phillips. The sale to Phillips was subject to a financing and security agreement between Martens and Coffman which Phillips assumed and agreed to pay. Part of the security agreement was a promissory note. After Phillips went broke, Mertens sued for the balance on Coffman's note. Coffman had told Phillips that the business was profitable and the equipment in good working order, and Phillips relied on these representations. They were false. Phillips raised the defense of fraud in the inducement. The defense was good because Mertens was not a holder in due course. He was a creditor beneficiary of the Coffman-Phillips agreement.

Conditional Delivery. As against a holder in due course, an individual who would be liable on the instrument cannot show that the instrument, absolute on its face, was delivered subject to an unperformed condition or that it was delivered for a specific purpose but was not used for it. If Sims makes out a check for Byers and delivers it to Richter with instructions not to deliver it until Byers delivers certain goods, but Richter delivers it to Byers, who then negotiates it to a holder in due course, Sims will have to pay on the check.

Improper Completion. If any term in a commercial paper is left blank, e.g., the payee or the amount, and the drawer then delivers the instrument to another to complete it, the drawer cannot raise the defense of improper completion against a holder in due course. In this case, the holder in due course may require payment from the drawer.

Payment or Part Payment. Upon payment of commercial paper the party making the payment should demand the surrender of the instrument. If the instrument is not surrendered, it may be further negotiated, and a later holder in due course would be able to demand payment successfully. A receipt is not adequate as proof of payment, because the subsequent holder in due course would have no notice of the receipt; whereas, surrender of the instrument would clearly prevent further negotiation.

Mitchell was the drawee of a ninety-day draft for $2,000, payable to Aldredge. Mitchell then sold Aldredge a trailer truck for $7,200 and allowed him credit for the $2,000 even though the draft was not due for thirty days. Aldredge said, "I'll mail the draft to you in a day or two." Aldredge had actually negotiated the draft to Brown, an innocent purchaser. When Brown presented it for payment on the due date, Mitchell denied liability because she had already paid it through a credit allowance on the truck. The defense that payment had been made was a limited defense and could not be used against an innocent purchaser.

If partial payment is made, the holder will be unlikely to surrender the instrument. In such a case the person making the payment should note the payment on the instrument, thereby giving notice to any subsequent transferee of the partial payment.

Nondelivery. Normally, a negotiable instrument which is fully or partially completed but is not delivered to the payee is not collectible by the payee. However, if the instrument is held by a holder in due course, payment of it may be required. For example, if one person makes out a note to another person and that other person takes the note from the maker's desk without the maker's permission and negotiates the note to an innocent purchaser, or holder in due course, the holder in due course would be entitled to recover the amount of the note against the maker. This is true in spite of the nondelivery of the note.

Theft. A thief may not normally pass good title; however, an exception is made when the thief conveys an instrument to a holder in due course. Such a purchaser will be able to enforce the obligation in spite of the previous theft of the paper. The thief or any ordinary holder cannot require payment of stolen paper.

Universal Defenses. Those defenses thought to be so important that they are preserved even against a holder in due course are "universal."

Minority. The fact that the defendant is a minor capable of avoiding agreements under contract law is a defense that may be raised against any holder.

Forgery. Except in cases where the forgery was made possible by the negligence of the defendant, forgery may be raised successfully against any holder. However, a forged signature operates as the signature of the forger in favor of a holder in due course.

Fraud as to the Nature of the Instrument or Its Material Terms. The defense that one was induced to sign an instrument when one did not know that it was in fact commercial paper is available against any holder. For example, an illiterate person who is told that a note is a receipt and thereby is induced to sign it may successfully raise this defense against any holder. This defense is not available, however, to competent individuals who negligently fail to read or give reasonable attention to the details of the documents they sign.

◆   Heritage, a blind man, was expecting delivery of goods to his home by the Atlex Delivery Service. When the goods arrived, the deliverer requested Heritage to sign papers which he maintained were needed receipts for the delivery service. In fact, they were promissory notes made out to the delivery van driver. Heritage will not be liable on the notes. Fraud as to the nature of the instrument is a universal defense.

Discharge in Bankruptcy Proceedings. Even holders in due course are subject to the defense that a discharge in bankruptcy has been granted.

Hybrid Defenses. There are several defenses which may be either universal or limited. These are:

1. Duress
2. Incapacity other than minority
3. Illegality
4. Alteration

Duress. Whether or not duress is a valid defense against a holder in due course depends upon whether the effect of such duress is to make the contract void or voidable. When the duress nullifies the contract, the defense is universal. When the duress merely makes the contract voidable at the option of the victim of the duress, the defense is limited.

Incapacity Other than Minority. In cases of incapacity other than minority, if the effect of the incapacity is to make the instrument a nullity, the defense is universal. If the effect of the incapacity does not make the instrument a nullity, the defense is limited.

Illegality. The fact that the law makes certain transactions illegal gives rise to a defense against an ordinary holder. Such a defense would be unavailable against a holder in due course unless the law making the transaction illegal also specifies that instruments based upon such transactions are unenforceable.

Alteration. If an instrument is altered, the instrument has no effect if the plaintiff is an ordinary holder. If the plaintiff is a holder in due course, the instrument can be sued upon according to its terms before it was altered. An "alteration" exists only if (1) a party to the instrument (2) fraudulently made (3) a material change. If any one of these elements is lacking, the modification of the instrument is not called an alteration and has no legal effect. As a practical matter, however, there may be some difficulty in proving just what the instrument said before it was modified.

Miscellaneous Matters

In addition to the defenses described above, it must be remembered that every lawsuit presents certain standard problems so that a defendant may, under appropriate circumstances, raise the defense that the suit is not brought in the proper court, that there was no service of process; or that the statute of limitations has run and bars suit. Any defendant in a suit on commercial paper can claim that the instrument is not negotiable; that the plaintiff is not the holder; and that the defendant is not a party liable for payment of the paper. If the holder claims that the defendant is secondarily liable for the payment of the face of the paper, the defendant may also show that the paper had not been properly presented to the primary party and that proper notice of default had not been given to the secondary party.

Questions

1. State in one sentence the chief advantage of being the holder in due course of commercial paper.

2. Is it any advantage to be the holder of a negotiable instrument even though one is not a holder in due course?

3. What is the difference between limited defenses and universal defenses?

4. Name and explain three limited defenses.

5. Name and explain three universal defenses.

6. What is the effect upon a holder in due course if the instrument was not completed nor delivered by the maker thereof but was subsequently filled in naming an inappropriate party as payee and specifying an unduly large sum?

7. When is duress a valid defense to a holder in due course?

8. What effect does alteration of an instrument have against a holder in due course?

Case Problems

1. Lucille Quazzo was grateful to Ada Shaw for some investment advice Ada had given to Lucille the previous year. Lucille executed a note for $1,000 payable to Ada. However, when the note became due, Lucille refused to pay. Ada filed suit. Lucille raised lack of consideration as a defense. Was this defense valid?

2. Matthew Roarke executed three promissory notes payable to the order of State Bank of Albany. Roarke defaulted on the notes, and the Bank sued for payment of them. Roark raised the defense of fraud as to the nature or essential terms of the instruments. He alleged that Maurice O'Connell, then a vice-president of the Bank, and Frank Kindlon conspired in a fraudulent scheme, that Kindlon misrepresented the nature of the instruments and their purpose when Roarke executed them at Kindlon's request. Was this defense good?

3. Dewey of Salem, Oregon, purchased a boat from Morse. At the time the contract was made the boat was supposedly in a boathouse on a lake in Idaho. Dewey gave a check for $3,500 in payment of the boat. Morse indorsed the check immediately to Wayne. A few hours after the sale, Morse received a wire informing him that the boathouse and the boat were destroyed in a fire the day before the sale. When she learned of this, Dewey stopped payment on the check. Wayne sued both Morse as indorser and Dewey as the drawer. Is either or both liable?

4. Garrett gave Brooks the following note:

Date _____
Six months after date I promise to pay E. Brooks or order, $1,572.84 with ____% interest from date in payment of one lot purchased by deed of even date and his promises to clear the lot of debris.
A. Garrett

Brooks induced Garrett to give him this note through fraudulent statements as to the value of the land. He sold the note to Chen, an innocent purchaser. Chen, in turn, sold it to Kim, who knew of the fraudulent nature of the transaction. Kim sued Garrett for the note, and Garrett attempted to plead fraud as a defense. Would the court permit her to offer this defense?

5. Mercantonio filled out a note payable to Mullins. It was complete in every respect except that the amount was omitted, pending a determination of the ex-

act amount. Through a mistake, Mercantonio's secretary mailed the note to Mullins, who, although she knew the proper amount was between $300 and $400, filled in the amount spaces for $1,000 and then sold it to Fortune, an innocent purchaser. Could Fortune collect the note from Mercantonio?

What would your answer be if it had been completed before Mullins obtained possession of it?

Summary Cases Part Five

Commercial Paper

1. Public Relations Enterprises, Inc., paid Melco Products Corporation for goods by means of personal money orders purchased from Nassau Trust Company and Republic National Bank of New York. When Melco presented them for payment, the banks dishonored them on the ground the Public had stopped payment. Melco sued the banks for payment, alleging that the banks had no right to stop payment on the personal money orders. Did they? [*Melco Products Corp. v. Public Relations Enterprises, Inc.,* 460 N.Y.S.2d 466 (N.Y. Sup. Ct.)]

2. Dallas County State Bank sold a personal money order on a forged check. It then stopped payment on the money order and refused to accept and pay it when it was presented by Northpark National Bank of Dallas. The money order had a checkwriting imprint, "Dallas County State Bank," as well as the name of the Bank printed on it. Northpark sued for payment. Dallas alleged it was not liable on the money order since its signature did not appear on it. Was it liable? [*Interfirst Bank Carrollton v. Northpark National Bank of Dallas,* 671 S.W.2d 100 (Tex. Ct. App.)]

3. The Board of Commissioners for the Pontchartrain Levee District executed a warrant to the State Comptroller payable to Farmer Construction Co., Inc. Farmer negotiated it to St. James Bank and Trust Co. Before the State Comptroller received it, the Board stopped payment, and the warrant was returned to St. James unpaid. St. James sued the Board, alleging it was a holder in due course. The Board defended that the warrant was not negotiable because it was payable out of a particular fund. Was the warrant conditional? [*St. James Bank & Trust Co. v. Board of Commissioners, Pontchartrain Levee District,* 354 So.2d 233 (La. Ct. App.)]

4. A check was drawn by the Havana Canning Company for $125, payable to George Wells. The check was regular in every detail except that in the lower left-hand corner were these words: "For berries to be delivered to us June 8th." This check was indorsed by George Wells to an innocent purchaser. The drawer wished to raise a defense to the payment of a breach of warranty which, being a failure of consideration, was a limited defense. In order to raise this defense, he had to establish that this check was nonnegotiable because of this notation. Did this notation make the order to pay conditional? [*First National Bank of Marianna v. Havana Canning Company,* 195 So. 188 (Fla.)]

5. Berry executed a promissory note payable to William C. Stepp. The note was in perfect order. Stepp indorsed the note before maturity as follows: "I hereby

transfer my right to this note over to W. E. McCullough. (signed) William C. Stepp." The maker failed to pay the note, and McCullough brought suit against Stepp, the indorser. Stepp's defense was that the indorsement was a qualified indorsement, and therefore, he was not liable, since the maker's only reason for not paying was insolvency. Was this a qualified indorsement? [*McCullough v. Stepp*, 85 S. E. 2d 159 (Ga. Ct. App.)]

6. Omega Electronics, Inc., executed a promissory note to the order of State Bank of Fisk. It was signed on the front by two officers of the corporation and on the back by five individuals. The note stated: "We, the makers, . . . endorsers and guarantors of this note, hereby severally waive presentment for payment, notice of nonpayment, protest and notice of protest." When the note was not paid, the Bank sued the individuals. They alleged they were not liable because they had not been given notice of dishonor and protest. Were they liable? [*State Bank of Fisk v. Omega Electronics, Inc.*, 634 S.W.2d 234, (Mo. Ct. App.)]

7. A check was drawn by Fellsway Motors, Inc., on October 25, made payable to Therrien. Therrien then drew a line through the "5" in "25" to make it look like Oct. 28. The line was in a different color of ink from the rest of the check, and the change in the number was perfectly evident. On October 29 Therrien indorsed the check to Manuel Medeiros for value and in good faith. Before the check was paid, payment was stopped by the drawer. The key question to be decided in the case was whether or not Medeiros was a holder in due course. [*Medeiros v. Fellsway Motors Inc.*, 96 N.E.2d 170 (Mass.)]

8. In August, 1949, Hier executed a negotiable note for $1,075, payable to the Washington Fixtures and Equipment Company. The note was to be paid in installments, the first installment to be due December 1, 1949, with a provision that if any installment was not paid on time, the entire balance should become due and payable at once. The first installment was not paid. On December 23, the payee indorsed the note to the Federal Glass Company, Inc., for value. When Hier was sued by the holder, he wished to plead fraud and a breach of warranty. The holder claimed he was not required to defend against such a defense. What fundamental error did some employee for the Federal Glass Company commit in this case? [*Hier v. Federal Glass Co., Inc.*, 102 A. 2d 840 (D.C.)]

9. Blas Garcia told Arthur and Lucy Casarez he was a representative of Albuquerque Fence Company, so they contracted with the Company to build a home for them. Blas introduced them to Cecil Garcia, who said he would make a loan for the home. The Garcias were in no way affiliated with Albuquerque. Cecil got a $25,000 loan from Rio Grande Valley Bank in the form of a cashier's check. The Casarezes signed a note, and Cecil indorsed the check: "Pay to the order of Lucy N. Casarez, Cecil Garcia." Lucy indorsed it: "Pay to the order of Albuquerque Fence Co., Lucy N. Casarez." She handed the check to Blas who indorsed the check: "Alb. Fence Co." Cecil signed his

own name under that and presented the check to Rio Grande in return for $5,000 and four cashier's checks for $5,000. The Casarezes sued Rio Grande, alleging the words "Pay to the order of Albuquerque Fence Co." constituted a special indorsement and the check could be negotiated only by indorsement by an authorized official of the company. Was this a valid assertion? [*Casarez v. Garcia*, 660 P.2d 598 (N.M. Ct. App.)]

10. An officer of Potpourri Publications, Inc., Gregory Gordon, signed a note for $7,000 to The Heights Bank and executed a Security Agreement for a $10,000 bond as security. Later Potpourri's checking account with the Bank was overdrawn but corrected by the deposit of the proceeds of the sale of the bond. The note was in default four days later. Clifford Lee, Gordon's brother-in-law, called Mr. Schafer, the chief operating officer of the Bank, about obtaining an $8,000 unsecured loan. Schafer later called Lee, told him he needed a favor, and asked him to come to the bank. Schafer asked Lee to cosign a note with Gordon. Lee refused. Schafer told Lee the note was fully secured by a $10,000 bond. Lee asked why he was needed if the loan was secured. Schafer said it would help him with the bank examiners and showed Lee a copy of the Security Agreement. Schafer stated, "You've made a loan request and I am going to help you out, too." After deliberating Lee agreed to cosign. Schafer produced a blank note which Lee refused to sign. Schafer then produced a renewal note signed by Gordon which stated: "This Note is secured by Security Agreement." Later Schafer told Lee the Bank's loan committee insisted on security for the $8,000 loan he wanted. Lee offered to post certificates of deposit of two other banks. Schafer insisted on the Bank's certificates of deposit as collateral, so Lee cashed in his certificates and established two $4,000 certificates at The Heights. Three months later Lee was told Gordon's note was in default. Lee told Schafer to sell the bond. Schafer told him there was none. The Bank told Lee if he did not pay the Gordon note, it would use the certificates of deposit to pay it, but it would ruin Lee's excellent credit rating. Lee paid the note and sued the Bank for reimbursement, alleging fraud in the inducement. Was it? [*Lee v. Heights Bank*, 446 N.E.2d 248 (Ill. App. Ct.)]

11. George Weast borrowed $140,000 from State National Bank of Maryland (SNB), and his wife, Ruth, cosigned for him. This debt later was in default, so George indorsed and delivered some notes made by Francis and Josephine Arnold and Randall Co. to the order of SNB. Payments were made on these notes for several years before default. Ruth and George got divorced. When Ruth paid off the amount owed on their debt, SNB indorsed the notes of the Arnolds and Randall to Ruth. She sued them for payment on the notes. They alleged she was subject to a defense regarding the transaction which gave rise to the notes. Ruth claimed to be a holder through a holder in due course, so the defense would not be valid against her. Was Ruth a holder through a holder in due course when the notes had been indorsed to her after default? [*Weast v. Arnold*, 474 A.2d 904 (Md.)]

12. South Carolina Insurance Company issued a draft to Kevlin Owens drawn on the account of Seibels, Bruce Group at South Carolina National Bank. Owens negotiated the draft to First National Bank of Denham Springs, which paid him the entire amount and delivered it to South Carolina National Bank. The insurance company alleged fraud in Owens' claim and issued a stop-payment order. South Carolina National Bank did not honor the draft. The draft stated it was payable as follows: "Upon acceptance, pay to the order of Kevlin Owens." South Carolina Insurance Company was a wholly owned subsidiary of Seibels, Bruce Group. Therefore, South Carolina was both drawer and drawee. First National sued South Carolina for payment. South Carolina said the words "upon acceptance" made the draft conditional, therefore the draft was not negotiable, First National is not a holder in due course, and the defense of fraud may be raised. Was the draft conditional? [*First National Bank of Denham Springs v. South Carolina Insurance Company,* 432 So. 2d 417 (La. Ct. App.)]

Part Six — Agency and Employment

Learning Objectives for Part Six

Agency and Employment

After studying this part you should be able to:

1. Explain the nature of an agency and identify the parties involved.

2. Distinguish between an agency and independent contractor or employer-employee relationships.

3. Describe the different classifications of agents and the corresponding authority of each.

4. Discuss how an agency is created.

5. Specify the duties an agent owes the principal and the principal owes the agent.

6. Determine when an agent may be personally liable.

7. Explain how an agency may be terminated, either by the parties or by operation of law.

8. Recognize an employment contract and describe how such a contract is created.

9. List the duties and liabilities of employers to their employees.

10. Name the duties an employee owes the employer.

11. Specify employers' defenses and the modifications that have been made to them.

12. Describe the four major provisions of the Federal Social Security Act.

13. Discuss the objectives and coverage of the Fair Labor Standards Act.

14. Discuss the major provisions of the Labor Management Relations Act, the Labor-Management Reporting and Disclosure Act, and the Civil Rights Act of 1964.

30

Creation of an Agency

Preview Cases

Robert Weeks was employed as an electrician by Howard P. Foley Company during construction of a power plant by Alabama Electric Cooperative, Inc. (AEC). He was injured when a scaffold collapsed. He sued AEC as the owner of the premises, alleging there was an employer–employee relationship, and AEC had breached its duty of care. By contract AEC had retained the right to supervise or inspect the work of each independent contractor to determine whether the work was being done according to the plans and specifications. Were AEC and Weeks in an employer–employee relationship?

Slaughter had a checking account with the Citizens Bank. The Bank was not authorized to honor any checks except those with Slaughter's signature. Over a period of six months Mrs. Slaughter signed her husband's name on dozens of checks and signed them: "by Mrs. Slaughter." Mr. Slaughter notified the bank to stop honoring his wife's checks and demanded that the bank restore to his account all checks drawn by her. Should the bank be so required?

When one party, known as a *principal,* appoints another party, known as an *agent,* to enter into contracts with third parties in the name of the principal, a contract of *agency* is formed. By this definition at least three parties are involved in every contract which an agent negotiates: the principal, the agent, and the third party. It is this making of a contract with a third person on behalf of the principal which distinguishes an agency from other employment relationships. The principal, the agent, or the third party may be an individual, a partnership, or a corporation.

Importance of Agency

Because of the magnitude and the complexity of our modern industry, many of the important details pertaining to business transactions must be delegated by the owners of businesses to agents for performance. The relation creating this delegation of powers is governed by the general principles of law pertaining to contracts.

Even in the performance of routine matters by individuals, agents are necessary in order to bring one person into a business contractual relationship with other persons. Thus, a farmer who sends an employee to town to have a piece of machinery repaired gives the latter the authority to enter into a contract that binds the farmer to the agreement.

What Powers May Be Delegated to an Agent?

As a general rule, a person may do through an agent all of those things which could otherwise be done by the person. There are, however, certain acts which are of such a personal nature that the courts will not permit them to be delegated to others. Some of the acts that are considered personal and that may not be performed by an agent are voting in a public election, executing a will, or serving on a jury.

What one may not lawfully do may not be done through another. Thus, no person can authorize an agent to commit a crime, to publish a libelous statement, to perpetrate a fraud, or to do any other act that is illegal, immoral, or opposed to the welfare of society.

Other Employment Relationships

There are two types of employment relationships other than agency relationships:

1. Independent contractor
2. Employer and employee, originally referred to in law as master and servant

Independent Contractor. An *independent contractor* is one who contracts to perform some tasks for a fixed fee but is independent of the control of the other contracting party as to the means by which the contract is performed except to the extent that the contract sets forth specifications and requirements to be followed. The independent contractor is merely held responsible for the proper performance of the contract. The contract does not create either a principal-agent relationship or an employer-employee relationship. The most usual type of independent contractor relationship is in the building trades.

Robert Weeks was employed as an electrician by Howard P. Foley Company during construction of a power plant by Alabama Electric Cooperative, Inc. (AEC). He was injured when a scaffold collapsed. He sued AEC as the owner of the premises, alleging there was an employer-employee relationship, and AEC had breached its duty of care. By contract AEC had retained the right to supervise or inspect the work of each independent contractor to determine whether the work was being done according to the plans and specifications. The court ruled this right did not include control over the employees of the contractors; thus, there was no employer-employee relationship.

There are many reasons why a contract of employment must not be confused with a contract of an independent contractor. An employer may be held liable for any injuries employees negligently cause to third parties. This is not true for injuries caused by independent contractors. Second, there are several laws employers must comply with relative to their employees. They must, for example, withhold social security taxes on their wages, pay a payroll tax for unemployment compensation, withhold federal income taxes, and, when properly demanded, bargain with their employees collectively. None of these laws apply when one contracts with independent contractors. Independent contractors are the employers of those employed by them to perform the contract.

Employer and Employee. An employee performs work for an employer and is under the employer's control both as to the work to be done and as to the manner in which it is to be done. The main differences between an employee and an agent are the degree of control which the employer or principal exercises over the employee or agent and the authority the agent has to bind the principal.

The main difference between an employee and an independent contractor is that the employer has power to control the doing of the work by the employee, whereas one contracting with an independent contractor does not have such control.

Classification of Agents

Agents may be classified as:

1. General agents
2. Special agents

General Agents. A *general agent* is one who is authorized to carry out the principal's business of a particular kind, or all the principal's business at a particular place even though it is not all of one kind. A purchasing agent and a bank cashier are examples of general agents who perform all of the principal's business of a particular kind. A manager who is in full charge of one branch of a chain of shoe stores is a general agent who transacts all of the principal's business at a particular place. In this capacity merchandise is bought and sold, help is employed, bills are paid, accounts are collected, and all other duties are performed. Such an agent has a wide scope of authority and the power to act without express direction from the principal.

A general agent has considerable authority beyond that expressly stated in the contract of employment. In addition to express authority a general agent has that authority which one in such a position customarily has.

Special Agents. A *special agent* is one who is authorized by a principal to transact some specific act or acts. Such an agent has only limited powers which may be used only for a specific purpose. The authorization may cover just one act, such as buying a house; or it may cover a series of acts which are mere repetitions, such as selling admission tickets to a movie.

Additional Types of Agents

There are several additional types of agents. Most of these are special agents, but because of the nature of their duties, their powers may exceed those of the ordinary special agent:

1. Factors
2. Factors del credere
3. Brokers
4. Attorneys in fact

Factors. A *factor* is one who receives possession of another's property for sale on commission. Commission merchants constitute the largest class of factors. Such merchants may sell in the name of the principal, but the usual practice is to sell in the merchant's own name. When the sale price is collected, the commission, or factorage, is deducted, and the balance is remitted to the principal. The third party as a rule is aware that the dealings are with an agent by the nature of the business or by the name of the business. The words "commission merchant" usually appear on all stationery. Commission merchants have the power to bind the principal for the customary terms of sale for the types of business they are doing. In this regard their powers are slightly greater than those of the ordinary special agent.

Factors Del Credere. A *factor del credere* is a commission merchant who sells on credit and guarantees to the principal that the purchase price will be paid by the purchaser or by the factor. This is a form of contract of guaranty, but the contract need not be in writing as required by the Statute of Frauds, since the agreement is a primary obligation of the factor.

Brokers. A *broker* is a special agent whose task is to bring the two contracting parties together. Unlike the factor, the broker does not have possession of the merchandise. In real estate and insurance a broker generally is the agent of the buyer rather than the seller. If the job is merely to find a buyer or, sometimes, a seller, the broker has no authority to bind the principal on any contract.

Attorneys in Fact. An *attorney in fact* is a general agent who has been appointed by a written authorization. The writing, which is intended to be shown to third persons, manifests that the agent has authority.

Extent of Authority

As a rule, a general agent has authority to transact several classes of acts: those clearly within the scope of the express authority, those customarily within such an agent's authority, and those outside of express authority which appear to third parties to be apparently within the scope of the agent's authority. Authority to act on behalf of another arises when by custom such agents ordinarily possess such powers. This is sometimes called *customary authority*. In addition, without regard to custom, the principal may have behaved in a way or made statements which caused the third person to believe that the agent has the authority. This is called *apparent authority*. For example, the Pardalos Insurance Company might advertise "For all your insurance problems see your local Pardalos Insurance agent." This would give the local Pardalos Insurance Company agent apparent authority to arrange any insurance matters even though actually they did not have such authority or had been told that certain kinds of cases had to be referred to the home office.

As to innocent third parties, the powers of a general agent may be far more extensive than those granted by the principal. Limitations upon an agent's authority are not binding upon a third party who has no knowledge of them; but a third party who knows of them is bound by them.

The owner of a radio shop employed Devaney to sell radios and instructed him to sell for cash only. If he disregarded this instruction and sold a radio on credit at reasonable terms of payment, the contract would have been binding upon the principal. Since it is the custom of radio shops in general to sell on credit, the purchaser had a right to presume that Devaney had authority to sell on credit. This is customary authority.

If Devaney had taken a car in payment of the radio and had agreed to pay the purchaser $150 for the difference in value, the shop owner would not have been bound. This would clearly have been beyond even the apparent scope of the agent's authority, and the purchaser would have had no right to assume that the agent had such authority.

In every case the person who would benefit by the existence of authority on the part of the alleged agent has the burden of proving the existence of authority. If a person appears to be the agent of another for the purpose of selling the car of that other person, the prospective purchaser must seek assurance from the principal as to the agent's authority.

Once the third party has learned the actual scope of an agent's express authority from the principal, it is clear that the agent has no greater authority than the principal's actions and statements indicate, together with such customary authority as would attach to the express authority given by the principal.

Who May Appoint an Agent?

All people who are legally competent to act for themselves may act through an agent. This rule is based upon the principle that whatever a person may do may be done through another. Hence corporations and partnerships, as well as individuals, may appoint agents.

The contract by which a minor appoints an agent to act for the minor is voidable. Some states hold that a minor's appointment of an agent to act is void.

Who May Act as an Agent?

Ordinarily, any person who has sufficient intelligence to carry out a principal's orders may be appointed to act as an agent. This is not a legal requirement but is a practical consideration of whether the principal is going to have the particular person act as agent. Corporations and partnerships may act as agents.

There are some types of transactions which cannot be performed by an agent unless certain requirements are met. For example, in many states a real estate agent must possess certain definite qualifications and must, in addition, secure a license to act in this capacity. Unless this is done, a person is disqualified to act as an agent in performing the duties of a real estate agent.

Creation of an Agency

There are several ways in which the relationship of agency may be created. Agencies are usually created by:

1. Appointment
2. Ratification
3. Estoppel
4. Necessity

Appointment. The usual way of creating an agency is by the statement of the principal to the agent. In most cases the contract may be either oral or written, formal or informal. There are some instances, however, where the appointment must be made in a particular form. The contract appointing an agent must be in writing if the agency is created to transfer title to real estate. Also, if an agent's authority is to extend beyond one year from the date of the contract, the contract is required by the Statute of Frauds to be in writing. If an agent is appointed to execute a formal contract, such as a bond, the contract of appointment must be formal.

A written instrument indicating the appointment of an agent is known as a *warrant* or *power of attorney*. If a power of attorney is to be recorded, it must also be acknowledged before a notary public or other officer authorized to take acknowledgments. An ordinary form of power of attorney is shown in Illustration 30-1.

Know All Men by These Presents

That I, Amelia Clermont

                                                        of Portland

County of Multnomah   *, State of* Oregon
have made, constituted and appointed, and by these presents do make, constitute and

appoint James Turner

                                                        of Vancouver

County of Clark   *, State of* Washington
my true and lawful attorney   *in fact, for me and in my name, place and stead,*
to manage, operate, and let my rental properties in the City of

Vancouver, County of Clark, State of Washington

giving and granting unto my said attorney   full power and authority to do and perform
all and every act and thing whatsoever requisite and necessary to be done in and about
the premises, as fully to all intents and purposes as I might or could do, if personally
present, with full power of substitution and revocation; hereby ratifying and confirming
all that my said attorney —— or his   *substitute —— shall lawfully do, or cause to be*
done, by virtue hereof.

In Witness Whereof,   *I have hereunto set my hand this* tenth   *day*
of July   *, 19* -- .   *Amelia Clermont*

Signed and acknowledged in presence of:
     Samuel Adamick
     Teresa Romano

ILLUS. 30-1. A Power of Attorney

Ratification. *Ratification* is the approval by one person of the unauthorized act of another done in the former's name. The unauthorized act may have been done by an assumed agent who purported to act as an agent without actual or apparent authority, or it may have been done by a real agent who exceeded actual and apparent authority. The supposed principal in such a case is not bound by the act unless and until it is ratified. The effect of the ratification is that the ratification relates back to the date of the act done by the assumed agent; hence, ratifying the act puts the assumed agent in the same position as if there had been authority to do the act at the time the act was done.

The essential elements of a valid ratification are:

1. The one who assumed the authority of an agent must have made it known to the third person that he or she was acting on behalf of the party who attempts to ratify the act.

2. The one attempting to ratify must have been capable of authorizing the act at the time the act was done. In some jurisdictions this rule is applied to corporations so that an act of a promoter cannot be ratified by a corporation that is formed subsequent to the time of the act. Other states have ignored this requirement in regard to ratification of the acts of corporate promoters.

3. The one attempting to ratify must be capable of authorizing the act at the time approval of the act is given.

4. The one attempting to ratify must have knowledge of all material facts.

5. The one attempting to ratify must approve the entire act.

6. The act that is ratified must be legal, although a forgery on commercial paper may be ratified by the person whose name was forged.

7. The ratification must be made before the third party has withdrawn from the transaction.

Estoppel. *Agency by estoppel* arises when a person by words or conduct leads another person to believe that a third party is an agent or has the authority to do particular acts. The principal who has made representations is bound to the extent of those representations for the purpose of preventing an injustice to parties who have been misled by the acts or the conduct of the principal.

Slaughter had a checking account with the Citizen's Bank. The bank was not authorized to honor any checks except those with Slaughter's signature. Over a period of six months Mrs. Slaughter signed her husband's name on dozens of checks and signed them: "by Mrs. Slaughter." Mr. Slaughter notified the bank to stop honoring his wife's checks and demanded that the bank restore to his account all checks drawn by her. The court held that because he allowed six months to pass without protesting, he was estopped to deny she had the authority to sign his name to checks. Had he protested as soon as he learned of the act, the bank would have had to make good the checks so drawn.

Necessity. The relationship of agency may be created by necessity. Parents are bound to support their minor children. If they fail to provide their children with necessaries, the parents' credit may be pledged for the children, even against their will. Agency by necessity may also arise from some unforeseen emergency. Thus, the driver of a bus operating between distant cities may pledge the owner's credit in order to have needed repairs made and may have the cost charged to the owner.

Questions

1. What is an agency?

2. Name the parties who are involved in a contract which an agent negotiates.

3. Why are most business transactions carried on by agents?

4. What acts can never be delegated to an agent?

5. Why is it important to distinguish between a contract with an independent contractor and an employment contract?

6. What is a general agent?

7. What is customary authority?

8. May corporations act as agents?

9. What is a power of attorney?

10. In order for a principal to ratify an unauthorized contract of an agent, must the agent have pretended to act for the principal?

11. How does an agency by estoppel arise?

Case Problems

1. McDowell was business manager for the WTUW radio station. Philips, representing himself as the agent of the Hartsfield Oil Company, presented to McDowell an advertising program to be aired by the station for two weeks. The charge agreed upon was $800. After the program was completed, McDowell sent a bill to the Hartsfield Oil Company. The company denied liability on the ground that Philips did not have the authority to place advertising contracts with the station. The facts showed that Philips' actual authority was to call on stations selling the Hartsfield products, to recruit new agents for the company, and to build goodwill for the oil company whenever possible. Was this authority broad enough to empower him to contract with a radio station for advertising campaigns?

2. Susan Blackmon was hired by Nelson, Hesse, Cyril, Weber & Sparrow as a secretary and later inquired of Ms. Steeves, the office manager, about coverage under the firm's group health insurance plan. She stated she told Steeves she needed surgery but would wait until she was covered. She further stated that Steeves told her upon completion of the application form that she would be included immediately, and Steeves made deductions from Blackmon's salary for premiums to start coverage that day. Eight days later, thinking she was covered, Blackmon had the surgery. Steeves had just mailed the application, and it was not approved until five days after the surgery. Blackmon sued the firm, alleging Steeves was its agent and was negligent in advising when the coverage would take effect. Was Steeves the firm's agent?

3. Hinton entered into a contract with Barnett whereby Barnett was to paint Hinton's building for $1,100, Barnett to furnish all materials and to pay for all labor. The work was to be completed within 30 days; otherwise, Barnett was free to work as he pleased. Barnett hired Dinkler to assist with the painting. A ladder on which Dinkler was standing broke; he fell to the sidewalk and was seriously injured. The latter was clearly not safe to use. Is Hinton liable to Dinkler for damages?

4. There were 55 transactions in which William Kirchberg contacted George Arakelian Farms, Inc., and ordered lettuce on behalf of his principal, Leonard O'Day. The custom in the business was for the orders to be oral. Arakelian would ship the lettuce for delivery to O'Day's customers. A bill of lading, signed by the carrier would be sent to Arakelian, which would prepare an invoice and send it and a copy of the bill of lading to O'Day. O'Day paid all but the last three invoices. They were paid by checks from O.K. Distributors Company, a firm owned by Kirchberg. Arakelian never dealt directly with O'Day. Unknown to Arakelian, O'Day and Kirchberg parted company. Twenty additional orders for lettuce were made by Kirchberg. Arakelian proceeded in its normal manner, and O'Day denied any connection with the 20 shipments. Arakelian sued him for payment of them. Was he liable?

5. Paulson employed Ferrer to sell an automobile repair shop and filling station she owned. Ferrer was specifically instructed to sell for cash only, with possession to be given to the buyer within 60 days. Ferrer entered into a contract with Laster to buy the business for one-third cash and the balance to be paid in three equal installments, with possession to be given in ten days. Paulson refused to sell on these terms. Is she bound on the contract the agent made for her?

6. Max Siegel was the assignee of a written lease of property owned by George and Emily Zeese. Siegel owned Trailer Mart, Inc., which did business on the property. After Trailer Mart took possession of the property, Siegel died. Eva Siegel, his widow and executrix, sent a letter to the Zeeses exercising an option to renew the lease for ten years. During the next four years, George Zeese visited the property on numerous occasions to observe the business,

and during this time Trailer Mart sent monthly rental checks to the Zeeses and paid the property taxes. The Zeeses then served a notice-to-quit on Trailer Mart, alleging Eva Siegel was not the agent of Trailer Mart when she exercised the option to renew the lease. Trailer Mart alleged that even if she was not an agent, it had ratified her acts. Had Trailer Mart renewed the lease?

7. Mr. and Mrs. Howard Anderson wanted to obtain a consolidation loan to reduce their monthly payments on their loans and consulted First National Bank of Pine City. Mrs. Anderson went to First National and brought home papers for Mr. Anderson to sign. He refused because there were unfilled blanks in the papers. Mrs. Anderson signed his name as well as her own to a note and mortgage deed on their home and delivered them to First National. When the Andersons fell behind in their payments on the note, First National began foreclosure proceedings. The Bank alleged Mr. Anderson ratified his wife's forgery by being silent and failing to notify it. Mr. Anderson stated he was silent because he was afraid his wife would be prosecuted for forgery. He had learned about her signing his name three months later and thought she had forged his name to a loan secured by personal property, not a mortgage. Had he ratified the forgery?

8. Knowles delivered two valuable antiques to Hruska, a licensed factor for antiques. Hruska sold the two items to Fort for $1,400. Knowles was dissatisfied with the price received and attempted to recover the items from Fort, claiming Hruska could not transfer title to them, since he was clearly not the owner. Is this contention sound?

9. Mary had an invitation to attend the Magnolia Ball, the leading social event on the college campus. She purchased a gown for the occasion for $510 and charged it to her father. Her father refused to pay for it on the basis that his daughter had no right to make the contract in his name. The store where the dress had been purchased contended Mary was her father's agent by necessity. Was she?

31

Operation and Termination of an Agency

Preview Cases

Hawkins was the manager of the Three Bar Ranch. The owner went on a world tour and left Hawkins in complete charge. Hawkins used the proceeds from the sale of cattle to buy and sell cattle at the public sales barns. His gross profits from these speculations amounted to $3,800, and his losses to $1,400, leaving a net profit of $2,400. When the principal returned and learned of these speculations, she demanded the $3,800 in profits. Is she entitled to recover this amount?

John Kennon, doing business as Kennon Adjustment Company, was hired by Commercial Standard Insurance Company to investigate a workers' compensation claim. There was no agreement as to the amount to be paid Kennon. After an award was made to the claimant, Kennon submitted a bill for more than three times the amount of the award. Commercial refused to pay that amount, and Kennon sued it. In the absence of an agreement for compensation, how much, if anything, must be paid an agent?

In a contract of agency, the law imposes upon the agent certain duties even though they are not set out in the contract. Likewise, the relationship of agency creates specific duties and obligations which the principal owes to an agent even though these are not specifically enumerated in the contract. In turn, the agency relationship imposes upon both principal and agent certain duties and obligations to third parties. An examination of these duties and obligations will reveal the importance of the relationship of agent and principal as well as the necessity for each party in the relationship to be fully cognizant of both the rights and duties which exist.

Agent's Duties to Principal

An agent owes the following important duties to the principal:

1. Loyalty and good faith
2. Obedience
3. Reasonable skill and diligence
4. Accounting
5. Information

Loyalty and Good Faith. The relationship of principal and agent is fiduciary in nature; that is, the principal must trust the agent to perform the duties according to contract. The relationship of agent and principal calls for a higher degree of faith and trust than do most contractual relationships. For this reason the law imposes upon agents the duty of loyalty and good faith and deprives them of their right to compensation, reimbursement, and indemnification when they prove disloyal to their principal or act in bad faith. The interests of the principal must be promoted by agents to the utmost of their ability.

Loyalty and good faith are abstract terms that give the courts wide latitude in interpreting what acts constitute bad faith or a breach of loyalty. Such acts as secretly owning an interest in a firm that competes with the principal, disclosing confidential information, selling to or buying from the agent without the knowledge of the principal, and acting simultaneously as the agent of a competitor are acts which the courts have held to be breaches of good faith. An agent who acts in bad faith not only may be discharged but the principal may also recover any damages which have been sustained. Also, the principal may recover any profits the agent has made while acting in bad faith even though the principal was not damaged by the act.

Hawkins was the manager of the Three Bar Ranch. The owner went on a world tour and left Hawkins in complete charge. Hawkins used the proceeds from the sale of cattle to buy and sell cattle at the public sales barns. His gross profits from these speculations amounted to $3,800, and his losses to $1,400, leaving a net profit of $2,400. When the principal returned and learned of these speculations, she demanded the $3,800 in profits. Hawkins was required to turn over $3,800 to the principal. He could not offset his losses against the profits. This is the penalty for a breach of good faith.

Obedience. An agent may have two types of instructions from the principal: one is routine and the other is discretionary. In all routine instructions the agent must carry them out to the letter as long as compliance would not defeat the purpose of the agency, be illegal, or perpetrate a fraud on others. An example of this is an instruction not to accept any payments made by check. The agent is liable for any losses incurred by reason of disobeying instructions. There is no justification for disobeying such instructions under any conditions.

If the instruction is a discretionary one, agents must use the best judgment of which they are capable. For example, if the agent is instructed to accept checks, there is no liability for a bad check when in the agent's judgment the drawer of the check was solvent and reliable. If an agent accepts a check which the agent has reason to believe is bad, the agent will be liable for any loss which the principal sustains by reason of this act.

Reasonable Skill and Diligence. One who acts as an agent must possess the skill required to perform the duties and must be diligent in performing the skill. There is an implied warranty that the agent has such skill and will exercise such diligence. Any breach of this warranty subjects the agent to a liability for damages for the loss by reason of the breach.

Because it is assumed that agents are appointed in reliance on their individual skills, talents, and judgment, it is not generally permissible for an agent to appoint subagents. This, of course, is not true if the agency agreement provides for the appointment of subagents, if the work delegated is merely clerical, or if the type of the agency is one in which it is customarily assumed that subagents would be appointed. Whenever the appointment of subagents is permissible, the agent must use skill and diligence in appointing competent subagents and remains liable to the principal for their breach of good faith or lack of skill.

Accounting. The duties of an agent include the keeping of a record of all money transactions pertaining to the agency. An accounting must be made to the principal for any of the principal's money and property that may come into the agent's possession. Money should be deposited in a bank in the name of the principal, preferably in a bank other than that in which the agent keeps personal funds. If the deposit is made in the name of the agent, any loss that may be caused by the failure of the bank will fall on the agent. Personal property of the principal must be kept separate from property of the agent.

Information. It is the duty of agents to keep principals informed of all facts pertinent to the agency that may enable the principals to protect their interests. In consequence, a principal's promise to pay a bonus to an agent for information secured by the agent in the performance of duties is unenforceable on the ground that the principal was entitled to the information anyway. The promise was therefore not supported by consideration.

Principal's Duties to the Agent

The principal has four important duties in respect to the agent:

1. Compensation
2. Reimbursement
3. Indemnification
4. Abidance by the terms of the contract

Compensation. The compensation due the agent is determined by the contract of employment. As in most other contracts, this provision may be either express or implied. If the amount is clearly and expressly stated, disputes seldom arise. If a person is asked to serve as an agent but no amount of compensation is stated, the agent is entitled to reasonable or customary compensation for services provided. This is true when an individual acts as an attorney or an accountant. If there are no customary rates of compensation, a reasonable rate will be fixed by the court according to the character of the services rendered. Frequently, the compensation is on a contingent basis, such as a percentage of the selling price, provided a sale is made. In such a case, the agent cannot collect compensation from the principal unless a sale is made.

John Kennon, doing business as Kennon Adjustment Company, was hired by Commercial Standard Insurance Company to investigate a workers' compensation claim. There was no agreement as to the amount to be paid Kennon. After an award was made to the claimant, Kennon submitted a bill for more than three times the amount of the award. Commercial refused to pay that amount, and Kennon sued it. The court held that in the absence of an agreement for compensation, there is an implied promise by a principal to pay an amount which is reasonable for such services rendered in the location where they were furnished.

Reimbursement. Any expenses incurred or disbursements made by the agent from personal funds as a necessary part of the agency are the liability of the principal. The agent is entitled to reimbursement. If, for example, the agent had to pay from personal funds a $100 truck repair bill before a trip on behalf of the principal could be continued, the agent would be entitled to reimbursement. If, on the other hand, a $50 fine for speeding had to be paid, the principal would not be required to reimburse this expense. Any expense incurred as a result of an unlawful act must be borne by the agent.

Indemnification. A contractual payment made by the agent for the principal is an expense of the principal. If the payment is made by the agent, not by reason of a contract but as a result of a loss or damage due to an accident, the principal must indemnify the agent. The principal must reimburse expenses and indemnify for losses and damages. If the principal directs the agent to sell goods in the stock room which already belong to the principal's customer, that customer can sue both the principal and the agent. If the agent is required to pay the customer damages, the agent can in turn sue the principal for giving the instructions which caused the loss.

Abidance by the Terms of the Contract. The principal must abide by the terms of the contract in all respects. Thus, the agent must be employed for the period stated in the contract unless there is justification for terminating the contract at an earlier date. If the cooperation or participation of the principal is required in order to enable the agent to perform duties, the principal must cooperate or participate to the extent required by the contract. For example, if the agent is to sell by sample and is to be paid a commission on all sales, samples must be furnished, and the opportunity to earn the fee or commission must be given. In real estate agencies this creates peculiar problems. If the owner of land merely lists land with the agent, either the owner or any other real estate agent may sell the property. In this case the first agent has no complaint. If the owner makes the first agent an exclusive agent for selling the land, the owner cannot list the property with another agent, for that would deprive the exclusive agent of the contractual opportunity to earn a commission. The owner, however, may sell the land. A third variant of this type of agency is the "exclusive sale" agency. In this case neither another agent nor the owner can sell the property while the agency remains in effect.

Agent's Liabilities to Third Parties

Ordinarily, whenever an agent performs duties, the principal is bound but not the agent. In relations with third parties, however, an agent may be personally liable on contracts and for wrongs in several ways:

1. Agents who contract in their own names and do not disclose the names of the principals become liable to the same extent as though they were the principals.

2. Agents may make themselves personally liable to third parties by an express agreement to be responsible.

3. People who assume to act for others without authority, or who exceed or materially depart from the authority that they were given, are personally liable to those with whom they do business. The latter situation may arise when agents are overzealous in effecting what they may think is a desirable contract.

4. Agents who sign contracts in their own names, will be held liable. The proper way for an agent to sign so as to bind only the principal is to sign "principal, by agent." A signing of the principal's name alone will

likewise protect the agent, although the third person may require the placing of the agent's name under the name of the principal so that at a later date it can be determined which agent had obtained the contract.

5. An agent is personally liable for fraud or any other wrongdoing, whether it was caused by disobedience, carelessness, or malice, or whether it was committed on the order of the principal.

Principal's Duties and Liabilities to Third Parties

The principal is ordinarily liable to third parties for contracts made within the actual or the apparent scope of the agent's authority. When the agent enters into an unauthorized contract that is not within the apparent scope of authority, the principal is not bound unless the contract is subsequently ratified.

The test of whether there is apparent authority is whether, on the basis of the conduct of the principal, a reasonable person would believe that the agent had the authority to make the particular contract. If the answer is in the affirmative, the principal is bound by the contract. For example, if the manager of a furniture store sells a suite of furniture on credit contrary to the authority granted, the principal is bound to fulfill the contract with the third party, provided the third party did not know of the limitation upon the agent's authority. The agent is then liable to the principal for any loss sustained.

The principal, as well as the agent, is liable for an injury to the person or the property of a third party that was caused by the negligence or the wrongful act of the agent in the course of employment. When the agent steps aside from the business of the principal and commits a wrong or injury to another, the principal is not liable unless the act is ratified.

Termination of an Agency by Acts of the Parties

An agency may be terminated by acts of the parties by:

1. Original agreement
2. Subsequent agreement
3. Revocation
4. Renunciation by the agent

Original Agreement. The contract creating the agency may specify a date for the termination of the agency. In that event, the agency is automatically terminated on that date. Most special agencies, such as a special agency to sell an automobile, are terminated because their purpose has been accomplished.

Subsequent Agreement. An agency may be terminated at any time by an agreement between the principal and the agent.

Revocation. The principal may revoke the agent's authority at any time, thereby terminating the agency. One must distinguish between the right to terminate the agency and the power to do so. The principal has the right to terminate the agency any time the agent breaches any material part of the contract of employment. If the agent, for example, fails to account for all money collected for the principal, the agent may be discharged, and the principal incurs no liability for breach of contract. The principal, on the other hand, has the power, with one exception, to revoke the agent's authority at any time. Under these circumstances, however, the principal becomes liable to the agent for any damages sustained by reason of an unjustifiable discharge. This is the agent's sole remedy. The agent cannot insist upon the right to continue to act as an agent even though nothing has been done to justify a termination before the end of the contract period.

The only exception to this rule of power to terminate occurs in the case of an agency coupled with an interest. Interest may take one of two forms: (1) interest in the authority and (2) interest in the subject matter. An agent has interest in the authority when authorized to act as an agent in collecting funds for the principal with an agreement that the agent is not to remit the collections to the principal but to apply them on a debt owed to the agent by the principal. In the second case, the agent has a lien on the property of the principal as security for a debt and is appointed as agent to sell the property and apply the proceeds on the debt.

The Cheyney Hardware Company owed Hanson $4,200. Hanson was appointed the agent for the Cheyney Hardware Company to collect certain accounts receivable for the principal, with instructions to keep the first $4,200 and remit the balance to the principal. After Hanson had collected $1,000, the principal attempted to discharge him. The principal cannot terminate this agency until Hanson has collected at least $4,200.

Renunciation. Like the principal, the agent has the power to renounce the agency at any time. An agent who abandons the agency without cause before the contract is fulfilled is liable to the principal for all losses due to the unjustified abandonment.

Termination by Operation of Law

An agency may also be terminated by operation of law. This may occur because of:

1. Subsequent illegality
2. Death or incapacity

3. Destruction
4. Bankruptcy
5. Dissolution
6. War

Subsequent Illegality. Subsequent illegality of the subject matter of the agency terminates the agency.

Death or Incapacity. Death or incapacity of either the principal or agent terminates the agency. For example, if the agent permanently loses the power of speech so that the principal's business cannot be performed, the agency is automatically terminated.

Destruction. Destruction of the subject matter, such as the destruction by fire of a house that was to be sold by the agent, terminates the agency.

Bankruptcy. Bankruptcy of the principal terminates the agency. In most cases bankruptcy of the agent does not terminate the agency.

Dissolution. Dissolution of a corporation terminates an agency in which the corporation is a party. This is similar to death, since a dissolution of a corporation is a complete termination of operation except for the activities necessary for liquidation.

War. When the country of the principal and that of the agent are at war against each other, the agent's authority is usually terminated or at least suspended until peace is restored. When war makes performance impossible, the agency is terminated.

Notice of Termination

When agencies are terminated by the acts of the principals, the principals must give notice to third parties with whom the agents have previously transacted business and who would be likely to deal with them as an agent.

When an agency is terminated by the operation of law, notice need not be given either to the agent or to third parties.

Questions

1. What duties does an agent owe the principal?

2. What two types of instructions may a principal give the agent?

3. When may an agent appoint subagents?

4. For what must an agent give an accounting to the principal?

5. If the agent and the principal do not set the amount of the agent's compensation at the time the contract is performed, on what basis is the amount determined if the agent and the principal cannot agree?

6. If an agent must pay agency expenses out of personal funds in order to complete the mission, what is the liability of the principal?

7. If an agent exceeds authority when contracting with a third party, who is held liable on the contract?

8. If an agent commits a fraudulent act on the instructions of the principal, who is liable to the third party for damages?

9. What is the principal's liability in regard to third parties for injuries caused by the negligent acts of agents?

10. When must notice of termination of an agency be given?

Case Problems

1. Heckman was an agent to sell Porter's country manor for $60,000. Johani contacted Heckman and asked him to find her a property of certain descriptions and agreed to pay him 5 percent of the purchase price if he found a desirable place. Without disclosing to Johani that he also was the agent to sell Porter's property, Heckman persuaded Johani to buy the Porter mansion. After the sale was consummated, Johani learned of Heckman's status as an agent for both parties and refused to pay Heckman his 5 percent commission. Must she pay?

2. The Scott Investment Company owned a housing project consisting of about 200 private dwellings. Langdon was the manager for this project. One of his duties was to keep each property properly insured. He was a secret partner with his mother-in-law in an insurance agency. He placed all insurance with this agency. There was no evidence that he purchased any more insurance than was necessary nor was there any excessive charge of any kind. When the principal learned of Langdon's ownership of the agency, it demanded his share of the profits on all policies placed on the 200 private dwellings. Was the Scott Investment Company entitled to these profits?

3. As the agent of Judy Hiller, Helen L. Lips Realty, Inc., negotiated the sale of Hiller's home and accepted checks totalling $2,400 as a deposit. Lips never cashed the checks. The purchaser refused to close the sale and then stopped payment on the checks. Hiller sued Lips for $2,400. Lips alleged that Hiller

had not stated a basis for a suit and moved to have it dismissed. Had Hiller presented grounds for a lawsuit?

4. Thomas and Cassandra Tackett were agents of Montgomery Ward. They would purchase merchandise from Wards, resell it to customers, and be paid commissions from Wards. The franchise agreement was terminated by Wards. In the resulting lawsuit, the Tacketts alleged wrongful termination. Many errors had been made by Wards in shipments, and while the policy of Wards was to act upon claims for credit within ten days, they were actually delaying some claims for months and refusing to pay some valid claims. The Tacketts withheld credits due Wards because of the trouble getting their claims approved. Several times they asked for an audit to settle the financial questions. When an auditor arrived without explanation, they assumed it was in response to their requests. Thomas told the auditor he was withholding credits because his claims were not properly approved. After the audit Thomas was asked to sign a statement agreeing to remit $1,586.49 to Wards. After signing, the agency was terminated. Was it wrongfully terminated?

5. Watson was employed by Whitworth as her agent at a salary of $15,000 a year plus expenses while traveling. Watson worked the first month, and during that time he filed an expense account of $75 for each day he worked, although some days he did not leave town. Whitworth discharged him and refused to pay him any salary or reimburse him for expenses. Watson sued for one year's salary plus one month's travel expense. Discuss their rights.

6. Welch was the general manager of a corporation. In addition to purchasing supplies for the corporaton she purchased an amount on her own account, which she then sold at a substantial profit. The corporation sued Welch for the profit she made. Was the corporation entitled to the profit?

7. Bak-a-Lum Corporation of America (BAL) had an agreement with Alcoa Building Products, Inc., by which BAL was the exclusive distributor in Northern New Jersey for ALCOA's aluminum siding. At a time when ALCOA had already secretly decided to terminate the exclusive nature of the distributorship, BAL, with ALCOA's knowledge, made a major expansion in its warehouse facilities at substantial expense. Just before the announcement of the termination, ALCOA's salespeople induced BAL to place an extremely heavy order. BAL sued ALCOA, alleging breach of good faith. Was there a breach of good faith?

32

Employer and Employee

Preview Cases

Under a written contract, Alex Mumford was employed by Hutton & Bourbonnais Company. The annual salary was to be increased in 60 and 90 days for satisfactory performance. In addition, Hutton was to advance money each month to Mumford's override account as follows: for the first year, 1 percent on all new accounts, and in the second and third years, 1/2 of 1 percent. At the end of the third year these were to become house accounts. Mumford was discharged, and he sued, alleging the employment contract was to be for three years. Was it?

Stair Glide manufactured elevator chairs which, if a gear stripped, would accelerate and throw their occupants out. Richard Dewey, employed by Stair Glide to weld and not to do engineering or design-concept work, heard about the problem through "shop talk." While at work, he had an idea for a safety device. He gathered some scrap material during lunch hour and built a model. He used the company welder and cutting torch as well as some of his own tools. Employees were allowed to take scrap home. At home, he made a drawing of his safety device. The next day he showed his drawing to Stair Glide officials and fully explained his idea and its operation. Stair Glide never returned his drawing but manufactured and used the device despite being told Dewey wanted compensation for the use of his idea. Dewey sued Stair Glide. Did Stair Glide have a shop right to the device?

Over a period of many decades the common law developed rules governing the relationship between an employer and employees, frequently called the master and servant relationship. Not only have the terms "master" and "servant" been largely abandoned but the laws governing their relationship have been greatly modified. In every state there are remnants of the common law which still apply to the employer-employee relationship. Many of its features dealing with safe working conditions and other aspects of the employment contract have been retained in modern labor legislation. These new laws do not cover all employees. In every state a very small number of employees still have their rights and duties determined largely by the common-law master-servant concept. The common law was slanted heavily in favor of the employer. This chapter deals with the common law and statutory modifications of it as they relate to employers and employees.

Creation of Employer and Employee Relationship

The relationship of employer and employee arises from a contract of employment, either express or implied. The common law allowed employers the right to hire whom they pleased and employees the right to freely choose their employers. The relationship of employer and employee could not be imposed upon anyone without consent. One who voluntarily performs the duties of a servant, cannot by that act subject the employer or householder to the liability of a master. But the relationship may be implied by conduct which demonstrates that the parties agree that one is the employer and the other the employee.

In the event an employee is discharged without cause, the employer must pay the wages due up to the end of the contract period. Seldom is the length of the contract period mentioned when the employer-employee relationship is created. In some jurisdictions, it is implied by the terms of compensation. An employee who is paid by the hour, may be discharged without liability at the end of any hour. If an employee is paid by the week or by the month, as is usually the case with many office employees, the term of employment is one week or one month as the case may be. With the monthly paid employees, the term of employment may depend upon the way the compensation is specified. If the quoted salary is $17,500 a year, the term of employment is one year, even though the employee is paid once a month. In other jurisdictions, employment at a set amount per week, month, or year does not constitute employment for any definite period, but is an indefinite hiring.

Under a written contract, Alex Mumford was employed by Hutton & Bourbonnais Company. The annual salary was to be increased in sixty and ninety days for satisfactory performance. In addition, Hutton was to advance money each month to Mumford's override account as follows: for the first year, 1 percent on all new accounts, and in the second and third years, 1/2 of 1 percent. At the end of the third year these were to become house accounts. Mumford was discharged, and he sued, alleging the employment contract was to be for three years. The court held that the time specified in the contract was just a formula for crediting the override account and did not establish a definite term of employment. Since the term was not specified, the contract was for an indefinite period and terminable at will.

The terms of the employer-employee contract, other than the compensation, are frequently not stated. They are determined by law, custom, and union contracts. In some cases, courts have held that statements in employers' written policy manuals are terms of employer-employee contracts.

Union Contracts

As indicated previously, the employer-employee relationship can come into existence only as the result of a contract, express or implied. Formerly the employer contracted individually with each employee. However, as the union movement developed and collective bargaining became commonplace, employers began agreeing to provisions of employment which applied to large numbers of employees. This agreement was between the employer and the union and was embodied in a signed contract between them. An agent of the employees, the union, speaks and contracts for all the employees collectively. As a general rule, a contract is still made individually with each employee, but the union contract binds the employer to recognize certain scales of union wages, hours of work, job classifications, and related matters.

Duties and Liabilities of the Employer

The employer under the common law had five well-defined duties:

1. Duty to exercise care
2. Duty to provide a reasonably safe place to work
3. Duty to provide safe tools and appliances
4. Duty to provide competent and sufficient employees for the task
5. Duty to instruct employees with reference to the dangerous nature of employment

Duty to Exercise Care. This rule imposes liability on employers if their negligence causes harm to an employee. The test whether employers have exercised proper care is whether they have done what a reasonable person would have done under the circumstances to avoid harm.

Duty to Provide a Reasonably Safe Place to Work. The employer is required to furnish every employee with a reasonably safe place to work. What is a safe place depends upon the nature of the work. Most states have statutes modifying the common law for hazardous industries.

Duty to Provide Safe Tools and Appliances. The tools furnished the employees by the employer must be safe. This rule applies also to the machinery and appliances.

Duty to Provide Competent and Sufficient Employees for the Task. Both the number of employees and their skill and experience affect the hazardous nature of many jobs. The employer is liable for all injuries to employees when the direct cause is due either to an insufficient number of workers or to the lack of skill of some of the workers.

Duty to Instruct Employees. In all positions where machinery, chemicals, electric appliances, and other production instruments are used, there are many hazards. The law requires the employer to give that degree of instruction to a new employee which a reasonable person would give under the circumstances to avoid reasonably foreseeable harm which could result from a failure to give such instructions.

Common-Law Defenses of the Employer

Under the common law, when an injured employee sued the employer, the employer could raise the following defenses:

1. The employee's contributory negligence
2. The act of a fellow servant
3. A risk assumed by the employee

Contributory Negligence Rule. The contributory negligence rule is that the employer can escape liability for breach of duty if it can be established that the employee's own negligence contributed to the accident. If the employee could have avoided the injury by the exercise of due diligence, there is no right to collect damages from the employer.

The Fellow-Servant Rule. The fellow-servant rule allows an employer to avoid liability by proving that the injury was caused by a fellow servant. A *fellow servant* is an employee who has the same status as another worker and is working with that employee. This rule has been abrogated or so severely limited that it is now very rarely of any significance.

Assumption-of-Risk Rule. Every type of employment in industry has some normal risks. The assumption-of-risk rule is that employees assume these normal risks by voluntarily accepting employment. Therefore, if the injury is due to the hazardous nature of the job, the employer cannot be held liable.

Statutory Modification of Common Law

The rising incidence of industrial accidents, due to the increasing use of more powerful machinery and the growth of the industrial labor population, led to a demand for statutory modification of the common-law rules relating to the liability of employers for industrial accidents.

For most kinds of employment, state workers' compensation statutes govern. They provide that the injured employee is entitled to compensation from the employer as long as the accident occurred in the course of employment from a risk involved in that employment. The employer is liable regardless of whether or not negligence was a cause of the accident.

Modification of Common-Law Defenses. One type of change was to modify by statute the defenses which an employer could assert when sued by an employee for damages. Under such statutes as the Federal Employers' Liability Act and the Federal Safety Appliance Act, which apply to common carriers engaged in interstate commerce, the plaintiff must still bring an action in a court and prove the negligence of the employer or other employees, but the burden of proving the case is made lighter by limitations on the employer's defenses. The employer is liable even if the employee is contributorily negligent; however, such negligence may diminish the amount of damages.

In many states the common-law defenses of employers whose employees are engaged in hazardous types of work have also been modified by statute.

Workers' Compensation. A more sweeping development has been made by the adoption of workers' compensation statutes in every state. With respect to certain industries or businesses, these statutes provide that an employee, or certain relatives of a deceased employee, are entitled to recover damages for the injury or death of the employee whenever the injury arose within the course of the employee's work from a risk involved in that work. In such a case compensation is paid without regard to whether the employer or the employee was negligent, although generally no compensation is allowed for a willfully self-inflicted injury or a harm sustained while intoxicated. However, the employer has the burden of proving that the injury was intentionally self-inflicted. The amount of recovery is limited and set in accordance with a prescribed schedule.

There has been a gradual widening of the workers' compensation statutes, either by amendment or by the adoption of special statutes, so that compensation today is generally recoverable for accident-inflicted injuries and occupational diseases. In some states compensation for occupational diseases is limited to those specified by name in the statute, such as silicosis, lead poisoning, or injury to health from radioactivity. In other states any disease arising from the occupation is compensable.

Workers' compensation proceedings differ from the common-law action for damages or an action for damages under an employer's liability statute in that the latter actions are brought in a court of law, whereas workers' compensation proceedings are brought before a special administrative agency or workers' compensation board. However, either party may appeal the agency's decision to the appropriate court of law.

Workers' compensation statutes do not bar an employee from suing another employee for the injury.

Occupational Safety and Health Act. In 1970, the Williams-Steiger Occupational Safety and Health Act was enacted to ensure safe and healthful working conditions. This federal law applies to every employer engaged in a business affecting interstate commerce except governments. The Occupational Safety and Health Administration (OSHA) administers the Act and issues standards which must be complied with by employers and employees. In order to ensure compliance with the standards, jobsite inspections are carried out by OSHA. Detailed records of work-related deaths, injuries, and illnesses are required to be maintained by employers. Fines are provided for violations of the Act, including penalties of up to $1,000 per day for failure to correct violations within the allotted time.

Liabilities of the Employer to Third Parties

The employer is liable under certain circumstances for injuries which are caused by employees to third parties. To be liable, the employee must have committed the injury in the course of employment. An employee, who, without any direction from the employer, injures a third party when the injury was not a result of the employment, is personally liable, but the employer is not. There is liability, however, if the employer ordered the act which caused the injury or had knowledge of the act and assented to it. Finally, the employer is liable for the torts of employees when these torts are due to personal negligence in not enforcing safe working procedures; providing safe equipment, such as trucks; or employing competent employees.

The Benten Wrecking Company instructed its employees not to throw timbers from the roof of the building it was wrecking unless one employee was on the ground to see that no one was in danger. The employees ignored this instruction and threw a large timber from the roof, injuring a person walking beside the building. The company was liable for this injury even though the employees ignored their instructions.

Employee's Duties to the Employer

The employee owes certain duties to the employer. Job duties must be performed faithfully and honestly. In skilled positions, the worker must perform the task with ordinary skill. Trade secrets or confidential information must not be revealed. In the event an employee breaches any of these duties, the employer's only practical remedy is to discharge the employee.

In the absence of an express or implied agreement to the contrary, inventions belong to the employee who devised them, even though the time and property of the employer were used in their discovery, provided that the employee was not employed for the express purpose of inventing the things or the processes which were discovered.

If the invention is discovered during working hours and with the employer's material and equipment, the employer has the right to use the invention without charge in the operation of the business. If the employee has obtained a patent for the invention, the employer must be granted a nonexclusive license to use the invention without the payment of royalty. This *shop right* of the employer does not give the right to make and sell machines that embody the employee's invention; it only entitles the employer to use the invention in the operation of the plant.

Stair Glide manufactured elevator chairs which, if a gear stripped, would accelerate and throw their occupants out. Richard Dewey, employed by Stair Glide to weld and not to do engineering or design-concept work, heard about the problem through "shop talk." While at work, he had an idea for a safety device. He gathered some scrap material during lunch hour and built a model. He used the company welder and cutting torch as well as some of his own tools. Employees were allowed to take scrap home. At home, he made a drawing of his safety device. The next day he showed his drawing to Stair Glide officials and fully explained his idea and its operation. Stair Glide never returned his drawing but manufactured and used the device despite being told Dewey wanted compensation for the use of his idea. Dewey sued Stair Glide. The court found he worked on his own time and at home where he fully developed his idea. He made only minimal use of Stair Glide's equipment, so Stair Glide did not have a shop right to the device.

When an employee is employed in order to secure certain results from experiments to be conducted by that employee, the courts hold that the inventions equitably belong to the employer on the ground either that there is a trust relation or that there is an implied agreement to make an assignment.

In any case, an employee may expressly agree that inventions made during employment will be the property of the employer. If such contracts are not clear and specific, the courts are inclined to rule against the employer. The employee may also agree to assign to the employer inventions made after the term of employment.

Federal Social Security Act

The Federal Social Security Act has four major provisions:

1. Old-age and survivors' insurance
2. Assistance to persons in financial need
3. Unemployment compensation
4. Disability and Medicare benefits

Old-Age and Survivors' Insurance. The first provision of the Social Security Act is for payment by the Social Security Board of decreasing term life insurance to the dependents of covered workers who die before the age of retirement. This is called Survivors' Benefits. If the workers live to a specified age and retire, then they and their spouses draw retirement annuities known as joint and survivor annuities. This is the old-age part of the provision. Both parts of the first provision are called insurance because they shift risks that life insurance companies will assume for a fee. The survivors' insurance covers the risk of the breadwinner's dying and leaving dependents without a source of income. The old-age benefits cover the risk of outliving one's savings after retirement. These are the same risks assumed by life insurance and annuity insurance contracts.

Who Is Covered? The Social Security Act was passed in 1935 and has been amended at almost every session of Congress since then. Today practically everyone except federal employees is covered by the life and annuity insurance provisions of the Act. Employees in state and local governments, including public school teachers, may be brought under the coverage of the Act by means of agreements between the state and the federal government. Before these workers can be covered by this agreement, a majority of the eligible employees must vote in favor of the coverage.

Farmers, professional people (such as lawyers), and self-employed business people are for the most part covered by this provision of the Act. Self-employed people who net less than $400 a year are excluded. Also specifically excluded are certain types of work of close relatives, such as a parent for a child, work by a child under twenty-one for parents, employment of a spouse by a spouse, but the Act covers self-employment by a spouse.

Eligibility for Retirement Benefits. To be eligible for retirement benefits, one must meet these requirements:

1. Be fully insured at the time of retirement
2. Be sixty-two years of age or older
3. After reaching the age of retirement, have applied for retirement benefits. If one elects to start drawing benefits at age sixty-two there is a penalty in the

form of a reduction in benefits, depending on how many months one is short of age sixty-five. To be entitled to the maximum retirement benefits, one must wait until age sixty-five to apply for them.

Eligibility for Survivors' Benefits. When a worker dies before achieving a fully insured status, the family is entitled to survivors' benefits if the deceased was currently insured at the time of death. A person is currently insured if at the time of death there are a specified number of quarters of coverage ending with the quarter in which the death takes place or in which old-age insurance benefits become available.

Assistance to Persons in Financial Need. People over sixty-five who are in financial need may be eligible for supplemental security income payments. These are monthly payments from the federal government. They are also made to people in financial need who are blind or disabled. This is a noncontributory system. Need is the only test, whereas with the old-age insurance need is not considered.

Unemployment Compensation. In handling unemployment compensation, the federal government cooperates with the states, which set up their own rules for the payment of unemployment benefits. Payments of unemployment compensation are made by the states and not by the federal government.

The unemployment compensation laws of the various states differ in many respects, although they tend to follow a common pattern. They are alike in providing for raising funds by levies upon employers. The costs of running the programs, however, are paid by the federal government.

The state unemployment compensation laws apply in general to workers in commerce and industry. Agricultural workers, domestic servants, government employees, and the employees of nonprofit organizations formed and operated exclusively for religious, charitable, literary, educational, scientific, or humane purposes may not be included under the laws.

In order to be eligible for benefits, a worker generally must meet the following requirements:

1. Be available for work and registered at an unemployment office
2. Have been employed for a certain length of time within a specified period in an employment covered by the state law
3. Be capable of working
4. Not have refused employment for which the worker is reasonably fitted
5. Not be self-employed
6. Not be out of work because of a strike or a lockout still in progress
7. Have served the required waiting period

Disability and Medicare Benefits. As part of the contributory portion of social security, monthly cash payments, called disability insurance ben-

efits, are available for disabled persons under the age of sixty-five and their families. A disabled person is someone who is unable to engage in any substantial gainful activity because of a medically determinable physical or mental impairment that is expected to end in death or has lasted or will last continually for twelve months. The amount of the benefits paid is the same as the amount the disabled person would receive as an old-age beneficiary.

Medicare is insurance designed to help pay a large portion of personal health care costs. Virtually everyone aged sixty-five and over may be covered by this contributory hospital and medical insurance plan. The program, however, covers only specified services.

Taxation to Finance the Plan. To pay the life insurance and the annuity insurance benefits of the Social Security Act, both the employer and the employee are taxed an equal percentage of all income earned in any one year up to a specified maximum. Since both the maximum income and the rate may be changed at any session of Congress, one needs to check current regulations. The unemployment compensation part of the Act is financed by a payroll tax. In most states this tax is borne entirely by the employer. The old-age assistance part of the Act is paid for by general taxation. No specific tax is levied to meet these payments.

Questions

1. How does the relationship of employer and employee arise?

2. If the length of the contract period is not mentioned when the employer-employee relationship is created, how is it determined?

3. What are the common-law duties of an employer?

4. Under the Federal Employers' Liability Act, does contributory negligence on the injured employee's part bar recovery?

5. What are the basic provisions of workers' compensation statutes with regard to injury or death of an employee?

6. What law was enacted to ensure safe and healthful working conditions?

7. When may an employer be liable for injuries to third parties caused by employees?

8. May an employer sue an employee for lack of loyalty and good faith?

9. Does an employee who invents some device on the employer's time have an exclusive right to it?

10. What workers or income recipients in America are not covered under the retirement part of the Social Security Act?

11. What are the general requirements for a person to be eligible for unemployment benefits under typical state laws governing unemployment compensation?

12. For what Social Security programs are employees taxed?

Case Problems

1. William Roundtree was a cab driver for Dotty Cab Co. He usually worked until 3 or 4 A.M. Dotty's radio dispatcher told him to pick up a fare on Bell Street. Two hours later his body was found a block away from the cab by the police. He and another person had been shot. The homicide was not solved. His dependents sought workers' compensation benefits. Was Roundtree's death sufficiently related to his employment that workers' compensation should have been awarded?

2. John Leffler was employed by Fluor Corporation in Iran. The employment agreement stated Fluor would provide housing and utilities. Leffler and his wife lived on the third floor of an apartment complex occupied by Fluor employees. There was a swimming pool beneath the balcony of their apartment. At a party, Leffler made a $20 bet with his new boss that he could dive off the balcony of the apartment into the pool. Leffler was a skilled high diver, but the balcony was 10 to 20 feet higher than any dive he had made. The next day Leffler dove from his balcony into the pool. He returned to the building, announcing he was the first person to dive from the third floor. At his apartment he complained of back and chest pain. He collapsed and was taken to the hospital, where he died. Death was due to a ruptured aorta as a result of the dive. Leffler's widow sought workers' compensation benefits. Should they be awarded?

3. Keller was color blind. He was employed by Koner to operate a crane. The foreman had a red light signal to notify the crane operator when to stop and a green light to tell him to proceed with the operation. While the red light was flashing, Keller continued to operate the crane, and as a direct result of this, House was injured. Is Koner liable for this injury?

4. Lawson was injured by the moving parts of a piece of machinery. The injury could not have happened had a guard been placed over the moving part. It developed that a guard had been provided but that it had been removed by the previous operator of the machine. Lawson was not aware a guard had ever been on the machine. Is Lawson entitled to damages under the common law?

5. Vigitron, Inc., manufactured and sold electronic flame safety controls for industrial boiler systems. The business involved trade secrets and confidential proprietary information. James Ferguson was employed to supervise all research and development. James Weeden was employed to develop new products and improve on flame safeguard controls. Vigitron started its "9003" project to develop an improved flame safeguard control box. The president of Vigitron told Ferguson about the project and asked him to keep it secret. Weeden worked on the project at home in response to instructions from Ferguson. Ferguson and Weeden formed a partnership to market electronic systems. Ferguson resigned from Vigitron, and the two attempted to sell to a distributor of Vigitron products a flame safeguard control device they had developed. The distributor told Vigitron, which then sued Ferguson and Weeden. To whom does the new control device belong?

6. The teachers of Clarke County wish to be covered by social security. The County School Board refuses to consider placing them under social security. What act, if any, can the teachers take to obtain coverage?

33

Labor Legislation

Preview Cases

The Fair Labor Standards Act permits employers to ask the Secretary of Labor for a waiver of child labor laws to employ ten- and eleven-year-olds to harvest certain crops. The waivers are to be granted if: "the employment . . . would not be deleterious to their health or well-being" and "the level and type of pesticides and other chemicals used would not have an adverse effect on the health or well-being of" the children. On the basis of a review of existing scientific literature, the Department of Labor issued a series of regulations approving certain pesticides for use a set time before harvesting by ten- and eleven-year-olds. Two private, nonprofit organizations representing farmworker families asked a court to rule that the approval of pesticide use violated the statutory waiver provision. None of the literature reviewed addressed the risk to children. Were the regulations valid?

The law firm of Humphreys, Hutcheson & Moseley represented Southern Silk Mills, Inc., which was facing an election to be conducted by the National Labor Relations Board (NLRB) to determine whether its employees would be represented by the Amalgamated Clothing and Textile Workers Union. Before the election, two attorneys from the firm made speeches to groups of Southern's employees to persuade them to vote against the union in the election. They were introduced as attorneys in the law firm representing Southern. The law firm refused to comply with the disclosure requirements of the Labor-Management Reporting and Disclosure Act. It alleged that the requirements did not apply because the intent of the law was to discourage secret persuader activities and that its relationship to Southern was announced before the presentation. Did the disclosure requirements apply to the law firm?

Since 1930, more laws dealing with industrial relations have been passed by the federal government than had been passed during the prior history of the Republic. Although these laws together with the court interpretations of them are for the most part beyond the scope of a course in business law, some basic knowledge of them is valuable. Covered in this chapter are the Fair Labor Standards Act, the Labor-Management Relations Act, the Labor-Management Reporting and Disclosure Act, the Civil Rights Act of 1964, and the Age Discrimination in Employment Act.

The Fair Labor Standards Act

The Fair Labor Standards Act had two major objectives. The first objective was to place a floor under wages so that all employees engaged in interstate commerce would be paid a minimum wage regardless of economic conditions. The second objective was to discourage a long work week and thus spread employment. The first objective was accomplished directly by setting a minimum wage, which by successive amendments has increased to a rate of $3.35 per hour. The second objective was achieved not by fixing the maximum number of hours to be worked each week but by requiring employers to pay time and a half for all hours over forty. An employer may work employees, other than children, any number of hours a week if the overtime wage is paid.

Exclusions from the Act. Not all workers are covered by the provisions of the Fair Labor Standards Act. There are various classes of exclusions; the following are examples:

1. Employees working for firms engaged in intrastate commerce are not covered by the Act. This is not a specific exclusion in the Act but is the result of the constitutional provision giving Congress power to regulate interstate commerce, not intrastate commerce.

2. A large number of employees who are engaged in interstate commerce are not covered by the Act, since certain businesses, such as agriculture, are specifically excluded. These exclusions are rather numerous. Other exclusions apply to the type of position rather than to the nature of the industry. Examples of this type of exclusion are executives, administrators, and outside salespeople.

3. The maximum-hours provisions do not apply to employees in that part of the transportation industry over which the Interstate Commerce Commission has control, to any employee engaged in the canning of fish, and to persons who are employed as outside buyers of poultry, eggs, cream, or milk in their natural state.

Child Labor Provisions. The Act forbids "oppressive child labor." The employment of children under sixteen years of age is for the most part prohibited. This rule does not apply to certain agricultural employment, to parents or guardians employing their children or wards, to children employed as actors, or to certain types of employment specified by the Secretary of Labor as being excepted by the regulations. Youth between the ages of sixteen and eighteen are not permitted to work in industries declared by the Secretary of Labor to be particularly hazardous to health.

◆   The Fair Labor Standards Act permits employers to ask the Secretary of Labor for a waiver of child labor laws to employ ten- and eleven-year-olds to harvest certain crops. The waivers are to be granted if: "the employment . . . would not be deleterious to their health or well-being" and "the level and type of pesticides and other chemicals used would not have an adverse effect on the health or well-being of" the children. On the basis of a review of existing scientific literature, the Department of Labor issued a series of regulations approving certain pesticides for use a set time before harvesting by ten- and eleven-year-olds. Two private, nonprofit organizations representing farmworker families asked a court to rule that the approval of pesticide use violated the statutory waiver provision. None of the literature reviewed addressed the risk to children. The court ruled the law did not require that waivers be issued so that safety standards, no matter how arbitrary, would be set. The regulations were invalid because of a lack of objective proof of safety.

Contingent Wages. Many types of employment call for the payment of wages on a commission basis or on a piece-rate basis. Many salespeople receive a commission on their sales rather than a salary. If the commissions earned in any one week are less than the minimum wages for the hours worked, then the employer must add to the commission enough to bring the total earnings to the minimum wage. The same is true for those on a piece-rate basis. These types of incentive wages are allowed, but they cannot be used to evade the minimum-wage provisions of the Act.

The National Labor Relations Act and The Labor-Management Relations Act

The National Labor Relations Act of 1935 (the Wagner Act), expanded by the federal Labor-Management Relations Act of 1947, also known as the Taft-Hartley Act, was aimed at creating bargaining equality between employers and employees. It requires that the employer recognize and bargain with (collective bargaining) the representative selected by the employees. The employees' representative is typically a union. The Act also sought to eliminate certain forms of conduct from the scene of labor negotiations and employment by condemning them as unfair practices.

With the following specific exceptions, the Act applies to all employers engaged in interstate commerce:

1. The railroad industry, which is under the Railway Labor Act of 1947
2. Agricultural laborers
3. Domestic servants

4. Supervisory employees, who are considered a part of management
5. Government employees

There are five major provisions of the Labor-Management Relations Act. These five provisions are:

1. Continuation of the National Labor Relations Board (NLRB) created by the National Labor Relations Act
2. A declaration as to the rights of employees
3. A declaration as to the rights of employers
4. A prohibition of employers' unfair labor practices
5. A prohibition of unfair union practices

The National Labor Relations Board. The Labor-Management Relations Act provides for continuation of the National Labor Relations Board of five members appointed by the President. This board hears employees' complaints of unfair labor practices and also employers' and employees' complaints of unfair union practices. If the board finds that an unfair practice exists, it has the power to seek an injunction to stop the practice. When a strike threatens national health or safety, the President may appoint a five-person board of inquiry and upon the basis of their findings may apply to the federal court for an injunction which will postpone the strike for eighty days. The NLRB conducts investigations of complaints of unfair labor practices and supervises elections to determine the bargaining representative for the employees within each bargaining unit. In case of dispute, the NLRB determines the size and nature of the bargaining unit. In addition to appointing the NLRB, the President appoints a general counsel. This general counsel is entirely independent of the board in prosecuting complaint cases but in most other matters acts as the chief legal advisor to the board.

A Declaration as to the Rights of Employees. The Labor-Management Relations Act sets forth the following rights which the employees have:

1. To organize
2. To bargain collectively through their own chosen agents
3. To engage in concerted action; that is, strike, for their mutual aid and protection
4. To join or not to join a union unless a majority of all workers vote for a union shop and the employer agrees thereto

A Declaration as to the Rights of Employers. The Labor-Management Relations Act gives the employer many important rights:

1. To petition for an investigation when questioning the union's right to speak for the employees

2. To refuse to bargain collectively with supervisory employees
3. To institute charges of unfair labor practices by the unions before the board
4. To sue unions for breaches of the union contract whether the breach is done in the name of the union or as an individual union member
5. To plead with workers to refrain from joining the union, provided no threats of reprisal or promises of benefits are used

A Prohibition of Employers' Unfair Labor Practices.

The chief acts which are declared to be unfair practices by employers are:

1. Interfering in the exercise of the rights granted employees by the Act
2. Refusing to bargain collectively with employees when they have legally selected a representative
3. Dominating or interfering with the formation or administration of any labor organization or contributing financial support to it
4. Discriminating against or favoring an employee in any way because of membership or lack of membership in the union, although an employee may be fired for nonmembership in a union when there is a valid union shop contract
5. Discriminating against an employee who has filed a complaint against the employer

When the National Labor Relations Board finds the employer guilty of any of these acts, it usually issues a "cease and desist order." If the cease and desist order is not effective, an injunction may be obtained.

A Prohibition of Unfair Union Practices.

The federal statute lists seven specific acts which unions and their leaders may not engage in:

1. Coercion or restraint of workers in the exercise of their rights under the Act
2. Picketing an employer to force bargaining with an uncertified union
3. Refusal to bargain collectively with the employer
4. Charging excessive initiation fees and discriminatory dues and fees of any kind
5. Barring a worker from the union for any reason except the nonpayment of dues
6. Secondary boycotts or strikes in violation of law or the contract, although certain exceptions are made in the construction and garment industries. A *secondary boycott* is an attempt to cause a third party to a labor dispute to stop dealing with the employer. The third party would normally be a customer or supplier of the employer. The most common ways the boycott is carried out are by a strike or by picketing.
7. Attempts to exact payment from employers for services not rendered

The Labor-Management Reporting and Disclosure Act

In 1959, Congress passed the Labor-Management Reporting and Disclosure Act, also called the Landrum-Griffin Act. The purpose of this Act was to protect union members from improper conduct by union officials. The Act contains a bill of rights for union members, it classifies additional actions as unfair labor practices, and it requires unions operating in interstate commerce and their officers and employers to file detailed public reports.

Bill of Rights. The bill of rights provisions guarantee union members the right to meet with other union members, to express any views or opinions at union meetings, and to express views on candidates for union office or business before the meeting.

Additional Unfair Labor Practices. In addition to the unfair labor practices outlawed by the Labor-Management Relations Act, the following acts are declared to be unfair labor practices by the Labor-Management Reporting and Disclosure Act:

1. Picketing by employees in order to extort money and for recognition when another union is the legally recognized bargaining agent and there is no question regarding union representation.

2. To close loopholes, an expanded range of activities defined as secondary boycotts, except in the garment industry.

3. "Hot cargo agreements," except in the construction and garment industries. A *hot cargo agreement* is an agreement between a union and an employer that the employer will not use nonunion materials.

Reporting Requirements. The very detailed reporting requirements of the act require unions to file copies of their bylaws and constitutions in addition to reports listing the name and title of each officer; the fees and dues required of members; and the membership qualifications, restrictions, benefits, and the like. Financial information required to be reported includes a complete listing of assets and liabilities, receipts and disbursements. The union reports must be signed by the officials of the union, and the information contained in them must be made available to the union members.

The officials of the union must each file a report indicating any financial interest in or benefit they have received from any employer whose employees the union represents. They must also report whether they have received any object of value from an employer.

In addition to the requirement of annual reports by the union and its officials, employers must file annual reports listing any expenditures made to influence anyone regarding union organizational or bargaining activities. Certain information must be disclosed by everyone involved in labor persuader activities. All these reports are public information and are available to anyone who requests them.

◆   The law firm of Humphreys, Hutcheson & Moseley represented Southern Silk Mills, Inc., which was facing an election to be conducted by the NLRB to determine whether its employees would be represented by the Amalgamated Clothing and Textile Workers Union. Before the election, two attorneys from the firm made speeches to groups of Southern's employees to persuade them to vote against the union in the election. They were introduced as attorneys in the law firm representing Southern. The law firm refused to comply with the disclosure requirements of the Labor-Management Reporting and Disclosure Act. It alleged that the requirements did not apply because the intent of the law was to discourage secret persuader activities and that its relationship to Southern was announced before the presentation. The court held the goal of the law was disclosure, and since the activities of the law firm were persuader activities, it must comply with the disclosure requirements.

The act also contains a number of additional provisions aimed at making unions more democratic and at protecting union funds from embezzlement and misappropriation.

Civil Rights Act of 1964

The federal Civil Rights Act of 1964 is designed to prevent job discrimination on the basis of race, color, religion, sex, or national origin. The act applies to every employer engaged in an industry affecting interstate commerce who has 15 or more employees. Labor unions with 15 or more members are subject to the act. It does not apply to the United States government or certain private membership clubs which are exempt from federal taxation.

This law makes it an unlawful employment practice for an employer to fail to hire, to discharge, or to in any way discriminate against anyone with respect to the terms, conditions, or privileges of employment because of the individual's race, color, religion, sex, or national origin. The employer also may not adversely affect an employee's status because of one of these factors. In addition, it is an unlawful employment practice for an employment agency or a labor organization to in any way discriminate, classify, limit, or segregate individuals on any one of these bases.

The act establishes the Equal Employment Opportunity Commission, which hears complaints alleging violations of this act. The complaints may be filed by individuals, or the EEOC itself may issue charges. If the EEOC determines the charge is true, it must seek by conference, conciliation, and persuasion to stop the violation. If this fails, the EEOC may bring an action in federal court.

The Age Discrimination in Employment Act

In order to protect persons in the forty- to seventy-year-old age group, the Age Discrimination in Employment Act was enacted. This statute prohibits discrimination by employment agencies, employers, or labor unions against persons aged forty to seventy. Employers are prohibited from failing to hire persons in this age group, and they may not limit, segregate, or classify their employees so as to discriminate against persons in this age group.

Questions

1. What are the two objectives of the Fair Labor Standards Act?

2. Are all workers covered by the Fair Labor Standards Act?

3. What was the chief purpose of the Labor-Management Relations Act?

4. What does the National Labor Relations Board do?

5. **a.** If an employer refuses to bargain collectively with employees, is this an unfair labor practice?
   b. Name some unfair labor practices by employers.

6. What law outlaws secondary boycotts?

7. What are the three major provisions of the Labor-Management Reporting and Disclosure Act?

8. If an employer discriminates against a woman what law, if any, is violated?

9. What law prohibits discrimination against older employees?

Case Problems

1. Williams Chemical Co. operated self-service gasoline stations and hired married couples to manage some stations where living quarters were located on the premises. Employees were instructed to keep the stations open 80 hours a week, but there was no written policy regarding the number of hours each employee was to work. Instructions about whether they were to work together or alone were vague. Generally, both spouses were on duty for the total number of hours the station was open. Paychecks were evenly split between them, and the time cards indicated that each had worked 40 hours. Only one person was needed to manage the station during a shift. The Secretary of Labor filed suit, alleging the husband-wife teams were entitled to back wages for all the hours they were at the stations. Should they get this back pay?

2. The Fenton Model Airplane Company made kits for model airplanes, boats, and cars. It sold some finished products. To make the finished products ready for sale, it contracted with high school and business college students to make the kits into finished products. Each student would take a given number of

kits home, and when they were returned finished, a fixed sum would be paid for each item. After several months John became dissatisfied with the amount he was earning and demanded that he be paid the minimum wage for the number of hours that he worked on the models. The company insisted that he was an independent contractor, and therefore, he was not entitled to the minimum wage. Is the company's contention correct?

3. The Independent Carpenters Union was a local union made up of all the employees of the Grace Sheet Metal Company who worked in any way with wood. The president of the company contributed $500 a month to the union so that it would not have to charge its members dues. Some of the members who wanted to be represented by the National Carpenters' Union, a dues-paying union, filed a complaint with the National Labor Relations Board, charging the company with an unfair labor practice. Is this an unfair labor practice?

4. A state statute limited the occupations women could engage in and the number of hours they could work. A group of employees brought suit against their employer, alleging the state statute violated the Civil Rights Act. Are the employees correct?

5. Walter Parcinski, a buyer aged sixty-three, was fired from his job at The Edward Malley Company after Malley was purchased by The Outlet Company. Malley was debt-ridden, and Outlet hoped to make it profitable by having buying handled through its central purchasing office. This arrangement meant eliminating Malley's buying staff, of which Parcinski was a member. The decision to eliminate the buyers was made prior to any consideration of their ages. Only four of thirty buyers were given new positions with Malley, and three of these four were within the protected age range of the Age Discrimination in Employment Act (ADEA). Parcinski sued under the ADEA. Was his discharge a violation of the Act?

6. Crawford owned a cotton gin and cotton storage company. At the peak of the cotton-picking season, she employed 20 or more workers, but only four employees had full-time work. Often when there was a long line of trucks waiting to have the cotton ginned, she would keep running until midnight. Some of the workers would work 14 hours a day. They brought suit to compel Crawford to pay them minimum wages and time and a half for overtime. Are they entitled to this relief?

Summary Cases for Part Six

Agency and Employment

1. In response to a newspaper ad, Helen Campbell looked at a car at Duncan's residence. She believed he was the only person who had owned the car and that the right door had been dented but was fixed and all right. She purchased the car, believing it was basically brand-new. After receiving her title and finding out the transferor was Hamilton Auto Company, she learned the car had not been a one-owner car owned by Duncan. The car had been totaled, sold as salvage, and transferred through a series of dealers. It was worth $3,000 less than she had paid, considering its actual condition. Had she known all this, she would not have bought it. Gordon Hamilton authorized Duncan to buy cars with drafts drawn on Hamilton Auto Company. The purchase was financed at a bank with Hamilton's credit. Title to the cars was in Hamilton's name, and Hamilton limited Duncan to buying three cars at any time. He was required to dispose of them within 30 days. Campbell sued Hamilton, alleging that his agent, Duncan, committed fraud. Should she recover? [*Campbell v. Hamilton*, 632 S.W.2d 633 (Tex. Ct. App.)]

2. Joseph and Frida Friedman owned adjoining lots, No. 3 and No. 5, with Leonard and Bernice Feldman. They retained Lam and Buchsbaum as their agent to sell the lots. Charles Samter, a salesman for Lam and Buchsbaum, showed Lot No. 3 to Victor and Barbara Kasser. The Friedmans had left the sale of the lots to Leonard Feldman, so Samter told Feldman the Kassers were interested in Lot No. 3. He asked Feldman to meet them at the lot to show them its dimensions. The meeting could not be arranged, but Feldman met Samter, gave him a plot plan, and paced off the lot's boundaries, which they staked off. Feldman told Samter the staking was probably a bit off, and any purchaser should have the lot surveyed. Samter showed the lot to the Kassers, pointed out the stakes, and gave them a copy of the plot plan. They bought the lot and built a house. The Friedmans got full title to adjoining Lot No. 5 and moved into the house there. They had parking pads built within the area designated by the stakes. A survey showed the Kassers' carport was 5.8 feet on Lot No. 5, and their driveway was up to 45 feet on the lot. The Friedmans sued to have removed the Kassers' carport, driveway, and so much of their house as was within 15 feet of Lot No. 5 in violation of zoning ordinance. Are the Friedmans bound by the property line as demonstrated by Samter? [*Friedman v. Kasser*, 481 A.2d 886 (Pa. Super. Ct.)]

3. Alfred S. Dale was the owner of an apartment building in Bismarck. He ordered some beds from Sears, Roebuck and Company. When the beds arrived, he contracted with Nelson to install one of them in one of the apartments. Claude Newman rented the apartment. The bed collapsed and Newman was

seriously injured. Nelson had not followed instructions in installing the bed. He used wood screws instead of the lag screws which the seller had recommended for the installation. This was the direct cause of the collapse. Was Nelson an employee of Dale or an independent contractor? [*Newman v. Sears Roebuck Co. and Dale*, 43 N.W.2d 411(N.D.)]

4. Mr. and Mrs. Miles contracted to buy a house and met with Frederick Russell, president of Perpetual Savings & Loan Company, to arrange a mortgage loan. The Mileses asked about a termite inspection and were told it was Perpetual's policy to require one and that these matters were usually handled by Perpetual. A termite inspection company was hired by Perpetual to inspect the house. For the closing, Russell prepared a real estate Disclosure/Settlement Statement indicating a termite inspection had been made. A copy was given to the Mileses. Later that day Russell was told the inspection showed termite infestation, and treatment would cost $460. Russell did not tell the Mileses. After they took possession of the house, they discovered the termite damage, which was estimated to cost $5,962.50 to repair. They sued Perpetual. It alleged that the obligation of a savings and loan to appraise property prior to approving a loan did not impose a duty to disclose to the buyer information about the property obtained from the appraisal. Was it liable? [*Miles v. Perpetual Savings & Loan Co.*, 388 N.E.2d 1364 (Ohio)]

5. Edrel Clinkenbeard contracted to have Central Southwest Oil Corporation help him participate in a lottery conducted by the Department of the Interior to award leases of federal land. Central was to select valuable tracts coming up for leasing, do the paper work required to enter Clinkenbeard's name, and notify him if he won a lease. Tom Allen, the president of Central, called to say Clinkenbeard had won a lease. Allen stated that the lease was not particularly valuable and that there had been few filings on it but offered Clinkenbeard $5,020 for it. Clinkenbeard finally agreed to assign the lease for $7,020 and an overriding royalty. Later Clinkenbeard found out the lease was one of the most heavily filed on in the lottery and was worth several times what Central paid him. He sued for rescission of the assignment, alleging that Central, as his agent, violated its duty to disclose material facts to him. Should he be allowed to rescind? [*Clinkenbeard v. Central Southwest Oil Corporation*, 526 F.2d 649 (5th Cir.)]

6. Harry Hager was the former minister of a church and was sued by the church for possession of the parsonage he occupied. Hager alleged that his contract of employment with the church provided for him to be their minister for his life; therefore, he was entitled to occupy the parsonage. The written contract of employment was not available, but a form copy's only provision which applied to the term of employment stated: "We promise and oblige ourselves . . . to pay you the sum of $ _____ in _____ payments Yearly and every year so long as you continue the minister of the Church." Did the contract provide that employment was for the duration of Hager's life? [*Bethany Reformed Church of Lynwood v. Hager*, 406 N.E.2d 93 (Ill. App. Ct.)]

7. While employed as a professor of food science and microbiology at the University of North Carolina, Marvin Speck, with the assistance of Stanley Gilliland, professor of food science, developed a new procedure by which lactobacillus acidophilus could be added to milk without causing a sour taste. Both were employed to teach and do research on the use of high temperature for pasteurization and sterilization of foods. It was in the course of this research that the new procedure was developed. The process was discovered at the University, and resources provided for their research by the University made it possible for them to discover it. They sued the University to share in the royalties from the commercial use of the process. Are they entitled to payment? [*Speck v. North Carolina Dairy Foundation*, 319 S.E.2d 139 (N.C.)]

8. Billy Forrester sued Roth's IGA Foodliner to recover unpaid overtime compensation. Officials of Roth's did not know Forrester had worked uncompensated overtime hours. Forrester admitted he did not mention unpaid overtime to any store official. He knew that overtime was to be reported on time sheets and that the store paid for such reported overtime. He was paid for all overtime he reported. He stated that if he had reported the additional overtime he claimed in the suit he would have been paid. Was Roth's in violation of the Fair Labor Standards Act? [*Forrester v. Roth's I.G.A. Foodliner, Incorporated*, 646 F.2d 413 (9th Cir.)]

9. The Duke Power Co. required all new employees and employees requesting a transfer to have a high school diploma or to have passed an intelligence test. These requirements were not directed at or intended to measure ability to learn or perform a particular job or category of jobs. Because of these requirements, a disproportionate number of black applicants were denied employment. A group of black employees brought an action charging discrimination under the 1964 Civil Rights Act. Were the requirements discriminatory? [*Griggs v. Duke Power Co.*, 401 U.S. 424]

10. John P. Finnegan was the driver of a truck for the New York Tribune, Inc. On his way to deliver a truckload of paper, he collided with a bus driven by Sauter. When Sauter got out of the bus, an argument ensued between Sauter and Finnegan. Finnegan became very angry and kicked Sauter in the face, causing a very painful injury. Sauter then sued the employer of Finnegan, the New York Tribune, Inc., for damages for this unprovoked assault. Was the employer liable for this act of its employee? [*Sauter v. New York Tribune, Inc. et al*, 113 N.E.2d 790 (N.Y.)]

Part Seven — Partnerships

Learning Objectives for Part Seven

Partnerships

After studying this part you should be able to:

1. Explain what a partnership is.

2. Distinguish between the types of partnerships.

3. Identify the different kinds of partners.

4. Describe how a partnership is created.

5. Determine the interest a partner has in partnership property.

6. Explain the difference between partnerships, joint-stock companies, and joint ventures.

7. Specify the duties the law imposes upon partners.

8. Identify the rights every partner has.

9. Discuss the potential liabilities of partners for the contracts and torts of other partners.

10. Distinguish between the powers every partner has and does not have.

11. Explain the difference between dissolution and termination of a partnership.

12. Describe the ways in which a partnership may be dissolved by the partners, by a court decree, or by operation of law.

13. Discuss the effects of dissolution of a partnership.

14. Specify when notice of dissolution is necessary.

15. Explain how partnership assets are distributed upon dissolution.

34

Formation of a Partnership

Preview Cases

Brothers George and Clarence Simandl owned 6.638 acres of land on which they operated a gas station, delicatessen, and magazine stand. Clarence conveyed his share of the land to George, and a year later George reconveyed the property to Clarence. The conveyances were to aid the brothers' ability to get credit. When 5.5 acres of the land were sold by Clarence to nonfamily members, the proceeds were divided equally between George and Clarence. They shared in the receipts of the businesses, and both signed contracts for the purchase of goods sold. The brothers made business decisions only after consulting each other, and each was able to bind the other. After they both died, George's widow sued for half the real property and business. Was there an implied partnership?

Brinkley was a retired merchant. While she was in business, she had bought vast quantities of merchandise from a particular wholesaler. Her credit with the wholesaler was excellent. Hartman, in the presence of the credit manager of the wholesale firm, said, "Brinkley and I have formed a partnership and will be ordering some merchandise from your firm soon." Brinkley did not deny this statement. Soon thereafter Hartman sent in an order amounting to more than $5,000 on 90 days' credit. The account was never paid and the wholesaler sued Brinkley. Is Brinkley liable?

A *partnership* is a voluntary association of two or more persons who have combined their money, property, or labor and skill, or some or all of them, for the purpose of carrying on as co-owners some lawful business for their joint profit.

The partnership must be formed for the purpose of operating a lawful business. If the business is unlawful, the attempt to form a partnership to operate such a business is ineffective. Furthermore, a partnership may not be formed for the purpose of conducting a lawful business in an illegal manner.

A hunting club, a sewing circle, a trade union, a chamber of commerce, or other nonprofit association cannot be treated as a partnership because the purpose of a partnership must be to conduct a trade, business, or profession for profit.

Advantages of the Partnership

By the operation of a partnership, capital and skill may be increased, labor may be made more efficient, the ratio of expenses per dollar of business may be reduced, and management may be improved. It is not certain that all of these advantages will accrue to every partnership, but the prospect of greater profits by reason of them is the incentive which leads to the formation of a partnership.

Disadvantages of the Partnership

The most important disadvantages are:

1. The unlimited liability of each partner for the debts of the partnership
2. The relative instability of the business because of the danger of dissolution by reason of the death or withdrawal of one of the partners
3. The divided authority among the partners, which may lead to disharmony

Classification of Partnerships

Partnerships may be classified as follows:

1. Ordinary, or general, partnerships
2. Limited partnerships
3. Trading and nontrading partnerships

Ordinary, or General, Partnerships.   When two or more persons voluntarily contract to pool their capital and skill to conduct some business undertaking for profit, with no limitations upon their rights and duties, an *ordinary partnership*, or *general partnership*, is created. This is the oldest type of business combination and is still widely used today. This type of business organization is governed by the Uniform Partnership Act in most states.* The purpose of this Act is to bring about uniformity in the partnership laws of the states.

---

*The Uniform Partnership Act has been adopted in all states except Louisiana.

Limited Partnerships. A *limited partnership* is one in which one or more partners have their liability for the firm's debts limited to the amount of their investment. This type of partnership cannot operate under either the common law or the Uniform Partnership Act.* Such a partnership cannot be formed without a specific state statute prescribing the conditions under which it can operate. If the limited partnership does not comply strictly with the enabling statute, the courts hold it to be an ordinary partnership.

Trading and Nontrading Partnerships. A *trading partnership* is one engaged in buying and selling merchandise. A *nontrading partnership* is one devoted to services, such as accounting, medicine, dentistry, law, and similar professional services. The chief reason for making the distinction is that the members in a nontrading partnership usually have considerably less apparent authority than the partners in a trading partnership. For example, one partner in a nontrading partnership cannot borrow money in the name of the firm and bind the firm. One dealing with a nontrading partnership is charged with considerably more responsibility in ascertaining the actual authority of the partners to bind the firm than is a person dealing with a trading partnership.

Who May Be Partners?

Since a partnership is based upon a contract, any person who is competent to make a contract is competent to be a partner. A minor may become a partner to the same extent to which a contract may be made about any other matter. Such contracts are voidable, but a minor acting as the agent of the other partner or partners can bind the partnership on contracts within the scope of the partnership business. A minor partner is subject to the liabilities of the partnership. There is a conflict of authority as to whether a minor who withdraws from a partnership can withdraw the entire contribution which was originally made or whether a proportion of any losses must first be deducted.

Kinds of Partners

The members of a partnership may be classified as follows:

1. General partner
2. Silent partner
3. Secret partner
4. Dormant partner
5. Nominal partner

---

*A Uniform Limited Partnership Act has been adopted in all states except Louisiana.

General Partner. A *general partner* is one who is actively and openly engaged in the business and is held out to everyone as a partner. Such a partner has unlimited liability in respect to the partnership debts. A general partner appears to the public as a full-fledged partner, assumes all the risks of the partnership, and does not have any limitation of rights. This is the usual type of partner.

Silent Partner. A *silent partner* is one who, though possibly known to the public as a partner, takes no active part in the management of the business. Such a partner's rights as a partner are limited to the sharing of the profits in the ratio agreed upon. As a general rule, there are two inducements to a person to invest money but to take no active part in the management. The inducements are limited liability and no share of the losses. This type of partner is frequently called a limited partner when known to the public as a partner.

Secret Partner. An active partner who attempts to conceal that fact from the public is a *secret partner*. This is done to try to escape the unlimited liability of a general partner but at the same time take an active part in the management of the business. Should such a partner's relationship to the firm become known to the public, however, unlimited liability cannot be escaped. The difference between silent partners and secret partners is that secret partners: (1) are unknown to the public and (2) take an active part in the management of the business. Secret partners may feign the status of employees or may work elsewhere, but they meet frequently with the other partners to discuss management problems.

Dormant Partner. A *dormant partner* (sometimes referred to as a *sleeping partner*) usually combines the characteristics of both the secret and the silent partner. A dormant partner is usually unknown to the public as a partner and takes no part in the management of the business of the firm. When known to the public as a partner, a dormant partner is liable for the debts of the firm to the same extent as a general partner. In return for limited liability so far as the other partners are able to effect it, a dormant partner foregoes the right to participate in the management of the firm. In addition, such a partner may agree to limit income to a reasonable return on investment, since no services are contributed.

Nominal Partner. *Nominal partners* hold themselves out as partners or permit others to do so. In fact, however, they are not partners, since they do not share in the management of the business nor in the profits; but in some instances they may be held liable as a partner.

Creation of a Partnership

A partnership is the result of a contract, express or implied, just as all other business commitments result from a contract. The partnership contract must meet the five tests of a valid contract as set out in Chapter 4. A partnership may also be created when two or more parties act in such a way as to lead third parties to believe that a partnership exists. This manner of formation is treated more fully under "Implied Partnership Agreements" and "Partnership by Estoppel" later in this chapter.

Articles of Partnership

The partners need not have a written agreement, but if they choose to, in the absence of a statute to the contrary, the written contract providing for the formation of a partnership need not be in a particular form. The written agreement is commonly known as the *partnership agreement* or *articles of partnership*. Articles of partnership will vary according to the needs of the particular situation, but ordinarily they should contain the following:

1. Date
2. Names of the partners
3. Nature and the duration of the business
4. Name and the location of the business
5. Individual contributions of the partners
6. Sharing of profits, losses, and responsibilities
7. Keeping of accounts
8. Duties of the partners
9. Amounts of withdrawals of money
10. Unusual restraints upon the partners
11. Provisions for dissolution and division of assets
12. Signatures of partners

Implied Partnership Agreements

A partnership arises whenever the persons in question enter into an agreement which satisfies the definition of a partnership. Thus, there is a partnership when three persons agree to contribute property and money to the running of a business as co-owners for the purpose of making a profit, even though they do not in fact call themselves partners. Conversely, the mere fact that persons say "we are partners now" does not establish a partnership if the elements of the definition of a partnership are not satisfied.

In many instances, it is not possible to prove exactly what happened, because of the death of witnesses or the destruction of records. Because of this, it is provided by the Uniform Partnership Act that proof that a person received a share of profits is *prima facie* evidence of a partnership. This means that in the absence of other evidence, it should be held that there was a partnership. This *prima facie* evidence can be overcome, and the conclusion then reached that there was no partnership, by showing that the share of profits was received as wages or as payment of a debt, interest on a loan, rent, or the purchase price of a business or goods.

Brothers George and Clarence Simandl owned 6.638 acres of land on which they operated a gas station, delicatessen, and magazine stand. Clarence conveyed his share of the land to George, and a year later George reconveyed the property to Clarence. The conveyances were to aid the brothers' ability to get credit. When 5.5 acres of the land were sold by Clarence to nonfamily members, the proceeds were divided equally between George and Clarence. They shared in the receipts of the businesses, and both signed contracts for the purchase of goods sold. The brothers made business decisions only after consulting each other, and each was able to bind the other. After they both died, George's widow sued for half the real property and business. The court said a partnership can be found when there was a sharing of net profits from a continuing business and each person is able to bind the business. This was a partnership.

Partnership by Estoppel

The conduct of persons who in fact are not partners could be such as to mislead other persons into thinking that they are partners. The situation is then the same as when a person misleads others into thinking that someone is an authorized agent. In a case of a false impression of a partnership, the law will frequently hold that the apparent partners are estopped from denying that a partnership exists; otherwise, third persons will be harmed by their conduct.

Brinkley was a retired merchant. While she was in business, she had bought vast quantities of merchandise from a particular wholesaler. Her credit with the wholesaler was excellent. Hartman, in the presence of the credit manager of the wholesale firm, said, "Brinkley and I have formed a partnership and will be ordering some merchandise from your firm soon." Brinkley did not deny this statement. Soon thereafter Hartman sent in an order amounting to more than $5,000 on 90 days' credit. The account was never paid and the wholesaler sued Brinkley. She is liable since her silence estops her from denying that a partnership exists.

Partnership Firm Name

A firm name is not a legal necessity or requirement for a partnership, but it is useful as a matter of convenience and for the purpose of identification. Any name that does not violate the rights of others or that is not contrary to law may be adopted by the firm and may be changed at will by agreement. In some states it is not permissible to use the name of a person who is not a member of the firm or to use the words "and Company" unless the term indicates an additional partner(s). Many of the states permit the use of fictitious or trade names, but require the firm to register its name, address, purpose, and the names and addresses of the partners.

At common law a partnership cannot bring a suit at law or be sued in the name of the firm, but by statute or court rule a partnership may sue or be sued either in the firm name or in the names of the partners. Under the common law, real property may be held only in the names of the partners, but under the Uniform Partnership Act any property, whether real or personal, may be owned either in the names of the partners or in the name of the firm.

Partner's Interest in Partnership Property

There are three classes of joint ownership of property. *Joint ownership* exists when the survivors of joint owners get full title to all the property upon the death of one.

In the case of *common ownership*, upon the death of one party, the surviving co-owners do not get title to the deceased owner's part. That share passes by will, or if there is no will, to the deceased's heirs. In both the joint and common ownerships, each owner can sell or give away the fractional share owned without the consent of the other owner or owners.

A partner is a *tenant* or *owner in partnership*. This type of ownership differs fundamentally from the other two types. A surviving partner does not get full ownership upon the death of the other partner, as is the case in joint ownership. One partner is not as free to sell an interest in partnership property, as is the case with both the joint and common ownership. The personal creditors of one partner cannot force the sale of specific pieces of property of the partnership to satisfy personal debts, nor can they force the sale of a fractional part of specific assets. The personal creditors of one partner can ask a court to appoint a receiver to collect the profits and any other money due the debtor partner from the partnership. Each partner owns and call sell only a pro rata interest in the partnership as an entity. The purchaser of one partner's share cannot demand acceptance as a partner by the other partners. The purchaser acquires only the right to receive the share of profits the partner would have received.

Joint-Stock Companies

A *joint-stock company* is in some respects similar to a partnership, but the ownership is indicated by shares of stock, as in a corporation. The ownership of these shares may be transferred without dissolving the association, thus overcoming one of the chief disadvantages of the general partnership. But shareholders in a joint-stock company do not have the authority to act for the firm. The joint stockholders are still liable, jointly and severally, for the debts of the firm while they are members, and for this reason, joint-stock companies do not offer the safeguards of a corporation. Joint-stock companies are permitted to operate in some states by special statutes authorizing them, or in some states, without statute, as common-law associations.

Joint Ventures

A *joint venture* is a business relationship in which two or more persons combine their labor or property for a single undertaking and share profits and losses equally or as otherwise agreed. For example, two friends enter into an agreement to get the rights to cut timber from a certain area and market the lumber. A joint venture is similar in many respects to a partnership, the primary difference being that a joint venture is for a single transaction, though its completion may take several years. A partnership is generally a continuing business.

Questions

1. For what purpose may a partnership be formed?

2. **a.** What are the advantages of a partnership?

   b. What are the disadvantages of a partnership?

3. What are the different classes of partnerships?

4. **a.** Who may be a partner?

   b. Can a minor be held to a partnership agreement?

5. What are the classifications of partners?

6. How is a partnership formed?

7. Can a partnership agreement be implied?

8. How might two or more parties be held to have formed a partnership when they had no intention to form one?

9. Are partnerships required to have a firm name?

10. Are the assets of a partnership subject to sale by a personal creditor of one of the partners?

Case Problems

1. Goldberg, in applying for credit, states that she is a partner in the firm of Goldberg and Rowan. Credit is extended to her on the basis of this assertion. Two months prior to this transaction, Goldberg had sold her interest in the firm to Rowan, but Rowan had retained Goldberg's name in the firm. Is Rowan liable on this debt after Goldberg defaults because of insolvency?

2. Wilton and Janet Jackson, husband and wife, and their adult son, Walter Jackson, filed a voluntary petition under the Bankruptcy Code. The petition purported to be a partnership filing. They operated a hog farm. Wilton and Janet, on the one hand, and Walter, on the other, were to share profits and losses equally. However, all the losses were absorbed by Wilton and Janet, and there never were any profits. Walter testified that his wife, Carol, was a member of the partnership, while his parents said she was not. The three could not agree on when the alleged partnership was formed. Was there a partnership?

3. Grider and Greene were partners in a CPA firm. One of their largest clients was in a tight financial situation. Grider offered to buy some stock the client owned by paying him one-third cash and giving him a 12-month note for the balance. The note was signed:

   Grider & Greene
   By Grider

   The stock became worthless, and Greene refused to pay any part of the note. Grider claims it is a partnership debt, since he made the deal to build goodwill for the firm. Must Greene pay his share of the note? *- no partnership, wasn't in business for buying stock*

4. Gordon was urged by McLain and Meyer to form a partnership. Gordon was profitably employed and did not wish to undertake a new enterprise. McLain and Meyer proposed that if she would invest $15,000 in the firm, they would make her a full-fledged member, would guarantee her 6 percent on her investment before they received any profits, and would not reveal to the public that she was a member of the firm. McLain and Meyer were to manage the business. The partnership was organized along the lines mentioned. The firm went bankrupt. A creditor learned of Gordon's relationship with McLain and Meyer and sued her as a partner. Is she liable? *yes; she is general partner & can manage*

5. The Second National Bank of Clearwater sued Donald and Betty Myrick on unpaid promissory notes. After obtaining a judgment, the Bank instructed the sheriff to levy on and sell the Myricks' interest in a partnership known as Port Richey Shopping Village. The Myricks alleged that because a person's interest in a partnership is personal property, the business could not be levied upon and sold. Should the Bank be able to have the business sold?

6. Perry, store manager for one of a chain of supermarkets, secretly entered into a partnership with Allen to operate an independent supermarket. He invested half the capital but took no part in the management of the firm. He was to receive 8 percent on his investment guaranteed and one fourth of any additional profits. The firm became insolvent, and the creditors learned of Perry's status. Perry claimed he was a limited partner, while the creditors contended he was a dormant partner. What was the significance of making this distinction?

7. Johnny Wood and Oscar Simmons created a partnership known as "Wood and Simmons Investments." On May 21, Wood deeded real property to "Johnny L. Wood and Oscar Harold Simmons d/b/a Wood and Simmons Investments, a partnership." The property was then leased to Quick-Stop Food Mart, Inc. In accordance with an agreement to dissolve the partnership, "Johnny L. Wood and wife, Zula Wood" conveyed to "Oscar Harold Simmons and wife, Jacqueline B. Simmons" by deed "all of their one-half undivided interest" in the property. Oscar then conveyed the property to Jacqueline, who alleged she owned the property and was entitled to eject Quick-Stop because it did not record its lease until after the property was deeded to her, Quick-Stop argued the May 21 deed conveyed title to the partnership in the partnership name, and since there was not a conveyance out in the partnership name, title was still in that name. Another tract of land was conveyed to "Wood and Simmons Investments, a partnership," without mention of Wood and Simmons individually. Is title to the property in Jacqueline Simmons or the partnership?

8. Richard Missan was hired as a lawyer by the firm of Gerald Schoenfeld and Bernard B. Jacobs. The firm received a large fee for work on an estate, and Missan sued, claiming a right to share in the fee as a partner. He alleged he was represented as a partner on the firm's letterhead, opinion letters, tax returns, professional directories, pension plan, and professional liability insurance policy. He also alleged that the parties had entered into an agreement admitting him as a member of the firm to receive a percentage of the profits. Schoenfeld and Jacobs submitted a written agreement which provided they would practice law as partners for one year. It also stated: "unless this agreement is extended by an agreement in writing . . . it shall terminate in all respects" and "This agreement constitutes the entire understanding among the parties." The agreement was executed many years before the suit and was not extended in writing. Schoenfeld and Jacobs contended Missan was barred from alleging an oral partnership agreement. Was he?

35

Operation of a Partnership

Preview Cases

Reed was a partner in the engineering firm of Reed and Dudley. Because of carelessness, as well as incompetency, Reed miscalculated the dimensions of steel piers for a bridge. As a result of this lack of care and skill, the firm was held liable for a $30,000 loss. Can the firm hold Reed liable?

For $260,500, Al Shacket and Leroy Helfman purchased options to buy land. They assigned the options to Hulett, Inc. Before Hulett closed the purchase of the land, Shacket and Helfman offered to buy the land for $525,000. After this offer was accepted, Shacket and Helfman assigned their purchase rights to a partnership they had with Harold Jaffa and Irving Taran, and the partnership bought the property from Hulett. The partnership agreement required Shacket and Helfman to transfer the property "at their cost." Jaffa and Taran sued, alleging Shacket and Helfman violated their duty to give to the other partners full and true information of all things affecting the partnership, because they failed to disclose that they had purchased the options for only $260,500. Shacket and Helfman alleged there is no violation of the duty to disclose information so long as there is no concealment of profit. Did Shacket and Helfman violate the duty to inform?

The law imposes upon each partner the utmost fidelity in all relationships with the other partners. If any partner is remiss in this duty, the other partners have several legal remedies to redress the wrong.

Duties of Partners *— similar to duties of agent*

The five most common duties which one partner owes to the others are:

1. Duty to exercise loyalty and good faith
2. Duty to use reasonable care and skill

3. Duty to conform to the partnership contract
4. Duty to keep records
5. Duty to inform

Duty to Exercise Loyalty and Good Faith.

Partners owe each other and the firm the utmost loyalty and good faith. Since each partner is an agent of the firm, the relationship of principal and agent prevails. This relationship is a fiduciary one, so strict fidelity to the interests of the firm must be observed at all times. No partner may take advantage of the copartners. Any personal profits earned directly as a result of one's connection with the partnership must be considered profits of the firm. If the personal interest or advantage of the partner conflicts with the advantage of the partnership, it is the duty of the partner to put the firm's interest above personal advantage. This duty lasts as long as the enterprise exists.

◆   Henry Slingerland and Raymond Hurley were partners under a written partnership agreement covering a real estate project. When the real estate was first purchased by the investors, the contract of sale did not indicate that $35,000 of partnership funds was used to pay off a prior debt owed by Hurley to the seller. Hurley alleged that since the seller would not sell without the debt's being paid, the $35,000 was a "necessary cost of doing business." The court held that the fact that the $35,000 payment was necessary to make the purchase did not excuse it. In all matters in which faith and trust are placed in a fiduciary, the fiduciary's conduct must be above reproach. Hurley had to repay the partnership the $35,000.

Duty to Use Reasonable Care and Skill.

Each partner must use reasonable care and skill in conducting the firm's business. Any loss resulting to the firm because of a partner's failure to use adequate care and skill in transacting business must be borne by that partner. If the partnership supplies expert services, such as accounting services or engineering services, then each partner must perform these services in a manner that will free the firm from liability for damages for improper services. However, honest mistakes and errors of judgment do not render a partner liable individually nor the partnership liable collectively.

◆   Reed was a partner in the engineering firm of Reed and Dudley. Because of carelessness, as well as incompetency, Reed miscalculated the dimensions of steel piers for a bridge. As a result of this lack of care and skill, the firm was held liable for a $30,000 loss. Reed in turn was personally liable to the firm for the loss.

Duty to Conform to the Partnership Contract.

Anyone who enters into a contractual relationship with another has a duty to abide by the terms of the contract. The partnership contract must be observed scrupulously because of the fiduciary status of the partnership type of business organization. Each partner has the power to do irreparable damage to the copartners if their trust is betrayed. For this reason, the law holds each partner to the utmost fidelity to the partnership agreement. Any violation of this agreement gives the other partners at least two rights: First, they can sue the offending partner for any loss resulting from the failure to abide by the partnership agreement; second, they may elect also to ask the court to decree a dissolution of the partnership. A trivial breach of the partnership agreement will not justify a dissolution, however.

Duty to Keep Records. Each partner must keep such records of partnership transactions as are required for an adequate accounting. If the partnership agreement provides for the type of records to be kept, a partner's duty is fulfilled when such records are kept, even though they may not be fully adequate. Since each partner must account to the partnership for all business transactions including purchases, sales, commission payments, and receipts, this accounting should be based upon written records.

Duty to Inform. Each partner has the duty to inform the other partners about matters relating to the partnership. On demand, true and full information of all things affecting the partnership must be rendered to any partner or the legal representative of any deceased partner or partner under legal disability.

For $260,500, Al Shacket and Leroy Helfman purchased options to buy land. They assigned the options to Hulett, Inc. Before Hulett closed the purchase of the land, Shaket and Helfman offered to buy the land for $525,000. After this offer was accepted, Shacket and Helfman assigned their purchase rights to a partnership they had with Harold Jaffa and Irving Taran, and the partnership bought the property from Hulett. The partnership agreement required Shacket and Helfman to transfer the property "at their cost." Jaffa and Taran sued, alleging Shacket and Helfman violated their duty to give to the other partners full and true information of all things affecting the partnership, because they failed to disclose that they had purchased the options for only $260,500. Shacket and Helfman alleged there is no violation of the duty to disclose information so long as there is no concealment of profit. The court held that information means all relevant information regardless of whether it relates to profit.

Rights of Partners

Every partner, in the absence of an agreement to the contrary, has five well-defined rights:

1. Right to participate in management
2. Right to inspect the books at all times
3. Right of contribution
4. Right to withdraw advances
5. Right to withdraw profits

Right to Participate in Management.

In the absence of a contract limiting these rights, each partner has the right by law to participate equally with the others in the management of the partnership business. Because the exercise of this right often leads to disharmony, it is considered one of the basic disadvantages of the partnership type of business organization; but it deserves to stand as a prime advantage because the investor maintains control over the investment, even though control may be exercised in a foolish manner. The right of each partner to a voice in management does not mean a dominant voice. With respect to most management decisions, regardless of importance, the majority vote of the individual partners is controlling. If the decision involves a basic change in the character of the enterprise or the partnership agreement so requires, the unanimous consent of the partners is required.

◆   Rex Hammons and Donald Ball began a business, Hammons Heating and Air Conditioning, in which Ball was not active. A few years later, Hammons and Ball moved their business from Raleigh to Laurel and adopted a new name, Shady Grove TV and Appliance. When they got into severe financial difficulties, they petitioned to have their debts discharged in bankruptcy. The Bankruptcy Court found that Hammons and Ball had established a new business under a new name at Laurel, with both serving as active partners. The appellate court, however, held that Ball's becoming active in the business did not mean that a new business was formed. Every partner has a right to participate in the management and conduct of the business.

Right to Inspect the Books.

Each partner must keep a clear record of all transactions performed for the firm, the firm's books must be available to all partners, and each partner must explain on request the significance of any record made that is not clear. All checks written must show the purpose for which they are written. There may be no business secrets among the partners.

Right of Contribution.

If one partner pays a firm debt or liability from personal funds, there is a right to contribution from each of the other partners.

The Uniform Partnership Act states that "the partnership must indemnify every partner in respect of payments made and personal liabilities reasonably incurred by him in the ordinary and proper conduct of its business or for the preservation of its business or property." The partner has no right, however, to indemnity or reimbursement when (1) acting in bad faith, (2) negligently causing the necessity for payment, or (3) previously agreeing to bear the expense alone.

Right to Withdraw Advances.

No partner is entitled to withdraw any part of the original investment without the consent of the other partners. If one partner, however, makes additional advances in the form of a loan, there is a right to withdraw this loan at any time after the due date. Also, a partner is entitled to interest on a loan unless there is an agreement to the contrary. A partner is not entitled to interest on the capital account. It is, therefore, desirable to keep each partner's capital account separate from that partner's loan account.

Right to Withdraw Profits. Each partner has the right to withdraw a share of the profits from the partnership at such time as specified by the partnership agreement or by express authorization by vote of the majority of the partners in the absence of a controlling provision in the partnership agreement.

The net profit after partners' salaries of the partnership of Carlton, Gutherie, and Knowles was $40,000. Knowles and Gutherie insist that the $40,000 be retained in the business for expansion to meet competition. Carlton insists upon withdrawing her share. She may not withdraw her share. The majority of the partners determine when profits may be distributed.

Liabilities of Partners

A partner's liabilities are of two kinds:

1. Liability for contracts
2. Liability for torts

Liability for Contracts. Every member of a general partnership is individually liable for all the enforceable debts of the firm. If one partner incurs a liability in the name of the firm that is beyond both the actual and apparent authority, there is personal liability for acting beyond the scope of authority, as in the case of an unauthorized agent; the firm is not liable for such unauthorized acts. The firm also is not liable for illegal contracts made by any member of the firm, since everyone is charged with knowledge of what is illegal. Thus, if a partner in a wholesale liquor firm contracted to sell an individual a case of whiskey, the contract would not be binding on the firm in a state where individual sales are illegal for wholesalers.

Liability for Torts. The partnership is liable for all torts committed by each partner if the torts are committed in the course of services to the partnership. If the liability arises because of the fault of the partner, the partnership and any partners can require indemnification for loss caused them.

Mrs. Luetkemeyer left some bearer bonds and other valuables with the partnership firm of Flannagan and Boyd for safekeeping. Boyd cashed some of the bonds and used the money for his personal benefit. The partnership was liable to Mrs. Luetkemeyer for the injury even though Boyd in turn would be liable to indemnify the partnership for the loss it sustains because of his conduct.

Nature of Partnership Liabilities

The partners are jointly liable on all partnership contractual liabilities unless the contract stipulates otherwise. They are jointly and severally liable on all tort liabilities. For joint liabilities, the partners must be sued jointly. If the firm's assets are inadequate to pay the debts or liabilities of the firm, the partners are, of course, liable individually for the full amount of debts or liabilities. If all the partners but one are insolvent, the remaining solvent partner must pay all the debts even though the judgment is against all of them. The partner who pays the debt has a right of contribution from the other partners but as a practical matter may be unable to collect from the other partners.

Withdrawing partners are liable for all partnership debts incurred up to the time they withdraw unless these partners are expressly released from liability by the creditors. New partners admitted to the firm are liable under the common law only for the debts incurred after admission unless they agreed otherwise. Under the Uniform Partnership Act, incoming partners are liable for all debts as fully as if they had been partners when the debt was incurred, except that this liability for old debts is limited to their investment in the partnership. Withdrawing partners may contract with incoming partners to pay all old debts, but this is not binding on creditors.

Powers of a Partner

A partner has any authority which is expressly given by the partnership agreement or by the action of the partnership. In addition, a partner has all powers which it is customary for partners to exercise in that kind of business in that particular community. As in the case of an agent, any limitation on the authority the partner would customarily possess is not binding upon a third person unless made known, although the firm is entitled to indemnity from the partner who causes the firm loss through violation of the limitation placed on the authority. Each partner in an ordinary trading partnership has the following customary or implied authority:

1. To compromise and release a claim against a third party
2. To receive payments and give receipts in the name of the firm
3. To employ or to discharge agents and employees whose services are needed in the transaction of the partnership business
4. To draw and indorse checks, to make notes, and to accept drafts

5. To insure the property of the partnership, to cancel insurance policies, or to give proof of loss and to collect the proceeds
6. To buy goods on credit or to sell goods in the regular course of business

Powers Not Implied

A partner does not have the implied power to do and must obtain express authorization for the following acts:

1. To assign the assets of the firm for the benefit of creditors
2. To indorse a negotiable instrument as an accommodation
3. To submit a partnership controversy for arbitration
4. To discharge a personal debt by agreeing that it will be set off against one due the firm
5. To dispose of the goodwill of the business, or to do any other act that would make impossible the continuance of the business

Sharing of Profits and Losses

The partnership agreement usually specifies the basis upon which the profits and the losses are to be shared. This proportion cannot be changed by a majority of the members of the firm. If the partnership agreement does not fix the ratio of sharing the profits and the losses, they will be shared equally and not in proportion to the contribution to the capital. In the absence of a provision in the partnership agreement to the contrary, the majority of the partners may order a division of the profits at any time.

Questions

1. What duties does a partner owe a copartner?

2. If one partner is able to make a personal profit as a result of membership in the firm, must this profit be shared with the other partners?

3. If A and B form a partnership for the purpose of operating a public accounting office, who is personally liable if A, through ignorance of accounting principles, loses $10,000 of the firm's money?

4. What records must a partner keep of the transactions performed for the partnership?

5. Is the right of each partner to participate in management equally with the other partners an advantage or disadvantage of partnerships?

6. If one partner makes a loan to the firm, when may this money be withdrawn without the consent of the other partners?

7. What are a partner's two kinds of potential liability for acts of other partners?

8. What debts is a withdrawing partner liable for?

9. Does a partner have the authority to indorse a negotiable instrument as an accommodation?

10. If the partnership contract does not set out the method of dividing profits and sharing losses, how are these allocated?

Case Problems

1. Hacket, Hammond, and Harper each invested $20,000 in an insurance agency. Each one was to handle a specified function of the business. Salaries of $1,200 each were to be drawn at the end of each month. After the partnership had operated for two years, during which time the net profits after salaries were $30,000, Hacket and Hammond wanted to retain all profits in the business and add a real estate agency. They would then enter into an ambitious suburban real estate development program. Hacket and Hammond were to handle these added duties and receive an additional $700 a month salary. Harper was to receive no increase. Harper refused to agree to these proposals. Hacket and Hammond insisted that the majority should rule and attempted to ignore Harper's objections. Could these changes be undertaken without Harper's consent?

2. Day, Dolwin, and Farmer operate a partnership engaged in the laundry and dry cleaning business. Each one has $40,000 invested in the business. In addition Day has loaned the business $10,000. At the end of the year the net profits are $25,000. Day and Farmer want to use the profits to install new machinery although the machinery they now have is good. The new machinery has a few modern gadgets which they think will tend to improve their profits. Cash equal to their allowance for depreciation account has been invested in common stock of various corporations. Dolwin insists this stock should be sold and used to purchase new machinery when necessary. He claims he needs his share of the profits to send his two daughters to school and insists upon withdrawing his profits. Does he have the right to do so?

3. C. R. Royal was a partner in Paseo Apartment Development Co. He sued the partnership, alleging the other partners refused to allow him access to the partnership books. In order to maintain the action, Royal had to show Griffis refused access to the books. Royal testified that Griffis had access to the books for an interim period, but it was not clear whether Royal requested to see them during that period. Griffis denied having custody of the books but

later testified that he packed them in cartons and sent them to another partner who was being audited by the IRS. When asked if he ever took custody of the books, he replied, "Never. They were sent to Dallas, and that is all I know about handling the books." Did Griffis refuse Royal access to the books?

4. Charles Gross withdrew from the partnership of Newburger, Loeb & Co. The partnership agreement required that at least 85 percent of the "partnership interest" of a withdrawn general partner remain in the firm, at the risk of the business, for one year following withdrawal. Under financial pressure, the remaining partners decided to transfer the assets of the partnership to a corporation. Gross and other withdrawn partners refused to consent to the transfer. The assets were transferred to a corporation anyway. In the resulting lawsuit, Gross alleged that the transfer was a breach of the fiduciary obligation of good faith, since without the withdrawn partners' consent, it violated state law. Did the partnership have a duty of good faith to the withdrawn partners?

5. Langford and Palmer were partners in a neon sign installation service. One of their best customers, the Sunset Drive-In Theater, needed credit to build a new drive-in theater in an adjoining town. Langford, without Palmer's knowledge or consent, indorsed in the name of the partnership as an accommodation indorser a note to the Citizens Bank for $15,000 with the owner of the Sunset Drive-In Theater as the maker. The note was never paid; the bank sued the partnership on the indorsement. Is the partnership liable? *No; not in ordinary course of business*

6. Pressman and Jordan owned and operated an insurance agency as a general partnership. Neal, an experienced underwriter for a large insurance company, was approached by Pressman to purchase the agency, since Jordan was sick and unable to work. Pressman, without Jordan's knowledge or consent, entered into a contract with Neal to sell the agency for $40,000. Neal paid one half down and agreed to pay the balance by turning over to Pressman and Jordan 10 percent of the commissions earned until the balance was paid. Neal resigned his position and operated the agency one month before Jordan learned of the sale. Jordan repudiated the contract and demanded that Neal restore control and management to the partnership. Discuss the rights of the parties.

7. Walter Zyck was injured in an automobile accident. He carried an insurance policy with Hartford Insurance Group to provide him compensation for loss of income resulting from his being unable to perform his job as a real estate salesman during his disability. Zyck and his wife had a partnership in the operation of a real estate agency. Zyck was primarily responsible for obtaining listings and making sales, but his wife held the brokerage license, and Zyck was licensed only as a salesman. Mrs. Zyck was at the office daily to supervise and discharge the normal duties associated with it. How should the shares of the profits of Zyck and his wife in the partnership be apportioned?

8. Pringle and Whyte were partners in a drug business. The partnership agreement provided that each partner might draw $250 each week as his share of

the profits of the business. Pringle became seriously ill, and as a result Whyte was compelled to work overtime to take care of the business. Because of the extra work he performed, Whyte drew a larger amount of money each week.

a. Did Whyte have the right to draw a larger sum?

b. If Whyte found it necessary to employ another person, would the wages of this person be considered an expense of the firm, or would they be deducted from the amount Pringle drew?

c. While Pringle was ill, was he entitled to as much of the profits as when he had worked all the time?

9. A partnership named Fort George Associates, by means of an Agreement of Sale signed by one of the partners, John Collins, agreed to sell a liquor license to International Restaurant Corporation, owned by Antonio Pinero. The agreement provided the sellers sold "the Class B Seven-Day Liquor License owned by them" for $12,500. When International did not make the payments for the license, the partnership sued it. Pinero counterclaimed, alleging the partnership and the partners were liable for fraud and deceit. The license had expired before the agreement was signed. If Collins is liable for punitive damages, are the partnership and the other partners also so liable?

10. Ronald Dreier withdrew from the law partnership of which he had been a member. The oral partnership agreement made no provision for withdrawal of a partner. Dreier sued his former partners for his share of the firm's earnings during the term of his membership. What should happen to fees which were unpaid or unbilled when Dreier withdrew?

36

Dissolution of a Partnership

Preview Cases

Gerald Olivet, Bennett Marcus, and Edgar Lucidi were members of Whittier Leasing Company, a partnership which engaged in sale–lease-back transactions with Whittier Hospital. The partnership would purchase equipment from the hospital and lease it back at favorable rates. The partnership was successful because seven of the partners (other than Olivet, Marcus, and Lucidi) were members of the board of directors of Whittier Hospital. These seven, together with the other two directors of the Hospital, formed a competing partnership, named Friendly Hills Leasing Company, which then got all the lease-back business of the Hospital. Olivet, Marcus, and Lucidi sued for dissolution of the Whittier partnership, alleging misconduct on the part of the other seven partners. Was this misconduct?

Sheldon Mandell, Howard Mandell, Jerome Mandell, and Norman Mandell were limited partners in Frontier Investment Associates with Centrum Frontier Corporation and William Thompson. Frontier's only asset was Park Place, an apartment building. To purchase Park Place, a $22,000,000 loan had been obtained from Continental Illinois National Bank. Continental had required the limited partners to pledge $1,600,000 in securities to guarantee the loan. Frontier managed Park Place for 17 months, during which time it suffered cash losses of $2,123,825. The losses were increasing because the floating interest rate on the loan had increased. There had been losses for all but two months of the 17-month operation. If the losses continued, they were to be paid by selling the $1,600,000 of securities pledged by the limited partners. The limited partners sued for dissolution. Should dissolution because of futility be ordered?

Dissolution of a partnership is the change in the relation of the partners caused by any partner ceasing to be associated in the carrying on of the business. If one member of a going partnership withdraws, the partnership relation is normally dissolved, and the partnership cannot thereafter do any new business. The partnership continues to exist for the limited purpose of winding up or cleaning up its outstanding obligations and business affairs and distributing its remaining assets to creditors and partners. After all this has been completed, the partnership is deemed terminated and goes out of existence.

If a partner wrongfully withdraws, the remaining partners may continue the business.

Dissolution by Acts of the Parties

A partnership is dissolved by act of the partners in these ways:

1. Agreement
2. Withdrawal or alienation
3. Expulsion

Agreement. At the time the partnership agreement is formed, the partners may fix the time when the partnership relation will cease. Unless the agreement is renewed or amended, the partnership is dissolved on the agreed date. If no date for the dissolution is fixed at the time the partnership is formed, the partners may by mutual agreement dissolve the partnership at any time. Even when a definite date is fixed in the original agreement, the partners may dissolve the partnership prior to that time. In this case the subsequent decision to dissolve the partnership is not binding as an agreement unless all the partners consent to the dissolution.

Sometimes no date is fixed for dissolving the partnership, but the agreement sets forth the purpose of the partnership, such as the construction of a building. In this event the partnership is dissolved as soon as the purpose has been achieved.

Withdrawal or Alienation. The withdrawal of one partner at any time and for any reason normally dissolves the partnership. In a partnership for a definite term, any partner has the power, but not the right, to withdraw at any time. A withdrawing partner is liable for any loss sustained by the other partners because of the withdrawal. If no dissolution date is fixed in the partnership agreement, a partner may withdraw at will without liability. After creditors are paid, the withdrawing partner is entitled to receive capital, undistributed profits, and any loan.

If a dissolution date is fixed in the partnership agreement or by subsequent agreement, the withdrawing partner breaches the contract by withdrawing prior to the agreed date. When a partner withdraws in violation of agreement, the damages which are caused the firm may be deducted from the distributive share of the assets of the partnership.

Closely related to withdrawal is the alienation of a partner's interest either by a voluntary sale or an involuntary sale to satisfy personal creditors. The sale does not of itself dissolve the partnership. But the purchaser does not become a partner by purchase, since the remaining partners cannot be compelled to accept as a partner anyone who might be "persona non grata" to them. The buying partner has a right to the capital and profits of the withdrawing partner, but not the right to participate in the management.

Expulsion. The partnership agreement may, and should, contain a clause providing for the expulsion of a member, especially if there are more than two members. This clause should spell out clearly the acts for which a member may be expelled and the method of settlement for such a partner's interest. The partnership agreement should also set forth that the remaining partners agree to continue the business if a partner is expelled; otherwise, it will be necessary to wind up the partnership business and distribute all the assets to the creditors and partners, thereby terminating the partnership existence.

Dissolution by Court Decree

Under certain circumstances a court may issue a decree dissolving a partnership. The chief reasons justifying such a decree are:

1. Insanity
2. Incapacity
3. Misconduct
4. Futility

Insanity of a Partner. A partner may obtain a decree of dissolution when another partner has been judicially declared insane or shown to be of unsound mind.

Incapacity of a Partner. If a partner develops an incapacity which makes it impossible for the partner to perform the services to the partnership which the original partnership agreement contemplated, a petition may be filed to terminate the partnership on that ground. A member of an accounting firm who goes blind would probably be incapacitated to the extent of justifying a dissolution. The court, not the partners, must be the judge in each case as to whether or not the partnership should be dissolved.

As a rule the incapacity must be permanent, not temporary. A temporary inability of one partner to perform duties is one of the risks which the other partners assumed when they formed the partnership and does not justify a court decree dissolving the partnership.

Misconduct. If one member of a partnership is guilty of misconduct that is prejudicial to the successful continuance of the business, the court may, upon proper application, decree a dissolution of the partnership. Typical illustrations of such misconduct are habitual drunkenness, dishonesty, persistent violation of the partnership agreement, irreconcilable discord among the partners as to major matters, and abandonment of the business by a partner.

◆   Gerald Olivet, Bennett Marcus, and Edgar Lucidi were members of Whittier Leasing Company, a partnership which engaged in sale–lease-back transactions with Whittier Hospital. The partnership would purchase equipment from the hospital and lease it back at favorable rates. The partnership was successful because seven of the partners (other than Olivet, Marcus, and Lucidi) were members of the board of directors of Whittier Hospital. These seven, together with the other two directors of the Hospital, formed a competing partnership, named Friendly Hills Leasing Company, which then got all the lease-back business of the Hospital. Olivet, Marcus, and Lucidi sued for dissolution of the Whittier partnership, alleging misconduct on the part of the other seven partners. The court held that if partners elect to compete with the partnership, the remaining partners are entitled to a court-ordered dissolution.

Futility. All business partnerships are conducted for the purpose of making a profit. When it is clear that this objective cannot be achieved, the court may decree a dissolution. One partner cannot compel the other members to assume continued losses after the success of the business becomes highly improbable and further operation appears futile. A temporarily unprofitable operation does not justify a dissolution. It is only when the objective reasonably appears impossible to attain that the court will issue a decree of dissolution.

◆   Sheldon Mandell, Howard Mandell, Jerome Mandell, and Norman Mandell were limited partners in Frontier Investment Associates with Centrum Frontier Corporation and William Thompson. Frontier's only asset was Park Place, an apartment building. To purchase Park Place, a $22,000,000 loan had been obtained from Continental Illinois National Bank. Continental had required the limited partners to pledge $1,600,000 in securities to guarantee the loan. Frontier managed Park Place for 17 months, during which time it suffered cash losses of $2,123,825. The losses were increasing because the floating interest rate on the loan had increased. There had been losses for all but two months of the 17-month operation. If the losses continued, they were to be paid by selling the $1,600,000 of securities pledged by the limited partners. They sued for dissolution. The court held that the history of losses indicated that profits were not to be expected in the future and ordered dissolution.

Dissolution by Operation of Law

Under certain well-defined circumstances, a partnership will be dissolved by operation of law; that is to say, it will be dissolved immediately upon the happening of the specified event. No decree of the court is necessary to dissolve the partnership. The most common examples are:

1. Death
2. Bankruptcy
3. Illegality

Death. The death of one member of a partnership automatically dissolves the partnership unless there is an agreement it shall not be dissolved. A representative of the deceased may act to protect the interest of the heirs but cannot act as a partner. This is true even when the partnership agreement provides that the partnership is not to be dissolved by the death of a member.

The partnership agreement can provide for an orderly process of dissolution upon the death of a member. Thus, a provision that the surviving partners shall have twelve months in which to liquidate the firm and pay the deceased partner's share to the heirs is binding.

Bankruptcy. Persons who have their debts discharged in bankruptcy are no longer responsible for paying most of their debts, including those connected with the partnership. Thus, the unlimited liability of the partner which would otherwise exist is in effect destroyed, and the partner is not a good credit risk. Because of this, the law regards bankruptcy of a partner as automatically terminating the partnership. The trustee in bankruptcy has the right to assume control of the debtor partner's share of the partnership business, but the trustee is not a partner. The trustee merely stands in the place of the partner to see that the creditors' interests are protected.

The bankruptcy of the partnership also terminates the partnership. It is impossible for the partnership to continue doing business when in the course of the bankruptcy proceeding all of its assets have been distributed to pay its creditors.

Illegality. Some types of business are legal when undertaken, but because of a change in the law, they later become illegal. If a partnership is formed to conduct a lawful business and later this type of business is declared illegal, then the partnership is automatically dissolved. If a partnership is formed for the purpose of operating an insurance underwriting business, the partnership is dissolved by a law restricting this type of business to corporations.

Smith and Combs formed a partnership to operate a tavern. Subsequent to the formation of the partnership, the county in which it was located voted in a local option election to prohibit the sale of alcoholic beverages within the county. Since the business was then illegal, the partnership was dissolved by operation of law.

Effects of Dissolution of a Partnership

Dissolution terminates the right of the partnership to exist and must be followed by the liquidation of the business. Existing contracts may be performed. New contracts cannot be made, except for minor contracts that are reasonably necessary for completion of existing contracts in a commercially reasonable manner. If a part of the assets of the firm are goods in process and additional raw materials must be purchased before the goods in process can be converted into finished goods, these raw materials may be purchased.

After dissolution, a third person making a contract with the partnership stands in much the same position as a person dealing with an agent whose authority has been revoked by the principal. If the transaction relates to winding up the business, the transaction is authorized and binds the partnership and all partners just as though there had not been a dissolution. If the contract constitutes new business, it is not authorized, and the liability of the partnership and of the individual partner so acting depends upon whether notice of dissolution has been properly given.

Dissolution does not relieve the partners of their duties to each other. These duties remain until the business is wound up.

Notice of Dissolution

When a partnership is dissolved, the change may not become known to creditors and other third parties who have done business with the old firm. For the protection of these third parties, the law requires that in certain cases they must be given actual notice of the dissolution. If notice is not given, every member of the old firm may be held liable for the acts of the former partners that are committed within the scope of the business.

Notice is usually given to customers and creditors by mail. It is sufficient to give the general public notice by publication. When a new partnership or corporation has been organized to continue the business after dissolution and termination of the original partnership, the notice of dissolution will also set forth this information as a matter of advertising. If the name of the dissolved partnership included the name of the withdrawing partner, this name should be removed from the firm name on all stationery so that the firm will no longer be liable for the contracts or torts of that person.

Notice of dissolution is usually not deemed necessary:

1. To those who were partners
2. When the partnernship was dissolved by the operation of law
3. When the partnership was dissolved by a judicial decree
4. When a dormant or a secret partner retired

Distribution of Assets

After the dissolution of a partnership, the partners are entitled to participate in the assets remaining after the debts are paid to creditors. The distribution of the remaining assets among the partners is usually made in the following order:

1. Partners who have advanced money to the firm or have incurred liabilities in its behalf are entitled to reimbursement.
2. Each partner is next entitled to the return of the capital that was contributed to the partnership.
3. Remaining assets are distributed equally, unless there is a provision in the partnership contract for an unequal distribution.

When a firm sustains a loss, the loss will be shared equally by the partners, unless there is an agreement to the contrary.

Questions

1. What is dissolution of a partnership?

2. If a partnership is to run five years, can one partner withdraw at the end of two years without incurring any liability to the other partners?

3. What are the rights of a person who buys a partner's interest in the firm?

4. Does expulsion of a partner require dissolution of the partnership?

5. If one member of a firm becomes ill and cannot perform a share of the work, what recourse do the other partners have?

6. What remedy can a court decree for misconduct of a partner?

7. When one member of a partnership dies, what effect does this have on the partnership?

8. If a partner's debts are discharged in bankruptcy, what effect has this upon the partnership?

9. After the termination of a partnership, how are the assets divided?

Case Problems

1. Metro U.S. Construction Corporation and James Riley were partners in Metro-Riley Associates, which owned an apartment complex. There were disputes between the partners, but a settlement agreement provided that Metro

would make a $125,000 loan to the partnership (the Metro Debt) due and payable in ten years. The partnership agreement was amended to add that if Metro loaned additional cash, "the amount of additional cash paid to the partnership shall be added to . . . the 'Metro Debt,' and repayment . . . shall be on the same terms and provisions." Metro loaned an additional $73,000 to the partnership. Metro was also to use all "excess depreciation" available for income tax purposes. The partners continued to disagree on the running of the business, and Metro filed suit to dissolve Metro-Riley, alleging that the $73,000 loan was payable on demand, that Metro-Riley did not have the cash to repay the loan, and that the partners could not agree on how to get the money to repay it; therefore, the business could be operated only at a loss and should be dissolved. Should it?

2. A partnership, the Lebanon Trotting Association, was to conduct the business of harness horse racing. The partnership agreement provided Lebanon should last for 20 years. The principal asset of Lebanon was a lease of a racetrack at the Warren County Fairgrounds, which lease extended beyond the term of the partnership. After the expiration of the 20 years Lebanon brought suit regarding the dissolution of the partnership. It was alleged that the fact that Lebanon entered into a lease which extended beyond the term of the partnership indicated an intention to continue it. Did it? *No.*

termination is different than dissolution

3. Chester S. and Margaret McDonald, husband and wife, operated a partnership with their four sons, Ronald, James, Chester R., and Robert. The parents were each to receive one-third of the profits, and each of the sons one-twelfth. The wills of the parents bequeathed their property equally among their four sons and two daughters. The father died, and Margaret, as executor, agreed with the sons that the father's estate would receive none of the partnership profits. Ronald later became the executor of the father's and Margaret's estates. The sons agreed the father's estate would continue to receive none of the profits, and Margaret's estate would receive one-fifth. The daughters received no profits of the business through the father's estate and one-sixth of one-fifth through Margaret's. In an action to dissolve the partnership, the daughters claim the executor is required to secure for the estate either interest on a deceased partner's share of ownership of the partnership or profits attributable to the continued use of that share. What, if anything, are the estates of the parents entitled to during winding up?

4. Smith, Combs, and Dennis were partners in a law firm. Smith was appointed judge of the Superior Court. There was a state law stating that it is illegal for an attorney who is also a judge to be a member of a law firm. The Stacy Furniture Company sold some office furniture and office equipment in the sum of $1,584.75 to the firm of "Smith, Combs, and Dennis," upon Combs' order. The debt was never paid, and the Stacy Furniture Company attempted to hold the partners personally liable, alleging no notice of termination was ever received. Are Smith and Dennis, either or both, personally liable for this account?

5. Andrews and Averitt operated a shoe store as a partnership. Andrews became seriously ill, and the court decreed a dissolution and a liquidation. The Snow Shoe Company sold $3,000 worth of shoes to the firm upon Averitt's order even though its manager, Henry Griffith, had notice of the dissolution. The account was never paid, and the Snow Shoe Company insisted upon the right of sharing in the firm assets along with other partnership creditors. Was it entitled to do so? *No*

6. Kelley, Love, and Marler form a partnership to operate a men's clothing store. The firm operates several years and is very profitable. Marler becomes insane and appears to be beyond hope of recovery. Marler's wife enters into a contract with Kelley and Love to dissolve the partnership. Kelley and Love pay her Marler's share of the partnership assets. Kelley and Love operate the new partnership for three years during which time their net profits are $36,000. Marler, having regained his sanity, now demands one third of these profits. Is he entitled to them?

7. Adams and Diehl conducted a printing establishment as a partnership under the name of The Economy Print Shop. Diehl withdrew, and Haley, the secretary-bookkeeper, was instructed to send notices of dissolution to all creditors. She did so but overlooked one paper company from which the partnership had in the past bought a considerable quantity of paper on credit. About two weeks after the dissolution, Adams ordered $1,000 worth of paper from the paper mill that had not received notice of dissolution. The order was made on a new type of order blank from which Diehl's name had been removed. Other than this, there was nothing to indicate any change in the business. The purchase price was never paid. Is Diehl liable for the bill?

Summary Cases for Part Seven

Partnerships

1. The Timely Investment Club (TIC), a partnership, was formed to educate the partners in investing and allow them to invest on a regular basis. The partnership agreement provided that when partners withdrew, TIC was required to redeem units of ownership of the withdrawing partners from the funds available. Eight partners withdrew. Was the partnership dissolved by their withdrawal? [*Cagnolatti v. Guinn*, 189 Cal. Rptr. 151 (Cal. Ct. App.)]

2. Paul Wright and John Termeer were partners in an auto repair business. Interstate Motors, Inc., brought in a car for repairs which was accepted by Wright, who then drove it to Houston and into a lake, causing significant damage. Is Termeer liable for Wright's negligence? [*Termeer v. Interstate Motors, Inc.*, 634 S.W.2d 12 (Tex. Ct. App.)]

3. Chet Ellingson, a licensed real estate broker, told Gregory Walsh that he owned real estate with "some partners" and that it was for sale. A buy-sell agreement was executed by Walsh and Ellingson, and Walsh gave Ellingson $1,000 in earnest money. The closing was set for April 5. Four Seasons Motor Inn owned the real estate with Ellingson as tenants in common. On April 5, Walsh told Ellingson he was ready to close, but Ellingson told Walsh he could not get his partners to sell. The real estate had a building on it which Ellingson managed. There had been a prior land holding between Ellingson and Four Seasons by which they had owned property as tenants in common and then sold it and divided the profits equally. Walsh sued for specific performance of the buy–sell agreement, alleging Ellingson had a partnership with Four Seasons and as an agent of the partnership bound it to sell. Was there a partnership? [*Walsh v. Ellingson Agency*, 613 P.2d 1381 (Mont.)]

4. Bernard Susman and members of the Asher family were partners in a real-estate business. They had a dispute concerning whether the partnership was to develop a portion of the property or whether it was to be sold to a developer. Their dispute became so heated the Ashers told Susman he was no longer a partner; changed the partnership tax returns to show Susman's interest was zero; kept him out of partnership business; refused to give him information concerning the business; and refused to account for expenses of the partnership. Susman sued for breach of the partnership agreement. Were the breaches serious enough to order dissolution? [*Susman v. Venture*, 449 N.E.2d 143 (Ill. App. Ct.)]

5. Harold, Jane, and Prudence Miller; Joanne and Theodore Lilley; Achsah Graham; Darrell Schroeder; and Miller Redwood Co. applied for a reduction in assessments on land to which they held title in a variety of combinations.

Harold and Jane were married, and Prudence, Achsah, and Joanne were their daughters. Theodore was Joanne's husband, and Darrell Schroeder is a key employee of the family lumber business. Miller Redwood was a wholly owned subsidiary of Stimson Lumber Company, at least 90 percent of which was owned by the individuals. A web of contractual rights bound the land together. The individuals regarded themselves as partners, operated their business jointly, and disbursed profits in accordance with their ownership interests. Was there a partnership? [*Cochran v. Board of Supervisors of Del Norte County*, 149 Cal. Rptr. 304 (Cal. Ct. App.)]

Part Eight — Corporations

Learning Objectives For Part Eight

Summary Cases for Part Eight

Learning Objectives for Part Eight

Corporations

After studying this part you should be able to:

1. Explain what a corporation is and why the corporate form of business is important.
2. Differentiate between corporations and partnerships.
3. List the different kinds and classifications of corporations.
4. Discuss how a corporation is formed and potential promoter liability.
5. Explain the powers a corporation has and the significance of ultra vires contracts.
6. Define stock.
7. Distinguish between common and preferred stock.
8. Discuss the significance of a prospectus.
9. Explain how stock can be sold and repurchased by a corporation.
10. Describe how stock is transferred.
11. Define dividends and explain how they may be paid.
12. Discuss the various laws regulating the sale of securities, exchanges, and brokers.
13. Discuss how a corporation is managed and the control of management by stockholders.
14. Specify the requirements for taking action at stockholders' meetings and how votes are cast.
15. Identify the rights of stockholders.
16. Explain the functions of the board of directors.
17. Describe how a corporation is dissolved.

37

Nature of a Corporation

Preview Cases

The charter of the Well Pump and Supply Company set forth that the corporation was "to engage in the boring of wells, installing pumps, selling pumps and supplies, and the servicing of these pumps." The board of directors planned to enter a contract with the Board of Supervisors of Buchanan County to hard surface three miles of county roads. Could a stockholder apply to the court for an injunction to prohibit the corporation from fulfilling the contract?

Bluegate Gardens made a contract to sell nursery supplies and insisted on making the contract out to Evergreen Nurseries, Inc., even though Bluegate Gardens knew the corporation was not yet formed. Simmons signed as president of Evergreen. The corporation was never formed, so Bluegate sued Simmons and the other promoters. Will Bluegate be able to recover from the promoters?

A *corporation* is "an association of individuals united for some common purpose, and permitted by law to use a common name and to change its members without dissolution of the association." This definition was given in an early decision by the Supreme Court of the United States and is still considered a satisfactory definition of the term "corporation." Unlike a partnership, a corporation need not be organized for the purpose of making and sharing profits. It may be organized for any lawful purpose, whether pleasure or profit.

A corporation is known in law as an "entity," that is, something that has a distinct existence separate and apart from the existence of its individual members. Chief Justice Marshall defined a corporation as "an artificial being, invisible, intangible, and existing only in contemplation of law." However, under certain circumstances, the courts may disregard the entity concept of the corporation and determine the case as though the individuals owning or running the corporation, and not the corporation, were involved.

A corporation is considered an artificial person that has been substituted for the natural persons who are responsible for its formation and who manage and control its affairs. Hence, when a corporation makes a contract, the contract is made by and in the name of this legal entity, the corporation, and not by and in the name of the individual members. It has almost all the rights and powers of an individual. It can sue and be sued, it can be fined for violating the law, and it has recourse to the Constitution to protect its liberties.

Importance of Corporations

Corporations have been in existence for a long time, but essentially they are the product of the modern era. The rapid expansion of industry from small shops to giant enterprises required large amounts of capital. Few people had enough money of their own to build a railroad or a great steel mill, and people hesitated to form partnerships with any but trusted acquaintances. In addition, even though four or five people did form a partnership, insufficient capital was still a major problem. The need was for hundreds or even thousands of people, each with a few hundred or a few thousand dollars, to pool their capital for concerted undertakings. The corporate form of business was well adapted to meet this need. It provided the necessary capital and freed investors from the risks and restraints of partnerships by specifically limiting each investor's liability to the original investment.

It is evident that our mass-production enterprises could not have expanded to their present size except through corporate financing. Small enterprises still offer opportunities; but experience has demonstrated that certain businesses that require much capital, such as a steel mill, an automobile manufacturer, or a railroad, can best be operated by a corporation.

Incorporation has become attractive to small businesses as a means of obtaining limited liability, as will be later discussed. Thus, many businesses that formerly would have been organized as a partnership are today corporations with the "partners" each owning an equal number of shares of the stock of the corporation. In many instances, the single proprietor of the small business has incorporated and owns all the stock of the corporation or virtually all, so as to be in effect a one-person corporation.

Differences Between Partnerships and Corporations

There are many differences between the law governing partnerships and that governing corporations. For the investor particularly, these differences are extremely important. For example, three people with $20,000 each can form a partnership with a capital of $60,000. We saw, however, in the chapters on partnership, how each partner risks losing not only this $20,000 but also almost everything else owned, since there is personal liability for all partnership debts. If a corporation is formed and each investor contributes $20,000, this amount is the maximum that can be lost, since there is no liability for the corporate debts beyond this investment.

This advantage of the corporation over the partnership is offset by at least one important disadvantage. In a partnership each partner has an equal voice in the management of the business. In a corporation the people who own or control a majority of the voting stock have not merely a dominant voice in management but the sole voice. If there are fifteen stockholders but one owns 51 percent of the voting stock, this stockholder is free to run the corporation as desired by the ability to dominate the board of directors and the corporate officers. People who invest their savings in a business in the hope of becoming "their own boss" will not find the corporate type of business organization the most desirable unless they can control a majority of the voting stock.

Public Corporations

Corporations may be classified as public and private. A *public corporation* is one formed to carry out some governmental functions, such as a city, a state university, or a public hospital. The powers and functions of public corporations may be much greater than those of private corporations conducted for profit. Public corporations may, for example, have the power to levy taxes, impose fines, and condemn property. Public corporations are created by the state primarily for the purpose of facilitating the administration of governmental functions.

Some public bodies, such as school boards, boards of county commissioners, and similar bodies are not true public corporations but have many similar powers, such as the right to sue and be sued; own, buy, and sell property; and to sign other contracts as an entity. They are called *public-service corporations* or *quasi public corporations*, quasi having the meaning "as if" or "in the nature of."

Private Corporations

Private corporations are those formed by private individuals to perform some nongovernmental function. They in turn are classified as:

1. Not-for-profit corporations
2. Profit corporations

Not-for-Profit Corporations. A *not-for-profit corporation* is one formed by private individuals for the purpose of conducting some charitable, educational, religious, social, or fraternal service. These corporations are not organized for profit, nor is membership in them evidenced by stock ownership. There is no stock issued. The corporation, however, is a legal entity like any other corporation, can sue and be sued as a corporation, can buy and sell property, and otherwise operate as any other corporation. Membership in these corporations is acquired by agreement between the charter members in the beginning and between the present members and new members thereafter.

Profit Corporations. A profit corporation is one organized to run a business and earn money. In terms of number and importance, stock corporations organized for profit constitute the chief type. Ownership in a *stock corporation* is represented by shares of stock. The extent of one's rights and liabilities is determined by the number of shares of stock owned and by the charter and the bylaws of the corporation.

A profit corporation which has a very small number of people who own stock in it is called a *close corporation* or a *closely held corporation*. Because the number of stockholders is so small, the stockholders normally expect to be and are active in the management of the business.

Classification by State of Incorporation

Corporations may be classified depending on where they were incorporated. Thus, we may classify corporations as domestic or foreign. A corporation is a *domestic corporation* in the state where it received its initial charter; it is a *foreign corporation* in all other states. If it is incorporated in another country, it may be referred to as an *alien corporation*.

Formation of a Corporation

The initial step of forming a corporation is usually taken by one who acts as the promoter. A lot of preliminary work must be done before the corporation comes into existence. The incorporation papers must be prepared, a registration statement may need to be drawn up and filed with the Securities and Exchange Commission (SEC) and the appropriate state officials, the stock must be sold, and many contracts entered into for the benefit of the proposed corporation. Filing with the SEC is not required in the case of smaller corporations. The corporation can be organized in any state the promoter chooses and then operate in any other state it chooses as a foreign corporation as long as it complies with the registration or other requirements of the other states.

Minor defects in the formation of a corporation may generally be ignored. In some instances the defect is of a sufficiently serious character that the attorney general of the state which approved the articles of incorporation of the corporation may obtain the cancellation or revocation of such articles. In other cases, the formation of the corporation is so defective that the existence of a corporation is ignored, and the persons organizing the corporation are held liable as partners or joint venturers.

Liability on Promoter's Contracts and Expenses

The corporation does not automatically become a party to contracts made by the promoter. After the corporation is organized it will ordinarily approve or adopt the contracts made by the promoter. The approval may be either express or by the corporation's conduct. Once approved, the corporation is deemed bound by such contracts and entitled to sue thereon.

The promoter may avoid personal liability on contracts made for the benefit of the corporation by including a provision in the contract that there is no personal liability if the corporation does not adopt or after the corporation does adopt the contract. In the absence of such a provision, it is a question of the wording of the contract whether the promoter is bound by the contract either pending the formation of the corporation or after it has come into existence.

Bluegate Gardens made a contract to sell nursery supplies and insisted on making the contract out to Evergreen Nurseries, Inc., even though Bluegate Gardens knew the corporation was not yet formed. Simmons signed as president of Evergreen. The corporation was never formed, so Bluegate sued Simmons and the other promoters. Bluegate lost, since the contract was made on behalf of the corporation and Bluegate had agreed to look to the corporation and not to the promoters for payment.

Along with the adoption of the promoter's contracts, the corporation may or may not adopt the expenses of the promoter in organization of the corporation. After it comes into existence, it is customary for the corporation to reimburse the promoter for all necessary expenses in forming the corporation. This may be done by a resolution passed by the board of directors.

Issue of Stock

When a new corporation is about to be formed, agreements to buy its stock will generally be made in advance of actual incorporation. In such a case the purchase agreement or subscription to stock by a prospective stockholder or investor, called a *subscriber*, is merely an offer to buy. In most jurisdictions this offer may be revoked anytime prior to acceptance.

The corporation is the offeree, and it cannot accept the subscription until the charter is issued. If the stock is to be sold by a corporation already in existence, it can accept all subscriptions immediately and make them binding contracts. If the promoter is to be paid by means of a stock option, the corporation can make such a contract with the promoter before any services are performed. Most state laws provide that a minimum amount of stock must be sold and paid for before the corporation can begin operations.

Once a valid subscription agreement is signed, the subscriber has rights in the corporation even if the stock certificates have not been received or issued.

◆

Richard Bielinski and Richard Miller prepared a written agreement for a corporation they were organizing. At a meeting of incorporators it was voted that the capital stock of the corporation would be 500 shares and that 100 shares each to Bielinski and Miller were to be issued for $1,000, cash. The corporation was formed, but at a board meeting, Bielinski resigned from the board and presidency because of illness. Pursuant to a law allowing a shareholder in a closely held corporation to seek judicial relief, Bielinski later filed suit to again have a say in running the corporation. The court found he was eligible to file suit because he was a subscriber to 50 percent of the stock. When he and Miller agreed to take and pay for 100 shares of stock they clearly expressed an intention to become subscribers. This subscription offer was impliedly accepted by the corporation. A valid subscription gives a subscriber the rights of a stockholder.

Articles of Incorporation

The written document setting forth the facts prescribed by law for the issuance of a certificate of incorporation or a charter and asserting that the corporation has complied with legal requirements is the *articles of incorporation*. Once approved by the state, the articles are the base on which rests all the authority of the corporation. This document is a contract between the corporation and the state. So long as the corporation complies with the terms of the contract, the state cannot alter the articles in any material way without obtaining the consent of the stockholders. The articles include such information as the name of the corporation, the names of the people forming the corporation (the incorporators), and the amount and types of stock the corporation is authorized to issue.

When the incorporators meet, elect a board of directors, and begin business, acceptance of the charter is presumed, and all parties are bound by it.

Powers of a Corporation

A corporation has powers expressly granted to it and powers which are deemed implied from or incidental to the powers which are expressly granted to it or which are essential to its existence as a corporation. The express powers are generally found in the statute or code under which the corporation is formed and to a lesser degree in the corporation's articles. In a few instances, powers of a corporation are set forth in the state constitution.

Incidental Powers. Certain powers that are always incidental to a corporate existence are:

1. To have a corporate name
2. To have a continuous existence
3. To buy, sell, and hold property
4. To make bylaws and regulations
5. To sue and be sued in the corporate name
6. To have and use a corporate seal

Corporate Name. A corporation must have a corporate name. The members may select any name they wish, provided it is not contrary to the statutes and is not already used by another firm or corporation within the state. Many of the states have statutes regulating corporate names, for example, by requiring the name to end with "Corporation," to be followed by the word "Incorporated," an abbreviation thereof, or other indication of corporate status.

Continuous Existence. The existence of the corporation is continuous for the period for which the charter is granted. This is one of the features of a corporation that makes this form of organization valuable. The death of a stockholder does not dissolve the organization. Sometimes this characteristic is referred to as perpetual, or continuous, succession.

Property Rights. A corporation has the right to buy, sell, and hold property that is necessary in its functioning as a corporation and that is not foreign to the purpose for which it was created.

Bylaws and Regulations. Rules and regulations are necessary to govern and to determine the future conduct of the organization. They must conform to the statutes and must not be contrary to public policy. These rules, called the corporation *bylaws*, are adopted by the corporation's board of directors.

Legal Actions. Another power that has long been considered incidental to corporate existence is the power to sue in the corporate name. Since a corporation may be composed of hundreds or thousands of stockholders, it would be a very cumbersome task, if not an impossible one, to secure the consent of all the stockholders each time a suit was to be brought by a corporation. A corporation may likewise be sued in the corporate name.

Corporate Seal. A corporation has the incidental power to have and to own a seal. Normally a corporation need not use a seal except (1) in executing written instruments that require the use of a seal when executed by natural individuals, or (2) in carrying out transactions where the use of the seal is required by special statutory requirements.

Implied Powers in General. In addition to the powers that are incidental to or expressly conferred upon all corporations, a corporation has the implied power to do all acts that are reasonably necessary for carrying out the purpose for which the corporation was formed. A corporation may borrow money and contract debts if such acts are necessary for the transaction of the corporate business. It may make, indorse, and accept negotiable instruments. It has the power to acquire and convey property and to mortgage or lease its property in case such transactions are necessary for carrying on its business. Modern corporation codes as a rule expressly list the various implied powers above described so that they are express powers.

Ultra Vires Contracts

Any contract entered into by a corporation that goes beyond its powers is called an *ultra vires contract.* As between the parties to the contract, that is, the corporation and the third person, the contract is generally regarded as being binding. However, a stockholder may bring an action to prevent the corporation from entering into such a contract or to recover damages from the directors or officers who have caused loss to the corporation by such contracts. In extreme cases, the attorney general of a state may obtain a court order revoking the articles of incorporation of the corporation if the improper acts are so frequent or so serious as to make it proper to impose such an extreme penalty.

The charter of the Well Pump and Supply Company set forth that the corporation was "to engage in the boring of wells, installing pumps, selling pumps and supplies, and the servicing of these pumps." The board of directors planned to enter into a contract with the Board of Supervisors of Buchanan County to hard surface three miles of county roads. The court upon application by a stockholder issued an injunction prohibiting the board from fulfilling this contract as it was an executory ultra vires contract.

Questions

1. What is a corporation?

2. What is the main difference between a corporation and a partnership?

3. If people wish to go into business for themselves so that they can "be their

own boss," are they more likely to achieve this objective as partners or as stockholders in a corporation? Explain.

4. What are the rights of the stockholders who control a majority of the voting stock in a corporation?

5. Does the ownership of 49 percent of the stock of a corporation automatically give a person a right to work for the corporation?

6. Is a promoter personally liable on contracts made for the benefit of a corporation?

7. What kinds of powers does a corporation have other than those expressly set out in its charter?

8. What action may the state take if a corporation engages in an ultra vires act?

Case Problems

1. Douglas McLeod, Lauren McLeod, and Allan Jones met with Edward Hamilton, the president of Peter Glenn Shops, Inc., and agreed that a corporation named Fashion Sports, Inc., would be formed, with the McLeods and Jones each owning 50 percent of the stock. Fashion Sports was to operate a ski shop. Glenn was to order and supply the company's inventory. The shop began operation, but Fashion Sports was never incorporated. Jones and the McLeods signed a note and Jones signed a renewal note for $30,000 which was used to pay for inventory from Glenn. Jones and the McLeods were supposed to invest $10,000 each, but never did. Hamilton became concerned, and a new agreement was reached that Hamilton would invest $5,000, Jones $5,000, and the McLeods $10,000. This was never done because credit from Glenn was cut off and the shop was closed. In a suit on the $30,000 note, Jones alleged Hamilton or Glenn, as promoters of Fashion Sports, should be liable for debts of the business. Should they?

2. Mr. and Mrs. Land and their daughter Joan proceeded to organize a family corporation to be known as The Right Way Laundry. The business began operating with all three parties actively engaged in carrying on the business while the incorporation papers were being drawn up. Neither the charter nor the certificate of incorporation was ever issued by the state, and no stockholders' meeting was ever held. Mr. Land borrowed $10,000 from the bank and signed the note:

> Right Way Laundry
> By Henry Land, President

The note was never paid, and the bank sued Mrs. Land as a partner. Was this a partnership?

3. L & S Boat Company, Inc., and Hydroswift requested a financing arrangement by which Hydroswift would sell boats to L & S, which would assign trust receipts to Westinghouse Credit, which would then advance money to Hydroswift. L & S was to keep boats in the showroom as security for payment, and when they were sold Westinghouse was to be paid. Westinghouse said it would not agree unless Hydroswift would, in writing, be a guaranty of the L & S account. A guaranty, signed by the president of Hydroswift, was delivered to Westinghouse, and on the basis of it business was carried on. L & S went bankrupt and Westinghouse sued Hydroswift. Hydroswift alleged the guaranty was invalid because it was not authorized by its board of directors, thus ultra vires. Was it binding?

4. Bisher and Furman formed a corporation to manufacture and market athletic equipment. They employed a stockbroker to obtain subscriptions to the $100,000 authorized capital stock. After all the stock had been fully subscribed, Bisher as copromoter, made contracts in the name of the corporation amounting to $11,000. Over half of the subscribers canceled their subscriptions. Since additional subscribers could not be found, the enterprise fell through. What serious blunder did Bisher and Furman commit?

5. Ten stockholders owned all of the stock in the Frost Tire Company, a company specializing in recapping tires. The company was only modestly successful. At a special stockholders' meeting, nine of the stockholders voted to sell all the assets of the tire recapping business and use the proceeds to start manufacturing "camel backs," the strip of rubber used to recap tires. The tenth stockholder brought suit to enjoin the corporation from engaging in this new enterprise. Is this procedure followed by the objecting stockholder proper?

6. Bill Weiss orally agreed to give Clifford Anderson temporary possession of a lot and building in exchange for monthly rental payments. For two years Anderson sent checks payable to and accepted by Weiss which constituted rental payments while Anderson was in possession. The first two checks were drawn on Capital Rentals & Import Repair and subsequent ones on Import Repair Self Service, Inc. Anderson's business, Import Repair & Body Shop, Inc., was not incorporated until five months after the lease began. Weiss alleged Anderson had not paid enough rent and sued him. Anderson alleged Import Repair Self Service, Inc., not he personally, should be liable for any rent due. Is Anderson liable?

7. A group of dairy farmers formed a corporation for the purpose of marketing milk and other dairy products. The charter stipulated that it was authorized to bottle and market whole milk in the city of Auburn. Soon the question arose as to whether or not the corporation could (a) buy milk from farmers other than the members; (b) make and sell ice cream; (c) make and sell butter and cheese; (d) buy and operate a freezer locker plant in conjunction with its milk plant; (e) buy a dairy farm in the name of the corporation to produce milk for

sale by the corporation; (f) operate a feed store for the convenience of the stockholders in purchasing dairy feed; (g) own and operate the Dairy Queen, a restaurant, selling only dairy products, such as ice cream, milk shakes, and other dishes consisting mainly of milk or milk products. Which of these powers were (1) express, (2) incidental or implied, or (3) not possessed by the corporation?

8. Perry Doyle had been in business under the name Doyle Plumbing Company for many years. Vincent J. Doyle organized a corporation named V. J. Doyle Plumbing Company, Inc. As the corporation's business grew, so did confusion caused by the similarity of names. It interfered with communications between the parties and the public. Perry Doyle asked a court to order V. J. Doyle Plumbing Company, Inc., not to use the name Doyle and the words "Plumbing" and "Company" in its corporate name and advertising. Should the corporation be prevented from using its corporate name?

9. Under an agreement with Indian Head Tennis Club, Inc., Steward Becker, Ltd., purchased 25 percent of the corporate stock for $150,000, with $75,000 to be paid in monthly installments. The shares were to be held in escrow until full payment was made. The agreement gave Becker all voting rights and the right to dividends from the shares. Becker sued for dissolution of the corporation, stating the shareholders were so divided that votes required for action by the board of directors could not be secured. The law under which it sued allowed the holders of stock to request dissolution. Should Becker be allowed to maintain the action?

10. Childs, Clyatt, and Collins formed a partnership dealing in antiques. Each invested $20,000 in the business. It was a very profitable enterprise but was endangered by the constant bickering among the three partners. As a solution to their problem, they incorporated, each taking $20,000-worth of stock in the corporation. In addition, the corporation was authorized to sell an additional $21,000-worth of stock, $7,000-worth for each stockholder. When Clyatt and Collins refused to buy any more stock, Child's mother-in-law bought the other shares. In electing a board of directors each of the original stockholders put up a separate slate. Child's slate won all places. The board of directors discharged Clyatt and Collins from their jobs and denied them all access to the business. From Clyatt's and Collins's point of view, did the corporate type of business organization overcome the so-called weaknesses of the partnership type?

11. A corporation was formed for the purpose of manufacturing and selling jewelry. It owned its own building. The directors found that they had more space than was needed for their business, and they decided to rent one of the floors for office purposes. One of the stockholders opposed the idea, contending that such an act would be ultra vires. Was the stockholder right in her contention in this case? Why?

38

Ownership of a Corporation

Preview Cases

The Glenrock Mining Corporation issued two classes of stock, common and preferred. The preference granted gave the preferred stockholders a prior right to the assets of the corporation on dissolution. The par value of the outstanding preferred stock totaled $300,000. The corporation assets on dissolution amounted to $425,000 after payment of debts. How should the $425,000 be allocated between the two classes of stockholders?

James Junker owned stock in Reco Investment Corporation. At a stockholders' meeting, Frederick Heisler, the attorney for Reco and the Road Equipment Company, Inc., suggested that since Reco could not pay a debt it owed to Road, the solution was to merge Reco into another company such as Road. The merger passed. The merger formula for exchanging Reco stock for Road stock used book values despite the fact Reco's property was located in an area where real estate values had greatly increased and the cost of building had greatly increased. Two months after the merger, Junker was notified that Road's annual report would show a loss. This had not been mentioned at the stockholders' meeting. Junker sued, alleging violation of the Federal Securities Act, which establishes a cause of action for a purchaser of securities against a person who sold the securities by means of oral communication that includes an untrue statement of material fact or omits a material fact required to render the statements not misleading. Did Heisler violate the Act?

The *capital stock* of the corporation is the declared money value of its outstanding stock. This stock is subscribed and paid for by the owners. It generally is not necessary that all the capital stock of a corporation be subscribed and paid for before the corporation begins operation. The amount of capital stock authorized in the charter cannot be altered without the consent of the state and a majority of the stockholders.

The capital stock is divided into units called *shares*. These shares may have any set, or par, value, usually $1, $10, or $100, or they may have no par value.

Ownership

Ownership in a stock corporation is achieved by acquiring title to one or more shares of stock. Owners are known as *shareholders* or *stockholders*. The shares of stock may be obtained by subscription either before or after the corporation is organized, or they may be obtained in other ways, such as by gift or purchase from another shareholder.

Stock Certificate

The amount of ownership, that is, the number of shares owned, is evidenced by a stock certificate. It shows on its face the number of shares represented, the par value of each share if there is a par value, and the signatures of the officers.

Kinds of Stock

Stock is divided into many classes. The classes are determined by the laws under which the corporation is organized and the articles of incorporation. The two principal classes of stock are:

1. Common stock
2. Preferred stock

Common Stock. *Common stock* is the simplest form of stock and the normal type of stock issued. If a corporation has issued 5,000 shares of common stock, the owner of 100 shares is entitled to 1/50 of the profits that are made available to the common stockholders. Unlike the partners in a partnership, the owners cannot receive the profits until they have been made available in the form of a dividend declared by the board of directors.

It is generally the right and responsibility of the common stockholders to elect the board of directors, which in turn hires the individuals who manage and operate the corporation. Unless selected as a director or appointed as an officer, a stockholder has no voice in the running of the corporation beyond the annual vote for the board of directors.

Common stockholders are also entitled to a share of the assets of a corporation when it is dissolved.

Preferred Stock. *Preferred stock* differs from common stock in that some sort of preference is granted to the holder of this stock. The preference may pertain to the division of dividends, to the division of assets upon dissolution, or to both of these.

The fact that particular stock is called preferred stock does not tell much about what preference the holder really has. It may be preferred as to assets only, which gives the holder no advantage except in the event of liquidation. It may be preferred as to dividends only, but not as to assets in the event of liquidation. The most common type is that which gives preference both as to dividends and assets. The stock may be first preferred, second preferred, or third preferred. The first preferred is given preference in the payment of dividends before the second preferred is entitled to anything. Likewise, the second preferred must be paid before the third preferred is entitled to receive a dividend.

The Glenrock Mining Corporation issued two classes of stock, common and preferred. The preference granted gave the preferred stockholders a prior right to the assets of the corporation on dissolution. The par value of the outstanding preferred stock totaled $300,000. The corporation assets on dissolution amounted to $425,000 after payment of debts. The $425,000 should be allocated between the stockholders as follows: The preferred stockholders should get the first $300,000 to be disbursed, leaving $125,000 to be divided among the owners of common stock.

The two rights usually given up by the preferred stockholders are the right to vote in stockholders' meetings and the right to participate in profits beyond the percentage fixed in the stock certificate.

When the stock is preferred as to dividends, this right may be cumulative or noncumulative. This fact is significant if the corporation operates at a loss in any given year or group of years. For example, a corporation that has $1,000,000 outstanding common stock and $1,000,000 outstanding 7 percent preferred stock operates at a loss for two years and then earns 21 percent net profit the third year. If *noncumulative preferred stock* has been issued, it is entitled to only one dividend of 7 percent; the common stock is entitled to the remaining 14 percent. If *cumulative preferred stock* has been issued, it is entitled to three preferences of 7 percent, or 21 percent in all, before the common stock is entitled to any dividend. Or if the company earns a net profit each year equal to only 7 percent on the preferred stock, the directors could, if the preferred stock is noncumulative, pass the dividend the first year and declare a 7 percent dividend on both the common and the preferred stocks for the second year. Since the directors are elected by the common stockholders, the common stockholders could easily elect directors who would act in ways to help the common stockholders as much as possible. For that reason the law is that preferred stock is cumulative unless specifically stated to be noncumulative. This is true, however, only when the corporation earns a profit but fails to declare a dividend. Unless the stock certificate expressly states that it is cumulative, the preference does not cumulate in the years during which the corporation operated at a loss.

Preferred stock may be participating or nonparticipating. Thus 7 percent *participating preferred stock* may pay considerably more than 7 percent annually; but if it is *nonparticipating preferred stock*, 7 percent annually would be the maximum to which the preferred stockholders would be entitled no matter how much the corporation earned. If the preferred stock is participating, it is entitled to share equally with the common stock in any further distribution of dividends made after the common shareholders have received dividends equal to those which the preferred shareholders have received by virtue of their stated preference. If the preferred stock is to participate, this right must be expressly stated in the stock certificate and articles of incorporation. The law presumes it is nonparticipating in the absence of a provision in the articles of incorporation to the contrary. If it does participate, it can do so only according to the terms of the articles of incorporation. The articles may provide that the preferred stock shall participate equally with the common stock, or it may provide, for example, that the preferred stock is entitled to an additional 1 percent for each additional 5 percent the common stock receives.

The Prospectus

The federal Securities Act of 1933 requires every corporation offering to the public a new issue of stock to provide a prospectus to every subscriber. Before the stock is sold, a registration statement must be submitted to the Federal Securities and Exchange Commission. The *prospectus* and registration statement must set forth the nature of the corporation, the type or types of stock to be issued, the selling price, and other pertinent information. If the promoter of a new corporation is to receive any stock options or other compensation in stock, this information must be set forth in the prospectus. A corporation is liable for a fraudulent prospectus.

The law allows the SEC to exempt certain stock offerings when the SEC determines registration is not necessary in the public interest and for the protection of investors. SEC regulations provide a simplified registration procedure for small public offerings.

Par-Value Stock and No-Par-Value Stock

Stock to which a face value, such as $25, $50, or $100, has been assigned and which has this value printed on the stock is *par-value stock*. Stock to which no face value has been assigned is *no-par-value stock*. Preferred stock usually has a par value, but common stock may be either par-value or no-par-value stock. The law requires that when par-value stock is issued in return for payment in money, property, or services, the par value of the stock must be equal in value to the money, property, or services. This relates only to the price at which the corporation may issue the stock to an original subscriber and has no effect upon the price which is paid as between a shareholder and a buyer thereafter. The price a buyer pays a shareholder is ordinarily the same as the market price, which may be more or less than the par value. If par-value stock is sold by the corporation at a discount, the purchaser is liable to subsequent creditors of the corporation for the discount.

No-par-value stock may be issued at any price; although some states do set a minimum price, such as $5, for which it can be issued.

Treasury Stock

If a corporation purchases stock that it has sold, this reacquired stock is referred to as *treasury stock*. When stock is first offered for sale, there may be less sales resistance encountered if the prospective purchaser can be assured that the corporation will repurchase the stock upon request. Treasury stock may also be reacquired by gift. The reacquired stock may be sold at any price fixed by the directors. Until it is resold, no dividends can be paid on it nor can it be voted.

The stock of the Mill Valley Corp. is owned equally by Sampson and Lawrence. Each owns 10,000 common shares. They have an agreement that if either one dies the corporation will buy his stock from his heirs for $5 per share. The corporation carries $50,000 in life insurance on each stockholder. Lawrence dies, and the corporation uses its $50,000 in life insurance proceeds to purchase Lawrence's stock. This stock is now treasury stock. Since Sampson now owns all of the outstanding stock, he is the sole owner of the corporation.

Watered Stock

When stock is issued as fully paid up, but the purchase price is paid with property of inflated values, it is said to be *watered stock*. If real estate actually worth $40,000 is paid for in stock having a par value of $100,000, the stock is watered to the extent of $60,000. Watering stock may be prohibited outright, but in any case it cannot be used to defraud creditors. In the event of insolvency, the creditors may sue the original recipients of watered stock for the difference between the par value and the actual purchase price. This may not be true, of course, if the creditors knew the stock was watered. Although creditors are allowed these rights, most state statutes do not prohibit the watering of stock by corporations other than public utility companies.

If the payment for stock is overvalued real estate, the extent of the watering can be determined with reasonable accuracy. If the payment is in the form of patents, trademarks, blueprints, or other similar assets, it may be difficult to fix the extent of the watering.

Transfer of Stock

A stock certificate indicates the manner in which the stock may be transferred to another party. On the back of the certificate is a blank form which the owner may use in making a transfer. The signature of the previous owner gives to the new holder full possession and the right to exchange the certificate for another made out by the corporation to the new owner. Whenever stock is transferred, the new owner should have the certificate exchanged for a new one showing the correct name so that the corporation's books will show the correct stockholders' names. Stockholders who are not so registered are not entitled to the rights and privileges of a stockholder and will not receive any dividends when they are declared.

Under the Uniform Stock Transfer Act, the unregistered holder of stock is entitled to the distribution that represents a return of capital. As under common law, the unregistered holder is not entitled to any distribution that represents a share of the profits.

Stock Options

A *stock option* is a contract entered into between a corporation and an individual which gives the individual the option for a stated period of time to purchase a prescribed number of shares of stock in the corporation at a given price. If the stock in a new corporation is sold to the public at $2 a share, the individual having the option must also pay $2 but may be given two, five, or even ten years in which to exercise the option. If the corporation succeeds, and the price of the stock goes up, the individual will of course want to exercise the option and buy at the low option price and then resell at the higher market price. If the corporation fails, the option does not have to be exercised. Existing corporations may give officials of the corporation an option to purchase a given number of shares of stock in lieu of a salary increase. If the market price of the stock rises, an official may make a capital gain by buying the stock, holding it the required time, and selling it. The income tax on a capital gain may be considerably less than that on other income. This type of compensation may be more attractive to top management officials than a straight increase in salary, enabling a corporation to retain their services at a lower cost than with a salary increase. If the stock is made available to all the corporation's employees, the option price may be less than the fair market value.

Dividends

The profits of a corporation belong to the corporation until the directors set them aside for distribution as *dividends*. Dividends may be paid in cash, stock, or other property.

A cash dividend usually can be paid out of retained earnings only, but there are two exceptions. A cash dividend may be paid out of donated or paid-in surplus. Also, for corporations with depleting assets, such as coal mines, oil companies, lumber companies, and similar industries, cash dividends may be paid out of capital.

Stock dividends may be in the corporation's own stock or in stock the corporation owns in another corporation. When in the corporation's own stock, they are usually declared out of retained earnings, but they can be paid out of other surplus accounts. A stock dividend of the corporation's own stock cannot be declared if there is no surplus of any kind, for this would result in stock watering. Dividends also may be paid in the form of property which the corporation manufactures, but this is seldom done.

The right to declare a dividend on either common or preferred stock depends entirely upon the discretion of the directors. The directors, however, must act reasonably and in good faith.

Once a cash dividend is declared, it cannot later be rescinded. It becomes a liability of the corporation the minute it is declared. A stock dividend, on the other hand, may be rescinded at any time prior to the issuance and delivery of the stock.

Blue-Sky Laws

The purpose of so-called *blue-sky laws* is to prevent fraud through the sale of worthless stocks and bonds. State blue-sky laws apply only to intrastate transactions.

These security laws vary from state to state. Some prescribe criminal penalties for engaging in prohibited transactions, and others require that dealers be licensed and that a state commission approve sales of securities before they are offered to the public.

Securities Act, 1933

Because the state blue-sky laws apply only to intrastate sales of securities, in 1933 the Congress passed the federal Securities Act to regulate the sale of securities in interstate commerce. Any corporation offering a new issue of securities for sale to the public must register them with the Securities and Exchange Commission (SEC) and issue a prospectus containing specified information. This act does not apply to the issuance of securities under $1,500,000 nor does the act regulate the sale or purchase of securities after they have been issued by the corporation.

In addition to filing the registration statement with the SEC, a corporation must furnish a prospectus to each purchaser of the securities. Full information must be given relative to the financial structure of the corporation. This information must include the types of securities outstanding, if any; the terms of the sale; bonus and profit-sharing arrangements; options to be created in regard to the securities; and any other data which the SEC may deem as required.

◆   James Junker owned stock in Reco Investment Corporation. At a stockholders' meeting, Frederick Heisler, the attorney for Reco and the Road Equipment Company, Inc., suggested that since Reco could not pay a debt it owed to Road, the solution was to merge Reco into another company such as Road. The merger passed. The merger formula for exchanging Reco stock for Road stock used book values despite the fact Reco's property was located in an area where real estate values had greatly increased and the cost of building had greatly increased. Two months after the merger Junker was notified that Road's annual report would show a loss. This had not been mentioned at the stockholders' meeting. Junker sued, alleging violation of the Federal Securities Act, which establishes a cause of action for a purchaser of securities against a person who sold the securities by means of oral communication that includes an untrue statement of material fact or omits a material fact required to render the statements not misleading. The court held that the exchange of Reco stock for Road stock by the merger made Junker a purchaser; Heisler's participation in the sales transaction was a substantial factor in causing the transaction to take place, so he was a seller, and he did violate the Act.

The registration statement must be signed by the company, its principal officers, and a majority of the board of directors. If either the registration statement or the prospectus contains misstatements or omissions, the Commission will not permit the securities to be offered for sale. If they are sold before the falsity of the information is ascertained, an investor may rescind the contract and sue for damages any individual who signed the registration statement. Any failure to comply with the law also subjects the responsible corporate officials to criminal prosecution.

Securities Exchange Act, 1934

The chief markets for the sale of securities after their initial offerings are the security exchanges and over-the-counter markets. In 1934 Congress passed the Securities Exchange Act to regulate such transactions. The Act requires the registration of stock exchanges, brokers, and dealers of securities traded in interstate commerce and SEC-regulated, publicly held corporations. Regulated corporations are also required to make periodic disclosure statements regarding corporate organization and financial structure.

Under rule making authority of the Securities Exchange Act, the SEC has declared it unlawful for any broker, dealer, or exchange to use the mails, interstate commerce, or any exchange facility to knowingly make an untrue statement of a material fact or engage in any other act which would defraud or deceive a person in the purchase or sale of any security. This provision applies to sellers as well as buyers.

Required by the Act are certain disclosures of trading by *insiders*— officers, directors, and owners of more than 10 percent of any class of securities of the corporation. Any profits made by an insider in connection with the purchase and sale of the corporation's securities within a six-month period may be recovered by the corporation or its stockholders suing in behalf of the corporation.

A 1975 amendment to this Act attempts to foster competition among securities brokers by reducing regulation of the brokerage industry.

Securities Protection Act of 1970

In order to protect investors when the stock broker or investment house with which they did business had severe financial difficulty which threatened financial loss to the customers, the Securities Protection Act was passed. This federal law requires generally that all registered brokers and dealers and the members of a national securities exchange contribute a portion of their gross revenue from the securities business to a fund regulated by the Securities Investor Protection Corporation (SIPC).

The SIPC is a nonprofit corporation whose members are the contributors to the fund. If the SIPC determines that any of its members has failed or is in danger of failing to meet its obligations to its customers, and there are any one of five other specified indications of its being in financial difficulty, the SIPC may apply to the appropriate court for a decree adjudicating the customers of such member in need of the protection provided by the Act. If the court finds the requisite financial problems, it will appoint a trustee for liquidation of the SIPC member. The SIPC fund may be used to pay certain customers' claims up to $50,000 for each customer.

Questions

1. Must all of the authorized stock of a corporation be sold before the corporation can begin business?

2. What evidences ownership of stock in a corporation?

3. What are the two principal classes of stock?

4. How do the stockholders of a corporation exercise control over the corporation?

5. What is a *prospectus*?

6. What is a *stock option*?

7. Who has the authority to declare dividends?

8. What law regulates the activities of securities exchanges?

Case Problems

1. Mrs. Dixon used the proceeds of her deceased husband's life insurance policies to purchase $50,000 worth of noncumulative 7 percent preferred stock in the belief that the $3,500 annual income from this investment would be adequate to support her. Over a ten-year period the corporation averaged 14 percent on its preferred stock, but during four years it earned no net profits and paid no dividends. Mrs. Dixon sued the corporation to compel it to pay these dividends. Was she entitled to dividends for the four years when the corporation operated at a loss?

2. Parrish, Mosteller, and Garrard operated a very profitable partnership in the wholesale meat business. Garrard died. Parrish and Mosteller persuaded Mrs. Garrard, who was the bookkeeper for the firm, to enter the partnership as a general partner. She accepted their offer, and her share of the profits in addition to her salary as bookkeeper gave her a very nice income. Parrish and Mosteller proposed that the partnership incorporate. Soon after the corporation was formed, Parrish and Mosteller, directors of the new corporation, decided not to pay any dividends and to use them instead to open up a new plant in another city. Mrs. Garrard protested so vehemently that they voted to discharge her as bookkeeper. She was then without any source of income. She brought suit to compel the directors to declare a dividend and also to restore her to her position as bookkeeper for the firm. Was she entitled to these remedies?

3. Rose Udoff was a stockholder in a corporation which had granted stock options to officers and employees. The directors of the corporation lowered the exercise price of the stock to the market price under the authority of and in accordance with the option plan. Udoff filed suit. Was the reduction in the price actionable as detrimental to the corporation?

4. John Greco was a shareholder in Tampa Wholesale Company, a corporation. He did not agree to an agreement by which Lucky Stores, Inc., was to acquire the assets of Tampa. He sued under a state law to receive the fair market value of his stock on the day preceding the date of the vote approving the agreement. Subsequent to the vote a dividend had been paid by Tampa, and Greco received a dividend check. The court ruled in his lawsuit that he was entitled to the fair market value of his stock. Is he allowed to keep the dividend?

5. Konter was the owner of 1,000 shares of stock for which she had paid only about 10 percent of their true value at the time the stock was issued. Later she sold 500 shares to Raul, who paid full value for the stock. The corporation became insolvent, and the creditors sued Raul, claiming that since his stock was 90 percent watered, he was personally liable. Was this correct?

6. Paul Joseph was employed by Wilson Leasing Company. He was told by Lawrence Wilson, the president of the corporation, that he would receive 10,000 shares of Class B stock at the same cost as the Wilson family. Later, Wilson told him he would receive 2,000 or 4,000 shares. Joseph quit because the amount was less than the 10,000 promised. Wilson asked if he would return to work if he got 10,000 shares. Joseph agreed, and Wilson sent a memo to his attorney which stated:

```
    Please arrange an immediate transfer of
2000 of my shares plus 1000 each from my
parents.
    Also draft an agreement to allow P. J. to
buy 2000 add'l shares on 9/30/70-9/30/71 &
9/30/72. At 9/30/72 he'll have 10,000 shares
of B convertible to 11,000 A--all bought at
our base cost.
```

Joseph paid for and received only 4,000 shares. He was asked to resign in May, 1972, before he had purchased any more stock. The value of the stock was $5 per share, and the base cost was 20 cents. Joseph sued for breach of the agreement, alleging it was a contract of sale. Wilson alleged it was a stock option granted as an incentive for continued employment, so future right to purchase stock was dependent on Joseph's continued employment. Was Joseph entitled to purchase any stock?

39

Management and Dissolution of a Corporation

Preview Cases

Washington Preferred Life Insurance Company called a stockholders' meeting to vote on a proposed merger. Notice of the meeting was mailed to stockholders of record and published in two legal newspapers. The published notice indicated that the meeting was to vote on the merger; that proxies, proxy statements, and notices were mailed to stockholders at their last known addresses; and that if anyone was a stockholder of record and had not received the material, inquiry should be made to the company at the address given. A week later Washington asked a court to appoint a representative for missing shareholders in accordance with state law. This law allowed for such appointment if addresses of the shareholders were lost or inadequate and if the purpose of the meeting required a two-thirds vote. The law stated that approval by the court of the representative's findings acted as an affirmative vote at the stockholders' meeting by the missing shareholders. The court appointed a representative, who approved the merger. James Watson, a Washington stockholder, asked the court to vacate the order of appointment because the notice to the allegedly missing stockholders was insufficient. The notice did not inform stockholders that if they did not attend the meeting, a person would be appointed to vote their shares. Was the notice inadequate?

At a meeting of the board of directors of the Sac River Mining Co., the board voted to loan $20,000 to Parsons, one of the board members. Allen, another board member, dissented vigorously, and her dissent was recorded in the minutes of the board. Parsons failed to pay back the loan. In an action by the stockholders against the members of the board, will Allen be liable?

Since a corporation is an artificial being, existing only in contemplation of law, it can perform business transactions only through actual persons, acting as agents. The directors as a group are both fiduciaries and agents.

To the corporation, they are trustees and are chargeable for breaches of trust. To third parties, directors as a group are agents of the corporation.

The board of directors selects the chief agents of the corporation, such as the president, the vice-president, the treasurer, and other officers, who perform the managerial functions. The board of directors is primarily a policy-making body. The chief executives in turn appoint subagents for all the administrative functions of the corporation. These subagents are agents of the corporation, however, not of the appointing executives.

The directors and officers manage the corporation. The stockholders indirectly control the board of directors, but neither the individual directors nor a stockholder, merely by reason of membership in the corporation, can act as an agent or exercise any managerial function.

Even a stockholder who owns 49 percent of the common stock of a corporation, has no more right to work or take a direct part in running the corporation than a stranger would have. Under partnership law, a person who owns even 1 percent of the partnership, has just as much right to work for the partnership and to participate in its management as any other partner.

Stockholders' Meetings

In order to make the will of the majority binding, the stockholders must act at a duly convened and properly conducted stockholders' meeting.

A regular meeting is usually held at the place and time specified in the articles of incorporation or in the bylaws; notice of the meeting is ordinarily not required. A special meeting may be called by the directors of the corporation or, in some instances, by a particular officer or a specified number of stockholders. Notice specifying the subjects to be discussed is always required for a special meeting.

Washington Preferred Life Insurance Company called a stockholders' meeting to vote on a proposed merger. Notice of the meeting was mailed to stockholders of record and published in two legal newspapers. The published notice indicated that the meeting was to vote on the merger; that proxies, proxy statements, and notices were mailed to stockholders at their last known addresses; and that if anyone was a stockholder of record and had not received the material, inquiry should be made to the company at the address given. A week later Washington asked a court to appoint a representative for missing shareholders in accordance with state law. This law allowed for such appointment if addresses of shareholders were lost or inadequate and if the purpose of the meeting required a two-thirds vote. The law stated that approval by the court of the representative's findings acted as an affirmative vote at the stockholders' meeting by the missing shareholders. The court appointed a representative who approved the merger. James Watson, a Washington stockholder, asked the court to vacate the order of appointment because the notice to the allegedly missing stockholders was insufficient. The court found that the notice did not inform stockholders that if they did not attend the meeting, a person would be appointed to vote their shares. Normally, absence from a stockholders' meeting constitutes a negative vote, so the notice was inadequate.

Meetings of the stockholders are theoretically a check upon the board of directors. If the directors do not carry out the will of the stockholders, a new board can be elected that will be amenable to the stockholders' wishes. This procedure is, in the absence of fraud or bad faith on the part of the directors, the only legal means by which the investors can exercise any control over their investment.

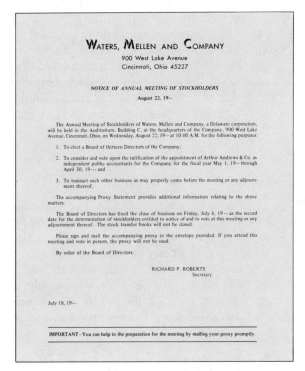

ILLUS. 39-1. A Notice of a Stockholders' Meeting

Quorum

A stockholders' meeting, in order to be valid, requires the presence of a quorum. At common law a *quorum* consisted of the stockholders actually assembled at a properly convened meeting. A majority of the votes cast by those present expressed the will of the stockholders. It is now ordinarily required by statutes, by bylaws, or by the articles of incorporation that a majority of the outstanding stock be represented at the stockholders' meeting in order to consitute a quorum. This representation may be either in person or by proxy.

Voting

The right of a stockholder to vote is the most important right, because this is the only way in which any control over investment in the corporation can be exercised. The right to vote is limited to those stockholders shown by the stockholders' record book. A person who purchases stock from an individual does not have the right to vote until the transfer has been made on the books of the corporation. Subscribers who have not fully paid for their stock are not, as a rule, permitted to vote.

The right to vote is controlled by state corporation laws. Voting and nonvoting common stock may be issued if the law permits.

There are two major classes of elections in which the stockholders vote: the annual election of directors and the elections to approve or disapprove some corporate policy which only the stockholders can authorize. Examples of some of these acts are consolidating with another corporation, dissolving, increasing the capital stock, and changing the number of directors.

Methods of Voting

Each stockholder normally has one vote for each share of common stock owned. In the election of a board of directors, the candidates receiving a majority of the stock actually voting win. In corporations with 500,000 stockholders, control of 10 percent of the stock is often sufficient to control the election. In all cases the owners of 51 percent of the stock can elect all the directors. This leaves the minority stockholders without any representation on the board of directors. To alleviate this situation, two legal devices are in existence which may give the minority stockholders a voice, but not a controlling voice, on the board of directors:

1. Cumulative voting
2. Voting trusts

Cumulative Voting. In some states the statutes provide that in the election of directors a stockholder may cast as many votes in the aggregate as are equal to the number of shares owned multiplied by the number of directors to be elected. This method of voting is called *cumulative voting*. Thus, if a stockholder owns ten shares and ten directors are to be elected, ten votes for each of the ten directors or one hundred votes for one director can be cast. As a result, under this plan of voting the minority stockholders may have some representation on the board of directors, although it is a minority.

Voting Trusts. Under a voting trust stockholders give up their voting privileges by transferring their stock to a trustee and receiving in return *voting trust certificates*. This is not primarily a device to give the minority stockholders a voice on the board of directors; but it does do that, and often in large corporations it gives them a controlling voice. Twenty percent of the stock always voted as a unit is more effective than individual voting. State laws frequently impose limitations on voting trusts, as by limiting the number of years that they may run.

Proxies

Under the common law only stockholders who were present in person were permitted to vote. Under the statutory law, the articles of incorporation, or the bylaws, stockholders who do not wish to attend a meeting and vote in person may authorize another to vote their stock for them. This right is called *voting by proxy*; the person who is authorized to vote for another is known as a *proxy*. The written authorization to vote is also called a proxy (see Illustration 39-2).

WATERS, MELLEN AND COMPANY
P R O X Y
ANNUAL MEETING AUGUST 22, 19--

KNOW ALL MEN BY THESE PRESENTS, That the undersigned shareholder of WATERS, MELLEN AND COMPANY hereby constitutes and appoints O. W. PRESCOTT, A. B. BROWN, and GEORGE CONNARS, and each of them, the true and lawful proxies of the undersigned, with several power of substitution and revocation, for and in the name of the undersigned, to attend the annual meeting of shareholders of said Company, to be held at the Main Office of the Company, 900 West Lake Avenue, Cincinnati, Ohio, on Thursday, August 22, 19--, at 10:00 o'clock A.M., Standard Time, and any and all adjournments of said meeting, receipt of the notice of which meeting, stating the purposes thereof, together with Proxy Statement, being hereby acknowledged by the undersigned, and to vote for the election of a Board of thirteen directors for the Company, to vote upon the ratification of the appointment of Arthur Andrews & Co. as independent public accountants for the fiscal year May 1, 19-- through April 30--, and to vote as they or he may deem proper upon all other matters that may lawfully come before said meeting or any adjournment thereof.

Signed the _____ 1*5* day of March

Wanda Klimecki

ILLUS. 39-2. A Proxy

As a rule, proxies are revocable at any time. If a stockholder should sign more than one proxy for the same stockholders' meeting, the proxy having the later date would be effective. A proxy may be good in some states for only a limited period of time. If the stockholder attends the stockholders' meeting in person, this acts as a revocation of the proxy.

◆   Robinson was a stockholder in the Southwest Smelting Corp. Six weeks before the annual meeting he received a notice of the upcoming meeting and a proxy in favor of the president of the company. Robinson signed the proxy and mailed it back. Forgetting about the proxy he went to the meeting and attempted to vote. He was allowed to vote in person since his appearance constituted a revocation of the proxy.

It is legal for the management of a corporation to solicit proxies for candidates selected by the board of directors. However, proxies secured by means of fraudulent representations to stockholders may not be voted.

Proxy Wars

If the stockholders are dissatisfied with the policies of the present board of directors, a new board may be elected. To elect a new board is often a difficult or impossible task. If one or even several people own a majority of the voting stock, there is no way the objecting stockholders can obtain a majority of the voting stock to ensure success. If the voting stock is widely held, and no group owns a majority of the voting stock, then the objecting stockholders at least have a chance to elect a new board. To do this a majority of the stock represented at a stockholders' meeting must be controlled by this dissatisfied group. To ensure this success, the leaders of the group will obtain proxies from stockholders who cannot attend the stockholders' meeting in person. The current board members will also attempt to secure proxies. This is known as a *proxy war*. The present board of directors is permitted in most instances to pay the cost of this solicitation from corporate funds. The "outsiders" generally must bear the cost of the proxy war out of their personal funds. If there are 1,000,000 shareholders, the cost of soliciting their proxies is enormous. For this reason proxy wars are seldom undertaken.

Rights of Stockholders

The stockholders of a corporation enjoy several important rights and privileges. Three of these rights have already been discussed. They are:

1. A stockholder has the right to receive a properly executed certificate as evidence of ownership of shares of stock.

2. A stockholder has the right to attend corporate meetings and to vote unless this right is denied by express agreement, the articles of incorporation, or statutory provisions.

3. A stockholder has the right to receive a proportionate share of the profits when profits are distributed as dividends.

In addition, each stockholder has the following rights:

4. The right to sell and transfer shares of stock

5. The right, when new stock is issued by the corporation, to subscribe for new shares in proportion to the shares that are owned. For example, a stockholder who owns 10 percent of the original capital stock, has a right to buy 10 percent of the shares added to the stock. If this were not true, stockholders could be deprived of their proportionate share in the accumulated surplus of the company. This is known as a *preemptive right*. Only stockholders have the right to vote to increase the capital stock.

6. The right to inspect the corporate books and to have the corporate books inspected by an attorney or an accountant. This right is not absolute, since most states have laws restricting the right. The tendency is for these laws to be drawn to protect the corporation from indiscriminate inspection, not to hamper a stockholder in this right.

7. The right, when the corporation is dissolved, to share pro rata in the assets that remain after all the obligations of the company have been paid. In the case of certain preferred stock, the shareholders may have a preference in the distribution of the corporate assets upon liquidation.

Directors

Every corporation is managed by a board of directors elected by the stockholders. Laws normally require every board to consist of at least three members; but if the number is in excess of three, the number, together with qualifications and manner of election, is fixed by the articles of incorporation and the bylaws of the corporation.

The directors, unlike the stockholders, cannot vote by proxy. Nor can they make corporate decisions as individual directors. All decisions must be made collectively and in a called meeting of the board.

The functions of the directors can be classified as:

1. Powers
2. Duties
3. Liabilities

Powers. The powers of the board of directors are limited by law, by the articles of incorporation, and by the bylaws. The directors have the power to manage and direct the corporation. They may do any legal act reasonably necessary to achieve the purpose of the corporation so long as this power is not expressly limited. They may elect and appoint officers and agents to act for the corporation, or they may delegate authority to any number of its members to so act. If a director obtains knowledge of something while acting in the course of employment and in the scope of authority with the corporation, the corporation is charged with this knowledge.

Duties. The directors are changed with the duty of establishing policies that will achieve the purpose of the corporation, selecting executives to carry out these policies, and supervising these executives to see that the policies are efficiently executed. They must act in person in exercising all discretionary power. The directors may delegate ministerial and routine duties to subagents, but the duty of determining all major corporate policies, except those reserved to the stockholders, must be assumed by the board of directors.

Liabilities. As fiduciaries of the corporation, the directors are liable for bad faith and for negligence. They are not liable for losses when they act with due diligence and reasonably sound judgment. Countless errors of judgment are made annually by directors in operating a complex business organization. Only when these errors result from negligence or a breach of good faith can a director be held personally liable.

The test of whether the directors failed to exercise due care depends upon whether they exercised the care which a reasonably prudent person would have exercised under the circumstances. If they did that, they were not negligent and are not liable for the loss which follows. The test of whether they acted in bad faith is whether they acted in a way which conflicted with the interests of the corporation. The corporate directors are under a duty of loyalty to the corporation similar to the duty of loyalty an agent has to a principal or a partner has to the partnership and the other partners.

Directors may be held liable for some acts without evidence of negligence or bad faith either because the act is illegal or bad faith is presumed. Paying dividends out of capital and ultra vires acts are illustrations of acts that are illegal. Loaning corporate funds to officers and directors is an act to which the court will impute bad faith.

The members of the board of directors are subject to civil and criminal liability in their corporate actions. That is to say, a person who is a director does not get any immunity or protection from the legal consequences of actions taken. Because of this, individual directors who do not agree with action taken by the other directors must be careful to protect themselves by having the minutes of the meeting of the directors show that they dissented from the board's action. Otherwise stated, every director who is present at a board meeting is conclusively presumed to have assented to the action taken unless positive action is taken to overcome this presumption. If the directors who are present and dissent have a record of their dissent entered in the minutes of the meeting, then they cannot be held liable for the acts of the majority.

◆   At a meeting of the board of directors of the Sac River Mining Co., the Board voted to loan $20,000 to Parsons, one of the board members. Allen, another board member, dissented vigorously, and her dissent was recorded in the minutes of the board. Parsons failed to pay back the loan. In an action by the stockholders against the members of the board, Allen was not liable because she dissented to the approval of the loan.

Officers

In addition to selecting and removing the officers of a corporation, the board of directors authorizes them to act on behalf of the corporation in carrying out the board's policies. Since the officers are the agents of the corporation, the principles of agency apply to their relationship with the corporation and define many of their rights and obligations.

State statutes may specify a few of the officers corporations must have. The corporation's bylaws will specify what additional officers the corporation must have and the duties of each officer. It is common for a corporation to have a president, vice-president, secretary, and treasurer. In small corporations, some of these offices may be combined. There may be additional officers such as assistant secretaries or treasurers, additional vice-presidents, and a chief executive officer. The chief executive officer is frequently the president or the chairman of the board of directors. Some positions are created or deleted by decision of the board of directors.

Corporate Combinations

When two corporations wish to combine, they frequently do so by means of a merger or a consolidation. A *merger* of two corporations occurs when they combine so that one survives and the other ceases to exist. One is absorbed into the other. A *consolidation* occurs when two corporations combine to form a new corporation. Both of the two previous corporations disappear.

It has become a rather common practice recently for a corporation to try to take over another corporation. This may be done by the acquiring corporation's making a formal tender offer, which is an offer to buy stock in the target corporation at a set price. Since attempts at takeovers usually cause the price of the stock of the target company to rise, the acquiring corporation may try to obtain the amount of stock it wants in its target through the purchase of large blocks of the target's stock. The purchase of a large amount of stock cannot be kept quiet for long, however, because the Securities Exchange Act requires any person who acquires 5 percent of any class of stock to file a schedule within ten days.

Dissolution

A corporation may terminate its existence by paying all its debts, distributing all remaining assets to the stockholders, and surrendering its articles of incorporation. The corporation then ceases to exist, and its dissolution is complete. This action may be voluntary on the part of the stockholders, or it may be involuntary by action of the court or state. The state may ask for a dissolution for any one of the following reasons:

1. Forfeiture or abuse of the corporate charter
2. Violation of the state laws
3. Fraud in the procurement of the charter
4. In some states, failure to pay specified taxes for a specified number of years

When a corporation dissolves, its existence is terminated for all purposes except to wind up its business. It is then incapable of suing, owning property, or forming contracts except for the purpose of converting its assets into cash and distributing the cash to the creditors and stockholders.

In the event that there are not enough assets to pay all creditors, the stockholders are not held personally liable. This is one of the chief advantages to business owners of a corporation over a sole proprietorship or partnership. It is an advantage from the stockholders' standpoint, but a disadvantage from the creditors' standpoint.

Questions

1. What is the only way that a corporation can perform business transactions?

2. What are the duties of the board of directors?

3. How many stockholders must be represented at a stockholders' meeting to constitute a quorum?

4. How do the stockholders exercise control over a corporation?

5. How many votes does each stockholder have?

6. What is cumulative voting?

7. What is a proxy?

8. Does every stockholder have the right to vote?

9. By what are the powers of the board of directors limited?

10. **a.** Under what conditions may the state order a dissolution of a corporation against the stockholders' objection?

    b. In the event of the dissolution of a corporation, how are the corporate assets distributed?

Case Problems

1. Jan Chin died owning the 300 outstanding shares of stock in Jan Chin, Inc., and by will left his property to his widow, Toy See Chin. Legal title to the

stock vested in his estate's executor, Donald Delahunt. At Toy Chin's request, Delahunt distributed 85 shares to her, and she gave them to her son, Chin Chak Ping and his children. Chin Chak Ping, the president of Jan Chin, Inc., called a meeting to elect directors. He and Toy Chin waived notice of the meeting. Delahunt was not notified of the meeting, and he did not attend. Toy Chin and Chin Chak Ping elected themselves directors and elected Chin Chak Ping to all the corporate offices. During the years, stock was issued to Toy Chin, who distributed 145 shares to her son and his family. Delahunt was never notified of any meetings and never attended any. Toy Chin died, and Delahunt assigned to her executor the stock he held. This executor brought a suit to cancel distribution of the 145 shares and have the election of directors and officers declared void, alleging that, as the beneficial owner, Toy Chin did not have the power to waive notice of the meeting and vote the stock. Did she?

2. Rooney was the president of the Frozen Food Lockers, Inc. The three-member board of directors loaned Rooney $15,000 from the corporate funds. Later, Rooney became bankrupt, and the corporation lost the entire loan. The stockholders brought suit against the board members personally for the loss. Were they liable?

3. Jerry Ward, a shareholder of Cook Inlet Region, Inc., sent a proxy solicitation to all shareholders. The solicitation started with a cartoon showing a group of Cook shareholders saying to management, "Hey! We want our money NOW." It further stated: "If we each want a big chunk of land then let's give it to ourselves 'NOW'" and "If we were to go ahead and sell just the coal for its estimated value that would be over three hundred thousand dollars . . . for every man, woman, and child owner of Cook." Ward received a large number of proxies from this solicitation. In the resulting lawsuit it was alleged that the proxy solicitation was materially false or misleading. Cook did not have large amounts of land it could distribute to shareholders, and there was no current prospect of selling coal reserves for anything like $300,000 per shareholder. Was the solicitation misleading?

4. O'Malley was the chief accountant for the Quitman Corporation, which had capital stock outstanding of $100,000 and retained earnings of $3,500. The board of directors declared a 2.5 percent dividend and instructed O'Malley to calculate the amount due and mail each stockholder a check. O'Malley, through an error, calculated the dividend at 25 percent instead of 2.5 percent. This resulted in a payment of dividend out of capital. Later, judgment creditors sued the directors personally for the amount of the dividend in excess of retained earnings. Were they liable?

5. Robert Nanney was a stockholder and president of Robert Nanney Chevrolet Co. The corporation was in financial trouble and owed money on loans personally endorsed by James Austin, the majority stockholder. Concerned about his personal liability, Austin took steps to liquidate the corporation. Nanney

hired Evans and Moses, a law firm, to defeat Austin's efforts to liquidate. Nanney and Austin settled their dispute. Nanney issued a check on the corporation, payable to Evans and Moses. There were two signature lines, but the check was signed only by Nanney. The check was not paid because two signatures were required. Evans and Moses sued the corporation for payment of the check. Austin, who had succeeded as president, testified Nanney did not have authority from the corporation to hire the firm or issue the check. Was the check valid?

6. Meeks was a stockholder in a corporation of 15,000 stockholders. The outstanding capital stock was $50,000,000; the retained earnings were $40,000,000. Meeks was dissatisfied with the operating policy of the corporation in retaining all profits for expansion instead of paying dividends. He started a proxy war to line up other stockholders who agreed with him. The board of directors retaliated by soliciting proxies at the corporation's expense. Meeks sought through legal action to enjoin the directors from spending corporate funds to solicit proxies. Will he succeed?

7. Henderson was a director on the board of directors of the Watson Corporation. Henderson also was a large stockholder in a competing firm. In a board of directors meeting, Henderson voted for a measure that was highly detrimental to the Watson Corporation but highly profitable for the competing firm. A stockholder in the Watson Corporation sought to make Henderson personally liable for the loss incurred by paying $50,000 for items worth only $10,000. Was he liable?

Summary Cases for Part Eight

Corporations

1. Darden, Doman & Stafford Associates (DDS), a partnership executed a renovation contract with "BUILDING DESIGN AND DEVELOPMENT INC. (In Formation) John A. Goodman, President." DDS knew the corporation was not in existence, but Goodman had told them he would form a corporation to limit his personal liability. The renovation was to be completed by October 15, and disputes were to be settled by arbitration. The first check in payment for the work was made out to "Building Design and Development Inc. — John Goodman." Goodman crossed out his name and indorsed it "Bldg. Design & Dev. Inc., John A. Goodman, Pres." and told DDS to make payments only to the corporation. The work was not finished by October 15 and DDS claimed it was of poor quality. A corporate license for Building Design and Development Inc. was issued on November 2. DDS served a demand for arbitration and named the corporation and Goodman. DDS testified it never agreed to make the contract only with the corporation; therefore, Goodman should be a party to the arbitration. Should he? [*Goodman v. Darden, Doman & Stafford Associates*, 670 P.2d 648 (Wash.)]

2. Jerold Murphy and three others were the incorporators and original stockholders of Country House, Inc. For nine years they all worked as full-time employees of Country House and were paid wages. Twice they were paid "bonuses" which were authorized when fiscal reports indicated sufficient corporate earnings. Murphy terminated his employment but kept his stock. After his termination, Country House paid stockholder-employees bonuses in addition to their wages. No dividends were ever paid. Murphy brought suit, alleging the bonuses were really dividends and, as a stockholder, money was due him, too. Were the payments dividends? [*Murphy v. Country House, Inc.*, 349 N.W.2d 289 (Minn. Ct. App.)]

3. United Electronics Co. (UED) borrowed money from Factors and Note Buyers and pledged stock it owned in Frost Controls Corp. UED defaulted on the loan, so Factors foreclosed. Factors offered the stock for sale publicly and then bought it itself. Frost's president, Authur Thomson, started a new company, which bought Frost's assets. UED sued Thomson and his new company. To win the lawsuit, UED had to have owned the Frost stock when Frost's assets were sold. To establish that it owned the stock at that time, UED tried to show the foreclosure sale was invalid because Factors, trying to sell the Frost stock, was an "underwriter" as defined in the Securities Act. UED alleged that Factors, with a view to the distribution of the securities, sold the stock for UED, which controlled Frost. Since the Frost stock was unregistered, it alleged the public foreclosure sale violated the Securities Act.

Did the sale violate the Securities Act? [*A.D.M. Corp. v. Thomson*, 707 F.2d 25 (1st Cir.)]

4. Glenn C. Shaw died on March 17 and by will bequeathed his property to the Abby Tarr–Glenn C. Shaw Foundation, a charitable, educational, and benevolent corporation. The Foundation was incorporated by his attorney on May 21. Shaw's heirs alleged that a bequest to a nonexistent charitable corporation is invalid and fails. Testamentary dispositions are assumed to take effect at the death of the testator, but a legal doctrine states a bequest made to a charitable corporation which is not in existence will not fail if there is an intention to devote the property to charitable purposes, not just to make a gift to a designated corporation. Shaw's will provided: "In the event any individual should prove themselves to be an heir at law and entitled to any portion of my estate then . . . I . . . bequeath to each such individual . . . the sum of One Dollar only, it being my intention and desire that . . . my entire estate should go to the above-named foundation." It also designated Shaw's attorney to handle "all other legal proceedings . . . including all legal and management services in connection with the handling of the Abby Tarr–Glen C. Shaw Foundation." Should the estate go to the corporation or the heirs? [*Matter of Estate of Shaw*, 620 P.2d 483, (Okla. Ct. App.)]

5. W. E. Groves and Lloyd Lindsey had a disagreement, and to settle it they signed an act of exchange. One of the provisions was that Groves transfer to Lindsey Groves' "ownership in Rosemound Improvement Association, Inc., represented by the following stock certificates." No certificates were described and none were signed over by Groves. Rosemound's charter provided: "Stock certificates herein shall not be transferable except back to the corporation." After the act of exchange was signed, the parties became dissatisfied, and the provisions were not all fulfilled. Groves sued to require Rosemound to recognize his right to vote at shareholders' meetings. Is Groves entitled to vote? [*Groves v. Rosemound Improvement Association, Inc.*, 413 So. 2d 925 (La. Ct. App.)]

6. Jack Alpert and others owned 26 percent of the stock of 79 Realty Corp., which had an office building as its principal asset. Another corporation, 28 William St. Corp., purchased more than two-thirds of 79 Realty's stock. The board of directors of 79 Realty was replaced, and the new board approved a merger of 28 William St. into 79 Realty. The minority shares would be cancelled, and title to the office building would end up in Madison 28 Associates, a partnership. The minority shareholders were to be paid the same price per share as had been paid to acquire the majority interest. The merger was to get more capital for necessary renovation and realize tax savings by owning as a partnership rather than as a corporation. The minority shareholders sued to rescind the merger. There was no showing of fraud, illegality, or self-dealing. Should the merger be rescinded? [*Alpert v. 28 Williams St. Corp.*, 457 N.Y.S.2d 4 (N.Y. App. Div.)]

Part Nine — Risk-Bearing Devices

Learning Objectives for Part Nine

Risk-Bearing Devices

After studying this part you should be able to:

1. Define insurance.
2. Distinguish between the two types of insurance companies.
3. Discuss the five aspects of the law of contracts which have special significance for insurance contracts.
4. Explain what life insurance is.
5. Differentiate among the different types of life insurance policies.
6. Explain the difference between life insurance and annuities.
7. Describe the two most common limitations on risks covered by life insurance.
8. Explain the rules regarding premium payment for life insurance policies.
9. Specify what is required in order to have an insurable interest in a person's life.
10. Describe what property insurance is.
11. Distinguish between the types of fires, loss from which are and are not covered by fire insurance.
12. Explain the requirements for having an insurable interest in property.
13. Describe the different types of fire insurance policies.
14. Explain the principle of coinsurance and its application to fire insurance policies.
15. Discuss the kinds of insurance included in physical damage insurance.
16. Identify the types of coverage afforded by public liability insurance.
17. Distinguish between contracts of guaranty and suretyship.
18. Discuss the rights of a surety and guarantor.
19. Name the acts that discharge a surety or guarantor.
20. Explain how secured credit sales are made and the rights of the parties.

40

Nature of Insurance

Preview Cases

Freddie Long obtained a life insurance policy from Mutual Benefit Life Insurance Company of New Jersey on which Richard Chisholm was the beneficiary. Question 15 in the application for the insurance asked if the applicant "had any surgery, treatment, observation or routine examination in doctor's office, hospital, clinic. . . ?" It instructed, "For routine physical examinations indicating only good health . . . state 'routine exams' beside your 'yes' answer." Long marked "yes" and stated "routine exams." Long died five months later in a car accident. Mutual denied Chisholm's claim for payment, stating that in answering Question 15 Long had failed to disclose that after an auto accident he had received hospital treatment for minor injuries for which the prognosis was good. Mutual's underwriting department indicated the injuries were of no underwriting concern. Was there concealment?

Crutchfield applied for a life insurance policy. On the application for insurance, the question was asked: "What is your occupation?" Crutchfield answered: "Airplane pilot." The insurance policy had a clause which stated that the company would not pay if the insured was an airplane pilot. The company issued the policy. One year later Crutchfield died of a heart attack, and the company refused to pay. Is the company obligated to pay?

It is the function of insurance to provide a fund of money when a loss covered by the policy is sustained. Life is full of unfavorable financial contingencies. Not every financial peril in life can be shifted by insurance, but many of the most common perils can be. *Insurance* is a contract whereby a party transfers a risk of financial loss to the risk bearer, the insurance company, for a fee.

Every insurance contract specifies the particular risk being transferred.

The name by which the policy is described is not controlling as to the coverage or protection of the policy. For example, a particular contract may carry the name "Personal Accident Insurance Policy," but this name may not clearly indicate the risk being assumed by the insurance company. A reading of the contract may reveal that the company will pay only if an accident occurs while the insured is in actual attendance in a public school. In such a case, in spite of the broad title of the policy, the premium paid covers only this much protection against a financial loss due to an accident, not the loss due to any accident.

Terms Used in Insurance

The company agreeing to compensate a person for a certain loss is known as the *insurer*, or sometimes as the *underwriter*; the person protected against the loss is known as the *insured*, or the *policyholder*. In life insurance the person who is to receive the benefits or the proceeds of the policy is known as the *beneficiary*.

Whenever a person purchases any kind of insurance, a contract with the insurance company is entered into. The written contract is commonly called a *policy*. The amount that the insurer agrees to pay in case of a loss is known as the *face* of the policy, and the consideration the insured pays for the protection is called the *premium*. The danger of a loss of, or injury to, property, life, or anything else, is called a *risk* or *peril*; when that danger may be covered by insurance, it is known as the *insurable risk*. Factors, such as fire, floods, and sleet, that contribute to the uncertainty are called *hazards*.

Types of Insurance Companies

There are two major types of insurance companies:

1. Stock companies
2. Mutual companies

Stock Companies. A *stock insurance company* is a corporation for which the original investment was made by stockholders and whose business is conducted by a board of directors. As in all other corporations, the stockholders elect the board of directors and receive the profits as dividends. Unlike other corporations, insurance companies must place a major portion of their original capital in a reserve account. As business volume increases, the reserve must be increased by setting aside part of the premiums.

Mutual Companies. In a *mutual insurance company* the policyholders are the members and owners and correspond to the stockholders in a stock company. In these companies the policyholders are both the insurer and the insured, but the corporation is a separate legal entity. A person who purchases a $10,000 fire insurance policy in a mutual company that has $10,000,000 insurance in force, owns 1/1,000 of the company and is entitled to share the profits in this ratio. Losses may also have to be shared in the same ratio if it is an *assessment mutual*. A policyholder is not subject to assessment where the policy makes no provision for it. In a stock company policyholders never share the losses.

In a nonassessment mutual insurance company, the policyholder's liability is limited to the amount of premium which the policy requires to be paid. The policyholder pays no more than a policyholder in a stock company. In an assessment mutual insurance company, however, the insured is liable for a pro rata share of the losses of the corporation without reference to the premium. If premiums are inadequate to pay all losses, the insured can be assessed for a pro rata share of the losses in excess of the premium.

Who May Be Insured

To become a policyholder, one must first have an insurable interest. The insurance contract is in its entirety an agreement to assume a specified risk. If the insured has no interest to protect, there can be no assumption of risk, and hence no insurance. The law covering insurable interest is different for life insurance and for property insurance.

To become an insured, an individual must also be competent to contract. Insurance is not a necessary; thus, a minor who wishes to disaffirm is not bound on insurance contracts. A minor who disaffirms a contract may demand the return of any money. Since insurance contracts provide protection only, this cannot be returned. Some states hold that because of this a minor can demand only the unearned premium for the unexpired portion of the policy.

Some Legal Aspects of the Insurance Contract

The laws applicable to contracts in general apply to insurance contracts. There are five aspects, however, that have special significance for insurance contracts:

1. Concealment
2. Representation
3. Warranty
4. Subrogation
5. Estoppel

Concealment. The nature of insurance is such that the insurer must rely upon the information supplied by the insured. This places upon the insured the responsibility of supplying all information pertinent to the risk. A willful failure to disclose this pertinent information is known as *concealment*. To affect the contract the concealed facts must be material; that is, they must relate to matters which would affect the insurer's decision to insure the insured, and the determination of the premium rate. Also, the concealment must be willful. The willful concealment of a material fact renders the contract voidable.

Freddie Long obtained a life insurance policy from Mutual Benefit Life Insurance Company of New Jersey on which Richard Chisholm was the beneficiary. Question 15 in the application for the insurance asked if the applicant "had any surgery, treatment, observation or routine examination in doctor's office, hospital, clinic . . . ?" It instructed, "For routine physical examinations indicating only good health . . . state 'routine exams' beside your 'yes' answer." Long marked "yes" and stated "routine exams." Long died five months later in a car accident. Mutual denied Chisholm's claim for payment, stating that in answering Question 15 Long had failed to disclose that after an auto accident he had received hospital treatment for minor injuries for which the prognosis was good. Mutual's underwriting department indicated the injuries were of no underwriting concern. The court held that Long had a routine examination and there was no concealment.

The rule of concealment does not apply with equal stringency to all types of insurance contracts. In fire insurance where the agent has an opportunity to inspect the property, the right of the insurance company to void the contract is waived. In ocean marine insurance there is concealment whenever pertinent information is withheld, even if there is no intent to defraud.

Representation. An oral or written misstatement of a material fact by the insured prior to the finalization of the contract is called a *false representation*. If the insured makes a false representation, the insurer may avoid the contract of insurance. This is true whether or not the insured made the misstatement purposely.

It is now usual for insurance policies to provide that if the age of the insured is misstated, the policy will not be voided; however, the sum paid on the policy "shall be that sum which the premium paid would have provided for had the age been correctly stated."

Gilmer owned a paper mill. She insured it in the amount of $100,000 as a paper mill against loss by fire. At the time she took out the policy, Gilmer was not using the building as a paper mill but had installed some stone burrs and was using the mill to grind wheat and corn into flour and cornmeal on the shares for farmers. This use was temporary while the paper business was depressed. While the mill was being used as a grist mill, it was totally destroyed by fire. The company refused to pay on the ground of misrepresentation. The court held this was not misrepresentation, since the mill was still a paper mill even though it was being used temporarily as a grist mill. Furthermore, the misrepresentation was not material, since a grist mill is less likely to burn than a paper mill and therefore involved a lesser risk.

Warranty. A *warranty* is a statement or promise of the insured which relates to the risk and appears in the contract or another document incorporated in the contract. If the statements are not true or the promises are not fulfilled, the insurer may declare the policy void.

There are several differences between warranties and representations. Warranties are included in the actual contract of insurance or are incorporated in it by reference, while representations are merely collateral or independent, such as oral statements or written statements appearing in the application for insurance or other writing separate from the actual contract of insurance.

Also, in order to void the contract of insurance, the false representations must concern a material fact, while the warranties may concern any fact or be any promise. A representation need only be substantially correct, while a warranty must be absolutely true or strictly performed.

Several states have enacted legislation which eliminates any distinction between warranties and representations and does not require a showing that the warranty is material or that the insured intended to defraud. A breached warranty does not void the policy. Even in states without such statutes, the courts are reluctant to find policies invalid and will construe warranties as representations whenever possible and interpret warranties strictly against the insurer so as to favor the insured.

Subrogation. In insurance, *subrogation* is the right of the insurer under certain circumstances to "step into the shoes" of the insured. Subrogation is particularly applicable to some types of automobile insurance. If the insurer pays a claim to the insured, under the law of subrogation the insurer is entitled to any claims which the insured had because of the loss. For example, *A* has a collision insurance policy on a car. *B* negligently damages the car. The insurance company will pay *A* but then has the right to sue *B* for indemnity.

Estoppel. Either party to an insurance contract may not be allowed to claim the benefit of a violation of the contract by the other party. Such a party is said to be *estopped* from claiming the benefit of such violation. An estoppel arises whenever a party, by statements or actions, leads another party to a conclusion which the latter relies upon and by which the latter would be harmed if the first party were allowed to show that the conclusion is not true. For example, if the insurer gives the insured a premium receipt, the insurer would be estopped from later asserting that the premium was not paid in accordance with the terms of the policy.

Crutchfield applied for a life insurance policy. On the application for insurance, the question was asked: "What is your occupation?" Crutchfield answered: "Airplane pilot." The insurance policy had a clause which stated that the company would not pay if the insured was an airplane pilot. The company issued the policy. One year later Crutchfield died of a heart attack, and the company refused to pay. The court held the company had waived this provision regarding airplane pilots.

Questions

1. Define *insurance*.

2. Does an "accident insurance policy" cover loss due to all accidents?

3. How does a mutual insurance company differ from a stock insurance company?

4. What two requirements must an individual meet to become an insured?

5. What is the effect of the insured's concealing material facts in applying for insurance?

6. What is the difference between a warranty and a representation?

7. What is *subrogation* as applied to insurance contracts?

8. What is *estoppel* as applied to insurance contracts?

Case Problems

1. Georgette owned and operated a storage business and carried fire insurance to cover about 50 percent of its value. Someone called her and told her that smoke was coming from the gable end of the building and that he believed it was on fire. Before going to the building, Georgette saw her insurance agent and placed another $50,000 fire policy on it but made no mention of the smoke and possible fire. It developed that there was no fire. About two weeks later, however, the building was destroyed by fire, and the company refused to pay on the second policy because it had learned of the circumstances under which it was purchased. Was the insurance company liable on this policy?

2. A fire insurance policy contained a clause that no provision of the policy could be waived by the agent except in writing and attached to the policy. One provision in the policy stated that manuscripts were not covered unless specifically named in the policy. Mitchell, an author, had a manuscript almost completed for a novel which she felt would be a best-seller. She called

her agent and asked that the manuscript be named in her household effects policy. The agent said that was not necessary and that the policy covered it. A fire destroyed Mitchell's home, and the manuscript was burned up. The company refused to pay for it. Was Mitchell entitled to collect for the value of the manuscript?

3. An application for life insurance asked the following questions: "Do you have or have you ever had or been treated for: . . . disorder of the stomach . . . any . . . mental disorder, . . ." "Have you ever been . . . counselled . . . because of . . . drug use?" and "Have you consulted any doctor or been hospitalized in the past five years for any reason. . . ." Roger Johnson answered them all in the negative, and a policy of insurance was issued by State Farm Life Insurance Co. A month later Johnson was killed in a car accident. He had been hospitalized for an intestinal disorder a year and a half before answering the questions. He had also taken Valium, and his doctor had counselled him regarding the fact he was taking too many drugs. State Farm refused to pay the insurance benefits, claiming misrepresentation. Was this misrepresentation?

4. Barbara Washington purchased two fire insurance policies on her home and contents from Interstate Fire Insurance Company. The application asked, "If this policy is issued, will the building be insured by any other policy?" It was answered "no." The application also stated, "NO APPLICATION WILL BE APPROVED . . . WHEN THE BUILDING OR CONTENTS TO BE INSURED ARE ALREADY INSURED" and "said answers . . . shall form the basis of a contract of fire insurance. . . ."

   After the agent prepared a premium payment book, he hung it on a nail at Washington's request. Hanging on the nail was a premium payment book for a fire insurance policy she had already purchased. A few days later she purchased another fire insurance policy, and ten days later her home was totally destroyed by fire. Interstate refused to pay, alleging misrepresentation. Was it?

5. Kevin Mulvihill bought a credit life insurance policy on the life of his wife. He had bought a car for her, and the insurance was to pay for the car in the event of her death. The insurance company did not ask for information concerning her health. Less than 3 weeks after the policy was obtained, she died of cancer. The company refused to pay, claiming Mulvihill had a duty to disclose his wife's terminal cancer. Did he?

6. A teenager, William Bertram, was in a fight with another boy, Clinton Griggs. Bertram promptly gave notice to his insurer, Franklin Mutual Insurance Company. Three months later Franklin sent an investigator to interview Bertram. Four months later, Griggs made a claim for injuries, and Bertram sent it to Franklin, which made no effort to find or interview other witnesses or to obtain a physical examination of Griggs. Twenty months after the fight, Griggs filed suit, and Bertram promptly sent the papers to Franklin. A month later, Franklin refused coverage because intentional torts were excluded by

the insurance policy. Bertram defended the action himself. He also alleged Franklin was liable to him on the basis of estoppel. He charged Franklin had a duty to promptly tell him that he might not be covered by the policy so that he could make his own investigation and preparation. Is Franklin liable?

7. Morrison, who owned three houses, asked his secretary to call the insurance agent and place a fire insurance policy on the one at 256 Cloverhurst. The agent asked her, "Is the house brick or frame?" She was not sure but thinking it made no difference, replied, "It is a brick building." It was in fact a frame building. The house was destroyed by fire, and the company refused to pay for the loss. Was Morrison entitled to collect?

41

Life and Annuity Insurance

Preview Cases

Eza Rozas had hospital and medical insurance with Louisiana Hospital Service, Inc. She had a severe headache and dizziness, was hospitalized, and was found to have two aneurysms and a large blood clot in her brain. Louisiana refused to pay her hospital bill because riders to her policy excluded coverage. The riders were stapled to her application for insurance which had been put inside the policy and given to her. Rozas alleged the riders were not effective because they were not physically attached to the policy. Were the riders effective?

A creditor insured the life of a debtor for the amount due her. Before the death of the insured, the debt was paid in full. After the insured died, the company refused to pay. Would it be required to pay?

Life insurance is a contract by which the insurer agrees to pay a specified sum or sums of money to a beneficiary upon the death of the insured. While it is generally obtained to protect the beneficiary from financial hardship resulting from the death of the insured, neither economic loss nor dependency upon the insured is necessary to be the beneficiary of a life insurance policy.

Types of Life Insurance Contracts

There are many different types of life insurance policies; the following are the most important:

1. Term insurance
2. Endowment insurance
3. Whole life insurance
4. Combinations, and other types

Term Insurance. As the name indicates, *term life insurance* contracts are those whereby the company assumes for a specified period of time the risk of the death of the insured. In this sense it is similar to a term fire insurance policy, or a term automobile insurance policy. This term may be for only one year; or it may be for five, ten, or even fifty years. The term must be stated in the policy. There are many variations of the term policies. In short-term policies, such as five years, the insured may, if the policy so provides, have the option of renewing it for another equal term without a physical examination. The cost is higher for each renewal period. This is called *renewable term insurance.* In nonrenewable term insurance the insured does not have the legal right to renew it unless the company consents to the renewal.

Term policies also may be either level term or decreasing term. In level term, the face of the policy is written in units of $1,000. The amount remains at this sum during the entire term of the policy. In decreasing term contracts, the policy may be written in multiples of $10 a month income. For example, a person aged twenty could purchase a decreasing term policy of ten units, or $100 a month, covering a period of 600 months, or 50 years. If the insured dies the first month after purchasing the policy, the beneficiary would draw $100 a month for 600 months, or $60,000 ultimately. If the insured dies at the end of 25 years, the beneficiary would draw $100 a month for 300 months, or $30,000 ultimately. Some decreasing term insurance is paid in a lump sum rather than periodically. Such insurance may be used, for example, to pay off a mortgage.

All term policies have one thing in common—they are pure life insurance. They shift the specific risk of loss as a result of death, and nothing more—just as a fire insurance policy shifts the risk of loss of property by fire, and nothing more.

Endowment Insurance. An *endowment insurance policy* is decreasing term insurance plus a savings account. Part of the premium pays for the insurance, and the remainder earns interest so that at the end of the term the total will equal the face amount of the policy. If the insured dies during the term of the policy, the beneficiary will collect the face. An insured who is still living at the end of the term, will collect the face unless a beneficiary has been designated to receive the amount.

Whole Life Insurance. In reality all life insurance contracts are either term insurance or endowment insurance. A whole life insurance policy is one that continues, assuming the premium is paid, until age 100 or death, whichever occurs first. If the insured is still living at age 100, the face of the policy is collected as an endowment. A whole life policy might correctly be defined as endowment insurance at age 100. As with all endowment policies, a whole life policy is reducing term insurance plus a savings account.

Whole life policies consist of several classes. A straight life policy is a whole life policy calling for the payment of the premium till death or age 100, whichever occurs first. For a person twenty years of age, this would be an 80-pay 80-year endowment. If the insured wants the same contract but wishes to limit the premiums to 20 years, the policy would be a 20-pay whole life policy, or a 20-pay 80-year endowment. Either term accurately describes the contract.

Combination and Other Types of Policies. The three basic life insurance contracts, term, endowment, and whole life, can be combined in an almost endless variety of combinations to create slightly different contracts. In the case of universal life insurance, any premiums paid which are more than the current cost of term insurance are put into a fund and earn interest. The fund can be withdrawn by the owner or paid to the beneficiary at the death of the insured. The Family Income Policy, for example, is merely a straight life policy with a twenty-year reducing term policy attached as a rider. A *rider* on an insurance policy is a clause or even a whole contract added to another contract to modify, extend, or limit the base contract. A rider must be clearly incorporated in, attached to, or referred to in the policy so that there is no doubt the parties wanted it to become a part of the policy.

In addition to the reducing term insurance, there are several other riders frequently found in life insurance policies. The disability income rider may be attached to any policy and pays an income to an insured who becomes disabled. Other riders are waiver of premium rider, which waives the annual premiums if the insured becomes disabled, and the double indemnity rider. By paying an additional premium, the insured can generally obtain a policy requiring the insurer to make a greater payment when death is caused by accidental means. This greater payment is customarily twice the ordinary amount of the policy and is hence described as "double indemnity."

◆ Eza Rozas had hospital and medical insurance with Louisiana Hospital Service, Inc. She had a severe headache and dizziness, was hospitalized, and was found to have two aneurysms and a large blood clot in her brain. Louisiana refused to pay her hospital bill because riders to her policy excluded coverage. The riders were stapled to her application for insurance which had been put inside the policy and given to her. Rozas alleged the riders were not effective because they were not physically attached to the policy. The court held that Rozas had the entire contract in her possession at all times and to require the riders to have been attached by staples, paper clips, or glue would be an absurd and unintended result.

Annuity Insurance

An annuity insurance contract pays the insured a monthly income from a specified age, generally age sixty-five, until death. It is a risk entirely unrelated to the risk assumed in a life insurance contract, even though both contracts are sold by life insurance companies. Someone has defined life insurance as shifting the risk of dying too soon and annuity insurance as shifting the risk of living too long, that is, outliving one's savings. An individual who is sixty-five years old and who has $50,000 and a life expectancy of seventy-two years of age could use up the $50,000 over the expected seven additional years of life if approximately $600 a month is used for living expenses. However, if the individual lives for more than seven years, there will be no money on which to live. An annuity insurance policy could be purchased for $50,000, and the monthly income would be guaranteed no matter how long the insured lives. If the annuity contract calls for the monthly payments to continue until the second of two insureds dies, it is called a *joint and survivor annuity*. This type of annuity is suitable for a couple who wish to extend their savings as long as either one is still living.

Limitation on Risks in Life Insurance Contracts

Policies of life insurance place various limitations upon the risk covered by the policy. The two most common limitations are: (1) suicide and (2) death from war activity.

Suicide. Life insurance policies commonly provide no payment for death by suicide. Such a provision is valid. Some suicide clauses stipulate that the company will not pay if death occurs by suicide, whether sane or insane, within two years from the date of the policy. If death is caused by suicide after the two-year period lapses, the company must pay.

Death from War Activity. The so-called "war clause" provides that if the insured dies as a consequence of war activity the company will not pay. If a member of the armed forces dies a natural death, the company must pay. The insurance company has the burden of proving that death was caused by war activity; if it cannot prove that such was the case, the insurer must pay the amount of the insurance.

◆ Raines was a bomber pilot. He had a $10,000 life insurance policy with a war clause. While over open water in the Pacific, he radioed his home base that he was being attacked by Japanese fighter planes. He was never heard from again, nor was any trace of his plane ever found. The court held that the insurance company had to pay, since the company could not prove he died as a result of war activity. The court pointed out that the pilot could have reached an island and died a natural death.

Payment of Premiums

The premiums must be paid within the time specified by the policy. If they are not paid when due, and the policy so provides, it will lapse either automatically or may be declared forfeited at the option of the insurer. If the premiums are to be paid annually, and the insured dies, the portion of premium unpaid for the year may be deducted from the proceeds. The policy or a statute of the state may provide that after a certain number of premiums have been paid, the policy will be extended for a specified time in case of nonpayment of a premium. Under such a condition a paid-up policy is sometimes issued for the term of the insurance but for a smaller amount. Sickness is no legal excuse for the nonpayment of premiums. In such a case the company may, if it so elects, extend the time of payment or take a promissory note for the amount of the premium. However, by the payment of an additional premium the insured may generally obtain a policy containing a waiver of premiums which becomes effective when the insured is disabled, with the result that if there is disability, the insured does not have to pay premiums for the period of time during which the disability exists.

Grace Period

All life insurance companies are required by law to provide a grace period of generally 30 or 31 days in every life insurance policy. This grace period gives the insured 30 or 31 days from the due date of the premium in which to pay it without the policy's lapsing. This provision is extremely important in life insurance contracts. Without this provision, if the insured through an oversight is one day late in paying the premium, the policy either would lapse or could be forfeited by the insured. If it is forfeited or lapsed, the insured may obtain a reinstatement of the policy but may sometimes be required to pass a new physical examination. An insured who wants to buy another policy, may have to pass a physical examination and will pay the higher rate for the current age.

Incontestability

Life insurance policies are made incontestable, either by statute or by the policies themselves, after a certain period of time, usually one or two years. After the expiration of the period of contestability, the insurance company usually cannot contest the validity of a claim on any ground except nonpayment of premiums.

Insurable Interest

In most states people can take out life insurance policies on their own lives and make any person they please the beneficiary. The beneficiary need not have an insurable interest in the insured's life.

When people insure another's life, however, and make themselves or someone else whom they select the beneficiary, they must have an insurable interest in the life of the insured at the time the policy is taken out.

A person has an insurable interest in the life of another when such a relationship exists between them that a reasonable expectation of benefit will be derived from the continued existence of the other person. The relationships most frequently giving rise to an insurable interest are those between parents and children, husband and wife, partner and copartner, and a creditor in the life of the debtor to the extent of the debt. This list is not exhaustive, as there are numerous other relationships which give rise to an insurable interest. With the exception of a creditor, if the insurable interest exists, the amount of insurance is irrelevant.

The insurable interest must exist at the time the policy of insurance is obtained. The fact that it does not exist at the time of the death of the insured is immaterial. Hence a policy naming the insured's spouse as beneficiary is valid even though prior to the insured's death the spouse obtained a divorce.

◆   A creditor insured the life of a debtor for the amount due her. Before the death of the insured, the debt was paid in full. The court held that the insurable interest which existed at the time the policy was taken out supported an action to recover against the insurance company after the death of the insured.

Change of Beneficiary

The modern form of life insurance policy reserves to the insured the right to change the beneficiary. Under such a policy, the insured may change the beneficiary at will, and this power of the insured is not affected by the fact that the beneficiary had paid the premiums on the policy.

The modern insurance policy permits the insured to name successive beneficiaries so that if the first beneficiary should die before the insured, the proceeds would pass to the second named or contingent beneficiary.

Assignment of the Policy

The policy of insurance may be assigned by the insured, either absolutely or as collateral security for a loan which the insured obtains from the assignee, such as a bank. The assignment does not affect the validity of the policy, since the hazard involved, namely the life of the insured, is not changed by the assignment. In many instances, the problem of assigning to a creditor is avoided by the insured's obtaining a loan directly from the insurer. The right to make such a loan is expressly reserved in the modern contract of insurance and no assignment of the policy is made in such case.

Distinct from an assignment by the insured is an assignment made by the beneficiary. If made before the death of the insured, the assignment by a beneficiary under a typical policy reserving to the insured the right to change the beneficiary is merely the transfer of the possibility that the beneficiary may receive the insurance proceeds in the event that the insured dies without changing beneficiaries. Under the basic principle that the rights of the assignee rise no higher than those of the assignor, the assignee of the beneficiary is subject to the same disadvantage as the named beneficiary that the insured may change beneficiaries. If the assignment is made after the insured has died, then the assignment is an ordinary assignment of an existing money claim; and, barring some defense, the beneficiary's assignee is then entitled to payment of the face amount of the policy.

Other Types of Insurance

There are several other types of insurance related to life insurance. They are health and accident insurance, hospitalization insurance, and group medical insurance. In these types of insurance the beneficiary is always the insured. The purpose is to protect the insured against loss or impairment of earning power or burdensome expenses rather than to protect someone who depends upon the insured for support.

Questions

1. Define *life insurance*.

2. What is term life insurance?

3. What is *decreasing term life insurance*? How does it differ from level-premium insurance?

4. What is a *rider* on a life insurance contract?

5. Define *annuity insurance*.

6. What are some limitations on risks that a life insurance company may provide?

7. What is the importance of a grace period in a life insurance policy?

8. When does a person have an insurable interest in the life of another?

9. Under what circumstances may the insured change the beneficiary of a policy?

10. May a policy of insurance be assigned?

Case Problems

1. Franklin Summers applied for life insurance, paid one month's premium, and received a Conditional Receipt for Advance Payment with Application for Life Insurance. The medical requirements of the application were completed on November 10, and by the terms of the Conditional Receipt, the policy became effective that day. The formal policy was issued on December 15. On November 18, two years later, Summers committed suicide. The suicide clause in the policy stated: "If the insured shall commit suicide . . . within two years from the Date of Issue of this contract, the amount payable will be limited to the premiums paid." "Date of Issue" was not defined in the policy. The company argued that date of issue meant the date of issue on the face of the policy. The beneficiary argued that date of issue meant the effective date of the policy; otherwise there would effectively be two policies, one during the conditional coverage period with no suicide clause and the formal policy. What was the date of issue?

2. The Masons, age twenty-six, have three children all under the age of six. Their income is $750 a month. They have the choice of insuring the breadwinner by purchasing a 20-pay life policy, face amount of $10,000, for an annual premium of $490 a year or a reducing term policy for $85,000 for $460 a year. The 20-pay life policy will build a substantial cash value in a few years; the term policy has no cash value. Which would you recommend that they buy?

3. Goff was treated over a period of three years by Dr. Richardson for serious stomach ulcers. She applied for a life insurance policy, and on the application was this question: "Have you been treated by a doctor for any illness during the past five years?" Goff answered "No." Three years after the policy was issued the insurance company learned of the false statement and brought suit to have the policy nullified. Will the company succeed?

4. On March 21, John D'Allessandro applied for life insurance with Durham Life Insurance Co. He signed an application, a copy of which was given him, indicating that he had not consulted a doctor or been hospitalized within five years and had no heart trouble, chest pains, or other health problem. He actually had been treated and hospitalized within five years for heart and kidney problems. The policy was issued July 1, and D'Allessandro died of coronary

artery disease on October 14. The incontestability clause in the policy stated: "no . . . statement shall be used in defense of a claim hereunder unless a copy of the instrument containing the statement has been furnished to the person making the claim." Durham furnished the beneficiary with a copy of the instrument after D'Allessandro died. She claimed the misrepresentations could not be raised by Durham because she had not been given a copy of the instrument before D'Allessandro died. Did the incontestability clause apply?

5. Sam Rich, Sylvera Rich Class, Charles Rich, and Mamie Rich were partners in an investment business. Class died and included in her estate were five life insurance policies on the life of Sam. The partnership agreement provided that upon the death of any partner, the partnership should terminate as to that partner, and the net worth of the partnership interest of the deceased partner should be paid to the deceased's personal representative. When, if ever, did Class have an insurable interest in Sam's life?

6. Hawkins purchased a $10,000 Family Income Policy with a 20-year decreasing term rider of $100 a month. In addition she had a double indemnity rider. Three years later she died in an automobile accident. How much will the beneficiary collect?

7. Matthew purchased a $200-a-month decreasing term life insurance policy. He was twenty-three when he purchased it for an annual premium of $225.80. He carried this policy until age thirty-five but through an oversight forgot to pay the premium on the due date. Three weeks later he learned of the oversight. The rate for this same policy at age 35 was $497.20. Can he still keep the $225.80 rate if he pays his premium immediately?

42

Property Insurance

Jordan carried fire insurance on his household effects at 1327 Ellis Street, a two-story frame building. He moved to 237 Beechwood Hills, a one-story stone building. He did not give notice of the move within the five days required. A fire damaged the furniture to the extent of $1,000. Did the company have to pay, since the new location carried a lower rate than the old?

Kevin Cumiskey leased property for a restaurant from Elizabeth Bradley. Cumiskey was required to insure the property to protect Bradley. The restaurant was opened for summers, and the property was insured in the name of Kevin Cumiskey, d/b/a "Chiripa's." Later the insurance lapsed, and the business was incorporated as K.S.J., Inc., with Kevin and his parents, Stephanie and John, as stockholders and officers. One summer Stephanie and John were to run the restaurant. They insured the property in the same name as previously. The restaurant consistently lost money, and a series of explosions and fire damaged the property. Circumstantial evidence indicated John had set the fire. The insurance company filed for a declaratory judgment, an action asking the court to decide the rights of the parties. Where an officer, director, stockholder, or managing agent deliberately sets a fire, the insurer has a good defense to a claim on the policy. Was the action proper in these circumstances?

Property insurance is a contract whereby the insurer, in return for a premium, agrees to reimburse the insured for loss or damage to specified property that is caused by the hazard covered. A contract of property insurance is one of indemnity that protects the policyholder from actual loss.

If a building actually worth $40,000 is insured for $45,000, the extra premiums which were paid for the last $5,000 worth of coverage do not provide any benefit for the insured, since $40,000, the actual value, is the maximum that can be collected in case of total loss. On the other hand, if the building is insured for only $20,000 and it is totally destroyed, the insurance company has to pay only $20,000. It will be seen from this that the maximum amount to be paid is fixed by the policy when the insurance is less than the value of the property. If the property is fully insured, the value of the property fixes the maximum.

Fire Insurance

Fire is the greatest cause of loss to property. Originally this was the only risk covered by insurance. As the additional types of property insurance developed, the same laws were applied to them that had been applied to fire insurance. Consequently, a thorough understanding of the laws of fire insurance is essential to understanding the basic laws governing all types of property insurance.

Losses Related to Fire

Normally, fire insurance covers damage to property caused only by what are known as hostile fires. A *hostile fire* is defined as one out of its normal place, while a *friendly fire* is one contained in the place where it is intended to be. Scorching, searing, singeing, smoke, and similar damages from a friendly fire are not covered under the fire policy. In order for there to be coverage by the fire policy, there must be an actual fire. Loss caused by heat without fire is not covered. In one case several thousand bales of cotton were under water during a flood. After the flood receded, heat in the bales of cotton was so intense smoke poured forth for days, but no flame was ever detected. The court held there was no fire.

Fire insurance also does not cover economic loss which results from a fire. A hostile fire may cause many losses other than to the property insured, yet the fire policy on the building and contents alone will not cover these losses. An example is the loss of profits while the building is being restored. This loss can be covered by a special policy called *business interruption insurance*. If one leases property on a long-term, favorable lease and the lease is canceled because of fire damage to the building, the tenant may have to pay a higher rent in new quarters. This increased rent loss can be covered by a *leasehold interest insurance policy* but not by a fire policy.

The typical fire policy may also cover the risks of loss by windstorm, explosion, smoke damage from a friendly fire, falling aircraft, water damage, riot and civil commotion, and many others. Each of these additional risks must be added to the fire policy by means of riders or extra clauses. This is commonly known as *extended coverage*.

Insurable Interest

One must have an insurable interest in the property at the time the policy is issued and at the time of the loss to be able to collect on a fire insurance policy. Ownership is, of course, the clearest type of insurable interest; but there are many other types of insurable interest. Insurable interest occurs when the insured would suffer a monetary loss by the destruction of the property. The most common types of insurable interest other than ownership are:

1. The mortgagee has an insurable interest in the property mortgaged to the extent of the mortgage.

2. When property is sold on the installment plan and the seller retains a security interest in it as security for the unpaid purchase price, the seller has an insurable interest in the property.

3. The bailee has an insurable interest in the property bailed to the extent of possible loss. The bailee's loss is from two sources. Compensation as provided for in the contract of bailment might be lost. Secondly, the bailee may be held legally liable to the owner if the loss is due to the bailee's negligence or to the negligence of the bailee's employees.

4. A partner has an insurable interest in the property owned by the firm to the extent of the possible loss.

5. A tenant has an insurable interest in property to the extent of the loss that would be suffered by damage or destruction of the property.

A change in title or possession of the insured property may destroy the insurable interest, which in turn may void the contract, because insurable interest must exist at the time of the loss.

The Fire Insurance Policy

The fire insurance policy will state a maximum amount which will be paid by the insurer. When only a maximum is stated, the policy is called an *open policy*, and in the event of partial or total loss, the insured must prove the actual loss which has been sustained. The policy may be a *valued policy*, in which case, instead of stating a maximum amount, it fixes values for the insured items of property. Once a covered total destruction of the property is shown, the insurer pays the total value. If there is only a partial loss, the insured under a valued policy must still prove the amount of loss, which amount cannot exceed the stated value of the property.

Dudley owned many valuable antiques. He carried a regular fire policy on his antiques in the amount of $100,000. A fire destroyed about half the antiques. After an extensive and expensive appraisal to ascertain the actual value of the items destroyed, he was able to collect $50,000. Had he carried a valued policy, he could have collected without an appraisal the stated value of the items totally destroyed.

Insurance policies also may be specific, blanket, or floating. A *specific policy* applies to one item only, such as one house. A *blanket policy* covers many items of the same kind in different places or different kinds of property in the same place, such as a building, fixtures, and merchandise in a single location. *Floating policies* are used for trucks, theatrical costumes, circus paraphernalia, and similar items which are not kept in a fixed location. A floating policy is also desirable for items that may be sent out for cleaning, such as rugs or clothes. Articles of jewelry and clothes that may be worn while traveling are also covered in a floating policy. A fire insurance policy on household effects covers for loss only at the named location. The purpose of the floating policy is to cover the loss no matter where the property is located at the time of the loss.

Another type of fire insurance policy of particular interest to merchants is the Reporting Form for Merchandise Inventory. This policy permits the merchant to report periodically, usually once a month, the amount of inventory on hand. This enables the merchant to carry full coverage at all times and still not be grossly over-insured during periods when inventory is low.

Description of the Property

Both personal and real property must be described with reasonable accuracy in order to identify the property and to inform the insurer of the nature of the risk involved. This description applies to both the nature of the property and its location. A description of a house as brick when it is actually asphalt brick siding is a misrepresentation. Personal property should be so described that in the event of loss, its value can be determined. One "piano" does not indicate the value of the piano. Also, the general description "living room furniture" may make it difficult to establish the value and the number of items. A complete inventory should be kept. In this event, such description as "household furniture" in the policy is adequate.

The location of the property is important because the location affects the risk. If personal property used in a brick house on a broad paved street is moved to a frame house on an out-of-the-way dirt road, the risk may be increased considerably. Express permission must always be obtained when property is moved except under a "floating" policy. Most fire policies sold today have a clause continuing the coverage at the new location for five days together with coverage during the moving trip. If a loss occurs during the five-day period, the company must pay, even though no notice has been given of the changed location. When property is by its nature not used at a fixed place, coverage will be provided in terms of use within a specified area, as within a radius of 50 miles from the home of the insured.

Jordan carried fire insurance on his household effects at 1327 Ellis Street, a two-story frame building. He moved to 237 Beechwood Hills, a one-story stone building. He did not give notice of the move within the five days required. A fire damaged the furniture to the extent of $1,000. The company did not have to pay, even though the new location carried a lower rate than the old.

Risk and Hazard

The insurance company assumes the risks caused by normal hazards. The insured must not commit any act which increases the risk. Negligence by the insured is a normal hazard unless so gross as to indicate a criminal intent. When a fire occurs, the insured must use all due diligence to minimize the loss. There is no responsibility for an increased risk over which the insured has no control or knowledge. The insured must remove household effects from the building if this can safely be done. The owner must do everything possible to minimize the loss by protecting the property from further damage from the elements. Any expense involved in doing this is recoverable as a part of the loss.

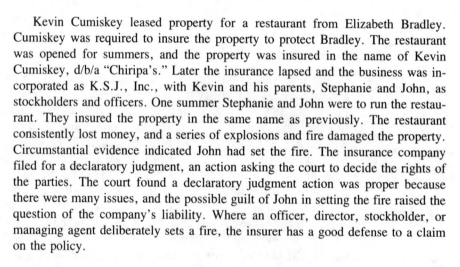

Kevin Cumiskey leased property for a restaurant from Elizabeth Bradley. Cumiskey was required to insure the property to protect Bradley. The restaurant was opened for summers, and the property was insured in the name of Kevin Cumiskey, d/b/a "Chiripa's." Later the insurance lapsed and the business was incorporated as K.S.J., Inc., with Kevin and his parents, Stephanie and John, as stockholders and officers. One summer Stephanie and John were to run the restaurant. They insured the property in the same name as previously. The restaurant consistently lost money, and a series of explosions and fire damaged the property. Circumstantial evidence indicated John had set the fire. The insurance company filed for a declaratory judgment, an action asking the court to decide the rights of the parties. The court found a declaratory judgment action was proper because there were many issues, and the possible guilt of John in setting the fire raised the question of the company's liability. Where an officer, director, stockholder, or managing agent deliberately sets a fire, the insurer has a good defense to a claim on the policy.

Coinsurance

Under the principle of *coinsurance* the insured recovers on a loss in the same ratio as the insurance bears to the amount of insurance which the company requires. Many policies contain an 80-percent coinsurance clause. This clause means that the insured may carry any amount of insurance up to the value of the property but that the company will not pay the full amount of a partial loss unless insurance for at least 80 percent of the value of the property is carried. If a building is worth $50,000 and the insured buys a policy for $20,000, the company under the 80-percent coinsurance clause will pay only half of the damage and never more than

$20,000. The 80 percent clause requires the insured to carry $40,000, or 80 percent of $50,000, to be fully protected from a partial loss. Since only half of this amount is carried, only half of the damage can be collected.

The coinsurance clause may be some percentage other than 80 percent. In burglary insurance it may be as low as 5 percent or 10 percent and on rare occasions as high as 100 percent in fire insurance.

Repairs and Replacements

Most insurance contracts give the insurer the option of paying the amount of loss or repairing or replacing the property. The amount the insurance company will pay for a loss will vary depending on whether market value or replacement cost is used to measure the amount of loss. Which measure is used will depend on the policy. If the property is repaired or replaced, materials of like kind and quality must be used. The work must be completed within a reasonable time. The option to replace is seldom exercised by the insurer. There also may be the option of the insurer's taking the property at an agreed valuation and then paying the insured the full value of the damaged property.

When there has been a total loss, if the insurer pays a sum equal to the damage and the insured restores the property to its original status, new insurance must normally be obtained to cover the replaced part, since the policy is normally cancelled when there has been a total loss. Such a clause is frequently provided in insurance policies covering residential property where the loss is limited to a relatively small amount. Policies covering large industrial plants, motels, apartment buildings, and similar structures seldom contain a restoration clause.

Cancellation and Termination of the Policy

Fire insurance policies permit each party to cancel by giving the other party notice. If a policy is canceled by the insured, a refund is made of the unearned premiums in excess of the short-term rate at which premiums would have been charged had the original contract of insurance been for such short term only. If at the end of six months the insured cancels a three-year policy costing $600, there will not be a refund of $500. The short-term rate for six months is considerably higher than one-sixth of a thirty-six month policy.

Questions

1. If one insures a fur coat for $2,000 against theft when its actual value is only $800, how much may the owner collect if the coat is stolen?

2. What is the greatest cause of loss to property?

3. What is extended coverage?

4. When must a person have an insurable interest before being able to collect under a fire insurance policy?

5. *A* delivers a deed to a house to *B* and is paid in full. At the time of the sale *A* has a $20,000 fire insurance policy on the house. What effect does the sale have on the insurance policy?

6. What is the difference between a valued fire insurance policy and an open policy?

7. How must one identify household furniture when household effects fire insurance is purchased?

8. When one insures property located at 256 Hope Street, what is the effect on the policy if the owner moves to a new location without notifying the insurance company?

Case Problems

1. John, the bookkeeper for the Anderson Department Store, had the responsibility for placing all the needed insurance to protect the firm from the major hazards. The firm's merchandise inventory fluctuated from $40,000 during the dull season to $120,000 at the peak of the rush season. The average was about $70,000. In order to be fully covered, John carried a fire policy for $120,000. What insurance knowledge would enable John to reduce the cost of this policy?

2. In the above case the Anderson Department Store sold several thousand dollars worth of television sets, suites of furniture, and other items on the installment plan with the seller retaining title until the merchandise was paid for. John placed no insurance on this merchandise. One customer owed the company $1,100 for furniture when her home was destroyed by fire. She carried no fire insurance on her household effects. How could the Anderson Department Store avoid similar losses in the future?

3. Arlene Schnitzer purchased from South Carolina Insurance Company two blanket insurance policies insuring five buildings for $2,136,000. One of the buildings was destroyed by fire. The policies stated: "THIS COMPANY SHALL BE LIABLE FOR NO GREATER PROPORTION OF . . . LOSS THAN THE AMOUNT OF INSURANCE SPECIFIED . . . BEARS TO THE PERCENTAGE SPECIFIED ON THE FIRST PAGE OF THIS POLICY ON THE ACTUAL CASH VALUE OF THE PROPERTY DESCRIBED . . . AT THE TIME OF LOSS, NOR FOR MORE THAN THE PROPORTION WHICH THE AMOUNT OF INSURANCE SPECIFIED . . . BEARS TO THE TOTAL IN-

SURANCE ON THE PROPERTY DESCRIBED . . . AT THE TIME OF LOSS." The percentage was 90 percent. The destroyed building was valued at $574,209, and the total value of the buildings was $3,887,499. Does the coinsurance clause apply?

4. Washington State Hop Producers, Inc., carried fire insurance with Harbor Insurance Company. Hop Producers discovered that 253 bales of hops in its warehouse were damaged by "browning." Browning is caused by heat generated by chemical oxidation. It may happen without flame, glow, or light, and none of those things were observed. The policy insured "against all direct loss by fire. . . ." When Harbor refused coverage, Hop Producers sued, alleging the hops were damaged by fire. Should they collect?

5. Hunt owned a factory building. It was rented to Sevede Dressmakers, Inc., for $1,000 a month. A fire caused a $12,000 loss to one section of the building. This section was immediately restored, but soon thereafter the entire building was destroyed by fire. Hunt carried a $100,000 fire insurance policy on the building, its full value. How much can she collect on this policy?

6. Hildegard and Lenard Price contracted to buy a house and lot, Lot 3, from Roy and Deanna Clemence, and the Prices took possession. The Clemences later refused to sell and a lawsuit resulted. The Prices bought a fire insurance policy from Trinity Universal Insurance Company, and the house was damaged by fire. The court held that the contract to buy the house was void for mutual mistake of fact. When Trinity would not pay for the fire loss, the Prices sued. Did the Prices have an insurable interest in the house?

7. Jerry gave his wife, Josephine, a fur coat as an anniversary present. The cost of the coat was $2,500. Jerry and Josephine had a fire insurance policy on their household effects in the amount of $2,000. Realizing that this amount was too low, especially since the value of their effects had been increased by $2,500, they increased the face of their policy to $5,000 and paid the additional premium. While visiting relatives, the relatives' home was destroyed by fire and the fur coat was burned up. Could Josephine collect for this loss on her insurance contract?

43

Automobile Insurance

Preview Cases

Cyrus See had an auto insurance policy with St. Paul Insurance Company which covered theft of equipment from his vehicle "only if the equipment at the time of the loss . . . was permanently installed in or upon" the vehicle. See had removed a citizens band radio and microphone from the mounting bracket on the dashboard of his truck and put them out of sight on the floor behind the driver's seat. To do this he had disconnected the electrical and aerial wires before leaving the truck. When he returned, the truck had been broken into, and the radio and microphone were missing. He sued St. Paul for the value of them. Was St. Paul liable for the value of the radio and microphone?

Graham had an automobile liability policy covering both bodily injury and property damage to others. In a collision with another car, the driver of the other car was seriously injured and her car wrecked. Graham's policy provided for coverage up to $15,000 for bodily injury and $5,000 for property damage. The injured driver offered to settle the claim out of court for $14,000. The insurance company rejected the offer and defended the claim in court. The court gave judgment against Graham for $30,000. How much is Graham obligated to pay? How much is the insurance company obligated to pay?

The laws dealing with automobile insurance can be best understood by discussing the major classes of insurance and their risks. The two major classes are physical damage insurance (including fire, theft, and collision) and public liability insurance (including bodily injury and property damage). To understand the law one must know what specific risk is assumed by the insurance carrier and the terms of the policy covering that specific risk. The term "automobile insurance" is loosely used to refer to insurance which the insured obtains to cover a car and the injuries which the insured and other members of the family may sustain and also liability insurance, which protects the insured from claims that third persons may make for injuries caused them or damage to their property caused by the insured.

Physical Damage Insurance

As the name implies, *physical damage insurance* covers the risks of injury or damage to the car itself. It includes:

1. Fire insurance
2. Theft insurance
3. Collision insurance
4. Comprehensive coverage

Fire Insurance. Much of the law of fire insurance discussed in the preceding chapter applies to automobile insurance. If the car is damaged or destroyed by the burning of any conveyance upon which the car is being transported, such as a barge, boat, or train, the fire policy covers this loss. Fire insurance can be obtained separately but is normally included in comprehensive coverage.

Theft Insurance. *Theft* is defined as taking another's property without the owner's consent with the intent to wrongfully deprive the owner of the property. Automobile theft insurance either by law or by contract normally covers a wide range of losses. Obtaining possession of a car and converting it to one's own use to the exclusion of or inconsistent with the rights of the owner is known as *conversion*. Taking another's car by force or threat of force is known as *robbery*. In some states the automobile theft policy is required by law to cover all these losses. The policy itself may define theft broadly enough to cover theft, conversion, larceny after trust, and robbery. Unless the policy is broadened either by law or by the wording of the policy, a theft policy covers only the wrongful deprivation of the car without claim of right.

Automobile theft insurance usually covers pilferage of any parts of the car but not articles or clothes left in the car. It also covers any damage done to the car either by theft or attempted theft. It does not cover loss of use of the car unless the policy specifically provides for this loss.

◆   Cyrus See had an auto insurance policy with St. Paul Insurance Company which covered theft of equipment from his vehicle "only if the equipment at the time of the loss . . . was permanently installed in or upon" the vehicle. See had removed a citizens band radio and microphone from the mounting bracket on the dashboard of his truck and put them out of sight on the floor behind the driver's seat. To do this he had disconnected the electrical and aerial wires before leaving the truck. When he returned, the truck had been broken into, and the radio and microphone were missing. He sued St. Paul for the value of them. The court held that they were not permanently installed in the truck at the time of the theft, so St. Paul was not liable.

Collision Insurance. The standard collision policy covers all damage to the car caused by a collision or upset. There is a collision whenever an object strikes the insured car or the car strikes an object. It is not required that both objects be automobiles nor that both be moving. Frequently collision policies require the collision to be "accidental." A rolling rock that crashed into the car while it was parked was held to be a collision. Likewise, there was a collision when a horse kicked the door of the insured automobile. It is generally held that there is no collision when the colliding object is a natural phenomenon, such as rain or hail.

Practically all collision policies provide that the policy is either void or suspended if a trailer is attached to the car unless insurance of the same kind carried on the car is placed on the trailer. The question of interpretation then arises as to what constitutes a "trailer." A small boat trailer and a small two-wheel trailer generally are not considered trailers, but horse or cattle trailers must be covered if they are attached.

If collision insurance but not fire is carried on the car, the policy will, in most states, pay both the fire loss and the collision loss occurring in the same wreck so long as the fire ensues after collision and is a direct result of the collision. A few states hold that even if the collision is the direct and proximate cause of the fire, the collision policy will not cover both losses. This is a minority view, however.

Most collision insurance policies have a deductible clause. It is possible to buy policies without any deductible clause, but the rates are extremely high. It is much cheaper for one to assume some of this risk.

If the insurance company pays the insured a claim for collision damage caused by someone else's negligence, under the law of subrogation the company has the right to sue this other party to the collision for the damages.

Comprehensive Coverage. Insurance companies will write automobile insurance covering almost every conceivable risk to a car: windstorm, earthquake, flood, strike, spray from trees, malicious mischief, submersion in water, acid from the battery, riot, glass breakage, hail, and falling aircraft. A *comprehensive policy* may include all of these risks plus fire and theft. A comprehensive policy covers only the hazards enumerated in the policy, and collision is normally excluded.

Public Liability Insurance

The second major division of automobile insurance is designed to protect third persons from bodily injury and property damage.

Bodily Injury Insurance. Insurance covering the risk of bodily injury to the insured's passengers, pedestrians, or the occupants of another car is designated bodily injury insurance. The insurance company obligates itself to pay any sum not exceeding the limit fixed in the policy for which the insured may be personally liable. If the insured is not liable for damages, the insurance company has no liability except the duty of defending the insured in court actions brought by injured persons. This type of insurance does not cover any injury to either the person or the property of the insured. Such loss is covered by other policies.

The coverage under the automobile liability policy is usually written as 10/20/5, 25/50/10, 100/300/15, or similar combinations. The first number indicates that the company will pay $10,000, $25,000, or $100,000, respectively, to any one person for bodily injury in any one accident. The middle number fixes the maximum amount the company will pay for bodily injury to more than one person in any one accident. The third figure sets the limit the company will pay for property damage. This usually is the damage to the other person's car but may include damage to any property belonging to someone other than the insured.

Under the "defense clause" the insurer agrees to defend the insured against any claim for damages. The insurer reserves the right to accept or reject any proffered settlement out of court.

Graham had an automobile liability policy covering both bodily injury and property injury to others. In a collision with another car, the driver of the other car was seriously injured and her car wrecked. Graham's policy provided for coverage up to $15,000 for bodily injury and $5,000 for property damage. The injured driver offered to settle the claim out of court for $14,000. The insurance company rejected the offer and defended the claim in court. The court gave judgment against Graham for $30,000. Graham had to pay all over and above his insurance. Had the insurance company settled out of court, Graham would not have had to pay anything. The insured has unlimited liability, but the insurer's liability is limited to the amount stated in the policy.

A bodily injury insurance policy does not cover accidents occurring while the car is being driven by a person who is under the age designated by state law. It may not cover accidents occurring while the car is rented or leased unless specifically covered, while the car is used to carry passengers for a consideration, while the car is used for any purpose other than that named in the policy, or while it is used outside the United States and Canada. Some policies exclude accidents while the car is being used for towing a trailer or any other vehicle used as a trailer. These are the ordinary exclusions. Policies may have additional exclusions of various kinds.

The insured is not permitted to settle claims or to incur expenses other than those for immediate medical help. In the event that the insurance company pays a loss, it is entitled to be subrogated to any rights that the insured has against others because of such losses.

Property Damage Insurance. In automobile property damage insurance the insurer agrees to pay, on behalf of the insured, all sums that the insured may be legally obligated to pay for damages arising out of the ownership, the maintenance, or the use of the automobile. The liability of the insurer, however, is limited as stated in the policy.

The policy usually provides that the insurer will not be liable in the event that the car is being operated, maintained, or used by any person in violation of any state or federal law as to age or occupation. The insurer is not liable for damage to property owned by, leased to, transported by, or in charge of the insured.

Medical Payments and Uninsured Motorist Insurance

In addition to physical damage and public liability insurance, there is insurance which covers injury to the insured or passengers in the insured's car. Medical payments cover bodily injury and are paid regardless of other insurance. Uninsured motorist coverage protects the insured when injury results from the negligence of another driver who does not have liability insurance.

Notice to the Insurer

In the event of an accident, it is the duty of the policyholder to give the insurer written notice and proof of loss regarding the damages resulting from the accident. The notice must identify the insured and give the names and addresses of the injured persons, the owner of the damaged property, and any available witnesses. It is also necessary to give information relative to the time, the place, and the detailed circumstances of the accident.

If a claim is made or a suit is brought against the insured, every demand, notice, or summons received must immediately be forwarded to the insurance company in order that the insurer may be able to make the proper legal defense. The insured must help secure any necessary information, evidence, and the presence of witnesses. In short, there must be the fullest cooperation with the insurer, who normally has the right to settle any claims or lawsuits as it deems best.

Recovery Even When at Fault

Normally the injured party must prove the driver of the car was negligent or at fault before the insured becomes liable. Frequently, both drivers are negligent. Formerly, the driver bringing suit had to come into court with "clean hands." If such a driver's own negligence contributed even slightly to the accident, no recovery could be had. This harsh rule has been replaced in most states by the *last clear chance* rule. This rule states that if one driver is negligent but the other driver had one last clear chance to avoid hitting the negligent driver and did not take it, then the driver who had the last clear chance is liable.

In a number of states the harshness of the common-law rule as to contributory negligence has also been modified by *comparative negligence* statutes which provide that the contributory negligence of the plaintiff reduces the recovery but does not completely bar recovery from a negligent defendant. That is to say, the negligence of each party is balanced against that of the other.

Some states have established *no-fault insurance*. Under this plan, insurance companies pay for injuries suffered by their insureds no matter who is at fault. This no-fault plan is used for a limited amount of damages. Above this amount the fault rules apply.

Financial Responsibility Laws

A few states have compulsory automobile liability insurance laws which require drivers to carry a certain amount of liability insurance. Most states have financial responsibility laws. These latter laws do not require one to have any insurance until the first accident. A person who then cannot prove the financial ability to pay any claims up to the amount fixed by law, usually $20,000, must buy insurance for this amount, that is 10/20/5 coverage. If one is required to carry insurance in order to be permitted to drive but no insurance company will sell a policy, then in many states the state insurance commissioner will assign this driver to an insurance company. The company must issue the policy under the "assigned risk" rule.

Questions

1. What are the two main classes of automobile insurance?

2. If John, the owner of a car, and four other young men drive to Jacksonville to attend a football game and each is to pay one fifth of the cost of the trip, is the insurer liable if the car is destroyed by fire during the trip?

3. Does automobile theft insurance cover pilferage of articles left in the car?

4. What is covered by collision insurance?

5. Why do most automobile collision insurance policies have a deductible clause?

6. Name eight causes of damage that may be covered by comprehensive insurance.

7. What two kinds of losses are covered by public liability insurance?

8. Is the insurer liable if an underage driver has an accident?

9. If a suit is brought, what must the insured do?

Case Problems

1. Sheila Blaylock bought a car for $8,500. Three months later she was informed by the police that the car had been stolen from its owner. They took the car and it was never returned. She filed suit against her insurance company, alleging it was liable on her comprehensive auto insurance. The policy stated it did "not apply to loss or damage . . . which may be caused by war, declared or undeclared, invasion, directly or indirectly, insurrection, civil war, military or usurped power, or to confiscation by duly constituted governmental or civil authority." Is the company liable?

2. John and Janet Kettle hooked their car to their house trailer and set out to tour the country. They carried full insurance on the car but none on the trailer. While crossing a mountain in West Virginia, the driver lost control of the car, and it plunged over the mountainside, completely demolishing both the car and the trailer. The insurance company refused to pay the damage for either the car or the trailer. Must it pay for the car?

3. Bennett, a truck driver for the Beck Bakery, struck a child with the company vehicle. The child was not hurt, and the police exonerated Bennett for the accident. Consequently, Anita Beck did not notify the insurance company of the accident. Six months later the boy's father sued the bakery for $10,000, alleging the boy suffered internal injuries. It cost Beck $800 to defend the suit even though she won it. Was the insurance company liable for the $800?

4. Leon D. McCormick & Sons, Inc., carried collision insurance on its dump truck with Auto-Owners Insurance Company. The truck was loaded with wet limestone, and the driver attempted to empty the load. The load emptied from the right-hand side of the truck first so that a large amount of wet limestone was on the left side of the dump bed. The uneven distribution caused the dump bed to twist. A rear hinge pin on the dump body broke, and the dump body tipped over onto the ground. The truck stayed upright. The policy covered damage to the vehicle "and its equipment caused by accidental collision with another object or by accidental upset." The dump body was within the definition of equipment. Auto-Owners refused to pay for the damage. Should it pay?

5. B. R. Justice owned a pickup truck which was insured by Government Employees Insurance Company. He bought a camper for use on the pickup. It was bolted on with chains and tighteners. Justice had an accident, and the pickup and camper were extensively damaged. Government refused to pay for the damage to the camper. The auto insurance policy provided coverage to "the automobile, including its equipment." Justice sued Government. Is Government liable for the damage to the camper?

6. Seabolt carried a 10/20/5 liability policy on his car. He negligently injured a child who was playing in the street. The father of the child offered to settle the claim for $9,000. Seabolt insisted the insurance company accept the offer, but the company refused. The father sued Seabolt and obtained judgment for $12,000. How much will the insurance company pay?

7. While driving a car owned by Roy Matheney, Alan Conley fell asleep and drove off the highway causing damage to the car. Alan was covered by automobile liability and collision coverage with Farmers Insurance Company of Arkansas. The policy stated it did not apply under Liability Insurance Coverage "to damage to . . . property . . . in charge of the insured other than a residence or private garage." Farmers denied liability, so Matheney sued it. He had already obtained a judgment against Conley, so Conley's liability was clear. Matheney argued that if a nonowner-driver is liable for negligence in causing collision damage, then his insurance policy ought to be interpreted, if possible, to cover him for such liability. Was Farmers liable?

8. Colbert was accident-prone. He had been in four serious car wrecks for which he had been held liable in each case. He was such a poor risk no company would sell him a policy. He did not have enough property to qualify for a driver's license under the state financial responsibility law. Is there any way he can be permitted to drive?

44

Security Devices

Preview Cases

Custom Leasing, Inc., a wholly owned subsidiary of Otoe County National Bank, purchased equipment from Carlson Stapler and Shippers Supply, Inc., to lease to Creative Buildings, Inc. Carlson executed a guaranty agreement for the lease. It provided: "in the event the LESSEE fails to perform . . . the DEALER agrees to Repossess the said equipment and therwith [sic] simultaneously pay the LESSOR" the amount remaining under the lease. Custom assigned the lease to Otoe, which improperly filed a financing statement. Creative filed a bankruptcy petition. Custom advised Carlson of the bankruptcy and made demand for the amount owing. The trustee in bankruptcy claimed the equipment on the basis of the improperly filed financing statement. It took thirteen months from Custom's demand until the bankruptcy court granted possession of the equipment to Otoe. During this time the value of the equipment decreased from more than the amount owing to $8,500 less. Otoe assigned the lease to Custom, which sued for the $8,500 and costs of obtaining possession from the trustee. What, if any, liability did Carlson have to Custom?

Pauline Fink bought a mobile home from Palmer Mobile Homes, Inc. Palmer retained a security interest which was assigned to Endicott Trust Company, which filed a financing statement as if the mobile home were a chattel. Fink bought real property from Wemco Corp. and gave Wemco a mortgage on the property. A crawl space was dug on the property, footings were installed, a cinder block pillar was cemented to the footings to support the home, a septic tank system was installed, and water and electric were run to it. The mobile home was delivered in two sections which were then bolted together. A roof cap was put over the joint and was cemented and nailed down. Siding was installed on the ends of the house and nailed over the joint in the two sections. Fink went bankrupt. Endicott claimed a security interest in the home. Did it have a perfected security interest?

There are two types of security devices which will be discussed in this chapter: guaranty and suretyship contracts, and secured credit sales.

Guaranty and Suretyship

A contract of guaranty or suretyship is an agreement whereby one party promises to be responsible for the debt, default, or obligation of another. Such contracts generally arise when one person assumes responsibility for the extension of credit to another, as in buying merchandise on credit or in borrowing money from a bank.

A person who is entrusted with money of another, such as a cashier, a bank teller, or a county treasurer, may be required to have someone guarantee the faithful performance of the duties. This, too, is a contract of suretyship, although it is commonly referred to as a *fidelity bond*.

Parties. There are three parties to a contract of guaranty or of suretyship. The party who undertakes to be responsible for another is the *guarantor,* or the *surety;* the party to whom the guaranty is given is the *creditor;* and the party who is primarily liable is the *principal debtor,* or simply the *principal*.

Distinctions. The words "surety" and "guarantor" are often used interchangeably; however, their legal usages are different. In a contract of suretyship the liability of the surety is coextensive with that of the principal debtor. The surety is directly and primarily responsible for the debt or obligation just as the primary debtor. The surety's obligation, then, is identical with the one for whom responsibility is assumed.

A guarantor's obligation is secondary to that of the principal debtor. There is a promise to pay only in the event that the principal defaults. The guarantor's obligation does not arise simultaneously with the principal's. The obligation is contingent upon the happening of another event, namely, the failure of the principal to pay.

For the most part, the law of suretyship applies with equal force to both paid sureties and accommodation sureties. In some instances, however, the contract of a paid surety will be interpreted strictly. Thus, in the case of acts claimed to discharge the surety, it is sometimes held that the paid surety must prove that it has actually been harmed by the conduct of the principal.

Importance of Making a Distinction. Three reasons why it is important to distinguish between a contract of guaranty and a contract of suretyship pertain to:

WATERS, MELLEN AND COMPANY
900 West Lake Avenue
Cincinnati, Ohio 45227

May 16, 19--

Ms. Norma Rae
201 E. Fifth Street
Campton, KY 41301

Dear Ms. Rae

In consideration of the letting of the premises
located at 861 South Street, this city, to Mr.
William H. Prost for a period of two years from
date, I hereby guarantee the punctual payment
of the rent and the faithful performance of the
covenants of the lease.

Very truly yours

Orvinne L. Meyer

Orvinne L. Meyer
Vice-President, Personnel

ILLUS. 44-1. A Letter of Guaranty

1. Form
2. Notice of default
3. Remedy

Form. Contracts of guaranty and suretyship have many similarities, but
the dissimilarities particularly need to be recognized. All the essential ele-

ments of a contract must be present in both. If the nature of the contract is such that it falls within the description of a contract of guaranty, it must be in writing; most contracts of suretyship may be oral.

The Uniform Commercial Code provides: "The promise to answer for the debt, default, or obligation of another must be in writing and be signed by the party to be charged or by his authorized agent." This provision applies only to a promise that creates a secondary obligation, that is, an obligation of guaranty, not to a promise that creates a primary obligation, that is, suretyship.

Notice of Default. Since sureties are primarily liable for the debt, it is not necessary to notify them if the debt is defaulted. Guarantors, on the other hand, must be notified by the creditor. Failure to give notice does not of itself discharge the guarantyship. A guarantor who is damaged by the failure to receive notice may offset the amount of the damage against the claim of the creditor.

Thomas Gentry was a guarantor on a promissory note executed by Baytown Sports Center, Inc., to Highlands State Bank. Sports Center defaulted on the note and Highlands foreclosed on the security. After foreclosure, there was a deficiency of $172,000 still owing on the note. Highlands filed suit against Gentry as guarantor. The trial court entered summary judgment against him. The appellate court held that in order to recover Highlands had to establish that notice had been given to Gentry. Since the court record did not show such notice the trial court ruling was reversed.

Remedy. In the case of suretyship, the surety assumes an original obligation. The surety is bound to pay if the other party does not. The reason that the other party does not pay is immaterial. Sureties are liable as fully and under the same conditions as if the debt were theirs from the beginning. The rule is different in many contracts of guaranty. If the guaranty is conditional, the guarantor is liable only if the other party cannot pay.

Arnold writes, "Let Brewer have a suit; if he is unable to pay you, I will." This guaranty depends upon Brewer's ability to pay. Therefore, the seller must make all reasonable efforts to collect from Brewer before collection can be made from Arnold. If Arnold had written, "Let Brewer have this suit, and I will pay you," an original obligation would have been created for which Arnold would have been personally liable. Therefore, Arnold would be deemed a surety if the understanding was that Brewer was to pay for the suit. The merchant could look to Arnold if Brewer merely did not pay, rather than if Brewer could not pay.

Rights of the Surety and the Guarantor. A guarantor and a surety have the following rights:

1. Indemnity
2. Subrogation
3. Contribution
4. Exoneration

Indemnity. A guarantor or surety who pays the debt or the obligation of the principal is entitled to be reimbursed by the principal. This right is known as the right of *indemnity*. The guarantor or the surety may be induced to pay the debt when it becomes due to avoid the accumulation of interest and other costs on the debt.

Subrogation. When the guarantor or the surety pays the debt of the principal, the claim of the creditor is automatically assigned to the guarantor or surety by operation of law. The payment also entitles the guarantor or surety to all property, liens, or securities that were held by the creditor to secure the payment of the debt. This right of subrogation does not arise until the creditor has been paid in full, but it does arise if the surety or the guarantor has paid a part of the debt and the principal has paid the remainder.

Clayton wished to borrow $2,000 from the Bank of Elbert. The bank required Clayton to get a surety to sign the note with him as well as to give it a mortgage on his truck. Reed agreed to become a surety for Clayton. When Clayton defaulted, Reed paid the debt and then attempted to foreclose on the mortgage on the truck. The court ruled Reed could do this under the rule of subrogation. Reed was subrogated to the bank's rights because she had paid the bank the amount of the debt.

Contribution. When two or more persons are jointly held liable for the debt, default, or obligation of a certain person, they are known as *coguarantors* or *cosureties*. Guarantors or sureties who have paid more than their proportionate share of the debt are entitled to recover from the other guarantors or sureties the amount in excess of their pro rata share of the loss. This right is known as the right of *contribution*. It does not arise until the surety or the guarantor has paid the debts in full or has otherwise settled the debt.

Exoneration. A surety or guarantor may call upon the creditor to proceed to compel the payment of the debt; otherwise the surety or guarantor will be released. This is known as the right of *exoneration*. The creditor may delay in pressing the debtor to pay because of the security of the suretyship. In cases where the debtor can pay, the surety is released, and the uncertainty concerning potential liability is eliminated.

Discharge of a Surety or a Guarantor. Both a surety and a guarantor may be discharged from their obligation by the usual methods of discharging any obligation, including performance, voluntary agreement, and bankruptcy. There are, however, some additional acts that will discharge the surety or the guarantor. These are:

1. Extension of time
2. Alteration of the terms of the contract
3. Loss or return of collateral by the creditor

Extension of Time. If the creditor extends the time of the debt without the consent of the surety or the guarantor and for a consideration, the surety or the guarantor is discharged from further liability.

Russell owed a note for $2,231 at the Bank of Omar. Lamar was surety on this note. When the note came due, the bank promised Russell it would renew the note if he would get Slack as an additional surety. This Russell did. Lamar did not consent to the renewal—in fact, she was not even aware of it. This extension of time released Lamar even though an added surety was to her advantage.

Alteration of the Terms of the Contract. Any material alteration of the contract by the creditor discharges the surety or the guarantor. The change must be prejudicial to the surety or the guarantor. A reduction in the interest rate has been held not to discharge the surety, while a change in the place of payment has been held to be an act justifying a discharge of the surety. A material change in a contract is in fact substituting a new contract for the old. The surety guaranteed the payment of the old contract, not the new one.

Loss or Return of Collateral by the Creditor. If the creditor through negligence loses or damages collateral security given to secure the debt, a surety or a guarantor is discharged. The same is true if the creditor returns to the debtor any collateral security. This collateral must be held for the benefit of the surety until the debtor pays the debt in full.

Custom Leasing, Inc., a wholly owned subsidiary of Otoe County National Bank, purchased equipment from Carlson Stapler and Shippers Supply, Inc., to lease to Creative Buildings, Inc. Carlson executed a guaranty agreement for the lease. It provided: "in the event the LESSEE fails to perform . . . the DEALER agrees to Repossess the said equipment at his own expense and therwith [sic] simultaneously pay the LESSOR forthwith an amount equal to the number of remaining months . . . thereof under Lease Agreement." Custom assigned the lease to Otoe, which improperly filed a financing statement. Creative filed a bankruptcy petition. Custom advised Carlson of the bankruptcy and made demand for the amount owing. The trustee in bankruptcy claimed the equipment on the basis of the improper filing of the financing statement. It took thirteen months from Custom's demand until the bankruptcy court granted possession of the equipment to Otoe. During this time the value of the equipment decreased from more than the amount owing to $8,500 less. Otoe assigned the lease to Custom, which sued for the $8,500 and costs of obtaining possession from the trustee. The court found that the action of Otoe in improperly filing the financing statement was the cause of the trustee refusing possession of the equipment and the delay and loss of value; therefore, Carlson was released from liability to the extent of the injury caused by Custom and Otoe.

Bonding Companies. In recent years *bonding companies* have taken over most of the business of guaranteeing the employer against losses due to the dishonesty of employees. These bonding companies are paid sureties as distinguished from unpaid sureties or guarantors. The bonding company's obligation arises from its written contract with the employer. This contract of indemnity sets out in detail the conditions under which the surety will be liable.

Secured Credit Sales

When goods are financed by someone other than the buyers (purchased on credit), one of the most convenient ways to protect creditors from loss is to allow them to have an interest in the goods. When sellers retain the right to repossess the items sold if the buyers breach the sales contracts, the transactions are *secured credit sales*. In such cases, the buyers obtain possession of the items and the risk of loss passes to them. Article 9 of the Uniform Commercial Code governs secured credit sales.

A security interest cannot attach or become enforceable until the buyer and seller agree it shall attach, value is given, and the buyer has the right to possess or use the item.

Security Agreement. A security interest is not enforceable unless the buyer has signed a security agreement. The *security agreement* is a written agreement, signed by the buyer, which describes the collateral, or the item sold, and usually contains the terms of payment and names of the parties.

Wayne's Furniture Mart sells Loretto $1,500 worth of furniture for $500 down and Loretto's promise to pay the remaining $1,000 in 24 monthly installments. Loretto signs a security agreement giving Wayne's the right to repossess the goods if he fails to fulfill the terms of the contract. After two months Loretto ceases to make any payments. In order to avoid losing the unpaid balance, the Furniture Mart repossesses the furniture.

Rights of the Seller. The rights of the seller, referred to as the secured party under the security agreement, may be transferred to a third person by assignment. In any sale, the buyer may have claims or defenses against the seller. In the case of consumer sales, the Federal Trade Commission requires the seller to include in the agreement a notice that any holder of the agreement is subject to all claims and defenses that the buyer could assert against the seller. Thus, the assignee would be subject to any claims or defenses. This protection for the buyer applies only to consumer transactions.

Rights of the Buyer. The buyer, also called the debtor, has the right to: transfer the collateral and require a determination of the amount owed.

Transfer of Collateral. Even though there is a security interest in the collateral, the debtor may transfer the collateral to others. Such a transfer will usually be subject to the security interest.

Determination of Amount Owed. A buyer who wishes may sign a statement indicating the amount of unpaid indebtedness believed to be owed as of a specified date and send it to the seller with the request that the statement be approved or corrected and returned.

Perfection of Security Interest. When the rights of the seller to the collateral are superior to those of third persons, the seller is said to have a *perfected security interest*. The use to which the collateral is put at the time of perfection of the security interest determines how the security interest is perfected.

Inventory and Equipment. Articles which are purchased with the intention of reselling or leasing them are called *inventory*. *Equipment* consists of goods which are used or purchased for use in a business, including farming or a profession. In order to have a perfected security interest in inventory or equipment, the seller must usually file a financing statement in the appropriate public office. However, filing need not be made when the law requires a security interest to be noted on the document of title to the goods, such as in the case of noting a lien on a title to a motor vehicle. Buyers of inventory sold in the regular course of business and for value acquire title free of the security interest. Any time an item subject to a security interest is sold at the direction of the secured party it is sold free of the security interest.

A *financing statement* is a writing signed by the debtor and the secured party which contains the address of the secured party, the mailing address of the debtor, and a statement indicating the types of or describing collateral. A copy of the security agreement may serve as a financing statement if it contains the required items.

Fixtures. Personal property which is attached to buildings or real estate is called a *fixture*. A security interest in fixtures is perfected by filing the financing statement in the office where a mortgage on the real estate involved would be filed or recorded.

Pauline Fink bought a mobile home from Palmer Mobile Homes, Inc. Palmer retained a security interest which was assigned to Endicott Trust Company, which filed a financing statement as if the mobile home were a chattel. Fink bought real property from Wemco Corp. and gave Wemco a mortgage on the property. A crawl space was dug on the property, footings were installed, a cinder block pillar was cemented to the footings to support the home, a septic tank system was installed, and water and electric were run to it. The mobile home was delivered in two sections which were then bolted together. A roof cap was put over the joint and was cemented and nailed down. Siding was installed on the ends of the house and nailed over the joint in the two sections. Fink went bankrupt. Endicott claimed a security interest in the home. The court held the home was so annexed to the realty as to become a part of it; therefore the mobile home was a fixture and the financing statement should have been filed in the office where real estate mortgages would be recorded. Endicott's filing was improper, which meant that the security interest was not perfected, so the rights of Endicott to the collateral were not superior to the rights of third persons.

Consumer Goods. Consumer goods are items used or bought primarily for personal, family, or household purposes. A security interest in consumer goods is perfected as soon as it attaches and without filing in most cases. It is not perfected, however, against a buyer who purchases the item without knowledge of the security interest, for value and for the buyer's own personal, family, or household use. The secured party can be protected against such a buyer only by filing a financing statement.

Duration of Filing. Filed financing statements are effective for five years from their date. However, a continuation statement may be filed which continues the effectiveness of the filing for five more years. Succeeding continuation statements may be filed, each of which lasts five years.

Effect of Default. Under the Uniform Commercial Code, the seller has certain rights if the buyer fails to pay according to the terms of the security agreement or otherwise breaches the contract. These rights include repossession and resale. The buyer is given the rights to redemption and an accounting.

Repossession. When the buyer has the right to possession of the collateral before making full payment and the buyer breaches the purchase contract, the seller may repossess, or take back, the collateral. If it can be done without a breach of the peace, the repossession may be made without any judicial proceedings. In any case, judicial action may be sought. The seller may retain the collateral in satisfaction of the debt unless the debtor, after being notified, objects.

Resale. After default, the seller may sell the collateral. A public or private sale may be used and any manner, time, place, and terms may be used as long as the disposition is commercially reasonable and done in good faith. Advance notice of the sale must be given to the debtor unless the goods are perishable. If the buyer has paid 60 percent or more of the cash price of the goods, the seller must resell the goods within 90 days after possession of them is taken unless the buyer, after default, has signed a statement waiving the right to require resale.

Redemption. At any time prior to the sale or the contracting to sell of the collateral, the buyer may redeem it by paying the amount owed and the expenses reasonably incurred by the seller in retaking and holding the collateral and preparing for the sale. This includes, if provided in the agreement, reasonable attorney's fees and legal expenses.

Accounting. After the sale of the collateral, the expenses of retaking and selling, the amount owed on the security interest, and all amounts owed on any subordinate security interests are paid in that order. If there is any surplus remaining, the seller must account to the buyer (pay over) for such surplus. If there is a deficiency, the buyer is liable for that amount.

Questions

1. What is the general nature of a contract of guaranty or suretyship?

2. What is the difference between a contract of guaranty and one of suretyship?

3. Must a contract of suretyship be in writing?

4. If the guarantor or the surety pays the debt of the principal, what is the right of reimbursement called?

5. When does the right of subrogation of the guarantor or surety arise?

6. What is the right of *contribution?*

7. What is the effect of the creditor's altering the contract?

8. If a creditor loses any collateral held as security for a debt on which there is a surety, what is the effect on the surety's liability?

9. What is a *secured credit sale?*

10. How is a security interest in equipment perfected?

11. What are the rights of a secured party upon default?

12. What are the rights of the debtor after default on a secured credit sale?

Case Problems

1. Robert Gandy was a guarantor on notes by U.S. National Mortgage Company to Park National Bank. The guaranty stated: "'indebtedness' . . . includes any and all advances, debts, obligations and liabilities . . . heretofore, now, or hereafter made . . ." and "This is a continuing guaranty relating to any indebtedness . . . which shall either continue the indebtedness or from time to time renew it. . . . This guaranty shall not apply to any indebtedness created after actual receipt by Bank of written notice of its revocation as to future transactions." A month later Gandy gave Park written notice of revocation. After that, Park extended the date of payment on the notes four times, on one extension increasing the rate of interest. When the notes were not paid, Park sued Gandy. Is he liable?

2. Farmers & Merchants Bank of Long Beach loaned $35,400 to Frank Hoffer to finance his tractor and trailer. Hoffer gave Farmers a security interest in them, and Farmers gave him the titles which had no binding notation of the liens. The vehicles were then registered with no notation of the liens on the titles. Hoffer filed a petition under Chapter 11 of the Bankruptcy Code, and Farmers sought to foreclose its security interest on the vehicles. Does Farmers have a perfected security interest in the tractor and trailer?

3. Flannagan entered into a contract with WGAU Radio Broadcasting Company to carry on an advertising campaign over a period of 60 days. The total cost was $6,000. The radio station required Flannagan to provide some guaranty of payment of the $6,000 before the advertising campaign could start. Gill, a wealthy friend of Flannagan, orally agreed "to be personally responsible for this debt if for any reason Flannagan fails to pay it." There were three witnesses to this oral contract. Flannagan failed to pay any part of the $6,000, and the radio corporation demanded that Gill pay. Was Gill liable for this debt?

4. Huntley was a guarantor on a debt of $700 which Bartlet owed to Whitley. The debt was long past due, and though Whitley had never legally extended the time of payment, he was in no hurry to sue Bartlet. Huntley was confident that Bartlet would pay and release him from the potential liability if suit was instituted. What right does Huntley have?

5. Bunch executed a security agreement covering 46 head of cattle. The agreement was then extended to cover 102 head. A cattle commission company sold 35 head, and Bunch gave the secured party the proceeds from the sale. Bunch then gave the secured party money from the sale of 56 head. Bunch and her son acquired more cattle which were subjected to the security agreement. Ultimately most of the cattle were sold, but not all the proceeds were given to the secured party. The bank (secured party) sued the commission company for the proceeds not turned over to it. Is the company liable?

6. General Insurance Company of America was surety on a bond running to the state as obligee to indemnify it for losses from the failure of any deputy registrar to faithfully perform the duties required by law. The bond stated, "the obligee shall notify the surety of any default . . . within a reasonable time after discovery . . . by the obligee" and "Within six months after discovery . . . of any default . . . the obligee shall file with the surety affirmative proof of loss. . . ." On May 6, the state auditor sent a claim memorandum to the attorney general regarding former deputy registrar Carol Shirk. Twenty-three months later a special counsel for the attorney general advised General that he had received the claim for collection eight months after the auditor's memo and four months later had secured a judgment against Shirk. This was General's first documentation from the state regarding the claim. The state sued General for payment on the bond. Is it liable?

7. Glenn McFadden bought a video cassette recorder on which Walloch TV & Appliances, Inc., held a security interest. At the time, McFadden occasionally used the recorder for business purposes, but more often for personal use. Sometime later, McFadden filed under Chapter 13 of the Bankruptcy Code, and Walloch filed a reclamation for the recorder, alleging it held a perfected security interest in the recorder. Walloch had not filed on the recorder with the secretary of state and the county clerk as was required for the perfection of a security interest in business equipment. Therefore the reclamation would be allowed only if the recorder were consumer goods and not business equipment. Was the recorder consumer goods or business equipment?

Summary Cases for Part Nine

Risk-Bearing Devices

1. Robert McCloskey obtained a life insurance policy from New York Life Insurance Company. The medical questionnaire asked, "Have you ever consulted a physician or . . . had or been treated for . . . heart attack . . . or any other disorder of the heart or blood vessels . . . or diabetes?" McCloskey answered no. He in fact had diabetes and had had a heart attack. A paramedical examination had revealed he was overweight, so the policy New York issued required a higher premium than was standard. Within a month of the issuance of the policy, McCloskey died. New York refused to pay on the policy, alleging misrepresentation. Was there misrepresentation? [*McCloskey v. New York Life Insurance Company*, 436 A.2d 690 (Pa. Super. Ct.)]

2. Evelyn Vlastos carried a fire insurance policy on her building. The policy included a section labeled Endorsement No. 4 which was incorporated into the policy and stated: "Warranted that the third floor is occupied as Janitor's residence." The building was destroyed by fire, and the insurers refused to pay on the policy, charging breach of warranty. Vlastos sued the insurers and after losing the case at trial appealed. She alleged there was no proof the provision in Endorsement No. 4 was a warranty, implying it was a representation. Which was it, and what difference would it make? [*Vlastos v. Sumitomo Marine & Fire Insurance Company (Europe) Ltd.*, 707 F.2d 775 (3rd Cir.)]

3. Merrimack Mutual Fire Insurance Company issued a fire insurance policy to James and Loree Stewart as owners with a mortgage clause requiring payment upon loss to Portland Savings Bank as mortgagee. The clause provided: "the mortgagee . . . shall notify this Company of any change of ownership . . . or increase of hazard. . . ." Portland later foreclosed on the property, and after the Stewarts' redemption period expired, it became the owner. It did not notify Merrimack of the foreclosure and its ownership before there was a fire loss. Merrimack denied coverage because Portland had not notified it of the change in ownership. The property was insured under Portland's master policy with Hartford Fire Insurance Company, which paid Portland for the loss and became subrogated to Portland's rights under the Merrimack policy. Was Merrimack liable under the policy? [*Hartford Fire Insurance Company v. Merrimack Mutual Fire Insurance Company*, 457 A.2d 410 (Me.)]

4. Rohde purchased an automobile public liability policy with a 20/50/5 coverage for each accident. The insured while driving negligently struck three motorcycles simultaneously. The drivers of the motorcycles were injured and their vehicles damaged. The total damages assessed were in excess of the limits of the policy if this was one accident. If there were three separate accidents, then the policy limits were adequate to cover all damages. Was this one accident or three accidents? [*Truck Insurance Company v. Rohde,* 303 P.2d 659 (Wash.)]

5. Bruener purchased a comprehensive automobile policy that specifically excluded collision damage. While driving on a wet pavement, Bruener lost control of his car when it skidded on the highway, finally coming to a violent stop when it hit the road embankment. The car was badly damaged. The question arose as to whether the direct and proximate cause of the damage was the skidding or whether the proximate cause was the collision with the road embankment. If it were the latter, then it came within the exclusion clause and the insurance company was not liable. Was the skidding the proximate cause of the damage? [*Bruener v. Twin City Fire Insurance Company,* 222 P. 2d 833 (Wash.)]

6. Sheila Kercher sued for dissolution of her marriage, and on November 3, the court issued an order restraining her husband "from transferring . . . or in any way disposing of any property except in the usual course of business or for the necessities of life." He had a term life insurance policy on which Kercher was the beneficiary and which gave him the right to change the beneficiary. On November 11, he changed the beneficiary to his mother, Helen Tallent, and on December 11, committed suicide. Should Kercher or Tallent receive the proceeds of the life insurance? [*Metropolitan Life Insurance Company v. Tallent,* 445 N.E.2d 990 (Ind.)]

7. C. E. Youse purchased a fire insurance policy on her household goods and personal property. She removed a valuable ring from her finger and laid it on the table with some cleansing tissue. By mistake the maid threw the tissue and the ring into the wastepaper basket and then threw the contents of the basket into a backyard incinerator. She lighted the contents of the incinerator intentionally, and the ensuing fire stayed within the incinerator. About one week later the ring was discovered in the ashes in the incinerator. It had sustained about $900 damage by the fire. The insurance company refused to pay on the ground this was a friendly fire. Was this a friendly fire or a hostile fire? [*Youse v. Employers Fire Insurance Company,* 238 P. 2d 472 (Kan.)]

8. A car driven by James Hilton struck a parked trash truck which extended onto the travel lane of the highway. Two people in the Hilton car received severe head lacerations, and the car was considerably damaged. The truck was owned by Joe Blakeney and insured by Safeco Insurance Company of America. At the scene, Blakeney saw the damage and injury, was issued a traffic summons, and was told by a police officer to file an accident report within ten days. Seven weeks later, an attorney for the Hiltons wrote the insurance agent who had written the Safeco policy and advised him of the accident. He prepared an accident report form and sent it to Safeco. Its policy stated: "written notice . . . with respect to the time, place and circumstances . . . and the names and addresses of the injured and of available witnesses, shall be given

by or for the insured to the company . . . as soon as practicable." Blakeney never notified anyone. Safeco denied coverage. Was it liable? [*Liberty Mutual Insurance Company v. Safeco Insurance Company*, 288 S.E.2d 469 (Va.)]

9. Devers Auto Sales financed its inventory with Thrift, Incorporated, which perfected its security interest in the inventory by filing a financing statement with the secretary of state in accordance with Article 9 of the UCC. The statement included a security interest in after-acquired inventory. A.D.E., Inc., agreed to sell three cars to Devers and gave it possession of them but not the titles. Thrift gave Devers the money for the cars, and Devers gave checks to A.D.E., but the checks were dishonored. Thrift took possession of Devers's inventory and demanded the titles from A.D.E. A.D.E. demanded the three cars. Did Thrift have a perfected security interest in the cars? [*Thrift, Inc. v. A.D.E., Inc.*, 454 N.E.2d 878 (Ind. Ct. App.)]

10. Smith sold a cruiser to Seal, who executed a security agreement and a note for $31,000 to the First National Bank of Linn Creek. A financing statement was filed by the bank. Seal decided not to keep the cruiser and asked Smith to sell it for him. Pieper bought it for $13,000 and his older boat. Smith applied the $13,000 to the note and told the bank it was received from the sale of the cruiser. Seal also told the bank he was going to sell the second boat. Five months later the bank repossessed the cruiser. Pieper sued for recovery of the cruiser. If the secured party has authorized a sale, the buyer takes free of the security interest. Was Pieper entitled to the cruiser? [*Pieper v. First National Bank of Linn Creek, Camdenton*, 453 S. W. 2d 926 (Mo.)]

Part Ten — Property

Learning Objectives for Part Ten

Property

After studying this part you should be able to:

1. Define property and name the two kinds of property.

2. Identify the real property estates.

3. Explain how title to property may be acquired.

4. Describe the means by which title to real estate is transferred.

5. Define an abstract of title and explain its significance when transferring real estate.

6. Define and discuss the effect of a mortgage.

7. Explain the duties and rights of a mortgagor.

8. Define and explain the effect of foreclosure.

9. Explain what a trust deed is and how it is used in real estate transactions.

10. Discuss what landlords and tenants are.

11. List the requirements for a valid lease.

12. Distinguish between the various types of tenancies.

13. Describe the rights and duties of tenants and landlords.

14. Explain how a lease may be terminated.

15. Describe what a will is, its characteristics, and the limitations on disposition of property.

16. Explain the formalities required for executing a will.

17. Name the ways in which a will may be revoked.

18. Discuss the procedure for probating a will and administering estates.

19. Identify the purposes for bankruptcy and who may file for it.

20. Describe the bankruptcy procedures and explain how property and debts are affected by them.

45

Nature of Property

Preview Cases

On August 12, Elwyn Groth sold all the Christmas trees growing on his land. He granted the buyers the right to enter upon the land to spray, prune, and care for the trees until they reached their appropriate growth. The buyers of the trees had the right to then harvest and remove the trees. Groth retained the right to sell any land on which there were no such trees and even land on which there were trees, but after they were harvested. About a year later, by warranty deed, Groth conveyed all the land to Ronald and Diane Stillson without reservation. The Stillsons alleged they did not have notice of the tree sale, so Groth asked the court to reform his deed to include a reservation of the trees. Christmas trees require care annually for six to eight years. Were the trees personal property or part of the land?

John Taylor bought a sewage treatment system which was manufactured by Multi-Flo, Inc. It was installed at Taylor's residence in August. In October he began to have problems with the system. Over the next three years, service and repairs were made by three different companies, and a few months later Taylor sued Multi-Flo, claiming the system was defective and had been since installation. In installing it, a hole was dug and the base leveled with sand. The unit was put into the hole and leveled. The inlet and outlet lines were then hooked up and the wiring system installed from the aerator to the alarm box. Backfill was then placed around the system. The trial court said the action was barred by a two-year statute of limitations on personal property. Was the system personal property or had it become a fixture?

Property is anything which may be owned, possessed, used, or disposed of. A person may enter into a contract with another to use property which does not belong to the person. The law protects not only the right to own property but also the right to use it. Property includes not only physical things but such things as money, notes, and bonds which give the right to acquire physical property or to use such property.

Property may be classified according to its movability. In this sense all property falls into one of two classes, real property and personal property. If it is not movable, it is real property; if it is movable property, it is personal property.

Real Property

Real property consists of land, which includes the actual soil, and all permanent attachments to the land, such as fences, walls, other additions and improvements, timber, and other growing things. It also includes minerals under the soil and the waters upon it. Through court interpretations we have accumulated a definite set of rules to guide us in distinguishing real property from personal property. The most important of these rules pertain to:

1. Trees and perennial crops
2. Rivers and streams
3. Fixtures

Trees and Perennial Crops. Trees that are growing on the land, orchards, vineyards, and perennial crops, such as clovers, grasses, and others that are not planted annually and cultivated, are classed as real property until they are severed from the land. When land is sold, if there is any doubt as to whether or not a particular item belongs to the land or is personal property, the parties should agree before the sale is completed just how the item is to be classed.

On August 12, Elwyn Groth sold all the Christmas trees growing on his land. He granted the buyers the right to enter upon the land to spray, prune, and care for the trees until they reached their appropriate growth. The buyers of the trees had the right to then harvest and remove the trees. Groth retained the right to sell any land on which there were no such trees and even land on which there were trees, but after they were harvested. About a year later, by warranty deed, Groth conveyed all the land to Ronald and Diane Stillson without reservation. The Stillsons alleged they did not have notice of the tree sale, so Groth asked the court to reform his deed to include a reservation of the trees. Christmas trees require care annually for six to eight years. The court held that the sale of the trees was the sale of a growing crop, and they were constructively severed from the land by the August 12 agreement. As personal property, they did not pass with the land.

Rivers and Streams. If a nonnavigable river flows through property, the person who owns the property owns the riverbed but not the water that flows over the bed. The water cannot be impounded or diverted to the property owner's own use in such a way as to deprive any neighbors of its use. If the river or the stream forms the boundary line, then the owner on each side of the river owns the land to the middle of the riverbed.

In most states where navigable rivers form the boundary, the owner of the adjoining land owns the land only to the low-water mark.

Fixtures. Personal property attached to land or a building is known as a fixture. Generally, a fixture becomes part of the real estate. To determine whether or not personal property has become real estate, one or more of the following four rules may be applied:

1. How securely is it attached? If the personal property is so securely attached that it cannot be removed without damaging the real property to which it is attached, then it ceases to be personal property. A tenant cannot remove fixtures when the lease expires.
2. What was the intention of the one installing the personal property? No matter what one's intention, the personal property becomes real property if it cannot be removed without damaging the property. But, if it is loosely attached and the person installing the fixture indicates the intention to make the fixture real property, then this intention is the controlling factor. Refrigerators have been held to be real property when apartments were rented unfurnished but contained refrigerators.
3. For what purpose was the fixture attached? The purpose for which the fixture is to be used may show the intention of the one annexing it.
4. Who installed the fixture? If the owner of a building installs personal property to the building, this usually indicates the intention to make it a permanent addition to the real property. If the tenant makes the same improvements, the presumption is that there was an intention to keep the fixture as personal property unless a contrary intention can be shown.

John Taylor bought a sewage treatment system which was manufactured by Multi-Flo, Inc. It was installed at Taylor's residence in August. In October he began to have problems with the system. Over the next three years, service and repairs were made by three different companies, and a few months later Taylor sued Multi-Flo, claiming the system was defective and had been since installation. In installing it, a hole was dug and the base leveled with sand. The unit was put into the hole and leveled. The inlet and outlet lines were then hooked up and the wiring system installed from the aerator to the alarm box. Backfill was then placed around the system. The trial court said the action was barred by a two-year statute of limitations on personal property. The appellate court held that where the product has become a fixture the two-year statute of limitations does not apply.

Personal Property

Personal property is any property or property right which is not classified as real property. An interest in real property other than a fee simple or a life estate (discussed below), such as a leasehold, is normally classified as personal property. Personal property includes movable physical property and notes, bonds, and all written evidences of debt. Personal property is divided into two classes:

1. Tangible
2. Intangible

Tangible Personal Property. *Tangible personal property* is personal property which can be seen, touched, and possessed. Animals, merchandise, furniture, annual growing crops, clothing, jewelry, and similar items are all classified as tangible personal property.

Intangible Personal Property. *Intangible personal property* consists of evidences of ownership of personal property. Some common forms of intangible personal property are checks, stocks, contracts, copyrights, and savings account certificates.

Estates in Property

An *estate* is the nature and extent of interest which a person has in real or personal property. The estate which a person has in property may be:

1. A fee simple estate, or
2. A life estate

Estate in Fee Simple. A *fee simple estate* is the largest and most complete right which one may possess in property. A fee simple owner of property, whether real or personal, has the right to possess the property forever. The owner of a fee simple estate may also sell, lease, or otherwise dispose of the property permanently or temporarily, and at the death of such owner, the property will pass to the persons provided for in the owner's will or, if there is no will, to the heirs at law.

A fee simple owner of land has the right to the surface of the land, the air above the land "all the way to heaven," and the subsoil beneath the surface all the way to the center of the earth. The courts have held, however, that the right to the air above the land is not absolute. An individual cannot prevent an airplane from flying over the land unless it flies too low. It is possible for a person to own the surface of the land only and not the minerals, oil, gas, and other valuable property under the topsoil. A person may also own the soil but not the timber.

Life Estate. One may have an estate in property by which the property is owned for a lifetime. This is known as a *life estate*. At the death of the owner, the title passes as directed by the original owner. The title may revert, or go back, to the grantor, the one who conveyed the life estate to the deceased, the interest of the grantor being called a *reversion*, or the property may go to someone other than the grantor, such interest being called a *remainder*.

John Dotson conveyed to his wife, Minnie, a life estate in all his real estate. At her death the property was to go to his three daughters in equal parts. The interest of the daughters was a remainder. Had the property at Minnie's death returned to her husband or to his estate, it would have been a reversion. In either case, the property right is real property, not personal property.

Methods of Acquiring Ownership

The title to property may be acquired by purchase, will, gift, descent, accession, accretion, confusion, creation, and adverse possession.

Purchase. Acquiring ownership through *purchase* is a common occurrence. The buyer pays the seller, and the seller conveys property to the buyer.

Will. The owner of property may convey title to another by *will*. Title is not transferred by will until the person who made the will dies and appropriate judicial proceedings have taken place.

Gift. A *gift* is a transfer made without consideration in return.

Descent. When a person dies intestate, that is without leaving a will, the person's heirs acquire title to the personal property according to the law of descent existing in the decedent's state and to the real property according to the law of descent in the state where the land is located.

Accession. *Accession* is the acquiring of property by means of the addition of personal property of another. If materials owned by two people are combined to form one product, the person who owned the major part of the materials owns the product. Accession includes the right to all which one's property produces, such as the produce of land.

Accretion. *Accretion* is the addition to land as a result of the gradual deposit by water of solids. It takes place most commonly when the boundary line of property is a stream, river, lake, or ocean. If one's land extends to the low water mark of a navigable stream, title to some land may be acquired by the river's shifting its flow. This occurs slowly by the deposit of silt. Also, the accretion may be the result of dredging or channeling of the river. If the silt and sand are thrown up on the riverbank thereby increasing the acreage of the upland contiguous to the river, the added acreage belongs to the owner of the upland.

Confusion. *Confusion* is the mixing of the goods of different owners so that the parts belonging to each owner cannot be identified and separated. Grain, lumber, oil, and coal are examples of the kinds of property that are susceptible to confusion. The property, belonging to different owners, may be mixed by common consent, by accident, or by the willful act of some wrongdoer.

When confusion of the property is brought about by common consent or by accident, each party will be deemed the owner of a proportionate part of the mass. If the confusion is willful, the title to the total mass passes to the innocent party, unless it can be clearly proven how much of the property of the one causing the confusion was mingled with that of the other person. If this cannot be done, the whole mass belongs to the other person.

Creation. One may acquire personal property by *creation*. This is true of inventions, paintings, musical compositions, and other intellectual productions. Title to these is made secure for a period of years through patents and copyrights.

The one who first applies for and obtains a patent gets title to the production. Creation alone does not give absolute title; it gives only the right to obtain absolute title by means of a patent. Songs, books, and other compositions which are fixed in any tangible medium of expression are protected by copyright from their creation. A copyright gives the owner the exclusive right to reproduce, copy, perform, or display the work or authorize another to do so. While the copyright protects from the creation of the work, the copyright must be registered in order to sue for infringement.

Adverse Possession. An individual may acquire title to real property by occupying the land for a period fixed by statute. This is known as *adverse possession*. The statutory period varies from seven years in some states to twenty-one in others. Occupancy must be continuous, open, hostile, visible, and exclusive. In colonial times this was known as "squatter's rights." To get title by adverse possession, one had to go one step further than the "squatter," that is, the adverse possession had to continue for the statutory period.

Possession for the statutory period then gave clear title to all the land one's color of title described. The color of title usually arises, but need not necessarily do so, from some defective document purporting to be a deed or a will or even a gift.

Mahan had used a path across certain land for quite a few years. Later Smithson purchased the land, and even later he attempted to prevent Mahan's use of the land. Mahan brought an action to establish his right to use the land, since he had already used the land for the statutory period. Smithson claimed Mahan's possession was not hostile, since Mahan had not excluded Smithson from also using the property. The court found that the claimant of an easement does not have to exclude the owner from the land for all purposes in order for the claimant's use to be hostile; therefore Mahan had established an easement.

Lost and Abandoned Property

The difference between abandoned and lost property lies in the intention of the owner to part with title to it. Property is considered to be *abandoned* when the owner actually discards it with no intention of reclaiming it. Property is considered to be *lost* when the owner, through negligence or accident, unintentionally leaves it somewhere.

A person who discovers and takes possession of property that has been abandoned and that has never been reclaimed by the owner acquires a right thereto. The prior owner, however, must have completely relinquished ownership.

The finder of lost property has a right of possession against all but the true owner; there is no right of possession against the true owner except in instances when the owner cannot be found through reasonable diligence on the part of the finder and certain statutory requirements are fulfilled. The finder of abandoned goods, however, has title to them and thus has an absolute right to possession.

In a few cases the courts have held that if an employee finds property in the course of the employment, the property belongs to the employer. Also, if property is mislaid, not lost, then the owner of the premises has first claim against all but the true owner. This is especially true of property left on trains, airplanes, in restaurants, and in hotels.

A number of states have enacted the Uniform Disposition of Unclaimed Property Act. This law provides that holders of property which the law presumes is abandoned turn over the property to the state.

Environmental Law

In recognition of the fact that the environment is the property of everyone, the federal and state governments have enacted legislation aimed at conserving and restoring our environment. The legislation is directed at four major problems: air pollution, water pollution, solid waste disposal, and strip mining. This area of the law is growing very rapidly.

The major federal legislation includes the Water Pollution Control Act, the Clean Air Act, and the National Environmental Policy Act (NEPA). The first two acts are designed to remedy problems with two specific types of pollution. The Environmental Policy Act seeks to establish a national environmental policy and requires all federal agencies to prepare environmental impact statements. These public statements detail the probable impact upon the environment of major proposed agency actions. If a federal agency does not comply with the requirements of NEPA, interested parties may request judicial review of the agency's impact statement and the procedures followed in developing it. The courts have included a wide range of associations and environmental organizations in the term "interested parties."

Almost all of the states have enacted some environmental protection legislation. Perhaps the most common problem to be attacked by state legislation is air pollution. The statutes enacted by the states vary greatly. A large number of states have established state agencies to regulate pollution and protect the environment. Anyone contemplating establishing a business which might affect the environment should investigate the applicable state laws and regulations.

Questions

1. What is *property*?

2. Are growing trees real or personal property?

3. What is a *fixture*?

4. If a tenant who has installed trade fixtures on the property moves away without removing the fixtures, to whom do the fixtures normally belong?

5. Name three types of intangible personal property.

6. What do we call the most complete right one can have in land?

7. How may the heirs obtain title to property of a person who has died intestate?

8. When is property considered abandoned?

9. What are the major problems which are the focus of environmental law?

Case Problems

1. Mr. and Mrs. Simmons lived in a mobile home which had been bought with community-property funds. The home was in a mobile home park where they rented a lot. Mrs. Simmons had title to the home. She went to Cooper's Mobile Homes, Inc., and signed a number of documents relating to the purchase of a new mobile home. She signed over the title certificate of the old home to Cooper's as a down payment on a new home, intending to move the old home off the lot. Mr. Simmons objected to the arrangement and said he would not

agree to it. Mrs. Simmons tried to cancel the agreement. The sale was never made, and Cooper's sued for breach of the contract to buy the new home. Mrs. Simmons alleged that the law which gives each spouse management authority over community property did not apply because the home was real property and both had to join in the conveyance. Was it real property?

2. A nonnavigable stream was the dividing line between O'Keefe's farm and Coppage's farm. The river at one spot ran along the edge of a rich field, the field all being on Coppage's side of the river. O'Keefe felled some trees across the river at the upper end of the field, inducing the river to swing to the opposite side of the field. O'Keefe claims this field under the law of accretion. Is he entitled to it? *No; he did it intentionally*

3. In 1767 and 1768, while he was the attorney for the King, William Hooper, who later signed the Declaration of Independence, signed and filed two indictments. They were purchased at an auction by B. C. West in 1974. The state sued to recover possession of them, alleging it was the lawful custodian of and had the right to possess all court records and documents of the state. By an act of the Colonial Assembly the chief justice was authorized to appoint clerks responsible for the safekeeping of records. West alleged the indictments were abandoned, and since he now had possession, he had title to them. Were the indictments abandoned?

4. In 1941, a tract of land owned by Elizabeth Selig and her husband was taken by the U.S. by eminent domain. The Declaration of Taking stated that a full fee simple title, subject only to easements for pipelines, roads, and utilities, was taken. Many years later Selig filed suit against the U.S., alleging the compensation paid in 1941 did not include compensation for the minerals. Who owned the minerals?

5. Eberhart owned a textile mill which manufactured cordage material from cotton. Brewer left with Eberhart 20 bales of cotton for storage. Eberhart used the 20 bales of cotton together with several hundred of his own and processed it into cordage. Brewer demanded all the finished cordage. Is she entitled to it? *No only prop. part*

6. The town of Hempstead attached street light fixtures to telephone poles owned by the New York Telephone Company. Under the provisions of state law the telephone company had an unconditional right to erect poles for its line on public streets and highways. When the telephone company sued Hempstead to require it to remove the light fixtures, the town alleged that the right to attach the fixtures to utility poles is an interest in real property and subject to the power of eminent domain. Is the telephone company's right to erect telephone poles an interest in real property?

46

Transfer of Real Property

Preview Cases

I. A. Rosenbaum conveyed land to T. S. McCaskey by quitclaim deed. The deed stated: "the grantor herein is to retain one-half of all oil, gas, and mineral rights in the above described lands. . . ." When this conveyance was made, Rosenbaum owned the surface and one-half of the mineral rights. After Rosenbaum died, his heirs sued to confirm title to the mineral rights. What did this deed convey to McCaskey?

Saul executed a general warranty deed conveying his home to his wife, Ilene. Since he did not want her to know of this act, he placed the deed in his safe deposit box. Only he had access to the box. Upon his death, the deed was discovered. John, Ilene's stepson, brought suit to have the deed nullified. Will the court declare the deed invalid?

The most common way of transferring title to real estate is by sale. In the ordinary case there will be a contract of sale followed by delivery of a deed. One may by means of a lease transfer a leasehold title giving the rights to the use and possession of land for a limited period. The extent of the interest transferred is determined by the provisions of the deed or the lease.

Even when title to real property is conveyed as a gift, the transfer must be evidenced by a deed. As soon as the deed is executed and delivered, title vests fully in the donee. Acceptance by the donee is presumed.

Deeds

A *deed* is a writing signed by the seller conveying title to real property. The law sets forth the form which the deed must have, and this form must be observed. The parties to the deed are the *grantor* or seller and the *grantee* or buyer. There are two principal types of deeds:

1. Quitclaim deeds
2. Warranty deeds

Quitclaim Deeds.   A *quitclaim deed* is just what the name implies. The grantor gives up any claim which the grantor may have to the real property. No warranty is made that the grantor has any claim.

In the absence of a statute or an agreement between the parties requiring a warranty deed, there is no reason why a quitclaim deed may not be used in making all conveyances of real property. The grantor's full and complete interest is as effectively transferred by a quitclaim deed as with a warranty deed. When buying real property, however, one does not always want to buy merely the interest which the grantor has. A buyer wants to buy a perfect and complete interest so that the title cannot be questioned by anyone. A quitclaim deed conveys only the interest of the grantor and no more. It contains no warranty that the grantor's title is good. In most real estate transactions, a quitclaim deed cannot be used because the contract will specify that a warranty deed must be delivered.

I. A. Rosenbaum conveyed land to T. S. McCaskey by quitclaim deed. The deed stated: "the grantor herein is to retain one-half of all oil, gas, and mineral rights in the above described lands. . . ." When this conveyance was made, Rosenbaum owned the surface and one-half of the mineral rights. After Rosenbaum died, his heirs sued to confirm title to the mineral rights. The court stated a quitclaim deed was only a conduit that passed the grantor's interest to the grantee. To find out what interest passed, it is necessary to determine what interest the grantor had to convey and take from it anything reserved in the quitclaim deed. This deed reserved a one-half interest in the mineral rights and conveyed what was left—the surface.

Warranty Deeds.   A *warranty deed* not only conveys the grantor's interest in the real property but, in addition, makes certain warranties or guarantees. The exact nature of the warranty or guarantee depends upon whether the deed is a general warranty or a special warranty deed.

A *general warranty deed*, an example of which is in Illustration 46-1, not only warrants that the grantor has good title to the real property but further warrants that the grantee "shall have quiet and peaceable possession, free from all encumbrances, and that the grantor will defend the grantee against all claims and demands from whomsoever made." This warranty, then, warrants that all prior grantors had good title and that there are no defects in any prior grantor's title. The grantee is not asked to assume any risks as the new owner of the property.

A *special warranty deed* warrants that the grantor has the right to sell the real property. There are no warranties of the genuineness of any prior grantor's title. This type of deed is used by trustees and sheriffs who sell land at a foreclosure sale. It is also used by executors and administrators. There is no reason why these officials should warrant anything other than that they have the legal right to sell whatever interest the owner has.

Characteristics of a Deed

Unless statutes provide otherwise, a deed usually has the following characteristics:

1. Parties
2. Consideration
3. Covenants
4. Description
5. Signature
6. Acknowledgment

Parties. The grantor and the grantee must be named in the deed. If the grantor is married, the grantor's name and that of a spouse should be written in the deed. If the grantor is unmarried, this fact should be indicated by using the word "single" or the phrase "a single person."

Consideration. The amount paid to the grantor for the property is the consideration. The payment may be in money or in money's worth. A statement of the consideration must be made in the deed, although the amount specified need not be the actual price paid. In some localities the practice is to indicate a nominal amount, as one dollar, although a much larger sum was actually paid. The reason for stating a nominal amount as the consideration is to keep the sale price from being a matter of public record.

Covenants. There may be as many covenants as the grantor and the grantee wish to include. Some of these are *affirmative covenants* whereby the grantee is obligated to do something, such as maintaining a driveway used in common with adjoining property. Others are *negative covenants* whereby the grantee agrees to refrain from doing something. Such covenants are very common in urban residential developments. The more common ones prohibit the grantee from using the property for business purposes and set forth the types of homes that can or cannot be built on the property. Most covenants run with the land and are binding upon all future owners.

Description. The property to be conveyed must be correctly described. Any description that will identify the property will suffice. Ordinarily,

WARRANTY DEED

Know All Men by These Presents:

That Donald C. Coson and Millicent M. Coson, his wife

of Butler *County,* Ohio

in consideration of the sum of Forty-five Thousand Dollars ($45,000)

to them *in hand paid by* Eugene F. Acknor, the grantee, the receipt of which is hereby acknowledged,

do *hereby* **Grant, Bargain, Sell and Convey**

to the said Eugene F. Acknor

h is *heirs*

and assigns forever, the following described **Real Estate** *situate in the* City *of* Hamilton *in the County of* Butler *and State of* Ohio
Lot No. 10, Section 14, Range 62, Randall Subdivision, being a portion of the estate of Horace E. Cresswell and Alice B. Cresswell

and all the **Estate, Right, Title and Interest** *of the said grantor* s *in and to said premises;* **To have and to hold** *the same, with all the privileges and appurtenances thereunto belonging, to said grantee* , his *heirs and assigns forever. And the said* Donald C. Coson and Millicent M. Coson

do *hereby* **Covenant and Warrant** *that the title so conveyed is* **Clear, Free and Unincumbered,** *and that* they *will* **Defend** *the same against all lawful claims of all persons whomsoever.*

In Witness Whereof, *the said grantor* s *have hereunto set* their *hand* s , *this* first *day of* December *in the year A. D. nineteen hundred and* --

Signed and acknowledged in presence of us:

..........*Michael R. Winer*.......... | ....*Donald C. Coson*..........
..........*Antonio C. Petricelle*.......... | ....*Millicent M. Coson*..........

State of Ohio, Butler **County, ss.**

On this first *day of* December *A. D. 19* -- *, before me, a* Notary Public *in and for said County, personally came* Donald C. Coson and Millicent M. Coson

the grantor s *in the foregoing deed, and* *acknowledged the signing thereof to be* their *voluntary act and deed.*

Witness *my official signature and seal on the day last above mentioned.*

Sarah M. Evans

Notary Public

ILLUS. 46-1. A General Warranty Deed

however, the description that was used in the deed by which the present owner acquired the title should be used if it is correct. The description may be by lots and blocks if the property is in a city; or it may be by metes and bounds or section, range, and township if the property is in a rural area.

Signature. The deed should be signed by the grantor in the place provided for the signature. If the grantor is married, the spouse also should sign for the purpose of giving up the statutory right of the spouse. In some states the signatures must be attested by a witness or witnesses. If the grantor is incapable of signing the deed, it may be executed by an agent, the grantor with assistance, or the grantor making a mark, thus:

Maria Smith
Witness of the mark of
Henry Finn

$$\text{Henry} \left\{ \begin{array}{c} \text{His} \\ \text{X} \\ \text{Mark} \end{array} \right\} \text{Finn}$$

Acknowledgment. The statutes in practically all the states require that the deed be formally acknowledged before a notary public or other officer authorized to take acknowledgments. The purpose of the acknowledgment is to make it possible for the deed to be recorded. After a deed has been recorded, it may be used as evidence in a court without further proof of its authenticity being given. Recording is not essential to the validity of the deed, but it is invaluable as security of the title of the grantee.

The *acknowledgment* is a declaration made by the properly authorized officer, in the form provided for that purpose, that the grantor has acknowledged the instrument as a free act and deed. In some states it is further required that the grantor understand the nature and effect of the deed or be personally known to the acknowledging officer. These facts are attested by the officer, who affixes an official seal, and are further evidenced by the certificate.

Delivery

A deed is ineffective until it has been delivered. *Delivery* consists of giving up possession and control over the deed. So long as the grantor maintains control over the deed and reserves the right to demand its return before the deed is delivered to the grantee, there has been no legal delivery. If the grantor executes a deed and leaves it with an attorney to deliver to the grantee, there has been no delivery until the attorney delivers the deed to the grantee. Since the attorney is the agent of the grantor, the grantor has the right to demand that the agent return the deed. If the grantor, however, delivers the deed to the grantee's attorney, then there has been an effective delivery.

Saul executed a general warranty deed conveying his home to his wife, Ilene. Since he did not want her to know of this act, he placed the deed in his safety deposit box. Only he had access to the box. Upon his death, the deed was discovered. John, Ilene's stepson, brought suit to have the deed nullified. He succeeded. There was never a valid delivery of the deed prior to Saul's death.

Recording

A deed need not be recorded in order to complete one's title. Title is complete as soon as the deed is delivered. Recording the deed protects the grantee against a second sale by the grantor and against any liens which may attach to the property while it is still recorded in the grantor's name.

When a deed is received for recording, the recording official will ordinarily be required to stamp the deed with the exact date and time that the deed is left for recording.

Abstract of Title

Before one buys real estate, it is advisable to have an abstract of title prepared. This is normally done by an abstract company, but it may be done by an attorney. The *abstract of title* gives a complete history of the real estate. It also shows whether or not there are any unpaid taxes and assessments, mortgages, or deeds of trust outstanding and any unpaid judgments or other unsatisfied liens of any type against the property. If an abstracting company makes the abstract, it is advisable to have an attorney read the abstract to see if it reveals any flaws in the title.

Title Insurance

Some defects in the title to real estate cannot be detected by an abstract. Some of the most common of these defects are forgery of signatures in prior conveyances; claims by adverse possession; incompetency to contract by any prior party; fraud; duress; undue influence; defective wills; loss of real property by accretion; and errors by title examiner, tax officials, surveyors, and many other public officials. A title insurance policy can be obtained that will cover these defects. The policy may expressly exclude any possible defects which the insurance company does not wish to be covered by the policy. With one premium, the insured is covered as long as the property is owned. The policy does not benefit a subsequent purchaser or a mortgagee.

Questions

1. What are the advantages and disadvantages of a quitclaim deed?

2. Define a *warranty deed*.

3. Who are the parties that must be named in a deed?

4. What description of property is sufficient in a deed?

5. Which party must sign a deed?

6. What is an *acknowledgment*?

7. When does a deed become effective?

8. a. Is it necessary to record a deed in order to complete one's title to the land?

   b. What does recording a deed do?

9. How may an owner of real property be protected against defects in title?

Case Problems

1. V.T.C. Lines, Inc., owned two pieces of real estate. On April 8 they were the subject of a deed to John Christian. The deed stated: "THIS DEED OF CONVEYANCE . . . between LOGAN MIDDLETON, President of the V.T.C. Lines Incorporated . . . party of the first part, and JOHN CHRISTIAN . . . party of the second part." It was signed by Logan Middleton, President V.T.C. Lines, Incorporated. The only other reference to the corporation was in the attestation clause, where Logan Middleton was again designated president of the corporation. The next day Jerry and Donald Johnson secured a judgment against V.T.C. On June 12 Christian and his wife conveyed a one-half interest in the property to Johnny Pace. The Johnsons tried to execute on the property. Who owns it?

2. Garlock purchased a house and lot. In a prior deed the grantor had inserted a covenant that the grantee would never use the property for commercial or business purposes. Such covenants were included by the original owner in the deeds for all the houses in that residential section. Garlock wished to set up a dry-cleaning establishment in the basement of her house. A neighbor brought suit to enjoin her from doing so. This action was based upon the original restrictive covenant. Was Garlock bound by this covenant?

3. Robert Young brought an action to quiet title to eighty acres of land in United States Survey 691 on Prince of Wales Island. William Shilts alleged that as the sole heir of Aaron Shellhouse, he was the record owner of part of the property. Alaska Industrial Company received a patent to U.S. Survey 691. It later conveyed six blocks of land in that survey to Shellhouse. The 200-foot-square blocks were located by reference to named streets and were "more paticularly described on Survey No. 691, made by Chas. S. Hubbell. . . ." That survey was not found, and the only plat did not indicate any lots or streets. The trial court determined the configuration of the lots from the street references in the deed and that the Shellhouse property was between Corner No. 1 and Point No. 2 on one of the exhibits and contained 400 feet of beachfront. Was the description in the deed adequate to convey the property?

4. R. S. Farrar executed a deed of real estate to Ann and Larry Shrewsbury on the same day an agreement was signed by which the Shrewsburys agreed to provide a home for Farrar for the rest of his life. After Farrar's death, his sons filed an action to set aside the deed for failure of consideration. Regarding consideration, the deed stated: "for and in consideration of the sum of One Dollar ($1.00), and other good and valuable consideration, cash in hand paid . . . the receipt of which is hereby acknowledged. . . ." Farrar lived with the Shrewsburys for four months and then lived elsewhere but visited them often on weekends and was always welcome at their home. Should the deed be cancelled for failure of consideration?

5. Stewart sold Stern a house and lot, executing a special warranty deed. About a year later Sprouse sued Stern to recover the property, claiming that the signature of the grantor of the property ten years earlier was forged. The person who sold the property to Stewart was not a party to the forgery. Must Stewart make good the loss to Stern? Would your answer be different if he had made a general warranty deed?

6. Holcomb executed a deed to his home, conveying all the property to his son John. The deed was delivered to John, but before he had it recorded, a brother, Roger, found the deed and burned it up. Before Holcomb could make another deed, he died; and John sought to have the court declare him the rightful owner of the house and lot. Was John entitled to the property?

7. Henry owned 600 acres of land which she had purchased by general warranty deed from Bell. She purchased title insurance on the property. She sold the land to Dawson and gave him a special warranty deed. She also agreed to assign the title insurance policy to Dawson. About two years after Dawson purchased the property, he learned an adjoining landowner claimed by adverse possession about 30 acres of the most valuable part of the land. In a court suit, the court awarded the 30 acres to the neighbor. What rights does Dawson have against Henry or the insurance company?

8. After Felix Dopieralla died, a sealed envelope containing a deed to his house was discovered in his home. The grantee on the deed was Pauline Adams. Adams stated Dopieralla had delivered the deed to her at the home of a friend, Mrs. Nielson. The deed was left with Nielson until she took a trip, when it was returned to Dopieralla. He lived in the house, exercised all rights of ownership over it, and paid the taxes on it. Was there a valid delivery of the deed to Adams?

47

Real Estate Mortgages

Preview Cases

Ralph and Florence Manning, husband and wife, executed a mortgage on land they owned as tenants in common to Farmers Trust and Savings Bank to secure a loan for $69,000. The mortgage contained an open-end, or dragnet, provision which stated: "This mortgage shall stand as security . . . for any and all future and additional advances made to the Mortgagors by the holder . . . in such . . . amounts so that the total . . . outstanding . . . shall not exceed $100,000 and Mortgagee is hereby given authority to make such future . . . advances to Mortgagors herein." Subsequently, Ralph alone borrowed a total of $31,000. None of the additional notes were signed by Florence. When one came due, Ralph offered Farmers checks in payment on the condition Farmers would loan the money to cover them. Farmers refused and sued, invoking an acceleration clause to declare the entire indebtedness due. It claimed that the mortgage secured the additional notes executed only by Ralph. Did it?

Earnestine and Henry Henderson executed a deed of trust on their home to the Farmers Home Administration (FmHA) as security for a loan. They defaulted on the loan, so FmHA accelerated the debt and foreclosed on the property. When sued for eviction, the Hendersons alleged the notice of foreclosure FmHA sent them misrepresented the law regarding what they had to pay to avoid foreclosure. The law stated: "the debtor . . . may at any time before a sale . . . stop a threatened sale . . . by paying the amount actually past due . . . rather than the amount accelerated." The amount past due was $1,200. The notice from FmHA stated: "The indebtedness . . . consists of . . . $8,585.77 plus interest of $477.77. . . . You are hereby notified that unless said indebtedness is paid in full within 20 days . . . the United States . . . will take action to foreclose. Any negotiation by the United States . . . of any remittance tendered by you . . . will not constitute a waiver of this acceleration or institution of foreclosure action." Was the notice faulty?

A *mortgage* is a lien given upon real estate to secure a debt. The mortgage is not the debt itself but the security for the debt. Land or any interest in land may be mortgaged. Land may be mortgaged separately from the improvements, or the improvements may be mortgaged apart from the land. A person who gives a mortgage as security for a loan is a *mortgagor*. A person who holds a mortgage as security for a debt is a *mortgagee*.

The mortgagor has possession of the property. In order for the mortgagee to obtain the benefit of the security, the mortgagee must take possession of the premises upon default or sell the mortgaged property at a foreclosure sale. In some states, the mortgagee may not take possession of the property upon default but may obtain the appointment of a receiver to collect the rents and income. If the sale of the property brings more than the debt and the costs, the mortgagor is entitled to receive the balance.

The Mortgage Contract

A mortgage must be in writing. The contract, as a rule, must have the same form as a deed; that is, it must be acknowledged. The mortgage, like all other contracts, sets forth the rights and the duties of the contracting parties.

A mortgage is usually given to raise money for the purchase price of real estate but may be given for other reasons. One may borrow money for any reason and secure the loan by a mortgage. One may assume a contingent liability for another, such as becoming a surety, and receive a mortgage as security.

The lien of the mortgage attaches to the property described in the mortgage. It is generally also provided that the lien attaches to additions thereafter made to the described property; for example, personal property which thereafter becomes a fixture is bound by the lien of the mortgage. A clause purporting to make the security clause of a mortgage cover future debts will be valid if the parties intended it to cover future debts.

Ralph and Florence Manning, husband and wife, executed a mortgage on land they owned as tenants in common to Farmers Trust and Savings Bank to secure a loan for $69,000. The mortgage contained an open-end, or dragnet, provision which stated: "This mortgage shall stand as security . . . for any and all future and additional advances made to the Mortgagors by the holder . . . in such . . . amounts so that the total . . . outstanding . . . shall not exceed $100,000 and Mortgagee is hereby given authority to make such future . . . advances to Mortgagors herein." Subsequently, Ralph alone borrowed a total of $31,000. None of the additional notes were signed by Florence. When one came due, Ralph offered Farmers checks in payment on the condition Farmers would loan the money to cover them. Farmers refused and sued, invoking an acceleration clause to declare the entire indebtedness due. It claimed the mortgage secured the additional notes executed only by Ralph. The court held that the express terms of the mortgage established it as security only on loans to both of the Mannings.

Recording

Depending upon the law of the state where the land is situated, the mortgage gives the mortgagee either a lien on the land or title to the land. The title or lien is divested or destroyed when the debt is paid. Recording the mortgage protects the mortgagee against subsequent creditors, since the public record is notice to the whole world as to the mortgagee's rights. There may be both a first mortgage and subsequent mortgages. The mortgage which is recorded first is normally given preference. This is not true when there is actual notice of a prior mortgage. However, a purchase money mortgage is given preference over other claims arising through the mortgagor. The mortgage is also recorded to notify subsequent purchasers that as much of the purchase price as is necessary to pay off the mortgage must be paid to the mortgagee.

Jarvis borrowed $10,000 from Sample and gave Sample a mortgage on her real estate to secure the debt. Sample forgot to record the mortgage. Anderson obtained a judgment of $5,000 against Jarvis and forced the sale of the real estate to pay off his judgment. The real estate was sold for $13,000. Sample sued to get $10,000 of the sale price, alleging that his mortgage was a first lien. The court found that since the mortgage was not recorded before Anderson obtained his judgment, Anderson was entitled to the full $5,000, and Sample was entitled to the remaining $8,000.

Duties of the Mortgagor

The mortgagor assumes three definite duties and liabilities when placing a mortgage upon real estate. These pertain to:

1. Interest and principal
2. Taxes, assessments, and insurance premiums
3. Security of the mortgagee

Interest and Principal. The mortgagor must make all payments of interest and principal as they become due. Most mortgages call for periodic payments, such as monthly, semiannual, or annual payments. These payments are used to pay all accrued interest to the date of payment, and the balance is applied on the principal. Other mortgages call for periodic payment of interest and for the payment of the entire principal at one time. In either case, a failure to pay either the periodic payments of interest and principal, or of interest only, is a default and gives the mortgagee the right to foreclose. Most mortgages contain a provision that if any interest or principal payments are not made when due or within a specified time after due the mortgagee may declare the entire principal immediately due. This is known as an *acceleration clause*.

If the mortgagor wishes to pay off the mortgage debt before the due date so as to save interest, that right must be reserved at the time the mortgage is given.

Taxes, Assessments, and Insurance Premiums. The mortgagor, who is the owner of the land regardless of the form of the mortgage, must continue to make all such payments as would be expected of an owner of land. The mortgagor must pay taxes and assessments. If this is not done, the mortgagee may pay them and compel a reimbursement from the mortgagor. If the mortgage contract requires the mortgagor to pay these charges, a failure to pay them becomes a default.

The law does not require the mortgagor to keep the property insured nor to insure it for the benefit of the mortgagee. This duty must be imposed on the mortgagor by contract. Both the mortgagor and the mortgagee have an insurable interest in the property to the extent of each one's interest or maximum loss.

Security of the Mortgagee. The mortgagor must do no act that will materially impair the security of the mortgagee. Cutting timber, tearing down buildings, and all acts that waste the assets impair the security and give the mortgagee the right to seek legal protection. Some state statutes provide that any one of these acts is equivalent to a default. This gives the mortgagee the right to foreclose. Other statutes provide only that the mortgagee may obtain an injunction in a court of equity enjoining any further impairment. Some states provide for the appointment of a receiver to prevent waste. Many state laws also make it a criminal offense to willfully impair the security of mortgaged property.

Rights of the Mortgagor

The mortgagor has four rights:

1. Possession of the property
2. Rents and profits
3. Cancellation of lien
4. Redemption

Possession of the Property. The mortgagor usually has the right to retain possession of the mortgaged property. Upon default the mortgagee usually may take possession to collect rents and profits. In some states possession cannot be taken, but the appointment of a receiver to collect rents and profits may be obtained.

Rents and Profits. The mortgagor is entitled to rents and profits. In the absence of an express agreement to the contrary, the mortgagor has the right to all rents and profits obtained from the mortgaged property. The mortgagor may retain the profits. This rule or any other rule may, of course, be superseded by a contract providing otherwise.

Cancellation of Lien. The mortgagor has the right to have the lien canceled on final payment. As soon as the mortgage is delivered to the mortgagee, it becomes a lien upon the mortgaged real estate. A mortgage lien is canceled by having the clerk in the recorder's office enter a notation, usually on the margin, certifying that the debt has been paid and that the lien is canceled. The mortgagee, not the mortgagor, must have this done. If this is not done, the mortgagor may institute court action to have this cloud removed from the title so that there may be a clear title.

Redemption. The mortgagor has the right to free the mortgaged property from the lien of the mortgage after default. This is the right of *redemption*. Statutes in many states prescribe a specific time after the foreclosure and sale when this right may be exercised. In order to redeem the property, the mortgagor must pay the amount of the mortgage and the costs of the sale.

Usually the right of redemption may be exercised only by a person whose interests will be affected by foreclosure. This includes the executor or administrator and heirs of the mortgagor, and frequently a second mortgagee.

Foreclosure

If the mortgagor fails to pay the debt secured by the mortgage when it becomes due, or fails to perform any of the other terms set forth in the mortgage, the mortgagee has the right to foreclose for the purpose of collecting the debt. *Foreclosure* usually consists of a sale of the mortgaged property made under an order of a court and generally by an officer of the court. The mortgagor must be properly notified of the foreclosure proceedings.

Foreclose literally means a legal proceeding to shut out all other claims. A first mortgage may not necessarily constitute a first claim on the proceeds of the sale. The cost of foreclosure and taxes always take precedence over the first mortgage. People who furnish materials for the construction of a house and workers who work on it have a claim under what is known as a *mechanics' lien* that takes precedence over a first mortgage. The foreclosure proceedings establish the existence of all prior claims and the order of their priority. Foreclosure proceedings are fixed by statutory law and therefore vary in different states.

If the proceeds of the sale of mortgaged property are greater than the amount of the debt and the expenses of foreclosure, the surplus must be given to the mortgagor. If a deficiency results, however, the mortgagee may secure a deficiency judgment for this amount. In that case the unpaid balance of the debt will stand as a claim against the mortgagor until the debt is paid.

Earnestine and Henry Henderson executed a deed of trust on their home to the Farmers Home Administration (FmHA) as security for a loan. They defaulted on the loan, so FmHA accelerated the debt and foreclosed on the property. When sued for eviction, the Hendersons alleged the notice of foreclosure FmHA sent them misrepresented the law regarding what they had to pay to avoid foreclosure. The law stated: "the debtor . . . may at any time before a sale . . . stop a threatened sale . . . by paying the amount actually past due . . . rather than the amount accelerated." The amount past due was $1,200. The notice from FmHA stated: "The indebtedness . . . consists of . . . $8,585.77 plus interest of $477.77. . . . You are hereby notified that unless said indebtedness is paid in full within 20 days . . . the United States . . . will take action to foreclose. Any negotiation by the United States . . . of any remittance tendered by you . . . will not constitute a waiver of this acceleration or institution of foreclosure action." This notice was faulty because it indicated that foreclosure could have been avoided only by payment of the entire amount owed. Notice is required to give debtors the opportunity to make the payments to avoid foreclosure. The incorrect notice negates the very reason for it.

Trust Deed

A trust deed is often used as a substitute for the ordinary form of mortgage for the purpose of securing a debt. A *trust deed* (sometimes called a *trust mortgage*) conveys the property to a disinterested third party, called a *trustee,* to be held in trust for the benefit of the creditor or creditors. If a default in payment occurs, the trustee must foreclose the property and apply the proceeds to the payment of the debt. The proceedings in the foreclosure of a trust deed are similar to those in the foreclosure of an ordinary mortgage. The right to redeem under a trust deed, when it exists, is similar to the right of redemption under a mortgage.

The trust deed may be employed when the mortgage debt is so large it is difficult or impossible to find one person or bank which is willing to lend so large a sum of money. By means of the trust deed the mortgage bond may be broken up into a large number of smaller bonds, generally $1,000 each, which are then purchased by individual investors.

In the event that the mortgagor defaults in the payments, the mortgagee who holds an ordinary mortgage can foreclose, that is, have the mortgaged property sold to satisfy the debt. In most states, however, the mortgagee must go into court and have a judicial foreclosure. In some states the trustee in a trust deed may sell the mortgaged property on the mortgagor's default outside of court without going through a time-consuming court foreclosure. Hence, the property can be more quickly sold at a trustee's sale.

Buying Mortgaged Property

It is a common practice to buy property on which there is a mortgage or a trust deed. The purchaser may agree to "assume the mortgage," that is, to be primarily liable for its payment. There is a difference between "assuming" the mortgage and buying the property "subject to the mortgage." In the first case the buyer agrees to be liable for the mortgage obligation as fully as the original mortgagor. If the property is taken "subject to the mortgage" and default occurs, the property may be lost, but no more. Observe how a knowledge of this point of law may be worth several thousand dollars:

♦   Ratcliffe sold Hurley a farm for $20,000, Hurley agreeing to pay $5,000 down and "assume a $15,000 mortgage." He held the farm a few years, during which time the value of farmland declined considerably. The mortgagee foreclosed on the mortgage and sold the farm for $9,000. This left an unpaid balance of $3,000 which Hurley was compelled to pay. Had he purchased the property "subject to the mortgage," he would not have had to pay the balance of $3,000.

The original mortgagor is not automatically released when mortgaged property is sold whether the purchaser assumed the mortgage or bought it subject to the mortgage. The mortgagor remains fully liable in both cases. A mortgagor may be released from the mortgage by novation. This occurs when the mortgagee extends the time of payment without the mortgagor's consent or when a written agreement to release the mortgagor is signed. Courts have held that the acceptance of an interest payment after the principal of the mortgage has become due constitutes an extension of the mortgage. If this is done without the mortgagor's consent, there is a full release from all liability under the mortgage.

Assignment of the Mortgage

The rights of the mortgagee under the mortgage agreement may be assigned. The assignee, that is, the purchaser, obtains no greater rights than the assignor had. To be protected, the assignee should require the assignor to produce an estoppel certificate signed by the mortgagor. This certificate should acknowledge that the mortgagor has no claims of any kind in connection with the mortgage. This would bar the mortgagor from subsequently claiming the right of offset.

The assignee of a mortgage should have this assignment recorded. In the event the mortgagee assigns the mortgage to more than one party, the one who records an assignment first has preference in case the proceeds are not adequate to pay both assignees.

Questions

1. **a.** Define a *mortgage*.

   b. Does the mortgagor lose possession of the mortgaged property at the time the mortgage is executed?

2. If two mortgages are executed on the same land, which mortgagee normally has priority?

3. What is an acceleration clause?

4. If there is a street assessment for $1,000 against mortgaged property, who must pay this, the mortgagor or the mortgagee?

5. What are the potential remedies if a mortgagor impairs the security of the mortgage?

6. When the mortgage is paid in full, how is this fact indicated in the record books in the county clerk's office?

7. How may the mortgagor redeem property after it has been sold under a foreclosure sale?

8. If the proceeds of a foreclosure sale of property are not enough to pay off the mortgage, how is the balance of the debt canceled?

9. What is the difference in the liability of the purchaser when mortgaged property is purchased "subject to the mortgage" and "assuming the mortgage"?

10. What are the rights of an assignee of a mortgage?

Case Problems

1. Johnson owned a farm which included ten acres of growing cotton. He borrowed $5,000 from Dupree and executed a real estate mortgage on his farm to secure the debt. The mortgage contained the usual clause that the mortgagor must not commit any act that would impair the mortgagee's security. It also provided that if the mortgagor sold any timber, pulpwood, or any other part of the real property, the net proceeds must be applied on the $5,000 note. Johnson later sold the cotton for $1,500 but spent the money for living expenses. Dupree brought suit to foreclose on the mortgage, claiming that Johnson had violated the contract. Was Dupree entitled to foreclose?

2. Jensen, who had some extra money to invest, agreed to lend Bowen on a first mortgage $15,000 with which Bowen was to build a house on a lot he owned. Jensen agreed to let Bowen have $3,000 to start and $3,000 a month as the construction progressed, the balance of the $15,000 to be loaned when the building was completed. About 30 days after the home was completed, Jensen and Bowen learned that the contractor had purchased on credit about $3,500 of materials for the house and had not paid for these materials out of the money Bowen paid him for building the house. In addition he owed $1,200 for labor that he had not paid. The materials supplier and the workers demanded that Bowen pay them. He had no money and could not pay. They threatened to sell the house unless Jensen paid them. Jensen contended his first mortgage took precedence over these items. Was this correct?

3. Turabo Shopping Center, Inc., owned and operated the Plaza del Carmen Shopping Center. In order to build it, Turabo had executed a mortgage to Chase Manhattan Bank. The mortgage provided that Chase was to be repaid by assignment of rent due Turabo from tenants of the Plaza. Chase instituted foreclosure proceedings and asked for the appointment of a receiver to manage the Plaza during the action. The value of the Plaza was probably not enough to cover the amount owed Chase, and three tenant companies run by the sister of Turabo's president paid no rent for a substantial time. Turabo allowed its lawyer to set up a restaurant without paying rent and withheld $100,000 in rent from Chase to defend the foreclosure action and get an appraisal to be used in that action. Should a receiver be appointed?

4. Billy and Yvonne Rogers owned 80 acres of land with a modest dwelling. There was a first mortgage on the property for $44,000. The entire property was worth about $60,000. Yvonne's father was retired. Billy and Yvonne deeded him and his wife two acres of land so that he could take what cash he had and build himself a modest house. Soon after the father-in-law completed his house, the country experienced a rather serious business recession. Real estate values declined about 25 percent. Billy lost his job and was unable to keep up his payments on the mortgage. The mortgagee foreclosed on the 78 acres and sold it at public auction. It brought only $35,000, leaving a balance on the mortgage of $7,000. The mortgagee threatened to sell the father-in-law's two acres and house if the father-in-law did not pay the $7,000. Was Billy and Yvonne's mortgage also a lien on the father-in-law's property?

5. The Henry S. Miller Company executed deeds of trust to Harold and Ruth Wood and Warren and Ruth Ann Wood to secure payment of notes. There was default, so the Woods foreclosed and bought the property at foreclosure. Later they paid ad valorem taxes assessed during the term of the mortgage and sued Miller for reimbursement. The deeds of trust stated: "the undersigned shall have no personal liability for the payment of the note secured hereby, and in the event of default, the holder of said note shall have the mortgaged property alone as security for payment of said note." The deeds of trust also stated: "if the undersigned shall fail . . . to pay such taxes, . . . said

taxes may be paid by the legal holder of said note, and sums so expended shall . . . become part of the debt hereby secured." Was Miller liable for reimbursement of the taxes?

6. On July 21, Steven Construction, Inc., executed a deed of real estate to Donald Kaplan. It was recorded on July 29. By deed dated July 24, Kaplan and his wife conveyed the property to Litwin Realty, a partnership. In the warranty clause this deed stated: "and except for unpaid balance of a certain mortgage to Government Savings & Loan Co. which the grantee assumes and agrees to pay." It was recorded the following February 10. A note and mortgage to Government by Kaplan and his wife in which they asserted they were the true and lawful owners were not executed until July 29 and were recorded on July 30. There was default on the note. Government sued the Kaplans and Litwin and the individual partners, on the basis of the assumption agreement in the deed, for payment and foreclosure of the mortgage. Was the assumption agreement binding on Litwin or the partners?

7. North purchased a home and agreed to pay $48,000 for it. She paid $10,000 down and assumed a $38,000 mortgage, which was to be paid off at the rate of $300 a month. The company for which North worked moved away, and North therefore lost her job. As a result she was unable to keep up the payments on the mortgage. The property was foreclosed and sold. The purchaser paid $30,000. This left an unpaid balance of $5,000. Was North liable for the payment of this $5,000?

8. Rankell had a ten-year mortgage on his home, to be paid at the rate of $175 a month. He was discharged from his job and defaulted on two monthly payments before he obtained another job. The mortgagee foreclosed immediately upon the first default. What were Rankell's rights?

9. American Bankers Life Assurance Company of Florida held a first mortgage on real property. Development International Corporation of Florida held a second mortgage. American Bankers then secured a third mortgage in reliance on a subordination agreement from Development yielding priority of its second mortgage to a "new mortgage." Prior to the subordination agreement, Development had made, and there was recorded, a collateral assignment of its mortgage to Security Mortgage Investors. Security later executed a general release to Development and assigned the second mortgage to Williams, Salomon, Kanner & Damian. There was default, and foreclosure proceedings resulted. American Bankers alleged its "new mortgage" had priority over Williams's second mortgage. Did it?

10. Poe was the mortgagor and Corkrell the mortgagee to the extent of $2,500 upon certain real estate. Poe, before the mortgage was paid, sold the mortgaged property to a corporation, and the corporation in turn conveyed the property to Burke, who assumed the mortgage. When Burke defaulted on the mortgage, Corkrell brought suit to foreclose and also to secure a deficiency judgment against both Poe and Burke. Was Burke liable for the deficiency?

48
Landlord and Tenant

Preview Cases

William H. Waldrop leased property from Erwin Siebert under a written lease for two years. The lease stated: "Lessor grants to Lessee the option to renew at the end of term for an additional term of Three (3) years, and year to year thereafter." The option for the additional three years was exercised. Prior to the expiration of that period, Waldrop notified Siebert he intended to renew the lease for a year and enclosed a check for the annual rent. Siebert returned the check and gave notice to quit. When sued for possession, Waldrop alleged the lease contained an option to renew from year to year forever. What was the effect of the option?

Watson rented an apartment on the first floor of a three-story apartment building. The occupants on the second floor over Watson's apartment loved music and dancing. Every night they and some friends danced until after midnight. The noise from the dancing was loud and continuous. Watson demanded that the landlord evict the tenants, but the landlord refused. Watson moved seven months before his lease expired. The landlord sued for the balance of the rent. Can the landlord recover?

The relation of landlord and tenant is created by a contract whereby one person agrees to lease land or a building to another. No special words or acts are necessary to create such an agreement unless the lease is for more than a year, in which case it must be in writing. The tenant's temporary possession of the premises and payment of rent for its use are the chief characteristics that determine the relation of landlord and tenant. The landlord is entitled to retake possession of the property at the end of the lease period.

The owner of the property is known as the *landlord* or *lessor*. The person who is given possession of the property is the *tenant* or *lessee*. The contract between the two parties is called a *lease* (see Illustration 48-1).

House Lease

THIS INDENTURE, *made the*   19th   *day of*   April   , 19 --

BETWEEN   Richard T. Mowbray   , *Lessor (whether one or more);*
Cincinnati, Ohio

AND   Edward J. and Doris R. Caldwell   , *Lessee (whether one or more);*
Cincinnati, Ohio

WITNESSETH: *That for and in consideration of the payments of the rents, and the performance of the covenants contained herein, on the part of the said Lessee, and in the manner hereinafter specified, said Lessor does hereby lease, demise and let, unto the said Lessee, that certain*   single-family   *dwelling house and its appurtenances situated at*   2668 Russel Road, Cincinnati, Ohio 45250

for the term of one (1) year   , *commencing on the*

1st   *day of*   May   , *19* -- , *and ending on the*

30th   *day of*   April   , *19* -- , *at the total rent or*

sum of   Six thousand ($6,000)   *Dollars,*

payable   monthly   *in advance on the*   1st   *day of each and every*

calendar month of said term in equal   monthly   *payments of*

Five hundred ($500)   *Dollars,*

AND *the said Lessee does hereby promise and agree to pay to the said Lessor the said rent, herein reserved in the manner herein specified.*
AND *not to let or sublet the whole or any part of said premises, nor to assign this lease, and not to make or suffer any alteration to be made therein without the written consent of the said Lessor. And it is further agreed, that the said Lessor shall not be called upon to make any improvements or repairs whatsoever upon the said premises, or any part thereof, but the said Lessee agrees to keep the same in good order and condition at* their own *expense.*

AND *it is agreed, that if any rent shall be due and unpaid or if default shall be made in any of the covenants herein contained, then it shall be lawful for the said Lessor to re-enter the said premises and to move all persons therefrom.*

AND THAT *at the expiration of the said term or any sooner determination of this lease the said Lessee will quit and surrender the premises hereby demised, in as good order and condition as reasonable use and wear thereof will permit, damage by the elements excepted. And if the Lessee shall hold over the said term with the consent, expressed or implied, of the Lessor, such holding shall be construed to be a tenancy only from month to month, and said Lessee will pay the rent as above stated for such term as* they *hold the same.*
Lessee *agrees to pay the water rate during the continuance of this lease.*

IN WITNESS WHEREOF: *the said parties have hereunto set their hands and seals the day and year first above written.*

Richard T. Mowbray   (Seal)

Edward J. Caldwell   (Seal)

Doris R. Caldwell   (Seal)

ILLUS. 48-1. A Lease

The amount the landlord is to receive for the use of the property is the *rent*.

A tenant is distinguished from a lodger or roomer in that the former has the exclusive legal possession of the property, while the latter has merely the right to use the premises subject to the control and supervision of the owner.

The Lease

The lease may be oral or written, express or implied, formal or simple, subject, however, to the general statutory requirements that a lease of land for a term longer than one year must be in writing. If a dispute arises between the tenant and the landlord over their rights and duties, the court will look to the terms of the lease and the general body of landlord and tenant law to determine the decision.

In order to avoid disputes, a lease should be in writing and should cover all terms of the contract. Such items as a clear identification of the property, the time and place of payment of rent, the notice required to vacate, the duration or the nature of the tenancy, and any specific provision desired by either party, such as the right of the landlord to show the property to prospective purchasers or agreement requiring the landlord to redecorate, should be included.

Types of Tenancies

There are four separate and distinct classes of tenancies, each having some rule of law governing it that does not apply to any other type of tenancy. The four classes of tenancies are:

1. Tenancy for years
2. Tenancy from year to year
3. Tenancy at will
4. Tenancy by sufferance

Tenancy for Years. A *tenancy for years* is any tenancy for a definite period of time, whether it be one month, one year, or 99 years. The termination date is fixed by the lease. The payment of the rent may be by the month even when the tenancy is for a specified number of years. Some states hold that no notice to terminate the tenancy is required when the termination date is fixed by the lease. Other states fix by statute the number of days' notice which must be given. The modern lease typically provides that it will continue to run on a year-to-year basis after the termination date, unless notice is given by the tenant to the landlord not less than a specified number of days before the termination date that the tenant intends to leave on that date.

William H. Waldrop leased property from Erwin Siebert under a written lease for two years. The lease stated: "Lessor grants to Lessee the option to renew at the end of term for an additional term of Three (3) years, and year to year thereafter."

The option for the additional three years was exercised. Prior to the expiration of that period, Waldrop notified Siebert he intended to renew the lease for a year and enclosed a check for the annual rent. Siebert returned the check and gave notice to quit. When sued for possession, Waldrop alleged the lease contained an option to renew from year to year forever. The court held that the option transformed the tenancy from a tenancy for years to a tenancy from year to year which was terminable by either party after proper notice.

Tenancy from Year to Year. When the tenancy is for an indefinite period of time with rent set at a yearly amount, it is known as a *tenancy from year to year*. Under such a tenancy, a tenant merely pays the rent periodically, and the lease lasts until proper notice of termination has been given. A tenancy of this kind may also be by the month or any other perod agreed upon. If by the month, it is called a tenancy from month to month. The length of the tenancy is usually determined by the nature of the rent stated or paid although there could be a tenancy from year to year with the rent paid quarterly or monthly.

Notice to terminate this type of tenancy must follow exactly the state law governing it. In a tenancy from month to month, notice is usually required thirty days before the rent due date.

Tenancy at Will. A *tenancy at will* exists when the tenant has possession of the property for an uncertain period. Either the tenant or the landlord can terminate the tenancy at will, since they are both required to agree to the tenancy. Of all the types of tenancies, this is the only one that is automatically terminated upon the death of the tenant or the landlord

Tenancy at Sufferance. When a tenant holds over the tenancy after the expiration of the lease without permission of the landlord, a *tenancy at sufferance* exists until the landlord elects to treat the tenant as a trespasser or as a tenant. The landlord may treat the tenant as a trespasser, sue for damages, and have the tenant removed by legal proceedings; or, if the landlord prefers, payment of the rent due for another period may be accepted and thus the tenant's possession may be recognized as rightful.

Rights of the Tenant

A lease gives the tenant certain rights, as follows:

1. Right to possession
2. Right to use the premises
3. Right to assign or sublease

Right to Possession. By signing the lease, the landlord warrants the right to lease the premises and that the tenant shall have possession during the period of the lease. During the term of the lease, tenants have the same right to exclusive possession of the premises as if they owned the property. If someone questions the owner's right to lease the property, the landlord must defend the tenant's right to exclusive possession. Failure of the landlord to give possession on time or to protect the tenant's rights subjects the landlord to liability for damages.

A particular cause of dispute between landlord and tenant is the existence of a nuisance that disturbs the tenant's quiet enjoyment of the property. Failure to remove dead rats from the wall, failure to stop disorderly conduct on the part of other tenants, and frequent and unnecessary entrances upon the property by the landlord or agents are examples of acts which the courts have held destroy the tenant's right to quiet enjoyment and constitute a breach of warranty on the part of the landlord.

If the nusiance existed at the time the tenant leased the property and the tenant was aware of its existence, the right to complain will be deemed to have been waived. Also, if the nuisance is one over which the landlord has no control, the tenant cannot avoid the contract even though the nuisance arose subsequent to the signing of the lease. If the landlord fails or refuses to abate a nuisance over which the landlord has control, the tenant not only may terminate the lease but may sue for damages. In other cases the tenant may seek an injunction compelling the landlord to abate a nuisance.

Watson rented an apartment on the first floor of a three-story apartment building. The occupants on the second floor over Watson's apartment loved music and dancing. Every night they and some friends danced until after midnight. The noise from the dancing was loud and continuous. Watson demanded that the landlord evict the tenants, but the landlord refused. Watson moved seven months before his lease expired. The court held he was not liable for the rent since the dancing and music were a nuisance. The court found Watson was justified in terminating the lease.

Right to Use the Premises. Unless this right is expressly restricted in the lease, the tenant has the right to use the premises in any way consistent with the nature of the property. A dwelling cannot be converted into a machine shop, nor can a clothing store be converted into a restaurant. Damage to leased property other than that which results from ordinary wear and tear is not permissible. In the case of farming land, the tenant may cut wood for personal use but not to sell.

Right to Assign or Sublease. If the tenant assigns the entire lease to another party who agrees to comply with its terms, including the payment of the rent to the landlord, this is an *assignment*. In *subleasing*, the tenant usually collects the rent from the subtenant and pays the landlord; in assignment, the rent is paid by the assignee directly to the landlord. Assignment must include the entire premises, although one may sublease to another person only a part of the property and retain the rest. Ordinarily the assigning or subleasing of the premises is prohibited in a written lease unless the lessor's written consent thereto is first obtained. Residential leases commonly restrict the use of the premises to the tenant and the immediate family or to a certain number of persons. Unless the lease expressly prohibits both assignment and subleasing, either may be done. If only subleasing is prohibited, then the lease may be assigned.

Closely related to subleasing is joint occupancy. A provision in the lease prohibiting subleasing does not forbid a contract for a joint occupancy. In joint occupancy the tenant does not give up exclusive control of any part of the premises. Another party is merely permitted to jointly occupy all or a part of the premises.

Duties of the Tenant

Duties of the tenant are:

1. To pay rent
2. To protect and preserve the premises

To Pay Rent. The tenant's main duty is to pay the rent. This payment must be made in money unless the contract provides otherwise, such as a share of the crops. The rent is not due until the end of the term, but leases almost universally provide for rent in advance.

It is a common practice for the landlord to appoint an agent for the purpose of collecting the rent. The death of the principal automatically terminates the principal-agent relationship. If rent is paid to the agent after this termination and the agent does not remit to the proper party, the rent must be paid again.

If the rent is not paid on time, the landlord may terminate the lease and order the tenant to vacate, or the landlord may permit the tenant to continue occupancy and sue for the rent. Under the common law the landlord could seize and hold any personal property found on the premises. This right has been either curtailed or abolished by statute.

To Protect and Preserve the Premises. The tenant must make all repairs necessary to prevent damage to or deterioration of the premises. There is no requirement to make repairs of a structural nature, however.

Rights of the Landlord

The landlord has three definite rights under the lease:

1. To regain possession
2. To enter upon the property to preserve it
3. To assign rights

To Regain Possession. Upon termination of the lease, the landlord has the right to regain peaceable possession of the premises. If this possession is refused, the most common remedy is to bring an *action of ejectment* in a court of law. Upon the successful completion of this suit the sheriff will forcibly remove the tenant and any property.

When the landlord repossesses the property, all permanent improvements and fixtures may be retained. The test is whether or not the improvements have become a part of the real estate. If they have, they cannot be removed.

To Enter upon the Property to Preserve It. The landlord has a right to enter upon the property to preserve it. Extensive renovations that interfere with the tenant's peaceable occupancy cannot be made. If the roof blows off or becomes leaky, the landlord may repair it or put on a new roof. This occasion cannot be used to add another story. A landlord who enters the property without permission may be treated as a stranger. There is no right to enter the premises to show the property to prospective purchasers or tenants unless this right is reserved in the lease.

To Assign Rights. The landlord has the right to assign the rights under the lease to a third party. The tenant cannot avoid any duties and obligations by reason of the assignment of the lease. Like all other assignments, the assignment does not release the assignor from the contract without the consent of the tenant. If, for example, the tenant was injured because of a concealed but defective water main cover, and the landlord knew of this condition, the landlord would be liable even though rights under the lease were assigned before the injury.

Duties of the Landlord

The lease imposes certain duties upon the landlord:

1. To pay taxes and assessments
2. To protect the tenant from concealed defects

To Pay Taxes and Assessments. Although the tenant occupies and uses the premises, the landlord must pay all taxes and special assessments. Sometimes the lease provides that the tenant shall pay the taxes. In such event, there is no liability for special assessments for sidewalks, street paving, and other improvements.

To Protect the Tenant from Concealed Defects. The landlord is liable to the tenant if the tenant is injured by concealed defects which were known or should have been reasonably known to the landlord at the time of giving the tenant possession of the premises. Such defects might be contamination from contagious germs, unfilled wells that are concealed, and rotten timbers in the dwelling. The tenant bears the risk of injury caused by defects which are apparent or reasonably discoverable upon inspection at the time that the tenant enters into possession. Most cities and many states have tenement laws that require the landlord to keep all rental property habitable and provided with adequate fire escapes. Any damage due to a failure to observe these laws may subject the landlord to liability for damages.

Termination of the Lease

A lease that is to exist for a fixed time automatically terminates upon the expiration of that period. The death of either party does not ordinarily affect the lease. If the leased property consists of rooms or apartments in a building and they are destroyed by fire or any other accidental cause, the lease is terminated without liability on the part of the tenant. In the case of leases of entire buildings, serious problems arise if the property is destroyed by fire, tornado, or other causes. Under the common law the tenant had to continue to pay rent even though the property was destroyed. Some states retain this rule while other states have modified it. A landlord who has a ten-year lease on a $100,000 building which is destroyed by fire one year after the lease is signed would not be inclined to rebuild if there is full fire insurance coverage. The landlord would find it more profitable to invest the $100,000 and continue to collect the rent. To prevent this, statutes may provide that if the landlord refuses to restore the property, the lease is canceled. The lease itself may contain a cancellation clause. If it does not, the tenant can carry fire insurance for the amount of possible loss. Even when the lease will thus terminate, the tenant will probably wish to carry fire insurance for personal property and, if the premises are used for a business purpose, may carry insurance to indemnify for business interruption or loss of business income.

The landlord may agree to the voluntary surrender of the possession of the premises before the lease expires. An abandonment of the premises without the consent of the landlord is not a surrender, however, but a breach of contract.

If the lease is to run from year to year or from month to month, the party wishing to terminate it must generally give the other party a written notice of this intention (see the examples in Illustrations 48-2 and 48-3). Statutes prescribe the time and the manner of giving notice; they may also specify other particulars, such as the grounds for a termination of the tenancy.

If either party fails to give proper notice, the other party may continue the tenancy for another period.

A tenant refusing to surrender possession of the property after the expi-

NOTICE TO LEAVE THE PREMISES

To Mr. C. Harold Whitmore

You will please take notice that I *want you to leave the premises you now occupy, and which*
you have rented of me *, situated and described as follows:*

Suite 4

Lakeview Apartment

Lake Shore Drive at Overview Street

in Cleveland *, County of* Cuyahoga *and State of* Ohio

Your compliance with this Notice by July 31

will prevent legal measures being taken by me *to obtain possession of the same, agreeably to law.*

Yours respectfully,

H. L. Simpson

May 1   19--

ILLUS. 48-2. A Landlord's Notice To Leave the Premises

To   Mr. George A. Hardwick

1719 Glenview Road, St. Louis, Missouri

Take notice that I shall on the 31st *day of* March *, 19--,*

quit the possession and remove from the premises located at

1292 Clarendon Road, St. Louis, Missouri

which I now hold as your tenant. This 2nd *day of* January *, 19--.*

John N. Richter

ILLUS. 48-3. A Tenant's Notice that the Tenant is Leaving the Premises

ration of the lease may be liable in a summary action brought by the landlord to regain possession. This is called a *forcible entry and detainer action*. In this matter the statutes of the different states have provided for the
quick recovery of real property by the one legally entitled to it.

Improvements

Tenants frequently make improvements during the life of the lease.
Many disputes arise as to the tenant's right to take these improvements af-

ter the lease is terminated. The test is whether an improvement has become a fixture, which must be left on the land, or whether it remains personal property. If a farm tenant builds a fence in the normal way, the fence is a fixture, and there is no right to remove it when the tenant leaves. A poultry house built in the usual way is a fixture and cannot be removed. In a similar case the tenant built the poultry house on sled-like runners. When ready to leave, the tenant hitched a team to the poultry house and took it away. The court held the shed had not become a fixture but remained personal property.

One may freely contract away rights or may waive them. In one case a tenant built a permanent frame house on leased property with the landlord's agreement that the house could be removed at the end of the lease. The landlord was bound by this contract.

Georg had leased an apartment for a year. After one month of occupancy he installed wall-to-wall carpeting. Upon termination of the lease Georg left the premises and desired to take the carpet with him. Since the carpeting is a fixture, it belongs to the landlord, and Georg cannot remove it.

Easements and Licenses

An *easement* is an interest in land, such as a right-of-way across another's land or the use of another's driveway. An easement is not a tenancy because there is no exclusive right of possession, as distinguished from the right of intermittent use. It is classified as an interest in land. It is created by deed or by adverse use for a period of time similar to that required for the acquisition of title by adverse possession.

A *license* is a right to do certain acts on the land but not a right to stay in possession of the land. A license does not create a leasehold interest and normally is terminated at will.

Questions

1. Must a lease be in writing?

2. What is a tenancy for a definite period of time called?

3. What rights does the tenant have when property is leased?

4. Explain the difference between subleasing and assigning.

5. Name three rights that a landlord has.

6. May a tenant refuse to let the landlord enter upon the premises during the period of the lease?

7. a. If a hurricane breaks all the windows in a dwelling, must the tenant replace these windows?

  b. If leased property is destroyed by fire, must the tenant continue to pay rent?

8. By what action may a landlord quickly recover the possession of property from a tenant who refuses to leave at the expiration of a lease?

9. If a tenant builds a garage on the property, may the garage be taken when the tenant moves? Explain.

10. What is an *easement*?

Case Problems

1. A storm blew the roof off a farmhouse. At her own expense the tenant immediately put on a new roof. The lease contract was silent about repairs. The tenant refused to pay any more rent until the rent equaled the cost of the roof. The landlord brought suit to evict the tenant for nonpayment of rent. Who was entitled to win the suit?

2. Ellis leased a house from Hunt. About one month after moving in, Ellis fell through the wooden floor of a back porch and was seriously injured. The floor was badly infested with termites, but this fact could not be detected by a casual inspection. Ellis sued Hunt for damages. Is she entitled to them?

3. Lawrence Frazier leased 26,000 acres of grazing land from Phillip Kern. The lease stated: "The Leasee shall not assign this lease or enter into any sublease without first obtaining the written consent of the Lessor." Frazier made an arrangement with Ronnie Bloxham to graze Bloxham's cattle at a fee of $7 per head. Frazier would control the range and movement of the cattle, supply salt and hay, repair fences and gates, and generally supervise the cattle. Bloxham was to supply hay if the winter was really bad, haul the cattle in and out, and take care of problem cattle. When Kern learned of this agreement, he sent a notice to declare a forfeiture, alleging Frazier had subleased or assigned the lease without written consent. Was the agreement a breach of the lease?

4. West leased a building for ten years to be used for a clothing store. The rent was $1,000 a month. There was no cancellation clause in the lease, and the state law followed the common law. Due to the rapid growth of the city, five years later similar property would rent for $1,500 a month. The building was damaged by fire so badly it could not be used until restored. (a) Must the landlord restore the property? (b) Must the tenant restore the property? (c) Could West protect himself for the monthly rent by carrying a fire insurance policy? (d) If there had been a clause providing for cancellation of the lease upon destruction of the premises, what would your answer to (c) be? (e) Under (d) would the landlord be inclined to cancel the lease? (f) If the landlord does cancel the lease, does West have an insurable interest to protect himself against having to pay $1,500 a month for the restored building?

5. By the terms of two agreements called leases, United Coin was to install, maintain, and service coin-operated laundry equipment in two apartment complexes. The agreements described the premises as "laundry space provided by OWNER . . . located in an area measuring approximately 10 feet by 10 feet in the 'Laundry area(s)' in the . . . building(s)." The owner of the complexes was to keep the laundry rooms clean and safely maintained. The complexes were sold to Craig Gibson, who removed United's equipment and installed some other. United sued Gibson, alleging breach of the "lease." Were the agreements leases?

6. State Warehouse Co., Inc., sued Standard Brands Incorporated for damages for failure to deliver possession of leased property at the commencement of the lease term. Standard alleged that the abatement of rent clause (which said that the tenant would not be required to pay rent if the premises were not fit for use) and the clause which granted State the right to cancel the lease under specified circumstances relieved Standard of its obligation to deliver possession. Did they?

49

Wills and Inheritances

Preview Cases

By the terms of her will, Eloise Williams devised her 103-acre "home place" to her nephews and nieces. The residue of the estate was bequeathed to the Masonic Home or Homes for Crippled Children. Three months before her death, Williams sold the "home place" and received an $80,000 note secured by a deed of trust. What effect does the sale of the property have on the devises?

A man gave his wife a $50,000 home which he had bought with money he had inherited from his parents. Shortly afterward, his wife died without leaving a will, survived only by her husband and her brother. How is the deceased's property to be distributed?

Title to all property, both real and personal, may be transferred by a will. A *will* is an instrument, prepared in the form prescribed by law, which provides for the disposition of a person's property to take effect after death.

The person making the will is called a *testator* (*testatrix* if a woman). Testators do not have to meet as high a standard of capacity to make a will as is required in order to make a contract. They must have the mental capacity at the time of making the will to know the natural objects of their bounty, understand the nature and extent of their property, understand that they are making a will, and have the ability to dispose of their property by means of a plan they have formulated. Even if they do not have the mental capacity to carry on a business or if unusual provisions in the will are made, this does not necessarily mean that they do not have capacity to make a will. A person who is insane lacks sufficient capacity; however, an insane person who has intervals of sanity has capacity during sane intervals to make a will. Any person, other than a minor, of sound mind ordinarily is competent to make a will. In a few states minors can, under limited circumstances, make a will.

Limitations on Disposition of Property

The right to dispose of property by will is a highly prized right and few restrictions are placed upon it. These restrictions are:

1. A spouse may elect to take that share of the property that would have been received had the deceased died without leaving a will, or the share provided by statute, if the spouse's will does not leave as large a share. This is called the right to take against the will.

Most state laws now provide that when an individual dies without leaving a will, a spouse is entitled to a set portion of all the property the deceased spouse owned at the time of death. The spouse's portion varies depending on the number of children or other heirs who survive. The surviving spouse in some states may also claim an interest in property conveyed by the deceased spouse during the marriage without the consent of the surviving spouse.

The right to take against the will can be barred by actions of the surviving spouse. If the surviving spouse is guilty of conduct which would have justified the deceased spouse in securing a divorce, the surviving spouse generally cannot elect to take against the will.

Except for the cases of a surviving spouse electing to take against the will and in some cases of a subsequent marriage, birth, or adoption, the testator may exclude or disinherit any person from receiving any portion of the estate. If the testator gives his entire estate to someone else, all persons who would inherit in the absence of a will are excluded. The testator does not even have to mention in a will those persons who are disinherited with the exception of children, nor does a nominal sum have to be left to those who are disinherited.

2. One cannot control by will the distribution of property in perpetuity or for all time. The common-law rule against perpetuities requires that an interest in property must vest, if at all, within 21 years after the death of persons living on the date the owner of the property creates the interest. When the interest is created by will, the date of creation is the date of death of the owner.

Terms Common to Wills

If the gift is real estate, the one receiving the gift (the beneficiary) is called the *devisee*; if it is personal property, the beneficiary is a *legatee*. A *devise* is real property given by will. A *bequest*, or a *legacy*, is a gift by will of personal property. The person named in a will as the one to administer the estate is an *executor*. One who dies without having made a will is said to die *intestate*. A person appointed by a court to settle the affairs of an intestate is an *administrator* (man) or an *administratrix* (woman).

Distinguishing Characteristics of a Will

A will has the following outstanding characteristics that distinguish it from many other legal instruments:

1. A will is construed by the courts with less technical strictness than a deed or any other kind of written document.

2. A will devising real property must be executed in conformity with the law of the state in which the property is situated. A will bequeathing personal property is governed by the law of the state in which the testator was domiciled at the time of death.

3. A will may be revoked at any time during the life of the testator.

Formalities

All states prescribe formalities for wills. These formalities must be strictly adhered to. A will is almost always required to be in writing and signed by the testator.

If a will is written in the testator's own handwriting and is dated, it need not be witnessed in a number of states. In many states the will must be witnessed by at least two, and in some states three, disinterested witnesses regardless of how it is written. The usual requirement is for the witnesses and the testator to sign in the presence of each other. Many states also require the testator to inform the witnesses that the instrument being signed is the testator's will. This is called *publication*.

When subscribing witnesses are required, they will be required at the time that the will is offered for probate to identify their signatures and the signature of the testator and to state that they were present when the signature was made. In states which do not require subscribing witnesses for a will, it is generally required that two persons identify the signature of the testator on the will, basing their opinion that it is the testator's signature upon their experience through prior correspondence or business records involving the testator's signature. A will executed in another jurisdiction is valid if correctly executed in the other jurisdiction. If a person's will is not drawn according to the legal requirements, the court may disregard it and the property may be disposed of in a manner entirely foreign to the testator's wishes.

Special Types of Wills

There are at least three special types of wills to meet special circumstances. First, there are *holographic wills*, which are written entirely in longhand by the testator. In some states there is no distinction between holographic and other wills. In other states variations of the general law of wills are established for holographic wills. In still other states holographic wills may not be recognized. Second, there are *nuncupative wills*, which are oral wills declared by the testator in the presence of witnesses. Usually such a will can only be made during the testator's last illness and only applies to personal property, and sometimes only a limited value of personal property may be so disposed. The witnesses frequently must reduce the will to writing within a specified number of days. Third, most states make special provision for soldiers and sailors. They are allowed to make oral or written wills of personal property without complying with the formalities required of other wills. These wills are in force even after the testator returns to civilian life. They must be revoked in the same manner as other wills.

The Wording of a Will

Any words that convey the intention of the testator are sufficient (see example in Illustration 49-1). No matter how rough and ungrammatical the language may be, if the intention of the testator can be ascertained, the court will order that the provisions of the will be carried out. Since the court will order the terms of a will to be carried out exactly, the wording of the will should express the exact wishes of the testator.

A well-to-do man, who had provided for his children previously, inserted into his will this provision: "To my brother, Kirby, I leave $8,000." By the time the testator died, his estate had shrunk from $80,000 to $10,000. He had intended to leave his brother one tenth of his estate; but because of the wording used in the will, his brother received almost the entire estate after the expenses were paid. The testator should have written, "To my brother, Kirby, I leave one tenth of my estate, which sum in no event is to exceed $8,000."

Revocation

A will may be revoked at any time prior to the death of the testator. The revocation may take any one of several forms.

Destruction or Alteration. If the testator deliberately destroys a will, this constitutes a revocation. If the testator merely alters the will, this may or may not revoke it, depending upon the nature and the extent of the alteration. If merely part of the will is obliterated, this in most states does not revoke the will.

Marriage and Divorce. If a single person makes a will and later marries, the marriage may revoke the will in whole or part, or the will may

WILL OF FRANK JOSEPH ROSE

I, Frank Joseph Rose, of the City of Chicago and State of Illinois, revoke all prior wills and codicils and declare that this is my will.

FIRST: If she survives me, I give to my beloved daughter, Anna Rose, now residing in Crestwood, Illinois, that certain piece of real estate, with all improvements thereon, situated at 341 Hudson Avenue, Crestwood, Illinois. If my daughter predeceases me, I give this real estate to my brother, James Earl Rose, now residing in Crestwood, Illinois.

SECOND: All the remainder and residue of my property I give to my beloved wife, Mary Ellen Rose, if she survives me. If my wife predeceases me, I give the remainder and residue of my property to my daughter, Anna. If both my wife and my daughter predecease me, I give the remainder and residue of my property to my brother, James.

THIRD: I hereby nominate and appoint my wife, Mary Ellen Rose, executrix of this will. If my wife is unable or unwilling to act as executrix, I nominate and appoint my daughter, Anna, executrix. I direct that neither Mary Ellen nor Anna be required to give bond or security for the performance of duties as executrix.

IN WITNESS WHEREOF, I have subscribed my name this tenth day of October, in the year nineteen hundred eighty-five.

Frank Joseph Rose
Frank Joseph Rose

We, the undersigned, certify that the foregoing instrument was, on the tenth day of October, signed and declared by Frank Joseph Rose to be his will, in the presence of us who, in his presence and in the presence of each other, have, at his request, hereunto signed our names as witnesses of the execution thereof, this tenth day of October, 1985.

Constance O. Moore residing at 4316 Cottage Grove Avenue
Chicago, Illinois 60600

Sarah J. King residing at 1313 East 63 Street
Chicago, Illinois 60600

Stewart S. Samuels residing at 2611 Elm Street
Joliet, Illinois 60400

ILLUS. 49-1. A Will

492

be presumed to be revoked unless it was made in contemplation of the marriage or made provision for a future spouse. In some states a marriage will not revoke a will completely, but only so that the spouse will get the estate that would have been received in the absence of a will. A divorce automatically revokes a will to the extent of the property left to the divorced spouse if there is a property settlement; otherwise, a divorce usually in no way affects the will.

Execution of a Later Will. The execution of a later will automatically revokes a prior will if the terms of the second will are inconsistent with the first will. If the second will merely changes a few provisions in the first will and leaves the bulk of it intact, then a second revokes the first will only to the extent of such inconsistency.

After-Born Child. A child may be born or adopted after the will is made. If the original will does not provide for subsequent children or no codicil is added to provide for the child, then this will revoke or partially revoke the will.

Abatement and Ademption

If a testator leaves $20,000 to his son John, $10,000 to his sister Mary, and a painting to his brother Adam, it is possible there will be both an abatement and an ademption in the will. When the will is probated, there may not be enough money after all debts are paid to comply with the terms of the will. If there is only $15,000 in cash left, then the cash gifts to John and Mary will *abate*. This means each will receive a proportionate share, in this case fifty percent, or $10,000 and $5,000 respectively. If the painting was sold, stolen, or destroyed before the death of the testator, then Adam would get nothing. The gift to him is *adeemed* since the property is not in existence at the time of the testator's death. He is not entitled to its cash value or any other substitute item of property.

By the terms of her will, Eloise Williams devised her 103-acre "home place" to her nephews and nieces. The residue of the estate was bequeathed to the Masonic Home or Homes for Crippled Children. Three months before her death, Williams sold the "home place" and received an $80,000 note secured by a deed of trust. The court held that the devise of the "home place" was adeemed by the sale, and the $80,000 note passed under the residuary clause of the will.

Probate of a Will

When a testator dies leaving a will, the will must be probated. Probate is a very simple process if there is no contest of the will. If the will does not name an executor, then upon petition of one of the beneficiaries the court will appoint an administrator.

If the will is contested, the court must hear the contest to determine if the will is valid. A contest of the will is to be distinguished from litigation over the meaning or interpretation to be given the will. If the contest alleges and proves fraud, undue influence, improper witnessing, mental incapacity of the testator, revocation of the will, or any other infirmity in the will affecting its legality, the will is nullified and the property of the testator distributed according to the law of descent described later in this chapter.

When Administration is Unnecessary

Of course, if an individual does not own any property at the time of death, there is no need for administration. Also, if all property is jointly owned with someone else who acquired the interest by right of survivorship, there is no need for administration.

Some states have special statutes allowing the administration procedures to be shortened when only a very small estate is involved. It is also possible in many states to have a *settlement agreement* by which the estate is divided without formal court proceedings if all the persons interested in the estate, relatives and creditors, can agree on the share each one is to receive.

Codicil

A *codicil* is a separate writing that modifies a will. Except for the part modified, the original will remains the same. A codicil must be executed with all the formalities of the original will.

Title by Descent

When a person dies intestate, the property is distributed in accordance with the state law of descent. Every state has such a law. Although these laws vary slightly, on the whole they provide as follows: The property of the intestate goes to any children subject to the rights of the surviving spouse. If there are no surviving children or grandchildren, the father and mother, as the next of kin, receive the property. If they are not living, the brothers and sisters become the next of kin; they are followed by grandparents, aunts and uncles, and so on. Some statutes permit any person related by blood to inherit when no nearer related relative exists. Other statutes do not permit those beyond first cousins to inherit. In any case, if there is not a proper person to inherit, the property passes to the state.

A man gave his wife a $50,000 home which he had bought with money he had inherited from his parents. Shortly afterward, his wife died without leaving a will, survived only by the husband and her brother. Under the state law, the brother was entitled to receive half of the house as his share of the wife's estate.

Title to real estate is passed by the administrator conveying by means of an administrator's deed. When approved by the court the grantee obtains good title to the property.

Per Capita and Per Stirpes Distribution

The lineal descendants of a decedent are the children and grandchildren. If all the children were living at the time of an intestate's death, and the spouse was dead, the property would be distributed *per capita*, meaning per head, or equally. If one child predeceased the intestate and left three surviving children, then the property would be divided into equal parts on the basis of the number of children the intestate had, and the dead child's part would then be divided into three equal parts with one of these parts going to each of the grandchildren. When this is done, the property is said to be divided *per stirpes*. If the deceased child left no children or other lineal descendants, then the surviving children of the intestate would take the deceased child's share.

Executors and Administrators

For the most part the duties and responsibilities of executors and administrators are similar, but there are two significant differences. (1) With but few exceptions anyone may be appointed an executor, but in the appointment of an administrator, there is, in some states, a clear order of priority. The surviving spouse has first priority, followed by children, grandchildren, parents, and brothers or sisters. (2) The executor may be excused by the testator from furnishing a bond, but an administrator must in all cases execute a bond guaranteeing the faithful performance of the duties.

The prime duty of executors and administrators is to preserve the estate and distribute it to the rightful parties. Any loss due to negligence, bad faith, or breach of trust subjects them to liability. They are required to act in good faith, with prudence, and within the powers conferred on them by will or by law. If any part of the estate is a going business, with only a few exceptions the business must be liquidated. A will may expressly provide that the executor continue the business; frequently the executor or administrator will obtain leave of court to continue the business for either a limited time or an indefinite time, depending largely upon the wishes of those entitled to receive the estate. Third parties dealing with executors and administrators are charged with knowledge of limitations upon their authority.

Questions

1. What is a *will*?

2. What restrictions are there upon one's right to leave property by will to anyone desired?

3. **a.** Do all states require all wills to be witnessed?

   b. How many witnesses are required to validate a will when witnesses are required?

4. What is publication?

5. What is a holographic will?

6. Does a second will automatically revoke a first will?

7. What is the difference between ademption and abatement?

8. Must a codicil be witnessed in the same way as a will?

9. What is the difference between distributing property per capita and per stirpes?

10. What is the major duty of executors and administrators?

Case Problems

1. Kirkland, sales manager for the Langford Furniture Company, received an order for furniture amounting to $10,285 from the John Quarles Furniture Mart. The order was signed by John Knowles, executor for John Quarles. Kirkland shipped the merchandise promptly. When the account was long past due, it was found that Quarles's will had never authorized Knowles to continue the business. The heirs of Quarles demanded that the bill not be paid. Kirkland sued both the estate and John Knowles, executor. There were no bondsmen. Knowles was insolvent. Could Kirkland look to the estate for his debt?

2. Tom Middlebrooks, twenty-nine and unmarried, made a will and left all his property, both personal and real, to his church since he had not planned to get married. Later he married Cynthia, but he failed to revoke his will. Over a period of twenty years he accumulated a considerable estate. After his death, the church pastor found the will and presented it to the court for probate since Tom had left his wife and children ample property by gift for their needs. Will the court order the property to be transferred to the church?

3. Lillian Burke did not sign her will on the line provided for her signature. She signed on one of the lines designed to be used by a witness at the end of the attestation clause following the line for her signature. After she signed her

name was typed into the attestation clause and the word "Testatrix" was typed above her signature. The will was contested. Was the will signed at the end by the testatrix?

4. Henry's mother died, leaving an estate of $200,000. Henry was named as the executor in the will. When the fire insurance policies on two houses belonging to the estate expired, Henry failed to have them renewed. Several months later one of the houses was totally destroyed by fire. The beneficiaries of the estate demanded that this loss be borne by Henry. Are they correct in their demand?

5. William Lamb executed a will witnessed by Grier Shotwell and Hilda Johnson. After Lamb's death there was a will contest. Johnson, the only living witness, testified either Lamb or Shotwell, his attorney, in Lamb's presence, referred to the document as Lamb's will. Lamb then signed the document. Was this sufficient publication?

6. Alice C. Little executed a will in conformity with the laws of the state in which she lived by having three witnesses. She then moved to another state and died. Her only heir was an infant daughter. The state in which she lived at the time of her death required only two witnesses. A petition for the probate of her will was made and proofs of will executed by two witnesses were filed with the court. The state in which she executed her will permitted probate upon the testimony of only one witness where there was no objection and where there was written consent of the heirs. Should the will be admitted to probate?

7. To write out her will Frances Black used three copies of a stationer's form designed to be used for a one-page will. In the clause at the top of each page she filled in her signature and residence. She also filled in the name and gender of her executor and used the appropriate blanks on the last page to give her city and state of residence and the date. She dated the top of the first page. The rest of the printed language was either stricken or ignored by her. She used almost all the remaining area on all three pages for a specific disposition of her estate. No other person's handwriting appeared on the three pages. The court denied probate of the will because Black "incorporated" portions of the form in her will so it was not entirely in her own handwriting. Should the will be admitted to probate?

50

Bankruptcy

Preview Cases

Veronica Scales filed a petition under Chapter 13 of the Bankruptcy Code. By the plan, she was to make weekly payments of $47.50 to the trustee for payment of claims. The form on which the plan was filed had blank spaces on which the amount of dividends to be paid secured and unsecured creditors was to be inserted but was not. At the confirmation hearing, Scales's lawyer advised that all secured and unsecured claims were to be fully paid over three years. Each claim in each of the two classes of creditors was to be treated alike. Peoples Financial Corporation, a secured creditor, alleged that the plan was so deficient that it was not a plan. Was the plan proposed sufficient to qualify as a Chapter 13 plan?

Baker, who filed a voluntary petition of bankruptcy, concealed the fact that she owned a substantial number of rare coins of high value. After a discharge in bankruptcy was granted, could one of Baker's prior creditors enforce his claim on the ground that Baker was not discharged because of her fraudulent concealment?

Bankruptcy is a judicial declaration as to a person's (the debtor's) financial condition. The federal bankruptcy law has two very definite purposes: to give the debtor a new start and to give creditors an equal chance in the collection of their claims

If an honest debtor is hopelessly insolvent, there may be a temptation to cease trying even to earn a living. Hope is a great stimulant to enterprise and honest endeavor. If hope vanishes, effort may diminish or even vanish. By permitting an insolvent debtor to give up all assets with a few minor exceptions and thereby get forgiveness of the debts, at least a new start can be made with the hope of success. The court prescribes an equitable settlement under the circumstances; and when these conditions are fully met, the debtor may resume full control of any business.

If one is insolvent, it is unfair to permit some unsecured creditors to get paid in full while others receive nothing. By appointing a trustee to take over the debtor's property and pay each creditor in proportion to a claim, a more equitable settlement is achieved. Not only is this arrangement more equitable, but it is also less wasteful and less expensive than for each creditor to sue the debtor in separate suits.

Who Can File A Petition for Bankruptcy

Today any person who lives in, has a residence, place of business, or property in the United States can be a debtor under the Bankruptcy Code except banks, insurance companies, savings and loan associations, and some municipalities. Rehabilitation proceedings may be instituted against all of these exempted institutions except municipalities, but the proceedings may not be had under the Bankruptcy Code. There are several Chapters under the Code and only specified persons may be debtors under the particular Chapters. Chapter 7, providing for liquidation, applies to any person; Chapter 9 applies to municipalities; Chapter 11, providing for reorganization, applies to any person; and Chapter 13 applies to individuals with regular income.

Kinds of Debtors

There are two kinds of debtors:

1. Voluntary
2. Involuntary

Voluntary Debtors. Anyone, except the institutions listed previously, may file a voluntary petition with the bankruptcy court under one of the four chapters of the Code. A husband and wife may file a petition for a joint case.

Involuntary Debtors. Under certain conditions one may be forced into involuntary bankruptcy. Generally if there are twelve or more creditors, three must join the petition. If there are fewer than twelve creditors, one may sign. The creditors who sign must have aggregate claims amounting to $5,000 in excess of any collateral held as security. Involuntary petitions may not be filed under chapters 9 or 13 or against farmers and charitable corporations.

A court will enter an order for relief when an involuntary bankruptcy petition is filed when either of the following two criteria are met:

1. The debtor is not paying debts as they become due, or

2. A custodian of the debtor's assets was established within 120 days preceding the filing of the involuntary petition.

The procedure in liquidating the estate is the same whether it is a voluntary bankruptcy proceeding or an involuntary one. The filing of a petition automatically stays the filing or continuation of proceedings against the debtor that could have been begun or were to recover a claim against the debtor that arose before the bankruptcy petition.

Procedure in a Bankruptcy Case

After the court issues an order for relief, the first step is to notify creditors and call a meeting of them. These creditors elect a trustee to take over all the assets of the debtor. The trustee steps into the shoes of the debtor and collects all debts due the debtor, preserves all physical assets, sues all delinquent creditors of the estate, and finally distributes all money realized according to a definite priority which will be discussed later in this chapter.

Exempt Property

The federal bankruptcy law lists property which will not be used to pay debts. In addition each state has laws exempting certain property from seizure for the payment of debts. The debtor is given a choice between federal or state exemptions unless state law specifies state exemptions must be used. The most common types of property that are excluded are a limited interest in a residence and vehicle, household effects, tools of the trade, such as a carpenter's tools, a dentist's equipment, and similar items within reasonable limits. The debtor may also exclude unmatured life insurance contracts owned other than credit life insurance.

Most states specifically exempt all necessary wearing apparel for the debtor and members of the family, such items as the family Bible, and all pictures of the members of the family even though some of these may be portraits of some value. Many of the federal exemptions set a limit on the value of items which may be excluded.

Included Property

Some property acquired by the debtor after the bankruptcy proceedings have been instituted is included in the debtor's estate and may be used for the payment of creditors. This is property acquired by inheritance, divorce, or as a beneficiary of life insurance within 180 days after the date of filing.

Also, if the debtor transfers property, normally within 90 days preceding the filing of the bankruptcy petition, to one creditor with the intent to prefer one creditor over another, the transfer may be set aside and the property included in the debtor's estate.

Business Reorganization

Bankruptcy proceedings under Chapter 7 result in the liquidation and distribution of the assets of an enterprise. Under Chapter 11 the national Bankruptcy Code provides a special rehabilitation system for businesses so that they may be reorganized rather than liquidated.

Reorganization proceedings may be voluntary or involuntary. Normally the debtor will be allowed to continue to run the business; however, a disinterested trustee may be appointed to run the business if there is mismanagement or in the interest of creditors. The debtor running its business is given the first right, for 120 days, to propose a rehabilitation plan indicating how much and how creditors will be paid. The court will confirm a plan if it is fair, equitable, feasible, has been proposed and accepted in good faith, and all the payments made or proposed are found to be reasonable. If no acceptable plan of reorganization can be worked out, the business may have to be liquidated under Chapter 7.

Chapter 13 Plans

If the debtor is an individual, a Chapter 13 plan may be worked out. This attempts to achieve the same advantages the business reorganization act gives to businesses. Any individual with a regular income, except a stock or commodity broker, who has unsecured debts of less than $100,000 and secured debts of less than $350,000 may file a petition under Chapter 13. This chapter is completely voluntary. Under the common law one unwilling creditor could prevent a composition among creditors of an insolvent debtor. Under the present law a majority of creditors can impose a settlement upon the dissenting minority. The debtor is as fully released from debts as under Chapter 7 of the Code. The purpose of these arrangements is to prevent the hardship of an immediate liquidation of all of the debtor's assets and to give the debtor the opportunity to develop a plan for the full or partial payment of debts over an extended period. This plan benefits the creditors because they are likely, in the long run, to receive a greater percentage of the money owed them. The plan may not pay unsecured creditors less than the amount they would receive under a Chapter 7 liquidation.

◆ Veronica Scales filed a petition under Chapter 13 of the Bankruptcy Code. By the plan, she was to make weekly payments of $47.50 to the trustee for payment of claims. The form on which the plan was filed had blank spaces on which the amount of dividends to be paid secured and unsecured creditors was to be inserted but was not. At the confirmation hearing, Scales's lawyer advised that all secured and unsecured claims were to be fully paid over three years. Each claim in each of the two classes of creditors was to be treated alike. Peoples Financial Corporation, a secured creditor, alleged that the plan was so deficient that it was not a plan. The court stated that it would have been better if the plan had listed the secured and unsecured creditors, indicated how much of their claims were to be paid, and stated the duration of the plan, but since these items were revealed at the first meeting of creditors, these defects in the plan were cured. The plan proposed was sufficient to qualify as a Chapter 13 plan.

Duties of the Debtor

The debtor must cooperate fully with the trustee. When requested, creditors meetings must be attended and all relevant evidence about debts due must be furnished. The debtor must file with the trustee a schedule of all assets and all liabilities. This schedule must be in sufficient detail so that the trustee can list the secured creditors, the partially secured creditors, and the unsecured creditors. Failure of the debtor to cooperate with the trustee and to obey all orders of the referee not only may prevent discharge from bankruptcy but may also subject the debtor to criminal prosecution for contempt of court.

Proof of Claims

All unsecured creditors in Chapter 7 cases must present proof of their claims to the trustee. Claims must generally be filed within 90 days after the date for the first meeting of creditors.

Reclamations

Frequently at the time debts are discharged, the debtor has property owned by others. This property takes the form of consigned or bailed goods, or property held as security for a loan. The true owner of the property is not technically a creditor of the bankrupt. The owner should file a reclamation claim for the specific property so that it may be returned.

A person in possession of a check drawn by the debtor may or may not be able to get it paid depending on the circumstances. If the check is an uncertified check, the holder is a mere creditor of the debtor and is not entitled to have it cashed. This is so because a check is not an assignment of the money on deposit, and the creditor merely holds the unpaid claim which the check was intended to discharge. If the check has been certified, the creditor has the obligation of the drawee bank on the check, which may be asserted in preference to proceeding upon the claim against the drawer of the check.

Priority of Claims

Claims of a bankrupt may be classified as fully secured claims, partially secured claims, and unsecured claims.

Fully secured creditors may have their claims satisfied in full from the proceeds of the assets which were used for security. If these assets sell for more than enough to satisfy the secured debts, the remainder of the proceeds must be surrendered to the trustee in bankruptcy of the debtor.

Partially secured creditors are those with a lien on some assets but not enough to satisfy the debts in full. The proceeds of the security held by a partially secured creditor are used to pay that claim; and, to the extent any portion of a debt remains unpaid, the creditor is entitled to claim as an unsecured creditor for the balance.

The claim with the highest priority is that for the administrative expenses of the bankruptcy proceedings (filing fees paid by creditors in involuntary proceedings, expenses of creditors in recovering property transferred or concealed by the debtor, and reasonable expenses of creditors in resisting a refused or set-aside composition). Additional priority claims include debts incurred after the filing of an involuntary petition and before an order of relief or appointment of a trustee, wage claims not exceeding $2,000 for any one wage earner, provided the wages were earned not more than three months prior to bankruptcy proceedings, fringe benefits for employees, claims by individuals who have deposited money with the debtor for undelivered personal, family, or household goods, and tax claims.

Debts Not Discharged

Certain obligations cannot be avoided by bankruptcy. The most important of these claims are:

1. Claims for alimony and child support
2. All taxes incurred within three years
3. Debts owed by reasons of embezzlement
4. Debts due on a judgment for intentional injury to others, such as a judgment obtained for assault and battery
5. Wages earned within three months of the bankruptcy proceedings
6. Debts incurred by means of fraud
7. Educational loans

There are some other circumstances under which certain debts are not discharged by bankruptcy, but the list above includes the most common ones.

Discharge of Indebtedness

If the debtor cooperates fully with the court and the trustee in bankruptcy and meets all other requirements for discharge of indebtedness, the discharge will be granted. The discharge voids any liability of the debtor on discharged debts and prevents any actions for collection of such debts.

◆ Baker, who filed a voluntary petition of bankruptcy, concealed the fact that she owned a substantial number of rare coins of high value. After a discharge in bankruptcy was granted, one of Baker's prior creditors sought to enforce his claim on the ground that Baker was not discharged because of her fraudulent concealment. The creditor prevailed.

Questions

1. State two purposes of the law of bankruptcy.

2. Who may file a petition under the Bankruptcy Code?

3. What is the difference between a voluntary and an involuntary filing under the Bankruptcy Code?

4. What are the two bases for entering an order of relief on an involuntary bankruptcy petition?

5. John, a debtor, had a portrait of his wife done by an artist of some note. At the time of the petition in bankruptcy, the portrait had a sale value of $500. Can he keep the portrait?

6. What procedure may be followed rather than liquidating a business which cannot pay its debts as they are due?

7. What are the duties of a debtor in bankruptcy proceedings?

8. What claim is given the highest priority in bankruptcy proceedings?

Case Problems

1. Henderson held a check drawn by Sellers for $700. She held this check two weeks before presenting it to the bank for payment. When she did present it, she was told that Sellers had his debts discharged in bankruptcy two days before, and for that reason the check could not be paid, although Sellers had ample funds in the bank to pay it. Henderson contended that by the check Sellers had assigned $700 to her before he had his debts discharged and therefore this $700 did not belong to Sellers. Was this contention correct?

2. Thomas and Joyce White filed a petition under Chapter 11 of the Bankruptcy Code. Midland Bank & Trust Company, which had two claims, objected to the plan as not being proposed in good faith. Under the plan, Midland's first claim was to be secured by the accounts receivable of Thomas's surveying business and was to be paid in monthly installments with 12 percent interest until paid in full. The second claim of $88,200, to be secured by a security

interest in an 87-acre farm, was to be paid over a ten-year term, and any funds from subdividing the land were to reduce the debt. There was testimony that in order to subdivide, a dirt road would have to be improved and water mains installed at a small cost. On the basis of the value of new projects in the surveying business, work in progress, accounts receivable, and general economic conditions, the business was projected to make enough money to provide the payments required on Midland's first claim. Was the plan proposed in good faith?

3. The three Hill brothers were laborers for Mayberry, a debtor. Mayberry owed each of them $300 earned in the last two months. Mayberry's assets amounted to only $7,000 after all costs of the bankruptcy proceedings were paid. His debts amounted to $11,000. How much were the Hill brothers able to collect?

4. O'Hara was in extreme financial difficulties and realized she could not avoid eventual bankruptcy. She accumulated $50,000 in cash by selling much of her property at a large discount. She then purchased a ten-year endowment insurance policy on herself and made her husband the beneficiary. She reserved the right to change the beneficiary. She paid for the policy with a single premium payment of $50,000. The creditors contended the cash value belonged to them, since the policy was purchased while insolvent and for the purpose of defrauding the creditors. Could the trustee demand that the cash surrender value of this policy be included in the debtor's assets?

5. When Charles Pettis filed an involuntary petition under Chapter 7 regarding International Teldata Corporation, the debt owed Pettis represented 52 percent of ITC's total debts. Another 30 percent was owed to insiders—officers of ITC. One officer testified that he and the other insider had voluntarily agreed to delay payment because ITC was unable to make payments on these debts. Pettis had obtained a judgment against ITC, but attempts at execution were unsuccessful. ITC argued it was paying all its debts when due except those owed Pettis and the insiders. Was ITC paying its debts as they became due?

6. Davis borrowed $5,000 from Harrell and deposited with him 125 shares of U.S. Steel common stock as collateral security. Before Davis paid the debt, Harrell's debts were discharged in bankruptcy. Should Davis file a reclamation or a proof of claim? Why?

7. Charles and Shirley Cunningham were the debtors in a proceeding under the Bankruptcy Code. They petitioned the bankruptcy court to grant them a divorce because, they alleged, the filing of a divorce petition against a debtor in a state court would violate the automatic stay of judicial proceedings against debtors provided in the Bankruptcy Code. Is a divorce proceeding stayed by filing under the Bankruptcy Code?

8. The Family Court entered an order directing Samuel Homyak to pay his wife, Linda, support. Later Samuel filed a divorce action, and Norman Essner was

Linda's attorney. The court which heard that action awarded Essner $900 for his fee. A month later, Homyak filed a petition under Chapter 7 of the Bankruptcy Code. After he was discharged, Essner filed a complaint to have his $900 claim declared nondischargeable because it was in the nature of alimony. Should this be a nondischargeable debt?

9. An involuntary bankruptcy petition was filed against Dr. McAlpin. Her offices were equipped with the most modern X-ray machines and other equipment, valued at $90,000. The state law stipulated that the tools of one's trade could not be attached by creditors, but the law was not specific as to what constituted tools of trade. Dr. McAlpin contended that none of her equipment need be turned over to the trustee in bankruptcy. The creditors contended that all but the bare minimum needed for general practice of medicine should be turned over. How much of this equipment could Dr. McAlpin keep?

Summary Cases for Part Ten

Property

1. Jacobson by oral contract sold some standing timber to Sorenson. Sorenson started immediately to cut and haul the timber. Since there was no time limit set on when the timber was to be removed, two years later much timber remained to be cut. Jacobson then served written notice on Sorenson that he had only ten days more to complete the contract. When the ten days expired, there were about 70,000 board feet of logs on the ground that had not been removed. Jacobson refused to let him haul these away even though Sorenson was willing to pay for them. The question was raised to what extent an oral contract for the sale of an interest in land can be enforced. Was this oral contract enforceable? [*Sorensen et al. v. Jacobson*, 232 P.2d 332 (Mont.)]

2. The Wade family owned the west half of Section 5, Township 7 North, Range 11 East in Newton County. Robert Grissom owned the east half of said section. Grissom claimed the west half by adverse possession and hired Jake Smith, Harvey Cleveland, and Bobby Gregory to cut timber from part of the west half. The timber was cut and delivered to Bay Springs Forest Products, Inc. The Wades sued Bay Springs to recover the value of the timber. Having determined that Grissom did not own the west half by adverse possession, the court had to consider the type of property the timber was. What was it? [*Bay Springs Forest Products, Inc. v. Wade*, 435 So. 2d 690 (Miss.)]

3. Cecil Carruth sent a letter to Paul McDaniel in which he agreed to deed McDaniel some land for $260,000. He stated that the deed would be delivered to McDaniel upon payment of the $30,000 down payment. Carruth later told McDaniel he was not going to sell him the land, and McDaniel filed suit for specific performance or conversion of his real estate. Carruth admitted he had told his lawyer to prepare a deed but denied signing it and instructing his lawyer to hold the deed until McDaniel paid the $30,000. McDaniel alleged a deed was executed and delivered for his benefit to the attorney and was either wrongfully taken or still in the possession of the attorney. Did the facts establish that McDaniel had title to the land? [*McDaniel v. Carruth*, 637 S.W.2d 498 (Tex.)]

4. Moretti, a pedestrian, received a very painful injury from an electric fan blade projecting from the outside of the wall of the building. The building was occupied by a tenant who installed the fan. The lease was on a month-to-month basis so that the landlord could have re-entered the premises for the purpose of removing the fan by giving the tenant 30 days' notice to vacate. He did not do this, nor did he order the tenant to remove the fan. Moretti

sued the landlord for damages for his injury. Is the landlord liable in this case for the injury to Moretti? [*Moretti v. C. S. Realty Co.*, 82 A. 2d 608 (R.I.)]

5. Arthur H. Kelley executed a deed to his home to his son. The deed was complete in every detail. When Kelly handed it to his son, he said, "Here is the deed to the home property. . . . The only request I want to make is that you do not record the deed until after my death." The father made many statements after this to the effect he had not given his son the property except on the condition that he die from a serious operation he was to undergo. The son's acts corroborated these statements by his failure to assume possession of the property, pay tax on it, or in any way assert ownership during his father's lifetime. Since a deed cannot serve as a will, this deed was not effective unless there was a delivery for the purpose of passing title. Was there a valid delivery? [*Kelley v. Bank of America, National Trust and Savings Association*, 246 P.2d 92 (Colo.)]

6. James and Wanda Hegland owned a condominium in Strawberry Commons Condominium Complex which they sold to Marilyn Fearing on a contract for deed. The Heglands left the property management to Fearing. She rented it to Gary Beavens. Strawberry was operated by an owners' association which assessed monthly dues. The dues for the Hegland–Fearing condominium became delinquent. The Declaration of Apartment Ownership contained a power of sale for assessment liens. The association filed a lien, and a notice of lien foreclosure was served on Beavens. Beavens told Fearing, but Hegland was not notified. The association bought the condominium at foreclosure for $1,200. The fair market value was $50,000. The association petitioned for a new certificate of title. The Heglands and Fearing argued the sale was invalid for inadequacy of price. Was it? [*Petition of Strawberry Commons Apartment*, 356 N.W.2d 401 (Minn.)]

7. B-L-S Construction Company, Inc., orally agreed to lease property to St. Stephen Knitwear, Inc., for four months at $4,500 a month. The parties had planned to sign a written lease but did not. St. Stephen paid one month's rent and then abandoned the property. B-L-S sued for the rent remaining under the oral lease. Was there a valid lease? [*B-L-S Construction Company, Inc. v. St. Stephen Knitwear, Inc.*, 281 S.E.2d 129 (S.C.)]

8. Robert Daly died, and his will was offered for probate. The first witness, Ronald Witkowski, stated he was employed by Daly and was called into Daly's office and asked to sign a document. Witkowski did not know what he was signing and was not told it was Daly's will. Daly did not sign it in his presence. The second witness, Leo Hodge, was also employed by Daly and asked to witness a document. Hodge insisted on knowing what he was signing, so Daly showed him the front which indicated it was Daly's will. Hodge was not sure whether Daly's signature was on the will or not. Daly's widow and three children, who were left very little by the will, filed objections to its

probate alleging it was not properly executed. Was it? [*Matter of Will of Daly*, 402 N.Y.S.2d 747 (N.Y.)]

9. On August 13, Dennis and Diane Rose borrowed $1,034.10 from Huntington National Bank. In order to obtain this unsecured loan the Roses omitted $2,900 in unsecured loans from the loan application. A month later, having made no payments on the loan, the Roses filed a petition under Chapter 13 of the Bankruptcy Code. Their plan called for them to pay the $220 difference between their monthly income and expenses to the trustee for three years and pay only 10 percent to unsecured creditors. Huntington objected to the plan on the ground of bad faith. Should Huntington recover only 10 percent? [*Matter of Rose*, 40 B.R. 178, (Bankr. S.D. Ohio)]

Glossary of Legal Terms

(Other legal terms are defined elsewhere in the text. Refer to the Index for them.)

A

Abandon: give up or leave employment; reliquish possession of personal property with intent to disclaim title.

Abrogate: recall or repeal; abolish.

Absolute liability: liability for an act that causes harm even though the doer was not at fault.

Abstract of title: history of the transfers of title to a given piece of land, briefly stating the parties to and the effect of all deeds, wills, and judicial proceedings relating to the land.

Acceleration clause: provision in a contract or any legal instrument that upon a certain event the time for the performance of specified obligations shall be advanced.

Acceptance: an accepted draft; the assent by the person on whom a draft is drawn to pay it when due.

Acceptor: one who assents to an order or a draft.

Accession: acquisition of title to property by virtue of the fact that it has been attached to property already owned.

Accessory after the fact: one who after the commission of a felony knowingly assists the felon.

Accessory before the fact: one who is absent at the commission of the crime but who aided and abetted its commission.

Accident: an event that occurs even though a reasonable person would not have foreseen its occurrence, because of which the law holds no one legally responsible for the harm caused.

Accommodation party: a person who signs a negotiable instrument as a favor to another.

Accord and satisfaction: an agreement made and executed in satisfaction of the rights one has acquired under a former contract.

Accretion: acquisition of title to additional land when the owner's land is built up by gradual deposits made by the natural action of water.

Acknowledgment: the admission of the execution of a writing made before a competent officer; the formal certificate made by an officer.

Acquittal: the action of a jury in a finding of not guilty.

Action: proceeding at law.

Act of God: an act of nature that is not reasonably foreseeable.

Adjudication: a judicial determination.

Administrative agency: a governmental commission or board given authority to regulate particular matters.

Administrator–administratrix: the person (man–woman) appointed by a court to take charge of the estate of a deceased person.

Adult: one who has reached full legal age.

Adverse possession: the hostile possession of real estate, which when actual, visible, notorious, exclusive, and continued for the required number of years, will place title to the land in the person in possession.

Affidavit: a voluntary sworn statement in writing.

Affirm: to declare to tell the truth under a penalty of perjury; to confirm.

Affirmative covenant: an express undertaking or promise in a contract or deed to do an act.

Agency: the relationship that exists between a person identified as a principal and another by virtue of which the latter may make contracts with third persons on behalf of the principal.

Agency coupled with an interest in the authority: an agency in which the agent has given a consideration or has paid for the right to exercise the authority.

Agency coupled with an interest in the subject matter: an agency in which for a consideration the agent is given an interest in the property with which the agent is dealing.

Agency shop: a union contract provision requiring that nonunion employees pay to the union the equivalent of union dues in order to retain their employment.

Agent: one who is authorized by the principal to make contracts with third persons on behalf of the principal.

Alien: a citizen of one country residing in another.

Alienate: to transfer voluntarily the title to real property.

Alimony: an allowance made to the dependent spouse living apart from the supporting spouse.

Allegation: a statement to be proved in a legal proceeding.

Alteration: any material change of the terms of a writing fraudulently made by a party thereto.

Ambiguity: doubtfulness; the state of having two or more possible meanings.

Annexation: attachment of personal property to realty in such a way as to make it become real property and part of the realty.

Annuity: a contract by which the insured pays a lump sum to the insurer and later receives fixed annual payments.

Annulment: the act of making void.

Answer: a written statement of the defendant's claim, as to the facts in a suit in equity; response.

Antedate: a date prior to the true one; an earlier date.

Anti-injunction acts: statutes prohibiting the use of injunctions in labor disputes except under exceptional circumstances; notably the Federal Norris-LaGuardia Act of 1932.

Appeal: taking the case to a reviewing court to determine whether the judgment of the lower court was correct.

Appellate jurisdiction: the power of a court to hear and decide a given class of cases on appeal from another court or administrative agency.

Arbitration: the settlement of disputed questions, whether of law or fact, by one or more arbitrators by whose decision the parties agree to be bound. Increasingly used as a procedure for labor dispute settlement.

Arraign: to accuse; to impeach; to read the charge of an indictment.

Assault: to attempt or threaten to do harm to another while having the apparent present ability to do so.

Assent: to consent; to concur.

Assets: property available for the payment of debts.

Assign: to transfer property or a right to another.

Assignee: one to whom property has been assigned.

Assignment: transfer of a right. Used in connection with personal property rights, as rights under a contract, a negotiable instrument, an insurance policy, or a mortgage.

Assumption of risk: the common-law rule

that an employee could not sue the employer for injuries caused by the ordinary risks of employment on the theory that the employee had assumed such risks by undertaking the work. Abolished in those areas governed by workers' compensation laws and most employers' liability statutes.

Attachment: the legal process by which property is seized in process of a debt settlement.

Attest: to bear witness.

Attorney: one legally appointed to act for another.

Attractive nuisance doctrine: a rule imposing liability on a landowner for injuries sustained by small children playing on the land when the landowner permits a condition to exist or maintains equipment that the landowner should realize would attract small children who could not realize the danger. The rule does not apply if an unreasonable burden would be imposed on the landowner in taking steps to protect the children.

Avoid: to make void; to annul.

Award: the decision of arbitrators.

B

Bad check laws: laws making it a crime to issue a bad check with intent to defraud.

Baggage: articles of necessity or personal convenience usually carried for personal use by passengers of common carriers.

Bail: security given for the appearance of a person in court.

Bailee's lien: a specific, possessory lien of the bailee on the goods for work done to them. Commonly extended by statute to any bailee's claim for compensation and eliminating the necessity of retention of possession.

Bailment: the relation that exists when personal property is delivered into the possession of another under an agreement, express or implied, that the identical property will be returned or will be disposed of in accordance with the agreement.

Bankruptcy: a procedure by which one unable to pay debts may have all assets in excess of an exemption claim surrendered to the court for administration and distribution to creditors. The debtor is then given a discharge that releases the debtor from the unpaid balance due on most debts.

Battery: the unlawful touching of another.

Bearer: the person in physical possession of a negotiable instrument payable to bearer.

Beneficiary: the person to whom the proceeds of a life insurance policy are payable, a person for whose benefit property is held in trust, or a person who is given property by a will.

Bequest: a gift of personal property by will.

Bilateral contract: a contract executory on both sides.

Bill of exchange (draft): an unconditional order in writing by one person upon another, signed by the person giving it, and ordering the person to whom it is directed to pay or deliver on demand or at a definite time a sum certain in money to order or to bearer.

Bill of lading: a document issued by a carrier showing the receipt of goods and the terms of the contract of transportation.

Bill of sale: a writing signed by the seller showing that the seller has sold to the buyer the personal property described.

Binder: a memorandum delivered to the insured stating the essential terms of a policy to be executed in the future, when it is agreed that the contract of insurance is to be effective before the written policy is executed.

Blank indorsement: an indorsement that does not state to whom the instrument is to be paid.

Blue-sky laws: statutes designed to protect the public from the sale of worthless stocks and bonds.

Boardinghouse keeper: one regularly engaged in the business of offering living accommodations to permanent lodgers or boarders as distinguished from transient guests.

Bona fide: in good faith; without deceit or fraud; genuine.

Bond: an obligation or promise in writing and sealed, generally of corporations, personal representatives, trustees; fidelity bonds.

Boycott: a combination of two or more persons to cause harm to another by refraining from patronizing or dealing with such other person in any way or inducing others to so refrain; commonly an incident of labor disputes.

Breach: in contracts, the violation of an agreement or obligation.

Brief: written or printed arguments or authorities furnished by a lawyer to a court.

Bulk sales acts: statutes to protect creditors of a bulk seller by preventing that seller from obtaining cash for the goods and then leaving the state. Notice must be given creditors, and the bulk sale buyer is liable to the seller's creditors if the statute is not satisfied. Expanded to "bulk transfers" under the UCC.

Burglary: the unlawful entering of a building with the intent to commit a felony.

Business trust: a form of business organization in which the owners of the property to be devoted to the business transfer the title of the property to trustees with full power to operate the business.

C

Cancellation: a crossing out of a part of an instrument or a destruction of all legal effect of the instrument, whether by act of party, upon breach by the other party, or pursuant to agreement or decree of court.

Capital: net assets of a corporation.

Capital stock: the declared money value of the outstanding stock of the corporation.

Case: an occurrence upon which an action in court is based.

Cash surrender value: the sum that will be paid the insured upon surrender of a policy to the insurer.

Cause of action: the right to damages or other judicial relief when a legally protected right of the plaintiff is violated by an unlawful act of the defendant.

Caveat emptor: let the buyer beware.

Cease and desist: an order to stop a practice, usually issued by a court or governmental agency.

Certificate of protest: a written statement by a notary public setting forth the fact that the holder had presented the commercial paper to the primary party and that the latter had failed to make payment.

Charter: the grant of authority from a government to exist as a corporation.

Chattel: any article of personal property.

Chattel mortgage: a security device by which the owner of personal property transfers the title to a creditor as security for the debt owed by the owner to the creditor.

Check: an order by a depositor on the bank to pay a sum of money to a payee; also defined as a bill of exchange drawn on a bank and payable on demand.

Circumstantial evidence: relates to circumstances surrounding the facts in dispute from which the trier of fact may deduce what had happened.

Civil action: in many states a simplified form of action combining all or many of the former common-law actions.

Civil court: a court with jurisdiction to hear and determine controversies relating to private rights and duties.

Client: one who employs a lawyer for legal matters.

Closed shop: a place of employment in which only union members may be employed. Now generally prohibited by statutes.

Code: a compilation of laws by public authority.

Collateral note: a note accompanied by collateral security.

Collateral security: a thing of value which

may be used to satisfy an obligation which is past due and unpaid.

Collective bargaining: the process by which the terms of employment are agreed upon through negotiations between the employer or employers within a given industry or industrial area and the union or the bargaining representative of the employees.

Collective bargaining unit: a group of employees who are by statute authorized to select a bargaining representative to represent all the employees within that unit in bargaining collectively with the employer.

Collusion: a secret agreement between two or more persons, designed to obtain an object forbidden by law or to defraud another.

Commission merchant: a bailee to whom goods are consigned for sale.

Common carrier: a carrier that holds out its facilities to serve the general public for compensation without discrimination.

Common law: the body of unwritten principles originally based on the usages and customs of the community which were recognized and enforced by the courts.

Common stock: stock that has no right or priority over any other stock of the corporation as to dividends or distribution of assets upon dissolution.

Community property: the cotenancy held by husband and wife in property acquired during their marriage under the law of some of the states, principally in the southwestern United States.

Competency: legal power, adequacy, or ability.

Complaint: the initial pleading filed by the plaintiff in many actions which in many states may be served as original process to acquire jurisdiction over the defendant.

Composition of creditors: an agreement among creditors that each shall accept a part payment as full payment in consideration of the other creditors doing the same.

Compromise: a settlement reached by mutual concessions.

Concealment: a withholding of information which one has a duty to reveal.

Conditional sale: a credit transaction by which the buyer purchases on credit and promises to pay the purchase price in installments, while the seller retains the title to the goods, together with the right of repossession upon default, until the condition of payment in full has been satisfied.

Conflict of laws: the body of law that determines the law of which state is to apply when two or more states are involved in the facts of a given case.

Confusion of goods: the mixing of goods of different owners that under certain circumstances results in one of the owners becoming the owner of all the goods.

Consanguinity: relationship by blood.

Consideration: the promise or performance by the other party that the promisor demands as the price of the promise.

Consignee: one to whom goods are shipped.

Consignment: a bailment made for the purpose of sale by the bailee. (Parties—consignor, consignee)

Consumer: one who purchases goods primarily for household, personal, or family use.

Contingent beneficiary: the person to whom the proceeds of a life insurance policy are payable in the event that the primary beneficiary dies before the insured.

Contingent liability: a responsibility to pay which usually does not arise until someone with primary liability defaults.

Contract: a binding agreement based upon the genuine assent of the parties, made for a lawful object, between competent parties, in the form required by law, and generally supported by consideration.

Contract carrier: a carrier which transports on the basis of individual contracts that it makes with each shipper.

Contract of record: name sometimes given to a judgment of a court.

Contract to sell: a contract to make a transfer of title in the future as contrasted with a present sale.

Contributory negligence: negligence of the plaintiff that contributes to the injury and at common law bars the plaintiff from recovery from the defendant although the defendant may have been more negligent than the plaintiff.

Conveyance: a transfer of an interest in land, ordinarily by the execution and delivery of a deed.

Cooperative: a group of two or more persons or enterprises that act through a common agent with respect to a common objective, as buying or selling.

Corporation: an artificial legal person or being created by law, which for many purposes is treated as a natural person.

Corporeal: material; tangible; substantial.

Counterclaim: a claim that the defendant in an action may make against the plaintiff.

Covenant: a promise contained in a conveyance or other instrument relating to real estate; a solemn compact.

Coverture: the status or condition of a woman during marriage.

Credit sale: the exchange of goods for a promise to pay later.

Crime: a violation of the law that is punished as an offense against the state or government.

Cumulative voting: a system of voting for directors in which each stockholder has as many votes as the number of voting shares owned multiplied by the number of directors to be elected, which votes can be distributed for the various candidates as desired.

Custody: care and control of property or a person.

D

Damages: a sum of money recovered to redress or make amends for the legal wrong or injury done.

Debt: an obligation to pay in money or goods.

Deceit: a device of false representation by which one person misleads another to the latter's injury.

Decree: the decision of a court of equity or admiralty.

Dedication: acquisition by the public or a government of title to land when it is given over by its owner to use by the public and such gift is accepted.

Deed: an instrument by which the grantor (owner of land) conveys or transfers the title to a grantee.

Default: the nonperformance of a duty or an obligation.

Defendant: a person against whom a suit is brought.

Defense: that which is relied upon by a defendant to defeat an action; the resistance to an attack.

Delegation: the transfer to another of the power to do an act.

Demurrage: a charge made by the carrier for the unreasonable detention of cars by the consignor or consignee.

Deposition: the testimony of a witness taken out of court before a person authorized to administer oaths.

Descent: hereditary succession to an estate.

Devise: a gift of real estate made by will.

Directors: the persons vested with control of the corporation, subject to the elective power of the shareholders.

Disability: incapacity for the performance of a legal act.

Discharge in bankruptcy: an order of the bankruptcy court discharging the debtor from the unpaid balance of most of the claims against him or her.

Discharge of contract: termination of a contract by performance, agreement, impossibility, acceptance of breach, or operation of law.

Dishonor by nonacceptance: the refusal of the drawee to accept a draft (bill of exchange).

Dishonor by nonpayment: the refusal to pay a commercial paper when properly presented for payment.

Divorce: the dissolution of the marriage ties.

Domestic bill of exchange: a draft drawn in one state and payable in the same or another state.

Domestic corporation: a corporation that has been incorporated by the state as opposed to incorporation by another state.

Domicile: the home of a person or the state of incorporation of a corporation, to be distinguished from a place where a person lives but which that person does not regard as home, or a state in which a corporation does business but in which it was not incorporated.

Double indemnity: a provision for payment of double the amount specified by the insurance contract if death is caused by an accident and occurs under specified circumstances.

Double jeopardy: the principle that a person who has once been placed in jeopardy by being brought to trial at which the proceedings progressed at least as far as having the jury sworn cannot thereafter be tried a second time for the same offense.

Draft: see bill of exchange.

Due care: the degree of care that a reasonable person would exercise to prevent the realization of harm, which under all the circumstances was reasonably foreseeable in the event that such care were not taken.

Due date: the time at which payment is required and after which payment is delinquent.

Duress: constraint or compulsion.

E

Easement: the right that one person has to use the land of another for a special purpose.

Eleemosynary corporation: a corporation organized for a charitable or benevolent purpose.

Embezzlement: the fraudulent appropriation of property by a person to whom it has been entrusted.

Emblements: growing crops that have been sown or planted.

Eminent domain: the power of a government and certain kinds of corporations to take private property against the objection of the owner, provided the taking is for a public purpose and just compensation is made therefor.

Enact: to make into a law.

Encumbrance: a right held by a third person in, or a lien or charge against, property, as a mortgage or judgment lien on land.

Equitable: just; fair; right; reasonable.

Equity: the body of principles that originally developed because of the inadequacy of the rules then applied by the common-law courts of England.

Erosion: the loss of land through a gradual washing away by tides or currents, with the owner losing title to the lost land.

Escrow: a conditional delivery of property or of a deed to a custodian or escrow holder, who in turn makes final delivery to the grantee or transferee when a specified condition has been satisfied.

Estate: an interest in property.

Estate in fee simple: the largest estate possible in which the owner has the absolute and entire interest in the land.

Estoppel: the principle by which a person is barred from pursuing a certain course of action or of disputing the truth of certain matters when the person's conduct has been such that it would be unjust to permit him or her to do so.

Eviction: the expulsion of an occupant of real property.

Evidence: that which is presented to the trier of fact as the basis on which the trier is to determine what happened.

Execution: the carrying out of a judgment of a court, generally directing that property owned by the defendant be sold and the proceeds first used to pay the execution or judgment creditor.

Executor–executrix: the person (man–woman) named by the maker of a will to carry out its provisions.

Ex parte: upon or from one side only.

Extradition: the surrender by one government to another of a person charged with a crime.

Extraordinary bailment: a bailment in which the bailee is subject to unusual duties and liabilities, as a hotelkeeper or common carrier.

F

Factor: a bailee to whom goods are consigned for sale.

Fair employment practice acts: statutes designed to eliminate discrimination in employment in terms of race, religion, national origin, or sex.

Fair labor standards acts: statutes, particularly the federal statute, designed to prevent excessive hours of employment and low pay, the employment of young children, and other unsound practices.

Featherbedding: the exaction of money for services not performed or not to be performed, which is made an unfair labor practice generally and a criminal offense in connection with radio broadcasting.

Fellow-servant rule: a common-law defense of the employer that barred an employee from suing an employer for injuries caused by a fellow employee.

Felony: a criminal offense that is punishable by confinement in prison or by death, or that is expressly stated by statute to be a felony.

Fiduciary: involving a relation of trust or confidence.

File: to make a matter of public record or notice by registering with the proper authorities.

Financial responsibility laws: statutes that require a driver involved in an automobile accident to prove financial responsibility in order to retain a driver's license, which responsibility may be shown by procuring public liability insurance in a specified minimum amount.

Firm offer: an offer stated to be held open for a specified time, which must be so held in some states even in the absence of an option contract, or under the UCC, with respect to merchants.

Fixture: personal property that has become so attached to or adapted to real estate that it has lost its character as personal property and is part of the real estate.

Forbearance: refraining from doing an act that it is legal to do.

Foreclosure: procedure for enforcing a mortgage resulting in the public sale of the mortgaged property and less commonly in merely barring the right of the mortgagor to redeem the property from the mortgage.

Foreign (international) bill of exchange: a bill of exchange made in one nation and payable in another.

Foreign corporation: a corporation incorporated under the laws of another state.

Forfeiture: the loss of some right or privilege.

Forgery: the fraudulent making or altering of an instrument that apparently creates or alters a legal liability of another.

Franchise: a right or privilege conferred by law.

Fraud: the making of a false statement of a past or existing fact with knowledge of its falsity or with reckless indifference as to its truth with the intent to cause another to rely thereon, and the other does rely thereon to his or her injury.

Fungible goods: goods of a homogenous nature of which any unit is the equivalent of any other unit or is treated as such by mercantile usage.

G

Garnishment: a process whereby a person's money or property which is held by another is applied to payment of the former's debt to a third person.

General partnership: a partnership in which the partners conduct as co-owners a business for profit, and each partner has a right to take part in the management of the business and has unlimited liability.

Grant: convey real property; an instrument by which such property has been conveyed, particularly in the case of a government.

Gratuitous bailment: a bailment in which the bailee does not receive any compensation or advantage.

Guarantor: one who undertakes the obligation of guaranty.

Guaranty: an undertaking to pay the debt of another if the creditor first sues the debtor and is unable to recover the debt from the debtor or principal.

Guardian: one who is responsible for the care of a person or property.

H

Hedging: the making of simultaneous contracts to purchase and to sell a particular commodity at a future date with the intention that the loss on one transaction will be offset by the gain on the other.

Heirs: those persons specified by statute to receive the estate of a decedent not disposed of by will.

Holder: the person in possession of a commercial paper payable to her or him as payee or indorsee, or the person in possession of a commercial paper payable to bearer.

Holder in due course: the holder of a commercial paper under such circumstances that the holder is treated as favored and is given an immunity from certain defenses.

Holder through a holder in due course: a person who does not meet the requirements of a holder in due course but is a holder of the paper after it was held by some prior party who was a holder in due course, and who is given the same rights as a holder in due course.

Holographic will: a will written by the testator in the testator's own hand.

Hotelkeeper: one regularly engaged in the business of offering living accommodations to all transient persons.

I

Implied contract: a contract expressed by conduct or implied or deduced from the facts. Also used to refer to a quasi-contract.

Incidental authority: authority of an agent that is reasonably necessary to execute the agent's express authority.

Incontestable clause: a provision that after the lapse of a specified time the insurer cannot dispute the policy on the ground of misrepresentation or fraud of the insured or similar wrongful conduct.

Indemnity: compensation for loss sustained.

Independent contractor: a contractor who undertakes to perform a specified task according to the terms of a contract but over whom the other contracting party has no control except as provided for by the contract.

Indictment: a formal accusation of crime made by a grand jury which accusation is then tried by a petty or trial jury.

Infant: any person not of full legal age.

Inheritance: the estate which passes from the decedent to the heirs.

Injunction: a judicial order or decree forbidding the doing of a certain act.

Insolvency: the state of being unable to pay one's debts as they become due.

Instrument: a written document.

Insurable interest: an interest in the nonoccurrence of the risk insured against, generally because such occurrence would cause financial loss, although sometimes merely because of the close relationship between the insured and the beneficiary.

Insurance: a plan of security against risks by charging the loss against a fund created by the payments made by policyholders.

Intangible personal property: an interest in an enterprise, such as an interest in a partnership or stock of a corporation, and claims against other persons, whether based on contract or tort.

International bill of exchange: an instrument made in one nation and payable in another.

Intestate: one who dies without having made a valid will.

Invalid: void, of no legal effect.

J

Joint and several contract: a contract in which two or more persons are jointly and severally obligated or are jointly and severally entitled to recover.

Joint contract: a contract in which two or more persons are jointly liable or jointly entitled to performance under the contract.

Joint stock company: an association in which the shares of the members are transferable and control is delegated to a group or board.

Joint tenancy: the estate held by two or more jointly with the right of survivorship between them.

Joint venture: a relationship in which two or more persons combine their labor or property for a single undertaking and share profits and losses equally unless otherwise agreed.

Judgment: a decision of a court.

Jurisdiction: the power of a court to hear and determine a given class of cases; the power to act over a particular defendant.

L

Land: earth

Lease: an agreement between the owner of property and a tenant by which the former agrees to give possession of the property to the latter in consideration of the payment of rent. (Parties—landlord or lessor, tenant or lessee)

Leasehold: the estate or interest which the tenant has in the land rented.

Legacy: a gift of personal property by will.

Legal: authorized or prescribed by law.

Legal tender: such form of money as the law recognizes as lawful and declares that a tender thereof in the proper

amount is a proper tender which the creditor cannot refuse.

Legatee: one to whom a legacy is given.

Levy: to take possession of property to satisfy a judgment.

Libel: defamation of another without legal justification.

License: a personal privilege to do some act or series of acts upon the land of another not amounting to an easement or a right of possession, as the placing of a sign thereon.

Lien: a right to control, hold, and retain, or enforce a charge against another's property as security for a debt or claim.

Life estate: an estate for the duration of a life.

Limited liability: loss of contributed capital as maximum liability.

Limited partnership: a partnership in which at least one partner has a liability limited to the loss of the capital contribution made to the partnership, and such a partner neither takes part in the management of the partnership nor appears to the public to be a partner.

Liquidated damages: the amount agreed upon in advance by the parties to a contract, to be paid in case of a breach.

Liquidation: the process of converting property into money whether of particular items of property or all the assets of a business.

Litigation: a suit at law, a judicial contest.

Lottery: any plan by which a consideration is given for a chance to win a prize.

M

Majority: of age, as contrasted with being a minor; more than half of any group, as a majority of stockholders.

Malfeasance: the doing of some wrongful act.

Malice: ill will towards some person.

Mechanics' lien: protection afforded by statute to various types of laborers and persons supplying materials, by giving them a lien on the building and land that has been improved or added to by them.

Merger: an absorption, union, or extinguishment of one contract or interest in another.

Merger of corporations: a combining of corporations by which one absorbs the other and continues to exist, preserving its original charter and identity while the other corporation ceases to exist.

Minor: any person not of full legal age.

Misdemeanor: a criminal offense which is neither treason nor a felony.

Misrepresentation: a false statement of fact although made innocently without any intent to deceive.

Monopoly: the condition of an industry when one or a few entities control the price or quality of a product.

Mortgage: an interest in land given by the owner to a creditor as security for the payment to the creditor of a debt, the nature of the interest depending upon the law of the state where the land is located. (Parties – mortgagor, mortgagee)

N

Negative covenant: an agreement in a deed to refrain from doing an act.

Negligence: the omission to do what a reasonable, prudent person would do, or doing what such a person would not have done.

Negotiable instruments: drafts, promissory notes, checks, and certificates of deposit in such form that greater rights may be acquired thereunder than by taking an assignment of a contract right.

Negotiation: the transfer of a negotiable instrument by indorsement and delivery by the person to whom then payable in the case of order paper, and by physical transfer in the case of bearer paper.

Nominal damages: a small sum given for the violation of a right where no actual loss has resulted.

Nominal partner: a person who in fact is not a partner but who holds himself or herself out as a partner or permits others to do so.

Notice of dishonor: notice given to parties secondarily liable that the primary party to the instrument has refused to accept the instrument or to make payment when it was properly presented for that purpose.

Novation: the discharge of a contract between two parties by their agreeing with a third person that such third person shall be substituted for one of the original parties to the contract, who shall thereupon be released.

Nuisance: something which wrongfully disturbs, annoys, or injures another.

Nuncupative will: an oral will made and declared by the testator in the presence of witnesses to be his or her will and generally made during the testator's last illness.

O

Obligation: a duty.

Occupation: taking and holding possession of property; a method of acquiring title to personal property which has been abandoned.

Open-end mortgage: a mortgage given to secure additional loans to be made in the future as well as the original loan.

Option contract: a contract to hold an offer to make a contract open for a fixed period of time.

Ordinance: a rule of law passed by the legislative body of a city.

P

Parole: the promise of a prisoner that in return for conditional freedom the prisoner will follow certain requirements.

Parol evidence rule: the rule that prohibits the introduction into evidence of oral or written statements made prior to or contemporaneously with the execution of a complete written contract, deed, or instrument, in the absence of clear proof of fraud, accident, or mistake.

Past consideration: something that has been performed in the past and which therefore cannot be consideration for a promise made in the present.

Patent: the grant to an inventor of an exclusive right to make and sell an invention for a term of years; a grant of privilege, property, or authority made by government to a private person.

Pawn: a pledge of tangible personal property.

Perjury: willful false testimony under oath in a judicial proceeding.

Perpetual succession: a phrase describing the continuing life of the corporation unaffected by the death of any stockholder or the transfer by stockholders of their stock.

Per se: in, through, or by itself.

Person: a term that includes both natural persons, or living people, and artificial persons, as corporations which are created by act of government.

Per stirpes: according to the root or by way of representation. Distribution among heirs related to the decedent in different degrees, the property being divided into lines of descent from the decedent and the share of each line then divided within the line by way of representation.

Picketing: the placing of persons outside of places of employment or distribution so that by words or banners they may inform the public of the existence of a labor dispute.

Plaintiff: one who brings an action in a court.

Pledge: a bailment given as security for the payment of a debt or the performance of an obligation owed to the pledgee. (Parties—pledgor, pledgee)

Police power: the power to govern; the power to adopt laws for the protection of the public health, welfare, safety, and morals.

Policy: the paper evidencing the contract of insurance.

Possession: exclusive domain and control of property.

Possessory lien: a right to retain possession of property of another as security for some debt or obligation owed the lienor which right continues only as long as possession is retained.

Postdate: to insert or place a later date on an instrument than the actual date on which it was executed.

Power of attorney: a written authorization to an agent by the principal.

Preferred stock: stock that has a priority or preference as to payment of dividends or upon liquidation, or both.

Prejudicial: something which substantially adversely affects one's rights.

Prescription: the acquisition of a right to use the land of another, as an easement, through the making of hostile, visible, and notorious use of the land, continuing for the period specified by the local law.

Price: the consideration for a sale of goods.

Prima facie: at first view, apparently true; on the first appearance.

Primary beneficiary: the person designated as the first one to receive the proceeds of a life insurance policy, as distinguished from a contingent beneficiary who will receive the proceeds only if the primary beneficiary dies before the insured.

Principal: one who employs an agent to act on his or her behalf; the person who in a suretyship is primarily liable to the third person or creditor.

Private carrier: a carrier owned by the shipper, such as a company's own fleet of trucks.

Privileged communication: information which the witness may refuse to testify to because of the relationship with the person furnishing the information, as husband-wife, attorney-client.

Privity: a succession or chain of relationship to the same thing or right, as a privity of contract, privity of estate, privity of possession.

Probate: a court having jurisdiction over estates.

Process: a writ or order of court generally used as a means of acquiring jurisdiction over the person of the defendant by serving the defendant with process.

Promissory estoppel: the doctrine that a promise will be enforced although not supported by consideration when the promisor should have reasonably expected that the promise would induce action or forbearance of a definite and substantial character on the part of the promisee, and injustice can only be avoided by enforcement of the promise.

Promissory note: an unconditional promise in writing made by one person to another, signed by the maker, engaging to pay on demand, or at a definite time, a sum certain in money to order or to bearer. (Parties—maker, payee)

Promoters: the persons who plan the formation of the corporation and sell or promote the idea to others.

Property: the rights and interests one has in anything subject to ownership.

Prosecute: to proceed against by legal means.

Protest: formal certification that proper presentment of a commercial paper was made to the primary party and that the primary party defaulted.

Proximate cause: the act which is the natural and reasonably foreseeable cause of the harm or event which occurs and injures the plaintiff.

Proximate damages: damages which in the ordinary course of events are the natural and reasonably foreseeable result of the defendant's violation of the plaintiff's rights.

Proxy: a written authorization by a shareholder to another person to vote the stock owned by the shareholder; the person who is the holder of such a written authorization.

Public domain: public or government-owned lands.

Punitive damages: damages in excess of those required to compensate the plaintiff for the wrong done, which are imposed in order to punish the defendant because of the particularly wanton or willful character of the wrongdoing.

Purchase-money mortgage: a mortgage given by the purchaser of land to the seller to secure the seller for the payment of the unpaid balance of the purchase price, which the seller purports to lend the purchaser.

Purchaser in good faith: a person who purchases without any notice or knowledge of any defect of title, misconduct, or defense.

Q

Qualified acceptance: an acceptance of a draft that varies the order of the bill in some way.

Qualified indorsement: an indorsement that includes words such as "without recourse" evidencing the intent of the indorser that he or she shall not be held liable for the failure of the primary party to pay the instrument.

Quantum meruit: an action brought for the value of the services rendered the defendant when there was no express contract as to the payment to be made.

Quasi: as if, as though it were, having the characteristics of; a modifier employed to indicate that the subject is to be treated as though it were in fact the noun which follows the word "quasi": as in quasi-contract, quasi-corporation, quasi-public corporation.

Quitclaim deed: a deed by which the grantor purports only to give up whatever right or title the grantor may have in the property without specifying or warranting that he or she is transferring any particular interest.

Quorum: the minimum number of persons, shares represented, or directors who must be present at a meeting in order that business may be lawfully transacted.

R

Ratification: confirming an act which was executed without authority or an act which was voidable.

Ratification by minor: the approval of a contract given by a minor after attaining majority.

Ratification of agency: the approval of the unauthorized act of an agent or of a person who is not an agent for any purpose after the act has been done, which has the same effect as though the act had been authorized before it was done.

Real property: land and all rights in land.

Realty: real property.

Reasonable care: that degree of care that a reasonable person would take under all the circumstances then known.

Recall: the process by which regulatory agencies demand that a manufacturer inform consumers of a product's defects and remedy them or replace the product.

Receiver: a person appointed by a court to take charge of property pending litigation.

Record: to file or make a matter of public record with the proper authority.

Redemption: the buying back of one's property which has been sold because of a default.

Referee: an impartial person selected by the parties or appointed by a court to determine facts or decide matters in dispute.

Referee in bankruptcy: a referee appointed by a bankruptcy court to hear and determine various matters relating to bankruptcy proceedings.

Reimbursement: the right of one paying money on behalf of another, which such other person should have paid, to re-

cover the amount of the payment from such other person.

Release: the surrender of relinquishment to another of a right, claim, interest, or estate.

Remedy: the action or procedure that is followed in order to enforce a right or to obtain damages for injury to a right.

Reorganization of corporation: procedure devised to restore insolvent corporations to financial stability through readjustment of debt and capital structure under the supervision of a bankruptcy court.

Replevin: an action to recover possession of property unlawfully detained.

Repossession: the power of the credit seller to take back goods because of the buyer's failure to meet the obligation specified in the credit agreement.

Representations: statements, whether oral or written, made to give the insurer the information which it needs in writing the insurance, and which if false and relating to a material fact will entitle the insurer to avoid the contract.

Representative capacity: action taken by one on behalf of another, as an executor acting on behalf of the decedent's estate, or action taken both on one's behalf and on behalf of others, as a stockholder bringing a representative action.

Rescission: cancelling, annulling, avoiding.

Reservation: the creation by the grantor of a right that did not exist before, which the grantor reserves or keeps upon making a conveyance of property.

Res ipsa loquitur: the rebuttable presumption that the thing speaks for itself when the circumstances are such that ordinarily the plaintiff could not have been injured had the defendant not been at fault.

Respondeat superior: the doctrine that the principal or employer is vicariously liable for the unauthorized torts committed by the agent or employee while acting within the scope of the agency or the course of the employment, respectively.

Restrictive covenants: covenants in a deed by which the grantee agrees to refrain from doing specified acts.

Restrictive indorsement: an indorsement that prohibits the further transfer, constitutes the indorsee the agent of the indorser, vests the title in the indorsee in trust for or to the use of some other person, is conditional, or states it is for collection or deposit.

Revocation: the annulment or cancellation of an instrument, act, or promise by one doing or making it.

Rider: a slip of paper executed by the insurer and intended to be attached to the insurance policy for the purpose of changing it in some respect.

Riparian rights: the right of a person through whose land runs a natural watercourse to use the water free from unreasonable pollution or diversion by the upper riparian owners and from blocking by lower riparian owners.

Risk: the peril or contingency against which the insured is protected by the contract of insurance.

S

Sale or return: a sale in which the title to the property passes to the buyer at the time of the transaction but the buyer is given the option of returning the property and restoring the title to the seller.

Scope of employment: the area within which the employee is authorized to act with the consequence that a tort committed while so acting imposes liability upon the employer.

Seal: at common law, an impression on wax or other material attached to the instrument. Under modern law, any mark not ordinarily part of the signature is a seal when so intended, including the letters "L. S." and the word "seal," or a pictorial representation of a seal.

Secret partner: a partner who takes an active part in the management of the partnership but is not known to the public as a partner.

Secured transaction: a credit sale of goods or a secured loan that provides special protection for the creditor.

Sentence: the penalty pronounced upon a person convicted of a crime.

Set off: the process in a case by which a defendant seeks to deduct from the plaintiff's claim amounts owed to the defendant by the plaintiff.

Severable contract: a contract the terms of which are such that one part may be separated or severed from the other, so that a default as to one part is not necessarily a default as to the entire contract.

Several contracts: separate or independent contracts made by different persons undertaking to perform the same obligation.

Severalty: sole ownership of property by one person.

Shareholder's action: an action brought by one or more shareholders on behalf of the shareholders generally and of the corporation to enforce a cause of action of the corporation against third persons.

Sight draft: a draft or bill of exchange payable on sight or when presented for payment.

Silent partner: a partner who takes no active part in the business, without regard to whether he or she is known to the public as a partner.

Sitdown strike: a strike in which the employees remain in the plant and refuse to allow the employer to operate it.

Slander: defamation of character by spoken words or gestures.

Slowdown: a slowing down of production by employees without actual stopping of work.

Special agent: an agent authorized to transact a specific transaction or to do a specific act.

Special damages: damages that do not necessarily result from the injury to the plaintiff but at the same time are not so remote that the defendant should not be held liable therefor, provided that the claim for special damages is properly made in the action.

Special indorsement: an indorsement that specifies the person to whom the instrument is indorsed.

Specific (identified) goods: goods which are so identified to the contract that no other goods may be delivered in performance of the contract.

Specific lien: the right of a creditor to hold particular property or assert a lien on any particular property of the debtor because of the creditor's having done work on or having some other association with the property, as distinguished from having a lien generally against the assets of the debtor merely because the debtor is indebted.

Specific performance: an action brought to compel the adverse party to perform a contract on the theory that merely suing for damages for its breach will not be an adequate remedy.

SS. or ss.: abbreviation for the Latin word scilicet, meaning, to wit; namely; that is to say.

Stare decisis: the principle that the decision of a court should serve as a guide or precedent and control the decision of a similar case in the future.

Statute of Frauds: a statute which, in order to prevent fraud through the use of perjured testimony, requires that certain types of transactions be evidenced in writing in order to be binding or enforceable.

Statute of Limitations: a statute that restricts the period of time within which an action may be brought.

Stop payment: an order by a depositor to a bank to refuse to make payment of the depositor's check when presented for payment.

Sublease: a transfer of the premises by the lessee to a third person, the sublessee or subtenant, for a period less than the term of the original lease.

Subpoena: a writ commanding a person to appear as a witness.

Subrogation: the right of a party secondarily liable to stand in the place of the creditor after making payment to the creditor and to enforce the creditor's right against the party primarily liable in order to obtain indemnity.

Subsidiary corporation: a corporation that is controlled by another corporation through the ownership by the latter of a controlling amount of the voting stock of the former.

Substantial performance: the equitable doctrine that a contractor substantially performing a contract in good faith is entitled to recover the contract price less damages for noncompletion or defective work.

Substantive law: the law that defines rights and liabilities.

Substitution: discharge of contracts by substituting another in its place.

Subtenant: one who rents the leased premises from the original tenant for a period of time less than the balance of the lease to the original tenant.

Suit: the prosecution of some claim in a court of justice.

Summons: a notice to a person to appear in court.

Suretyship: an undertaking to pay the debt or be liable for the default of another.

Surrender: the yielding up of the tenant's leasehold estate to the lessor in consequence of which the lease terminates.

Survivorship: the right by which a surviving joint tenant or tenant by the entireties acquires the interest of the predeceasing tenant automatically upon death of the predeceasing tenant.

Syndicate: an association of individuals formed to conduct a particular business transaction, generally of a financial nature.

T

Tenancy at sufferance: the holding over by a tenant after the lease has expired without the permission of the landlord and prior to the time that the landlord has elected to treat the person as a trespasser or a tenant.

Tenancy at will: the holding of land for an indefinite period that may be terminated at any time by the landlord or by the landlord and tenant acting together.

Tenancy for years: a tenancy for a fixed period of time, even though the time is less than a year.

Tenancy from year to year: a tenancy which continues indefinitely from year to year until terminated.

Tenancy in common: the relation that exists when two or more persons own undivided interests in property.

Tender of payment: an unconditional offer to pay the exact amount of money due at the time and place specified by the contract.

Tender of performance: an unconditional offer to perform at the time and in the manner specified by the contract.

Testamentary: designed to take effect at death, as by disposing of property or appointing an executor.

Testate: the condition of leaving a will upon death.

Testator–testatrix: a person (man–woman) who makes a will.

Testimony: the answers of witnesses under oath to questions given at the time of the trial.

Third-party beneficiary: a third person whom the parties to a contract intend to benefit by the making of the contract.

Time draft: a bill of exchange payable at a stated time after sight or a stated period after a certain date.

Title: evidence of ownership in property.

Title insurance: a form of insurance by which the insurer insures the buyer of real property against the risk of loss should the title acquired from the seller be defective in any way.

Tort: a private injury or wrong arising from a breach of a duty created by law.

Trade acceptance: a draft or bill of exchange drawn by the seller of goods on the purchaser at the time of sale and accepted by the purchaser.

Trade fixtures: articles of personal property which have been attached to the freehold by a tenant and which are used for or are necessary to the carrying on of the tenant's trade.

Trademark: a name, device, or symbol used by a manufacturer or seller to distinguish his or her goods from those of other persons.

Trade name: a name under which a business is carried on and, if fictitious, it must be registered.

Treasury stock: stock of the corporation which the corporation has reacquired.

Trespass: an unwarranted invasion of another's right.

Trust: a transfer of property by one person to another with the understanding or declaration that such property be held for the benefit of another, or the holding of property by the owner in trust for another, upon a declaration of trust, without a transfer to another person.

Trust deed: a form of deed which transfers the trust property to the trustee for the purposes therein stated, particularly used as a form of mortgage when the trustee is to hold the title to the mortgagor's land in trust for the benefit of the mortgage bondholders.

Trustee: one who holds property for the benefit of another.

Trustee in bankruptcy: an impartial person elected to administer the bankrupt's estate.

U

Ultra vires: an act or contract which the corporation does not have authority to do or make.

Underwriter: an insurer.

Undisclosed principal: a principal on whose behalf an agent acts without disclosing to the third person the fact that he or she is an agent nor the identity of the principal.

Undue influence: the influence that is asserted upon another person by one who dominates that person.

Unfair competition: the wrong of employing competitive methods that have been declared unfair by statute or an administrative agency.

Unfair labor practice acts: statutes that prohibit certain labor practices and declare them to be unfair labor practices.

Unilateral: one-sided, applied to contracts where only one party's promise is still unperformed.

Unincorporated association: a combination of two or more persons for the furtherance of a common nonprofit purpose.

Union contract: a contract between a labor union and an employer or group of employers prescribing the general terms of employment of workers by the latter.

Union shop: a place of employment where nonunion workers may be employed for a trial period of not more than 30 days after which the nonunion worker must join the union or be discharged.

Universal agent: an agent authorized by the principal to do all acts that can lawfully be delegated to a representative.

Usury: the lending of money at greater than the maximum rate allowed by law.

V

Valid: legal.

Venue: the place where the trial is held.

Verdict: a decision rendered by a jury.

Void: no legal effect and not binding on anyone.

Voidable: a transaction that may be set aside by one party because of fraud or similar reason but which is binding on the other party until the injured party elects to set the contract aside.

Voting trust: the transfer by two or more persons of their shares of stock of a corporation to a trustee who is to vote the shares and act for such shareholders.

W

Waiver: the voluntary surrender or relinquishment of a right or privilege.

Warehouser: a person regularly engaged in the business of storing the goods of others for compensation. If the warehouser holds himself or herself out to serve the public without discrimination, he or she is a public warehouser.

Warehouse receipt: a receipt issued by the warehouser for goods stored. Regulated by the UCC, which clothes the receipt with some degree of negotiability.

Warranty deed: a deed by which the grantor conveys a specific estate or interest to the grantee and covenants that she or he has transferred the estate or interest by making one or more of the covenants of title.

Waste: damage or destruction to property done or permitted by a tenant.

Watered stock: stock issued by a corporation as fully paid when in fact it is not.

Will: an instrument executed with the formality required by law, by which a person makes a disposition of property to take effect upon his or her death.

Witness: a person who gives testimony in court; one who sees a document executed and signs his or her name thereto.

Workers' compensation: a system providing for payments to workers because they have been injured from a risk arising out of the course of their employment while they were employed at their employment or have contracted an occupational disease in that manner, payment being made without consideration of the negligence of any party.

Works of charity: in connection with Sunday laws, acts involved in religious worship or aiding persons in distress.

Works of necessity: in connection with

Sunday laws, acts that must be done at the particular time in order to save life, health, or property.

Writ: a formal written command issued by a court of law.

Z

Zoning restrictions: restrictions imposed by government on the use of property for the advancement of the general welfare.

Index

529